THIRD EDITION

Comprehensive Classroom Management

Motivating and Managing Students

VERNON F. JONES
Lewis and Clark College

LOUISE S. JONES
Beaverton School District

ALLYN AND BACON   Boston / London / Sydney / Toronto

To Vern's first mentors, Jere Brophy, whose excellent work continues to inform us, and Dan Duke, a valued friend and scholar; to the hundreds of teachers whose ideas and responses to the materials in the book have enriched its content and been a source of professional and personal satisfaction; and to our children, Sarah and Garrett, who teach us so much and bring us so much happiness.

Copyright © 1990, 1986 by Allyn and Bacon
A Division of Simon & Schuster, Inc.
160 Gould Street
Needham Heights, MA 02194

A previous edition was published under the title *Responsible Classroom Discipline*, copyright © 1981 by Allyn and Bacon, Inc.

Text on pages 146 and 329 is from Vernon F. Jones, *Adolescents with Behavior Problems: Strategies for Teaching, Counseling, and Parent Involvement*, pp. 71–72, 76–78. Copyright © 1980 by Allyn and Bacon. Reprinted with permission.

Quotes on pages 65, 99, 111–12, 210, 398–399 are published by permission of Transaction Publishers, from *Successful Schools for Young Adolescents*, by Joan Lipsitz. Copyright © 1984 by Transaction Publishers.

Series Editor: Sean W. Wakely
Production Administrator: Annette Joseph
Editorial-Production Service: Grace Sheldrick, Wordsworth Associates
Cover Administrator: Linda K. Dickinson
Cover Designer: Susan Slovinsky
Manufacturing Buyer: Tamara McCracken

Library of Congress Cataloging-in-Publication Data

Jones, Vernon F., 1945–
    Comprehensive classroom management : motivating and managing
students / Vernon F. Jones, Louise S. Jones. — 3rd ed.
      p. cm.
    Bibliography: p.
    Includes index.
    ISBN 0-205-12088-1
    1. Classroom management. 2. Interaction analysis in education.
3. Motivation in education. 4. School discipline. I. Jones,
Louise S., 1949– . II. Title.
LB3013.J66 1989
371.1′024—dc20
                              89–34676
                                 CIP

Printed in the United States of America

10 9 8 7 6   94 93 92

Contents

Preface

PURPOSE

In March 1984, a 10-member Panel on the Preparation of Beginning Teachers, chaired by Ernest L. Boyer, president of the Carnegie Foundation for the Advancement of Teaching, issued a report listing 3 major areas of expertise needed by beginning teachers:

1. Knowledge of how to manage a classroom.
2. Knowledge of subject matter.
3. Understanding of their students' sociological backgrounds.

A publication from the Association for Supervision and Curriculum Development entitled *Effective Schools and Classrooms: A Research-Based Perspective* (Squires, Huitt, & Segars, 1983) stated that effective teachers—those whose students demonstrate consistently high levels of achievement—possess skills in

1. Planning, or getting ready for classroom activities;
2. Management, which has to do with controlling students' behavior; and
3. Instruction, which concerns providing for or guiding students' learning. (p.10)

Walter Doyle (1986), in his comprehensive chapter in *Handbook of Research on Teaching,* explained that the classroom teacher's role involves two major functions: establishing order and facilitating learning. Regardless of changes that may be made in the education system, schooling in the United States will not improve significantly unless teachers develop skill in the widely varied teaching methods generally described as classroom management.

Fortunately, technology in classroom management has kept pace with the increasing demands placed on teachers. Research in classroom management has grown explosively in the last 20 years. Most teachers trained in the 1960s learned only such simple prescriptions as ''don't smile until Christmas'' or ''don't grin until Thanksgiving.'' By 1990, however, thousands of articles and hundreds of thoughtful research projects focused on student behavior and learning. The concept of school discipline, which had concentrated on dealing with inevitable student misbehavior, was replaced by the concept of classroom management, which emphasized methods of facilitating positive student behavior and achievement.

Unfortunately, too few teachers have been provided with clear, usable materials that enable them to develop essential knowledge in classroom organization and student motivation and management. In a recent NEA special report, *Conditions and Resources of Teaching* (NEA, 1988), teachers rated undergraduate education courses and inservice training as the 2 least effective sources of job-related knowledge and skills. Graduate courses fared only slightly better, rating tenth of the 14 sources listed. *Comprehensive*

FIGURE P.1 Putting Research and Theory into Practice

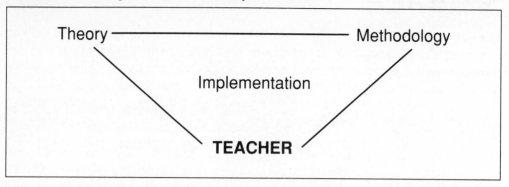

Classroom Management, third edition, fills this need. This text provides college faculty, inservice educators, teachers-in-training, and experienced teachers with practical, research-supported, effective methods for increasing student motivation and improving student behavior and thereby for increasing students' learning and a positive sense of themselves as lifelong learners.

In this book, the authors call on their combined 36 years of experience in teaching, public school administration, and teacher education. *Comprehensive Classroom Management* provides the most current theory and methodology in managing classes effectively so that students will choose to be productively involved in instructional activities. However, we realize that the teacher is the key ingredient in implementing this material (see Figure P.1).

We can provide research-proven methods and the theory that supports their use in schools and classrooms, but the teacher is the portion of the triangle that controls initiative. We realize that making change in the classroom is difficult and risky and that making changes in the school is even more difficult. However, we strongly believe (and the best current educational research supports) that in order to create schools that will help an increasing number of at-risk students succeed in life, educators must implement many of the methods presented throughout this book. We acknowledge and respect that teachers must consider each new approach in light of their personal style and teaching situation; we also know that the methods in this book have proven effective for thousands of teachers in diverse settings. Inaction is no longer professionally responsible. Thoughtful, reflective decision making before implementing a new approach is the sign of a competent professional.

AUDIENCE

This book is for teachers, counselors, administrators, school psychologists, and special educators. Its comprehensive and research-based presentation offers practical ideas for creating positive classroom and school climates, organizing and managing classrooms, improving instruction, dealing with classroom discipline problems, and developing school-wide discipline programs. These ideas enable educators in their various roles to understand the broad issues and skills involved in effective management, instruction, and discipline and to work collegially in responding to unproductive student behavior.

APPROACH

Materials used to train teachers and administrators have too often focused on isolated aspects of effective instruction and management. To develop a realistic, workable approach to classroom management, educators have had to seek out and integrate information from literally dozens of sources—each of which has claimed to provide "the answer." This third edition of *Comprehensive Classroom Management* offers a thorough research-based synthesis of current knowledge in effective classroom management, instruction, and school-wide student management.

"Recent research makes it clear that successful classroom management involves not merely responding effectively when problems occur, but preventing problems from occurring frequently" (Brophy, 1983, p. 23). Extensive review of the research and our own experiences in classrooms highlights five major factors or skill areas involved in effective classroom management:

1. Developing a solid understanding of students' personal/psychological and learning needs.
2. Establishing positive teacher-student and peer relationships that help meet students' basic psychological needs.
3. Implementing instructional methods that facilitate optimal learning by responding to the academic needs of individual students and the classroom group.
4. Using organizational and group management methods that maximize on-task student behavior.
5. Using a wide range of counseling and behavioral methods that involve students in examining and correcting their inappropriate behavior.

This emphasis on providing a variety of specific methods to consider does not, however, imply that teachers should implement these methods by rote. We believe that teachers should (and will) implement recommendations selectively, attending to their own teaching styles, learning goals, students' needs, and other context variables. Because we have always been deeply involved in schools and in teacher training, it seems obvious that research "can extend the range of hypotheses (alternative strategies) considered and sensitize the teacher to the possible consequences of his/her actions" (Good & Power, 1976, p. 47). However, research cannot prescribe a universal set of methods that will be effective in all instances.

The importance of encouraging teachers to consider context variables, including instructional goals and students' age, socioeconomic level, and cognitive skills, has been pointed out by a number of writers and researchers (Darling-Hammond, Wise, & Pease, 1983; Doyle, 1979; Soar, 1983; Zumwalt, 1983). As Brophy and Evertson (1976) state,

> Effective teaching requires the ability to implement a very large number of diagnostic, instructional, managerial, and therapeutic skills, tailoring behavior in specific contexts and situations to the specific needs of the moment. Effective teachers not only must be able to do a large number of things; they also must be able to recognize which of the many things they know how to do applies at a given moment and be able to follow through by performing the behavior effectively. (p. 139)

Any writer (or reader) must be cautious about how research is used as a framework for making practical decisions. In determining the methods to be presented in this book and the research used to support and expand these methods, we have made numerous choices. These choices are based on extensive study of the available research; on personal and professional acquaintance with leading researchers and writers in the field; and on our own experience as regular classroom teachers, special educators, public school administrator, pre- and inservice teacher trainers, psychologist, and researcher. Our decisions are also based on Elliot Eisner's (1984) ideas about translating educational research into useful prescriptions for practitioners. Responsible use of research, according to Eisner, requires that the educator should "have examined a body of research studies, extracted generalizations, determined that the theory is supported by the evidence, and then used the theory as a tool for shaping decisions" (p. 448). He also suggests that people involved in educational research (and, we trust, in prescription and training) should have "an intimate acquaintance with life in classrooms" (p. 450). The material presented throughout this book meets these criteria.

The methods have been used by us and by numerous teachers whom we have taught and with whom we have worked during the past 20 years. During the past 8 years, the methods have been field-tested by teachers in hundreds of classrooms evenly divided among primary, intermediate, middle, and high school settings. These settings include classrooms in inner-city, rural, and suburban schools.

ORGANIZATION OF THE TEXT

Comprehensive Classroom Management, third edition, is divided into five parts. Part I presents an overview of the history and key concepts associated with classroom management and its relationship to students' basic personal and psychological needs. This overview provides a theoretical foundation for understanding and thoughtfully implementing the practical suggestions in later chapters. Part II focuses on interpersonal relationships in the classroom and on the interaction between school and home as key factors influencing students' behavior and achievement. Part III examines motivation and instruction as major variables influencing student behavior. Part IV provides numerous research-supported, practical strategies for improving classroom organization and management. Part V presents methods for working with individual students who experience ongoing and/or serious behavior problems.

The book and chapter organization helps readers implement the content into their classroom management process. Chapter 1 presents an overview of classroom management that can help the reader understand the issue of classroom management. Each subsequent chapter begins with an overview of the chapter's topic and presents data to support the value of teachers' changing to incorporate the specific ideas presented throughout the chapter. This overview is followed by specific methods teachers can consider as alternatives to how they currently manage their classroom. Each chapter concludes with activities to help the reader implement the skills presented in the chapter and evaluate the results.

USING THIS BOOK

Many of you are reading *Comprehensive Classroom Management* as part of a university course in which class discussions, assignments, and summary projects can help you implement the material into a classroom. Some of you may select this book as a professional growth activity outside the context of a college or inservice course. With particular sensitivity to these readers, we offer the following suggestions for incorporating the material into a personal system of classroom management.

First, decisions in classroom management are most effective when they are based on a clear concept of what you wish to accomplish. Therefore, it is important to have a cogent philosophy outlining your goals for the students. Second, if you are currently teaching, be aware that you are already using many effective strategies. Give yourself credit for the many successful methods you have invented or learned. In many cases, new methods you choose to incorporate will enhance rather than replace your existing methods. This does not mean, of course, that you have an effective classroom management plan merely because students are quiet. As suggested, your plan needs to be evaluated in light of clearly stated goals about students' academic and personal growth. Third, do not try to accomplish too much at once. You can monitor and evaluate new methods more effectively if you try them one or two at a time. In addition, too many changes are stressful on teachers and students alike. Fourth, try to develop a method for assessing the effect of a new strategy. Were students more attentive? Did they complete more work? Fifth, keep in mind that there is no *one* way to manage a classroom. The ideas in *Comprehensive Classroom Management* are not intended as recipes to follow verbatim; rather, they are a wide variety of research-supported methods, each of which can be implemented into a teacher's existing classroom management plan. You should select methods with which you are comfortable and that respond to your students' developmental and educational needs.

One way of using this book is to select individual methods you find exciting and try them out in your classroom. Teachers agree that this approach provides a realistic, enjoyable, and effective way to implement new ideas. Teachers also tell us that this approach is more beneficial and enjoyable when they team up with two or three other teachers who are reading the book and share the results of various classroom changes. This sharing reinforces new methods, suggests why methods may not work as well as you hoped, and offers ideas for selecting methods you had not considered but that have worked effectively for a colleague.

A related approach to using this book involves assessing your own teaching and classroom environment to determine specific methods you believe will improve student learning and behavior. You can do this by completing several forms provided in the book and asking for student feedback. Especially helpful are forms in Figure 2.5, Figure 3.6, Figure 6.6, Activity 6.2, Activity 7.2, Activity 9.3, Figure 9.10, and Figure 9.11. Examine your responses to these forms and determine areas in which changes in your classroom instruction and management might bring about positive changes in students' behavior. Again, many teachers inform us that this process is more enjoyable and productive when shared with colleagues.

A third and more general approach is first to state your general concept of or approach to classroom management before reading this book or becoming involved in a class that uses it. Then, complete this statement: "Specific methods I have used to ensure positive student behavior include . . . ." When you have completed your work with this book, write a response to this statement: "Having read the material in *Comprehensive Classroom Management,* third edition, my philosophy of classroom management is . . . ." Then complete this statement: "Specific methods I would like to incorporate in order to increase positive student behavior and learning in my class include . . . ." Then, list the new methods in the order you would like to implement them. Keeping in mind that you are busy and that too many changes are stressful to both teachers and students, select two methods you can implement in the next two weeks and two you would like to implement the next time you begin a class with a new group of students. This process will provide you with a specific and realistic agenda for professional growth in the area of classroom mangement.

We hope that you enjoy the process of change and that it enriches your professional life and enhances your students' learning and personal development.

THE THIRD EDITION

This third edition of *Comprehensive Classroom Management* includes several new chapters and numerous new methods stemming from the teacher and school effectiveness research completed in the past four years. Specific changes include:

- The book's increased emphasis on secondary education, with many new ideas and case studies.
- Numerous case studies to demonstrate teachers' use of the methods presented throughout the book.
- Many new practical forms.
- Many ideas for dealing with disruptive students, including a systems approach to working with students prior to referral for special education placement.
- A new chapter on a systems approach to deal with student discipline problems.
- A new chapter on student motivation.
- A major focus on methods that work with at-risk students.
- New design features that make the book easier to read.
- Updated chapter bibliographies providing a rich source of reference material for the interested student and professional.

ACKNOWLEDGMENTS

We wish to acknowledge the many teachers whose application of the methods presented in *Comprehensive Classroom Management* have validated their effectiveness. Specifically, we thank Susan Foster, Mark Gaulke, Dean Long, Marjorie Miller Tonole, and Terri Vann for allowing us to use student behavior change projects they completed in our graduate classes. We also thank Marty Voge for providing us with Figure 11.8. Our special appreciation goes to Cory Dunn for his assistance in developing Figure 1.4, his work in developing the concept of the curriculum of responsibility, his sharing of the Think–Feel–Act model to problem solving and the associated case study presented here, and his work on the systems approach. We have learned a great deal from working with Cory during the past six years.

Our thanks also go to the following educators for their thoughtful comments: Karen A. Bosch, Old Dominion University; Kathryn Castle, Oklahoma State University; Charles P. Doyle, DePaul University; Peter J. Gilman, Hardin-Simmons University; and George Miller, Western Michigan University. And thanks to Grace Sheldrick, Wordsworth Associates, for her editorial/production assistance.

PART I

Foundations of Comprehensive Classroom Management

Theory and practice in classroom management have improved dramatically during the past two decades. Unfortunately, practical methods presented to teachers have often been simplistic and piecemeal. Because of public and teacher concern over discipline problems, new ideas have too often been quickly marketed as panaceas. Rather than helping teachers understand the issues in effective classroom management and the relationship among various strategies, most published materials have presented unidimensional approaches to small aspects of classroom management. These methods have usually failed to affect students' behavior significantly or have solved only a few of the teacher's problems with discipline. When this occurs, teachers are left with a sense of frustration and impotence. They must either blame themselves or ask if the profession has anything meaningful to offer in the way of ideas on classroom management.

Part I is directed toward alleviating the confusion associated with the topic of classroom management. In this section we examine the major causes of unproductive student behavior and provide a theoretical and philosophical foundation from which to examine approaches to encouraging positive student behavior and achievement and responding to disruptive behavior. In chapter 1 we place the concept of classroom management in perspective by examining the extent of the problem, considering the reasons for an increase in problems associated with student behavior, describing the history of classroom management, defining comprehensive classroom management, and discussing the relationship between classroom management and the teacher's professional needs. In chapter 2 we examine students' personal needs that must be met for them to become productively involved in the learning process. Discussions of classroom management have until recently placed too much emphasis on controlling unproductive student behavior and too little on creating environments that encourage productive behavior. The concepts in chapter 2 provide a foundation for refocusing attention on preventive interventions.

After completing Part I you should understand why discipline problems arise and the factors that can be examined and impacted in order to reduce these problems. This perspective provides a basis for employing the preventive and corrective strategies described throughout the book. Perhaps more important, this understanding will enable you to analyze your own classroom or school environment creatively and to evaluate how you might implement the ideas presented in this book or create new solutions for dealing with the behavior problems that occur in your school.

CHAPTER 1

Classroom Management in Perspective

Almost all surveys of teacher effectiveness report that classroom management skills are of primary importance in determining teaching success, whether it is measured by student learning or by ratings. Thus, management skills are crucial and fundamental. A teacher who is grossly inadequate in classroom management skills is probably not going to accomplish much.

/ Jere Brophy and Carolyn Evertson (1976)
Learning from Teaching

The concept of classroom management is broader than the notion of student discipline. It includes all the things teachers must do to foster student involvement and cooperation in classroom activities and to establish a productive working environment.

/ Julie Sanford, Edmund Emmer, and Barbara Clements,
"Improving Classroom Management"
Educational Leadership, April 1983

Student behavior problems have for years been a major concern of teachers, administrators, and parents. National concern about students' achievement has intensified public interest in schools and students' behavior. Although teachers face the task of educating many students whose home and community environments are disruptive, research demonstrates that teachers' skills in managing classrooms are a major factor influencing students' motivation, achievement, and behavior. The concept of discipline, with its emphasis on dealing with inevitable misbehavior among students, has been replaced by a more comprehensive body of knowledge on how to increase students' achievement by preventing management problems.

EXTENT OF THE PROBLEM

The issue of student behavior has been a longstanding concern of laypersons and educators. Since its inception in 1969, the annual Gallup Poll of the Public's Attitudes toward the Public Schools has found school discipline to be the public's primary educational concern on 16 of 20 occasions. From 1986 through 1988 discipline was viewed as second to drug use as the biggest problems facing the U.S. public schools.

Teachers echo the public's concern about student behavior. In a 1987 study conducted for the Center for Education Statistics, 44 percent of public school teachers reported more disruptive classroom behavior in their schools than five years earlier, and 28 percent indicated that problems were about the same. Almost one-third of teachers (29 percent) stated that they had seriously considered leaving teaching because of student misbehavior, and teachers estimated that about 7 percent of their students were habitual behavior problems. Not surprisingly, 27 percent of teachers stated that student behavior greatly interfered with effective teaching. In June 1989 the second Gallup Phi Delta Kappa Poll of Teachers' Attitude toward the Public Schools reported that 50 percent of the teachers surveyed rated the discipline problems in their community as "very serious" or "fairly serious" (up 1 percent from 1984). Even though 93 percent of teachers in the study reported that their school had a written discipline policy, 34 percent regarded it as too lenient, 28 percent said it was not comprehensive, and 50 percent stated that it was not applied consistently.

Every five years since 1956 the NEA has conducted research on the status of the public school teacher in the United States. The most recent poll reports that from 1966 to the present time, discipline problems and negative attitudes of students have ranked second or third as the factor that hindered them in providing the best service to students. Therefore, it is not surprising that a study on problems listed by beginning teachers shows classroom discipline first, followed by problems with motivating students (Veenman, 1984).

These findings also are no surprise, considering the amount of time teachers are involved in managing students' behavior. Gump (1967) reported that approximately half of teachers' actions involved instruction. The remainder of teachers' behavior involved such management functions as organizing and arranging students for instruction (23 percent), dealing with misbehavior (14 percent), and handling individual problems (12 percent). A study (Wragg, 1984) of 36 British teachers observed during 213 lesson hours in classes of mixed ability found that 54 percent of teachers' behavior involved management functions. Doyle (1986) presents an impressive review of research indicating the interdependence of management and instruction functions. Simply stated, students' learning is directly related to classroom order.

The Regular Education Initiative, which focuses on increasing the extent to which handicapped students are educated in regular classrooms, requires that teachers improve their classroom management skills. Research indicates that teachers spend significantly more time instructing and managing these special students and have between 60 percent and 90 percent more interactions with them than with students not identified under the law (Thompson, White, & Morgan, 1982).

Also, the increasing number of at-risk students attending school places a premium on teachers with effective classroom management skills. A recent study conducted by the University of Washington School of Medicine (Trupin et al., 1987) reported that nearly

7 percent of the children in Washington (state) public schools may be seriously emotionally disturbed. Most of these children receive little or no treatment for their problems, and at times their behaviors create serious problems for teachers. In order to work effectively with groups of children and to find professional fulfillment in their jobs, teachers increasingly need skills in helping children to develop positive and supportive peer relationships in classrooms, in establishing behavior and academic norms supportive of on-task behavior and achievement, in motivating students to learn, and in responding effectively to disruptive behavior.

School administrators share teachers' and parents' concerns. In a 1986 survey conducted by the Center for Statistics, U.S. Department of Education, two-thirds of the junior and senior high school principals stated that even though school discipline was less of a problem than five years ago, it was still a major problem, and 12 percent stated that discipline problems in their schools were worse. Administrators also reported suspending an average of 10 students out of every 100 each year for disciplinary reasons. Principals reported a similarly high rate for students being placed in in-school alternatives to suspension. In summarizing the current data on school discipline problems, Moles (1987) states:

> The main conclusion remains. There has been no progressive worsening of school crime during the 70s and 80s according to these national data on student and teacher victimization. What increases there were occurred in the late 1970s in attacks on teachers and damage to their personal property. For theft and all other offenses against students, crimes in schools as reported by the victims remained essentially level or declined in the 1970s and 80s. (p. 26)

Even though violent student misbehavior was the focus of concern during the 1970s and continues to be an important issue, students' achievement became the focus during the 1980s. Studies such as *A Nation at Risk: The Report of the National Commission on Excellence in Education* and John Goodlad's *A Place Called School* (1984) aroused public concern about the quality of education in the United States. Consequently, classroom management has increasingly been seen as vital because of its relationship to students' learning.

Regardless of whether disruptive behavior or low achievement troubles us most, students' attendance and the number of students who fail to graduate provide additional cause for alarm. A 1986 longitudinal study of U.S. high school students conducted by the National Center for Educational Statistics indicated that 25 percent of students drop out of school before graduation. Dropout rates vary dramatically according to students' racial or ethnic group and geographic location. Dropout rates are 42 percent for American Indians, 40 percent for Hispanic students, 25 percent for blacks, 14 percent for whites, and 10 percent for Asian and Pacific Island students. Dropout rates in East Los Angeles are 60 percent, and 50 percent of students in Boston and 45 percent of students in Washington, D.C., drop out of school. More than 35 percent of students drop out of school in 10 states; 10 other states have fewer than 20 percent of students drop out. Additionally, on any given day, 1 in 12 students is absent from school; this figure is nearly 1 in 5 in some large cities. In a study of 56 schools, Gottfredson (1983) found that 31 percent of black male students had been suspended at least once during the previous term.

Obviously it is insufficient merely to document the severity of student behavior problems. Educators must understand why these problems arise. The two basic reasons classroom management continues to be a major problem in our schools are these: First, teachers are asked to instruct a wide range of students, many of whom come to school with varying degrees of emotional distress and inadequate personal skills. Second, despite significant research and the associated dramatic increase in methods for effectively motivating and managing students, many teachers have received only a limited amount of useful information about how to organize and manage classrooms effectively in order to maximize productive student learning and behavior. The following sections examine why student behavior continues to be a major problem in U.S. schools and presents a conceptual framework for understanding the steps that can be taken to reduce the problem dramatically.

SOCIAL FACTORS INFLUENCING STUDENTS' BEHAVIOR

Although teachers cannot immediately or directly alter the social factors that create students' problems, understanding them does enable teachers to place students' failure and disruptive behavior in perspective and to create environments that reduce rather than intensify their effects. When discussing the problem of disruptive or disturbed student behavior, teachers often ask why these problems seem to have increased during the past decade. Indeed, as education and psychology have developed an increasingly sophisticated body of knowledge, teachers have entered the classroom better trained than before. There is little question that today's teachers better understand such topics as human development and the learning process than did teachers 10 years ago. Therefore, although unproductive student behavior is often a response to factors within schools and classrooms, it seems reasonable to assume that today's school environments are, in general, more supportive of students' needs and more conducive to learning than they were 10 or 20 years ago. Consequently, though improving teachers' skills remains a major component in combating unproductive student behavior, other variables must be considered in order to develop a comprehensive understanding of the intensified problems of classroom discipline.

More than 40 percent of today's schoolchildren will live in a single-parent family by the time they reach age 18. Fourteen percent of students in U.S. schools were born to unmarried parents, 30 percent are latchkey children, 20 percent live in poverty, 15 percent speak a native language other than English, 700,000 schoolchildren are homeless, and 15 percent have physical or mental handicaps. "The United States has the highest child poverty rate of eight major industrialized countries . . . and the Child Welfare League of America reports over 2 ¼ million abused or neglected children" (Somans, 1988, p. 2). Only 7 percent of today's schoolchildren live in families that were considered typical 25 years ago: two-parent families with one working parent.

The lack of a stable family creates stress for children and makes them less able to cope effectively with the academic and social demands of a school setting. During the past decade, runaways have doubled from 1 to 2 million youth and suicides in the United States are 8 times those of Japan. In addition, even homes that may look like safe, prosperous, nurturing environments often create stress for children as working parents expect children to take on major family responsibilities without adult supervision and encourage children to become involved in numerous out-of-school activities. Indeed, studies indicate that young people who commit suicide are often high achievers unable to handle the stress of fast-paced lives and high expectations for achievement in multiple tasks.

Students' increased use of drug and alcohol is certainly partially a response to the increasingly stressful lives they live, and substance abuse is another social factor that reduces the time, energy, and ability of students to attend to academic tasks. In the United States, 56 million people report family trouble related to alcoholism (Gress, 1988), and schools are increasingly asked to identify students at risk because of substance abuse.

> Children are beginning alcohol use at an early age: the average beginning age is 12.5. . . . One-half of high school students are classified as regular drinkers; one of three drinks heavily at least once a week; one of four students in high school has a serious drinking problem; approximately four million youth under the age of 17 are alcoholics. . . . Some 80 percent of high school seniors have used marijuana, and two-thirds of American children will have used an illicit drug other than marijuana and alcohol before they graduate from high school. (Horton, 1988, p. 5)

According to the University of Michigan's Institute for Social Research, youth in the United States have the highest rate of drug use of any industrialized nation. More than 57 percent of seniors graduating in 1988 stated that they had tried an illegal drug, and more than one-third stated they had tried an illegal drug other than marijuana.

Given these figures, it is perhaps not surprising that the twentieth Annual Gallup Poll on the Public's Attitudes toward the Public Schools (Gallup & Elam, 1988) reported that when asked to identify the biggest problems facing local schools, 32 percent of those interviewed said "use of drugs by students." The 1988 poll was the third consecutive year in which the public rated drug use first and discipline second as the biggest problems in U.S. schools.

Student drug use illustrates the importance of considering both social and school variables as factors influencing student behavior and learning. Certainly, educators are not solely or even primarily responsible for this problem that affects them so profoundly. Conversely, schools often provide learning environments that fail to engage a large segment of students actively and meaningfully. This situation possibly increases the likelihood that students will abuse substances during school hours and will choose substance abuse rather than involvement in school-based activities.

SCHOOL FACTORS INFLUENCING STUDENTS' LEARNING AND BEHAVIOR

Even while social factors have made the teacher's job more difficult, recent studies indicate that teachers and schools make a dramatic difference in the lives of many children. The extent to which students learn academic material, how they feel about themselves as learners, and how responsibly they behave are significantly influenced by what happens in schools. *Teachers have control over many factors that significantly influence the achievement and behavior of students.* Schools and teachers working with similar student populations differ dramatically in their ability to help students develop desirable behavior and increase students' achievement. Mortimore and Sammons (1987) summarize their extensive research on factors that influence students' academic and social gains:

> In our measurement of reading progress, we found the school to be about six times more important than backgrounds (factors of age, sex, social class, and race). For written math and

writing, the difference is tenfold. The analyses of speech and of the social outcomes also confirm the overriding importance of school. . . . It is the policies and processes within the control of the principal and teachers that are crucial. These factors can be changed and improved. (p. 6)

This finding is similar in many ways to that reported by William Wayson and Gay Su Pinnell (1982) following their studies of schools varying in amounts of discipline problems experienced:

> When discipline problems occur in school, they can more often be traced to dysfunctions in the interpersonal climate and organizational patterns of the school than to malfunctions in the individual. In short, misbehaving students are often reacting in a predictable and even sensible way to the school as it affects them and as they have learned to perceive it and react to it. We are not blaming the teacher, the principal, or the custodian for student misbehavior. But we would have them see that the system of roles and relationships in which they engage are often to blame for misbehavior. In most cases, better behavior may be taught more easily by altering patterns of roles and relationships in the school organization than by viewing and treating the student as a pathological problem. (p. 117)

These sentiments have recently been highlighted by such noted writers and researchers as Elliot Eisner (1988), William Glasser (1988), John Goodlad (in Goodlad & Oakes, 1988), and Ted Sizer (1988). To make significant changes in student learning and behavior, we must seriously look at a broad range of variables in the school setting and embrace opportunities for changing our teaching behavior and how schools are structured.

Findings from several major national studies place this matter in an interesting perspective. In his book *A Place Called School*, John Goodlad (1984) provides strong support for the necessity of viewing student behavior problems as more than a response to poorly controlled classrooms. In summarizing the findings, Goodlad (1983a) states that the students

> scarcely ever speculated on meanings, discussed alternative interpretations or engaged in projects calling for collaborative effort. Most of the time they listened or worked alone. The topics of the curriculum, it appears to me, were something to be acquired, not something to be explored, reckoned with, and converted into personal meaning and development. (p. 468)

In another summary of the study, Goodlad (1983b) stresses the two major problems associated with instructional practices that fail to emphasize varied learning goals and instructional strategies.

> The dominant instructional practices we observed in more than 1,000 classrooms (and which most staff development programs emphasize) appear to provide few opportunities for students to engage in the behaviors implied by the more exalted academic purposes of education, to say nothing of those other goals of citizenship, civility, and creativity to which state documents claim commitment. . . . (p. 553)
>
> Being a spectator not only deprives one of participation, but also leaves one's mind free for unrelated activity. If academic learning does not engage students, something else will. (p. 554)

Additional observational studies have confirmed Goodlad's findings. In *Horace's Compromise,* Ted Sizer (1984) states, "No more important finding has emerged from the inquiries of our study than that the American high school student, as student, is all too often docile, compliant, and without initiative" (p. 54). This sentiment is reinforced by Ernest Boyer (1983) in his *High School: A Report on Secondary Education in America* and also by Joan Lipsitz's (1984) study of effective middle schools, presented in her *Successful Schools for Young Adolescents.*

Walter Doyle's (1983) examination of academic work suggests that teachers often select methods of instruction that, while focusing on rote learning, are easily managed in terms of maintaining control. Also, some teachers handle the problem of classroom control by excluding students of lower ability from active participation in classroom activities or by reinforcing incorrect answers by these students in order to maintain a smooth classroom flow. A comprehensive, realistic examination of students' behavior must consider not only methods of classroom organization and management that increase students' attending behavior and basic skill acquisition, but also instructional factors that provide students with a sense of meaningful involvement in the school and community as well as encouraging thoughtful and creative examination of issues presented in a meaningful, dynamic curriculum.

Students' attitudes toward school are another strong indication that school factors contribute greatly to students' academic and behavior problems. When Jane Norman and Myron Harris (1981) surveyed 160,000 teenagers for their book *The Private Life of the American Teenager,* they discovered that only 42 percent of the students described school as "necessary," 21 percent found it "interesting," and 27 percent said school was "boring." Additionally, 60 percent of the students said they studied primarily to pass tests rather than to learn. Another study conducted by the National Center for Educational Statistics reported that more than half of the high school seniors sampled found their part-time jobs more enjoyable than school. When John Goodlad (1983a) asked students to identify the best thing about school, 34.9 percent said "friends," 13.4 percent said "sports," 7 percent said "classes," 4.1 percent said "teachers," and 8 percent said "nothing." Given these findings, we should not be surprised that more than 55 percent of teenagers state they cheat in school (Norman & Harris, 1981).

CLASSROOM MANAGEMENT: AN HISTORICAL PERSPECTIVE

Because approaches to classroom management have changed so dramatically since 1975, teachers have been bombarded with a wide range of methods for responding to unproductive student behavior. However, due to the newness of research and prescription in the area of classroom management, most teachers have received relatively poor training. Brophy and Rohrkemper (1981) observed and interviewed 44 teachers from inner-city schools in a large metropolitan school district and 54 teachers in a small city. Most of the teachers had 10 or more years of experience, and half were nominated by their principals as outstanding in working with problem students. The researchers found that few of the teachers had any preservice or inservice training in classroom management. The study also reported that few of the teachers (including those rated most effective) had a clear, consistent philosophy or understanding of how to manage their classrooms. Instead, they tended to rely on an unsystematic bag-of-tricks approach developed through experience.

Because teachers have been presented with numerous competing and sometimes conflicting methods, they are not likely to develop a thoughtful, well-articulated, and effective classroom management system unless they can develop a perspective on the various methods and use this as a basis for developing their own philosophy and practice. To help the reader develop a professionally accurate and useful perspective, the following section describes four classroom management concepts and methods presented to teachers during the past three decades.

The Counseling Approach

During the 1960s and through much of the 1970s, the emphasis in dealing with student behavior was on discipline. The little training teachers received focused on what to do after students misbehaved. Because the emphasis in psychology during the late 1960s and early 1970s was on personal growth and awareness, most methods focused on understanding students' problems and helping them better understand themselves and work cooperatively with adults to develop more productive behaviors.

One of the earliest and most widely used models was William Glasser's Reality Therapy (1965). Glasser's model derived from the belief that young people need caring professionals willing to help them take responsibility for their behavior and develop plans aimed at altering unproductive conduct. Rudolf Dreikurs and his associates (1971) developed a somewhat more clinical model based on the belief that acting-out children were making poor choices because of inappropriate notions of how to meet their basic need to be accepted. Dreikurs proposed a variety of methods for responding to children's misconduct, depending on the goal of the behavior. His model provided teachers and parents with strategies for identifying the causes of students' misbehavior, responding to misbehavior with logical consequences, and running family and classroom meetings.

Emphasis on humanistic psychology was most obvious in the models of self-concept theorists. Initially summarized by LaBenne and Green (1969) and Purkey (1970), this work focused on the relationships among positive student self-concepts, students' learning, and productive behavior. This work was extended to a more practical program for teachers by Tom Gordon (1974), whose *Teacher Effectiveness Training* provided them with techniques for responding to students' misbehavior with open communication and attempts at mutually solving problems.

Behavioristic Methods

As social uneasiness rose about disruptive behavior of youth, the focus of classroom discipline moved in the direction of teacher control. This increased attention to discipline was associated with the development and popularization of behavioristic methodology. Beginning in the mid-1970s, most courses aimed at helping teachers cope with disruptive student behavior focused almost exclusively on behavior-modification techniques. Teachers were taught to ignore inappropriate behavior while reinforcing appropriate behavior, to write contracts with recalcitrant students, and to use time-out procedures. This emphasis on control was most systematically presented to teachers in Lee Canter's (1976) *Assertive*

Discipline. Teachers learned to state clear general behavioral expectations, quietly and consistently to punish disruptive students, and to provide group reinforcement for on-task behavior.

Teacher-Effectiveness Research

While counseling and control-oriented approaches vied for popularity, a new emphasis on classroom management was developing during the 1970s. This new direction emphasized not what teachers did in response to student misconduct, but rather how teachers prevented or contributed to students' misbehavior. This research, later labeled *teacher effectiveness,* has focused attention on three sets of teacher behaviors that influence students' behavior and learning: (1) teachers' skill in organizing and managing classroom activities, (2) teachers' skills in presenting instructional material, and (3) teacher-student relationships.

Teachers' Organizational and Management Skills
A study that initially displayed the importance of teachers' organizational and management skills was reported in Jacob Kounin's 1970 book, *Discipline and Group Management in Classrooms.* Kounin and his colleagues videotaped thousands of hours in classrooms that ran smoothly with a minimum of disruptive behavior and classrooms in which students were frequently inattentive and disruptive. The videotapes were then systematically analyzed to determine what teachers in these two very different types of classrooms did differently when students misbehaved. The results showed no systematic differences. Effective classroom managers were not notably different from poor classroom managers in their ways of responding to students' misbehavior. Further analysis, however, demonstrated clear and significant differences between how effective and ineffective classroom managers behaved prior to students' misbehavior. Effective classroom managers used various teaching methods that prevented disruptive student behavior.

The Texas Teacher Effectiveness Study was a second landmark study dealing with organizing and managing behavior. In this study, reported in *Learning from Teaching* by Jere Brophy and Carolyn Evertson (1976), the researchers observed 59 teachers over 2 years. Teachers were selected to provide two groups whose students differed consistently in performance on standardized achievement tests. Classroom observations focused on teachers' behaviors previously suggested as being related to effective teaching. The results of the study supported Kounin's findings on effective behaviors that prevented disruption and facilitated learning by creating smoothly run classrooms.

The findings of Kounin and Brophy and Evertson were expanded by Emmer, Evertson, and Anderson (1980) in the Classroom Organization and Effective Teaching Project carried out at the Research and Development Center for Teacher Education at the University of Texas at Austin. In the first of a series of studies, these researchers observed 28 third-grade classrooms during the first several weeks of school. The research findings showed that the smooth functioning found in effective teachers' classrooms throughout the school year mostly resulted from effective planning and organization during the first few weeks of school. Effective classroom managers provided students with clear instruction in desirable classroom behavior and carefully monitored students' performance—reteaching behaviors that students had not mastered. Effective teachers also made consequences for misbehavior clear and applied these consistently. This study was followed by research in junior high school classrooms (Evertson, 1985; Evertson & Emmer, 1982a) that verified the importance that early planning and instruction in appropriate behavior have in secondary school settings.

Instructional Skills

A second area of investigation on teachers' behavior that prevents disruptive student behavior and enhances learning examines how material is presented to students. The earliest and most lasting work on this subject has been conducted by Madeline Hunter. For nearly two decades her ITIP (Instructional Theory into Practice) program has attempted to translate findings in educational psychology into practical strategies that improve instruction. Though her work emphasizes some of the skills pointed out by researchers interested in classroom organization and teacher-student relationships, her major contribution is in helping teachers understand the need to develop clear instructional goals, state these to students, provide effective direct instruction, and monitor students' progress.

This research has been expanded by studies that have examined the relationship between various teacher instructional patterns and students' achievement. These studies, often called *process-product research* because they examine correlations between instructional processes and student outcomes or products, are thoughtfully reviewed by Rosenshine (1983) and Good (1983). The third edition of the *Handbook of Research on Teaching* (Wittcock, 1986) contains an excellent series of chapters on this topic. Criticism of this line of research has focused on the fact that no one behavior group or group of behaviors of teachers is related to students' achievement with all ages and types of students and for all learning outcomes. Subsequently, some writers (Darling-Hammond, Wise, & Pease, 1983; Doyle, 1979; Soar & Soar, 1986; Zumwalt, 1982) warn against placing too much emphasis on specific teacher skills. These writers suggest that although teachers should be familiar with the results of process-product research, they must use these findings selectively, taking into account the unique characteristics of the students with whom they work and the educational goals they espouse.

A second field of study examines the relative merits of competitive, cooperative, and individualized instruction. This work, carried out by Roger and David Johnson of the University of Minnesota, demonstrates that cooperative learning activities are associated with many desirable learning outcomes. Students who work cooperatively on learning tasks tend to relate more positively to their peers, to view learning as more positive, and to learn more information (Johnson & Johnson, 1983, 1987). Additional work in cooperative team learning was carried out by Slavin (1983a, 1983b, 1987, 1988), who developed the Teams-Games-Tournaments approach, and by Sharan (1980, 1987) and Sharan and Sharan (1987).

Another area of study is the variability in how students learn best and how teachers can adjust instruction to respond to students' individual learning styles. This work, carried out by Rita Dunn (Dunn, 1983, 1989; Dunn & Dunn, 1978), Joseph Renzulli (1983), Anthony Gregorc (1982), and others shows that when teachers allow students to study in environments conducive to learning and use approaches to learning that are most productive for each student, the students learn much more effectively and behave appropriately. In their *Models of Teaching,* Bruce Joyce and Marsha Weil describe many types of instructional methods that respond to different learning goals and students' learning styles. Joyce and Weil (1986) write that despite the fearsome troubles besetting education, there presently exists a really delightful and vigorous array of approaches to teaching that can be used to transform the world of schools if only we could employ them.

We believe that strength in education resides in the intelligent use of this powerful variety of approaches—matching them to different goals and adapting them to the students' styles and characteristics. Competence in teaching stems from the capacity to reach out to differing children and to create a rich and multi-dimensional environment for them. (p. xxiii)

Teacher-Student Relationships

The third major research area within the teacher-effectiveness paradigm focuses on the effect teacher-student interactions have on students' achievement and behavior. This field of study can be divided into two basic parts: (1) studies exploring the influence of the frequency and quality of teacher-student interactions on students' achievement, and (2) studies emphasizing the personal, affective dimension of teacher-student relationships and their effect on students' attitudes and, to a lessor degree, achievement.

Robert Rosenthal and Leonore Jacobson's *Pygmalion in the Classroom* (1968) generated tremendous interest in the influence teacher-student relationships have on students' achievement. These authors report that teachers' expectations for students' performance became self-fulfilling prophecies. In other words, students seem to perform as teachers expect them to. The important question became what specifically teachers do to communicate high or low expectations to students. This question was initially studied by Brophy and Good (1971, 1974) at the University of Texas. This research has been replicated and expanded (Wineburg, 1987), including examination of attribution theory and factors related to teachers' sense of control (Cooper & Good, 1983).

The second area of study involves the affective quality of teacher-student relationships and its effect on students' attitudes and self-concepts. This research was first widely reported in the late 1960s and early 1970s in books such as LaBenne and Green's *Educational Implications of Self-Concept Theory* (1969) and William Purkey's *Self Concept and School Achievement* (1970). Although interpersonal relationships in the classroom were emphasized less during the mid-1970s, research and practical ideas on this subject received more attention in the early 1980s (Purkey & Novak, 1984).

Studies building on those cited demonstrate that when teachers are provided information about skills associated with effective teaching and receive feedback on how their behavior in the classroom matches criteria for effective teaching, they can become much more effective teachers (Good & Grouws, 1979; Fitzpatrick, 1982; Sanford, Emmer, & Clements, 1983; Showers, Joyce, & Bennett, 1987; Stallings, 1983).

TEACHER TRAINING IN CLASSROOM MANAGEMENT

The wide variety of approaches to classroom management has created a situation in which training in classroom management often involves both introducing teachers to theoretical approaches to classroom discipline (Charles, 1989; Duke & Meckel, 1984; Wolfgang & Glickman, 1986) and providing tips on how to implement these approaches in a classroom. There are, however, several major problems with this method. First, little research evidence supports such models as assertive discipline, teacher effectiveness training, Adlerian-based approaches, or even reality therapy. In a recent review of the research on several leading approaches to classroom discipline, Emmer and Aussiker (1987) reported that "results of the review provide only limited support for teacher training in the models" (p. i). Second, because these methods provide teachers with responses to student misconduct but do not deal with preventing behavior problems or increasing student motivation and learning, they are only a small aspect of effective classroom management.

Methods that focus on isolated models emphasizing responding to disruptive behavior seem to suggest that unproductive student behavior is inevitable. This orientation tends to suggest a limited view of teachers' options in altering classroom environments to increase positive student behavior and learning. In summarizing their findings on popular models of discipline, Emmer and Aussiker (1987) state, "It is concluded that training in one or more of these models should be viewed as supplemental to a more comprehensive approach to discipline and management" (p. i.).

Another approach to training teachers in classroom management focuses on providing a limited number of specific methods supported by substantive research. Unfortunately, in our opinion, this training is deceptive because it provides teachers with only a piece of a complex yet manageable puzzle. Teachers need more than simple prescriptions. They need to understand the complexity of effectively managing and instructing students and to be prepared to make important decisions based on a thorough understanding of the professional knowledge available in the 1990s.

Recent research indicates that the most effective method of responding to disruptive student behavior involves combining preventive classroom management and instructional approaches with corrective methods. A major research project conducted at the Center for Social Welfare Research at the School of Social Work, University of Washington (Hawkins, Doueck, & Lishner, 1988), provides support for a comprehensive approach to classroom management. The project was designed to determine methods to improve the behavior and increase the achievement of low achievers at risk for serious and extended behavioral problems. The project involved providing teachers working with high at-risk seventh-grade students with an in-service package involving proactive classroom management methods, interactive teaching, and cooperative learning. Student attitudes, behavior, and achievement in these classes were compared to those of students taught by teachers who did not receive the training. Results indicated that low-achieving, at-risk students in the experimental classrooms had more positive attitudes toward subject matter, felt more involved in school, had greater expectations for continued school success, and had less serious misbehavior than did students in the control group. This research supports a comprehensive approach to classroom management in which the teacher uses methods to improve peer relationships, instruction, and classroom organization and management.

Research from the Institute for Research on Teaching at Michigan State University indicates that the more effective teachers accept responsibility for student learning and behavior rather than blaming students. These teachers examine their instruction to determine whether students understand and find meaning in their work. They also view aggressive student behavior not as an unmanageable psychological problem but as a behavioral problem requiring resocialization and skill training to help the student learn alternative methods for dealing with stressful or conflicting situations.

COMPREHENSIVE CLASSROOM MANAGEMENT: AN ALTERNATIVE FOR THE 1990S

As we discuss in the previous section, researchers and writers have approached student behavior problems from a variety of perspectives. Figure 1.1 highlights the key approaches to managing student behavior and the writers associated with each approach. The research conducted and the methods suggested by these educators have contributed much to teachers' ability to manage classrooms effectively.

Unfortunately, because schools of education are constricted in the hours available for education courses and because school districts have limited resources, both preservice and inservice education concerning classroom management too often focus on the work of one or two or these educators or provide a theoretical review of several individuals' work. In many preservice education programs, classroom management is presented as a brief unit in a methods or educational psychology class. Inservice presentations on the topic also are often scheduled for only a few hours, thus requiring consultants to teach a few tricks or only one aspect of classroom management, as if they were presenting the answer to teachers' problems. This approach leaves teachers with only a piece of a complex and critical puzzle. When these limited techniques fail to help teachers significantly, the teachers must assume that something is wrong with either themselves or their use of the new methods or that no one really knows how teachers can manage classrooms effectively. The results frequently are confusion, frustration, and ineffectiveness in managing classrooms and individual students' behavior.

Research on staff development suggests that to implement new material into their classrooms, teachers need both a solid theoretical understanding of the material and practice in specific methods or strategies. Therefore, it is extremely important that before attempting to develop or improve your classroom management skills, you have a clear understanding of their scope. Extensive reviews of the research (Brophy, 1983, 1986c; Doyle, 1986; and Jones, 1982, 1989) and our own experience in classrooms and schools suggest five major factors or skill areas associated with effective classroom management.

First, *classroom management should be based on solid understanding of current research and theory in classroom management and on students' personal and psychological needs.* Our experience in teaching classroom-management courses and consulting with schools suggests that, despite extensive worry about students' achievement and misbehavior, very few teachers understand why problems exist or the relationship between the problem and their own professional behavior. An analysis of data from the 1984 Gallup Poll of Teachers' Attitudes toward the Public Schools shows that

> teachers blame disciplinary problems on outside influences—specifically, the courts, lack of respect for authority, and especially lack of discipline in the home, which is mentioned by virtually all teachers (94 percent). Only about one-third of the teachers feel that teachers themselves are at fault. (Gallup, 1984, p. 99)

Once teachers understand students' needs and how these needs are related to behavior, the next step in developing a well-managed classroom is to use teaching methods that enhance learning and positive behavior by ensuring that students' personal needs are met in the classroom. Therefore, a second factor is, *classroom management depends on establishing positive teacher-student and peer relationships that help meet students' basic*

FIGURE 1.1 Continuum of Classroom Management Strategies

Chapters 3, 4, 5	Chapters 8, 9	Chapters 6, 7	Chapter 10	Chapter 11	Chapter 12
Interpersonal relationships	Classroom organization and management	Instruction	Problem solving	Behavioristic	School-wide discipline
Jack Canfield & Harold Wells	Jere Brophy	Walter Doyle	Rudolf Dreikurs	Wesley Becker	Lee Canter
Thomas Gordon	Edmond Emmer	Rita Dunn	William Glasser	Lee Canter	Daniel Duke
William Purkey	Carolyn Evertson	Thomas Good	Thomas Gordon	Frank Hewett	William Glasser
Richard & Patricia Schmuck	Thomas Good	Madeline Hunter	Frank Maple	Daniel O'Leary	William Wayson
	Madeline Hunter	David & Roger Johnson	Robert Spaulding	Hill Walker	
	Jacob Kounin	Bruce Joyce			
	Jane Stallings	Bernice McCarthy			
		Robert Slavin			
		Jane Stallings			

psychological needs. Creating more desirable student behavior by concentrating on establishing positive, supportive classroom environments is based on a concept presented by numerous psychologists and educators: Individuals learn more effectively in environments that meet their basic personal and psychological needs.

Although the creation of positive relationships in classrooms can significantly improve student behavior and achievement, research and our own observations increasingly support the importance of instructional excellence. Thus, the third factor in effective classroom management is, *comprehensive classroom management involves using instructional methods that facilitate optimal learning by responding to the academic needs of individual students and the classroom group.* This aspect of classroom management is based on the idea that

> low motivation, negative self attitudes, and failure are largely the result of improper learning conditions. According to this learning-theory analysis, we should be able to alter a student's failure rate by changing the conditions of classroom learning and, as a consequence, increase his motivation to succeed. (Covington & Beery, 1976, pp. 12, 13)

Most classrooms house 25 to 35 students. Teachers are responsible for orchestrating the movement, attention, and learning of varied students in a limited space. Therefore, regardless of how well a teacher understands students' needs, creates a positive emotional climate, and effectively provides instruction, organizational skills are critical. Consequently, the fourth factor is, *comprehensive classroom management involves using organizational and group management methods that maximize on-task student behavior.* Order and control should not, of course, be viewed as the ultimate goal of effective classroom management, yet they are important means to the end of enhancing students' academic interest and achievement. Teachers' organizational and instructional skills interact to influence students' achievement. Kounin (1970) reported that student task involvement ranged from 98.7 percent for the most successful teacher in his sample to 25 percent for the least effective. Numerous additional studies emphasize the relationship between on-task behavior and achievement. Therefore, though teachers must consider providing variety and choice in instructional tasks (Soar, 1983), it is desirable to emphasize strong control in the form of desired student behavior. Doyle (1986) summarizes this relationship between behavior control and instruction:

> The data reviewed in this chapter suggest, however, that the solution to the tension between management and instruction may require a greater emphasis on management. In other words, solving the instructional problems of low ability students cannot be done by de-emphasizing management or by designing more complex instructional arrangements for the classroom. Indeed, such "solutions" are likely to increase the problems they are designed to rectify. A more appropriate answer to the problem would seem to involve improved knowledge and training in management so that teachers can be free to concentrate on instructional solutions to learning problems. (p. 418)

Studies have indicated that decisions teachers make in an effort to maintain order significantly affect the type and quality of academic work and therefore the quality of students' achievement (Buike, 1981; Doyle, 1983; Duffy & McIntyre, 1982). Specifically, teachers often select lecture material and seatwork focusing on rote learning because these classroom activities are more easily managed. Goodlad (1983a) highlights this relationship between order and instruction:

> Our data reveal that the teachers we studied were aware of the desirability of having students participate in setting their goals, making choices, solving problems, working cooperatively with peers, and so on. But these views were tempered by conflicting ones having largely to do with maintaining control. Those time-honored practices that appeared to help maintain control won out. (pp. 469, 470)

Because of this emphasis on the preventive, instructional aspects of classroom management, a significant portion of this book focuses on strategies for creating positive learning environments and using instructional methods that respond effectively to students' needs. Although it is difficult to calculate how much inappropriate classroom behavior can be reduced by using such methods, 75 percent may be a conservative estimate. Employing effective organizational and instructional methods and creating a positive classroom environment will reduce minor classroom disruptions, which not only creates a better learning environment, but also assists teachers in identifying students with severe problems and provides more time for working with these students. Finally, unless teachers use effective teaching methods, more direct behavior-change interventions will have limited long-term effectiveness.

The creation of positive, supportive classroom environments characterized by effective teaching skills will go a long way toward reducing behavior problems and increasing students' achievement. Anyone who has taught or worked with behavior-problem children is aware, however, that some children will, at least for a time, behave inappropriately in even the most productive learning environments. Consequently, teachers need a repertoire of problem-solving skills to support their instructional skills. The final factor in management is, *classroom management involves the ability to use a wide range of counseling and behavioral methods that involve students in examining and correcting their inappropriate behavior.*

Many teachers will say that they do not have the time to use in-depth counseling strategies; we believe this statement is generally accurate and realistic. Teachers cannot be expected to administer sophisticated psychological diagnostic instruments or use in-depth counseling strategies within the classroom. On the other hand, many relatively simple yet effective approaches are available for helping children examine and change their behaviors. Because, as we have seen, teachers are increasingly faced with the task of teaching children who require special assistance, it has become necessary that teachers acquire problem-solving and behavior-management techniques.

These five basic factors and their relationships to the chapter organization of this book are depicted in Figure 1.2. Even though teachers will want to examine methods associated with each factor, changes aimed at creating more positive student behavior should proceed in the hierarchic order suggested in Figure 1.2. When faced with problems concerning students' classroom behavior, teachers too often begin to intervene at the upper end of the hierarchy without laying a foundation by developing prerequisite knowledge and using preventive interventions. When they do, interventions will, at best, cause a limited, short-term improvement in students' behavior and may create greater student resentment and alienation.

As indicated by the topics listed in Figure 1.2, this book is designed to offer a comprehensive and hierarchic presentation of classroom management. Considerable sup-

FIGURE 1.2 Skills the Teacher Needs to Develop Comprehensive Classroom Management

Correction	*Factor 5*	
(Chapters 10–12)	Helping students evaluate and correct unproductive behavior	Schoolwide student management programs Implementing behavioristic techniques Using problem-solving methods
Prevention	*Factor 4*	
(Chapters 3–9)	Organization and management (Chapters 8, 9)	Beginning the school year Implementing methods that maximize on-task student behavior
	Factor 3 Motivation and instruction (Chapters 6, 7)	Incorporating teaching methods that motivate students by responding to their learning needs
	Factor 2 Interpersonal relationships (Chapters 3–5)	Working with parents Creating positive peer relationships Establishing positive teacher-student relationships
Theoretical Foundation	*Factor 1*	
(Chapters 1, 2)	Developing a sound theoretical foundation	Understanding classroom management Understanding students' personal needs

port exists for this approach (Doyle, 1986; Emmer & Aussiker, 1987; Jones, 1986). This approach also has been supported by previously mentioned work at the Center for Social Welfare Research at the School of Social Work, University of Washington, and at the Institute for Research on Teaching at Michigan State University. In addition, studies conducted by the National Center for the Study of Corporal Punishment and Alternatives in the Schools (Hyman & D'Alessandro, 1984) to examine effective programs for training teachers to discipline students verify the importance of the skills described in this book. Their analysis of effective programs gives seven general techniques for motivating students and helping them deal with discipline problems:

1. Providing feedback to students about their behaviors, feelings, and ideas;
2. Using diagnostic strategies to better understand students and student-teacher interactions;

3. Modifying the classroom climate;
4. Applying techniques of behavior modification;
5. Using democratic procedures for solving classroom problems;
6. Expressing emotions appropriately; and
7. Using therapeutic approaches to behavioral problems (p. 43).

PLACING CLASSROOM MANAGEMENT IN PERSPECTIVE

A discussion of classroom management is not complete without recognizing teachers' limitations in dealing with disruptive student behavior. When unproductive student behavior is a response to lack of appropriate instructional materials, negative classroom environment, lack of peer support, or temporary crisis in a child's life, changes in the classroom environment will often immediately and significantly change students' behavior. Unfortunately, in a few children, unproductive behaviors are an indication of serious personality disorders that cannot be immediately altered by changes in environment or limited counseling intervention. When working with these children, we must place our interventions in proper perspective to avoid becoming discouraged. It is important to do everything possible to provide a positive learning environment and to help such children control their behavior. Realize, however, that even psychotherapists are not always able to help children who display severe behavior disorders. Similarly, residential treatment centers are often only modestly successful in working with such children.

The Curriculum of Responsibility

The concept of a curriculum of responsibility (Figure 1.3) has helped many teachers place classroom management and instruction in its proper perspective. This concept suggests that both teachers and students have major responsibilities within the school environment. Teachers are responsible for creating positive, supportive, clearly structured learning environments. Students cannot be expected to respond responsibly in a confusing, arbitrary, irresponsible environment. However, when teachers have met this responsibility, they have the right to expect students to behave responsibly within this environment.

Teachers' Responsibilities
First, teachers are responsible for ensuring that students feel accepted and supported rather than isolated or intimidated in the classroom. This responsibility involves creating teacher-

FIGURE 1.3 Curriculum of Responsibility

Relationships		
Knowledge		
Limits	}	Educators' Responsibility
Options		
Choices	}	Students' Responsibility
Consequences		

student and peer relationships that are positive and supportive for all students. Second, teachers are responsible for ensuring that students understand the school environment. Students need to know how the classroom will operate (classroom procedures) and why these procedures exist. Students need to know the specific expectations each teacher has for student behavior. For example, some teachers feel strongly about students talking when someone else in the room is speaking. Some teachers are particularly sensitive to what they define as inappropriate language. Students can be expected to act responsibly in settings in which they are clear about the values and expectations held by the people in charge. Students also need to understand the academic procedures, such as what will be learned, why this learning is being presented, how their work will be assessed, and why instructional decisions are made.

Third, teachers are responsible for ensuring that students know the limits within the classroom and school. Students need to know what will occur if they choose not to follow classroom and school rules and procedures.

Students also need to know the limits placed on teachers. Teachers do not determine the entire curriculum. Teachers do not have an unlimited amount of time to work with individual students, grade papers, or plan lessons. It is important that, in a positive manner, teachers discuss these limits so students can better understand teacher decisions.

Fourth, teachers are responsible for providing students with options. When students have difficulties learning or behaving responsibly, teachers need to assist them or help them obtain assistance. In the case of academic difficulties, this responsibility might involve tutorial time from the teacher or a peer, referral to another resource in the building, or modifications in the work presented to the student. For students whose home environment and/or work schedule makes it difficult to complete homework, this teacher responsibility may involve assistance in scheduling time and in finding effective places to complete work. Teachers need to help students experiencing behavioral difficulties resolve the matter through problem solving, developing new skills, or support from another peer or adult.

Within a responsible, productive environment students are responsible for the choices they make and thus for the consequences these choices elicit. Students choose whether to be productively involved in instructional activities, to attend class, to complete homework, and to follow classroom and school rules. When students make good choices, they should encounter positive consequences. When they make poor choices, they need to receive consequences that help them develop new skills and/or make better choices.

Developing Programs That Meet the Needs of Students At Risk

Like teachers, school district personnel at all levels are increasingly being asked to clarify their roles in serving students who are at-risk for school failure. The authors have spent much of the past three years developing programs for at-risk students. Our work has included actual classroom involvement with students in programs we have helped establish and extensive training of administrators and teams of teachers in methods for working with these students. Our reading of the research and extensive work with these children suggests four major areas in which school district staff can implement program development in order to meet the needs of at-risk students more effectively.

First, a major focus must be placed on improving teachers' skills in classroom management and instruction. Teaching at-risk students requires greater skills than does teaching students who come to school motivated to learn and with a majority of personal and emotional needs met. Much as physicians must constantly upgrade their skills and specialists must develop extra skills to serve their patients' unique needs, teachers working with at-risk students need to incorporate a variety of current management and instructional methods into their repertoire. Because we believe improved teacher skills are an essential and basic component of any school program for better serving at-risk students, most of this book (chapters 1 through 9) focuses on concepts and methods to assist teachers in this important task. Recent studies clearly point to the benefits to at-risk students when teachers use the methods suggested in these chapters (Firestone, 1989; Freiberg, 1989; Hamby, 1989; Hawkins, Doueck, & Lishner, 1988; Johnson & Johnson, 1987; Jones, 1986; Lehr & Harris, 1988; Leinhardt & Bickel, 1987; Madden, Slavin, Karweit, & Livermon, 1989; Slavin & Madden, 1989). It is extremely important to realize that meeting the educational needs of at-risk students does not detract from the educational experience of even the most gifted students. While at-risk students may receive the greatest benefits from the implementation of new methods described throughout this book, with very few exceptions these methods simultaneously benefit all students.

The second aspect of effective school programs for at-risk students involves how educators respond to problem behavior. As suggested in the next section, a focus on instruction and skill development rather than on control characterizes school programs that better serve the needs of at-risk students. Chapters 10 through 12 present a wide variety of methods for helping behavior-problem students learn new skills and demonstrate increased responsibility.

The third component of an effective school program consists of the special programs developed to meet the unique needs of seriously at-risk students. As discussed in chapter 12, special programs can provide important and necessary assistance for students struggling to succeed in school. It is imperative, however, that the creation of special programs not become a substitute for implementing changes in the two previously mentioned areas. Special programs must support and supplement—not replace—instructional and management changes that help at-risk students.

The fourth aspect of programs for at-risk students involves school-community communication and program coordination. Many at-risk students come from home settings that seriously affect their ability to function well in school. In such cases it is important that individuals skilled in coordinating community assistance for children and their families be available to ensure that support is provided to these families. This work, in turn, will be most effective when it is coordinated with school-based efforts to meet these students' needs. Chapter 12 briefly discusses this concept and suggests directions for program implementation.

Effective Classroom Management versus Control

Some researchers on school effectiveness (Edmonds, 1982) and some approaches to classroom management (Assertive Discipline) have placed almost exclusive emphasis on student on-task behavior and achievement of basic skills. Classroom management and instructional skills that enhance these student behaviors tend to emphasize a high degree of classroom structure and the use of extrinsic rewards to increase students' motivation. Research (Rim & Coller, 1979; Soar, 1983) suggests, however, that an intermediate amount of control is associated with the greatest student gains in achievement. That is, too little or too much control of either students' behavior or students' responsibility for the learning task limits their achievement.

Another reason for avoiding too great an emphasis on controlling students' behavior and enhancing achievement-test scores is that this emphasis fails to address important issues about the goals of public education in our society. Research indicates that for simple, low cognitive–level tasks, greater teacher control is desirable. Thus, if the goal is to learn the multiplication tables, greater teacher control of learning activities and students' behavior may result in increased learning. When students are involved in solving complex problems or in creative production, however, less teacher control is associated with better outcomes (Johnson & Johnson, 1987; Soar & Soar, 1972, 1975). Jencke and Peck (1976) reinforce this concept:

> If teachers supply immediate reinforcement, they must pay the cost of having students learn to rely on rewards that are external to the problem situation itself. This cost may be worth incurring if the teacher is merely attempting to get children to efficiently commit facts to memory. However, the price may be too high when students are learning new concepts or if they are engaged in problem-solving or pattern-searching. (p. 33)

Corno (1979) reported that although increased classroom structure was associated with student gains in achieving basic learning tasks, it was associated with lower scores in creativity. Similarly, Soar and Soar (1980) found that the degree of students' attention to a task was positively related to low cognitive-level learning but negatively related to high cognitive–level learning. Apparently, creative production requires time merely to "sit and think," as opposed to working diligently as it is normally defined by research in on-task student behavior.

These studies are supported by research (Brophy, 1981; Rowe, 1974; Stallings & Kaskowitz, 1974) suggesting that high levels of teacher praise are associated with increased basic skill achievement but with decreased creativity and less student independence, persistence, and self-confidence. When teachers use praise to reinforce on-task behavior and simple, correct answers, students respond by producing more of these responses at the expense of more creative, independent work.

If we wish to enhance students' independence, responsibility, creativity, and motivation, we must use classroom-management strategies that do more than use rewards and punishments to increase on-task behavior and high scores on achievement tests. Structure, praise, and reinforcement are important tools that do help many, if not all, students in learning basic skills, yet they are not the best techniques for helping all students to reach all learning goals.

Doyle (1984) found that student achievement may be higher when teachers continue to focus on instruction despite small amounts of disruptive student behavior. There appears to be a fine line between maintaining an orderly classroom and doing so at the expense of instruction.

Finally, our own experience strongly suggests that a focus on control often creates at least two undesirable responses. First, rather than emphasizing classroom and school factors that may be influencing student behavior, a focus on control reinforces teachers' viewing student behavior problems primarily as an issue of gaining control of recalcitrant students. This orientation seems to run counter to the large body of research indicating that some teachers and schools are very effective at facilitating student learning and positive behavior whereas some are much less effective. Second, the research on punishment clearly indicates that aggression tends to beget aggression. For many of the most difficult-to-manage students at whom a power orientation is directed, a focus on power and control tends to evoke aggressive, hostile, or withdrawal behavior. In short, the use of power is often effective at intimidating students who need control least and is seldom effective with students whose behavior is most unproductive.

Effective classroom managers use the skills suggested in Figure 1.2 to create positive, supportive, well-structured classrooms and actively engage students in meaningful learning activities. Effective classroom managers maintain order through their effective classroom management and instruction rather than with authoritarian control methods.

Meeting Teachers' Needs: Establishing a Systems Approach to Responding Effectively to Student Behavior Problems

Teachers' professional needs fall into three general categories: (1) possessing the skills to motivate and manage students in a manner that allows teachers to experience success and professional fulfillment, (2) receiving personal and professional support from their teaching colleagues, and (3) receiving support from administrators and other support personnel.

Whether the reader's goal is to make significant changes in his or her approach to managing a classroom or to learn a few new techniques for working with a particularly difficult student, the quality of professional support available in the school setting will significantly affect that reader's ability to reach the goal. Teaching is a demanding job, and teachers need encouragement, suggestions, and expressions of personal interest and support from their colleagues. Numerous writers have emphasized that teachers are able to work more effectively with students when the teachers themselves are treated as professionals and experience the school environment as being safe and supportive. Research indicates a significant relationship among teachers' positive feelings about themselves, their teaching, and such factors as students' achievement (Aspy & Buhler, 1975), students' statements about teachers' effectiveness (Usher & Hanke, 1971), and how students view themselves in a classroom (Landry, 1974).

Support from colleagues may take the form of sharing materials, helping colleagues by taking their duty when they are not feeling well, listening with interest, providing ideas for dealing with a difficult parent or student, or reinforcing a colleague's efforts. Discussing this type of support, Schmuck and Schmuck (1974) emphasize the relationship between teachers' needs for personal and professional support and their ability to work effectively with children.

> First, the security, comfort, and stimulation that teachers receive from their colleagues increase the amount of personal esteem they bring to interactions with students and the amount of energy they have for working closely with students. Second, staff interactions offer models to students that represent the actual climate of the school. (p. 124)

Marc Robert (1976) also mentions the importance of meeting teachers' needs for support from their colleagues.

> I believe that no great "humanization" breakthrough between student and teacher will occur unless an organized and concerted effort is made to develop and maintain some realistic human support systems within which staff members can help each other feel good about their personal and professional effectiveness. (p. 44)

Despite their best intentions, teachers can become frustrated by the persistent unproductive or irresponsible behavior of a student or group of students. When this occurs, teachers may have difficulty analyzing the classroom situation and developing new strategies for working with the students. At this point, teachers benefit from the assistance of colleagues who can see the situation from a new and different perspective and can offer suggestions for working with the student(s). As discussed in chapter 12, teacher assistance teams can provide teachers with ideas and support for working with students who are demonstrating ongoing and/or serious learning and behavior problems and can also increase the support teachers experience (Chalfant, VanDusen Pysh, & Moultrie, 1979).

During the past decade, much attention has been paid to the value of colleagues' serving as instructional coaches for teachers seeking to improve their skills (Joyce & Clift, 1984; Showers, Joyce, & Bennett, 1987). Teachers need time to observe colleagues who are skilled in a teaching method, to attempt new methods while being observed by a colleague, and to discuss the results. The importance of providing this type of collegial support is accentuated by the fact that teacher training programs often fail to prepare teachers adequately in current classroom management or instructional methods. Likewise, in many cases neither support provided during the early years of teaching (Arends, 1982; Wise, Darling-Hammond, & Berry, 1988) nor standard inservice programs (Gall, Haisley, Baker, & Perez, 1982; Joyce, Bush, & McKibbin, 1981; Mertens & Yarger, 1981) provide teachers with meaningful training.

The second category of teachers' needs is administrative and specialist support. This support includes provision of materials and supplies, involvement in formulating curricular and schoolwide student management, support for advanced training, support for innovative instructional activities, and support in the form of positive feedback as well as specific, nonjudgmental professional criticism. The extensive body of research in school effectiveness and instructional leadership consistently points to the importance of administrators' providing these forms of support for teachers (De Bevoise, 1984). When these aids are not available, teachers will be much less effective in the classroom. Specialists in learning and behavior who assist in developing effective programs for children with special learning needs should also be available.

Some students will test even the most well designed classroom management system implemented within the most positive learning environment. When this occurs, teachers need assistance from administrators and other special support personnel as part of a well-designed schoolwide student management plan. During the 1980s teachers became increasingly aware of the importance of formalizing such support. An example of this approach is the following 1988–1989 contract between the West Linn School District No. 3Jt, Clackamas County, Oregon, and the Willamette Falls Bargaining Council.

Article 5—Student Discipline

A. *General*

Definition of duties and responsibilities of all administrators, coordinators, supervisors, and other personnel pertaining to student discipline shall be reduced to writing by the District, and presented to each teacher at the start of each school year. Such definition of the duties and responsibilities of personnel is a retained right of the District.

B. *Procedure*

Teachers may temporarily exclude a student from the classroom when in the judgement of the teacher the student's behavior is seriously disrupting the instructional program. When a student is so excluded, the following procedure will be utilized:

1. The student will be sent to the building office. Prior to requesting that the student be placed back in the classroom, the principal or designee will meet with the teacher to discuss the referral and the conditions for the student's return.
2. If the teacher does not agree to place the student back in the classroom at the principal's or designee's request, the student will not be allowed back in the class pending completion of this procedure.
3. In the event the teacher and principal or designee disagree, the matter will be referred as soon as possible to the Superintendent. A conference will be arranged with the teacher, principal or designee and Superintendent. The decision of the Superintendent will be final.
4. The parties agree that in such matters a speedy resolution of any disagreement is of paramount importance. The parties agree that a good faith effort will be made to arrange and meet with the Superintendent as soon as possible; even if it means meeting outside the regular workday. If the Superintendent is not available to meet as per this section, this meeting will be conducted by the Assistant Superintendent. If neither is available, it will be conducted by another certified central office administrator.

[From West Linn School District and Willamette Falls Bargaining Council]

Students who repeatedly violate classroom rules may need the assistance of specialists within the school setting or community. Initially, these specialists can make additional suggestions for teacher interventions in the classroom. Eventually, some students may need to be placed in a more structured setting, where they can obtain more systematic and consistent interventions to help them develop and demonstrate new skills. The model in Figure 1.4 outlines the responsibilities of various educators and support personnel at different steps of unproductive student behavior. The key concept in this model is that teachers are initially responsible for the majority of inappropriate student behavior. However, when students continue to behave unproductively, despite teachers' use of proven classroom management and instruction methods, teachers and students will be best served when the school system has developed clear guidelines concerning the assistance that will be provided to teachers.

The majority of the methods presented throughout this book focus on what teachers can do to motivate and manage students more effectively (Step 1 in Figure 1.4). Teachers

FIGURE 1.4 Continuum of Services for Managing Student Behavior

Step	Responsibility	Procedure	Resources
#1	Classroom teacher	Regular classroom placement	The teacher uses instructional and classroom management methods that incorporate best-accepted practices.
#2	Classroom teacher and school staff	Regular classroom and referral to school resources	This step involves advice and support from colleagues, involvement of the school support staff, or student referral into a systematic schoolwide student management (discipline) system.
#3	Classroom teacher, school staff, and district staff	Regular classroom placement and request for district resources	The district provides consultation resources, such as a special educator, school psychologist, or behavior specialist.
#4	Classroom teacher, school staff, and district staff	Request for special education evaluation and eligibility decision. Placement in a special building program and/or regular classroom	The multidisciplinary team determines eligibility, the IEP team determines the placement and programming, and the special education staff provides and coordinates services.
#5	School staff, special education, district staff, and community resources	Placement within district resources and referral to community resources	District and community resources are called in for assistance.

and administrators should understand that implementing the concepts and methods presented in this book will be facilitated when teachers receive strong support from colleagues and administrators. As discussed in detail in chapter 12, school systems can best support teachers and provide important services and safeguards for the children they serve when they have clearly delineated and widely disseminated procedures for obtaining assistance in responding to students with special needs.

SUMMARY

Teachers continue to experience persistent and often serious problems managing students' classroom behavior. Given the increasing numbers of students who will enter U.S. schools at risk for school failure, it seems likely that throughout the 1990s teachers will continually need to upgrade their skills in motivating and managing students.

Fortunately, research in classroom management has expanded dramatically during the past 15 years. Teachers no longer need to depend on simplistic advice for or unidimensional answers to the complex tasks of motivating and managing students. During the 1990s, teachers will have exciting opportunities for better understanding and influencing the factors that affect student behavior and learning. Teachers can draw on an expanding body of methods that will enable them to create more positive, supportive classroom environments, better organize and instruct their students, and more effectively respond to the behavior of students who misbehave even in supportive, well-managed classrooms characterized by clear, meaningful instruction. The efficacy of new methods can be enhanced if teachers have a clear philosophy of classroom management and understand their own responsibilities and those of their students and the school support personnel. Finally, school systems can better assist students with serious behavior problems if all educators within the system understand the methods to be followed in responding to unproductive student behavior.

RECOMMENDED READING

Alschuler, A. (1980). *School discipline: A socially literate solution.* New York: McGraw-Hill.

Brophy, J., & Evertson, C. (1976). *Learning from teaching: A developmental perspective.* Boston: Allyn and Bacon.

Duke, D. (1984). *Teaching: The imperiled profession.* Albany: State University of New York Press.

Elkind, D. (1981). *The hurried child: Growing up too fast too soon.* Reading, Mass.: Addison-Wesley.

Glasser, W. (1969). *Schools without failure.* New York: Harper and Row.

Good, T., & Brophy, J. (1987). *Looking in classrooms,* 4th ed. New York: Harper and Row.

Goodlad, J. (1984). *A place called school.* New York: McGraw-Hill.

Hahn, A., Danzberger, J., & Lefkowitz, B. (1987). *Dropouts in America: Enough is known for action.* Washington, D.C.: Institute for Educational Leadership.

Henry, J. (1963). *Culture against man.* New York: Random House.

Jones, V. (1980). *Adolescents with behavior problems: Strategies for teaching, counseling, and parent involvement.* Boston: Allyn and Bacon.

Kounin, J. (1970). *Discipline and group management in classrooms.* New York: Holt, Rinehart and Winston.

Lehr, J., & Harris, H. (1988). *At-risk, low-achieving students in the classroom.* Washington, D.C.: NEA.

Lipsitz, J. (1984). *Successful schools for young adolescents.* New Brunswick, N.J.: Transaction Books.

McManus, M. (In press). *Troublesome behavior in the classroom: A teacher's survival guide.* London: Routledge.

Maeroff, G. (1982). *Don't blame the kids: The trouble with America's public schools.* New York: McGraw-Hill.

Mongon, D., & Hart, S. (In press). *Improving classroom behaviour: Making a difference.* London: Cassell PLC.

Purkey, W., & Novack, J. (1984). *Inviting school success: A self-concept approach to teaching and learning,* 2nd ed. Belmont, Calif.: Wadsworth.

Rutter, M., Maughan, B., Montimore, P., Ouston, J., & Smith, A. (1979). *Fifteen thousand hours.* Cambridge, Mass.: Harvard University Press.

Schmuck, R., & Schmuck, P. (1974). *A humanistic psychology of education: Making the school everybody's house.* Palo Alto, Calif.: National Press Books.

Silberman, C. (1970). *Crisis in the classroom: The remaking of American education.* New York: Random House.

Sizer, T. (1984). *Horace's compromise: The dilemma of the American high school.* Boston: Houghton Mifflin.

CHAPTER 2

Understanding Students' Basic Psychological Needs

Conflict between students and teachers is caused largely by misunderstanding. It is primarily a failure to communicate effectively with each other and understand each other's goals, wants and needs.

/ Mick McManus (in press)
Troublesome Behaviour in the Classroom: A Teacher's Survival Guide

The needs for safety, belongingness, love relations, and for respect can be satisfied only by other people, i.e., only from outside the person. This means considerable dependence on the environment.

/ Abraham Maslow (1968)
Toward a Psychology of Being

When discipline problems occur in school, they can more often be traced to dysfunctions in the interpersonal climate and organizational patterns of the school than to malfunctions in the individual. In short, misbehaving students are often reacting in a predictable and even sensible way to the school as it affects them and as they have learned to perceive it and react to it.

/ William Wayson and Gayson Pinnell (1981) in D. Duke (ed.)
Helping Teachers Manage Classrooms

Students behave appropriately and learn more effectively in environments that meet their basic personal and psychological needs. All students learn best in school settings in which they are comfortable and feel safe and accepted. In addition, students' needs vary somewhat according to their age, and effective teachers create classroom settings and use instructional strategies that meet their students' unique needs. Students' academic failure and misbehavior can be understood—and subsequently prevented or corrected—by examining classroom and school environments to determine which student needs are not being met.

Teachers are frequently frustrated by their inability to determine the source of disruptive student behavior that detracts from students' learning. When asked to describe why children misbehave, teachers often include in their responses such factors as poor attitude, poor home environment, lower-than-average IQ, lack of parental support for school, or medical or emotional problems. In a 1987 report entitled *NEA Research/Gallup Opinion Polls: Public and K–12 Teacher Members,* teachers overwhelmingly stated their belief that parents and society are responsible for discipline problems occurring in schools. Eighty-one percent of the teachers polled stated that parents and society had major responsibility; only 7 percent believed that schools had major responsibility, and 12 percent thought schools shared responsibility equally with parents and society. Interestingly, only 58 percent of the public polled believed that parents and society were the major causes of student discipline problems; 21 percent believed the schools had major responsibility, and 21 percent believed responsibility was shared equally.

It is also important and somewhat disturbing to note that 64 percent of teachers polled stated that because the problem is at home, there is not much more schools can do to bring about improved student behavior. This conclusion suggests that teachers can merely coax or bribe these students into behaving more appropriately or remove or punish these children when misbehavior occurs. Teachers may thus absolve themselves of responsibility for students' misbehavior. In this scheme, teachers are merely a reactive force. They must put a finger in the dike when confronted with unpredictable forces over which they have little control.

Even though it is true that student behavior is influenced by factors outside the control of the school, studies on school and teacher effectiveness have demonstrated that teachers and schools have a major impact on how students behave and learn and on how they feel about themselves. Therefore, another approach to analyzing unproductive or irresponsible student behavior is to believe that almost all students can function productively in a classroom and to consider what classroom variables can positively affect student learning and behavior. Much of this book provides specific methods teachers have used to create such environments. We believe, however, that professional educators must understand why these techniques are effective rather than merely use them as gimmicks that positively influence student behavior. Consider for a moment that you were taking a child with a stomachache to see a physician. How would you react if, without examining the child, the physician indicated that an appendectomy would be performed? When you asked why the physician intended to perform the operation, the doctor indicated that the previous summer he had taken a class on appendectomies, had been told the operation was helpful to all children, and had demonstrated skill in performing it. It is likely that you would seek another opinion and would perhaps even report the incident to the appropriate source.

Consider, however, how often teachers take such courses as Assertive Discipline (that place no emphasis on research or on the relationship between student needs and the recommended interventions) and simply implement the new methods without first analyzing the situation to consider what is causing the problems and whether other less control-oriented interventions methods could be implemented. Given the quality of research in the fields of classroom management and instruction, it is somewhat surprising that more teachers do not face lawsuits for malpractice.

Teachers are involved daily in creating the atmosphere in which children spend approximately one-fourth of their waking lives. Although this necessity obviously places considerable responsibility on the teacher, it simultaneously imparts a positive, creative dimension into teachers' professional lives. Teachers are not faced with the prospect of merely reacting to student behaviors over which they have no control. On the contrary, by creating environments that respond sensitively to students' needs, teachers can ensure that most student behavior will be positive and goal directed.

The reader may wonder whether an emphasis on students' needs means subjugating teachers' needs or expectations. It is important to realize that meeting children's needs does not mean that adults do not provide structure, expect high-quality performance, or hold students accountable for their behavior. Indeed, these factors are part of environments that meet students' needs.

The necessity for presenting a chapter on students' psychological needs and focusing a portion of this book on strategies for creating positive classroom environments is based on the unfortunate but very real fact that classroom environments often fail to meet students' basic needs. Too many children who enter school excited and eager to learn leave school feeling unliked and unsuccessful. After conducting a survey of more than 600 students in grades 3 through 11, Morse writes:

> Eighty-four percent of the third-graders were proud of their school work, while only 53 percent of the eleventh-graders felt the same way. In the low grades, 93 percent felt they were doing the best work they could; only 37 percent of the seniors felt this way. Without regard to their achievement quotients and the fact that the failures tend to drop out, the older pupils who remained in school came to feel they were doing inadequate work. Again, over half the young children said they were doing as well in school as they would like, but only 22 percent of the eleventh-graders felt this way. About 40 percent of the pupils often felt upset in school; and with regard to achievement, 20 percent said their teacher made them feel "not good enough." Over 40 percent reported they often became discouraged in school and this discouragement too increased with age. (Morse, 1964, p. 198)

Similar results are reported by Cormany (1975), based on a study in which the Pennsylvania Department of Education surveyed students' feelings about school. Cormany reports that although 64.4 percent of the kindergarten children expressed positive feelings about school, only 12.8 percent of sixth graders reported such feelings. A variety of other studies support the findings that, as children become older and progress through the grades, they often develop poorer self-esteem and less positive attitudes toward school (Landry & Edeburn, 1974; Stanwyck & Felker, 1974; Yamamoto, Thomas, & Karnes, 1969). A survey of more than 8,000 students in grades 5 through 9 reports a similar change in students' attitudes and behavior (Currence, 1984). Results showed that 61 percent of fifth graders said they "try their best at school," compared with only 30 percent of the ninth graders. Similarly, while 60 percent of fifth, sixth, and seventh graders said they never cheated, only 33 percent of ninth graders said this.

It can be argued that children simply become more critical as they grow older; but there is more than enough evidence in other works (Glasser, 1988; Goodlad, 1984; Mortimore & Sammons, 1987; Purkey & Novak, 1984; Rutter et al., 1979; Sizer, 1984) and in our own experience in schools to suggest that at least a significant amount of this negativism and the associated acting-out or withdrawal behavior is a response to school settings that fail to meet students' needs. Teachers certainly do not mean to create such environments and are often not even aware that they are doing so. Most teachers sincerely wish to provide an optimal learning environment for their students. Unfortunately, many teachers are hampered by a combination of limited skills resulting from ineffective teacher training programs and the multiple demands placed on them. This book cannot alter the latter situation, but it does provide teachers with skills that enable them to cope with these demands more effectively.

This chapter describes the basic psychological needs that must be met for students to behave in a positive, productive manner. No attempt is made to present an in-depth description of any one theorist's work or to describe child and adolescent development. Rather, the chapter highlights needs that, when met within the school setting, enhance positive teacher and student behavior and thereby facilitate learning.

The effectiveness of any teaching strategy or behavior-change approach is influenced by the degree to which it responds to students' needs. Similarly, when a teacher's behavior elicits an unproductive student response, it is likely that the student lacks necessary skills to respond as the teacher would like and/or that the teacher has in some way infringed on, or failed to provide a productive means of obtaining, an important student need. In a fascinating analysis of why students drop out of traditional educational settings, Quigley (1987) proposes that it is less the content of schoolwork and instead the extent to which the school environment responds to how the student has learned to view learning, meaning, and participation in his or her environment. In most cases dropping out is related to how people relate to one another and to the quality of independence and respect provided to the student within the learning environment.

In a similar vein, Mick McManus, in his forthcoming British publication *Troublesome Behaviour in the Classroom: A Teacher's Survival Guide,* writes: "I have argued that pupils' disruptive behaviour may result from understandable perceptions, beliefs and intentions; and that understanding and accepting this insulates the teacher from personal hurts, permits the possibility of communication, and gains, however slowly, the pupils' attention and respect" (p. 170). He goes on to state that "the solution to the problem of conflict is to convince pupils, through an accepting relationship, that they are persons of value: both teachers and pupils need to acknowledge each other as persons and not seek refuge in the categories of (authoritarian) teacher or (intransigent) pupil" (p. 136). Indeed, a popular theme in current British writing about behavior-problem students is the importance of understanding the students' perspective and realizing that doing so allows us to consider changes that may need to be made within the school or classroom if at-risk students are to have a positive learning experience. For example, Hargreaves (1982) argues that what teachers interpret as disruptive behavior may in fact be students' legitimate criticism of schooling as it affects them. He states that schools do not treat lower-level students with dignity and that students' response is to reject the schooling process.

THEORETICAL PERSPECTIVES

When faced with unproductive student behavior, teachers may in their frustration make statements such as, "I don't understand why he does that," "She did that for no reason," or, "What would you expect given his family." Numerous writers have, however, noted that all behavior is caused either by environmental factors or by the individual attempting to meet a need.

One approach to understanding children's unproductive school behavior suggests that most unproductive student behavior is a response to children not having their basic needs met within the environment in which the misbehavior occurs (Maslow, 1968). Considerable theoretical work and research support this contention. Furthermore, our own experiences with children of various ages in widely varied settings consistently confirm this explanation of children's unproductive behavior. This explanation has the advantage of placing the teacher in a creative, exciting position. Rather than simply reacting to uncontrollable forces, the teacher controls a wide variety of factors that influence children's behavior.

This view of teachers as able to influence students' behavior positively is supported by research and theory presented by the behavioristic approach and by social psychology. Behaviorism views individual behavior as determined by the pattern of rewards and punishments to which the person is exposed. Teachers often experience frustration when working with students whose history at home or in school or both has included limited reinforcement for desirable school behaviors and considerable reinforcement for behaviors inappropriate in the school. Teachers can, however, learn to teach and reinforce appropriate behaviors systematically. Teachers also can enlist peers in reinforcing positive behaviors. The works of Bandura (1969) and Bronfenbrenner (1970) highlight the social psychologists' view that students' behavior is heavily influenced by the values and behaviors modeled by individuals who are significant in children's lives. Children learn a great deal by modeling others' behavior. Research suggests that children are more likely to model individuals who (1) are perceived as having a high degree of competence, status, and control over resources, (2) have provided previous support and reinforcement, and (3) play a prominent role in the students' daily life. Because teachers have the potential for possessing these qualities, they can, by thoughtful modeling, significantly affect students' behavior. Similarly, by helping to create classroom norms and procedures that encourage students to behave in a positive, supportive manner, teachers can create settings in which the majority of students serve as effective models for the few students who may initially lack desirable attitudes and behaviors.

Another way to view unproductive student behavior is to see it as a skill deficit. This model suggests that students who act aggressively on the playground lack skills to make appropriate contact with peers, to handle the inevitable frustrations and conflicts that arise, and to solve problems. Similarly, students who act out during instructional time may lack skills in understanding or organizing the work, using self-talk to handle frustration, or knowing how to obtain assistance.

This social, cognitive skill deficit model suggests that students need more than reinforcement for appropriate behavior and negative consequences for inappropriate behavior. In addition, students need to be taught social and work skills in the same manner that they are taught reading or math skills. Indeed, it is interesting that when students have serious difficulties reading, they are referred to a specialist who works intensively with them for an extended period of time. Educators do not expect students to learn to read by being placed in time out or otherwise isolated from classmates. Likewise, teachers seldom expect students with reading difficulties to be at grade level after only a few sessions with the reading specialist. However, when students experience difficulties with their behavior, educators often isolate them, provide little or no instruction in how to behave appropriately, and expect one or two visits to a counselor or principal to resolve the problem and ensure that the child has the skills necessary to function as effectively as his or her classmates. If we accept student behavior problems as representing skill deficits, this is not realistic. Instead, educators must respond to unproductive student behavior by creating opportunities for students to develop much needed skills.

Various writers have attempted to categorize and describe basic psychological needs that exist for children at different stages of their development. Understanding these needs can help educators better understand student behavior. This understanding allows us to become less emotional and defensive about unproductive student behavior and instead to consider ways to alter this behavior by more effectively meeting students' needs within our classrooms and schools. Instead of asking, ''Why does he or she do this to me?'' we can ask, ''What needs are not being met for this student in my classroom?'' and ''Can I make any adjustments that will help this student better meet these needs so he or she can experience success in my class?''

Rudolf Dreikurs

Basing his work on the concepts developed by the Viennese psychiatrist Alfred Adler, Dreikurs (1972) centered his ideas for working with children on the belief that their basic need is to be socially accepted.

> We should realize that a misbehaving child is only a discouraged child trying to find his place; he is acting on the faulty logic that his misbehaviour will give him the social acceptance which he desires. (Dreikurs & Cassel, 1972, p. 32)

Dreikurs describes four goals associated with children's misbehavior: attention-getting, power, revenge, and displays of inadequacy. He suggests that ''when a child is deprived of the opportunity to gain status through his useful contributions, he usually seeks proof of his status in class through getting attention'' (1972, p. 34). If adults are ineffective at responding to this attention-getting, Dreikurs indicates that students will seek power. If this response is thwarted by the teachers' own power methods, Dreikurs believes that students will become deeply discouraged and seek revenge. Finally, Dreikurs suggests that ''a child who has tried passive destructive forms of attention-getting in order to achieve the feeling of 'belonging' may eventually become so deeply discouraged that he gives up all hope of significance and expects only failure and defeat'' (Dreikurs & Pearl, 1972, p. 39). In *Discipline without Tears* (Dreikurs & Cassel, 1972) and *Maintaining Sanity in the Classroom* (Dreikurs, Grunwald, & Pepper, 1971), Dreikurs suggests methods for assisting teachers in identifying which of the four mistaken goals the child is seeking and ways teachers can respond to children to help them return to positive involvement in the regular classroom.

Erik Erikson

In his well-known conceptualization of the eight stages of man, Erikson (1963) postulates that elementary-age children are in the stage he labels "Industry versus Inferiority." During this stage, children must move away from playing make-believe and develop an ability to produce things. Children must learn to do something well and to develop a sense of their own competence. Erikson describes the essence of this stage:

> And while all children need their hours and days of make-believe in games, they all, sooner or later, become dissatisfied and disgruntled without a sense of being able to make things and make them well and even perfectly: it is this that I have called the sense of industry. . . . For nothing less is at stake than the development and maintenance in children of a positive identification of those who know things and know how to do things. (Erikson, 1968, pp. 123, 125)

In Erikson's writing we can see the dual emphasis on viewing oneself as competent and on having this competence verified and expanded through meaningful contact with other people. Teachers can assist in meeting these student developmental needs by ensuring that all students (1) understand the work they are being asked to do, (2) can successfully complete the work they are given, (3) monitor and chart their progress, and (4) receive positive feedback from other people for their efforts and accomplishments. Similarly, students need to understand teachers' behavior expectations, to be allowed to practice these when necessary, and to receive assistance in and reinforcement for developing these behaviors when they are not skills the students currently possess. Many of the ideas presented in chapters 6 through 11 will help the reader create a classroom setting in which this can be accomplished.

In addition to understanding theories that deal with children's needs, upper-grade elementary or middle school teachers must be aware of the unique needs of adolescents. The physical onset of adolescence is occurring at an earlier age. In addition, children are becoming more sophisticated at an earlier age due to the availability of television and of adults' tendency to encourage sophisticated behavior in children. Consequently, fifth- and especially sixth-grade teachers find themselves dealing with students who are experiencing the early stages of adolescence.

Erikson describes the next developmental stage—that experienced by young adolescents—as the search for a sense of identity. During the initial phase of this stage (ages 11 to 13) there is a dramatic increase in self-consciousness and a lowered self-esteem. Young adolescents feel onstage, as if everyone is observing them. Elkind (1967) labels this the "imaginary audience." Young adolescents also view themselves and their personal problems as unique and cannot understand that other people are experiencing similar feelings. Elkind labels this concept the "personal fable."

This means that even though secondary teachers often feel pressure to cover material and complete the curriculum, student learning and behavior can be enhanced when teachers take time to create a classroom climate in which adolescents feel comfortable with their teacher and peers and engage in cooperative learning activities that allow for supportive peer interactions. This climate serves to reduce the students' sense of self-consciousness and isolation, which releases energy for productive learning.

Young adolescents are also beginning to challenge previously accepted beliefs and values. With the gradual increase in their ability to consider abstract ideas and better understand the concepts of past and future, adolescents began to view their world more subjectively and critically (Kohlberg, 1976; Piaget, 1970). Therefore, adolescents have a basic need to examine ideas, rules, and decisions critically. They are likely to question why they must study a topic, complete an assignment, or follow a rule that does not apply to the adults who share their environment. This often frustrating behavior increases as students move through midadolescence (ages 14 to 16) and become somewhat less absorbed in ego-centric, self-oriented matters and more interested in their relationship to others and in better understanding and controlling their environment. Students during grades 8 through 10 are often testing their new personal, physical, and cognitive skills by challenging rules or adult behavior they view as illogical or indefensible. During these early and midadolescent years, students need fair, clearly articulated structure and adults who are personally strong and flexible enough to become involved in openly discussing questions adolescents have about subject matter, teaching techniques, and school rules and procedures (Jones, 1980).

Stanley Coopersmith

Another useful concept on students' needs is offered by Coopersmith (1967). In his research on the factors associated with self-esteem, Coopersmith found that in order to possess high self-esteem, individuals need to experience a sense of significance, competence, and power. Significance can best be defined as the sense of being valued that an individual attains from involvement in a positive two-way relationship in which both parties sincerely care about each other. Competence is developed by being able to perform a socially valued task as well as or better than others at one's age level. For example, winning a free-throw shooting competition involving her peers would provide a fifth-grader with a sense of competence. Being able to tie her shoe or add one-digit figures would provide her with a much smaller sense of competence. Finally, power refers to an ability to control one's environment.

Like Erikson, Coopersmith's research indicates that students need to experience a sense of trust and personal involvement as well as a sense of accomplishment or competence if their needs are to be met. Coopersmith also notes that in order for individuals to feel good about themselves and their environment they must experience a sense of power or control. Students who clearly understand classroom rules and procedures and who understand what is to be learned and why it might be useful to them will experience a sense of power. Likewise, students experience a sense of power when they are allowed to choose a topic of special interest to study, provide input into how the classroom is arranged, or understand their own learning style and its relationship to their learning and teacher decision making.

William Glasser

For nearly three decades William Glasser has crusaded for increasing the sense of efficacy and power students experience. In his most recent book, *Control Theory in the Classroom*, Glasser (1986) states, "Our behavior is always our best attempt at the time to satisfy at least five powerful forces which, because they are built into our genetic structure, are best called basic needs" (p. 14). Glasser described the five basic needs as "(1) to survive and reproduce, (2) to belong and love, (3) to *gain power*, (4) to be free, and (5) to have fun." (Glasser, 1986, p. 22). Glasser indicates that students will function productively only in school environments that allow them to experience a sense of control or power over their learning.

Even though Glasser argues strongly and articulately for providing all students with a sense of power, he notes that this need is particularly important and most often frustrated in secondary schools:

> Secondary schools have many more losers than winners because there is more failure, more competition, more emphasis on memorization and less on thinking than there is in most elementary schools. It is this lack of access to power in the academic classes that is so frustrating to students because it comes just at the time when students are beginning to experience the increased need for power which is part of the normal biology of adolescence.
>
> Now, wanting more power, they have access to less because it is all but impossible for any but a few high-achieving students to gain any sense of personal power from the work they do in a traditional high school classroom. (Glasser, 1986, p. 63)

David Elkind

In *The Hurried Child*, Elkind (1981a) adds an interesting dimension to the topic of children's psychological needs. He states that relationships among all individuals, but especially between children and adults, involve basic patterns of dealing with each other. He describes these patterns as implicit contracts and notes that they are constantly changing. He further comments that children's needs are met when contracts change in response to changing personal and cognitive skills demonstrated by children, but that contracts must not change primarily in response to adults' needs.

Elkind describes three basic contracts between adults and children: (1) responsibility-freedom, (2) achievement-support, and (3) loyalty-commitment. The freedom-responsibility contract refers to adults' "sensitively monitor[ing] the child's level of intellectual, social, and emotional development in order to provide the appropriate free-doms and opportunities for the exercise of responsibility" (p. 124). The achievement-support contract refers to adults' expecting age-appropriate achievements and providing the necessary personal and material support to help children reach expected goals. The loyalty-commitment contract emphasizes adults' expectations that children will respond with loyalty and acceptance of adults because of the time, effort, and energy adults give. Although Elkind focuses on the parent-child relationship, these contractual areas apply to all adult-child relationships.

Elkind's key concept related to contracts is that they are frequently violated by adults and that this violation causes stress for youngsters. Violation of the freedom-responsibility contract occurs when adults fail to reward responsibility with freedom. For example, when students act responsibly in making a reasonable request of a teacher or administrator and are met with disrespect, this contract has been violated. Likewise, students who have demonstrated skill in directing portions of their own learning but are not allowed to do so experience frustration and stress through violation of the responsibility-freedom contract. The achievement-support contract is violated when adults do not provide adequate support for students' achievement. The low-achieving student who receives few opportunities to respond in class, little assistance in answering questions, and less reinforcement for appropriate answers is not receiving support commensurate with desired and potential achievement. Difficulties in the loyalty-commitment contract occur when children, especially adolescents, fail to provide adults with indications of loyalty commensurate with the efforts or commitment that adults see themselves as having made. When adults respond with removal of commitment, giving up on or criticizing the student, rather than by understanding and discussing the problem, contract violation occurs. This condition is more likely to happen with low-achieving students who may not immediately repay teachers for what appear to be considerable amounts of time and effort.

Joan Lipsitz

While serving as director of the Center for Early Adolescence at the University of North Carolina at Chapel Hill, Joan Lipsitz wrote extensively on the needs of early adolescence. She noted that adults often fail to understand this age group, which leads to classroom management and instructional decisions that cause a considerable amount of the unproductive behavior that so frequently frustrates teachers who work with this age group. Lipsitz emphasizes the importance of developing school environments that meet young adolescents' developmental needs. These needs include:

1. The need for diversity,
2. The need for opportunities for self-exploration and self-definition,
3. The need for meaningful participation in school and community,
4. The need for positive social interaction with peers and adults,
5. The need for physical activity,
6. The need for competence and achievement,
7. The need for structure and clear limits. (Dorman, 1981, p. 1)

Joan Lipsitz's thoughtful book, *Successful Schools for Young Adolescents* (1984), examines four schools that have successfully met these needs. Schools interested in assessing their effectiveness in responding to these needs as well as in creating more productive learning environments for young adolescents can refer to Lipsitz's book and also can use Dorman's *Middle Grades Assessment Program* (1981).

Abraham Maslow

Although each theoretical conceptualization described in the previous section provides a valuable increment of insight into children's needs, Maslow's concept of the basic human needs incorporates the key components of many theories in a form that allows teachers systematically to assess and respond to students' needs. Maslow suggests that there is a hierarchy of basic human needs and that lower-level needs generally take precedence over higher-order needs. His hierarchy of needs, which has been divided in a variety of ways, includes these components:

> Self-actualization
> Self-respect
> Belongingness and affection
> Safety and security
> Physiological needs

Maslow's theoretical position is that people are basically good and that they have an innate need to be competent and accepted. Unproductive behavior is therefore not viewed as an indication of a bad child but rather as a reaction to the frustration associated with being in a situation in which one's basic needs are not being met. Maslow further suggests that these basic needs cannot be met without assistance from other people. Finally, he postulates that only when the basic needs are met can the individual become motivated by self-actualization or the need to take risks, learn, and attain one's fullest potential.

The major goal of our educational system is to help children develop demonstrable academic and social skills and the related ability to solve meaningful problems. Within the school environment, then, children are expected to demonstrate new understandings and new ways of perceiving and manipulating their environment. Therefore, in a real sense, the school's primary goal requires students to be involved in the process of self-actualization. Maslow's theory suggests, however, that children will not be able to accomplish this task unless the environment first provides adequately for lower-level needs. The message is clear. If we expect students to perform appropriate academic tasks, we must first create environments that meet children's basic needs. Conversely, if we fail to meet these needs, we can expect that children will become frustrated and anxious and will behave in an unproductive manner.

Physiological Needs

It is easy for teachers to pass over the importance of meeting students' physiological needs. Because schools provide shelter, heat, and food that is certainly adequate and is more substantial than many children receive at home, it is perhaps natural to assume that students' physiological needs are being met. Nevertheless, schools may fail to respond sensitively in many subtle ways to students' physiological needs and thereby unwittingly cause varying degrees of unproductive students' behavior.

In extensive work on students' learning styles, Rita Dunn (1978, 1983, 1987, 1989; Dunn & Dunn, 1978) identified 26 variables that influence students' learning. Examining the elements described, we find that these 10 deal directly with physiological factors: (1) sound, (2) light, (3) temperature, (4) design, (5) auditory learning preference, (6) kinesthetic learning preference, (7) visual learning preference, (8) intake, (9) time, and (10) mobility. Students vary significantly in the amount of sound and light that is optimal for learning. As many schools have realized, students respond more productively when they have had an adequate breakfast. We recall working with a fifth-grade boy whose only nutrition between the evening meal and his school lunch was a bottle of cola. A change in the student's eating habits brought about a dramatic improvement in his behavior.

Likewise, some students (and many adults) are unable to function effectively if they must work for several hours with nothing to eat or drink. Teachers should consider that students who eat breakfast at seven or eight o'clock must often wait at least four hours between meals. Teachers also need to be sensitive to any visual or auditory deficits experienced by a student and to alter classroom structures to respond to these factors. Teachers should also attempt to develop classroom procedures that include a simple, unembarrassing method for students to leave the room quietly to use the lavatory.

These are fairly obvious examples of physiological needs. There are other more subtle factors that adults frequently fail to recognize. For example, studies involving both primates (Harlow, 1958) and infants (Casler, 1965; Dennis, 1960) indicate that touch is an important physiological and psychological need. Direct classroom research in this area is lacking, but we suggest that touch is a real need for children and that there is a relationship between meeting this need and productive student behavior.

Another physiological factor is the degree to which the classroom environment provides a comfortable, stimulating atmosphere for students. Simple adjustment in standard furniture is common, yet it is less common for teachers to respond to the fact that some students need quite different seating, such as a chair, table, or the floor. Similarly, teachers who frequently move around the room may forget that their students are expected to remain relatively immobile for much of the school day. Though some students may adapt to this requirement of schooling, others learn less effectively or misbehave, partly because they cannot cope with behavioral expectations that violate their basic need to move. Teachers of preadolescents and young adolescents must be particularly sensitive to students' needs for mobility and social interaction. Research (Goodlad, 1984) indicates that students are seldom actively involved in the learning process. This expectation of passive, immobile behavior is a major cause of acting-out behavior in many middle schools and junior high schools.

Readers can undoubtedly envision a room in their home that has been decorated to provide a relaxing, comfortable place to study, sew, or enjoy family activities. As adults, we go to considerable lengths to create environments that we find pleasant. Although children have much less control over the physical aspects of their environment, they too feel more comfortable and can be more productive in environments that provide comfort and stimulation. Classrooms should be colorful and should include a variety of visually interesting materials, such as posters and mobiles, as well as a comfortable corner in which students can relax and read or discuss problems, or to which they can move when they need a respite from the tasks associated with a busy school day. Some teachers enjoy collecting and displaying such materials. It also is important to encourage students to incorporate materials that they bring from home. Students' input can also include having them decorate the walls or having their artwork displayed on classroom walls and in hallways.

Although teachers normally associate comfort and physiological needs with the physical aspects of the classroom, the pacing of learning activities is also a significant factor. All teachers experience days when the pace is so demanding that at the end of the day they retreat to a long jog, a hot bath, or two aspirins. We often forget, though, that students are also faced with numerous academic and social tasks each day. In fact, the strain associated with the pace of classroom activities may be more pronounced for children, for they are generally not controlling the pace. It is therefore important that teachers provide time other than the traditional lunch and recess breaks (which sometimes prove to be more tension-producing than are academic activities) for children to relax and synthesize their learning. This time may be particularly important for slow learners. Within the normal academic program of the school day, these children may never complete all their assignments and thus need adults to provide opportunities to relax and reflect on what they have learned.

Although the classroom is certainly the hub of a student's school day, it is important to examine other aspects of school environments for situations in which physiological needs may not be met. Perhaps the best example of such settings is the school cafeteria. Most elementary and many secondary school cafeterias consist of long tables with attached benches. Although this arrangement is economical, relatively indestructible, and easy to move, it also tends to create a noisy, crowded, uncomfortable, impersonal atmosphere. A variety of small tables would provide a calmer, more relaxing lunch break for students. To verify the difference between these two environments, we encourage the reader to spend, if possible, several lunch periods in each setting. Each time the authors spend time in a traditional lunchroom environment, we come away with a fresh appreciation for why teachers often find that students return from their lunch break in anything but a relaxed state.

Safety and Security Needs

Certainly the most basic aspect of safety and security is that students feel safe from physical harm when going to and from school and when they are in the school or on the playground. It is very important that schools respond to this need by providing adequate supervision by caring adults and by developing procedures for working effectively with children to confront situations in which this need is not being met. In addition to ensuring that students are safe from physical abuse by peers, schools must ensure that students are safe from physical abuse by adults. Several days before writing this portion of the book, one of the authors witnessed a teacher towering over a second-grade student and screaming angrily. The child had lowered himself to the floor and cowered in a near fetal position. The teacher concluded her tirade by screaming at the child that if he repeated his misbehavior she would paddle him soundly. This incident took place in an upper middle-class school and was a response to the student's violating a minor school rule. One cannot help but wonder how many times a day a scene like this occurs. If teachers wish to create schools in which children experience a sense of physical and psychological safety, they must ensure that their behavior and that of their colleagues does not violate this important human need.

Though it is paramount that teachers create school environments in which students feel safe from physical harm, it is also important to attend to students' needs to feel safe from unnecessary and unproductive psychological pressures. Unfortunately, it is often difficult for adults directly and immediately to pinpoint factors that may be causing subtle pressure for students. An excellent example occurred several years ago in a school district in Oregon. Much to their credit, district administrators became worried about what they perceived as a negative attitude among a significant number of their young schoolchildren. The district subsequently sought the services of an outside agency to examine the situation. The consultants decided initially to examine the ratio of positive to negative statements made by teachers. They began their intervention by simply asking children in second-grade classrooms to answer yes or no to the question, ''Do you like school?'' As indicated in the fourth column of Figure 2.1, at the beginning of the school year, most students in all classes responded yes to this question. The consultants discovered, however, that, for

FIGURE 2.1 Influence of Positive and Negative Teacher Statements on Students' Feelings about School

	Pre 2 weeks after start of school (September 20–27)			Post January 22–24		
Teacher	Pos.	Neg.	Students responding yes to: "Do you like school?"	Pos.	Neg.	Students responding yes to: "Do you like school?"
1	.72	28	90%	.76	24	90%
2	.34	66	90%	.33	67	20%
3	.66	34	80%	.70	30	70%
4	.69	31	90%	.65	35	80%
5	.54	46	100%	.61	39	20%
6	.80	20	100%	.87	13	100%
7	.22	78	90%	.19	81	.20%
8	.64	36	70%	.64	36	40%
9	.79	21	100%	.77	23	100%
10	.92	08	80%	.89	11	90%
11	.52	48	100%	.63	37	60%
12	.73	27	90%	.65	35	90%
13	.45	55	90%	.61	39	80%
14	.67	33	80%	.73	27	80%
15	.58	42	90%	.60	40	70%
16	.51	49	60%	.58	42	10%
17	.76	24	70%	.77	23	70%

Personal correspondence with Bud Fredericks, Teaching Research, Monmouth, Oregon.

students who experienced classrooms characterized by a low rate of positive teacher verbalizations, these positive feelings about school changed dramatically within the first 15 weeks of school.

More specifically, in the eight classes in which teachers provided less than 65 percent positive statements, the percentage of students responding that they liked school dropped an alarming 48 percent during the 15 weeks. In the 7 classrooms in which 70 percent or more of the teachers' statements were positive, though, students' responses to the question of whether they liked school remained, on the average, exactly the same after 15 weeks of school. These data suggest that children are much less comfortable in classroom environments characterized by a low rate of positive teacher statements, probably because students frequently feel attacked and punished under such conditions, which significantly reduces their psychological safety. In their sensitive and creative book, *Inviting School Success,* Purkey and Novak (1984) reinforce this concept by poignantly emphasizing that the quality of the learning environment is significantly influenced by the degree to which teachers' supportive, inviting statements outweigh their critical, uninviting statements.

Psychological safety can also be enhanced by applying instructional methods ensuring that students are given work they feel able to master and by ensuring that students understand and take part in the evaluation process. Students will not experience a sense of safety and security when they are involved in classrooms in which they have little understanding of, or control over, their environment and yet in which their ability to function must be judged daily.

Need for Belonging and Affection

Experiencing a sense of belonging and affection is an extremely important psychological need. In addition to being important in itself, this sense is a key ingredient in feelings of both safety and respect of others. We have all, at one time or another, been in a situation in which we felt we did not belong and that other people in the environment did not feel affection for us. Put the book aside for a moment and try to visualize one such situation. See if you can focus on how you felt about being in that situation. How did you feel about remaining in or returning to that situation? Would you want to work in that environment? If you were required to work in such an environment, how do you think it would influence your performance and behavior?

Teachers must realize that children experience these same feelings when they are involved in settings in which they do not feel they belong. Indeed, because their sense of self is less well defined and consequently more dependent on outside influences, it is likely that children experience lack of belonging with more intensity than do most adults. Children who feel that they do not belong are likely to withdraw or to seek attention through unproductive behaviors. It is no surprise that research suggests that individuals' behavior in a group setting is significantly influenced by the degree to which the person views other group members as liking him or her.

> Although educators generally have not considered student friendships relevant to individual students' cognitive and affective development, our research evidence . . . and experience indicate that they are related. In fact, the friendships classmates have for one another, along with their willingness to help and support one another, represent important ingredients for the enhancement of individual academic achievement. Moreover, learning groups in which friendship and influence are dispersed among many peers have more supportive work norms and are more cohesive than groups in which the friendship and influence processes are hierarchical. Strong relationships with others are not only valuable in themselves; they also can enhance cognitive development in the classroom. (Schmuck & Schmuck, 1974, p. 101)

The peer group is very important to students, and the extent to which students experience acceptance or rejection from the group can dramatically influence their behavior.

> Positive interpersonal relations among students [are] necessary both for effective problem solving in groups and for general classroom enjoyment of instructional activity. The psychological security and safety necessary for open exploration of instructional tasks is based upon feelings of being accepted, liked, and supported by fellow students. Class cohesion is based upon positive interpersonal relationships among students. (Johnson & Johnson, 1975, p. 188)

While writing this chapter, one of the authors conducted a workshop with the leadership team of a high school that was experiencing attendance problems with minority students bused to the school. After discussing a wide range of teacher-student relationship and instructional factors, the staff agreed that a significant cause of the problem was that students in the school—and especially those bused to school—did not know the other students in their classes. The staff agreed that attendance could not be significantly improved unless nonattending students felt more comfortable and wanted in their classes.

Although the sense of belonging resulting from peers' statements can be extremely important, it is equally, if not more, important that students feel accepted and respected by their teachers. Because children are highly dependent on adults for satisfaction of many of their basic needs, the respect they receive from adults affects them in a major way. Patterson (1973) states this reality powerfully: "The concepts which the teacher has of the children become the concepts which the children come to have of themselves" (p. 125)

The therapeutic value inherent in providing individuals with a sense of being cared for and respected is sensitively presented by Carl Rogers and his colleagues. In describing the essential ingredients of a relationship that facilitates positive personal growth and learning, Rogers states,

> There is another attitude which stands out in those who are successful in facilitating learning. . . . I think of it as prizing the learner, prizing his feelings, his opinions, his person. It is a caring for the learner, but a non-possessive caring. It is an acceptance of this other individual as a separate person, having worth in his own right. (Rogers, 1969, p. 109)

Need for Self-Esteem

Self-esteem has been defined in various ways, but it can, perhaps, best be described as a general positive or negative view one holds of oneself. Therefore, whether a child has a positive self-esteem will be heavily influenced by the extent to which the previously discussed needs have been met. All individuals have a strong need to experience a sense of significance, competence, and power, and thereby to have basically positive self-esteem. Unfortunately, young people often find that they are unable to acquire these ingredients through socially acceptable channels. This situation occurs when parents fail to provide love and support and when schools do not foster positive personal relationships, fail to develop instructional patterns that enable each child to experience success, and consistently place all power in the hands of adults. In such situations, youngsters attempt to acquire significance, competence, and power by methods that adults find less desirable and that are almost always ultimately less beneficial to the youngster.

An excellent example of the powerful influence self-esteem can have on an individual's behavior is reported by Combs, Avila, and Purkey (1971) in *Helping Relationships*. These authors describe an incident in which what a young man believed about himself significantly influenced his school performance.

> What a boy believes about himself is really important. We had a student at Greeley who scored in the 98 percentile on the entrance test, and he thought that he had a 98 IQ. And because he thought he was an average kid, he knew college would be hard for him. He almost failed in his first term. He went home and told his parents, "I don't believe I'm college caliber," and the parents took him back to school and talked with the college counselor. When he found out that 98 percentile score meant that he had a 140 IQ, he was able to do "A" work before the year was over. (p. 43)

Many research findings support the fact that, at all grade levels, students with high self-concepts achieve more effectively than do those with poor self-concepts. Studies in elementary schools (Campbell, 1967; Farls, 1967; Williams & Cole, 1968), junior high schools (Brookover, Patterson, & Thomas, 1965), high schools (Farquhar, 1968; Gowan, 1960), and college (Brunkan & Sheni, 1966; Irwin, 1967) all indicate varying degrees of positive correlation between positive self-concept and successful school achievement. If we wish to help all students become effective learners, we must create classroom settings that facilitate the development of positive self-esteem. This task involves creating warm, safe environments in which students feel they belong and are an accepted part of the group. It also involves using instructional strategies that help students clearly understand the learning goals, become actively involved in the learning process, and experience success.

Need for Self-Actualization

In Maslow's conceptualization, self-actualization refers to each person's intrinsic need to reach his or her potential and to express himself or herself completely and creatively.

> So far as motivational status is concerned, healthy people have sufficiently gratified their basic needs for safety, belongingness, love, respect and self-esteem so that they are motivated primarily by trends to self actualization (defined as ongoing actualization of potentials, capacities, and talents). . . . (Maslow, 1968, p. 25)

The existence of this need is seen in children's curiosity, in their need to understand their environment, and in their need to express themselves creatively, whether by building a treehouse or painting a picture. Therefore, though it is important for schools to meet students' basic needs, it is also important to provide settings that encourage this higher-level self-need. This can be accomplished by varied strategies, including allowing students to choose special learning projects, encouraging individual goal setting and self-evaluation, stimulating class discussions, and encouraging students to constructively challenge both academic and procedural issues.

A number of writers have emphasized that we live in a rapidly changing society in which the knowledge and skills that adults possess will often be dated by the time children reach adulthood. It appears therefore that the most effective and useful skills teachers can help children acquire are skills in creatively analyzing situations and making effective decisions. These skills are closely related to the need to experience self-actualization. Educators should attempt to develop schools that meet students' basic needs, simultaneously providing them with opportunities to experience learning activities associated with self-actualization.

NEEDS OF STUDENTS AT RISK

Concern for students at risk has become a major theme in American education. The term *at risk* has generally referred to students who are likely to drop out of school. The Business Advisory Commission of the Education Commission of the States (ECS) has extended this concept to include youngsters who are likely not to make successful transitions to becoming productive adults.

FIGURE 2.2 Indicators of At-Risk Youth Cited in Current Literature

Category	Indicator
Background Characteristics	Single-parent family
	Teenage mother
	Youth employment
	Ethnic origin
	Poverty status
	Limited English speaking
	Parents' education
	Low birth weight
	Latchkey children
School Performance	Low grades
	Low test scores
	Learning disabled
	Illiteracy
	Attendance, tardiness
	Suspension, expulsion
	Remedial or vocational track
	Participation in school activities
Social Behavior	Drug/alcohol abuse
	Arrests
	Suicide attempts
	Self-esteem
	Attitudes toward school
	Effort in school

From R. Gabriel and P. Anderson, *Identifying At-Risk Youth in the Northwest States: A Regional Database* (Portland, Ore.: Northwest Regional Educational Laboratory, 1987), p. 3.

Even though it is difficult to determine the exact nature of children who are at risk, a variety of factors have been determined to be associated with students being at risk. Figure 2.2 presents these indicators as determined by a research review conducted by the Northwest Regional Educational Laboratory.

We believe that even though early identification of at-risk students is an important issue, identification is not the central issue facing school personnel. Most teachers and counselors know which students are at risk for failing school and/or for making a poor transition to adult life. The real issue becomes what can be done to assist these students. As with their lower-risk peers, the authors believe that programs or interventions developed to assist at-risk youth will be most effective when they are based on an understanding of the basic skill deficits and needs of these youth. Even though much work needs to be done in identifying the specific personal and emotional needs of students at-risk, it is becoming increasingly clear that the most seriously at-risk students come from home environments characterized by "negativism, harsh discipline practices, inconsistency, lack of structure, and lower levels of competence in parenting skills" (Ramsey & Walker, 1988), and that the severity of these factors is significantly related to the severity of the students' school problems. Because they have spent time in families characterized by confusion and lack of support, at-risk students enter school with some important skill deficits. The literature as well as our work with these children suggest the following six major areas of concern:

1. A history of poor adult-child relationships with its accompanying need for positive, supportive relationships,

2. A tendency to lack a sense of personal efficacy or power and the associated need to experience this by better understanding the learning process and developing a sense of personal responsibility and power,

3. A closely related focus on external factors as influencing their behavior and the need to learn to accept responsibility for their behavior and to see how they can control their own learning and behavior,

4. Low self-esteem, especially related to such school behaviors as achievement and peer friendships and the need to develop and validate a positive self-esteem through positive social interactions and school success,

5. A poorly developed sense of social cognition—an inability to understand others' feelings or points of view and take this into account when making decisions and the need to learn to understand others' responses and to work cooperatively with others,

6. Poor problem-solving skills and the need to develop these skills as a means to enhance self-efficacy and self-esteem as well as to develop an important life-long skill.

While the condition of being at risk has major social implications, it is also a factor related to the quality of schooling in our society. The coordinator of the At-Risk Research Project of The National Center on Effective Secondary Schools reinforces this concept:

> We have to face the fact that the condition of being at risk is partially generated by the school. The problems these kids bring to school are exacerbated by the way they're treated by the discipline system and the ways teachers interact with them. There is also a substantially detrimental effect caused by the lack of interesting and engaging experiences to which they will be able to respond. (Turnbaugh, 1986, p. 8)

This concept was recently echoed by British writers Mongon and Hart (in press):

> Schools must accept their own responsibility for examining how the dynamics of schooling may be contributing to "problem behaviour," and what might be done both to ease the problems pupils are currently experiencing and, where possible, to prevent the same problems arising with the next generation of pupils. (p. 218)

Research findings indicate that low-socioeconomic-status (SES) and minority students differ from their higher SES counterparts in that they need greater psychological support and praise (Brophy & Evertson, 1974; Soar & Soar, 1975; Solomon & Kendall, 1976), clearer classroom structure (Brophy & Evertson, 1974; Moskowitz & Hayman, 1976; Soar, 1983; Sanford & Evertson, 1981), and more active involvement in the learning process (Aronson et al., 1978; Goodlad & Oakes, 1988; Kagan, 1980). These findings as well as comments by skilled inner-city teachers who reviewed and field tested the methods presented throughout this book suggest that although all students benefit from teachers' implementing these methods, they are critical when teaching students at risk.

We believe that the student needs presented in this chapter, particularly the needs of students at risk, can be effectively met by teachers who choose to implement the methods presented throughout this book. This belief is supported by the fact that much of the research on effective schools and teacher effectiveness on which these methods are based was conducted in schools with many at-risk students. Furthermore, in order better to respond to the needs of students at risk, the materials in this book expand on the school effectiveness research by including a greater emphasis on students' personal and social skill development as well as increasing students' motivation to learn and their sense of understanding and influencing their classroom and school environment.

Teachers often are concerned that if they attempt to meet the needs of students experiencing behavior and learning problems, they will shortchange the students behaving appropriately and learning. We believe that the methods that help the troubled, at-risk student almost always create a more positive learning environment for other students. In a recent study of suspension and expulsions from various schools serving similar student populations, Galloway and Goodwin (1987) found that (1) whether a student is considered disruptive or maladjusted depends at least as much on factors within the school as on factors within the pupil or the family, and (2) schools meeting the needs of their most disruptive students are also more successful with all students in the school. Mongon and Hart (in press) support this concept:

> Even for those whose behaviour reflects difficult or stressful circumstances that lie outside our sphere of influence, a sensitive "curricular" response can, as Hanko (1985) has so effectively illustrated, not only have a beneficial effect upon the particular child for whom it was intended, but have the spin-off effect of enhancing the curriculum for the whole class. Instead of being a debilitating drain on our resources, the challenge of "problem behaviour" can thus become an opportunity for us as teachers to use our skills and professional judgement creatively, and find solutions which may potentially improve learning opportunities for all. (p. 222)

NEEDS OF EXCEPTIONAL STUDENTS

The emphasis on placing students in the least restrictive educational environment and the lack of funds available to provide special education services to students ensure that regular classroom teachers will continue to be responsible for a large portion of exceptional children's education. The use of effective classroom management methods influences all students but has a particularly strong impact on exceptional students. Emotionally disturbed students are more responsive to negative teacher or peer responses and require classroom environments in which relationships are characterized by safety and support (Epanchin & Paul, 1982; Jones, 1980; Wood, 1975). These students also benefit from structured environments in which academic and behavioral expectations and consequences are clearly taught, monitored, and implemented (Haring & Phillips, 1972; Kerr & Nelson, 1983; Walker, 1979). Learning disabled students also benefit from supportive, well-structured environments. In addition, these students have special needs for instructional methods and materials that meet their unique learning needs (Dunn, 1983, 1989; Smith, 1983; Weber, 1982).

Although often ignored, gifted students also have unique learning needs that are best served by teachers using the classroom management methods described throughout this book (Jones, 1983a). Because many gifted students possess a questioning attitude, skepticism, and sense of their own power (Seagoe, 1974) and because they have intensified needs to learn problem-solving skills, participate in decision making, and set and evaluate goals (Culross, 1982), they are especially resentful of and harmed by classroom management methods that emphasize rigid teacher control.

In working with exceptional students, you will be called on to use a wider range of teaching skills than with students who display more normative behavior. In fact, the teaching methods presented throughout this book are those used by effective special education teachers. Interestingly, these methods not only enable teachers to manage and instruct a wide range of exceptional students effectively, they also improve the behavior and achievement of the more typical students.

Educators are understandably concerned and frustrated when they encounter students whose needs seem more extensive than those of most students. Polly Nichols (1984) developed an interesting and useful model for considering how educators need to respond differently to students who vary in their personal needs and developmental level. As shown in Figure 2.3, Nichols believes that students can generally be classified into one of four groups. Autonomous students effectively meet their personal and learning needs in school settings and are often a joy to teach. Reactive students "have the skills in their repertoire to manage life in the mainstream, but they do so inconsistently; they react to external and internal stimuli by acting out, withdrawing, or avoiding school. They will do well for one teacher and be terrors for another; they do well for three days and do battle on the fourth, all for reasons that 'were not their fault' " (Nichols, 1984, p. 53). Reactive students often do not understand their schoolwork and lack prerequisite skills for completing work. They also frequently lack skills for getting along with other students, for controlling their emotions, and for problem solving. Therefore, these students need assistance in understanding their environment and in developing new skills that will enable them to meet their needs in school settings.

Self-centered students lack the ability to understand others' point of view and to comprehend the impact their behaviors have on others. They have often come from abusive or drug-affected families and require considerable assistance in developing new skills and altered self-perceptions. Teachers who have these students in their classroom often require assistance from other sources, and these students are frequently candidates for special education services. Dysfunctional students are generally not served in regular education classrooms. This category includes children who are autistic and seriously emotionally disturbed.

The important point Nichols makes in presenting her model is that when working with students who are experiencing behavior problems, teachers must go down the up staircase. Teachers will be most effective when they use with all students the methods described as being effective for autonomous students. When students fail to respond to these more proactive methods that place a priority on students' being internally motivated and responsible for their own behavior, teachers will need to develop the skills to use methods described as needed for reactive students. "For example, social approval is not used only with autonomous students; on level two, social approval plus activities, privileges and progress charts will be used to reinforce desired behaviors, and so on down to level four" (Nichols, 1984, p. 53). While Nichols's model suggests that reactive students receive

FIGURE 2.3 Down the Up Staircase: Step Up/Step Down Model

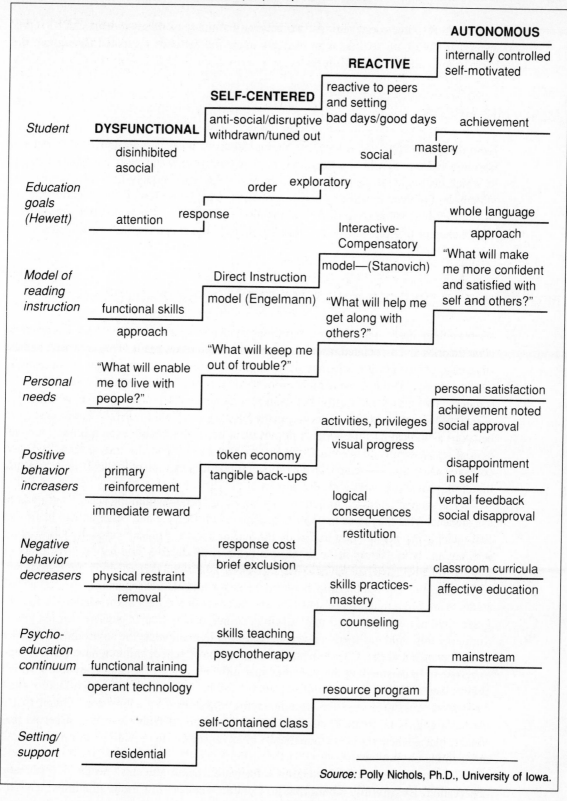

Source: Polly Nichols, Ph.D., University of Iowa.

services in resource room settings, we believe that many of these students can be served in regular classroom settings with teachers using the methods presented throughout this book to meet these students' needs.

ACADEMIC NEEDS

Even though meeting youngsters' psychological needs will make a dramatic difference in how they behave, in school settings it is also imperative that educators consider the extent to which instructional methods respond to needs that are uniquely important when individuals are involved in learning new information. Chapter 6 presents these learning needs as key variables influencing student motivation and learning. The material is presented in a later chapter in order that it may directly precede the chapter on effective instructional methods.

METHODS FOR DISCOVERING STUDENTS' PERSONAL NEEDS

We have three basic methods for determining students' needs. First, teachers can examine what theories and associated research results say about those needs. This approach has the advantage of providing teachers with information based on a large sample of students in varied settings. Perhaps even more important, this method is relatively free from the teachers' own biases and needs. For example, the teacher who does not feel comfortable allowing students to take an active part in the learning process may, in fact, interpret student behavior as indicating that students do not want or cannot handle even a limited amount of this responsibility. Theoretical statements that have stood the test of time and data collected using sound research designs are not influenced by such individual biases and may therefore provide us with a clearer picture.

The second approach to determining students' needs within the school setting is to ask students what they need in order to feel more comfortable and better able to learn. An individual is the world's best expert on himself or herself. Students basically know better than anyone what factors make them comfortable, productive, and happy. It is a fact of life that students have had fewer experiences than adults and consequently are less knowledgeable about the relationship between behavior and its consequences. Nevertheless, students are often much more sensitive and aware than teachers acknowledge. A fourth-grade child has been involved in observing and influencing human behavior for ten years. Similarly, this child has spent ten years attempting to manipulate the environment in order to meet personal needs. Consequently, even elementary school children have considerable expertise in understanding the variables that influence their behavior. They know which environmental factors create comfort, safety, and belongingness and which factors elicit discomfort, rejection, and the accompanying withdrawal or aggression. Given that a teacher's goal is to create environments that facilitate students' learning, it seems reasonable that teachers should systematically involve students in providing information about the learning environment.

The third method for obtaining information about students' needs is systematic observation. By carefully monitoring how children behave in various situations, teachers can learn a great deal about unmet student needs. One of the authors recently taught a child who often appeared very sluggish, unmotivated, and slow in both speech and comprehension. At times, however, the student was quite animated and aware. Before making a referral, and following an uninformative parent conference, the author began collecting data on the relationship between the student's behavior and food consumption. The student consistently seemed more animated after lunch. Data also revealed a consistent pattern between mornings when the student seemed sluggish and those when he reported having no breakfast or merely a cookie or a similarly poor breakfast. When the mother was shown these data, she reported that the child had hypoglycemia. This realization led to a discussion that culminated in the mother's agreeing to provide the necessary morning diet, and this change was followed by significant improvement in the child's behavior.

A young teacher provided another example of the benefits associated with carefully observing students' behavior as a means of assessing students' needs. When describing a student's behavior, the teacher noted that the student did not get along well with his peers and that this unmet need was very likely to be the cause of his problem. A more thorough examination of the boy's behavior, however, indicated that he had few negative peer contacts in situations such as recess or at lunch when fights might be expected. Instead, nearly all his negative peer contacts occurred when the class was involved in seatwork. Therefore, though it was quite possible that a need for belongingness influenced the boy's behavior, a more appropriate initial intervention involved responding to his academic needs by providing him with seatwork that he could complete successfully.

ACTIVITIES FOR EXAMINING STUDENTS' PERSONAL NEEDS

This section presents several activities that can be used to examine students' personal/psychological needs within the classroom. The first three activities are based on the theoretical work described earlier in the chapter and therefore stem from the first method of determining students' needs. The fourth activity directly involves students in providing teachers with information about students' needs in a classroom setting. Because chapter 11 includes a section on collection of data, activities for incorporating this third approach to assessing students' needs are included there.

ACTIVITY 2.1 Responding to Students' Basic Needs—Examining the Classroom Setting

Because this activity will require some time and thought, select a time when you can work relatively uninterrupted for perhaps an hour. Begin by writing the words *Physiological Needs* at the top of a sheet of paper. Now list two ways in which you ensure that these needs are being met in your classroom. Be specific when listing the factors. For example: The teacher provides five minutes of calm music and silent reading following lunch. Next, list two situations in the classroom that might hinder meeting students' physiological needs. Continue this activity by following the steps above for each of the remaining four needs presented by Maslow. If you are not currently teaching full time, complete this activity by selecting a classroom you have observed recently. Finally, after reading chapters 3 through 9, return to this activity and describe two specific changes that could be made in the classroom in order to meet each of the five student needs more effectively.

ACTIVITY 2.2 Responding to Students' Basic Needs—Examining an Individual Case

Select a student who is having particular difficulty in behaving appropriately in class. List at least one specific example to indicate how each of Maslow's needs is not being met in the classroom or school environment.

It is possible that you may not be able to list an example under one particular need but may be able to list three or four examples under another. The important point is that this activity will assist you in thoughtfully considering the student's actions in light of his or her needs. After completing chapters 3 through 9, return to this activity and list at least one method that can be used to ensure that each need is met for this child.

ACTIVITY 2.3 Examining Various Perspectives to a Behavior Problem

Select an incident in which a student misbehaved to such an extent that you had to send him or her to the office. Before continuing this activity, write down the punishment or consequence you would expect the student to receive for this act.

On a separate sheet of paper write a ½- to 1-page statement indicating how each of the following individuals would describe the incident leading to the referral: (1) yourself, (2) the student involved, (3) a student-centered counselor, and (4) the administrator who heard both your and the student's points of view.

At the bottom of each paper, write a brief statement indicating what you think each individual would suggest as the solution or resolution to this situation.

Having completed this exercise, write a statement concerning how you believe the situation should be responded to or resolved.

ACTIVITY 2.4 Discovering Students' Own Thoughts about Their Needs

This activity provides students with an opportunity to describe the extent to which their needs are being met in the classroom. The questionnaire presented in Figure 2.4 has been used in a variety of classrooms. We encourage you to use this form or to alter it in any manner that will provide a more accurate tool for determining students' needs.

Once you have prepared an instrument for obtaining information from students, set aside a suitable amount of time for introducing and administering the questionnaire. Be sure to prepare the students adequately by briefly discussing your reasons for seeking their ideas and sincerely expressing your desire that they take the activity seriously and feel free to provide honest responses.

The reader who has requested written feedback from students is aware of how easy it is simply to scan the material for any positive or negative comments, feel good about

FIGURE 2.4 Students' Psychological Needs Assessment Questionnaire

Check the appropriate box.	Always	Most of the time	Sometimes	Seldom	Never
Your thoughts about our class					

Physiological

1. Do you eat a good breakfast each morning?
2. Does your teacher touch you enough?
3. Can you see the blackboard and screen from where you are sitting?
4. Do I talk loud and clearly enough for you to hear?
5. Do you have time to relax during the day?
6. Do you have enough time to complete your assignments?
7. Do we go slowly enough in class?
8. Do you need a study period at the end of the day?
9. Is the room a quiet place to work?

Safety and Security

10. Are your grades fair?
11. Does each day in this class seem organized?
12. Do you understand the school and classroom rules?
13. Is the discipline used in this classroom fair?
14. Can you say what you'd like to in this class?
15. Do you feel free enough to ask me questions?
16. Can you trust your teacher?
17. Can you get help when you need it?
18. Are you happy when you take your report card home?

Love and Belonging

19. Is the room a happy place to be?
20. Do you think that the students in this class like you?

(continued)

FIGURE 2.4 (continued)

Check the appropriate box. Your thoughts about our class	Always	Most of the time	Sometimes	Seldom	Never
21. Am I friendly and do I smile at you?					
22. Do I take time with you each day?					
23. Does your teacher show that she or he likes you?					
24. Do you feel that I listen to you when you have a problem?					
25. Do I praise you when you deserve it?					
26. Do other students respect your property?					
27. Do other students care about how well you do in school?					
28. Do I listen to your suggestions?					
Self-Esteem					
29. Do you feel involved in this class?					
30. Do you feel proud when you share a project with the class?					
31. Do you take part in class discussions?					
32. Do you follow the classroom rules?					
33. Do you help other students learn?					
34. Are you a good student?					
35. In which subject area do you feel most successful?					
Self-Actualization					
36. Are you able to study things that interest you?					
37. Can you use what you learn in school?					
38. Do you have a chance to be creative in your schoolwork?					
39. Do you like to continue your studies at home on your own?					
40. Are you excited about what you are learning in school?					

having asked for feedback, and file the material away. There are two problems with this approach to responding to student feedback. First, by merely scanning the feedback you may either fail to notice subtle but consistent feedback or overreact to several negative statements that are not representative of the feelings expressed by the majority of students. If you receive a piece of negative feedback from only one or two students, you may want to discuss the findings with the students (if students have signed their names) or to consider why a few students responded as they did (it may simply be that the student(s) had a bad experience immediately preceding the administration of the questionnaire). It is unlikely, however, that you would want to make a major change in the classroom, or even raise the issue with the entire class. On the other hand, if three-fourths of the class respond that they would like a change, it is important that the issue be thoughtfully examined and discussed with the class. Unless student feedback is clearly summarized and tabulated, it is easy to confuse major issues that need attention with comments from a few students that are taken too personally and blown out of proportion.

A second danger associated with merely scanning student feedback is that unless the results are shared with students and obvious responses are made to their suggestions, students begin to feel that the activity is not meaningful and that their input is not valued. Consequently, it is advisable to create a method for displaying the results so that they can be shared with students. The easiest approach is often to tally the results. Figure 2.5 provides the tallied results obtained by using the first nine questions on the student feedback form presented in Figure 2.4.

FIGURE 2.5 Results of Administering a Student-Needs Questionnaire

Your thoughts about our class	Always	Most of the time	Sometimes	Seldom	Never
1. Do you eat a good breakfast each morning?	////	ℍℍ ℍℍ	ℍℍ /	////	
2. Does your teacher touch you enough?	ℍℍ ℍℍ	ℍℍ	ℍℍ /	//	//
3. Can you see the blackboard and screen from where you are sitting?	ℍℍ ℍℍ ////	ℍℍ /	//	//	
4. Do I talk loud and clearly enough for you to hear?	ℍℍ ℍℍ ℍℍ ///	ℍℍ //	//		
5. Do you have time to relax during the day?	///	ℍℍ ////	ℍℍ ///	//	////
6. Do you have enough time to complete your assignments?	ℍℍ //	ℍℍ ℍℍ /	///	//	
7. Do we go slowly enough in class?	ℍℍ	ℍℍ ℍℍ //	////	//	
8. Do you need a study period at the end of the day?	///	ℍℍ //	ℍℍ //	ℍℍ //	/
9. Is the room a quiet place to work?	//	ℍℍ ////	ℍℍ ////	//	///

ACTIVITY 2.5 Interpreting and Responding to Student Feedback

After developing and administering a student feedback form and summarizing the results, you should interpret the results and decide what changes, if any, need to be made. The following tasks and questions will help facilitate this process.

List the three statements students marked most frequently in the two most positive categories. For each of these statements, write one factor in the classroom that contributes to this positive student reaction.

List the three statements students marked most often in the lowest categories. For each of these statements, write one factor in the classroom that contributes to this negative student reaction. After completing chapters 3 through 9, return to the activity and, following each classroom factor, list one change (including teacher's behavior) that could be made in the classroom to reduce or eliminate this factor.

Complete this activity by listing three things you learned about your students' needs based on the results of the questionnaire.

A simple tally enables you to see where changes may be needed, as well as areas that students view as strengths. An interesting extension to tallying data is to determine a numerical average score for each item. When using a five-choice rating scale, as in Figure 2.4, a score of five can be assigned for each student who marked the most positive response, a score of four can be given for the second response, and so on. The scores can be added and then divided by the number of students completing the form in order to achieve a class score for each item. Therefore, the results shown in Figure 2.5 indicate that the class score for item 1 in Figure 2.4 is 3.6. Obtaining a class score for each item allows you to compare students' attitudes and feelings at different times throughout the school year. For example, if you responded to a low score on item 1 by teaching a unit on nutrition or sending a letter home to all parents about students' breakfasts, you could check the results of the intervention by administering the questionnaire again after several weeks and comparing the class scores on item 1 to see whether a change had taken place.

SUMMARY

Many teachers view their lack of ability to understand and effectively respond to unproductive student behavior as a major cause of job-related stress and personal frustration. Anyone who has taught has heard a colleague say in exasperation, "I just don't understand why Johnny acts that way." Chapter 2 presents the important concept that student behavior can be understood by considering basic psychological needs students bring to the school setting. In many if not most cases when students act unproductively at school they are responding to the fact that basic needs are not being met in the school setting. Unproductive school behavior is more frequent among students whose basic needs are not being met at home and in the community. Nevertheless, the problems outside of school are often not the major cause of the student's school difficulties, nor does their presence absolve us of our responsibility to create learning environments that meet students' basic needs.

Throughout much of the 1980s school improvement projects focused heavily on improving the quality of instruction. During the late 1980s educators became increasingly aware of the number of at-risk students who enter school without the personal support and positive self-esteem needed to succeed. All students will experience greater success when they are educated in settings that meet their basic needs, but this factor is critical for students who enter school with many needs unmet.

RECOMMENDED READING

Allers, R. (1982). *Divorce, children, and the school*. Princeton, N.J.: Princeton Book Company.

Coopersmith, S. (1967). *The antecedents of self-esteem*. San Francisco: W. H. Freeman.

Dreikurs, R., Grunwald, B., & Pepper, F. (1971). *Maintaining sanity in the classroom: Illustrated teaching techniques*. New York: Harper and Row.

Elkind, D. (1981). *The hurried child: Growing up too fast too soon*. Reading, Mass.: Addison-Wesley.

Englander, M. (1986). *Strategies for classroom discipline*. New York: Praeger.

Erikson, E. (1963). *Childhood and society*, 2nd ed. New York: Norton.

Erikson, E. (1968). *Identity, youth, and crisis*. New York: Norton.

Glasser, W. (1969). *Schools without failure*. New York: Harper and Row.

Glasser, W. (1985). *Control theory in the classroom*. New York: Harper and Row.

Gordon, T. (1974). *Teacher effectiveness training*. New York: Wyden.

Holt, J. (1979). *The underachieving school*. New York: Pitman.

Jones, V. (1980). *Adolescents with behavior problems: Strategies for teaching, counseling, and parent involvement*. Boston: Allyn and Bacon.

Maslow, A. (1968). *Toward a psychology of being*. New York: Van Nostrand.

Morse, W. (1985). *The education and treatment of socio-emotionally impaired children and youth*. Syracuse, N.Y.: Syracuse University Press.

Phlegar, J. (1987). *Good beginnings for young children: Early identification of high-risk youth and programs that promote success*. Andover, Mass.: Regional Laboratory for Educational Improvement of the Northeast and Islands.

Purkey, W., & Novak, J. (1984). *Inviting school success: A self-concept approach to teaching and learning*, 2nd ed. Belmont, Calif.: Wadsworth.

Spaulding, R. & Spaulding, C. (1982). *Research-based classroom management*. San Jose, Calif.: Maple Press.

Willis, H. (1987). *Students at risk: A review of conditions, circumstances, indicators, and educational implications*. Elmhurst, Ill.: North Central Regional Educational Laboratory.

Wood, M. (1975). *Developmental therapy*. Baltimore: University Park Press.

PART II

Creating Positive Interpersonal Relationships in the Classroom

An ounce of prevention is worth a pound of cure: this statement is the key to effective classroom management. A large percentage of classroom problems can be prevented by creating positive, safe classroom environments. Books on classroom management too often focus on techniques for modifying individual students' behavior through a system of rewards and punishments while failing to acknowledge the vital role the social atmosphere plays in influencing students' behavior. Unfortunately, this major oversight frequently creates situations in which students are manipulated into behaving appropriately in environments that do not meet their basic psychological or academic needs. This approach is not only thoughtless and unfair to students, but it also creates a situation in which the new behavior is maintained only as long as desired rewards are present. Therefore, we can understand why programs based solely on behavioristic interventions have had limited success in generalizing behavior change to new environments.

Part II focuses on specific methods for preventing unproductive student behavior by creating positive interpersonal relationships in the classroom and throughout the school. These methods are important because they help create environments in which students feel happy and excited about learning. This atmosphere, in turn, tends to elicit more positive student behavior and to facilitate learning. Because the school's primary goal is to transmit knowledge, it seems logical to assume that schools should create learning environments that allow all students to view the acquisition of knowledge as an exciting, enjoyable activity. Unless we create such environments, we will continue to find that many students see learning as a solemn and difficult task to be engaged in only when appropriate rewards or punishments exist and to be terminated as soon as possible. In a democratic society characterized by amazingly rapid change, this attitude creates not only poor mental health but also citizens who cannot adequately govern themselves.

Educators should be aware of the dangers inherent in the completely unsubstantiated belief that time spent in creating classrooms in which students feel involved, safe, and happy could somehow be better spent in additional instructional time. As we discuss in Part I, students' academic performance is enhanced when we take time to respond to their personal and psychological needs. Research (Purkey & Novak, 1984; Johnson & Johnson, 1987; Soar, 1983; Walberg & Waxman, 1983) indicates that positive affect is associated with improved student attitudes and higher-level thinking skills. Another important reason for blending academic and personal-social skill building is that if schools' goals include preparing young people to be involved citizens, activities aimed at developing a sound base of knowledge must be balanced with skills in interpersonal relations and problem solving.

Chapter 3 examines two pivotal aspects of teacher-student relationships: (1) the personal, affective quality of these relationships, and (2) how we communicate expectations to students. Chapter 4 focuses on the quality of peer relationships within classrooms. The chapter provides numerous activities for enhancing positive, cooperative peer relationships. Parents can do much to encourage positive student attitudes toward school, and chapter 5 examines methods you can use to create positive, supportive relationships with parents.

CHAPTER 3

Establishing Positive Teacher-Student Relationships

What research findings and student reports on the importance of self-regard mean for educators is that many common classroom problems such as student disruption, inattention, apathy, and anxiety probably indicate negative self-regard on the part of the students exhibiting such behavior.

/ William Purkey and John Novak (1984)
Inviting School Success

It seems to the writer that the most important single factor in establishing sound mental health is the relationship that is built up between the teacher and his or her pupils.

/ Virginia Axline (1947)
Play Therapy

Teachers retain their effectiveness as professional persons only so long as they remain warmly human, sensitive to the personal needs of children, and skillful in establishing effective relationships with them.

/ Robert Bush (1954)
The Teacher-Pupil Relationship

The quality of teacher-student relationships dramatically affects whether students' personal needs are met in the classroom. Students spend nearly a quarter of their waking lives between ages 6 and 17 with teachers. Because teachers are responsible for evaluating students' work and controlling the quality of life in the classroom, they are powerful adult figures in students' lives. Effective teachers understand the influence they have on students and use this influence positively.

A significant body of research indicates that academic achievement and students' behavior are influenced by the quality of the teacher-student relationship. Students prefer teachers who are warm and friendly (Rosenshine, 1970; Norman & Harris, 1981). More important, positive teacher-student relationships, in which teachers use the skills described in this chapter, are associated with more positive student responses to school (Aspy & Roebuck, 1977; Norman & Harris, 1981) and with increased academic achievement (Aspy, 1969, 1972; Aspy & Roebuck, 1977; Brookover et al., 1978; Brophy & Evertson, 1976; Davidson & Lang, 1960; Hefele, 1971; Kleinfield, 1975; Soar, 1977; Stallings, 1975; Stoffer, 1970). Davidson and Lang (1960) reported that students who felt liked by their teachers had higher academic achievement and more productive classroom behavior than did students who felt their teachers held them in lower regard. Similarly, Morrison and McIntyre (1969) reported that 73 percent of the low-achieving students in their study perceived their teachers as thinking poorly of them, but only 10 percent of high achievers held such beliefs. When examining students' adjustment, Truax and Tatum (1966) found that children adjusted more positively to school, teachers, and peers when teachers displayed empathy and positive regard for children.

An excellent example of the importance of combining acceptance with respect for students was reported by Kleinfeld (1972) in a powerful analysis of teachers' interactions with Eskimo and Indian students who had recently moved to urban settings. Kleinfeld found that teachers who were effective with these children were able to combine showing a personal interest in the students with demands for solid academic achievement. Summarizing her findings, she states:

> The essence of the instructional style which elicits a high level of intellectual performance from village Indian and Eskimo students is to create an extremely warm personal relationship and to actively demand a level of academic work which the student does not suspect he can attain. Village students thus interpret the teacher's demandingness not as bossiness or hostility, but rather as another expression of his personal concern, and meeting the teacher's academic standards becomes their reciprocal obligation in an intensely personal relationship. (Kleinfeld, 1972, p. 34)

Support for the importance of improving teacher-student relationships can also be found in numerous studies indicating that teachers demonstrate a low rate of positive statements when working with children (Brophy, 1981; Greenwood & Hops, 1976; Luce & Hoge, 1978; Thomas, Presland, Grant, & Glynn, 1978; White, 1975).

In general, praise for appropriate and desired behavior is a rare event, particularly between adult and child. Studies of natural rates of teacher praise and approval to individual children have shown them to be extremely low in an absolute sense and also in relation to other categories of teacher behavior. (Walker, 1979, p. 95)

In her *Successful Schools for Young Adolescents,* Joan Lipsitz (1984) remarked that successful schools for this age group provide a warm, personal environment. Describing these schools, Lipsitz writes:

Gradually, students gain increasing amounts of independence. They remain, however, in a highly personalized environment. The nature of the schools' organizational structure establishes continuity in adult-child relationships and opportunities for the lives of students and adults to cross in mutually meaningful ways. In each school, students express their appreciation for being cared about and known. They are actively aware of being liked, which is notable only because, in most schools, young adolescents are generally disliked. (p. 181)

Taken together, this research points to a need for teachers to learn and conscientiously apply skills in relating more positively to their students.

Fortunately, research (Aspy & Roebuck, 1977) demonstrates that teachers' behavior in the area of interpersonal relationships can be significantly changed by inservice training. Furthermore, these changes can positively affect students' attendance, achievement, and self-concept.

In examining children's behavior from a behavioristic perspective, we can say that teachers control the consequences (rewards and punishments) that influence children's behavior during a significant number of hours each day. Because we selectively reinforce desired behaviors, we have a major influence on students' behavior. The quality of the teacher-student relationship significantly influences the value children place on reinforcers controlled by the teacher. Behavioristic concepts stress the importance of social reinforcement (praise) and specify that when tangible or token reinforcers are needed to influence students' behavior, we must pair these with social reinforcement so that the child gradually begins to respond to our praise. How well students respond either to concrete reinforcers dispensed by the teacher or to teachers' praise, however, is based on the quality of the teacher-student relationship.

THE TEACHER AS MODEL

Modeling theory provides another reason to be concerned about the quality of the teacher-student relationship. Children learn a great deal by watching adults. Much of children's behavior is developed by emulating the behaviors of adults who play significant roles in their lives.

One of the most salient developments in American social psychology during the past decade has been what for many laymen appears as a demonstration of the obvious; namely, children learn by watching others. Or, to put the issue in more provocative form: the behavior of others is contagious. (Bronfenbrenner, 1970, p. 124)

Social learning theorists have shown that individuals learn many things primarily by observing and modeling the behavior of others. Research (Bandura, 1969, 1977) indicates that individuals are more likely to model the behavior of people whom they view as possessing competence and control over resources, and who are a major source of control, support, and reinforcement. Because teachers possess these characteristics, they are in an excellent position to serve as models for their students. Studies also suggest that people are more likely to model the behavior of others in unfamiliar situations in which rules and expected behaviors have not been established. Because the beginning of the school year is the time when many students experience the classroom as most uncomfortable and unclear, it is important that early in the school year we model behaviors we wish them to emulate. On several occasions when we have presented information about current educational research to professionals in fields other than education, someone in the audience has commented that the research on the importance of the first few days of school coincides with their own experiences. These professionals relate that in their own public school experiences they knew after only a few school days if the teacher was someone who would run a well-organized class and whom they could respect. One participant recently recalled that teachers usually got back what they gave out. If they were well organized and treated students warmly and politely, students responded in kind.

We must realize that our influence as models continues throughout the school year. In many schools, student turnover is high, and the many students who transfer into the school have their initial and most influential contacts with the teacher at times other than the first days of school. Teachers frequently comment that transfer students often gravitate to a less-than-ideal group of students. If we wish to have new students accept our values, we must make a special effort to provide them with an adult model who demonstrates competence and warm care for the new student. A few minutes of extra time spent going over classroom procedures and meeting privately with the students to discuss their work and offer assistance can dramatically increase the likelihood that they will model us rather than the behavior of any potentially negative group of peers.

Bronfenbrenner also reported that young people are more likely to model behavior that is exhibited by several adults. Furthermore, youngsters tend to model behaviors if they think adults benefit from the performance of these behaviors. These factors demonstrate the importance of creating schools in which a large percentage of adults demonstrate the skills and attitudes described in this chapter and in which teachers are reinforced by their peers and administrators for exhibiting these skills.

Before presenting specific approaches for improving teacher-student relationships, we must place this issue in a proper perspective. The quality of teacher-student relationships has great influence on the amount of productive or disruptive behavior students display in a school setting. By improving the quality of our interactions with students, we can significantly increase the amount of productive student behavior. Creating positive teacher-student relationships, however, will obviously not solve all classroom problems. We must be careful not to confuse the importance of establishing positive teacher-student relationships with the belief that all classroom problems can be solved by love and understanding. Regardless of how concerned, positive, and fair a teacher is, students frequently misbehave in classes that are poorly organized and in which students are not provided with appropriate and interesting instructional tasks.

ESTABLISHING EFFECTIVE RELATIONSHIPS WITH STUDENTS

As anyone who has taught for very long realizes, students need and want positive teacher behavior to be associated with firmness, realistic limits, and competent teaching. The ability to blend warmth and caring with realistic limits is frequently a difficult task for young teachers. Unfortunately, this confusion is occasionally intensified by advice suggesting that beginning teachers should be less warm toward and more distant from their students. The main issue is not whether teachers should be less warm or friendly, but that they must stimultaneously assert both their right to be treated with respect and their responsibility for ensuring that students treat each other with kindness. Warmth and concern can exist side by side with firmness. Indeed, effective teaching involves blending these vital ingredients.

Before presenting specific communication skills that help teachers develop open, effective relationships with students, it is important to consider the general issue of how teachers can most effectively relate to their students. In his classic book *Teacher Effectiveness Training*, Thomas Gordon (1974) writes:

> The relationship between a teacher and a student is good when it has (1) *Openness* or *Transparency*, so each is able to risk directness and honesty with the other; (2) *Caring*, when each knows that he is valued by the other; (3) *Interdependence* (as opposed to dependency) of one on the other; (4) *Separateness*, to allow each to grow and to develop his uniqueness, creativity, and individuality; (5) *Mutual Needs Meeting*, so that neither's needs are met at the expense of the other's needs. (p. 24)

Creating Open, Professionally Appropriate Dialogue with Students

Although the specific decisions teachers make concerning their relationships with students vary depending on their students' age, the basic themes related to teacher-student relationships are similar across grade levels. One important question involves deciding how open and involved a teacher wishes to be with students. In an earlier work (Jones, 1980) one of us wrote that teachers can select from among three general types of teacher-student relationships. Although teacher-student relationships vary on numerous dimensions, a primary factor involves the level of openness we choose. We can choose a teacher-student relationship characterized by:

1. Almost complete openness, in which we share a wide range of personal concerns and values with students,

2. Openness related to our reactions to and feelings about the school environment, with limited sharing of aspects reflecting our out-of-school life, and

3. An almost exclusive focus on a role-bound relationship; that is, we share no personal feelings or reactions, but merely perform our instructional duties.

The first type of teacher-student relationship is frequently chosen by teachers working in informal settings with older students. For example, teachers in secondary alternative schools may choose very open, self-disclosing relationships with their students. These relationships may be very effective in some settings, but they are generally not the best practice in most school settings. Not surprisingly, beginning teachers often grapple with whether they should be involved in very open, personal relationships with their students. They may wonder about the extent to which they should join in with students, share students' interests, use student slang, and so on. Our experience suggests that students respond best to adults who are comfortable with themselves, their values, and their personal preferences and who, when appropriate, can share these nonjudgmentally with students. Consequently, if a teacher enjoys the same music as many students do, discussing it with students offers a format for relaxed, personal interaction. Likewise, when our preferences or values differ, encouraging a two-way exchange of ideas can prove stimulating and educational to both the students and ourselves.

We should, however, avoid becoming overly involved in students' interests or activities outside of school, particularly those of us who are secondary teachers. Adolescents are working at developing their own identity and generally view adulthood as a positive stage in which individuals have reached desired personal and social adjustment. Consequently, adolescents are confused by adults who show intense interest in students' social activities and interests. It confuses them to see adults who appear to want to be similar to young people or a part of their peer group. If adults do not have something more interesting or valuable to offer, a major goal of adolescence—moving toward partnership in the adult community—is devalued. Students need to know that we have interesting lives apart from them and that we find life stimulating and challenging in some ways that are different from theirs. At the same time, they need us to be interested enough in them and open enough with our own values to share our ideas with them and engage them in discussions of personal as well as academic matters.

These issues highlight the value of establishing the second type of teacher-student relationship—one in which we share our reactions to and feelings about occurrences within the school setting and share with students limited aspects of our out-of-school life. Teachers who choose this type of relationship will often share with students occurrences involving their children, recreational activities, or cultural events they have attended. These teachers will also show considerable openness in discussing their feelings about events in the classroom.

Many years ago John Holt discussed the concept of natural as opposed to arbitrary or role-bound authority. He stated that virtually all teachers have natural authority, which is the authority based on their knowledge of the subject matter, their ability to develop effective and exciting learning activities, their control of important resources, and their ability to manage effectively and facilitate the classroom group. Students are impressed with this type of authority. One need only observe young people at athletic camps to see how extremely impressed they are with natural authority and how it can motivate positive, on-task behavior. Teachers also possess role-bound authority. This is the authority based on their role as teacher and includes their ability unilaterally to reward and punish student behavior. Holt suggests that these two types of authority are in opposition; that is, the more natural authority one uses, the less one needs to use role-bound authority; conversely, the more role-bound authority one uses, the less students can observe or will be responsive to one's natural authority.

The importance of being open enough to allow students to know us as people was highlighted for one of the authors during his experiences teaching behavior-disordered junior high school students. Discussions with students indicated that a number of students in the school were involved in shoplifting from a large chain store near the school. However, these same students frequently visited a leather shop where the proprietor kept money, tools, and leather on the outer counter while he worked in a back room. When asked why they stole from the chain store but not the leather worker, the students expressed some surprise and indicated emphatically that they knew this man and they did not steal from "real people." This incident emphasized an important issue in dealing with young people. They often react negatively to and abuse people whom they view as merely roles, but they less often create problems for individuals whom they know and understand.

In addition to letting students know us as people, we can model a degree of openness to our own students' verbal expressions of concerns and feelings in our classrooms. An excellent example of effective modeling occurred several years ago when we visited the classroom of an extremely effective teacher. The eighth-grade students in his class were actively involved in a science project and the room buzzed with noise and interest. A boy called across the room to his friend, John, and requested that John throw him the scissors. John immediately obliged, and the airborne scissors narrowly missed hitting another student. Rather than shouting at John, the teacher walked over to him and put his hand on John's shoulder. He proceeded to share with John the fact that the near miss had frightened him because he cared about and felt responsible for the students in his class. He then asked John if in the future he would carry the scissors across the room. The teacher then spoke briefly with the boy who had requested the scissors and with the student who had narrowly missed being hit. At the end of the period the teacher took time to review the importance of the classroom procedure regarding scissors and had students demonstrate the correct procedure.

After class the teacher explained why his intervention had been so calm and personal. He stated that young adolescents are involved in so many changes that their egos are very fragile and they personalize almost everything. He went on to say that his goal was to provide the student with information in a manner that would enhance the likelihood that the student would listen. Had he yelled at the student or made an example of him in front of the class, the student probably would have responded by focusing on the teacher's mean behavior rather than by examining his own behavior. The teacher stated that by admitting to his own feeling and sharing it with the student, he had provided the student with valuable information without making him defensive.

This incident is an excellent example of a skilled teacher's ability spontaneously to synthesize a working knowledge of adolescent development with practical communication skills. The result of this synthesis was that the teacher was able to respond in a way that facilitated the student's personal growth while modeling emotional control and sensitivity to the student's feelings.

A central theme of this book is that effective classroom managers are aware of classroom processes and are willing and able to engage students in assessing and adjusting classroom procedures and instructional methods. This act involves not only our own awareness and self-analysis, but also involving students in open dialogue and problem solving.

An interesting example of the decision we must make about openness to student feedback occurred while this book was being written. A student-teacher being supervised by one of us was challenged by a student in his sophomore biology class. Frustrated by his inability to understand a lecture, the student stood up at the back of the class and stated loudly, "This class stinks!" Rather than sending the student to the office, the teacher responded by stating that, though he wished the student would share his frustration in a more polite manner, he was glad that he was able to state his anger rather than not come to class. The teacher proceeded to inform the student that he would like to discuss the student's concern, but that first he needed to determine whether it was shared by a majority of the class or only by a few students. The teacher's inquiry indicated that only three students shared this concern. Therefore, the teacher indicated that it made more sense for him and the three students to work together to consider how to make the class better for them. The student responded positively, and several discussions led to a positive resolution.

An interesting sidelight to this story involved the supervising teacher's reaction. This teacher strongly supported the third approach to teacher-student relationships. He stated that teachers cannot afford to be open with students or to discuss classroom instructional or behavioral matters. Instead, he believed that teachers must always be in authoritarian command of the classroom and that students must be required to do what teachers expect with no questions asked. The student-teacher who very effectively used an open response experienced considerable pressure from the school setting to become socialized to accepting the third type of response.

An optional manner for handling this situation within the context of the second type of teacher-student relationship was offered by a skilled junior high school physical education teacher. She indicated that even though she supports the concept of teachers being open about their reactions to classroom events, she felt that students can be taught that the teacher will not allow abusive language or direct confrontation of a teacher in front of a class. She believes that students should know ahead of time that when this occurs they will be politely but firmly required to leave the class, knowing also that at a later time they will have an opportunity to discuss their concerns and behaviors with the teacher.

The different reactions chosen by the teachers in this example exemplify the decision we must make concerning the type of openness to students' input we select. Certainly, each teacher must operate at a degree of openness that is personally comfortable. Nevertheless, the second type of openness enhances students' sense of ownership in, and impact on, the classroom environment and thus can improve classroom management and student motivation. Teachers who wish to begin the school year with a rather closed, role-bound teacher-student relationship may wish to consider ways gradually to increase the degree to which they interact with students in an open and meaningful manner on topics related to classroom organization, management, and instruction.

Our experience supervising beginning teachers suggests that young teachers' concerns about teacher-student relationships are frequently confounded by conflicting messages they receive from the university and public school sites. People responsible for supervising young teachers can facilitate the transition into this demanding but rewarding profession by encouraging dialogue by all concerned about the quality of teacher-student relationships.

Systematically Building Better Relationships

Even though using the second type of teacher-student relationship will generally enhance the rapport teachers can establish with students, it is sometime desirable for teachers to act more systematically in developing positive teacher-student relationships. We can express our interest in and concern for students by (1) monitoring the quality of our relationships with students, with a focus on maintaining a high rate of positive statements; (2) creating opportunities for personal discussions with them; and (3) demonstrating our interest in activities that are important to them.

Maintain a High Ratio of Positive to Negative Statements

Children are sensitive to praise and criticism given by adults. Unfortunately, many teachers find that disruptive behavior is more noticeable and therefore respond to it more frequently than to on-task behvavior. As indicated in Figure 2.1, frequent negative remarks by the teacher are usually accompanied by students' dislike for school. Though we often fall into the trap of believing that critical remarks will improve students' behavior, research suggests that the opposite is true.

> In one study we took a good class and made it into a bad one for a few weeks by having the teacher no longer praise the children. When the teacher no longer praised the children, off-task behavior increased from 8.7 percent to 25.5 percent. The teacher criticized off-task behavior and did not praise on-task behavior. When the teacher was asked to increase her criticism from 5 times in 20 minutes to 16 times in 20 minutes, the children showed even more off-task behavior. Off-task behavior increased to an average of 31.2 percent, and on some days was over 50 percent. Attention to that off-task behavior increased its occurrence when no praise was given for working. Introduction of praise back into the classroom restored good working behavior. (Becker, Engelmann, & Thomas, 1975, p. 69)

Most children need and want attention from their teacher. If they find that it is easier to obtain this attention by negative actions, they will understandably increase the frequency of such behavior. Unfortunately, this interchange not only negatively affects the student's self-concept, but it also creates a ripple effect that often produces a generally negative classroom atmosphere. In a real sense teachers in such cases are actually responsible for increasing unproductive student behavior.

In a more positive vein, attending to on-task behavior and increasing the ratio of positive to negative statements can increase on-task behavior and can rapidly create a more positive classroom environment. In his *Inviting School Success*, William Purkey (1978) discusses the benefits of teachers' sending inviting rather than disinviting statements to students. In defining these terms Purkey writes:

> As used here, an invitation is a summary description of message—verbal and nonverbal, formal and informal—continuously transmitted to students with the intention of informing them that they are responsible, able, and valuable. Conversely, a disinvitation is intended to tell them that they are irresponsible, incapable, and worthless. (p. 3)

Purkey explains the importance of inviting statements:

> Rather than viewing students as physical objects to be moved about like puppets on strings, the teacher's primary role is to see students in essentially positive ways and to invite them to behave accordingly. Students, like all of us, greatly benefit from others who see and communicate to them the positive traits and potentials that they may not see in themselves. . . .

Judging by what we now know about school life, an invitational approach to education very likely increases the probability of student success and happiness in the classroom. (pp. vi, vii)

In their book *Inviting School Success*, Purkey and Novak (1984) set forth four types of teacher behaviors toward students:

1. Intentionally disinviting
2. Unintentionally disinviting
3. Unintentionally inviting
4. Intentionally inviting

An example of an intentionally disinviting behavior would be the teacher who on the first day of school privately singles out a student whose sibling had been a particular problem several years earlier and informs the child that if he is anything like his brother, this will be a very difficult year for him. Even though this teacher statement is intentional and intended to motivate the student to behave properly, the student receives it as punitive, unfair, and disinviting. An example of an unintentionally disinviting statement was provided by a high school vice-principal. He stated that the day before final exam week began, he observed a student requesting assistance from a teacher. The teacher's response, ''Don't worry, you haven't got a chance of passing the test anyway,'' was devastating but probably unintentionally disinviting.

Teachers make many inviting comments to students. For example, teachers often greet students at the door, state how glad they are to see a student, and respond positively to the quality of student work. Some of this inviting behavior occurs unintentionally because teachers are positive people who care about their students. On other occasions, teachers consciously consider the impact of positive invitations and intentionally invite students to be positively involved in their classes. An excellent example of intentionally invitational behavior and its relationship to teacher openness with students was shared with the authors by a high school English teacher. One day the teacher experienced a small crisis before arriving at school. The first two periods went fairly well. However, the teacher became tired and anxious as the day went on and was concerned about teaching his unruly third-period class. At the end of the second period one of his better junior English students asked for some assistance. The teacher stated that he was not feeling well and asked the student if he would assist the teacher. The student was glad to help and the teacher suggested that they both stand at the door, greet the incoming students, and make a statement about what an interesting class this was going to be. The teacher reported that when the bell rang and he turned to the class, every student was seated and attentively focused on the front of the class—an unheard of reaction from these students. The teacher then noticed two sets of students who were not in his third period class. They informed him that they had heard this was going to be an interesting class and had decided to attend. Two of the students had even obtained permission from their third-period teacher. The English teacher reported that after clarifying the issue of the additional students he had one of the most rewarding instructional experiences in some time.

In addition to their value in increasing positive student attitudes, invitational interactions provide the basis for creating teacher-student relationships that facilitate the use of corrective interventions described in chapters 10 and 11. An excellent example of this concept was provided by a student-teacher with whom one of us was working during the final editing of this book. The student-teacher was working with one of the most disruptive third-graders we have encountered. Each day the boy was involved in many instances of aggressive behavior toward peers and insubordination to adults. Because the school's assertive discipline program had only increased the student's acting-out behavior, and because the boy's parents would not allow the school to provide special education services, the principal was considering expelling the student.

The student-teacher decided to work with the student as part of her assignment in a classroom management course. In so doing, she was asked to attempt many of the methods described throughout this book and was encouraged to work consistently (and persistently) on establishing rapport with the student. The student's initial responses were extremely negative. He frequently and vividly informed the student-teacher that he hated teachers (a value reinforced by his parents) and that he wanted nothing to do with her. But the teacher persisted. She discovered that the boy's mother raised show dogs, and she watched a cable television show from New York in which the mother's dog took second place in a national competition. The student-teacher discussed this event with the student and attempted to discover other aspects of the boy's life. One day when a professional athlete with the same name as the boy's was traded, the teacher laminated the article in plastic and placed it on the bulletin board with a large red arrow pointing to it. The class was understandably curious, and the boy received considerable attention. Gradually, he increased his willingness to work cooperatively with the teacher. Although he would not become involved in problem solving, he did agree to a contract that was associated with considerable changes in behavior. Although the dramatic improvement in the student's behavior required behavioristic methods, these were not effective until the student was willing to work with the teacher. The improved relationship made possible other interventions that led to important changes.

Communicating High Expectations

How teachers communicate their expectations about how well students will do in the classroom is an important and well-documented factor in teacher-student relationships. School effectiveness research (Brookover et al., 1979; Edmonds, 1979; Mortimore & Sammons, 1987; Rutter et al., 1979) has consistently pointed to teachers' high expectations of students' performance as a key factor associated with students' achievement. In a variety of subtle and not-so-subtle ways, we communicate to some students that they are bright, capable, and responsible, while other students receive the message that they are dull, incapable, and irresponsible. It is obvious that our behaviors that create positive expectations almost always enhance the teacher-student relationship, and those that indicate negative expectations not only create poor relationships but also create poor self-concepts and reduce learning.

Our expectations of students are influenced by a variety of factors other than actual performance or behavior. Frericks (1974) found that teachers viewing a group of students labeled low in ability described the students' behavior more negatively than did teachers who viewed the same students but were told they were observing ''regular students in a normal classroom.'' Spencer-Hall (1981) reported that some students nominated for a citizen-of-the-year reward had misbehavior rates as high as that of any student in the class.

Teachers are obviously influenced by how students present themselves or are labeled, as well as by students' behavior.

Results from classroom interaction studies indicate that teachers generally respond more favorably to students they perceive as high achievers. High-achieving students receive more response opportunities (Brophy & Good, 1971), are given more time to answer questions (Rowe, 1974; Bozsik, 1982), receive more positive nonverbal feedback such as smiles, nods, and winks (Chaikin, Sigler, & Derlega, 1974), and are less likely to be ignored (Willis, 1970). Cooper and Good (1983) provide this list of common ways in which teachers respond differently to high- and low-achieving students.

1. Seating low-expectation students far from the teacher and/or seating them in a group.
2. Paying less attention to lows in academic situations (smiling less often and maintaining less eye contact).
3. Calling on lows less often to answer classroom questions or to make public demonstrations.
4. Waiting less time for lows to answer questions.
5. Not staying with lows in failure situations (i.e., providing fewer clues, asking fewer follow-up questions).
6. Criticizing lows more frequently than highs for incorrect public responses.
7. Praising lows less frequently than highs after successful public responses.
8. Praising lows more frequently than highs for marginal or inadequate public responses.
9. Providing lows with less accurate and less detailed feedback than highs.
10. Failing to provide lows with feedback about their responses as often as highs.
11. Demanding less work and effort from lows than from highs.
12. Interrupting performance of lows more frequently than highs. (p. 10)

In reviewing the research on expectation effects, Brophy (1983) cites studies suggesting that "teacher expectations do have self-fulfilling-prophecy effects on student-achievement levels, but that these effects make only a 5 to 10 percent difference, on the average" (p. 635). Brophy goes on to state:

These conclusions clearly imply that even ideal teacher education related to the topic of teacher expectations will not work miracles in our schools, but they do not imply that the topic is unimportant. Even a 5 percent difference in educational outcomes is an important difference, the more so as it is compounded across school years. Furthermore, the presentation so far has been confined to consideration of the average effect across all teachers of expectations concerning student achievement. The story becomes much more complicated, and the implications for teacher education much more obvious, when we turn attention to other kinds of expectations and to differences among teachers in predisposition to expectation effects. (p. 635)

We must realize that the concept of holding high expectations for all students does not mean that we should provide identical treatment for all students. To a considerable extent, the differential treatment students receive from teachers is a logical and often thoughtful response to individual student needs. Nevertheless, teachers should become aware of the potential for allowing successful students to dominate classroom interactions. Brophy (1983) sheds light on this important issue:

> Clearly, if teachers merely react consistently to the student behavior that confronts them, group statistics will reveal that the high expectation students receive more response opportunities (because they volunteer and call out more often), have more academic and fewer procedural or behavioral interactions with the teacher (because they are oriented more toward academic learning, can work more independently without supervision, and seldom become disruptive), receive more praise (because they succeed academically more often), and receive less criticism (because they show less classroom disruption and academic failure). (p. 637)

It is often desirable that we initiate a higher percentage of our academic contacts with low-achieving students during individual or small-group instruction. Similarly, especially when introducing new material to younger children, we should try to maximize the percentage of correct responses so that students do not become confused by competing, inaccurate information. The critical issue is that we must become aware of ways in which we respond differently to various types of students and thoughtfully and systematically implement differential interaction patterns that support individual student and group learning. Figure 3.1 presents guidelines teachers can follow to minimize the negative effects of teacher expectations.

As teachers we need to be aware of the importance of communicating positive expectations to all students. Periodically, we need to (1) collect data about how we interact with students in our classes, (2) analyze the data to see if we are using primarily supportive or critical statements, (3) determine whether we are responding differently (more critically or less often) to some students, and (4) attempt to alter our patterns of interaction so that we communicate high expectations to all students.

Creating Opportunities for Personal Discussions

As in any relationship, it is helpful to have time to get to know one another without the interruptions occasioned by day-to-day events. The following sections discuss ideas for creating such opportunities within the context of the teacher-student relationship. Your decision about which activities to use will depend on the grade level you teach and the time and energy you wish to employ in developing positive teacher-student relationships.

Demonstrating Our Interest in Students' Activities
An important way to indicate our concern for students and to enjoy our relationships with them is to take time to attend the activities in which they are involved. We have consistently found that parents are extremely appreciative of and impressed with teachers' attendance at student activities. Additionally, we have found that such attendance often is associated with dramatic improvement of the students whose activities were attended.

Eating Lunch with Students
Most teacher-student contact occurs in the presence of 25 to 30 other children. Unless they take the initiative by staying after school, students may never have individual private time with their teacher. One way to provide this personal time is to have lunch in the classroom

FIGURE 3.1 Guidelines for Avoiding the Negative Effects of Teacher Expectations

Use information from tests, cumulative folders, and other teachers very carefully.

Some teachers avoid reading cumulative folders for several weeks at the beginning of the year.

Be critical and objective about the reports you hear from other teachers, especially "horror stories" told in the teachers' lounge.

Be flexible in your use of grouping strategies.

Review work of students in different groups often and experiment with new groupings.

Use different groupings for different subjects.

Use mixed-ability groups in cooperative exercises when all students can handle the same material.

Make sure all the students are challenged.

Avoid saying, "This is easy, I know you can do it."

Offer a wide range of problems, and encourage all students to try a few of the harder ones for extra credit. Try to find something positive about these attempts.

Be especially careful about how you respond to low-achieving students during class discussions.

Give them prompts, clues, and time to answer.

Give ample praise for good answers.

Call on low achievers as often as high achievers.

Use materials that show a wide range of ethnic groups.

Check readers and library books. Is there ethnic diversity?

Ask your librarian to find multiethnic stories, filmstrips, etc.

If few materials are available, ask students to research and create their own, based on community or family resources.

Be fair in evaluation and disciplinary procedures.

Make sure equal offenses merit equal punishment. Find out from students in an anonymous questionnaire whether you seem to be favoring certain individuals.

Try to grade student work without knowing the identity of the student. Ask another teacher to give you a "second opinion" from time to time.

Communicate to all students that you believe they can learn—and mean it.

Return papers that do not meet standards with specific suggestions for improvements.

If students do not have the answers immediately, wait, probe, and then help them think through an answer.

Involve all students in learning tasks and in privileges.

Use some system for calling on or contacting students to make sure you give each student practice in reading, speaking, and answering questions.

Keep track of who gets to do what job. Are some students always on the list while others seldom make it?

Monitor your nonverbal behavior.
Do you lean away or stand farther away from some students? Do some students get smiles when they approach your desk while others get only frowns?
Do you avoid touching some students?
Does your tone of voice vary with different students?

From Anita Woolfolk, *Educational Psychology* 3/e, © 1987, pp. 340–341. Reproduced by permission of Prentice-Hall, Inc., Englewood Cliffs, New Jersey.

with individual students. This time can be arranged by providing a sign-up sheet so that students who are interested can reserve a time to eat lunch alone with you. You and the student can use the lunch period to share personal interests. You should be willing to listen to the student's concerns about personal or school problems, but the time together should not be used as a conference in which you discuss the student's schoolwork or behavior.

Arranging Interviews

Anyone who has taught young children for several years has experienced an instance in which a student appeared surprised to see the teacher in a nonschool setting, such as the grocery store. Children often view the teacher solely as a teacher and are quite unaware of our interests and life outside the school setting. One approach for making you seem more real is to allow the children to interview you. You can expand this activity by having your spouse or older children visit the classroom and be interviewed by the class.

Sending Letters and Notes to Students

Beginning the school year with a personal letter from you is an effective technique for establishing rapport with students. A positive individualized letter placed on each student's desk informs each student that you are happy to have him or her in class, eager to get to know him or her, and excited about the upcoming school year. Notes given to students throughout the school year can enhance the personal relationship between you and the student. Appropriate times for expressing thoughts or providing information by notes or letters include when a student has been successful at a new or difficult task, when a student's behavior has improved, when a personal matter seems to be worrying a student, and on a student's birthday. Students also appreciate receiving a note or a get-well card along with their homework when they are sick and must miss school for several days.

Using a Suggestion Box

Students often perceive their teacher as relatively uninterested in their ideas about the classroom. Although we may view this situation as undesirable, it is to some degree an understandable response to the reality that we have primary responsibility for creating an appropriate classroom environment. One method that indicates our interest in students' ideas is to display a suggestion box and encourage students to write ideas for making the class a better place in which to learn. This approach can be expanded to include holding class meetings in which students discuss their ideas and concerns about the classroom. When classroom meetings are used, having students place agenda items on the board can replace the suggestion box. Either way, our willingness to request, accept, and respond to students' suggestions can be an effective method for improving teacher-student rapport.

Joining in School and Community Events

Schools often organize special events such as hat days, carnivals, and bike rodeos. Similarly, communities have picnics, carnivals, and other social events. We can demonstrate our interest in students and our own enjoyment of a good time by becoming involved in these activities. Schools can also organize special events or displays that give students a chance to view teachers in a personal light and increase positive teacher-student interaction. We have both worked in buildings where a childhood picture of each staff member was displayed and students attempted to match the teachers with the childhood pictures. Similarly, we have taught in schools where a bulletin board was arranged so that teachers and students could publicly write positive statements to other students or teachers. Our involvement in activities such as these helps create a positive school atmosphere and thereby significantly reduce unproductive student behavior.

Joining in Playground Games

Students enjoy having teachers participate in their playground activities. There are few better ways for us to show our humanness and to demonstrate that we enjoy our students than occasionally to share in their recess activities. Not only can this activity enhance teacher-student relationships, but it can also provide us with an excellent form of relaxation. The physical activity and the opportunity to interact with children in a relaxed and nonacademic setting can provide a refreshing break in the school day. One way to formalize this type of teacher-student interaction is to develop several opportunities for friendly athletic competition between students and teachers.

Making Birthday Cards

A birthday is a special day for children. A thoughtful way to respond to children's excitement is to make a card when each student has a birthday. The card can include a birthday greeting as well as a positive statement about some aspect of the student's work or behavior.

Introducing New Students to Adults in the School

Several schools with which we work have developed a creative method for introducing new children to school personnel. A new student is given a booklet in which they are to obtain the signatures of key adults in the building, such as the principal, secretary, librarian, custodian, cook, and playground assistant. When each adult signs the book, he or she gives the child a gift, such as an eraser, pencil, cookie, or a positive note. By the end of the second day, the child has met a variety of caring adults, and these adults know there is a new student who will need special invitations for a few weeks as he or she makes the adjustment into a new school setting.

USING EFFECTIVE COMMUNICATION SKILLS

Teachers who choose to discuss classroom issues with students and to elicit student feedback about classroom events will benefit from a variety of specific communication skills that enhance open interpersonal relationships. Teachers can use the communication skills described in the following sections regardless of the type of teacher-student relationship they choose. If you choose a more open, interactive classroom management style, however, you will find these skills particularly important in effectively developing your classroom management skills.

The importance of using effective communication skills cannot be overemphasized. They are the foundation for good classroom management. Unless we use effective communication skills, all other attempts at creating a well-managed, positive learning environment will be severely limited and usually short-lived. Caring interpersonal interactions are essential in meeting such important individual needs as safety and security, belongingness, and self-esteem.

In addition to creating relationships that meet essential student needs, using effective communication skills benefits us by allowing us to meet our own needs more effectively and simultaneously to achieve our professional goals. Using the skills presented in this section enables us to:

1. Be warm and friendly and enjoy relationships with students,
2. Express our own needs and wants clearly within the classroom,
3. Better understand and accept students and experience more positive feelings toward them, and
4. Create situations in which students feel understood and cared for and therefore respond more positively to us and to their peers.

Communication skills can be divided into the two categories of sending skills and receiving skills. Sending skills are commonly used when speaking to someone. Receiving skills are techniques that can be used to become a more effective listener.

Before examining the communication skills presented in this section, realize that the effective use of these skills is based on specific beliefs about children and the goals and roles adults choose to follow when working with children. The use of communication skills is based on these four premises:

1. We wish to share with students responsibility for resolving problems.
2. We believe that students are, for the most part, responsible individuals when the atmosphere is conducive to their being so.
3. We accept that there can be more than one perspective to a problem and consider perspectives other than our own to be valid.
4. We do not perceive our objective in a teacher-student confrontation as being ''to win.''

When considering whether to use the methods described in the following sections, the reader must realize that they are skills intended to help teachers implement open, type-two interactions with students. These methods will be of little value to teachers who wish to establish or maintain closed, authoritarian type-three relationships with students.

Sending Skills

Sending skills fall into three general categories: (1) skills in confronting students about behaviors they need to change, (2) skills in providing students with feedback about their academic performance, and (3) skills in presenting positive expectations to students. To highlight their most common use, each skill is presented separately. It is obvious, however, that the three skills are interrelated and particularly that the skills for confronting student behavior will, in most interactions, enhance the quality of the teacher-student relationship.

Skills for Confronting Inappropriate or Disruptive Behavior

DEAL IN THE PRESENT. Information is more useful when it is shared at the earliest appropriate opportunity. Young people are very "now" oriented. It is unfair and ineffective to bring up issues after several days have elapsed. Therefore, though it may be necessary to wait until you can speak with the student alone or until the student has better control of his or her emotions, it is best to discuss important matters as soon after they occur as possible.

TALK DIRECTLY TO STUDENTS RATHER THAN ABOUT THEM. Adults have a tendency to talk to parents or colleagues about students rather than talking directly to the student. The assumption seems to be that students could not understand or would be overpowered by the information. Our experiences strongly contradict these beliefs. Indeed, it appears that students suffer more from worrying about what has been said about them than they do from receiving skillfully presented direct feedback. By talking directly to students, we show respect for them while ensuring that they receive accurate (rather than second-hand) information about adults' feelings.

SPEAK COURTEOUSLY. Nothing does more to create positive interactions than using simple courtesy statements such as "thank you," "please," and "excuse me." Because teachers serve as important models for students, their interactions with them should include more (certainly not less) frequent use of courtesies than do their interactions with other adults.

MAKE EYE CONTACT AND BE AWARE OF NONVERBAL MESSAGES. An old saying states that children often respond more to what adults do than to what they say. Because young people are so dependent on adults, they become adept at reading adults' nonverbal messages. It is therefore important that we attempt to make our nonverbal messages congruent with our verbal messages. If you are talking to a student but looking over his or her shoulder, the student will find it difficult to believe that you feel positive about her or him and are sincerely concerned. Similarly, when we shout that we are not angry with a class, the students will be more likely to listen to the tone of voice than to the words.

TAKE RESPONSIBILITY FOR STATEMENTS BY USING THE PERSONAL PRONOUN *I*. It is hard to underestimate the importance and value of "I" messages. Students who experience consistent and/or serious behavior problems are often deficient in social cognition skills. Simply stated, they are not as capable as their peers of understanding and appreciating others' points of view. For example, they may not understand why a teacher is bothered by their talking out or why, despite their aggressive or rude behavior, their peers do not wish to play with them.

Just as many students learn to read before entering school, many children learn to understand others' perspectives through the use of language employed at home. Students who have not had these opportunities will, just like students who enter school unable to decode letters and sounds, need learning experiences that help them develop important social cognition skills. "I" messages are one method of providing this important assistance.

In their *Discovering Your Teaching Self*, Curwin and Fuhrmann (1975) provide a succinct and sensitive statement about this skill:

> Meaningful communication between people (the communication between adults and children is of special interest to us) often breaks down because one party (or both) continually tells the other what's wrong with him rather than identifying how he himself is feeling in the situation. When I tell someone what's wrong with him, I virtually take away from him all responsibility for himself. Since I know what is wrong, I also know how to "correct" it. Thus I leave him powerless and probably defensive. (p. 196)

If we say to a student, "You are being disruptive," or "You're late again!" the student is likely to feel attacked and defensive. If, however, we say, "It distracts me and I feel uncomfortable when you talk while I am talking (or when you come in late)," the student has been provided with some useful information about his or her effect on other people. Similarly, using the pronoun *we* is unfairly ganging up against a student. When confronted with statements beginning with "we feel" or "the entire class believes," the student is likely to feel attacked and defeated. Though they are flexible, children are also very sensitive and need to be confronted by one person at a time. Furthermore, because each of us is an expert on only our own feelings, it appears reasonable that each of us should share our own feelings and dispense with the pronoun *we*.

In his *Teacher Effectiveness Training* (TET), Thomas Gordon (1974) writes that when expressing a concern about students' behavior that affects the teacher, the teacher should employ an "I" message consisting of three components: (1) the personal pronoun *I*, (2) the feeling the teacher is experiencing, and (3) the effect the student's behavior is having on the teacher. For example, a typical teacher's response to a student's interruption might be, "If you can't stop interrupting me, you can leave the room." If we used an "I" message in this situation, we might say, "When you interrupt me I become frustrated because I get distracted and have difficulty helping the other students."

Because "I" messages express personal feelings and often deal with student behaviors that require change, it is best to send them privately. We should do so especially when we are dealing with adolescents. Adolescents, being particularly sensitive to peer pressure, will often respond to even the most thoughtful public criticism defensively. Because most adolescents value being treated as adults, though, they will usually respond positively to private expressions of our concern.

Another, less open, way to send an "I" message involves politely yet firmly expressing a demand using the first person singular. Therefore, if a student began talking to another student during a teacher's presentation, the teacher might say in a nonthreatening manner, "I expect students to listen quietly while someone in this class speaks." Although this type of "I" message will more likely elicit a defensive response from older students, it is a clear, straightforward way to present your expectations.

MAKE STATEMENTS RATHER THAN ASKING QUESTIONS. When children misbehave, they are frequently bombarded with questions. This approach leaves the child feeling intimidated and defensive. Questions such as "Are you feeling all right?" "Would you like to leave the room for a few minutes?" or "Can I help?" can be extremely productive. Teachers should, however, be aware of opportunities for replacing questions with statements. Consider the different feelings a child might have on coming late to class and hearing "Where have you been?" compared to "I was concerned when you were late because we have to leave on our field trip in five minutes." It is important to keep in mind that questions are often important tools for helping children understand and change their behavior. Asking students what they were doing or how their behavior helped them is an important component in solving problems. Questions often misdirect students from taking responsibility for their own behavior, however, while creating defensiveness. Therefore, when dealing with students' behaviors, use questions sparingly and in the context of a problem-solving approach.

Skills for Giving Specific, Descriptive Feedback

Studies indicate that teachers are not particularly effective at using feedback to students. When providing students with feedback about their academic performance it is useful to ask ourselves three questions: "How much?", "To whom?", and "What type?" The answer to the first question is probably somewhat more but not too much.

Based on results of a three-year study involving data collection in more than 100 fourth-,-sixth-, and eighth-grade classrooms, Sadker and Sadker (1985) express concern about the quantity and quality of teachers' feedback to students. These researchers found that teachers demonstrated low rates of specific positive feedback or criticism and high rates of acceptance. "Acceptance included teacher comments that implied that student performance was correct and appropriate . . . (Examples include: "O.K.," "uh-huh," "I see," or simply teacher silence)" (Sadker & Sadker, 1985, p. 360). The Sadkers' main interpretation of their findings was that teacher feedback was too bland. They found that "In two-thirds of the classrooms observed, teachers never clearly indicated that a student answer was incorrect" (p. 360). Similarly, only 11 percent of teacher feedback involved praise, and in more than one-fourth of the classrooms, teachers never praised students' answers. These findings regarding the general lack of critical or specific feedback are reinforced by data reported by Goodlad (1984) indicating that 20 percent of both elementary and secondary students stated that they were neither informed nor corrected following a mistake.

The answer to the second question, "To whom should effective feedback be provided?" is closely related to the issue of expectation effects. Positive, prescriptive feedback needs to be more evenly distributed so that it is provided not only to high-achieving students or to students with the social skills to elicit this feedback. In fact, research (Brophy & Evertson, 1976; Good, Ebmeier, & Beckerman, 1978; Soar, 1975; Stallings, 1975) indicates that positive feedback is more effective with lower-SES students and low-achieving students—the students who research suggests receive the least positive feedback.

The answer to the question "What type of feedback is most effective?" is the key question. One of the most important communication skills teachers can use is specific, clear, descriptive feedback that helps students take responsibility for their successes. Research on attribution theory (Anderson & Prawat, 1983; Weiner, 1979) indicates that students attribute their success or failure to ability, effort, luck, or difficulty of task. If students attribute their success or failure to effort, they are able to view their performance as influenced by factors within their control (an internal locus of control) and are therefore able to expect success in similar situations if they make the effort (Andrews & Debus, 1978; Harter & Connell, 1981). When failure is attributed, however, to ability, luck, or difficulty of task, students feel less control over results and begin to believe that making a concerted effort in the future will have little effect on the outcome. Praise that helps students focus on factors within their control that influenced performance allows students to develop an internal locus of control.

Unfortunately, on occasions when they are successful, low-achieving students tend to credit luck or the ease of task for this success. Higher-achieving students, however, tend to credit their effort and ability for their success. Teachers can alter children's perceptions of their control over success or failure by using feedback more effectively. In an interesting study, Dweck (1975) showed that elementary students who viewed school learning as extremely hopeless could change this belief by receiving training sessions in which they were given both success and failure, and when failing were informed that their failure was due to lack of effort. Students who received this training responded to failure by persisting and implementing problem-solving strategies to resolve their dilemma. Schunk (1983) studied elementary students' responses to positive feedback and stated that simply providing students with statements about their effort may suggest to students that they do not have the ability to complete the task without extensive effort. It seems that the most effective feedback provides students with information that they possess the ability to achieve success and that they will need to expend effort to do the task well.

By becoming more skilled in providing students with useful positive feedback, teachers can help students take credit for their successes and develop a better appreciation for their ability to control the school environment in positive ways. O'Leary and O'Leary (1977) state that to serve as an effective reinforcer, feedback to students (they use the term *praise*) must have three qualities:

1. *Contingency:* Praise must immediately follow desired behaviors rather than being applied simply as a general motivator. Anderson et al. (1979) found that teachers failed to use praise contingently because the rate of praise following reading turns that contained mistakes was similar to the rate following correct responses.

2. *Specificity:* Praise should describe the specific behavior being reinforced. Again, Anderson et al. (1979) suggest that teachers needed improvement in this area. Their data showed that teachers were specific in only 5 percent of their praise for academic work and in 40 percent of their praise for behavior.

3. *Credibility:* Praise should be appropriate for the situation and the individual. Older, high-achieving students are aware that praise is used primarily for motivation and encouragement and may find praise unnecessary and even insulting.

Perhaps the most useful information on the effective use of positive feedback to students was presented by Brophy (1981). Figure 3.2 presents Brophy's summary of research findings on the effective use of feedback (he also uses the word *praise*).

FIGURE 3.2 Guidelines for Effective Praise

Effective praise	Ineffective praise
1. is delivered contingently	1. is delivered randomly or unsystematically
2. specifies the particulars of the accomplishment	2. is restricted to global positive reactions
3. shows spontaneity, variety, and other signs of credibility: suggests clear attention to the student's accomplishment	3. shows a bland uniformity that suggests a conditioned response made with minimal attention
4. rewards attainment of specified performance criteria (which can include effort criteria)	4. rewards mere participation without consideration of performance processes or outcomes
5. provides information to students about their competence or the value of their accomplishment	5. provides no information at all or gives students information about their status
6. orients students toward better appreciation of their own task-related behavior and thinking about problem solving	6. orients students toward comparing themselves with others and thinking about competing
7. uses student's own prior accomplishments as the context for describing present accomplishments	7. uses the accomplishments of peers as the context for describing students' present accomplishments
8. is given in recognition of noteworthy effort or success at difficult (for this student) tasks	8. is given without regard to the effort expended or the meaning of the accomplishment (for this student)
9. attritubes success to effort and ability, implying that similar successes can be expected in the future	9. attributes success to ability alone or to external factors such as luck or (easy) task difficulty
10. fosters endogenous attributions (students believe they expend effort on task because they enjoy it and/or want to develop task-relevant skills)	10. fosters exogenous attributions (students believe they expend effort on the task for external reasons—to please the teacher, win a competition or reward, etc.)
11. focuses students' attention on their own task-relevant behavior	11. focuses students' attention on the teacher as an external authority figure who is manipulating them
12. fosters appreciation of, and desirable attributions about, task-relevant behavior after the process is completed	12. intrudes into the ongoing process, distracting attention from task-relevant behavior

From Jere E. Brophy, "Teacher Praise: A Functional Analysis." *Review of Educational Research* (Spring 1981): *51*, 32. Washington, D.C.: American Educational Research Association, 1981. Reprinted by permission.

Receiving Skills

Listening skills are extremely important; when used effectively they create relationships that allow students to feel significant, accepted, respected, and able to take responsibility for their own behavior. By effectively using listening skills, adults help youngsters clarify their feelings and resolve their own conflicts. Unfortunately, adults all too often provide quick answers for children rather than carefully listening in order to help the youngsters clarify the problem and then aid them in developing a solution.

William Glasser (1988) recently stated that students' attempts to have someone listen to them is the source of nearly 95 percent of discipline problems in school. Speaking of student behavior problems in schools, Glasser wrote, "I believe that frustration of the need for power, even more than the need for belonging, is at the core of today's difficulties" (1988, p. 40). Glasser notes that there are three levels at which students can satisfy their need for power of involvement in the school environment. First, students simply need to believe that someone whom they respect will listen to them. At the second level, someone listens and accepts the validity of the student's statement or concern. The third and highest level involves an adult's stating that the student's idea may be worth implementing.

Stop for a moment and reflect on the last several situations when a student came to you with a problem or expressed a strong emotion. What did you do? If you are like most adults, at least half of the time you provided a quick answer to the problem or attempted to stop the expression of emotion by providing assurances or by suggesting that the student should not be expressing the emotion. Both of these responses are commonly used because they require a minimum of time and effort and prevent adults from having to deal with a youngster's emotions. When adults consistently provide answers, however, they subtly inform students that they do not care enough really to listen to them and do not trust their ability to resolve their own conflicts.

Before examining the major listening skills, we must clarify an important point. There are numerous instances (perhaps even a significant majority) during a school day when a student is merely requesting information. If a student requests permission to leave the room or asks for clarification of directions, it is appropriate simply to provide the information. However, when students share personal problems, express confusion with their work, or display emotions, it is often most effective initially to use one or more of the listening skills discussed in this section.

The primary goal of using listening skills is to help students express their real concern, need, or want. Students often initially make general, angry statements that disguise their real concerns. A student who says, "I hate this class," might be feeling frustration at his or her inability to understand the material or concern over lack of acceptance by peers. By using the methods described in the following pages, you can help the student clarify the underlying problem. Once the problem has been exposed, you must switch from merely listening to an active role in helping the student examine and solve the problem.

Empathic, Nonevaluative Listening

This skill involves providing the speaker with a sense that she or he has been clearly heard and that the feelings expressed are acceptable. Several major benefits can be derived from using these skills. First, students learn that their feelings are acceptable, which reduces the tension and anxiety associated with having to hide one's true feelings. This act in turn makes students feel more accepted. Second, when thoughts and feelings can be expressed openly and are received nonjudgmentally, students are much less likely to express feelings through unproductive behaviors. Acting-out in the classroom, vandalism, and truancy are often indirect methods of dealing with feelings that could not be expressed openly and directly. Third, when adults listen nonevaluatively they provide young people with an opportunity to examine and clarify feelings that are often confusing and frightening. This exchange frequently enables youngsters to understand a situation and to consider approaches to coping with the situation effectively.

There are two basic approaches to nonevaluative listening. First, the listener can simply acknowledge the speaker's statement by looking at him or her and making oral responses such as "M-hm," "Yes," "Uh-uh," "I see," and "I understand." This form of listening encourages the speaker to continue talking by indicating that the listener is attentive and involved. Obviously, this type of response is least effective when used in isolation; most children wish to hear more than a simple acknowledgment.

The second method for using empathic, nonevaluative listening is commonly called *paraphrasing, active listening,* or *reflecting.* In their *Learning Together and Alone,* Johnson and Johnson (1975) present seven guidelines for using this skill.

General Guidelines for Paraphrasing

1. Restate the sender's expressed ideas and feelings in your own words rather than mimicking or parroting her exact words.

2. Preface paraphrased remarks with, "You think . . . ," "Your position is . . . ," "It seems to you that . . . ," "You feel that . . . ," and so on.

3. Avoid any indication of approval or disapproval.

4. Make your nonverbal messages congruent with your verbal paraphrasing; look attentive, interested, and open to the sender's ideas and feelings, and show that you are concentrating upon what the sender is trying to communicate.

5. State as accurately as possible what you heard the sender say and describe the feelings and attitudes involved.

6. Do not add to or subtract from the sender's message.

7. Put yourself in the sender's shoes and try to understand what it is he is feeling and what his message means. (p. 102)

Paraphrasing has the advantage of making the speaker feel listened to while allowing the listener to be somewhat more involved than is possible when using only acknowledging responses. Furthermore, by providing a summary of the speaker's statement, the listener may help the child clarify his or her thoughts or feelings. If the paraphrased statement is not congruent with what the speaker wanted to say, the speaker has an opportunity to correct the listener's paraphrase and thereby clarify the initial statement.

One word of caution about the use of paraphrasing: Students may say that they do not like having someone repeat what they have just said. This response is more common in the upper elementary and secondary grades than among young children. If students frequently indicate that they view your statements as parroting their own, you will either need to reduce the amount of paraphrasing used or try to use responses that vary slightly from the student's original statement. Activity 3.9 provides several methods for helping you improve and diversify skills in empathic, nonevaluative listening.

Activities for Improving Sending Skills

It is easy to react positively to ideas and yet never take the time or risk to incorporate these into our repertoire. The activities presented below can help you practice the sending skills discussed in this section. Even teachers who frequently use these skills will find that the structured practice will improve their awareness of and fluency in implementing these skills.

ACTIVITY 3.1 Talking Directly to Children Rather Than about Them

1. During a two-day period, list every statement (positive or negative) you make to an adult about a child.
2. In front of each statement, write either "yes" or "no" to indicate whether the content of the statement was shared with the child.
3. For each statement with a "no" placed in front of it, write out a statement that you could have made to the child.

ACTIVITY 3.2 Monitoring Courteous Remarks

1. Make a tally of the courteous remarks you make to students during a one-day period. You may want to carry a counter or a small note pad.
2. If you used fewer than 25 such statements (recall that research indicates that elementary teachers have approximately 1,000 interactions with children each day and that secondary teachers have nearly 500), try to double the number the next day.
3. Briefly write (or discuss with a colleague) how it felt to increase the number of courteous statements. Did your students respond any differently the second day?

ACTIVITY 3.3 Sending "I" Messages

1. To test your knowledge of "I" messages, change each of these five statements into an "I" message:
   a. Late again! What's the matter with you?
   b. I don't want to hear another word out of anyone.
   c. No book again? How do you expect to learn anything?
   d. How can you be so inconsiderate as to stand there drinking water for so long when you know other children want a drink?
   e. If you get in trouble on the playground one more time you can miss the rest of your recesses this month!
   If you have difficulty with this task, consult a colleague or refer to Thomas Gordon's *TET: Teacher Effectiveness Training.*

(continued)

ACTIVITY 3.3 (continued)

2. Tape-record your classroom for at least 1 hour. While listening to the tape, list all the "I" messages you sent and all the "you" or "we" messages you sent. Next, change all the "you" or "we" statements to "I" messages. Finally, repeat the activity and try to increase the ratio of "I" to "you" or "we" statements.

ACTIVITY 3.4 Giving Useful Oral Feedback

Change each of these general statements into a statement that provides the student with specific, nonevaluative feedback.
1. That's a nice picture, Susan.
2. Jimmy, your behavior on the playground was terrible.
3. Class, you were very rude during the assembly.
4. Erin, your penmanship has improved a lot since the last writing assignment.
5. Bill, if you keep disrupting the class I will send you to the principal's office.
Write a specific example of effective and ineffective praise for each of the 12 aspects of praise listed in Figure 3.2.

From the list of 12 aspects of effective praise, select 3 you believe would be most helpful in improving the quality of your praise. If you are currently working with students, use each of these at least once a day over a 5-day period.

ACTIVITY 3.5 Improving Your Positive-Negative Ratio

1. Have a student or colleague tally the positive and negative statements you make during a minimum of two hours of instructional time. Try to include several types of lessons and do not code more than 30 minutes at a time. Especially when using students to tally remarks, it is helpful to define positive and negative statements and to provide the coder with a list of commonly used positive and negative remarks. Neutral remarks such as statements related to instruction or comments such as "Okay," "All right," or "Yes" should not be coded.
2. If your ratio of positive to negative statements was less than 3 to 1, repeat the activity and try to focus on responding positively to productive student behavior. Following a period in which your ratio was very high, ask the students to evaluate the lesson.
3. Write 10 inviting statements that you could use in your teaching. During the next 2 teaching days, make at least 10 inviting statements each day.
   Inviting statements: Examples
   a. I really enjoyed your presentation. Would you be willing to share it with the other fifth-grade class?
   b. I'm really glad you're back and feeling better.
   c. I'm very glad you are in my class this year.

   d. Those are two good causes; can you think of any more?

   e. Would you like some help with that work?

Inviting Statements: Your list

a.	f.
b.	g.
c.	h.
d.	i.
e.	j.

Activities for Monitoring Teachers' Expectations

The activities that follow are examples of methods we can use to examine our interactions with low- and high-achieving students. You can use these data as a reference for considering whether your differential interactions are supporting optimal learning for all students or are inadvertently disadvantageous to low-achieving students.

Additional information and activities dealing with communication of teachers' expectations can be found in a packaged inservice program entitled "Teacher Expectations and Student Achievement" (TESA) (Kerman & Martin, 1980). Many teachers with whom the authors have worked have found this material extremely valuable both in increasing their positive expectations for lower-achieving students and for enhancing professional dialogue and sharing among staff members within the school.

Before beginning the activities listed below you should know that research indicates that when teachers are made aware of how they treat students differentially and are involved in monitoring their teacher-student interactions, inequitable interactions can be eliminated (Good & Brophy, 1974; Sadker & Sadker, 1985).

ACTIVITY 3.6 Monitoring Students' Response Opportunities

List the four highest- and four lowest-achieving students in your class. Place these students' names in the form provided in Figure 3.3. Have a colleague tally your interactions with these students during at least two half-hour periods when the class is involved in group instruction.

This activity can also be completed by presenting the observer with a seating chart and a label for each type of teacher-student interaction on which you wish to obtain data. An observer might be asked to observe several students and to tally the number of times they were asked a question, given assistance in answering a question, criticized, praised, or volunteered an answer. Figure 3.4 is a sample of the data you might collect using this procedure.

After examining the results, respond to these statements:

Two things I learned about my interactions with these students were . . .

Two things I will try to do differently the next time I teach a large group lesson are . . .

FIGURE 3.3 Monitoring Teaching-Student Dyadic Interactions

Student's name	Student volunteers answer	Teacher asks student a question			Teacher assists student	Teacher praises student	Teacher criticizes student	Teacher calls on another student
			Student response					
			correct	partially correct	incorrect				

FIGURE 3.4 Monitoring Teacher-Student Interactions

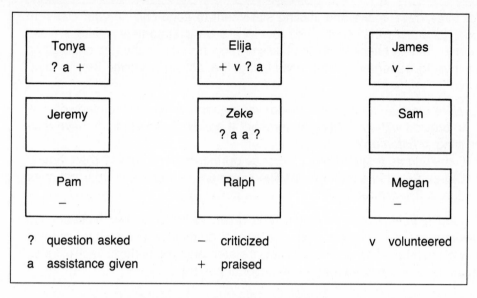

Tonya ? a +	Elija + v ? a	James v –
Jeremy	Zeke ? a a ?	Sam
Pam –	Ralph	Megan –

?   question asked   –   criticized   v   volunteered

a   assistance given   +   praised

ACTIVITY 3.7 Mapping a Teacher's Classroom Movement

Draw a map of your classroom, including location of the furniture. Ask a colleague to come into your classroom during a period of at least half an hour when the class will be involved in seatwork and you will be free to assist students. Have the observer mark your movement with a solid line during the entire observation. The observer should place a number by each place where you stop. To record the amount of time spent at each spot, have the observer place a tally mark next to the number for every 15 seconds that you remain in that spot.

After examining the walking map, answer these questions:

1. Where did you spend the most time? Least time?
2. Were any students ignored? Were there specific reasons for not interacting with these students?
3. Did the classroom arrangement influence your movement? How?
4. What changes, if any, would you make in your walking pattern during this type of instruction?
5. What changes, if any, would you make in your classroom arrangement?

Teachers who frequently use lecture or large-group discussions almost inevitably look at one area of the class much more than others. Almost all teachers have some blind spot. While teaching, one of us almost always sits with his left leg on his right knee. Because this position twists the body to the right, students on the left side of the class are often ignored. The author periodically asks his students to tally the number of contacts he has with students from each side of the class in order to make him more aware of (and accountable for) his behavior.

ACTIVITY 3.8 Balancing Positive Statements

For three days, make one inviting statement to each child in your class. In order to ensure that each child receives such a statement, make a class list and place a check by each child's name when he or she has been given an inviting statement. After completing the activity, answer these questions:

1. Were there some students whom you had to consciously remind yourself to provide with an inviting statement? If so, did these students have anything in common?
2. Did students respond any differently during the three days? If so, how?
3. Did any students make a positive comment to you about your behavior during these three days?

A good supplement to this activity is again to list your four highest- and lowest-achieving students. Ask a colleague, an aide, or even the principal to tally the number of positive and negative statements you make to each of these students during two half-hour instructional periods.

Student's name	Positive comments	Negative comments
High achievers		
1.		
2.		
3.		
4.		
Low achievers		
1.		
2.		
3.		
4.		

After completing this activity, answer these questions:

1. What do the data indicate about how you respond to high- as opposed to low-achieving students?
2. Did you find yourself behaving differently because you were being observed? If so, what did you do differently?
3. Did any of the eight students appear to respond differently than usual while you were observed? If so, how did their behavior change?

Activities for Improving Receiving Skills

The demanding pace of the school day places real demands on teachers' ability to listen carefully to student concerns. Nevertheless, the act of carefully listening to students can considerably reduce classroom problems and is imperative as a prerequisite to effective problem solving. The activities that follow are designed to help you take time to implement effective listening skills.

ACTIVITY 3.9 Practicing Listening Skills

To examine and improve your skills in using paraphrasing, imagine that each of the following statements has just been said to you. Write two responses to each of the ten statements. In the first response, simply paraphrase the statement without mimicking the student's words. In the second response, add a feeling component.

a. Someone stole my lunch ticket!
b. This work is too hard.
c. Can we have ten extra minutes of recess?
d. Bill has had the book for two days.
e. I hate you!
f. I didn't get into trouble in music class today.
g. Nobody in the class likes me.
h. Do I have to take my report card home?
i. I never get to take the roll.
j. Mary is always picking on me.

During one school day, list five statements children make to you and five questions they ask you that could best be responded to by empathic, nonevaluative listening. When the list is complete, write a response to each of the ten student statements.

EVALUATING THE QUALITY OF TEACHER-STUDENT RELATIONSHIPS

Before implementing any of the varied behaviors that you can use to create more positive teacher-student relationships, you should evaluate the current quality of your own interactions with students. Just as effective teaching involves both a diagnostic and a prescriptive component, any decision to alter our behavior can be helped by first assessing the students' reaction to the current behavior. This approach enables us to focus changes in areas in which students' feedback suggests that changes may be needed in order to improve teacher-student relationships. Figures 3.5, 3.6, and 3.7 present forms that many teachers have found useful in assessing the quality of their relationships with their students.

The questionnaire in Figure 3.5 has been used by many teachers in grades 3 through 9. Teachers who want to use a similar format for children who cannot read can modify the form to look more like Figure 3.6 and read the questions to the students. Numerous elementary teachers have also used Figure 3.7.

Although information collected by individual teachers provides more specific information, when students work with several teachers each day it is useful periodically to assess students' general attitude toward adults in the school. Many student attitude surveys include items that provide a school staff with such information. While working on this book, one of us conducted a school assessment for a middle school that was experiencing significant problems with students' achievement, students' behavior, and community support. As part of the assessment, students were asked to complete the DEMOS D scale (a dropout-prediction scale developed by George Demos). Figure 3.8 shows the results of the items directly related to the quality of teacher-student relationships.

FIGURE 3.5 Questionnaire

Check the appropriate box	Home run	3rd base	2nd base	1st base	Strike-out!
1. Am I courteous toward you?					
2. Do I treat the students fairly?					
3. Am I honest?					
4. Do I touch you?					
5. Do you seem excited about my teaching?					
6. Do I talk over problems with you?					
7. Are you praised for your work?					
8. Am I patient and understanding?					
9. Do I keep my temper?					
10. Do I listen to you when you want to talk?					
11. Am I polite?					
12. Do you think that I like you?					
13. Am I too strict with the class?					
14. Do I seem happy?					
15. Am I willing to admit I am wrong?					
16. Can you trust me?					
17. Do I embarrass you?					
18. Do I listen to your suggestions?					
19. Do I expect too much from you?					
20. Do I smile at you?					
21. Am I friendly?					
22. Am I a good sport?					
23. Do I have a sense of humor?					
24. Do I show appreciation for special things you do?					
25. Do I encourage you?					
26. Can you ask me questions?					
27. Do I have any nervous habits?					
28. Do I help you when you need it?					
29. Do I give you helpful feedback?					
30. Do I look at you when I talk to you?					
31. Do I share my feelings?					
32. Do I think you can do your work?					

Thank you for completing this questionnaire. Your responses help me evaluate my teaching.

COMMENTS

thank you!

FIGURE 3.6 Elementary School Teacher Feedback Form

1. Do I listen to you?			
2. Do I help you enough?			
3. Do I care about you?			
4. Do I help you feel good about learning?			
5. Do I seem happy when I teach?			

(continued)

96 / Creating Positive Interpersonal Relationships in the Classroom

6. Do I think you can do your work?			
7. Can you share your good and bad feelings with me?			
8. Am I polite?			
9. Am I fair?			
10. Do you know what I want you to do?			
11. Do I help you understand why we are doing each activity in class?			
12. Do I call on you enough in class?			
13. Do I let you know when you have done good work?			
14. Are you excited about what I teach you?			

The data presented in Figure 3.8 show a dramatic pattern of students who have spent more time in the school perceiving teachers as less understanding, caring, helpful, and fair professionals. Though slight decreases in students' attitudes might be expected as youngsters move into early and mid-adolescence, our work in middle schools suggests that significant changes are unusual. When such changes do occur, they are inevitably associated with lower achievement and greater student misbehavior.

FIGURE 3.7 Teacher-Student Relationship Evaluation Form

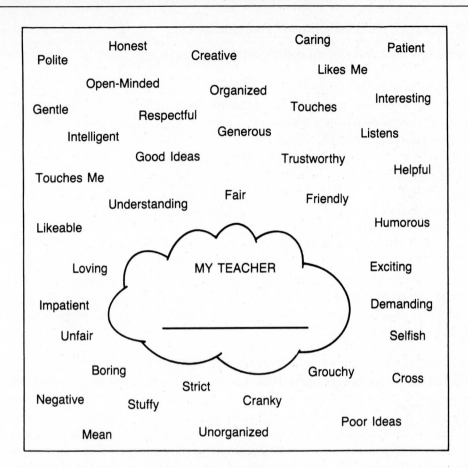

Honest
Caring
Patient
Polite
Creative
Likes Me
Open-Minded
Organized
Interesting
Gentle
Respectful
Touches
Intelligent
Generous
Listens
Good Ideas
Trustworthy
Helpful
Touches Me
Understanding
Fair
Friendly
Likeable
Humorous
Loving
MY TEACHER
Exciting
Impatient
Demanding
Unfair
Selfish
Boring
Grouchy
Cross
Strict
Negative
Stuffy
Cranky
Poor Ideas
Mean
Unorganized

Circle the words that describe your teacher.

Circle in red if the words describe your teacher most of the time.
Circle in blue if the words describe your teacher sometimes.
Circle in green if the words seldom describe your teacher.
Circle in orange if the words never describe your teacher.

FIGURE 3.8 Students' Perceptions of Teachers: Percentage of Students Responding "Nearly Always" or "Most of the Time"

Question	6th grade	7th grade	8th grade
Teachers understand the problems of students	37	33	20
Teachers care about students	76	43	41
The principal and vice-principal help the students	43	32	21
Teachers pick on some students	25	40	51
Teachers give most of their help and attention to the good students	31	36	51
A student can get help from a teacher	50	43	25

ACTIVITY 3.10   Evaluating the Teacher-Student Relationship

Have every student in your class(es) complete the forms in Figures 3.6 or 3.7 or a similar form you devise.

Tabulate the results so that you have a summary of all students' responses. Keep in mind that one or two low statements may indicate that a change is needed with only several students. Five or more low statements suggest, though, that a major change may help to improve your relationships with students.

After tabulating the results, complete these statements:

I learned that . . .
I was surprised that . . .
I was pleased that . . .
I was disappointed that . . .
I would like to change the fact that . . .

The results of this survey led the staff to include in their school-improvement plans considerable effort to incorporate many of the skills discussed in this chapter. Tentative results indicate that these changes have significantly influenced students' attitudes, achievement, and behavior.

ASSESSING THE EFFECT OF ATTEMPTS TO IMPROVE TEACHER-STUDENT RELATIONSHIPS

Although it is easy to read about new ideas but not take time to implement them, we may also become excited about new ideas and fail to assess whether implementing the ideas did in fact have the desired results. The final activity in this chapter reminds you to attend to both of these potential pitfalls.

ACTIVITY 3.11   Assessing the Effect of Attempts to Improve Teacher-Student Relationships

Complete each of the activities presented in this chapter. In addition, implement at least three of the activities for improving teacher-student rapport.

When these activities have been completed, repeat Activity 3.10 and compare the results. From these results, complete these statements.

My students now see me as more . . .
My students now see me as less . . .
My feelings toward my students have changed in that I now . . .
I particularly like the fact that . . .
I will certainly continue . . .

SUMMARY

Positive, supportive teacher-student relationships are important for all students. However, they become a critical factor influencing the behavior and achievement of students who are experiencing academic and behavioral difficulties. These at-risk students come to school with greater needs for adults who model positive adult behavior and provide students with positive, inviting statements, high expectations, and feedback that helps them learn to take credit for their successes.

The learning process is a highly interactive, personal, and ego-involving activity. Students cannot reach their potential in school unless adults positively invite them to do so. In summarizing her findings on particularly effective middle schools, Joan Lipsitz (1984) wrote:

> Most striking is the level of caring in the schools. In the careful assignment of students to teachers and houses, in counseling, on school-sponsored trips, in home visits, in teachers' use of personal time with students for weekend canoeing expeditions, baseball games, and jazz combos, hours upon hours are spent in and outside of school on behalf of the personal welfare of the students. This level of caring, which we all need and flourish under, is especially important for a vulnerable age group. (p. 181)

We believe that even though not all teachers wish to be as involved as those in the middle schools Lipsitz found to be most supportive of student personal growth and achievement, we can all work to improve the quality of adult-student relationships in schools. In so doing, we can make schools more positive and enjoyable learning environments for both adults and young people.

RECOMMENDED READING

Alberti, R., & Emmons, M. (1974). *Your perfect right,* 2nd ed. San Luis Obispo, Calif.: Impact.

Brophy, J., & Good, T. (1986). Teacher behavior and student achievement. In M. Wittrock (Ed.), *Handbook of research on teaching,* 3rd ed. New York: Macmillan.

Combs, A. (1982). *A personal approach to teaching beliefs that make a difference.* Boston: Allyn and Bacon.

Dusek, J. (Ed.) (1985). *Teacher expectations.* Hillsdale, N.J.: Erlbaum.

Gazda, G. (1973). *Human relations development: A manual for educators.* Boston: Allyn and Bacon.

Ginott, H. (1972). *Teacher and child.* New York: Macmillan.

Gordon, T. (1974). *Teaching effectiveness training.* New York: Peter H. Wyden.

Hurt, H., Scott, M., & McCroskey, J. (1978). *Communication in the classroom.* Reading, Mass.: Addison-Wesley.

Jones, V. (1980). *Adolescents with behavior problems: Strategies for teaching, counseling, and parent involvement.* Boston: Allyn and Bacon.

Jourard, S. (1971). *The transparent self.* New York: D. Van Nostrand.

Kraft, A. (1975). *The living classroom: Putting humanistic education into practice.* New York: Harper and Row.

Lang, A., & Jacobowski, P. (1976). *Responsible assertive behavior: Cognitive/behavioral procedures for trainers.* Champaign, Ill.: Research Press.

Liberman, R., King, L., DeRisi, W., & McCann, M. (1975). *Personal effectiveness: Guiding people to assert themselves and improve their social skills.* Champaign, Ill.: Research Press.

Purkey, W. & Novack, J. (1984). *Inviting school success: A self-concept approach to teaching and learning.* Belmont, Calif.: Wadsworth.

Rogers, C. (1961). *On becoming a person.* Boston: Houghton Mifflin.

Schmuck, R., & Schmuck, P. (1983). *Group processes in the classroom.* Dubuque, Iowa: William C. Brown.

Seiler, W., Schuelke, D., & Lieb-Brilhart, B. (1984). *Communication for the contemporary classroom.* New York: Holt, Rinehart and Winston.

CHAPTER 4

Creating Positive Peer Relationships

Classrooms that have a climate of competitiveness, hostility and alienation cause anxiety and discomfort and do not facilitate the intellectual development of many students. Classrooms in which students and teachers support one another facilitate the development of self-esteem and the satisfaction of fundamental motives. They also provide the opportunity for students to use their intellectual capacities to their fullest.

/ Richard Schmuck and Patricia Schmuck (1983)
Group Processes in the Classroom

Positive interpersonal relations among students are necessary both for problem solving in groups and for general classroom enjoyment of instructional activity. The psycho-logical security and safety necessary for open exploration of instructional tasks is based upon feelings of being accepted, liked, and supported by fellow students. Class cohesion is based upon positive interpersonal relationships among students.

/ David Johnson and Roger Johnson (1975)
Learning Together and Alone:
Cooperation, Competition, and Individualization

Peers play an important role in determining the quality of the learning environment. With today's increased emphasis on students' achievement, teachers are often hesitant to allocate time for creating positive peer relationships in the classroom. In addition, teacher education programs seldom provide teachers with specific skills for developing positive, supportive group norms. A considerable body of research indicates, however, that time spent creating a positive peer group can eliminate much misbehavior and can provide a classroom climate that enhances students' achievement.

Peer relationships influence students' achievement in several ways. First, peer attitudes toward achievement affect students' academic aspirations and school behavior (Coleman, 1966; Lewis & St. John, 1974; Rutter et al., 1979; Sharan & Sharan, 1976). Second, the quality of peer relationships and personal support in classrooms affects the degree to which students' personal needs are met and, subsequently, their ability to be productively involved in the learning process (Lewis & St. John, 1974; Schmuck, 1963, 1966). Finally, peer relationships can directly affect achievement through cooperative learning activities (Johnson & Johnson, 1987; Johnson, Marayama, Johnson, Nelson, & Skon, 1981; Slavin, 1983a, 1988).

Anyone who has worked with groups of students has witnessed the role peers play in influencing students' behavior. When discussing the differences between confronting an adolescent in front of the group and having a private talk with the student, teachers frequently remark that it seems as if they are dealing with two completely different students. We should not be surprised that students' feelings and behaviors are significantly influenced by their classmates. During the school year, students spend more than 1,000 hours with their classmates. And, because most elementary school classrooms are composed of children who live near one another, friendships and conflicts that develop in the classroom often influence youngsters' lives outside the school. Peer pressure is somewhat less complex and extensive for early primary-grade children whose egocentricity reduces the influence of their peers. Nevertheless, at all grade levels the values, norms, and behaviors of the group significantly affect individual students' feelings of safety, belongingness, respect for others, and self-esteem.

In their *Group Processes in the Classroom*, Richard and Patricia Schmuck (1983) write of the classroom group's importance:

> The classroom clearly offers a setting in which high levels of feeling exist daily and wherein covert psychological dynamics often come into play. As students interact, and students and teachers relate, they communicate—however indirectly—their feelings about one another. Such gestures of affect influence how students view themselves, their abilities, their likability, and their general worth. Morever, feelings, evaluations, or defenses about oneself make up students' self-esteem and have impact on the degree to which they use their intelligence and the manner in which they form their current educational aspirations. (p. 24)

UNDERSTANDING THE CLASSROOM GROUP

The classroom by nature elicits many interactions and feelings. By placing 25 to 35 individuals in a 30-by-30-foot room, schools create a highly interactive environment. Peer interaction is a natural and desirable aspect of almost all learning environments. Group instruction is used both because it is frequently more expedient and because a good education involves learning how to function as a group member. The group's influence is intensified by the competition found in most classrooms. Students compete for the highest test scores, strive to move into a higher reading group, or run for class office. Even when we use individualized programs that deemphasize competition, students have numerous opportunities to compare their work to that of their classmates. It is understandable and perhaps unavoidable that classrooms are characterized by a fairly high level of interaction and the accompanying spontaneous interchange of feelings.

Although teachers often express concern and frustration over the negative aspects of peer pressure, the peer group can be a positive and supportive factor in the classroom. When students feel liked by their peers and when interactions are characterized by thoughtfulness and helpfulness, students experience a sense of safety and security, belongingness and affection, significance, respect of others, and power. Students are then able to concentrate more fully on learning and are willing to take greater risks in attempting to master new skills. Consequently, it is extremely important that we implement strategies that encourage development of positive, supportive peer interactions in the classroom.

It is beyond the scope of this book to examine group dynamics thoroughly, but we must realize that groups, like individuals, have needs that must be met before the group can function effectively. If the classroom group is to function in a supportive, goal-directed manner, we must initially set aside time for activities that enable students to know each other, develop a feeling of being included, and create diverse friendship patterns. Only after these feelings have been developed can a group of students proceed to respond optimally to the learning goals of the classroom.

A large body of both theory and research supports these observations. Several major theories of group development support the concept that interpersonal issues must be clarified before groups can begin to function effectively in meeting their task goals. Tuckman (1965) and Schmuck and Schmuck (1983) observe that the functions groups serve can be divided into interpersonal and task functions. This two-stage theory of group development and functioning is supported by work with classroom groups (Runkel, Lawrence, Oldfield, Rider, & Clark, 1971). Schutz's theory (1966) states that during the early stages of a group's development, members care primarily about being included in the group. Discussing this aspect of group dynamics in their *Group Processes in the Classroom*, Schmuck and Schmuck (1975) write:

> Issues of interpersonal inclusion characterize the beginning of a group's life. In the classroom, the students and teacher confront one another's presence and raise questions such as: How will I fit in here? Who will accept me? Who will reject me? What do I have to do to be accepted? Academic work cannot easily be accomplished until these questions of inclusion are answered satisfactorily. (p. 171)

Gibb's (1964) theory of group dynamics also supports the importance of initially dealing with interpersonal issues. Gibb states that groups begin to function effectively only after members feel accepted and develop a sense of interpersonal trust. He says that, following resolution of this primary issue, groups move on to the issues of making decisions and group norms and goals.

Much research also suggests that group norms greatly influence individual students' behavior. The Coleman Report (1966) is perhaps the best-known study of the effect of peer norms. This study, commissioned by the U.S. Office of Education and directed by James Coleman, was an attempt to determine the factors that influenced school achievement among high school students. Coleman's data suggest that factors such as funds available for equipment and salaries, the racial makeup of the school, and the teachers' educational level make little difference in determining students' achievement. Instead, the major factors are the socioeconomic composition and achievement orientation of fellow students. When students attend schools in which academic achievement is valued, their interest in academic endeavors and their academic achievement increase. Similarly, attendance at schools in which academic performance is not valued tends to decrease students' academic interest and achievement. Coleman's study has been criticized on several grounds, yet it appears that peers' attitudes do account for a significant amount of variance in students' achievement.

In a closely related study, Lewis and St. John (1974) attempted to determine the variables that influenced achievement of black students in classrooms in which the majority of students were white. Their research showed that higher achievement among black students was related to norms that stressed both achievement and acceptance of black students within the classroom. The results indicated that the presence of high-achieving white students was not significantly sufficient to enhance academic achievement among the black students. It appeared that this factor has to be combined with white students' accepting their black peers as friends.

Other studies (Alexander & Campbell, 1964; Hargreaves, 1967; McDill, Rigsby, & Meyers, 1969) reaffirm that students are heavily influenced by the attitudes and information of their peers. Berenda's (1950) study examined the extent to which 7- to 13-year-old children would respond to group pressure by contradicting material they could clearly see was correct. The experiment involved placing each child in a room with the 8 highest-achieving students in the child's class. The 8 peers were instructed to give incorrect responses to comparisons of the lengths of two lines. The results showed that 57 percent of the 7- to 10-year-olds and 46 percent of the 13-year-olds agreed with obviously wrong answers provided by their peers. This powerful influence of peer conformity is partially explained by the fact that

> individuals rely on group norms to guide them, especially when they are unsure about social reality. . . . For students especially there is a pull toward the peer group to make the complex world of the school more understandable. . . .
> Students feel insecure when their personal response is in opposition to a group norm. (Schmuck & Schmuck, 1975, p. 121)

Group values and norms so deeply influence the individual student's behavior that we can expect that the student's self-esteem will be significantly affected by the group, and that the student's self-image will mirror the group's attitudes about the student (Mannheim, 1957). Similarly, research (McGinley & McGinley, 1970; Stevens, 1971) suggests a correlation among the student's popularity, self-esteem, and achievement. Although the influence of these factors undoubtedly is complex, most teachers would agree that students who are well liked by the group generally feel better about themselves and tend to function more productively in the classroom. The influence of positive group feelings on learning is directly supported by studies from various grade levels indicating that students' achievement is higher in classrooms characterized by diverse, positive peer relationships (Muldoon, 1955; Schmuck, 1966; Walberg & Anderson, 1968).

This work has been supported by studies on cooperative learning. Students involved in cooperative learning activities in which they study with peers and their efforts produce benefits for peers as well as for themselves perform higher on standardized tests of mathematics, reading, and language and also do better on tasks involving higher level thinking than when they study alone (Slavin, 1983b, 1987, 1988; Slavin, Madden, & Leavey, 1984). Slavin (1987) summarizes the results of studies on the benefits of students working cooperatively:

> When cooperative learning methods provide group goals based on the learning of all members, the effects on student achievement are remarkably consistent. Of 38 studies of at least four weeks' duration comparing cooperative methods of this type to traditional control methods, 33 found significantly greater achievement for the cooperatively taught classes, and 5 found no significant differences. (p. 10)

Similarly, researchers at the National Center on Effective Secondary Schools at the University of Wisconsin–Madison synthesized the research on cooperative learning and students' academic success in secondary schools. With the exception of one technique (the jigsaw method), cooperative learning was found to be more successful in more than 75 percent of the studies. Research indicates that cooperative learning appears to be less effective when used in high school settings. Our own work in helping high school teachers implement cooperative learning suggests that cooperative learning is very effective, especially in increasing the motivation and learning of at-risk students when teachers (1) take time to help students understand the reasons behind their decision to implement this new method, (2) help students become better acquainted, and (3) assist students in developing skills for working in groups.

Studies also indicate that cooperative learning can be an effective technique for helping students be accepted into and function effectively in classrooms. Good and Brophy (1987) highlight the social/affective benefits associated with cooperative learning:

> Effects on outcomes other than achievement are even more impressive. Cooperative learning arrangements promote friendship choices and prosocial patterns of interaction among students who differ in achievement, sex, race or ethnicity, and they promote the acceptance of mainstreamed handicapped students by their nonhandicapped classmates. Cooperative methods also frequently have positive effects, and rarely have negative effects, on affective outcomes such as self-esteem, academic self-confidence, liking for the class, liking and feeling liked by classmates, and various measures of empathy and social cooperation. (p. 438)

As we discuss in chapter 9, cooperative learning involves more than having students like each other and support each other's efforts. However, the creation of positive peer relationships in classrooms and in the small cooperative working groups is an essential ingredient to successful learning in classrooms and these groups (Johnson & Johnson, 1987; Johnson, Johnson, & Johnson-Holubec, 1986).

The relationship among positive group norms, diverse liking patterns, and productive student behavior and achievement is a major incentive for teachers to develop skills in creating positive peer relationships in the classroom, but we have a second important reason for acquiring these skills. Today's students live in a world that is increasingly urban and in which people are more and more interdependent. The time when the average person lived in relative isolation and was basically self-sufficient is long past. Individuals depend on others for needed goods and services as well as for meeting emotional needs. Likewise, individuals are rediscovering the importance of coming together in order to combat social problems ranging from burglary to an energy crisis. This increased interdependence can also be seen in the move away from the Renaissance scholar toward increased specialization. In producing anything from automobiles to ideas, individuals focus on an ever more specialized aspect of their work and must cooperate with other people in order to create increasingly sophisticated products.

If schools are to prepare students for a society characterized by interdependence and cooperative effort, they must provide students with frequent and meaningful experiences in functioning cooperatively in groups. Rather than continually stressing competition and individual learning, teachers must use cooperative group work in the classroom. More than three decades ago, John Dewey emphasized that life in a classroom should mirror the processes students will face in society. He wrote too that the goal of schooling is to provide students with skills that will enable them to create a better living situation.

It is likely that many teachers who read this chapter will be concerned that the time taken to help students know and work effectively with their peers is time taken away from instruction. This is an important issue. As teachers, our primary responsibility is to help students develop skills in the subject matter for which we are responsible. We must also realize, however, that we are responsible for understanding and implementing the most current research and instructional methodology for helping all students develop mastery of the content. We believe the evidence clearly indicates that taking time to establish a safe, supportive classroom group in which students know each other and support each other's learning will significantly enhance student learning. We can either take a small but significant amount of time to help the relationships in our classrooms run smoothly or we can risk spending extensive time and energy on responding to problems caused by students feeling isolated, unable to receive assistance, uninvolved, and unwanted.

The activities presented throughout the remainder of the chapter can help the reader create a more positive, supportive classroom environment. They can also help students develop work norms and personal skills that will serve them well in their future roles as parent, spouse, friend, and worker.

ACQUAINTANCE ACTIVITIES

You can undoubtedly recall experiencing discomfort when walking into a party or other group setting knowing very few individuals. Compare this feeling with those elicited when you walk into a room filled with acquaintances and friends. People usually feel more relaxed and comfortable in discussions or other activities with people they know. Students experience similar feelings. The new student who is confronted by 30 unfamiliar faces is likely to respond either by withdrawing until the environment becomes more familiar or by acting-out as a means of controlling the environment by eliciting an expected response.

Several years ago, one of us was contacted by a teacher who was experiencing much frustration because the students in his sophomore English class were not becoming involved in group discussions. Furthermore, the teacher said absenteeism in class was relatively high and students were not handing in the number of assignments he had expected. The teacher, a hardworking, dynamic young man, indicated that the material being read and discussed seemed to be of high interest and that he had made a special effort to relate aspects of the literature to students' lives. Students were seated in a circle and open discussion was encouraged.

While discussing this situation, I asked the teacher whether students in the class knew each other. The teacher seemed surprised by the question and indicated that because the students came from only two feeder schools and had been in his class for nearly six months, he assumed they were well acquainted. The students' behavior suggested, however, that they felt some discomfort, and the teacher agreed to assess how well they knew one another. He was surprised to discover that only a quarter of the students in his class knew the first names of more than half of their peers. He discussed this figure with the class and explained his decision to allocate time to activities that would help students become better acquainted. Following these activities, he again collected data on attendance, percentage of assignments handed in, and students' participation in class discussions. All three variables showed changes that were statistically significant at the .01 level. These results were so striking that the teacher's English department decided to incorporate a peer-acquaintance unit into the first nine weeks of the school year.

The peer-acquaintance activities described below include several that were used by the teacher described in the previous paragraph. These activities are designed to help students get better acquainted with one another so that they will feel safe and secure and will therefore become more actively engaged in the learning process. As students become better acquainted, the likelihood that they will interact with and be influenced by a wider range of students increases and cliquish behavior decreases.

The Name Chain
A name chain is the most effective method for helping students learn each other's names. These steps can make this activity run smoothly.

1. Ask the students to sit in a circle so that each one can comfortably see all the students in the group.

2. Clearly explain the reasons for being involved in the activity. You might say that one benefit of knowing everyone's name is that this increases their knowledge of the environment and thereby makes them more comfortable and more likely to become actively involved. Similarly, you may indicate that knowing other students' names will enable students to greet each other in a friendlier, more relaxed manner, which will have a tendency to make both the classroom and the school a more positive place.

3. Ask the students if they have any questions about why they are being asked to do the activity.

4. Explain to the students that each person will be asked to say his or her first name and tell the group one thing about himself or herself. They may choose to tell the group something they like to do, something interesting that happened to them recently, how they are feeling, and so on. Inform the class that they will be asked to repeat each student's name and the statement he or she has made. They will begin with the person who spoke first and stop when they have given their name and have said something about themselves. The first student may say, "I'm Bob, and I went to the beach this weekend." The next would say, "That's Bob (or you're Bob), and he (or you) went to the beach last weekend. I'm Sandy, and I enjoy backpacking." Because we are faced with the difficult task of learning a large number of names and because having an adult remember their names seems particularly important to adolescents, it is best to have you be the last person to speak. You will therefore be able to list each student's name and what they have shared with the class.

5. Have everyone take a paper and pencil and change seats. Ask the students to start with a designated individual and go clockwise around the circle, writing down each person's name. It is not necessary to have them list what each student shared.

6. Ask for a volunteer who will begin with the person designated as the starting place and slowly give the name of each person in the circle. This recital serves as an opportunity for students to check the accuracy of their list and to learn the names of any students they might have missed.

It is important to provide followup for this activity. For example, for several days following the activity you may want to attempt to go around the class listing each student's name or ask for a volunteer to do so. We must continue to be aware of whether students are remembering names and continue to emphasize the value of knowing names. If you ask students to work in groups, you may suggest that they make sure they know each member's name before beginning the group activity. Teachers too often involve students in activities and then fail to follow-up with behavior that reinforces the learning derived from and the values implied by the activity.

What's in a Name?

This activity is excellent as a first-acquaintance activity or as an activity following a name chain. Students are placed in groups of five or six. Briefly lead a discussion on the value of names. You might include comments about how names may reflect a cultural heritage, refer to a loved relative, or be chosen because a parent liked the name. The discussion can also focus on how names may evoke positive or negative feelings, depending on how each of us likes our name or what people do with the name. Then, tell the class that the activity involves sharing some things about the students' names as a way of becoming better acquainted. Ask students to tell these facts about their name:

1. State their full name.
2. How did they get their name? For example, were they named for someone? Does the name represent a family heritage or nationality?
3. Do they have any nicknames? Who calls them by this name? Do they like the nickname(s)?
4. Do people change their name in any way? For example, is it often shortened and so on? How do they feel about this?
5. Do they like their name? If not, what name would they prefer?
6. What name do they want used in the class?

After all groups have finished, one student in each group can volunteer to introduce each member of the small group to the entire class. They do so by giving the name each student wants to be called in the class.

Know Your Classmates

Each student will need a ditto sheet entitled ''Know Your Classmates'' and a pencil or pen. Ask students to find a person in the class who fits each description listed on the sheet and to obtain the person's signature on the line in front of the description. To encourage students to interact with numerous peers, inform them that they cannot have the same person sign their sheet more than twice. Figure 4.1 is an example of this activity. The descriptions can be adapted to fit the specific interests of children at different ages and in different settings.

Interviews
Interviews are an excellent means for students to become better acquainted with each other. This activity will often foster new friendships and feelings of self-importance. Lack of information about others is often a major barrier to establishing new friendships. When children do not know their peers, they tend to make assumptions and develop unrealistic fears or unfounded biases. As students interview each other, they learn new and exciting information about their peers. This knowledge, in turn, promotes diversified friendship patterns in the classroom.

FIGURE 4.1 Know Your Classmates

Name_____

Collect the signatures of the appropriate persons:

_____ 1. A person whose birthday is in the same month as yours.
_____ 2. A person who has red hair.
_____ 3. A person whom you don't know very well.
_____ 4. A person who has an interesting hobby. What is it?_____
_____
_____ 5. A person with freckles.
_____ 6. A person whose favorite color is yellow.
_____ 7. A person who loves to read.
_____ 8. A person who takes gymnastic lessons.
_____ 9. A person who is left-handed.
_____ 10. A person with naturally curly hair.
_____ 11. A person who has a dog. The dog's name is _____.
_____ 12. A person who belongs to a Scouting troop.
_____ 13. A person shorter than you.
_____ 14. A person taller than you.
_____ 15. A person with the same color shirt or dress as you are wearing.
_____ 16. A person who plays an instrument. What instrument?_____
_____
_____ 17. A person who traveled out of the state this summer. Where?__
_____
_____ 18. A person who wants to play professional sports when he or she grows up. Which one?_____
_____ 19. A person with more than four children in the family. How many?
_____
_____ 20. A person who plays soccer.
_____ 21. A person with braces on his or her teeth.
_____ 22. A person who rides horseback.

We can use interviews in the classroom in many ways. One method involves introducing the interviewing process by having students list ten questions that would help them know a classmate better. This list provides some examples of questions that might be asked by 9-year-olds:

1. What is your favorite color?
2. What is your favorite sport to play? to watch?
3. What are you proudest of?
4. Do you have any pets? If so, what are their names?
5. What is your favorite professional team in football? basketball? baseball?
6. What kinds of foods do you like to eat?
7. If you could go anyplace on a vacation, where would you go? Why?
8. Do you take any lessons?
9. Do you have any hobbies?
10. Do you like your first name? If not, what would you change it to?

We write these questions on the chalkboard and tell the students each to choose a person whom they do not know very well and, using the ten questions as a guide, learn as much as they can about their partner. After ten minutes ask each pair to separate but stay within viewing distance and draw their partner. These portraits are later shared and displayed. The next step consists of the pairs drawing a map of how to walk to each other's homes (only students old enough to understand the streets in their neighborhood). The final step is for each student to share the information about their partner with the rest of the class. Because you are a group member, you should participate in this activity.

Another approach to interviewing also begins by developing a list of questions students might ask each other. These questions are written on the board and referred to as students interview each other in pairs. After these questions have been asked, each pair of students joins with another pair. The four children share the new information they have learned about their partners. After a few minutes ask the class to reconvene and each person to share five things about his or her partner with the class.

A third interviewing technique has a student sit in a place of honor at the front of the classroom. The student is asked questions by the other class members. Students enjoy being in the limelight and often state that this is their favorite approach to interviewing.

A final interviewing approach has several students serve as reporters. They interview their peers and obtain such information as where students were born; the number of members in their family; a student's favorite television show, food, color, or animal; a special hobby or pet; any unusual places they have traveled to; and students' future goals. The teacher tabulates the information and either duplicates it and gives it to each student or makes a large chart in the hall for other classes to read.

The results of these interviewing activities can often be seen in new friendships and more open communication in the classroom. This atmosphere in turn makes the classroom a safer and more relaxed learning environment for students.

Guess Who?

An acquaintance activity used by a number of secondary teachers gives students an opportunity to discover how well they know their peers. The steps for setting up this activity are:

1. Briefly describe the activity to the students and elicit their willingness to take part in the activity.

2. Ask students to write brief (two- or three-line) statements about themselves, which can include facts about their personal history, family, hobbies, and so forth.

3. Collect all the autobiographical statements.

4. Ask each student to take out paper and pencil. Read each description and ask the students (you, too, should be involved) to write the name of the student who they believe wrote the description.

5. After all the descriptions have been read, reread them and ask the authors to identify themselves. Ask the students to indicate on the list whether they made the correct choice. Upon completing the task, you can ask students to indicate the number of their peers whom they correctly identified. These results can be used to initiate a discussion about the degree to which class members have become acquainted.

6. An interesting alternative to this activity is to have students write brief statements that include one false statement about themselves. Then give the class the student's name and personal description and ask them to decide which statement is false. This activity can be performed by the entire group or can be developed as a contest between two groups.

7. A second variation of this activity is to have each student write a poem or riddle about himself or herself. These poems are put into a box. Each student draws a poem from the box and reads it aloud to the class. From the information on the poem the class tries to identify the author of the poem. As a followup, each student could draw a self-portrait that could be placed on a bulletin board with his or her poem below it.

Dyads

This acquaintance activity involves providing students with an opportunity to spend several minutes getting to know someone with whom they are not well acquainted. This activity is most beneficial when it gives students a chance to interact both with peers whom they would like to get to know better and with peers whom they might initially not choose to meet. These are the specific methods for involving students in this activity.

1. Explain the reasons for using the activity. Inform the participants that it provides them with an opportunity to sit down and talk to several peers whom they do not know well. Be sure to give the students a chance to question and discuss the activity.

2. Ask the students to stand in a circle so they can see all members of the group. Then ask them to look around the group and see whether there are people whom they would like to get to know better. This may be a person whom they have not met but would like to meet or a person whom they know a little and would like to get to know better. At this stage in the activity it is helpful to point out that picking someone does not mean you want to date that person or become a best friend. It simply means he or she is a person whom you do not know well.

3. Suggest that each person determine several people whom they would like to meet, because the person they choose may be chosen by someone else. Here it is helpful to state that a situation sometimes arises in which the last few people remaining already know each other. This situation can be handled in two ways. First, these individuals can simply form dyads and get to know each other better. Second, these adolescents can each join a dyad that includes two people whom they do not know well. Because the activity is much less effective if groups are larger than three, limit their size.

4. Before having students make their selection, inform them that their task is simply to spend four or five minutes getting to know the person they choose or who chooses them. It is useful to tell the students that they can learn something about themselves by paying attention to how they choose or are chosen. For example, if they turn their back slightly, look at their feet, and think, "I'm not very interesting, no one will choose me," they may be creating a situation in which they are less likely to be chosen. Also inform the class that because this is not an easy task, they may have a tendency to take the easy way out by choosing their best friend. Point out that even though it may be easier, they may be cheating both themselves and other students out of some interesting learning.

5. Inform the students that they can now choose someone and that they will be called back together in about five minutes.

6. About one minute before the time is up, inform the students that they have about one minute to complete their conversation.

7. When the students are once again in the large group, ask them how the activity went and how they felt. Allow several minutes for this discussion and then, unless they found the activity very difficult and do not want to try it again, ask them to once again look around the group and choose a person whom they would like to get to know better. Depending on the time available, the leader's goals, and the students' interest, this activity can be repeated any number of times. If the students indicate that the activity was difficult and they do not want to continue, follow-up by asking what they found difficult. Their difficulty may stem from such factors as well-formed cliques that need to be dealt with in order to create an open, safe environment.

8. One interesting alteration that teachers and group leaders find beneficial is to have the students select someone whom they might normally not get to know. Indicate that this does not mean that they do not like the person, but simply that that person might be a little more difficult for them to approach. It is helpful to provide the students with examples and for teachers to share their own concerns about meeting certain types of people. The leader might say that when he or she was in high school, he was not athletic, and therefore, he found it difficult to approach the so-called jocks. He might also say that people tend to have difficulty approaching someone they have never met or who has interests different from their own. Though this version of the activity is more difficult, it does have payoffs in reducing tensions and expanding the pattern of students' interactions.

Having students know and feel supported by their peers is valuable at all grade levels, but it may be particularly critical as young people move through early adolescence. Students in grades 6 through 8 are experiencing rapid cognitive and physical changes. This is a time of heightened self-consciousness and decreased self-esteem. Consequently, students learn much more effectively in environments in which teacher-student and peer relationships are characterized by warmth, support, and stability. Schools for young adolescents should not only use a wide range of acquaintance activities, but should also be organized so that students spend a sizable portion of the school day with students and teachers whom they know. Joan Lipsitz (1984) describes successful schools for young adolescents:

The groups of students are small enough that, as the teachers and paraprofessionals in the schools say, they know the students' moods and do not make the interpersonal mistakes that would be unavoidable in large, more impersonal settings. The students are secure in being known, and staff members are relaxed because of their deep familiarity with the students and their confidence in dealing with them. . . . The schools have adopted policies that strengthen and stabilize peer groupings by extending the time students remain together, both during the day and also over a period of several years. . . . Antisocial behavior that results from the randomness and brevity of student groupings in most secondary schools is substantially reduced in these schools. (p. 182)

If you are interested in incorporating additional acquaintance activities into your lesson plans, you can find numerous resources. Among those we have found most useful are Bailey and Kackley, *Positive Alternatives to Student Suspensions* (1980); David Johnson's *Reaching Out* (1986); Jack Canfield and Harold Wells's *One Hundred Ways to Enhance Self-Concept in the Classroom* (1976); Nickerson et al., *Miraculous Me* (1980); and Michele and Craig Borda's *Self-Esteem: A Classroom Affair* (1978).

ACTIVITIES FOR ESTABLISHING A COHESIVE GROUP

Group cohesiveness refers to the extent to which a group experiences a sense of identity, oneness, and esprit de corps. Cohesive groups are characterized by warm, friendly interactions among all members rather than by positive interchanges limited to small cliques within the group. Cohesive groups provide settings in which students feel safe, experience a sense of belonging, and view themselves as being liked and respected by others. Research (Lewis & St. John, 1974; Schmuck, 1966) indicates that students who are accepted by their classmates have more positive attitudes toward school and are more likely to achieve closer to their potential than are students who feel rejected and isolated. These findings are supported by research (Combs & Taylor, 1952) that indicates that students perform less effectively when they feel threatened by the environment.

> Cohesiveness is correlated with the productivity of a group, provided the norms are supportive of production. Cohesive groups are more goal-directed than noncohesive groups, and as long as the goals of the individuals are in line with productivity, cohesiveness is a facilitating factor. Classroom groups which have strong goals have satisfied students. Moreover, students who know what is expected of them and who are involved and close to their peers in pursuing educational goals are more satisfied than students in classrooms that are disorganized and fragmented. (Schmuck & Schmuck, 1974, p. 31)

Group cohesiveness and a positive group identity do not develop simply because students spend time together. Rather, positive feelings about being a group member are developed by making the group seem attractive, distinguishing it from other groups, involving the group in cooperative enterprises, and helping students view themselves as an important component in the group. The activities described in this section are designed to accomplish these goals. The activities are most effective when used in association with acquaintance activities and with activities for creating diverse liking patterns.

Activities aimed at creating a cohesive classroom group will be most effective when introduced at the beginning of the school year. One important reason for developing group cohesion early in the school year is that cohesive groups are desirable only if the group's norms support your learning goals. If you can begin the year by establishing a positive group feeling while creating norms that support academic achievement and productive behavior, the school year will be pleasant and productive.

Activities for Elementary School Classrooms

Ways of Having a Happy Classroom

Focusing on the positive qualities of a classroom sets a tone for the entire year. In the fall we can ask students to list things they can do to make the classroom a happy place to be. Students can be encouraged to describe ways of positively interacting with each other, ideas for having fun in the classroom, and so on. The students' ideas can be written on a large sheet of paper and posted in the classroom. Every month students can be asked whether they are acting in accordance with the ideas expressed on the chart and they can evaluate each item to see if it is still applicable. New ideas may be added at any time.

Group Contributions

To establish a cohesive classroom it is important that students focus on their contributions to the group. We can enhance this theme by creating a bulletin board. Give each child paper, pencil, and crayons and ask him or her to draw a picture of himself or herself. After these have been completed, ask students to think about what contribution they can make to the group. After you have led a short discussion to clarify the concept and provide students with ideas, give them a strip of paper and tell them to write down their contribution. Collect the pictures and contributions and mount them on a bulletin board for all to see. This is an excellent way of reinforcing the facts that everyone can contribute to the classroom and that the classroom will be a better place if all contribute some of their special talents.

Classroom Arrangements

Developing a comfortable classroom environment can enhance students' motivation and provide opportunities for increasing their sense of competence and power. It is desirable to involve students in decisions about the classroom arrangement whenever possible. Give them a basic floor plan of the room including all built-ins. Then ask them to sketch in the desks and any other movable furniture. The arrangements can be displayed and the students and you can choose the floor plan with which all would be most comfortable. By giving students responsibility for a room arrangement, we indicate our respect for their judgment and they gain a sense of significance, competence, and power.

Students can also be active in decorating the room. They can be encouraged to bring posters from home, take part in designing bulletin-board displays, and determine the types of plants they would like in the room. Increased student involvement in organizing and decorating the room is almost always associated with an intensified group feeling, higher motivation, and reduced vandalism.

Class Spirit

At the beginning of the school year most students are excited and motivated. Teachers can take advantage of this excitement by establishing a class spirit that creates a bond among the students. Many activities throughout the year can revolve around this class spirit.

To create a class spirit, teacher and students discuss the kinds of group identity they would like to develop and formulate a list. The list might include a class animal, name, flower, insect, song, flag, color, cheer, game, cartoon character, sport, bird, and poem. Suggestions are welcomed, and eventually students vote to determine their choices in each category. When the class spirit is completed it is displayed proudly in a prominent place in the room.

It is very important to reinforce this activity by using parts of the class spirit whenever possible throughout the year. For example, when sending a newsletter to parents we might draw several of the class symbols on the letter and mimeograph the newsletter onto paper that is the class color. Similarly, stating the class cheer before special sporting events or singing the class song at the close of each week continues to enhance class spirit.

Class History

An effective activity that helps mold students into a cohesive group is development of a class history or class yearbook. When approached with this idea in the fall, students are always overwhelmingly in favor of making a class history.

Four to six students are chosen either by the teacher or by their peers to write the history, and all students are encouraged to contribute ideas. Every month the history writers meet and decide what events, assemblies, new lessons, and so on they wish to incorporate into their class history. The historians then divide the writing assignments. At the end of the year students have a collection of the year's events. In addition to these events the class history can include poems written by students, a student directory of addresses and phone numbers, an autograph page, a page about students' thoughts on the year, and a letter written to the students by the teacher. The class history helps create a sense of group purposefulness and commitment and is a memorable treasure for each student.

Photo Album

Whenever a special event occurs, capture the moment in a photograph. Students can become actively involved by learning to use a camera. Pictures taken by students can be accompanied by written statements and put on the bulletin board until replaced by a picture and description of a new event. The old material can then be placed in the class photo album and some of the written material can be incorporated into the class history.

The photo album can be shown to parents during scheduled conferences or when a parent drops by the school. Parents enjoy seeing pictures of their children involved in special school activities. This sharing enhances parent interest in their child's school experience and increases parental support for the teacher and the school. When a particularly good picture of a child is obtained, the teacher can make a copy and send it to the parents along with a short note. Parents appreciate this thoughtful gesture, and their increased interest in their child's classroom experience helps their child develop a sense of pride and commitment.

When there are a few moments left in a day, it is enjoyable to recall several of the special events by looking at the pictures in the class photo album. This is an effective means of reinforcing a sense of identity and creating positive feelings about the class.

Opening and Closing Questions

Students arrive at school with many different feelings and needs. Some students may arrive in an irritable mood resulting from an argument with a younger brother or lack of a proper breakfast. Another student's favorite goldfish may have died, while another child may be happy because it is his or her birthday. It is often hard for students to make the transition from home to school. Therefore it is important that students be given a few minutes at the beginning of each day to share any events that are significant to them.

Students are asked to meet in a circle. The teacher then asks whether any person needs or wants to share anything. A student who has just broken his or her foot may need someone to carry his or her lunch tray, while another student whose dog just died may need some care and understanding. Teachers also have days when they are tired or not feeling well and therefore would like the students to be particularly quiet and helpful during the day. When students are treated kindly and their needs are accepted and respected, they will respond to your needs and desires.

For students who are less comfortable sharing their needs in a group, an optional activity is to have them write down their needs and place them in a box or bag. You can check several times during the day to see whether any child has put a need in the box.

The end of the school day can be an important time to establish closure on any issues that occurred during the day. Questions such as, ''What did you learn today?'' ''How do you feel about the day?'' or ''What did you like and dislike about today?'' often evoke serious discussion. It is advisable to allow at least 10 minutes for this session. Taking time at the end of each day encourages students to examine what they have accomplished and also helps to ensure that the day will end on a positive note.

Special Days

Creating special days allows students to have some influence over their environment while enhancing a sense of group identity. Special days might include a day on which everyone wears the same color, a day for wearing favorite buttons, a day when students wear their baseball, soccer, ice skating, or Scout uniforms, a day for dressing as students did during the fifties, and a day when everyone wears his or her favorite hat. You can add to the special day by relating various subjects to the day's theme. Math problems to solve batting averages could be included on uniform day, music of famous singers during the rock'n'roll era might be discussed and listened to during music class on fifties day, or students might read stories involving hats on hat day.

My School Bulletin Board

Creating a cohesive group is very important, but it is often useful to expand this concept beyond the classroom. One way to do so is to have students make a hall display or bulletin board with the theme ''What I Like about My School.'' Use pictures, essays, or a collage. This activity enhances school spirit and focuses on the positive aspects of a school. This concept can be extended to include a large hall mural with the same theme to which each class contributes their ideas about why they like their school.

Baby Pictures Bulletin Board

An activity that enhances group or school cohesiveness is the display of teachers' or students' baby pictures. A contest can be held to determine which students can correctly identify the teachers' or students' baby pictures. Students enjoy this activity and it often leads to increased dialogue between students and teachers and among students.

A somewhat similar activity is to display samples of students' or teachers' hobbies in the main showcase. Students and teachers can try to match the hobby with the person involved. This activity can be used to generate positive feelings and a sense of esprit de corps either within the classroom or throughout the school.

Activities for Secondary Classrooms

Because secondary school students spend considerably less time in one classroom group, most secondary teachers will choose to incorporate only one or two of the types of activities described in the previous section. A teacher of Junior Writing and American Literature recently shared with us one technique for incorporating group cohesiveness activities. During the first week of school she has the class brainstorm ways in which individuals contribute to the class as a whole. These are listed on the chalkboard and may include such statements as:

> Breaking the ice
> Listening carefully and quietly
> Making perceptive observations
> Contributing their own experiences
> Bringing the group back to the topic being discussed
> Asking someone to clarify a point
> Summarizing
> Asking questions

This material is used to stimulate a discussion about how there are many ways of contributing to a class and that students will differ in their contributions. About a week later, pass out slips of paper with the name of a student on each slip. Each student in the class receives one slip and is asked to write one positive comment about a contribution the student listed on the slip has made to the class. The slips are handed in, and students volunteer to read several of them.

Two additional and complementary methods can be used with secondary classes to enhance group cohesiveness. We can involve students in cooperative-learning activities. Cooperative learning is described by Johnson, Johnson, and Johnson-Holubec (1987) in *Learning Together and Alone* and *Circles of Learning*. Cooperative learning involves students working together to attain a goal. This activity may include group projects in which all students obtain the same grade for work completed, cooperative studying for an exam, cooperatively obtaining material to be used individually, or generating creative ideas.

Because they have limited time with their students, most secondary teachers emphasize cooperative learning or other academic learning activities as the basis for creating positive peer relationships that enhance students' motivation and achievement. It is important to keep in mind, though, that these activities will be more successful when students have first been taught basic group skills. Students enjoy activities aimed at teaching these skills, and you will find numerous materials available for developing these skills.

We have found several activities and processes particularly valuable in helping secondary students develop skills in functioning as supportive, effective group members. The process includes involving students in an activity that requires cooperation to reach a goal, followed by systematically discussing the behaviors that facilitated the group activity. The game five squares (Figure 4.2) is perhaps the best activity for stimulating this student learning. As described in Figure 4.2, students are placed in groups of five, and each group is given the task of passing puzzle pieces until each group member has an equal-sized square in front of him or her. Tell students that groups who complete their task can quietly observe groups still at work. Finally, if one or more groups has difficulty completing the task, members of these groups can raise a hand, signaling that they would like to be replaced by a student from a group that has completed the task. This student then joins the group still working and continues to follow the rules. The addition of a new member who has seen the correct pattern will usually facilitate quick task completion.

FIGURE 4.2 The Five-Squares Game

Preparation of Puzzle

A puzzle set consists of five envelopes containing pieces of stiff paper cut into patterns that will form six-inch squares, as shown in the diagram. Cut the squares into parts and lightly pencil the letters *a* through *j* as shown below. Then mark the envelopes *A* through *E* and distribute the pieces thus:

Envelope A – j, h, e
B – a, a, a, c
C – a, j
D – d, f
E – g, b, f, c

  Erase from the pieces the lowercase letters and write instead the envelope letters *A* through *E*, so that the pieces can easily be returned for reuse.

  Several combinations of the pieces will form one or two squares, but only one combination will form five squares.

Instructions for Students

Each person should have an envelope containing pieces for forming squares. At the signal, the task of the group is to form five squares of equal size. The task is not complete until everyone has before him or her a perfect square and all the squares are of the same size. These are the rules: (1) No member may speak, (2) No member may signal in any way that he or she wants a card, (3) Members may give cards to others.

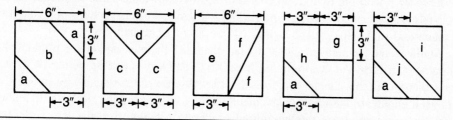

When all groups have completed the task, you can involve students in discussing the groups' functioning. On a chalkboard or butcher paper, make columns labeled "Behaviors that facilitated task completion" and "Behaviors that hindered the group." Then ask students, without mentioning names, to describe behaviors that helped their group complete their task. Next, students can list behaviors that blocked their group. Then lead a discussion on group behavior. Interestingly, this activity may also highlight additional factors related to establishing effective learning environments. For example, when using the activity recently, a student in one of our classes indicated that he had experienced considerable anxiety when other students began watching his group. This comment led to a productive discussion on the advantages and disadvantages of anxiety in learning and a further discussion on how anxiety could be limited in the class.

Even though this activity requires most of a class period, we and dozens of secondary teachers with whom we have worked find that the benefits in terms of students' understanding how groups operate and appreciating the value of involving everyone in group activities far outweigh the time cost.

Group skill-building activities have the advantage of serving several functions. While teaching students the behaviors associated with effective group work, they help students become better acquainted and can increase the feeling of group cohesiveness. Additional group skill-building activities can be found in the books listed in the Recommended Reading at the end of this chapter.

We can also enhance group cohesiveness by involving students in shared decision making about classroom organizational factors or problems. As discussed in chapter 9, students can cooperatively develop classroom rules and procedures. Also work with students to resolve problems that arise. We recently spoke with a friend who reported working with his junior English class to resolve the problem of student papers being late. The teacher reported that more than half his class worked part time and several teachers were requiring that major projects be due on the same day. The teacher and his students collected data on due dates for each student's assignments and developed a series of due dates that was approved by all students in the class.

ACTIVITIES FOR ENHANCING DIVERSE LIKING PATTERNS

You have undoubtedly been involved in groups in which everyone was comfortable with and enjoyed every group member. Whether it was an extended family, school staff, religious group, or group of close friends, you probably looked forward to being with this group and found that the group supported personal and intellectual growth. Compare this experience with working in a group characterized by cliquishness and numerous isolated individuals. Anyone who has been unfortunate enough to work in such a group knows that it is much less supportive of creativity, risk taking, and productivity.

Students are similar to adults in that they are happier and more productive in environments that provide warmth and friendship. The Lewis and St. John (1974) study discussed earlier in this chapter indicates that the presence of high-achieving students was not in itself enough to increase achievement among lower-achieving students. In addition to being exposed to norms that supported academic achievement, the lower-achieving students needed to be accepted as friends by their classmates. When students feel liked by their peers they experience a sense of significance, belonging, safety, and respect of others. Unless these basic personal needs are met, students will have less energy to expend in learning.

The activities described in this section increase the likelihood that all children in the classroom will be liked and accepted by their peers. Though it is important to use several of these activities early in the school year, we should reinforce positive peer interactions by using activities such as these at least two or three times a month throughout the school year.

As with the activities connected with group cohesiveness, elementary and middle school teachers will be most likely to use the specific activities described in this section. Because teachers in grades K–8 work with groups of students longer, it is appropriate that they spend more time involving students in activities encouraging positive peer relationships and improved self-esteem. Secondary teachers will find that by incorporating the methods described in the previous section, student friendships will become more widespread and cliquishness will be reduced. These results are more likely to occur if elementary and middle school teachers have used activities such as those found on the following pages.

Friendship Bulletin Board

''The only way to have a friend is to be one,'' can be the theme of a bulletin board in the hall. This bulletin board can take many forms. One method is to have students draw pictures of friends doing things together and to share with the class what they are doing. A second approach is to make a collage of friends and write words around the collage about the qualities a friend has. Another method is either to have students draw self-portraits or to pair students and have each person draw or make a silhouette of his or her partner.

Students can then put feelings that describe themselves or their partner into words in the heart of the silhouette. Thoughts and ideas the students have can be put in the brain. By the hands and feet of the silhouette, students can draw in things that they can do well. These can be mounted and each person can write a paragraph about why the partner is a friend.

This activity introduces the concept that children in the class can be friends. It also encourages children to begin to consider positive characteristics of their classmates. These concepts provide a basis for establishing a safe, positive environment characterized by diverse liking patterns.

Good Deeds Tree

To build on the theme of helping others, a large paper tree or branch is placed on the bulletin board. Students are asked to pay special attention to the nice things people say and do. Whenever they see something nice being done, students write down what happened on a leaf made of green paper and pin it to the tree. The result is a tree full of leaves and a room filled with happy children.

Variations of this activity can be created by using pumpkins in a pumpkin patch at Halloween or shamrocks in a field near St. Patrick's Day. When working with children who cannot write their responses, we can set aside several times a day to ask children to list nice things they have seen or heard. We can write these on the appropriate paper and allow the children to pin them on the bulletin board.

Wanted Posters

Another activity that helps create an environment of warmth and friendship is construction of wanted posters. Students are given a piece of parchment paper. They burn the edge of the paper to make it look like a poster from the old West and print the word "WANTED" on the paper. Next the student mounts a picture of himself or herself in the center and writes the phrase, "For a friend because . . ." underneath the picture. Around the picture each student writes words describing the qualities that make them a good friend. A piece of tagboard or brown construction paper can be used as a backing or support. A discussion about friendship and an opportunity to share the posters should follow this activity.

Warm Fuzzies

People enjoy receiving compliments. Everyone likes to receive positive attention and recognition in the form of a warm smile, physical touch, or kind word. Unfortunately, children often receive more criticism and frowns than compliments and smiles. In response to this situation Claude Steiner (1977) wrote a children's book entitled *The Warm Fuzzy Tale*. This delightful story can be read to students of all ages. After reading the story you can lead a discussion that helps students clearly understand the concepts of warm fuzzies and cold pricklies and how they make people feel. Following this discussion, students will often initiate the idea of giving warm fuzzies to each other.

One approach to helping children learn to be more positive with their classmates is actually to make warm fuzzies. Warm fuzzies can be made by wrapping yarn around one's fingers several times. The wrapped yarn is then tied in the middle and the ends are cut off. The ends are then fluffed up and a warm fuzzy has been created. After students have made a warm fuzzy they are asked to think of a reason they deserve a warm fuzzy. Students are encouraged to share their reasons. Each student then keeps his or her first fuzzy. The class should continue making fuzzies until each child has between five and ten fuzzies. To conclude this activity students can be asked to give a fuzzy to a friend. When giving a fuzzy students are asked to tell the reason it is being given. Even though the teacher may choose to set time aside daily to hand out fuzzies, students should also be encouraged to give a fuzzy whenever they wish.

Another way to give warm fuzzies is to have a Fuzzy Box where students place positive notes about their peers (students often choose to attach a warm fuzzy to their note). These notes can be read aloud during the last few minutes of the day. Students enjoy receiving compliments in front of their peers.

Friendship Kites

This activity is an opportunity for students to share some positive thoughts about other students. Spring is usually kite season, and so students make personal paper kites. To implement this activity, students will need four sheets of construction paper: one 12-by-18-inch white sheet for the kite and three 9-by-12-inch sheets of any other color. The three colored sheets can be used to make paper flowers or other designs. Students will also need crepe paper streamers cut and twisted and stapled to the kite. To complete the project they will need string, glue, scissors, a ruler, a pencil, and felt pens or crayons.

Once the kites have been constructed they are passed around the room and each student writes a positive statement about the designer on each kite. The kites can then be displayed for several days. In addition to reinforcing a diverse liking pattern, this activity helps increase students' feelings of worth and self-esteem.

Valentine Booklets

Another activity that encourages sharing positive feelings is creating Valentine booklets. Give each child a Valentine's Day booklet cut in the shape of a heart. The front and rear covers are red hearts, and the inside pages are white hearts. There should be as many white heart pages as there are members in the class (including the teacher). A booklet is created by punching each heart and attaching the pages with string.

Students sit in a circle with their Valentine booklets on their laps. Ask the children to "pass to the right." Students then write a nice phrase about the person whose booklet they receive. When you or the timekeeper see that each child has finished writing, speak the phrase, "pass to the right" again. This activity continues until each individual has his or her own booklet. It takes about one hour to complete, but the results are worth the time spent. Students enjoy this activity and are often seen reading through their booklets when they need a lift.

This activity can be used in association with a variety of special days. Shamrock books can be used on St. Patrick's Day, and the words "I am lucky to know Scott because . . ." written on the outside. Similarly, booklets can be developed around the theme of being thankful at Thanksgiving, and special qualities each student possesses that will help him or her succeed can be used as a theme on a holiday celebrating the birthday of a famous person.

Secret-Pal Books

Positive communication is vital in a classroom. The secret-pal book activity is a strategy for increasing positive communication. Every Monday each child draws the name of another student. During the week, the students observe the nice things that they see their secret pal doing and write these in their secret-pal book. These books can be made of colored construction paper cover and plain newsprint pages. Students can be encouraged to decorate the books by drawing pictures, writing positive adjectives that describe their secret pal, or writing a word that begins with each letter of the child's name; e.g., Brian—B = brave, R = responsible, I = interesting, A = athletic, N = neat. On Friday, students reveal their secret pals and present them with their books. Students enjoy this activity very much and always look forward to finding out who will be their new secret pal.

A daily variation in the week-long secret-pal books involves having children write their own names on a "secret-pal smiley face." These faces are placed in a basket and each child draws one, making sure that it is not his or her own name. Throughout the day, each child watches his or her secret pal and writes down two or three friendly or helpful things he or she observes the secret pal doing. At the end of the day the secret pal are revealed and the smiley faces may be taken home.

Discovering Me

This activity gives students an opportunity to interact positively with each other and enhances their self-esteem. Each student draws a class member's name from a hat. Beneath the drawn name the student writes a positive adjective to describe the class member. When everyone has finished writing an adjective the papers are pinned to students' backs. Each student may ask another student three questions that can be answered only with yes or no. Each child continues asking questions until he or she has guessed the adjective pinned to his or her back, at which time they sit down. Students enjoy this type of peer involvement.

"I" Booklet

Each child cuts eight capital *I* letters out of colored construction paper. The student uses the first *I* to decorate a cover using his or her name in colored cutout pieces of construction paper. On the first page of the book the child focuses on his or her name by writing it in as many unusual ways as possible. On the second page of the "I" booklet the student illustrates such favorite things as food, toys, colors, friends, television shows, and so on. On the third page the students draw pictures of things they like to experience with each of their five senses. On page 4, ask students to think about the seasons and what they enjoy doing on the weekends during the various seasons. They can either cut out pictures or draw favorite activities for each season. The next page is devoted to pictures of family, their house, a special friend, pets, and something special their family enjoys doing, such as camping. On the sixth page of the book the *I* is divided into black and white, representing night and day. Students draw several things they do during the day and several things they do in the evening. Page 7 focuses on facts about the student, such as age, height, address, brothers and sisters, or pets. On the last page students write a poem about themselves, list positive words that describe them, or write a story about themselves. When all the *I* pages are completed they can be assembled to form an "I" booklet. These booklets should be shared with other classmates. Unlimited topics can be chosen to form an "I" booklet, and topics should be adjusted according to the grade level. For primary students we could have a laminated person in blue jeans but without hair or eye color. Each week a student's name is drawn and the child colors in his or her eyes and hair on the laminated figure. The chosen child adds patches to the blue jeans with titles such as height, weight, favorite color, favorite food, phone number, address, or friends, and fills in the patch with the designated information.

Positive Bombardment

Positive self-concepts are sustained and strengthened in an atmosphere of trust and security. When this type of environment has been established, a positive bombardment can be effectively used. This activity can be implemented in a variety of ways. One technique is to have a child seated on a stool in a circle. The students take turns sharing reasons they like or respect the person being bombarded.

Once students have become familiar with this activity and have learned how to give specific positive feedback, the positive bombardments can take place in small groups. Students can now assume greater responsibility for the activity, and more children can become involved in a shorter time.

Another alternative is to choose a theme such as "I felt really happy when you . . ." or "You really are a friend because . . ." and have students complete this phrase as they talk to the person being bombarded. Positive bombardments can also be used as an ending to class discussions or class meetings. For example, children can be asked to make one nice statement to the person seated on either side of them.

Good Citizen Award

One special award that helps students focus on the nice things that are done for others is the Good Citizen Award. Students are asked to pay attention to the sensitive and thoughtful responses their peers make to each other. At the end of the day students share their observations and the class decides who should receive the honor of Good Citizen for the day. The chosen citizen receives a special certificate, and the child's name is added to the Good Citizens' list. This is a simple way to build strong positive feelings within a classroom.

Student Directory

Almost all students have special interests and abilities about which they feel confident. When students feel comfortable in the classroom, they will often be excited about sharing their expertise with their peers. The creation of a student directory is an activity designed to help students identify their strengths and encourage them to use each other as resources.

Students are asked to identify the activities or skills they believe they perform effectively enough to teach another child. These topics should not be limited to school subjects. They may include skills such as basketball dribbling, downhill skiing, working with dogs, model rocketry, borrowing in subtraction, organizing desks, writing a report, or calligraphy. These lists are collected, tabulated, and placed in alphabetical order with the name(s) of the student(s) listed after each skill. The student directory is typed and mimeographed, and each student receives a copy. A directory is also placed in the front of the room for use by the students. The directory can be a valuable tool for a child who needs assistance with a topic. Students will often use this directory as a way to improve their skills by asking an expert to help them.

The "I Can" Can

This activity provides students with a visible means of becoming aware of their successes and achievements. We give each child a soup or coffee can and ask them to decorate the cans in some way that represents themselves, such as favorite color, activities, or hobbies. Next, students write the words *I CAN* on their can. Each time a student masters a new skill, he or she writes the mastered skill on a piece of paper, rolls it up like a scroll, ties it with ribbon, and places it in the can. Periodically the students should take their cans home and share their successes with their parents.

Social-Skill Training Programs

Another increasingly popular approach to creating positive peer relationships and integrating isolated or aggressive children into their peer group involves implementing social skills and problem-solving training activities with the entire class (Akita & Mooney, 1982; Cartledge & Milburn, 1978; Jackson, Jackson, & Monroe, 1983; LeCroy, 1983; Goldstein, Sprafkin, Gershaw, & Klein, 1980; McGinnis & Goldstein, 1984; Waksman, Mesmere, & Waksman, 1988; Walker et al., 1983). In its simplest form, social-skill training can be accomplished by instructing students in many of the skills described in chapters 3, 4, and 10 of this book. For example, we could instruct children in sending ''I'' messages and warm fuzzies. Students could practice these skills as a group and be encouraged to use them frequently in their daily classroom interactions. Similarly, we can teach students active listening (chapter 3) and problem-solving skills (chapter 10).

Social-skill training can also be implemented with one of several curricular programs now available. Recently we heard about an inner-city middle school that needed to reduce suspensions of minority students. Investigating the cause of suspensions, the administration discovered that most were in response to students' fights. Further investigation suggested that most fights began with students becoming involved in verbal putdowns. The staff decided to approach this problem by teaching all students in the school some basic communication and problem-solving skills. Each home room was scheduled for one full day of training in a program developed by the school district. Teachers joined their students and also received special training so that they could encourage students to use the new skills.

Followup after six months and one year showed a nearly 50 percent reduction in suspensions for fighting.

Rose (1983) states several advantages to using social-skill training in the classroom or other school-group setting. First, youngsters generally find a group setting more attractive than individual work. Second, a group makes better use of the teacher's or counselor's time. Third, the group provides diverse models and an opportunity for students to receive feedback from peers. Fourth, the group provides an opportunity for students to teach each other, thus facilitating development of their own social competence.

We have worked with numerous schools whose faculties have chosen to implement social-skill training in their curriculum. Most frequently, these have been middle schools and junior high schools whose faculties were interested in reducing the anxiety and conflicts that occur when students from several small neighborhood schools are combined into a larger school.

SCHOOL CLIMATE

Improving the classroom climate by systematically monitoring and improving the quality of teacher-student and peer relationships will do much to create positive student behavior and increased achievement. Students' and teachers' attitudes and behavior are also affected, however, by the quality of life in the school at large. An increasing body of research points to the importance of school climate (Anderson, 1982).

The importance of classroom and school climate was emphasized by John Goodlad in his *Study of Schooling*. He and his colleagues studied 38 schools in 7 regions across the country. The study involved interviews with all 38 principals, 1,350 teachers, 8,624 parents, and 17,163 students, as well as intensive observations in 1,016 classrooms (Goodlad, 1984). Analyzing the results of this study, Goodlad reports that schools differed very little in the type of instruction found within classes. He reports, though, that differences in student achievement were found. Goodlad (1983b) summarizes these findings.

> I have used the adjectives, "healthy," "satisfying," and "renewing" to describe schools in our sample that pay more than average attention to the quality of interactions among those inhabiting the school and to the physical and social context in which those interactions occur. . . . Schools differed in their ability to create an academic ambience, but the differences appear to be more related to school and classroom climate factors than to methods of teaching per se. (p. 555)

More specifically, Wayson and Pinnell (1982) cite a variety of studies to support their contention that "eight features of schools have a strong relationship to the quality of discipline" (p. 118).

1. Patterns of communication, problem solving, and decision making.
2. Patterns of authority and status.
3. Procedures for developing and implementing rules.
4. Student belongingness.
5. Relationships with parents and community forces.

6. Processes for dealing with personal problems.
7. Curriculum and instructional practices.
8. The physical environment. (p. 118)

In their study of 12 London high schools, reported in *Fifteen Thousand Hours*, Rutter and his colleagues (1979) reported that a variety of schoolwide factors differentiated schools with positive student behavior and high achievement from schools facing serious problems in these areas. Factors within the school's control that significantly influenced students' behavior and performance included the degree to which teachers emphasized academic achievement; teachers' organizational, instructional, and classroom-management skills; high teacher expectations about students' performance; teachers' willingness to see students about problems at any time; an emphasis on rewards rather than punishments; teachers' involvement in decision making and the associated consistency in teachers' expectations and behavior; and students' involvement in positions of responsibility within the school. Rutter and his associates concluded that

> the pattern of findings suggested that not only were pupils influenced by the way they were dealt with as individuals, but also there was a group influence resulting from the ethos of the school as a social institution. (p. 205)

The factors described by Wayson, Pinnell, and Rutter and his colleagues have also been reported in two books whose authors conducted ecological analyses of effective secondary schools. Joan Lipsitz's (1984) analysis of four high-quality middle schools reported in *Successful Schools for Young Adolescents* and Sarah Lawrence Lightfoot's (1983) study of six high schools, *The Good High School,* offer thoughtful portraits of secondary schools that are serving youths well.

Educators interested in assessing their school's climate can turn to an ever-larger number of instruments and procedures (Bebermeyer, 1982; Dorman, 1981; Howard, 1981; Kelley, 1980, 1981; Lindelow & Mazzarella, 1981; Squires, 1983; Wood & Johnson, 1982). We have used Dorman's (1981) *Middle Grades Assessment Program* with several schools and found it to be extremely helpful in assisting middle-school staff in determining directions for improving the quality of their school's climate.

The important point is that teachers should work together to consider not only how their classroom management and instruction influence students' behavior and achievement, but also how the school environment can be altered to encourage positive student attitudes. This can prove to be an exciting, cooperative project that effectively and creatively uses teachers' creativity and concern for students. We have taught in and worked with schools in which a committee consisting of students and teachers was established to generate ideas for improving school climate. Figure 4.3 offers some examples of positive school-climate activities instigated by these committees.

ACTIVITIES FOR EXAMINING PEER RELATIONSHIPS IN THE CLASSROOM

There are two basic methods of determining the degree to which children in the class are accepted by and feel involved in the classroom group. One method is the sociometric test

FIGURE 4.3 Activities for Creating a Positive School Climate

1. Take pictures of students (including those with a history of school problems) involved in positive behavior. Enlarge these and post them in the hallway.
2. Hold assemblies at least each quarter to reinforce positive student accomplishments. Emphasize improvement as well as standard excellent achievement.
3. Involve students in beautifying the school. Plant flowers around the outside of the school.
4. Provide a space in the hallway where teachers can post positive comments about students and students can write positive statements about their teachers.
5. Create an award (a stuffed turtle or giraffe works nicely) to be presented each week to the staff member who "stuck their neck out" to help students. The award can initially be given by the school climate committee with subsequent selection made by the previous recipient.
6. Involve students and staff in a fund-raising activity, such as a jog-a-thon, with proceeds going to a local charity or other worthy cause.
7. Rather than have an attendance officer call absent students, have an adult with whom the student relates well call.
8. Involve the entire school in a day-long evaluation of the school, with ideas generated to resolve problems and make the school even better.
9. Set aside some time each day or week when everyone in the school stops what they are doing and reads quietly.
10. At the end of each day, have everyone in the school write on a three-by-five-inch card one positive experience they had that day.
11. Release teachers to spend a day experiencing the same schedule as a student who is having an unsuccessful school experience. Have the teachers report to the faculty what they saw, how they felt, and any suggestions they have for making the school a better place for their student to learn.
12. Encourage the school staff to write notes to their colleagues whenever they observe a colleague involved in an especially helpful or thoughtful interaction with a student or staff member.

for determining which students are most frequently chosen by other students as desired work or play partners. To collect these data, students can be asked to list (younger children may tell you their choices) the two students in the classroom with whom they would like to eat lunch, work on a school project, or do some other activity.

In *Group Processes in the Classroom*, Schmuck and Schmuck (1983) provide more methods for collecting this type of sociometric data. A sociogram can also be developed by actually observing a class for a time and recording every instance in which a child has a positive or negative interaction with another child. This method has the advantage of providing an indication of the actual interaction patterns in a classroom.

The second method for determining students' feelings about their position in the classroom group as well as their general feelings about the group is to develop a questionnaire that allows them to report their feelings about the group. The advantage of this approach is that it can provide more detailed information than is available through a sociometric test or observation. The main problem with this approach is that students must experience fairly high trust before they will accurately report the information. Even during the initial stages of group development, however, this approach will often reveal useful information. Figure 4.4 is an example of a questionnaire that can be used at several grade levels.

Once we have discovered the dynamics in the classroom, the next step is to implement activities that create more positive peer relationships and group norms. There are several methods for developing positive peer relationships in the classroom. We can begin the school year by helping students become better acquainted with their peers. This endeavor can be accompanied by activities that create a class spirit and positive group identity. Throughout the year we can support these activities by involving students in other activities aimed at building friendships. We can also enhance positive peer relationships by implementing instructional strategies, such as peer tutoring and group projects, which reinforce the value of supportive, cooperative learning. Finally, we can use problem-solving approaches focused on helping peers resolve their own conflicts.

ASSESSING THE EFFECT OF IMPLEMENTING ACTIVITIES FOR IMPROVING PEER RELATIONSHIPS IN THE CLASSROOM

Whenever a teacher implements a new academic or behavior-change program, it is important periodically to assess its effectiveness. Educators too often use new ideas because they appear interesting or educational and fail to determine whether the new program meets its stated goals. The following activity will help you assess the outcomes of implementing the procedures described throughout this chapter.

ACTIVITY 4.1 Assessing the Effect of Implementing New Peer-Relationship Activities

Select and implement at least three activities from each of the three approaches to improving peer relationships. These activities can be selected from those described in this chapter or from the resources listed at the end of the chapter. Secondary teachers will want to select several acquaintance activities and to involve students in several cooperative activities.

Both prior to and after implementing these activities, administer Figure 4.4, a similar figure, or use a sociogram. Compare the results obtained earlier with the new data. Summarize this comparison by completing these statements:

The number of students who were not selected by any of their peers changed from ____ to ____.
I was surprised to find that . . .
I was happy that . . .
More students stated that they . . .
Fewer students stated that they . . .
My thoughts about improving peer relationships in the classroom are that . . .

FIGURE 4.4 Group Assessment Questionnaire

Please answer these questions as carefully as you can.

1. Do you like being in this class? ____ ____
                                      Yes   No
   Why? _____

2. Would you say that you are a leader or a follower in this class?
   (Circle your answer in red)   Leader   Follower

3. Would you rather be the opposite of the answer that you gave in question 2?
   (Circle your answer in green)   Yes   No   Maybe

4. Do you listen to people in our class?
   (Circle your answer in yellow)   Usually   Sometimes   Seldom

5. Do other children listen to you when you are talking? ____ ____
                                                          Yes   No

6. Are you comfortable helping people in this class?

                                          ____   ____   _____
                                          Yes   No   Sometimes

7. Are you comfortable asking for help from class members?

                                          ____   ____   _____
                                          Yes   No   Sometimes

8. Name three things that you contribute to our group.
   a.
   b.
   c.   Help?!!

9. Name two things you would like to contribute to our group.
   a.
   b.

10. How do you feel about the students in your class?
                    ____   I like all the students
    (check in blue) ____   I like most of the students
                    ____   I like only a few students

11. Do the students like you?
                      ____   Most of the students like me.
    (check in orange) ____   Some of the students like me.
                      ____   I don't think the students like me very much.

12. Do you have friends to sit with at lunch? ____ ____
                                               Yes   No

13. When you are at recess, do members of this class let you play with them?

                                     ____ ____ _____
                                     Yes   No Sometimes

14. If you could change one thing about the people in this class, what would you change?_____
_____

Thank you for filling out this questionnaire for me.

SUMMARY

Prior to the recent focus on cooperative learning, the quality of peer relationships was perhaps the most underestimated factor influencing student behavior and achievement. The emphasis on achievement test scores and the associated concern with covering content led even teachers who valued and were comfortable with their role in creating positive peer relationships to view time spent on building positive, supportive peer relationships as a luxury they could not afford. Many lessons learned in school programs for at-risk children and youth during the late 1960s and 1970s were apparently forgotten with the focus on on-task behavior, direct instruction, and achievement test scores.

Fortunately, recent research on cooperative learning has again provided impetus for teachers to consider the creation of positive peer relationships as an important variable influencing student behavior and learning. We hope that during the 1990s teachers are increasingly provided with information about the importance of selecting a range of methods for creating classroom environments supportive of high student achievement. The recent concern about at-risk students should help ensure that a greater emphasis is placed on meeting students' personal needs both as a critically important goal in itself and as a prerequisite to higher achievement.

RECOMMENDED READING

Beane, J., & Lipka, R. (1984). *Self-concept, self-esteem and the curriculum.* Boston: Allyn and Bacon.

Berger, T. (1971). *I have feelings.* New York: Behavioral Publications.

Berger, T. (1971). *Reach, touch and teach.* New York: McGraw-Hill.

Borba, M., & Borba, C. (1982). *Self-esteem: A classroom affair.* Vol. 2. Minneapolis: Winston Press.

Borda, M., & Borda, C. (1978). *Self-esteem: A classroom affair. 101 ways to help children like themselves.* Minneapolis: Winston Press.

Brown, G. (1971). *Human teaching for human learning: An introduction to confluent education*. New York: Viking Press.

Burns, M. (1976). *The book of think*. Boston: Little, Brown.

Canfield, J., & Wells, H. (1976). *100 ways to enhance self-concept in the classroom*. Englewood Cliffs, N.J.: Prentice-Hall.

Castillo, G. (1974). *Left-handed teaching: Lessons in affective education*. New York: Praeger.

Chase, L. (1975). *The other side of the report card*. Pacific Palisades, Calif.: Goodyear.

Covington, M., & Beery, R. (1976). *Self-worth and school learning*. New York: Holt, Rinehart and Winston.

Daniel, B., & Daniel, C. (1978). *Warm smiles, happy faces*. Carthage, Ill.: Good Apple.

Dinkmeyer, D. (1973). *Developing an understanding of self and others (DUSO)*. Circle Pines, Minn.: American Guidance Service.

Eberle, B., & Hall, R. (1975). *Affective education guidebook: Classroom activities in the realm of feelings*. Buffalo, N.Y.: DOK.

Farnette, C., Forte, I., & Loss, B. (1977). *I've got me and I'm glad: A self-awareness activity book*. Nashville, Tenn.: Incentive.

Freed, A. (1973). *T. A. for tots*. Sacramento, Calif.: Jalmar.

Goldstein, A. (1980). *Skillstreaming the adolescent: A structured learning approach to teaching prosocial skills*. Champaign, Ill.: Research.

Jensen, J., & Cooley, S. (1982). *The elementary guidance connection*. Springfield, Ill.: Charles C Thomas.

Johnson, D. (1986). *Reaching out: Interpersonal effectiveness and self-actualization*, 3rd ed. Englewood Cliffs, N.J.: Prentice-Hall.

Johnson, D., & Johnson, F. (1987). *Joining together: Group theory and skills*, 3rd ed. Englewood Cliffs, N.J.: Prentice-Hall.

LaBenne, W., & Greene, B. (1969). *Educational implications of self-concept theory*. Pacific Palisades, Calif.: Goodyear.

Lalli, J. (1984). *Feelings alphabet: An album of emotions from A to Z*. Rolling Hills Estates, Calif.: B. L. Winch.

McElmurry, M. (1983). *Belonging*. Carthage, Ill.: Good Apple.

McElmurry, M. (1981). *Caring*. Carthage, Ill.: Good Apple.

McElmurry, M. (1981). *Feelings*. Carthage, Ill.: Good Apple.

Nickerson, C., Lollis, C., & Porter, E. (1980). *Miraculous me*. Seattle: Comprehensive Health Education Foundation.

Pincus, D. (1983). *Sharing*. Carthage, Ill.: Good Apple.

Plum, L. (1980). *Flights of fantasy*. Carthage, Ill.: Good Apple.

Polland, B. (1975). *Feelings, inside you and outloud too*. Millbrae, Calif.: Celestial Arts.

Purkey, W. (1970). *Self-concept and school achievement*. Englewood Cliffs, N.J.: Prentice-Hall.

Purkey, W., & Novak, J. (1984). *Inviting school success: A self-concept approach to teaching and learning*, 2nd ed. Belmont, Calif.: Wadsworth.

Rainbow activities: Fifty multi-cultural human relations experiences. (1977). South El Monte, Calif.: Creative Teaching Press.

Richards, J., & Standley, M. (1982). *Dealing with feelings*. Santa Barbara, Calif.: Learning Works.

Schwartz, L. (1976). *The month to month me*. Santa Barbara, Calif.: Learning Works.

Simon, S. B., Howe, L. W., & Kirschenbaum, H. (1972). *Values clarification: A handbook of practical strategies*. New York: Hart.

Stanford, G., & Roark, A. (1974). *Human interaction in education*. Boston: Allyn and Bacon.

Stanish, B. (1982). *Connecting rainbows*. Carthage, Ill.: Good Apple.

Stanish, B. (1977). *Sunflowering, thinking, feeling, doing activities for creative expression*. Carthage, Ill.: Good Apple.

Stevens, J. P. (1973). *Awareness:* New York: Bantam Books.

Stevens, J. P. (1971). *Awareness: Exploring, experimenting, experiencing*. Moab, Utah: Real People Press.

Thayer, L. (Ed.) (1976). *Affective education: Strategies for experiential learning*. La Jolla, Calif.: University Associates.

Vacha, E. (1979). *Improving the classroom social climate*. New York: Holt, Rinehart and Winston.

Waksman, S., & Messmer, C. (1979). *Social skills training: A manual for teaching assertive behaviors to children and adolescents*. Portland, Ore.: Enrichment Press

CHAPTER 5

Working with Parents

Research has shown that parents and family are critical factors in children's education, particularly for those who are at risk of dropping out of school. Numerous studies demonstrate that the influence and support given by the family may directly affect the behavior of children in school, their grades, and the probability that they will finish high school.

/ Paul Haley and Karen Berry (1988)
Home and School as Partners

What are optimal conditions for a parent-teacher conference? A quiet corner, protection from interruptions and a teacher who listens. The words exchanged during the conference may be forgotten, but the mood of the meeting will linger on. It will decide the subsequent attitudes and actions of the parents.

/ Haim Ginott (1972)
Teacher and Child

Parents are the most important and influential adults in students' lives. Even at the secondary school level, parents' attitudes toward school dramatically affect students' feelings and behavior. With few exceptions, parents want to know about their children's progress and to have their youngsters be successful in school. Parents are delighted to hear that their youngsters are performing well and expect to be informed immediately when problems arise. Effective teachers accept the important role parents play in students' lives and implement methods for communicating positively with parents.

Although a teacher's primary role is to work with students, for several reasons, teachers find that an important and rewarding role includes their work with parents. First, children's attitudes about school are influenced by their parents (Coleman, 1966; Simpson, 1962). When parents feel good about their child's teacher and school, the youngster is more likely to receive encouragement and reinforcement for desirable school behavior. Second, because parents are, most often, legally responsible for their children, they should be kept informed about their children's behavior and academic performance. Third, parents can be valuable resources for teachers. They can volunteer time to tutor students, assist teachers by typing or mimeographing materials, or share their expertise on special topics with students. Finally, in a limited number of instances the rewards and punishments available in school are not powerful enough to elicit desirable behavior from a youngster. When this occurs, school personnel need to involve parents in developing a behavior-change program for the student.

Even though teachers can derive numerous benefits from interacting with parents, many teachers indicate that parent contacts are a difficult and relatively undesirable aspect of teaching. Teachers' discomfort in working with parents is based on several factors. First, parent contacts are often time consuming and energy draining. When teachers have worked with students for 7 hours and had approximately one thousand interchanges (Jackson, 1968), it is understandably difficult to be enthusiastic about additional school-related interactions. Similarly, by the end of the day teachers are usually tired and face several hours of grading and planning. Time spent contacting parents means that a larger amount of this work must be completed at home in the evening. Teachers also find parent contacts difficult because local funding of education makes parents aware that they pay for their children's education and they therefore believe they should be able to monitor teachers' performance. This situation is intensified because the teaching profession has never been viewed with the awe or respect bestowed on such professions as medicine or the law. Perhaps because all parents have been students, they believe themselves knowledgeable about what their youngster needs in order to function effectively in school. These factors cause many teachers to be somewhat intimidated by parents and therefore to minimize their parent contacts.

These factors increase the likelihood that contacts with parents will be seen as a necessary task rather than an enjoyable sidelight. Teachers can, however, develop attitudes and skills that will make parent contacts much more enjoyable and productive. This chapter provides methods for making positive contacts with parents throughout the school year, implementing effective parent conferences, and handling parent confrontations. In chapter 11 we present methods for involving parents in helping us deal with students' consistent or extremely disruptive behavior.

As with most classroom-management methods, each of us must decide how much time and effort we wish to invest in working with parents. Elementary school teachers are expected to maintain frequent contact with parents, and children at this age generally respond well to parents' encouragement. At the middle school and junior high school level, most teachers will, because they work with between 80 and 150 students, choose to implement only a few of the ideas presented in this chapter.

However, the authors and most secondary teachers with whom we have worked have found that the benefits of teacher-parent communication can be obtained with minimal contact and by using methods that are pleasant and not very time consuming. As students move into the upper middle school and high school grades, they can and should become more responsible for their own behavior, and parent contacts can become primarily informational in nature. Nevertheless, most students enjoy having parents informed of their activities and successes, and parents of students at every grade level should be informed when students are experiencing serious or persistent problems.

KEEPING PARENTS INFORMED

Importance of Early Contacts

Obtaining parental support is facilitated by familiarizing parents with our instructional goals and classroom methods as soon as possible. Parents are no different from children or teachers. They are more likely to feel positive about and support issues they clearly understand and have had an opportunity to discuss. Parents who perceive themselves as being treated warmly and respectfully by us and who are familiar with our instructional goals and classroom-management procedures are much more likely to encourage student achievement and support us if problems arise.

By introducing parents to the curriculum and major classroom procedures early in the year, we are also able to work with the parents before any worries about their child's achievement or behavior make contacts less positive. A major reason for teachers' concerns about parental contacts is that, except for parent-teacher conferences, most teacher-parent contacts focus on negative student behavior. When our initial interaction with the parents is positive, we are more likely to feel comfortable contacting the parents as soon as their involvement appears necessary. Relationships based on infrequent interactions are seldom as warm and comfortable as those in which contacts are more frequent. Therefore, if we wish to feel comfortable in our contacts with parents, we must instigate relatively frequent, positive contacts with them. Contacts with parents are an excellent example of the idea that an ounce of prevention is worth a pound of cure. In this section we offer several suggestions for initiating such contacts.

Methods for Obtaining Parental Support

There are many approaches to developing parental support for student achievement and positive classroom behaviors. The ideas presented here are among those that we and teachers with whom we have worked have found particularly useful. We encourage you to modify these methods creatively in order to develop an approach best suited to your situation.

An Introductory Letter

Perhaps the easiest approach for making the initial contact is to send a letter to each student's parent(s). Because the letter will include information that you will want to present personally to students, it is best to send the letter so that it arrives one or two days after school begins. In the letter you can introduce yourself, state your interest in developing positive teacher-parent contacts, and invite the parents to attend a back-to-school night or similar event in which you and they have an opportunity to meet and discuss the school year. Figure 5.1 is an example of an introductory letter.

The Initial Meeting

It is very important that we attempt to meet parents as soon as possible. The most expedient approach to meeting between 30 and 150 parents seems to be to provide an evening when parents are invited to visit their child's classroom(s) and discuss our approach to instruction and classroom management. It is helpful if the school supports this concept by arranging a formal back-to-school night. If this opportunity is not available, though, it is worth our effort to arrange such an event for ourselves and any colleagues who may be interested. Our experience also suggests that it is sometimes necessary to arrange an alternative meeting time for parents who are unable to attend an evening session. Information about the times that are most convenient for parents can be obtained by requesting this information in the initial letter sent to parents.

FIGURE 5.1 Introductory Letter to Parents

(Date)

Dear Parents,

With school under way, I'd like to take a moment of your time to welcome you to the fourth grade and to introduce myself. My name is Mrs. Louise Jones and I have taught in the Beaverton School District for 19 years in both open and self-contained classrooms. I completed my undergraduate work at Oregon State University and received my Masters Degree from Lewis and Clark College.

I am very interested in making this a successful and happy school year for you and your child. To ensure this success, we must keep the lines of communication open. I respect the fact that you know your child very well, and so when either you or your child feel worried, please contact me. Likewise, if there is an activity or project that you enjoy, please let me know. I am available at school until 4:00 P.M. each day. I will be contacting you throughout the year about projects, upcoming events, the nice things I see your child doing, and problems, if any arise.

In a few weeks our school will have its annual Back-to-School Night. At that time I will discuss in detail the academic program, my discipline procedures, grading, and my goals and expectations for the year. There will also be a display of books and materials that your child will be using during the year. I encourage you to attend this special evening, because it will give you an opportunity to understand the fourth-grade program and to become better acquainted with the room and materials that your child will be using throughout the coming year.

Sincerely,
Mrs. Louise Jones

Prior to the initial meeting with parents it is important for elementary teachers to make a telephone contact in which we report something positive about the child and obtain the parents' commitment to attend the parent orientation meeting. This telephone contact also breaks the ice and sets the stage for future telephone conversations.

First impressions are extremely important—especially when a relationship involves sporadic and somewhat role-bound interactions—and it is imperative that we do everything possible to create a positive initial meeting. In addition to the obvious factors of being well-groomed and personable, the teacher should be well organized and the classroom should look interesting and include a personal touch. Parents are very impressed by competence. We can start the meeting on a positive note by placing an outline of the evening's topics on the board. Figure 5.2 provides an example of an outline for a parent orientation meeting. This outline can be accompanied by a folder for each parent, including:

1. A description of the curriculum for the grade level,
2. An introductory letter about yourself that includes professional background and a philosophy of education,
3. A class schedule,
4. A handout describing the emotional and social characteristics of a child at the grade level,
5. A list of special projects that may require some parental assistance,
6. A statement of your classroom-management procedures,
7. Book ideas for book reports, and
8. A parent resource form eliciting information about what parents can offer to the class.

By providing parents with written information, we indicate that the information is important. A folder also creates ready-made notes and thus increases the likelihood that parents will learn and recall the information presented.

Another popular idea is to display the textbooks the students will be using throughout the year. This exhibit is most effective if we place a card beside each book indicating the subject, an overview of the topics covered in the book, and why the book is being used.

We can also facilitate a positive meeting by providing a personal touch. There are obviously as many ways to do so as there are creative teachers. One activity that is fun is to have each child make a silhouette of her or his head or a life-size outline of her or his body. The silhouette can be placed on the desk, and the outline seated in the child's chair. The parent(s) can then be asked to find their child's seat. Children can also write a note to their parent(s) to indicate several things they would like their parent(s) to see in the classroom.

During the parent orientation we can discuss our approach to classroom management. Parents can be provided with copies of the classroom rules, and we can discuss how both minor problems and consistent behavior problems will be handled. For example, we can outline the use of class meetings, describe the problem-solving approach that will be used, and discuss behavior contracts. We should also make a clear statement on when parents will be contacted about students' behavior.

Similarly, we should clearly outline the instructional methods that will be used to help the students. We can discuss the class schedule and indicate the types of instruction that

FIGURE 5.2 Outline for Parent Orientation Meeting

I. Introducing the Teacher
   A. College training and degrees earned.
   B. Professional experience:
      1. length of teaching experience,
      2. type of classroom—open vs. self-contained.
II. Social and Personal Expectations for Students during the Year
   A. Students will develop responsibility:
      1. for themselves,
      2. for their property,
      3. for their assignments.
   B. Students will learn to respect their peers' successes and weaknesses.
   C. Students will develop a feeling of pride for their accomplishments.
   D. Emphasis will be placed on maintaining and improving self-concept:
      1. focus on the positive at school,
      2. encourage parents to reinforce positive behavior at home.
   E. Students will learn to work harmoniously in groups: emphasis on sharing.
   F. Emphasis will be placed on teaching students the skills to communicate openly with each other and adults.
III. Academic Curriculum and Goals
   A. Students will increase their learning by one grade level in all subject areas by the end of the school year.
   B. A short discussion on the major topics covered in each academic subject:
      1. Reading
      2. Math
      3. Language Arts
      4. Handwriting
      5. Spelling
      6. Social Studies
      7. Science
      8. Physical Education
      9. Music
      10. Library
IV. Emphasis Will Be Placed on Organizational Skills
   A. Notebooks will be organized by subjects and returned papers will be filed under the proper heading.
   B. Spiral notebooks will contain students' creative-writing work.
   C. Desks will remain neat and orderly.
V. Grading System
   A. Students' grades are determined by the marks: 0 – outstanding; S – satisfactory; N – needs improvement.
   B. Report cards are given four times a year.
   C. Conferences are held in the fall and spring quarters.

VI. Students Will Have Homework under These Conditions:
   A. To reinforce a weak skill area.
   B. To reinforce a new concept: short practice on the multiplication factor or weekly spelling word list.
   C. When students have failed to use their academic time wisely in school.
   D. Students are encouraged to read for a few minutes each night.
VII. Students Will Be Assigned Three Major Projects during the Year
   A. Parents will be informed by letter.
   B. The date on which the project is due will be set realistically so that it will not interfere with family obligations.
   C. Students are encouraged to start the projects when they are assigned.
VIII. Discipline Procedure
   A. Parents will be contacted when necessary.
   B. Parents are given a copy of the Class Rules.
IX. Teachers' Comments on the Student's Study Habits So Far This Year
X. Miscellaneous Comments
   A. Mark all clothing with the student's full name.
   B. Keep emergency card current.
   C. Please send a note when your child has been ill, is riding a different bus home, or is leaving before the end of the school day.

will be used in teaching each topic. We might inform the parents that during reading their children will be grouped by ability and will receive numerous homework assignments. We can discuss the types of homework students will be assigned and describe how parents can best respond to the homework. You may want to state that should students ever be confused and overly concerned about a particular homework assignment, the student or parent is welcome to call you at home for assistance. Our experience indicates that though parents appreciate and are impressed by this offer, teachers receive very few evening phone calls about assignments.

When discussing academic work, we will want to describe the various special services, such as reading or gifted programs, that are available for providing students with individualized instruction outside the classroom. Similarly, we should discuss how individual differences are attended to in the classroom. Along these lines, it is helpful to outline the grading system that will be used and to discuss such issues as whether grades will reflect improvement or performance measured against some external standard. We will also want to describe any special instructional methods such as peer tutoring, individual goal setting, or group projects. Finally, parents can be informed that they will receive letters from us announcing any special projects or assignments that may require that they provide their child with some assistance. By clarifying the academic program and informing parents when and how they will be involved in helping their children, we can begin to create an accepting, supportive parent response.

We should also inform parents that they can expect to receive telephone calls and notes when their child has had a particularly good day or done something new or especially interesting. Similarly, the parents should be informed that they will also be notified when problems arise so that they are aware of what is happening. Teachers can make this process easier and more comfortable for themselves and parents by obtaining information concerning the most convenient time to contact each parent. We can indicate that although we accept the responsibility for providing an exciting educational experience and helping the students to learn social skills and responsibility, the most effective approach to motivating student learning and dealing with any problems that arise is for the home and school to work together effectively.

Followup

We must not wait too long before reinforcing the ideas presented in the orientation meeting. We can do so by arranging to involve parents in an instructional activity within a week or two following the meeting. The involvement may include an assignment in which parents are asked to help their children obtain information. We might ask the students to develop a family tree or to interview their parents for a career day. Another followup activity involves sending positive notes to parents about improvements or achievements their children have made in the specific areas discussed during the orientation meeting.

An additional aspect of followup is contacting parents who did not attend an orientation session. One approach is to send the parents their folder along with a letter stating that they were missed and inviting them to schedule a time to visit the classroom and discuss the material in the folder. It is helpful to call parents who do not respond and ask them whether they had any questions about the material they received. Although such contacts do require additional time, they are worth the effort, for they create a foundation for increased parental support.

Continuing Teacher-Parent Communication

All parents care about their children, and virtually all parents want their children to be successful at school. Therefore, it is important to keep parents continually informed about their child's progress in your class.

We should also contact parents when a child consistently begins to act out in class, falls behind in schoolwork and may need special assistance, or needs to complete some work at home. As in any relationship, it is better to deal with problems when they first arise than to wait until a crisis has occurred. Parents are justified in their annoyance when they attend a conference and discover that their child has been behind for six or eight weeks. Though it is true that some parents either do not care or cannot provide assistance in working with their child, it is important that we hold positive expectations. It is surprising how often parents with a reputation for lack of concern or for ineptness in helping their child can respond productively when contacted early and treated thoughtfully. There is an important distinction between teachers' constantly calling parents for support and calling parents to provide them with information. Parents have a right to expect teachers to handle minor problems and seek professional assistance in coping with major problems. Parents should be informed, however, when minor problems such as incomplete assignments or failure to bring supplies become frequent occurrences. Similarly, parents should be informed when major behavior or academic problems arise.

One method of communicating with parents is to send informational letters about upcoming areas of study, field trips, and long-term projects their child will be asked to complete, or newsletters about class happenings. Parents appreciate receiving information regularly, and a bimonthly or monthly letter seems most appropriate.

Another approach is to have students make personalized stationery during the first weeks of school. They can design their own patterns and decorate their stationery using felt pens, charcoal, paint, or any other art medium. We can use this stationery to send positive notes home about the student. It is best if elementary teachers send a positive note home at least twice a term. Most teachers find it helpful to record when notes were sent as well as the content of the notes. In this way we can send notes to all students and focus on different positive events each time a note is sent for each child.

Phone calls are another method for contacting parents. Teachers who call each child's parent(s) at least once before scheduling the initial conference and at least once a term thereafter find that parent-teacher contacts are more relaxed and enjoyable. Teachers often shy away from parents who have a reputation for being difficult to deal with. These, however, are the parents whom we should make the most effort to know. Parents appreciate knowing that their child's teacher cares enough to make a phone call, and the most critical parent will frequently become a supporter of the teacher who takes time to call. When making phone calls, always begin and end the conversation with a positive statement about the child. We should also ask the parent how the child is reacting to school and whether the parent has any information that might assist us in making the school experience more productive for the child. Like children, parents respond more positively when given a sense of competence and power.

Parents can also be contacted informally when we attend extracurricular activities in which their child is involved. We have found this strategy to be particularly effective with the parents of students who are doing poorly in school. On a number of occasions we have made concerted efforts to attend athletic performances of students involved in persistent school misbehavior and have found that when the parents saw concrete evidence of our concern for their child they became much more involved in encouraging the student to behave responsibly in school.

A final method for keeping parents informed is to ask them to serve as volunteers in the classroom. Parents are more likely to support us if they understand and feel a part of what goes on at school. Many parents of behavior-problem students had negative experiences when they were in school. Consequently, they respond negatively to and are often intimidated by teachers. Involving these parents in a positive manner in the classroom can do a great deal to alleviate these negative feelings. Parent volunteers who are treated with respect by teachers almost always become strong supporters of the teacher. As anyone who has worked with parent volunteers knows, we will initially need to spend time discussing the volunteer's role and helping volunteers understand and respond consistently to our instructional and discipline style. We will also need to recognize situations in which a parent's style of interacting with children may contradict our methods. In such cases, we may wish to channel the volunteer's efforts into support activities that involve minimal contact with students.

PARENT CONFERENCES

For most teachers, parent conferences are a required form of parent contact. Parent conferences can play a vital role in eliciting parents' support for us and can help us work with students who are experiencing difficulties. Unfortunately, a poorly organized or otherwise negative conference can create or intensify parental dissatisfaction. This dissatisfaction will frequently be reflected in students' behavior. Furthermore, coping with parental criticism diverts valuable teacher time and energy. Therefore, parent conferences have a real influence on classroom discipline.

By thoughtfully preparing for a conference and implementing a well-organized conference, we can reduce our own anxiety about conferring with parents while increasing the likelihood that parents will leave the conference feeling positive about and supportive of us. In this section we offer suggestions for improving skills in conferring with parents.

Preparing for a Conference

Because teacher, parent, and student all care about the outcome of a teacher-parent conference, we must consider how best to prepare each of these individuals for the conference. A conference will be more comfortable and productive when each person involved (the student is integrally involved even if he or she is not present) is prepared for the conference.

Preparing Students

The first steps in preparing students are to discuss the goals of conferences and to allow children to ask questions and express their concerns. Students need to know why their parents are being given a report and what will happen at the conference. The next step is to provide students with an opportunity to evaluate their own work. Because the primary goal of periodic teacher-parent conferences is to clarify and communicate students' accomplishments, it is logical that students should be involved in this process. Providing students with an opportunity to evaluate their own work also reduces their anxiety about the type of information their parents will be receiving. Self-evaluation provides children with a sense of significance, competence, and power.

There are several approaches to involving students in self-evaluation. The most specific and valuable method is to allow students to fill out a report card on themselves. The easiest and most effective method of developing a self-evaluation report card is to ask students to rate themselves on the same items on which the district or school requires us to rate students. Figure 5.3 is an example of such a form. Once the student has completed a self-evaluation form (younger children or students who have difficulty with reading will require assistance in completing a form), we can schedule time to discuss the results individually with each student. We should inform the students that this conference will allow the teacher and student to discuss any discrepancies between the teacher's and student's evaluation. It is extremely important to discuss these differences. Student resentment and hostility are often the outcomes of a conference in which parents are given negative information about a student before this information has been systematically discussed with the student. The implications for classroom management are obvious and dramatic. Students will treat their teacher and peers with greater kindness and respect when they feel they have been treated fairly.

Another method that can be incorporated with a self-evaluation report card is to have students examine their behavior and academic achievements compared with their stated goals. If students have been involved in writing goals for the grading period, they can be asked to write a short statement about the degree to which they have met these goals. This

FIGURE 5.3 Self-Evaluation Report Card

Name _____

Reading
1. Approximately how many pages of outside reading have you done this term?_____
2. Have you done as good a job on outside reading as you could have? _____
3. Have you kept up your daily assignments in your workbook and reading text?_____
4. What grade do you deserve in reading?
   grade: _____   effort: _____

Math
1. Have you worked hard to get all your assignments done on time? _____
2. Are there any of the multiplication tables that you are not sure of? _____ If so, which ones?_____
3. Are there any areas of math that you are not clear about or need more help in? _____
4. What grade do you deserve this term in math?
   grade: _____   effort: _____

Spelling
1. Have you studied your list words each week?_____
2. Have you been completing your workbook assignments each week on time? _____
3. Do you think you remember the words that you learn to spell each week?
   _____
4. How well do you spell your words in your creative writing and on daily assignments?
   superior   very good   fair   poor   (Circle one)
5. What grade should you receive for spelling this term?
   grade: _____   effort: _____

Cursive Writing
1. What grade do you feel you have earned this term in cursive writing?
   grade: _____   effort: _____
2. What do you need to work on?_____

Science, Social Studies, and Art
What grade would you give yourself in each of these areas for this term?
Please give a reason for each grade.
Science: grade: _____   effort: _____

(continued)

FIGURE 5.3 (*continued*)

Reason _____

Social Studies: grade: _____   effort: _____

Reason _____

Art: grade: _____   effort: _____

Reason _____

What areas are you doing well in at school? _____

What do you need to work on? _____
_____

In what ways do you feel you have grown personally this year?
_____

Please evaluate your study habits and personal growth, using these ratings.

+ = outstanding growth

= = okay or satisfactory growth

✔ = need to improve in this area

Put the appropriate mark on each line below.

Study Habits

_____ Following directions

_____ Completing assignments on time

_____ Working well in (your) a group

_____ Working well alone

_____ Listening well to whomever is speaking

_____ Showing neatness in your work and desk

_____ Assuming responsibility for your work

Personal Growth Areas

_____ Considering other people's feelings

_____ Following school rules in a positive way

_____ Taking care of your personal belongings

_____ Controlling your own behavior

_____ Being able to accept responsibility for your own actions

_____ Being able to get along well with others

Is there anything that you would like to share with me about yourself or your work?_____
_____

Is there anything you would like me to write on your report card or share with your parents?_____

Do you have any comments about my teaching this term?_____
_____
_____

Other comments that might be helpful for me to know?_____
_____

Thank you for your help!

procedure not only places their learning and subsequent grade in perspective but also reinforces the concept of students' responsibility for their own learning.

Preparing Parents

There are two basic methods for preparing parents for a teacher-parent conference. First, as discussed earlier, we should already have had several positive contacts with the parents. These contacts ideally include a back-to-school night, a phone call, and several notes sent home on their child's progress. Second, about one week before the conference we should send the parent(s) a note reminding them of the conference and providing them with an agenda for the conference. Figure 5.4 provides an example of such a note and outline.

Teacher Preparation

We are responsible for providing the parent(s) with clearly presented information in the context of a positive, comfortable interaction. The three basic steps in accomplishing this goal are these: First, as discussed in the preceding paragraphs, we should adequately prepare the student and parent(s) for the conference. Second, we should acquire and clearly organize important information about the student. Third, we should create a comfortable, relaxed environment.

Parents are impressed with data. Data indicate that we have invested time and energy in preparing for a conference. Data also testify directly to our professional competence.

FIGURE 5.4 Agenda for a Parent Conference

Dear Mr. and Mrs. Smith:

I am looking forward to our conference on Wednesday, November 6, at 3:30 P.M. In order to help us use the time most effectively I will try to follow the agenda listed below. I hope that this list will cover all areas you would like to discuss. If you have any special questions, it might be helpful to jot them down prior to the conference.

Conference Agenda
1. Share positive personal qualities about the student.
2. Read student's self-evaluation.
3. Discuss the report card and examine samples of the student's work.
4. Discuss the student's behavior and peer relationships.
5. Time for any final parent questions or concerns.
6. Summarize the conference by discussing the student's strengths, weaknesses, and areas that need improvement.

Sincerely,

Mrs. Johnson
3rd Grade Teacher

By focusing on specific data, we quickly move ourselves out of the parents' conception of teachers as professional babysitters and into the category of skilled professional educator. Data also have the obvious advantage of objectifying a discussion. The presence of data greatly diminishes the likelihood that a conference will turn into a debate over whether a student's grade is fair or whether a student's behavior really warrants concern.

Data also provide protection for the educator. Data provide a record of the student's academic progress and behavior as well as of our attempts to make thoughtful interventions aimed at improving skills and behaviors. The availability of data prevents us from being accused of exaggerating a problem, picking on a student, or not having attempted to solve the problem ourselves. Regardless of how competent we may be, lack of specific information significantly undermines our position when working with parents. Consequently, well-organized data are a necessary component of any parent conference and are especially important when a conference focuses on dealing with inappropriate student behavior or poor student achievement.

The four major types of data that are useful in a parent conference are:

1. Data on the students' and parents' feelings about the class;
2. Data on students' behavior and the results of attempts to improve the behavior;
3. Data on the student's academic work;
4. Data on conferences with colleagues and specialists aimed at developing a solution to any matter that is a problem.

It is helpful to acquire information about how the parents view the school year as progressing for their child. By requesting this information, we acknowledge the importance of the parents' concerns and ideas. Information about the parents' perceptions of their child's reactions to school and the parents' own wishes can also enable us to be better prepared for the conference. Figures 5.5 and 5.6 provide an example of a cover letter and parent questionnaire used by intermediate-grade teachers.

FIGURE 5.5 Cover Letter to Preconference Parent Questionnaire

Dear Parents,

I am attempting to make parent conferences more productive for myself, your child, and you.

In order to do so, I would like to have as much information as possible for the conference. You can help me by responding to the questions on the attached sheet. If there are any questions that you do not care to answer, please feel free to leave them blank. I would very much appreciate your returning this questionnaire to me at least one day before the conference. If that is not possible, please bring it to the conference with you.

I appreciate the time you are taking to help make this a rewarding conference for all of us.

I look forward to seeing you next week.

Miss Wilson

FIGURE 5.6 Preconference Parent Questionnaire

Please complete this questionnaire and return it as soon as possible. Thank you.

Name: _____

1. My child's general attitude toward school this year is _____
   _____

2. My child expresses most interest in school in _____
   _____

3. My child's greatest concern in school seems to be _____
   _____

4. Some things my child does very well are (these do not have to pertain to school)
   a. _____   d. _____
   b. _____   e. _____
   c. _____   f. _____

5. An area I would like to see my child work especially hard in is _____
   _____

6. Please list some positive qualities that your child has so that we can discuss good qualities at school (such as: trustworthy, patient, understanding, punctual) _____
   _____

7. Something I have wondered about this year is _____
   _____

8. Some things my child would like to do but has never done are _____
   _____

9. Some things that seem difficult for my child are (not necessarily school work: example, doing small tasks with fingers) _____
   _____

10. Something my child would like to do in school is _____
    _____

11. Several subjects that my child seems to enjoy are (include interests and hobbies) _____
    _____

12. I would appreciate any suggestions or comments you have that would help me work more effectively with your child. _____
    _____
    _____
    _____

Thank you for taking time to complete this questionnaire.

Data on a student's behavior will be necessary only when conferring with parents whose child is having serious behavior problems. In such cases we should present the parents with specific data on the child's behavior and our approaches to helping the child in improving the behavior.

Because the school's primary function is to provide students with basic academic skills, the teacher-parent conference should heavily emphasize informing parents about their child's academic progress. We should prepare for each conference by readying a folder that includes samples of the student's work in each major subject. The folder should include specific examples that will help the parent understand any areas in which the student is having particular difficulties.

If the data on the student's academic progress indicate that the student is not functioning well, we should be prepared to provide the parent(s) with examples of ways in which the student's academic program has been adjusted in order to meet the student's special needs. If we have worked with specialists in developing an individualized program, it is helpful to provide information about these conferences. We can do so by using a standard form to record the results of such conferences. Figure 5.7 is an example of a form you can use for this purpose.

FIGURE 5.7   Teacher-Specialist Conference Form

Consultant's name _____   Date _____

Consultant's position or role _____
Reasons for holding the conference:

Goals for the conference:

Information obtained:

Decision(s) reached:

Additional comments:

_____

From Vernon F. Jones, *Adolescents with Behavior Problems: Strategies for Teaching, Counseling, and Parent Involvement*, p. 274. © 1980 by Allyn and Bacon. Reprinted with permission.

There are several advantages to presenting this type of data. Data concerning professional consultation speak to the teacher's concern and resourcefulness. Furthermore, they indicate to the parents that their child's problem is not simply a personality conflict with a teacher or the result of an incompetent teacher's having difficulty teaching their slightly energetic student. Another advantage to having consulted with specialists is that this procedure should present the parents with clearer and more thorough data. Especially in the area of academic difficulties, classroom teachers often have limited skills in diagnosing the specific factors that may be causing a student's problems. By consulting specialists, we can not only provide the parents with more detailed information, but can also simultaneously acquire information that can assist in developing a more appropriate academic program for the student.

It is helpful to provide parents with a conference summary. This review can focus the conference and can also refresh our minds, for we often hold several consecutive conferences. The parent should be given the summary sheet at the end of the conference. Figure 5.8 is an example of a conference summary form.

Once we have prepared students and parents and have collected and developed the important data, the final preparation involves creating a comfortable conference setting. If possible, the conference should be held at a round table so that neither party is in a dominant position. The atmosphere can be made more relaxed by placing some flowers on the table and having cookies and coffee available. The agenda should be placed on the board or on a large sheet of butcher paper as a reminder for both parties. Parents also appreciate knowing what topics and skills have been covered during the term. A piece of paper listing these skills can be placed next to the agenda for reference during the conference. Pencil and paper should be provided so the parent(s) can take notes during the conference.

Providing an Effective Conference

If we have prepared effectively, the actual conference will usually be quite easy and comfortable. After greeting the parent(s) warmly and chatting for a moment about any positive topic, we should begin the conference by sharing several positive personal qualities the child displays at school. We can encourage the parent(s) to discuss any aspects of the student's behavior they have enjoyed or been particularly pleased with recently. The next step is to ask the parent(s) to read the student's self-evaluation report card and any other material the student has written about his or her progress during the term. Students often are so critical of their own work that this is an interesting and sensitive preparation for any critical comments we may need to make. Once they have read their child's own critical evaluation, parents are less likely to question our statements about areas in which their child needs improvement.

Many parents are concerned about their child's report card, so that the next step is to discuss the actual report card and examine specific examples of the student's work. When doing so, we should initially focus on positive aspects of the student's work. Parents respond well to the "sandwich theory of feedback," in which critical comments are sandwiched between positive comments about their child. Another strategy is to introduce an area that needs improvement with the statement, "I would like to encourage your child to. . . ." By focusing on the positive, we can minimize parental defensiveness and criticism.

FIGURE 5.8 Conference Summary Form

Student's Name: _____

Academic Achievement

Reading

Doing well in: _____
Needs to work on: _____

Math
Average of math scores: _____   _____
                              tests   daily work

Strong areas: _____
Needs to improve on: _____

Other subjects: _____
_____

Behavior and Personal Characteristics
Positive personal qualities that I see in your child: _____
_____

Improvement needed in: _____
_____

Comments about how your child is relating to his or her classmates: _____
_____

Final Comments
You could help at home by: _____
_____
_____

Any additional comments: _____
_____
_____
_____

Once academic matters have been discussed, we can focus on the student's behavior and peer relationships. It is important to discuss positive aspects of the student's behavior as well as aspects that require improvement. Also, if the student has experienced serious behavior problems, we must provide the parent(s) with specific data on the student's behavior and efforts to assist the student in changing behavior. During this portion of the conference it may be appropriate to invite the principal or any other specialists to join in the discussion. The last section in this chapter provides specific strategies for conferring with parents of seriously acting-out children.

After we have discussed the student's academic progress and behavior, the parent(s) should be encouraged to ask questions and make comments. If the parents do not have any questions, we can help them focus on their thoughts and concerns by referring to any pertinent items on the preconference parent questionnaire (Figure 5.6).

We can conclude the conference by summarizing the student's academic and behavior strengths and weaknesses. Goals for improvement can be written down (Figure 5.9), and we can discuss any ways in which the parents can assist the child at home. These should be listed on the conference summary form (Figure 5.8). We should discuss any followup contacts that appear desirable based on the information discussed during the conference, and we should express sincere appreciation for the parents' efforts and input.

The final step in implementing an effective conference is to ask parents to evaluate the conference (Figure 5.10). This evaluation provides us with valuable information about aspects of the conference that parents find most and least beneficial. Perhaps equally important, by requesting an evaluation we conclude the conference with an activity that acknowledges the parents' value and provides them with a sense of competence and power.

METHODS FOR SECONDARY TEACHERS

As stated at the beginning of this chapter, secondary teachers usually have fewer direct parent contacts than do their elementary school counterparts. Most secondary schools do not require parent conferences for all students, nor do they expect teachers to maintain continuing contact with their students' parents. Nevertheless, our own experience and reports from numerous teachers suggest that secondary teachers too often underestimate both the value and feasibility of steady parent contacts. Teachers who have placed an emphasis on positive, proactive interactions with parents by using the following cost-effective methods for communicating with parents report increased parental support and improved student attitudes toward academic activities.

Introductory Letters

We can provide parents with a wide range of information by sending home a form letter describing selected aspects of our learning goals, instructional methods, and classroom procedures. A letter might include a course syllabus or similar list of topics to be covered and specific skills the students will learn. We may also comment on the specific teaching methods we will use during the course. For example, if we use group work or projects, we might describe the activities in which students will be involved as well as the educational rationale for using these methods. We may also comment on our grading procedures and our decision on when to inform parents about lack of student progress. And we can describe the methods we will use in responding to disruptive student behavior. When doing so, we must preface this material by suggesting that such behavior is not anticipated, because the

FIGURE 5.9 Plan for Improvement

PLAN FOR IMPROVEMENT

STUDENT'S NAME: _____

TEACHER'S NAME: _____

PARENT'S NAME: _____

DATE: _____

AREA TO BE IMPROVED: _____

_____

THE TEACHER WILL: _____

_____

THE STUDENT WILL: _____

_____

THE PARENT WILL: _____

_____

LONG-RANGE GOAL: _____

_____

FIGURE 5.10 Conference Evaluation Form

Would you please take a moment to evaluate our conference? This review helps me as I plan our next one.

Excellent	10	_____	
	9	_____	
	8	_____	
	7	_____	Please check the appropriate line.
	6	_____	
Average	5	_____	
	4	_____	
	3	_____	
	2	_____	
Poor	1	_____	

Was there a subject that you especially appreciated my sharing or that was very helpful to you?
Was there an area we neglected to discuss that you feel I should have brought up?
Do you have any other comments to share?

combination of interesting and effective instruction and our commitment to assist students will make it unlikely that these methods will prove necessary.

Newsletters

A newsletter is an expedient way to keep large numbers of parents informed. Because most secondary teachers have three separate preparations, a newsletter sent every three weeks for each class requires a teacher to write one newsletter each week. The newsletter can involve less than a page, describing subjects currently being taught, projects due, films being shown, and so on. We can also use this opportunity to jot a personal note on newsletters to parents whose child is experiencing noteworthy success or problems.

Progress Reports

Many schools require that teachers notify parents at midterm of each nine-week period if their child is earning lower than a *C* grade. You can readily develop your own form for immediately contacting parents whose children are beginning to experience academic or behavioral problems. Because this form should be sent when students are just beginning to experience a problem, you should summarize the steps you will be taking to help the student. This form need not initially require you to write; you can simply list the methods you systematically use.

DEALING EFFECTIVELY WITH PARENTS' CRITICISM AND CONFRONTATION

Anyone who has taught for several years has had to deal with an angry or critical parent. Many teachers state that, along with classroom discipline, this type of confrontation is perhaps the least desirable aspect of teaching. Although there is no foolproof method for dealing with an angry parent, there are several strategies we can use to cope with such situations in an effective, professional manner.

1. Greet the parent in a pleasant manner. It is more difficult for parents to remain critical and aggressive if you seem glad to see them.

2. Use active listening to defuse the parent's emotions. Becoming defensive or initially arguing with the parent will usually only intensify the parent's emotions. By using phrases such as "I appreciate your concern, . . ." or "I can see that you are really concerned about this," you can help the parent feel understood. This tactic will gradually enable the parent to calm down and replace angry or frightened feelings with more positive and productive feelings.

3. Look genuinely interested and listen carefully. This attitude also helps the parent feel accepted and will gradually reduce negative or intense feelings.

4. Present a calm, professional manner. Stand erect, look at the parent, and remain calm. Just as students respond more effectively to teachers who remain calm and in charge during a crisis (Brophy & Evertson, 1976; Kounin, 1970), parents need the structure provided by a calm response.

5. Ask the parent what he or she wishes to accomplish. One method of structuring a confrontation conference is by questioning the parent: "I appreciate your concern. What would you like to accomplish with our discussion today?" This approach helps focus the parent's energy and moves the conference away from a gripe session into a potentially productive problem-solving conference.

6. Set a time limit if necessary. If your time is limited, it is important to inform the parent. Do so by stating, "I have 20 minutes before I have to be back with my class. Let's see how far we can get in solving the problem in that time. If we need more time, I will be glad to schedule a conference as soon as possible."

7. Ask the parent whether the student is aware of the problem. Because the student is the most important person involved, it is important to clarify how he or she feels about the issue being raised by the parent. This question also slows the parent down and creates a more productive focus for the conference. Furthermore, the question helps introduce the issue of the student's responsibility for any problem that may exist.

8. Be honest. When confronted by parents, it is easy to understate the seriousness of a problem or to accept too much responsibility for a problem that is largely something the child must work on. We must maintain our professional integrity and set the stage for future conferences by initially presenting an honest and clear statement of the problem.

9. Emphasize specific data. Data are simultaneously one of your best professional tools and your best defense. If a parent angrily states that his daughter did well in math last year but is having difficulty this year, the most logical and effective approach is to examine data on the student's math skills.

10. Tell the parent specifically what will be done to deal with the problem. Parents have a right to know what the teacher will do to alleviate a difficulty. Furthermore, critical parents can often become strong supporters if they learn that they will be listened to, shown data, and presented with a plan. If the parent's worry was not justified, the plan may involve a follow-up conference to examine the results of the current program. If, however, the parent highlighted an area that required attention, developing a plan shows respect for the parent's concern and competence on your part.

INVOLVEMENT WITH PARENTS OF HANDICAPPED CHILDREN

With the passage of PL 94–142, teachers became more frequently and formally involved in working with parents of handicapped students. As awareness about various handicapping conditions increased, more handicapped students were placed in public schools, more services became available to help them, and teachers found themselves referring more students for these services. Referral forms vary from district to district, but usually include requests for this information:

> Date of referral
> Name of person making referral
> Parent's name, address, and phone number
> Student's current placement
> Reason for referral
> Examples of attempts to correct problem
> Responses of student to such efforts. (Meyen 1982, p. 69)

Although parents need not be contacted until their permission is required for the educational evaluation, they should be notified as soon as we perceive a problem, so that teacher-parent communication will be open throughout our efforts to assist the student and during the referral process. Steady communication with the parents better prepares them to participate productively in the decision on placement and in creating an individualized education program (IEP).

> They are also able to share information that can be of value, and can allow insight into any cultural and language differences that may be contributing to the student's difficulty. Effective communication between home and school is an effective way to help gain a total picture of the child's needs and to prevent disagreements and misunderstandings that too often have led to delays in needed services. (Meyen, 1982, p. 70)

In addition to involvement in the referral process, PL 94–142, Section 121a. 344, states that the student's teacher(s) will, along with the parents, other school personnel, and, when appropriate, the student, be involved in an IEP conference to determine the specific special services needed to assist the student. The formats employed vary from state to state, but most IEPs include:

1. A statement of the child's present levels of educational performance, including academic achievement, social adaptation, prevocational and vocational skills, psychomotor skills and self-help skills;

2. A statement of annual goals which describes the educational performance to be achieved by the end of the school year under the child's individualized education program;

3. A statement of short-term instructional objectives, which must be measurable, intermediate steps between the present level of educational performance and the annual goals;

4. A statement of specific educational services needed by the child (determined without regard to the availability of services), including a description of:
    a. all special education and related services needed to meet the unique needs of the child, including the type of physical education program of the child, and
    b. any special instructional media and materials which are needed;

5. The date when those services will begin and length of time the services will be given;

6. A description of the extent to which the child will participate in regular education programs;

7. Objective criteria, evaluation procedures, and schedules for determining, at least annually, whether the short-term instructional objectives are being achieved;

8. A justification for the type of educational placement that the child will have; and

9. A list of the individuals who are responsible for implementing the individualized education program. (Heward & Orlansky, 1980, pp. 20, 21)

Our involvement does not end with participation in developing an IEP. In many cases, a portion of the student's special educational program will be carried out in the regular classroom. It is likely that this placement will involve us in periodic contacts with the student's parents and school support personnel. Although we need to be aware of these requirements, we need not be intimidated by them. If you use the skills presented in this chapter, you will find most relationships with parents to be a positive and productive aspect of your professional role.

PLACING SCHOOL-HOME INTERACTION IN PERSPECTIVE

A chapter on teacher-student contacts is not complete without clarifying the parameters of school-home contacts. As mentioned throughout this chapter, when teachers take a pro-active approach by providing early positive and informative contacts with parents, teacher-parent interactions can be a positive, enjoyable aspect of a teacher's job. Similarly, when teachers develop skills for calmly and professionally responding to parents' concerns, even potentially negative interactions with parents can become less stressful and can serve to initiate greater parent understanding and support.

Unfortunately, the high rate of divorce, substance abuse, poverty, family mobility, and two working parents have all created a society in which an increasing number of at-risk students live in homes characterized by ineffective parenting and stress. Many parents lack the preparation, emotional stability, time, and support to provide effective parenting. This means that many students come to school anxious or upset about situations that have occurred at home.

Our responsibility as teachers is to use methods such as those described throughout this book that create positive, caring, supportive, well-structured environments for all students. As discussed in chapter 12, teachers are also responsible for obtaining the help of other teachers and school support personnel in developing special methods for working with students who experience ongoing problems. This is the extent of our responsibilities as teachers. Teachers are not mental health specialists and cannot be expected to provide parent training or to help parents obtain resources for resolving family problems.

Even though teachers' responsibilities in working with parents are limited, school staffs can provide varied assistance to parents. Schools are the one societal institution with which all children and parents come into contact. School personnel thus are often the first to become aware of problems, and parents may be more likely to seek assistance from schools than from social service agencies. Schools can provide an important service to parents and children by offering limited direct services and by referring families to other community resources. School counselors are an obvious source of direct services to parents and children. Many elementary schools have child development specialists who work with the most seriously at-risk children and their parents. Unfortunately, many elementary schools do not have counselors. Given the frequency and depth of personal problems facing many elementary children, it seems critical that elementary schools provide counselors who can help children work through emotional conflicts and develop personal/social skills they have not learned at home. Unless these services are available, some of our most needy children will be hampered by emotional problems that will seriously limit their obtaining essential learning.

Another type of assistance to families can be classes on parenting skills. Many schools offer parents periodic seminars or classes on methods of effective parenting. Because virtually all parents have some contact with their child's school, and because for most parents the stigma of attending a session at their child's school is less than attending a mental health clinic class, the schools are an important resource for providing parenting skills. Schools with whom we have worked have successfully used the *Parent Effectiveness Training* and *Systematic Teaching for Effective Parenting (STEP)* materials as tools for helping parents develop basic parenting skills. The authors have provided numerous parent training sessions and classes and have consistently found parents to be appreciative and pleased with the applicability of their new skills.

Schools can provide another important support service for parents and families in turmoil. Many schools with whom we work have begun to contract a social worker or other social service professional to serve as a liaison between the home, family, and community for children who are experiencing ongoing school problems in association with serious home problems. Mental health agencies employ systems and language different from those used by school personnel; therefore, someone familiar with these systems can use these resources more effectively. A school-community liaison can serve as a resource for educators and parents and can help obtain much needed community services for children and their families. Even though schools are not responsible for resolving all problems faced by the students they help educate, they do have an obligation to identify and provide effective referrals for children experiencing stress and trauma that are influencing their ability to benefit from the educational environment. Additional suggestions and references for increasing home-school cooperation and support can be found in *Home and School as Partners: Helping Parents Help Their Children* by Paul Haley and Karen Berry (1988), published by the Regional Laboratory for Educational Improvement of the Northeast and Islands (290 S. Main St., Andover, MA 01810).

Reporting child abuse is a special issue in home-school relationships. An educator's responsibility for reporting child abuse is an example of the coordination of school and community resources to help children and their families.

> Child abuse and neglect is recognized as a problem of epidemic proportions, both nationally and in Oregon. The number of identified child victims in Oregon has grown at an alarming rate; more than 385 percent increase from 1980 to 1985. In spite of the skyrocketing numbers of reports, national studies indicate that only a small percent of maltreated children are reported to child protection agencies. (Roberts, 1986, p. 7)

To help abused children, states have enacted legislation that requires educators to report child abuse. In Oregon, educators are required to report suspected physical abuse, neglect, mental injury or emotional abuse, sexual abuse, and sexual exploitation. Oregon law also provides the professional who makes the report with safeguards against legal prosecution.

418.762–Immunity of persons making reports in good faith.

> Anyone participating in good faith in the making of a report pursuant to ORS 418.750 to 418.760 and who has reasonable grounds for the making thereof, shall have immunity from any liability, civil or criminal, that might otherwise be incurred or imposed with respect to the making or content of such report. Any such participant shall have the same immunity with respect to participating in any judicial proceeding resulting from such report.

All teachers and administrators should become familiar with the child-abuse laws in their state and the reporting and followup procedures used by their district. Many districts have developed working relationships with community children's service agencies responsible for handling reported child abuse to ensure that proper followup is provided and to coordinate efforts to help the child cope with the temporary emotional stress often associated with this type of report.

ASSESSING PARENT CONTACTS

Awareness is almost always the first step in changing one's behavior. Before deciding whether to take the time and risks involved in trying new behaviors, most people choose to examine their present behavior. Activity 5.1 provides you with an opportunity to examine your current parent contacts. It also offers several ideas for systematically improving these contacts.

ACTIVITY 5.1   Assessing and Improving Parent Contacts

Assessing your parent contacts

To assess the current level of your contact with parents, answer these questions:

1. How many informational letters have you sent out to every parent so far this year?_____
2. What percentage of your students' parents have received a positive phone call about their child's work or behavior?_____
3. What percentage of your students' parents have received a positive note about their child's work or behavior?_____
4. How many students in your class are experiencing what you would define as significant academic or behavior problems?_____
5. How many parents of these students have you talked to about the problem and your approach to dealing with it?_____
6. How many parents have served as volunteers in your classroom this year?
_____
7. How many hours a week is a parent present in your classroom?_____

Improving your parent contacts

1. Send an informational letter to your students' parents. After two weeks evaluate this effort by answering these questions:
   a. How many parents made a positive comment about the letter?_____
   b. How many students said something positive about the letter?_____
   c. List two advantages to sending the letter:
      (1) _____
      (2) _____
   d. List any disadvantages associated with sending the letter.

2. Over a two-week period, send a positive note home with each child in your class. After two weeks evaluate this effort by answering these questions:
   a. How many parents made a positive comment about the note? _____
   b. How many students said something positive about the note? _____
   c. List two advantages to sending the note:
      (1) _____
      (2) _____
   d. List any disadvantages associated with sending the note.

IMPLEMENTING AND ASSESSING NEW METHODS

Having examined a variety of methods for preparing and implementing parent conferences, the next step is to select specific methods you believe would make your next set of conferences more productive and enjoyable. If you are somewhat tentative about a new method, you might wish to use it with several parents with whom you are most comfortable.

ACTIVITY 5.2 Implementing and Assessing New Methods

Select one method for improving student, parent, and teacher preparation. Write these on a sheet of paper and make a specific statement about how you will implement each method. Next, select one method from the section on implementing an effective conference.

During your next series of parent conferences, implement each of the methods you have selected. After the conferences are completed, evaluate the new methods by completing these statements for each new approach:

The most beneficial aspect of this new approach was . . .
Another advantage was that . . .
Parents' response to this approach was . . .
Students' response was . . .
One difficulty with this new approach was . . .
I felt more comfortable when using this method because . . .

SUMMARY

Teachers often underestimate the power parents give to teachers. As teachers who have children in school, the authors are acutely aware of the value of parent-teacher contacts. Like virtually all parents, we are deeply concerned about our children's progress in handling new social and academic expectations. Teachers provide parents with input concerning how intelligent and skilled their children are and how well they are getting along with others. These are extremely important facts to almost all parents. Indeed, the defensiveness you may experience when working with parents of children who are struggling in school is due in large part to the importance parents place on the information you are giving them and to the difficulty they have accepting negative information about their child.

Because information about their children's school progress is so important to parents, it is necessary that this information be shared on a regular basis. As teachers, we can establish more positive, supportive teacher-parent relationships when we initially inform parents about the curriculum, instruction, and classroom management to which their child will be exposed. This needs to be followed by periodic updates about classroom activities and student progress. In addition, any time a student begins to have an academic or behavioral problem, we should contact the parent as soon as it appears that the matter cannot be quickly and smoothly resolved between us and the student.

Teacher-parent contacts can be time-consuming and, like all aspects of our profession, require practice before we become comfortable and adept at them. They can, however, be among the most rewarding aspects of our teaching experience and can have a significant impact on the most important and rewarding aspect of our job—seeing improvement in the quality of student behavior and learning.

RECOMMENDED READING

Books on Teacher-Parent Contacts

Bailard, V., & Strang, R. (1964). *Parent-teacher conferences.* New York: McGraw-Hill.

Gordon, I., & Breivogel, W. (1976). *Building effective home-school relationships.* Boston: Allyn and Bacon.

Heffernan, H., & Todd, V. (1969). *Elementary teachers' guide to working with parents.* West Nyack, N.Y.: Parker.

Jones, V. (1980). *Adolescents with behavior problems: Strategies for teaching, counseling, and parent involvement.* Boston: Allyn and Bacon.

Kelley, E. (1974). *Parent-teacher interaction: A special education perspective.* Seattle, Wash.: Special Child Publications. A Division of Bernie Straub Publishing Company, Inc.

Losen, S., & Diament, B. (1979). *Parent conferences in the schools: Procedures for developing effective partnership.* Boston: Allyn and Bacon.

Rutherford, R., & Edgar, E. (1979). *Teachers and parents: A guide to interaction and cooperation.* Boston: Allyn and Bacon.

Wilson, G., & Wingate, B. (1974). *Parents and teachers: Humanistic educational techniques to facilitate communication between parents and staff of educational programs.* Atlanta, Ga.: Humanities Press.

Books That Teachers Can Give Parents as References for Parenting Skills

Blechman, E. (1985). *Solving child behavior problems at home and at school.* Champaign, Ill.: Research Press.

Dinkmeyer, D., McKay, G., & McKay, J. (1987). *New beginnings: Skills for single parents and stepfamily parents.* Champaign, Ill.: Research Press.

Ehly, S., Conoley, J., & Rosenthal, D. (1985). *Working with parents of exceptional children.* Columbus, Ohio: Merrill.

Faber, A., & Mazlish, E. (1982). *How to talk so kids will listen and listen so kids will talk.* New York: Avon.

Faber, A., & Mazlish, E. (1987). *Siblings without rivalry.* New York: W. W. Norton & Co.

Ginott, H. (1965). *Between parent and child: New solutions to old problems.* New York: Macmillan.

Gordon, T. (1970). *Parent effectiveness training: The tested way to raise responsible children.* New York: Wyden.

Haley, P., & Berry, K. (1988). *Home and school partnerships: Helping parents help their children.* Andover, Mass. The Regional Laboratory for Educational Improvement of the Northeast and Islands.

Kroth, R., & Otteni, H. (1985). *Communicating with parents of exceptional children,* 2nd ed. Denver, Colo.: Love Publishing Co.

Pogrebin, L. (1980). *Growing up free: Raising your child in the 80s.* New York: Bantam Books.

Rich, D. (1987). *School and families: Issues and actions.* Washington, D.C.: National Education Association.

Rotter, J., Robinson, E., & Fey, M. (1988). *Parent-teacher conferences,* 2nd ed. Washington, D.C.: NEA.

Sloane, H. (1979). *The good kid book: How to solve the 16 most common behavior problems.* Champaign, Ill.: Research Press.

Swick, K., & Duff, E. (1979). *Parenting.* Washington, D.C.: National Education Association.

Wagonseller, B., & McDowell, R. (1979). *You and your child: A common sense approach to successful parenting.* Champaign, Ill.: Research Press.

Increasing Student Motivation and Learning by Implementing Instructional Methods That Meet Students' Academic Needs

During the 1980s, the concepts of allocated time and on-task behavior were a major focus for educational research and practice. These remain important topics; in addition, the issues of student motivation, productive time, and interactive instruction will receive major attention during the first half of the 1990s. Concern about at-risk students will focus on how to motivate and actively engage these students in learning activities as well as how to manage them.

Part III presents current theory and practice on student motivation and effective instruction. Chapter 6 examines current research on motivation to learn and indicates the relationship between this research and classroom practice. Teachers faced with students who come to school lacking strong parental expectations and support for academic achievement need a solid understanding of applied motivation theory. Our experience indicates that many teachers lack this basic understanding of student motivation. Teachers have too often been provided with methods for teaching without understanding how these methods relate to student motivation. These teachers then become frustrated technicians rather than the creative decision makers they would like to be. Our experience indicates that when provided with new information on student motivation and given the opportunity to use it as the basis for considering instructional methods, teachers are excited about the changes in their teaching and the accompanying changes in student behavior and learning.

Chapter 7 presents a discussion of and practical suggestions for implementing a variety of instructional methods proven effective in increasing student motivation and learning. This chapter responds to the large and growing body of data indicating that many students find schools confusing, boring, meaningless places in which to learn. We present methods for altering this situation by clarifying instruction, increasing meaningful student involvement in the learning process, and using teaching methods that respond to individual students' needs. Ideas for teaching young adolescents and gifted students are included in chapter 7.

CHAPTER 6

Enhancing Students' Motivation to Learn

Thus low motivation, negative self-attitudes, and failure are largely the result of improper learning conditions. According to this learning theory analysis, we should be able to alter a student's failure rate by changing the conditions of classroom learning and, as a consequence, increase his motivation to succeed. Actually there is considerable experimental evidence on this point.

/   Martin Covington and Richard Beery (1976)
Self-Worth and School Learning

Being a spectator not only deprives one of participation but also leaves one's mind free for unrelated activity. If academic learning does not engage students, something else will.

/   John Goodlad (1983b)
Phi Delta Kappan, "A Study of Schooling"

Typically, the information offered to teachers about motivational strategies focuses on controlling performance rather than on stimulating motivation to learn, and emphasizes the use of incentives, rewards, and grades rather than strategies designed to stimulate students to generate learning goals and the cognitive and metacognitive strategies to accomplish them.

/   Jere Brophy (1986b)
Socializing Students' Motivation to Learn

If learning activities could be made more interesting, involving and accessible to all, then problems of any kind, whether learning difficulties, behavioural difficulties or a combination of the two, would be less likely to arise. Our first focus of "support" should thus be the curriculum rather than the individual.

/ Denis Mogon and Susan Hart (in press)
Improving Classroom Behaviour: Making a Difference

Recent studies have demonstrated that students learn best and behave more appropriately in classroom settings that meet their learning needs. Students' misbehavior and failure can often be traced to failure to create an educational environment conducive to learning. Educators have also begun to appreciate that students vary in the type of classroom structure and instruction that best facilitate their learning. Understanding the instructional needs of an individual child or group of children provides teachers with information essential for creating a positive learning environment.

Although meeting students' personal needs (as discussed in chapter 2) provides a foundation for creating environments supportive of personal growth and learning, closely related and equally important needs exist within environments that are specifically designed to help children acquire academic knowledge. Many students meet their needs for autonomy, competence, self-esteem, and self-actualization by successfully completing classroom activities and assignments. Understanding the research on motivation and its relationship to student academic needs enables teachers to implement instruction that results in students' obtaining feelings of worth within the school setting.

When frustrated by students' failure to pay attention, complete assignments, or attend class, it is tempting to blame factors outside the classroom. As discussed in chapter 1, studies indicate that teachers generally blame family and community factors for students' lack of motivation to learn. Our own experience and reading of the research suggests another explanation, however. We have never met a student who was unmotivated to learn. We have met many students who were unmotivated in certain settings but highly motivated in others. We have met many students who were motivated when their learning needs were met but appeared unmotivated when they were not. Consider how you would feel if you were placed in a third-year, second-semester medical school program and told that your future success would be influenced by how you performed. Most of us would search for ways to withdraw from or deny the value of this anxiety-provoking, stressful situation. More concretely, consider how you respond in a college course, inservice workshop, or meeting in which the content seems irrelevant or boring or when you are not asked to be actively involved. In our nearly 40 years of attending faculty meetings, we have seen numerous examples of teacher behavior that looked similar to the behavior of the at-risk students about whom we are all concerned.

Studies indicate that students are highly motivated by the desire to demonstrate their competence (Hahn, Danzberger, & Lefkowitz, 1987). Many students who appear unmotivated in school have a desire to demonstrate competence as learners. An Oregon Department of Education study documented that 77 percent of students who leave school before graduation plan to obtain further schooling within three years, and that over 60 percent do pursue additional schooling within this time. Virtually all students want to learn new information and demonstrate competence as learners. Unfortunately, too many classroom learning environments fail to meet these students' learning needs, and the students cannot cope with their continued frustration and failure.

Rather than focusing our discussion on motivation as a theoretical construct, we emphasize applied motivational research, which we relate to specific student academic needs. This decision is based on several factors. First, "although there is a large body of theory and research on the general topic of motivation, only a small portion of it applies specifically to the subtopic of motivation to learn in the classroom" (Brophy, 1986b, p. 7). Second, teachers inform us that they frequently find it difficult to translate theory and research on motivation into the practical reality of making decisions in their classrooms. Third, we believe that focusing on students' needs places the student at the center of the issue; this clarifies for teachers the options available to them for increasing student motivation. Following a brief discussion of motivation in the classroom, this chapter is organized around a series of student academic needs that, when met, increase student motivation and learning. The importance of each academic need is supported by a body of research; this material is presented along with specific ideas for using this research to increase student motivation and learning.

AN OVERVIEW OF MOTIVATION IN THE CLASSROOM SETTING

Teachers often express concern and frustration about students' lack of motivation. The good news for teachers is that research suggests that

> student motivation to learn is an acquired competence developed through general experience but stimulated most directly through modeling, communication of expectations, and direct instruction or socialization by others (especially parents and teachers). . . . According to this view, teachers are not merely reactors to whatever motivational patterns their students had developed before entering the classrooms but rather are active socialization agents capable of stimulating the general development of student motivation to learn and its activation in particular situations. (Brophy, 1987, pp. 40, 41)

Therefore, teachers who respond effectively to students' personal and academic needs will find that even though not all students will become college-bound scholars, a wide range of low-achieving and at-risk students can become actively, positively, and productively involved in learning within regular classroom settings.

Teachers with whom we work find it helpful to understand the general basis or conceptual framework from which we operate when thinking about motivation and its relationship to students' academic needs. Like many other writers, our view of motivation incorporates the expectation × value theory (Feather, 1982). This model suggests that the extent to which people become actively and productively involved in an activity is based on (1) whether they believe they can be successful at the task and (2) the degree to which they value the rewards associated with successful task completion. We add a third variable—climate, or the quality of relationships within the task setting during the time the people are engaged in the task. Thus, the formula becomes:

$$\text{motivation} = \text{expectation} \times \text{value} \times \text{climate}.$$

Because it is described as a multiplicative function, this model suggests that students will not be motivated unless all three components are present, that is, they (a) expect they can accomplish a task, (b) find value in the task, and (c) complete the task in an environment supportive of their basic personal needs (see chapter 2).

Adelman and Taylor (1983) present a similar concept of motivation. They suggest that with students who have a history of school failure it is often essential initially to focus on issues of motivation and then to emphasize a program designed to develop basic skills.

> Whatever the instigating cause, an individual who has been deficient in basic skills for a significant period of time is likely to have strong feelings and thoughts about many learning activities. The feelings may include anxiety, fear, frustration, and anger; the cognitions may include *expectations* of "failure" and *devaluation* of academic learning opportunities. (p. 102)

These feelings, expectations, and devaluing are similar to the concepts of climate, expectation, and value.

The second concept that organizes our thinking about motivation is Eccles and Wigfield's (1985) idea that three types of value may be associated with a task: (1) intrinsic value—the simple interest or enjoyment associated with engaging in a task; (2) attainment value—the value of obtaining achievement, notoriety, or influence through accomplishing a task; and (3) utility value—the benefits to one's career or other personal goals associated with performing a task successfully. This threefold concept suggests that teachers need to ensure that at least one type of value is present if students are to be motivated by the task.

STUDENTS' ACADEMIC NEEDS

As mentioned, we have found it useful to relate motivation research and theory to student needs. The academic needs listed in Figure 6.1 that serve as the foundation for this chapter are based on our own categorization of research on student motivation and learning. This list has been validated and expanded by lists generated by more than 400 teachers. We encourage you to review the literature and reflect on your experiences with students and to consider this list in light of your ongoing professional reading and experience.

It is informative to compare the academic needs in Figure 6.1 to a recent summary of research on strategies for motivating students to learn by Jere Brophy. Figure 6.2 presents 33 principles of motivation based on Brophy's research review. In parentheses beside each motivation principle is the student academic need to which the principle lends support or can be presented as an example. Brophy's review provides a strong validation for the 13 academic needs that are the basis for this chapter.

Additional validity for the list of academic needs can be found in Wehlage's (1983) analyses of a number of programs particularly successful with marginal students. According to Wehlage, programs for marginal students

FIGURE 6.1 Students' Academic Needs

1. Understand and value the learning goals
2. Understand the learning process
3. Be actively involved in the learning process
4. Relate subject matter to their own lives
5. Control the learning environment by setting goals or following their own interests
6. Experience success
7. Receive realistic and immediate feedback that enhances self-efficacy
8. Receive rewards for performance gains
9. See learning modeled by adults as an exciting and rewarding activity
10. Experience an appropriate amount of structure
11. Have time to integrate learning
12. Have positive contact with peers
13. Receive instruction matched to their cognitive and skill level and learning style

1. Should offer "optimal challenge with manageable conflict"
2. Should provide a young person an opportunity to exercise initiative and responsibility
3. Should provide the young person with a task that has integrity (i.e., is not "make-work") and thus reinforces the person's sense of dignity
4. Should provide the young person with "a sense of competence and success"
5. Must engage the student in reflection about their experiences (pp. 38–40)

Our review of the research, our own research (Jones, 1986), and our experience as teachers indicate that when teaching methods respond effectively to the student academic needs in Figure 6.1, students' learning is significantly increased and misbehavior is dramatically decreased. When these academic needs are met, students can meet the personal needs that are prerequisite for effective learning. The academic needs focus on providing students with a sense of feeling safe and secure and of developing a sense of competence and efficacy in their school environment. This sense of efficacy and empowerment can be developed by helping students better understand teachers' decisions about the purpose and meaning of instruction, by giving students opportunities to make decisions and set goals, by helping students monitor their own progress, and by creating safe, supportive environments.

The remainder of this chapter examines each of the 13 needs. In many cases, we provide specific methods for responding to a need within the classroom. In some cases, the reader is referred to the next chapter on teaching methods for a detailed look at a method that responds to a particular need. Increasing the degree to which each need is met will increase student motivation and learning. Nevertheless, based on your own teaching situation, you will make important decisions about the specific needs you wish to focus on in order to create a more productive learning environment for your students.

FIGURE 6.2 Highlights of Research on Strategies for Motivating Students to Learn

(The numbers in parentheses are added and refer to the 13 student academic needs in Figure 6.1)

Essential Preconditions
1. Supportive environment (1)
2. Appropriate level of challenge difficulty (2)
3. Meaningful learning objectives (2)
4. Moderation/optimal use

Motivating by Maintaining Success Expectations
5. Program for success (6)
6. Teach goal setting, performance appraisal and self-reinforcement (5, 7)
7. Help students to recognize linkages between effort and outcome (7)
8. Provide remedial socialization (5, 7)

Motivating by Supplying Extrinsic Incentives
9. Offer rewards for good (or improved) performance (8)
10. Structure appropriate competition (8, 10, 12)
11. Call attention to the instrumental value of academic activities (1, 4)

Motivating by Capitalizing on Students' Intrinsic Motivation
12. Adapt tasks to students' interest (5)
13. Induce novelty/variety elements
14. Allow opportunities to make choices or autonomous organizers (6)
15. Provide opportunities for students to respond actively (3)
16. Provide immediate feedback to student responses (7)
17. Allow students to create finished products (10, 11, 13)
18. Include fantasy or simulation elements
19. Incorporate game-like features (3, 4)
20. Include higher-level objectives and divergent questions (13)
21. Provide opportunities to interact with peers (12)

Stimulating Student Motivation to Learn
22. Model interest in learning and motivation to learn (9)
23. Communicate desirable expectations and attributions about students motivation to learn (1, 9)
24. Minimize students' performance anxiety during learning activities (1, 5, 6, 11, 12, 13)
25. Project intensity (9)
26. Project enthusiasm (9)
27. Induce task interest or appreciation (4, 5, 9)
28. Induce curiosity or suspense
29. Induce dissonance or cognitive conflict (1, 10)

30. Make abstract content more personal, concrete or familiar (1, 2, 4, 5, 12, 13)
31. Induce students to generate their own motivation to learn (1, 2, 3, 4, 5, 12, 13)
32. State learning objectives and provide advance decisions (5)
33. Model task-related thinking and problem solving (9)

Understand and Value the Learning Goals

People are more likely to become involved in activities that have a clear goal. You can undoubtedly recall sitting through a meeting that seemed to have no direction or purpose. Compare the feelings generated by this type of situation to those from a meeting in which goals were clearly stated and the activities moved smoothly toward reaching the stated goals. Similarly, children will derive more satisfaction and enjoyment from an activity that has a definite aim. Compare a child who merely bounces a basketball against a wall to the youngster who is shooting baskets. The child will remain involved in the latter activity much longer because it includes a designated goal. Walter Doyle (1983) writes that

> the quality of the time students spend engaged in academic work depends on the tasks they are expected to accomplish and the extent to which students understand what they are doing. It is essential, therefore, that direct instruction include explicit attention to meaning and not simply focus on engagement as an end in itself. (p. 189)

To no one's surprise, research indicates that students ranging from middle-class college students (Bryan & Locke, 1967) to lower-class elementary school children (Kennedy, 1968) achieve better when they are presented with specific learning goals.

Unfortunately, many if not most students do not really understand why they are involved in a learning activity. They study to obtain good grades, please their parents or teacher, or avoid punishment. Research suggests that this lack of understanding and meaning begins early in school. Anderson and her colleagues (1984) interviewed first-grade students about the seatwork they had done. They found that many low-achieving students did not know how to complete the tasks and that few students at any level really understood why they had done them. Nevertheless, rather than ask important questions of the teacher, low-achieving students seemed concerned about completing the assignments and often used rather random methods of completing their tasks. As one first-grader told the researchers, "I don't know what it means, but I did it." (Anderson, Brubaker, Alleman-Brooks, & Duffy, 1984, p. 20). Even though high-achieving students completed the work, they gave little evidence of understanding the purpose of the assignments. They described the purpose of the assignments as "It's just our work" but consistently failed to indicate specific material they were learning or skills they were practicing. In discussing this study, Brophy stated that analysis of the teachers' presentations of assignments to the students suggested that teacher failure to call attention to the purposes and meanings of these assignments was a major reason for the students' low quality of engagement in them. Most presentations included procedural directions or special hints (Pay attention to the underlined words), but only 5 percent explicitly described the purpose of the assignment in terms of the content being taught. (Brophy, 1986, p. 11)

In another study, Rohrkemper and Bershon (1984) asked elementary students to describe what they were thinking about while they completed their assignments. Two of the 49 students mentioned their concern with finishing (perhaps so they could go to recess); 45 were trying to get the right answer; and only 2 mentioned anything related to understanding the content.

We are reminded of a story told by a college student in an introductory education course. During her field experience she observed a second-grade boy spend most of his morning looking out the window. Finally she decided to approach the boy and ask him if she could assist him. The boy said that he knew how to do the work. When she asked why he was not doing it, he pointed to a girl in the next row. "See her," he stated. "She has done nine of these worksheets this morning and when she's done she will get another one. I think I will just take my time." As parents of an elementary school child, we are consistently dismayed at her lack of understanding of the reasons for the material presented in school. However, when provided with clear explanations, she seems interested and able to explain in her own words the reasons for her work.

Unfortunately, this is characteristic not only of elementary students who lack formal operational thinking and thus require considerable assistance in understanding the reason for the work they are asked to complete. For many secondary school students, school becomes a game. As one adolescent stated:

School is just like roulette or something. You can't just ask: Well, what's the point of it? The point of it is to do it, to get through and get into college. But you have to figure the system or you can't win, because the odds are all on the house's side. (Silberman, 1970, pp. 146–147)

It is no surprise that 55 percent of 160,000 teenagers sampled by Norman and Harris for *The Private Life of the American Teenager* (1981) stated that they cheated in school.

At one point we observed an eighth-grade boy working on an English assignment involving selecting adverb phrases embedded in a paragraph. His strategy was to find a phrase, look back at the model, check for similarity, and then, if it matched, write the phrase on his paper. When asked what he was doing, the boy responded, "I have absolutely no idea, but I had better have it done tomorrow when class starts."

These observations are not surprising in light of research on how teachers present learning tasks to students. Brophy and his colleagues (Brophy, Rohrkemper, Rashed, & Goldberger, 1983) examined teacher statements while presenting new assignments in six intermediate classrooms. During the presentation of 165 tasks, not once did a teacher indicate that the task would help the children develop skills that would be useful or enjoyable. In only 3 percent of the introductions did the teachers express personal enthusiasm for the task; in only 3 percent did they relate the material to students' personal lives or interests; and only 1 percent of the task introductions included a statement about the teacher's personal experiences or beliefs that illustrated the importance of the task. In analyzing these teacher presentations of instructional tasks in intermediate-grade mathematics and reading groups, Brophy states:

> The task introductions made by teachers observed in this study probably did not have much impact on student motivation to learn because: a) statements likely to stimulate student motivation to learn did not occur often enough; b) when they did occur, they were usually too short and sketchy to do much good; and c) whatever good they might have done was probably negated by other statements likely to undermine motivation to learn. (Brophy, 1986b, p. 13)

Research suggests that teachers can learn to present clear goal statements associated with comments intended to increase student motivation to learn. In a recent study, Roehler, Duffy, and Meloth (1987) reported that teachers could learn to give students specific explanations concerning the purpose of instructional activities. Results indicated that students taught by these teachers demonstrated significantly greater understanding of and appreciation for the purpose of the instruction.

Understand the Learning Process

Associated with the importance of teachers' clarifying instructional goals and objectives is the concept of teachers' helping students better understand the educational process. In our society, many people view the medical profession as the standard of professionalism. In this profession, the practitioner is almost always seen as having a lot of information that is too sophisticated for the client. Therefore, instead of discussing the process of their diagnosis, many physicians provide the solution or prescription. It is unfortunate that this standard has existed because it provides a model that, while perhaps beneficial in the medical profession, certainly fails to translate to many other professions. The teaching profession is one in which the more the teaching role is demystified and clarified for the clients (students), the better they will be able to care for their own long-term learning needs. The analogy in the medical profession is the area of preventive medicine, in which the idea is to inform clients so they themselves may be involved in maintaining their physical health.

Ideally, students who graduate from high school should be able to pass a university course in educational psychology. Students who for 12 or 13 years have been informed of their teachers' instructional decisions would be well-educated in the learning process. Indeed, the concept that teachers need only subject-matter knowledge might be realistic if students were involved in a learning experience that provided them with excellent information about the learning process. Currently, however, anyone who has taught able college freshmen who are interested in becoming educators knows that even these students know virtually nothing about human learning. They are often either students who have played the school game well and are excited about sharing their excitement with other people or students who believe they were taught ineffectively and wish to provide other people with a higher percentage of effective teaching.

Students' motivation can be increased dramatically by providing them with information about the learning process. Students can learn how individuals differ in their preferred learning style, that different learning tasks are conducive to certain learning outcomes, and that, ideally, teachers select instructional activities to support specific learning outcomes and student learning styles. Following a recent presentation, a veteran high school teacher commented that within one class period it was difficult to use different instructional activities and assignments with students varying in ability because the students complained about doing different work. When asked if he had discussed his thinking and decision about instructional methods with his students, he responded that he had not. The teacher followed the suggestion that he discuss his instructional goals and decisions with the students. Several weeks later he commented that it felt like he had a "new class." He reported that students were more positive and were turning in more work. Furthermore, he reported that students were enthusiastic about his attempts to provide varied instructional methods with different student groups.

In addition to increasing students' motivation, the act of instructing students about the learning process can help teachers improve their instruction. In order to inform students about instructional decisions, we must be clear about these choices. Because many teachers are not skilled at correctly matching instructional methods to learning outcomes (Doyle, 1983), attempting to give students explanations for such choices will provide us with important motivation to develop, and practice, a critical teaching skill. When working with a beginning high school English teacher recently, one of us noticed that the teacher seemed to focus exclusively on factual-level questions. Although students in the upper middle-class school were generally well behaved, students in this class were only moderately attentive and were frequently observed completing work other than English. When asked to describe her learning goals, the teacher listed several higher-level concepts, and she seemed surprised to hear that her instructional methods were not those that could be expected to reach these goals. The teacher was encouraged first to clarify her goals; second to consider learning activities (including altering her questioning strategies) that would facilitate this learning; and finally to share her goals and instructional decisions with students. This procedure proved very helpful to the teacher, and her sophomore students responded enthusiastically to the increased clarity.

In addition to increasing the clarity of learning goals and their relationship to instructional methods, teaching students about the learning process helps teachers evaluate learning more effectively. If we select one learning goal as being able to list concepts from Greek mythology that describe universal human flaws and their influence on history, students know they must go beyond basic story-line facts and incorporate ideas generated in class. We know that evaluation of student learning must involve questions aimed at the concept and generalization level, although these need to be supported by specific facts from the material students have read. This clarity of goals, teaching methods, and the evaluation process make learning less a game of student versus teacher. This cooperation in turn increases students' motivation, reduces students' frustration, and enhances achievement.

The following chapters contain many specific methods for helping students more clearly understand teachers' educational goals and better understand the learning process. For example, Madeline Hunter's ITIP material reviewed in chapter 7 emphasizes clarifying instructional goals. The material on learning styles in chapter 7 can help students better understand the learning process and teachers' instructional decisions. Likewise, the material in chapter 9 on involving students in developing classroom rules, teaching classroom procedures, and clarifying for students the consequences of violating rules and procedures provide specific methods for helping students better understand teachers' decisions in creating an orderly learning environment.

Be Actively Involved in the Learning Process

You have probably been involved in a variety of learning experiences characterized by an almost total lack of learner participation. Over the years we have noticed that teachers-'behavior at faculty meetings often resembles students' behavior that teachers find annoying. We should consider our own response to lack of involvement before punishing the same behavior in students. As George Leonard wrote in *Education and Ecstasy* (1968), "No environment can strongly affect a person unless it is strongly interactive" (p. 39).

When considering the issue of increasing students' involvement in the classroom, it is interesting how limited this involvement actually is. Summarizing his findings on classroom interactions, Flanders (1963) presented the law often called "the rule of two-thirds." His findings indicate that someone is talking during approximately two-thirds of class time, about two-thirds of the talking is done by the teacher, and nearly two-thirds of the talk is spent giving directions, expressing opinions and facts, and criticizing students. Numerous research studies have supported Flanders's finding that the teachers monopolize verbal interchanges in the classroom. Based on observations of first-, sixth-, and eleventh-grade teachers, Adams and Biddle (1970) report that teachers were the dominant factor in 84 percent of classroom interactions. Hudgins and Ahlbrand (1969) report similar findings based on their work in seventh- and ninth-grade classrooms. Studies in both elementary schools (Flanders, 1963) and secondary schools (Bellack, Kliebard, Hyman, & Smith, 1966; Gallagher, 1965) indicate that students often do little more than respond to teachers' factual questions. More recently, Goodlad's (1984) Study of Schooling found that, across all grade levels, teachers talked three times as much as students. Goodlad's study paints a clear picture of uninvolved students who sit listening to the teacher or who are involved in seatwork.

Research also indicates that students' feelings are seldom dealt with in classroom settings. Adams and Biddle (1970) reported that less than .5 percent of verbalizations in the classrooms they studied focused on feelings or interpersonal relations. Similarly, after collecting data in a large number of classrooms, Flanders and Amidon (1967) reported that the acceptance of feelings accounted for only .005 percent of the verbal exchanges in classrooms. Goodlad's (1983a) data support these findings. He concluded that "affect—either positive or negative—was virtually absent. What we observed could only be described as neutral, or perhaps 'flat' is a better adjective" (p. 467).

Summarizing his extensive, systematic study of education in a sample of 38 schools, Goodlad (1983a) writes:

> Teachers appear to teach within a very limited repertoire of pedagogical alternatives, emphasizing their own talk and the monitoring of seatwork. The customary pedagogy places the teacher very much in control. Few activities call for or even permit active student planning, follow-through and evaluation. (p. 467)

Regardless of whether one views learning as based on reinforcement of appropriate responses, modeling, or reconstruction of cognitive concepts, learning will take place only when the learner is actively involved in attempting new skills. Piaget (1977) emphasizes that, especially for young children, learning must involve doing. Children tend to learn what they do rather than what they see or hear.

> Good pedagogy must involve presenting the child with situations in which he himself experiments, in the broadest sense of that term—trying things out to see what happens, manipulating things, manipulating symbols, posing questions and seeking his own answers, reconciling what he finds one time and what he finds at another, comparing his findings with those of other children. (Duckworth, 1964, p. 2)

Studies completed at the Center for Early Adolescence suggest that this age group, along with primary-age children, requires particular emphasis on active participation in the learning process. The *Middle Grades Assessment Program* (Dorman, 1981), designed to help schools for young adolescents assess the effectiveness of their instruction, asks schools to assess the extent to which:

18. Teacher encourages students to ask questions of each other as well as of the teacher.
19. Teacher builds on students' comments and ideas.
30. Students are actively engaged in activities, manipulating materials and objects. They are not just listening.
42. In many classrooms, small groups of students are working independently on projects or assignments.
46. Students and teachers relate what they are learning in class to field trips or visits into the community that they are planning or have completed. (pp. 44–46)

It is interesting to note that during the 1930s a team of educators and psychologists carried out a major study to assess the value of active student involvement in the learning process (Aikin, 1942; Chamberlain, 1942). The program, called The Eight Year Study, involved working with 30 secondary schools dramatically to increase interdisciplinary study and the use of diverse teaching methods such as small groups, cooperative learning, and simulation. The results of the comparison showed that, in college, students from the experimental schools:

1. Earned a slightly higher total grade average;
2. Earned higher grade averages in all subject fields except foreign language;
3. Specialized in the same academic fields as did the comparison students;
4. Did not differ from the comparison group in the number of times they were placed on probation;
5. Received slightly more academic honors in each year;
6. Were more often judged to possess a high degree of intellectual curiosity and drive;
7. Were more often judged to be precise, systematic, and objective in their thinking;
8. Were more often judged to have developed clear or well-formulated ideas concerning the meaning of education—especially in the first two years in college;
9. More often demonstrated a high degree of resourcefulness in meeting new situations;
10. Did not differ from the comparison group in ability to plan their time effectively;

11. Had about the same problems of adjustment as the comparison group, but approached their solutions with greater effectiveness;
12. Participated somewhat more frequently, and more often enjoyed appreciative experiences in the arts;
13. Participated more in all organized student groups except religious and "service" activities;
14. Earned in each college year a higher percentage of non-academic honors (officeship in organizations, election to managerial societies, athletic insignia, leading roles in dramatic and musical presentations);
15. Did not differ from the comparison group in the quality of adjustment to their contemporaries;
16. Differed only slightly from the comparison group in the kinds of judgments about their schooling;
17. Had a somewhat better orientation toward the choice of a vocation;
18. Demonstrated a more active concern for what was going on in the world. (Aikin, 1942, pp. 111–112)

One reality of modern living is that children spend a lot of time watching television. Preschool children watch television for nearly four hours a day, and elementary school children watch as much as six hours a day (Friedrich & Stein, 1973).

By the time a child is 18, he or she has spent 11,000 hours in school—and 15,000 hours watching television. The average 18-year-old has used up the equivalent of more than two full years of his life mummified in front of the TV set. (Torgerson, 1977, p. 4)

This extensive television viewing strongly influences teachers and the educational process. During their many hours in front of the television set, children are passive recipients of information. The medium provides a colorful, diverse, entertaining array of programs aimed at holding children's interest. It is therefore no surprise that we often find it difficult to hold students' attention during passive learning activities. Most teachers do not have the flair, energy, or diversity to match the motivational/entertainment quality to which students have become accustomed. Therefore, it is not surprising that students often tune out while we present material to them. Students have learned by years of turning the television's channel during boring programs or advertisements that it is possible to tune out less-than-interesting input.

Television does provide passive entertainment, but it is not capable of meeting children's needs to be actively and personally involved in the learning process. Students may often become bored and restless during periods of passive learning; conversely, they can become stimulated and intense when actively and emotionally involved in their own learning. When lessons require passive learning, they should be short and interesting. Misbehavior is also significantly less during lessons that involve students in using higher levels of cognitive skills, incorporate students' feelings, and relate material to their own lives.

The curriculum can be a positive force in classroom control. As a matter of fact the most constructive approach to discipline is through the curriculum. Learning that is interesting and provides a sense of growing power and accomplishment is the best means of classroom control. (Tanner, 1978, p. 43)

Robert White's (1959) theory of competence motivation and DeCharms's (1968, 1976) work relating this theory to the educational setting further emphasize the importance of actively involving students in the learning process. These writers report that individuals seek to control their own behavior and to resist consistent external control over their behavior. DeCharms's major thesis is that students who are involved in directing their own learning will produce better work and will enjoy their work more than will students who are merely responding obediently in order to receive reinforcement. DeCharms (1976) writes that schools should provide children with small but real choices and that this effort should be associated with adults' expectations that students will act responsibly.

Rotter's (1954, 1966) theory and research, related to locus of control, reinforces the concept that students should be meaningfully involved in the learning process. Students who possess an internal locus of control believe that their own efforts determine their success or failure, and external locus of control students believe that outside forces have a major influence on outcomes. Research indicates that students who possess an internal locus of control are more likely to achieve academic success. Furthermore, studies (Bar-Tal, Bar-Tal, & Leinhardt, 1975; Chandler, 1975; Chapin & Dyck, 1976; Fowler & Peterson, 1981) indicate that children can develop an internal locus of control by being involved in learning environments in which they are provided with responsibility and choice.

Teachers can increase active student involvement in the learning process in many ways. Chapter 7 presents a number of methods, including (1) cooperative learning, (2) 4-MAT lesson planning, (3) individual goal setting and data recording, and (4) peer tutoring. The methods for summarizing lessons present in chapter 8 provide additional suggestions.

Relate Subject Matter to Their Own Lives

Unfortunately, students all too often do not view their schoolwork as pertaining to their needs or interests, and consequently experience feelings similar to those just described. This situation may be intensified for students who find that they have difficulty understanding the material. Consider how you would feel if you were required to take a course in advanced biochemistry or quantum theory. It is likely that your frustration over the irrelevance of the subject to your life would be compounded by your inadequacies in understanding the material. Many children experience similar frustration and impotence as they struggle to learn material that seems neither related to their lives nor within their ability to master. Examining the reasons for school failure, William Glasser (1969) describes this factor poignantly.

With increasing frequency from grade one through the end of graduate school, much of what is required is either totally or partially irrelevant to the world around them as they see it. Thus both excess memorization and increasing irrelevance cause them to withdraw into failure or strike out. (p. 30)

McClelland's theory and subsequent research on achievement motivation (McClelland, Atkinson, Clark, & Lowell, 1953; McClelland & Alschuler, 1971) suggests that individuals will be more highly motivated to achieve if they can be shown how their efforts relate to their everyday lives. Ausubel's (1968) concept of the value of meaningful learning supports the importance of relating subject matter to pertinent issues in students' lives. When the material being learned cannot be related to existing cognitive structures, retention is limited (Dooling & Mullet, 1973). Stinchcombe (1964) concisely states the results associated with learning that fails to relate to students' lives:

> When a student realizes that he does not achieve status increment from improved current performance, current performance loses meaning. The student becomes hedonistic because he does not visualize achievement of long-run goals through current self-restraint. He reacts negatively to a conformity that offers nothing concrete. He claims autonomy from adults because their authority does not promise him a satisfactory future. (Stinchcombe, 1964, pp. 5, 6)

If we want students to remember information, we must help them to relate the information to some meaningful event or idea in their lives. It is much more difficult initially to learn and retain nonsense syllables than it is to learn meaningful information. Material is forgotten not because the brain fails to retain the information, but because the information is not retrievable due to interference from other associations that are more accurate, important, or relevant. "Frequent quizzes and oral questions may be effective . . . for short-term memory but inefficient for long-term retention. Making the subject intrinsically interesting, however, is even more attractive" (Walberg, 1988, p. 79).

That students' motivation, learning, and retention are enhanced by relating material to events within their lives is certainly a major reason for ensuring that subject matter meets this criterion. It is equally important to realize, however, that if children are to develop the skills that will enable them sensitively to operate a democratic social system, they need to have more than just the knowledge of facts. They need to know how to make decisions about current issues and how to weigh values against facts. This wisdom is not learned through an education that is based primarily on memorization and an emphasis on improving scores on standardized tests. Rather, it is learned by applying knowledge to meaningful issues in children's lives. Philosopher John Dewey stated this concept clearly:

> What avail is it to win prescribed amounts of information about geography and history, to win ability to read and write, if in the process the individual loses his own soul: loses his appreciation of things worth while, of the values to which they are relative; if he loses desire to apply what he has learned and, above all, loses the ability to extract meaning from his future experiences as they occur? (Dewey, 1963, p. 50)

In his examination of the impact of demographic changes on education and its implications for an increasing number of at-risk students in our schools, Hodgkinson (1985) highlights the importance of helping students understand the relationship between their schoolwork and the world outside school. In commenting about successful dropout programs he noted, "When the relation between education and work becomes clear, most of these potential drop-outs can be motivated to stay in school and perform at a higher level" (p. 12). Several sections in chapter 7 provide specific methods for more clearly relating subject matter to students' lives.

Take Responsibility for Their Own Learning by Setting Goals and/or Following Their Own Interests

Student motivation and learning are significantly enhanced when students understand teacher-developed learning goals, the reasons for these goals, and the possible application of the learning. In addition, however, an impressive body of research indicates that student learning is also enhanced when students have an opportunity to be involved in selecting learning material and establishing learning goals. Students need opportunities to delve into topics they find exciting and interesting. Anyone who has worked with students has seen and been impressed by the energy and enthusiasm they display when searching for information associated with a topic they find interesting. Similarly, we have, on numerous occasions, been amazed by the extent and sophistication of students' knowledge of these self-chosen topics. Although it may not be in the students' best interest to allow them to learn only about topics of their own choosing, it is equally if not more destructive to fail to reinforce and support their self-initiated inquiries.

It is interesting that, after reading the autobiographies and biographies of 400 of the most famous people of the twentieth century, Goertzel and Goertzel (1962) commented that nearly 60 percent of these people experienced major school problems, and many intensely disliked school. It is probable that many school problems these individuals experienced were related to the schools' demand for conformity and reinforcement of learning unrelated to students' special interests. Torrance (1960), a leading researcher in creativity in the schools, stated that schools tend to suppress creativity in order to increase conformity.

One probable factor leading to students' decreased satisfaction with school as they progress through the grades (Flanders, Morrison, & Brode, 1968) is that students learn that they must study what they are told rather than what interests them. Morris (1978) provides a similar analysis:

> The reasons for this are complex. However, the drop might be minimized by a careful examination and involvement of children's interests (not what teachers think children's interests are) in the curriculum. (Morris, 1978, p. 242)

William Glasser (1969) reflected on this view of school instruction and its influence on students' motivation and behavior: "Both excess memorization and increasing irrelevance cause them to withdraw into failure or strike out in delinquent acts" (p. 30).

Swift and Spivack (1975) present a similar prescription for teaching at-risk students:

> Relating children's interests and ideas to classroom activities is probably a useful procedure for all children. However, for inattentive youngsters such an interplay of interest and classroom

is paramount for decreasing the distraction caused by preoccupation with thoughts, ideas, interests, or activities which pull their attention away from the classroom. (Swift & Spivack, 1975, p. 21)

In an interesting study, Asher and Markell (1974) found that even though fifth-grade girls were much better readers than boys when reading low-interest materials, boys read as well as girls when both were given high-interest material.

Students' motivation to learn seems related to their sense of feeling in control of the learning environment. Deci, Nezlek, and Sheinman (1981) report that students in classrooms in which teachers are less controlling score higher on intrinsic motivation. Pascarella, Walberg, Junker, and Haertel (1981) found that greater control over the learning environment is associated with greater interest in subject matter.

DeCharms (1984) presents the concept of personal causation as a way to explain the impact that choice has on student behavior and learning. He compares the experience of being a pawn and feeling externally controlled and pushed around to that of being an origin and feeling in control of one's actions. DeCharms states that students who feel more like origins will experience greater intrinsic motivation that, as mentioned earlier, appears to be associated with greater learning gains. Notice the similarity between this concept and Glasser's (1988) statement that most behavior problems in schools are caused by students' sense of a lack of power.

Mahoney (1974) found that students enjoy school more and achieve better when they are allowed to make choices during their school day. Several additional studies support the value of providing students with a sense of choice and control over the learning environment. Matheny and Edwards (1974) evaluated the impact of increasing students' choices and responsibility for learning in 25 classrooms in grades 1 through 7. Teachers were provided with inservice training to (1) allow students more choice in deciding when assignments would be completed, (2) have students score their own work, (3) use individual conferences with students to evalaute progress, (4) develop learning centers, and (5) use learning contracts with students. The results indicated that teacher implementation of these strategies was associated with higher student reading gains and increased student perception of controlling their learning outcomes.

In two interesting studies, DeCharms (1976, 1984) involved teachers of sixth- and seventh-grade minority students in setting their own goals and making decisions about how to reach these goals. A major emphasis was on students' feeling a sense of personal responsibility for meeting or failing to meet their goals. Results of these studies indicate that student achievement gains were greater for students in the goal-setting classes than in the control group and that despite the fact that no followup interventions occurred during the following years, students in the experimental group continued to have a higher achievement rate and had a higher rate of graduation from high school. Similar results have been found when providing a similar experience to mainstreamed handicapped high school students (Maher, 1987). Wlodkowski (1978) mentioned several benefits associated with academic goal setting:

> The advantage of this method is that it brings the future into the present and allows the student to become aware of what it is necessary to do in order to have a successful learning experience. . . . With the goal-setting model, the student knows that she/he is in command and can

calculate what to do to avoid wasting time or experiencing self-defeat. Thus, before even beginning the learning task, the student knows that his/her effort will be worthwhile and has an actual sense that there is a good probability for success. (p. 54)

Bandura suggests that goal setting is particularly effective when students set achievable, short-term, or proximal goals. Bandura and Schunk (1981) used three different types of goal structures with three groups of elementary students involved in completing subtraction problems. One group was asked to complete one set of problems each session (proximal goal); one group was told to complete all seven sets by the end of the sessions; and one group was provided with no statement concerning a goal. Students presented with a specific, short-term goal scored highest on motivation and subtraction skills, whereas students given a long-term goal scored no better than students presented with no goal at all.

One important caveat related to goal setting involves the important distinction between learning goals and performance goals (Dweck, 1986). Students who focus on learning goals view the purpose of studying to gain competence in specific skills, whereas students who focus on performance goals seek to obtain rewards and positive judgments about their work. Students who focus on learning goals tend to persist when confronted with failure and tend to compare their work less with other students because their goal is to improve their own ability (Nichols, 1984). Students who focus on performance goals, however, become easily discouraged. Therefore, when setting goals it is important for teachers to help students establish specific individualized goals while emphasizing the interest and practical value of the material being mastered.

The concept of student responsibility and choice does not mean that students should be provided with a shopping-mall approach to education. Rather, it suggests that throughout the school day students benefit from being involved in making decisions about what aspects of the content they will emphasize or how they will study materials adults have deemed meaningful. The ways to provide students with a sense of choice and control over the learning environment generally fall into the categories of choice about (1) what material to work on, (2) when work will be accomplished, (3) how it will be completed, (4) the level of difficulty of the assignment, (5) self-correcting and self-monitoring of work, and (6) individual goal setting. Many sections in chapters 7, 9, 10, and 11 provide specific methods for enhancing students' sense of control by using these techniques. Sections in chapter 7 focus on incorporating students' interests, academic goal setting, self-evaluation, and learning centers; chapter 9 offers material on establishing rules; chapter 10 presents the problem-solving methods; and chapter 11 presents the self-monitoring and curriculum of responsibility contract.

Experience Success

None of us enjoys being in a setting in which we consistently fail. Most adults can recall situations in which they responded to failure by dropping an activity and attempting something at which they were more adept. To a large degree, this behavior was influenced by the need to view oneself as competent. Success experiences are instrumental in developing feelings of self-worth and confidence in attempting new activities.

It is through achievement that academic self-confidence grows, and increased confidence in turn promotes achievement through inspiring further learning. In short, confidence and competence must increase together for either to prosper. When they do not grow apace, students are likely to suffer. (Covington & Beery, 1976, p. 5)

Teacher-effectiveness research suggests that students' learning is increased when they experience high rates of success in completing tasks. When the teacher is available to monitor and assist students, success rates of 70 to 80 percent are desirable (Brophy & Evertson, 1976). When students are expected to work on their own, success rates of 95 to 100 percent are desirable (Fisher et al., 1980). Studies suggest that when students are given inappropriate tasks, the tasks are much more likely to be too difficult than too easy (Fisher et al., 1980; Gambrell, Wilson, & Gantt, 1981; Jorgenson, 1977).

Following successful experiences, individuals tend to raise their expectations and set higher goals, whereas failure is met with lowered aspirations (Diggory, 1966). Success or failure also influences individuals' self-evaluations (Wylie, 1961). Studies also indicate that praising students' work produces greater performance gains than does criticism (Costello, 1964; Page, 1958) and that the positive effects in self-rating and performance tend to spread to areas related to those in which praise was provided for success experience (Maehr, 1976).

Students who have a history of school failure and are concerned about future failure are at a distinct disadvantage. Tobias (1979) suggests that highly anxious students divide their attention between the material being taught and their concerns about failure, or being criticized or embarrassed. These students are involved in a downward spiral because they miss considerable amounts of information due to their anxiety (Hill & Wigfield, 1984). Covington has characterized this situation as a "double-edged sword." If these students try, they look stupid. However, if they do not try, they are viewed negatively by the teacher. The power associated with preventing feelings of humiliation and incompetence is supported by the fact that many students choose a teacher's frustration and criticism about their behavior rather than risk another academic failure (Covington, Spratt, & Omelich, 1980).

Students who experience a low rate of school success are more likely to have an external locus of control. Students who believe that their past failures were caused by lack of ability are less likely to anticipate future success and are therefore less likely to exert effort (Bar-Tal, 1979). In extreme cases, this can lead to learned helplessness, in which the students feel that nothing that they do matters. Students who can be helped to establish higher expectations and a sense of personal control in the learning environment will make greater gains in achievement. These gains can be accomplished by providing students with opportunities for success in small steps, by setting specific learning goals, and by having students monitor and chart their own progress. They then can see that even though they may not be in the top 50 percent compared to their peers, they are making significant personal progress.

If we fail to provide students with activities in which they can succeed, we should expect that they will withdraw or act out. Because children have a basic need to experience a sense of competence, they will reject settings and activities that attest to their failure and will, instead, become involved in activities at which they can be successful. These alternative behaviors often include actions adults consider unproductive. Such actions, however, are often merely attempts to display competence and receive acknowledgment in the only way a student has found successful.

Methods presented in chapter 7 that can help students experience higher rates of success include cooperative learning, setting individual goals, evaluting one's own learning, peer tutoring, and effective teacher monitoring and reteaching.

Receive Realistic and Immediate Feedback That Enhances Self-Efficacy

Closely associated with the need for success experiences is the need to receive immediate and specific feedback. Because students care about being successful, it is important that they receive feedback clearly designating the extent to which they have succeeded at a task. Several studies (Burrows, 1973; Collins, 1971) show that students' achievement is enhanced by providing them with information about their current level of performance (based on results of diagnostic tests), followed by specific learning tasks aimed at mastering the material.

In fact, students most concerned about failing are most in need of immediate feedback; without it, they tend to judge their performance as unacceptable (Meunier & Rule, 1967). Page (1958) found that supportive comments, accompanied by statements about specific strengths and weaknesses in students' work, were more effective in improving students' performance than were either grades or brief positive comments. Butler and Nisan (1986) compared student responses to papers with either substantive comments and no grade or grades with no comments. Students who received comments more frequently stated that they (1) found the task more interesting, (2) worked on the task because they were interested in the material, and (3) attributed their success on the task to their interest and effort.

The quality of feedback is important because it affects students' perceptions of themselves as learners. Stipek (1988) stresses the importance of students receiving feedback that helps them see their progress: "Unless students actually perceive themselves to be making process in acquiring skills or new knowledge, they will not feel efficacious, even if they are rewarded for their efforts and even if their performance is better than others" (p. 94).

Not all feedback is effective in improving students' performance. Studies show that hostile or extensive criticism creates negative attitudes and lowers achievement, creativity, and classroom control (Brophy & Evertson, 1976; Dunkin & Biddle, 1974; Flanders, 1970; Rosenshine, 1976). Praise is often overused and is not a powerful reinforcer for many children (Brophy, 1981; Ware, 1978). Praise can be an effective form of feedback when it provides students with specific information about the quality of their work and the effort made to complete the work. Praise is, however, often misused. Teachers frequently praise incorrect answers (Anderson, Evertson, & Brophy, 1979; Mehan, 1974), and this false praise is more often given to lower-achieving students (Brookover et al., 1978; Kleinfeld, 1975; Weinstein, 1976). "To the extent that praise is important, the key to its effectiveness lies in its quality rather than its frequency. Effective teachers know both when and how to praise" (Good & Brophy, 1984, p. 193).

Rosenholtz and Simpson (1984) examined classroom variables that affect how students view their ability. They categorize classrooms as unidimensional (creating a sense that ability is a stable characteristic and in which students know who has and does not have ability) and multidimensional (in which ability is not nearly as stratified). In unidimensional classrooms, feedback is provided in such a way that students can easily compare their work with others. For example, charts indicating the level of student performance are placed on the walls, and exemplary work and the names of students whose work is missing or needs redoing are prominently displayed. These authors suggest that to encourage students to see ability as a trait or factor that is flexible and related to effort, teachers should make feedback and evaluation a more private matter.

Effective feedback provides students with important benchmarks. It enables students better to understand where they are in relation to achieving goals, the amount of progress they have made toward a goal, and what they need to do to continue or improve on their progress. Effective feedback also communicates that the teacher believes the student can reach predetermined goals, that the student's effort is a major factor influencing the outcome, and that how a student's progress compares to that of other students is not a major factor.

The material on praise in chapter 2 provides helpful hints on how to apply positive feedback effectively to enhance student motivation. The section in chapter 8 on providing useful feedback and evaluation and the section on goal setting in chapter 7 offer additional suggestions for increasing student motivation by meeting this academic need.

Receive Appropriate Rewards for Performance Gains

"Rewards are one proven way to motivate students to put forth effort, especially when the rewards are offered in advance as incentives for striving to reach specified levels of performance" (Good & Brophy, 1987, p. 319). Rewards are obviously not needed for tasks that have a high degree of intrinsic appeal based on the pleasure of the task or the obvious utility value associated with the task, but they are sometimes necessary to stimulate effort on tasks a student finds difficult or tedious. Consider your own behavior when facing a task that holds little intrinsic value—such as marking a series of exams, balancing a checkbook, or scrubbing the floor. You perhaps enhance your motivation to complete such tasks by determining some form of reinforcer that will be available on completion of the task. Because students have limited access to or control over such reinforcers within the school environment, it is sometimes necessary for us to provide them.

Anyone who has taken an introductory psychology class is familiar with the benefits of reinforcers. Events that are followed by a reinforcer trend to be repeated; this fact has obvious application for educators. Students who are struggling in school and obtain few of the more natural reinforcers associated with academic achievement (grades, teacher praise, status and its associated privileges, enhanced self-esteem) often require an external reinforcer to stimulate their initial involvement in important academic activities. For more than two decades, special educators have realized the value of this concept and have used reinforcements to motivate student interest in learning activities. These specialists as well as regular classroom teachers have, for example, found that contracts that provide students with incentives for specific behaviors can have dramatic positive effects on students' on-task behavior and achievement gains.

When considering the value of rewards for performance gains, however, educators need to consider several important problems associated with the use of rewards. First, more than 75 published studies indicate that external rewards can reduce intrinsic interest in a task (Morgan, 1984). Children who receive a reward for participating in an activity frequently show less interest in the activity. Therefore, rewards should be used only when other attempts such as altering the approach to presenting the material, individual goal setting, and other motivational and instructional strategies have failed. Good and Brophy (1987) summarize this concern:

> Extrinsic motivational strategies can be effective in certain circumstances, but teachers should not rely on them too heavily. If students are preoccupied with rewards or competition, they may not pay as much attention as they should to what they are supposed to be learning and may not appreciate its value. The quality of task engagement and ultimately the quality of performance or achievement are highest when students perceive themselves to be engaged in a task for their own reasons (intrinsic motivation) than when they perceive themselves to be engaged in order to please an authority figure, obtain a reward, escape punishment, or respond to some other extrinsic motivational pressure. (p. 322)

We are particularly concerned when we see teachers unknowingly use reinforcement in their daily manner of instruction. For example, teachers often make such statements as, "You can use the learning center when you finish the work"; "If you finish we will go outside." These comments send a message that learning is not motivating and requires reinforcement to encourage engagement. When this message becomes inculcated into a teacher's way of talking to students it is likely that the children learn more from this than from teacher statements about the value of the material. This result seems particularly likely given teachers' low rates of statements concerning the value of academic work (Brophy & Kher, 1986).

A second issue concerning rewards is that they appear to be most useful when they simultaneously reinforce performance and provide feedback about mastery of the material (Bandura, 1982; Lepper, 1981; Deci, 1975). Lepper (1981) states that rewards used to obtain control (e.g., "do what I say and you will be rewarded") tend to reduce intrinsic motivation. However, when rewards are provided based on a student's reaching a designated performance criterion (e.g., "let's agree on a goal and when you reach this you will be rewarded"), they are less likely to undermine interest. Nevertheless, as suggested by reinforcement theory, even this is dependent on the student's being able to obtain the reward. Rewards that are offered but not obtained have a negative impact on motivation and effort.

Chapter 11 offers specific methods for using rewards to enhance student performance and improve student behavior. The bibliography at the end of chapter 11 cites additional sources that emphasize this approach to motivation.

View Learning Modeled by Adults as an Exciting and Rewarding Activity

As mentioned in chapter 3, teachers possess many characteristics that make their behavior likely to be modeled. Therefore, teachers should carefully consider how they model an interest in and excitement about learning. Brophy (1987) lists 33 strategies for motivating students to learn. Four of these support the value of effective teacher modeling: (1) model interest in learning and motivation to learn, (2) project intensity, (3) project enthusiasm, and (4) model task-related thinking and problem solving.

During a workshop presented by one of the authors while writing this chapter, a group of middle-school teachers were asked about their approaches to beginning lessons. A number of the teachers admitted that they showed little enthusiasm when introducing lessons. They listed such comments as "OK, it's Monday again, let's get going," "Here we go again," and "Turn to page 185" as their introductory comments. In further discussing ways to interest students in learning, these teachers listed several factors involving teacher modeling, including making positive statements about their own learning activities, their positive and supportive reactions to students' questions, whether they model learning in the school setting, and their reactions to students' comments about learning. For example, teachers can mention books they are reading, plays they attended, courses they have taken, or new learning experiences, such as learning to repair an electrical outlet or build a piece of furniture.

We are consistently impressed with how frequently students are surprised that teachers continue to take courses and be involved in the learning process. This seems to suggest that many students see learning as a task assigned to young people and relatively unrelated to the practical world. One of the authors recalls a junior high school student who expressed surprise that the author had a small library of education books in his classroom. The student asked many questions about the books and eventually read most of them, frequently stopping by after school to discuss the content with the author.

Teachers can also model positive attitudes about learning by how they respond to student questions. Questions can be addressed with enthusiasm, curiosity, and interest. A teacher might say, "That's an interesting question, I'd never thought about that aspect of it," or "I don't know the answer to that but it is an interesting question. Would you be willing to look into that and share with us what you find?" Students benefit from seeing that teachers enjoy the learning process and are stimulated by new ideas.

Teachers can model the excitement of learning as well as the intellectual openness and rigor associated with meaningful learning by expressing interest and enthusiasm in answering students' tough questions or critical comments about content and instruction. Students often ask why material has to be learned or comment about the lack of value in the information being studied. Teachers can accept these as important comments and questions and an opportunity to relate learning to students' lives, can discuss why they have made a curricular or instructional decision, and can present ways the student can think about the learning process. One of the authors recently heard a teacher respond to the question of why Shakespeare was being studied by stating that the material had been listed in the course description and the students had signed up for the course. Another teacher presented with this challenge might say, "That is an important question that needs to be addressed before we delve into studying this material." In addition, the teacher could involve the class in working in small groups to develop a list of why Shakespeare is studied. This activity could be followed by a discussion of how curricular materials are selected or why the teacher believes this material has value to students in the 1990s.

Experience a Safe, Well-Organized Learning Environment

Given the number of students who come from home environments characterized by a lack of support, safety, and consistency, it is imperative that teachers develop clear expectations about student behavior and academic performance. These expectations should include the statement that the teacher will fulfill her or his responsibility to ensure that other students will not interfere with a student's right to feel safe, supported, and able to learn in a calm learning environment. Students also need to understand how the classroom will operate, how problems will be resolved, and how they will be involved in influencing classroom structures—including curricular and instructional decisions.

Interestingly, Fagot (1973) and Hamilton and Gordon (1978) found that preschool children persisted less on tasks if their teachers were extremely directive and intrusive. Stipek (1988) makes this important point about teachers' efforts to structure the learning environment:

> The point is not that children should not be helped. Rather, help needs to be given in a way that enables students to complete tasks on their own. A poor product completed on one's own may contribute more to self-confidence and intrinsic motivation to attempt similar tasks in the future than a good product for which the student cannot take responsibility. (p. 64)

One way teachers can provide productive structure is by helping students better understand and be more prepared for test situations. When students see tests as powerful measures of their abilities and competence, low achievers are likely to withdraw and students who define their value in terms of school success may be extremely anxious. Teachers can increase the motivation of low achievers and minimize the anxiety of all students by helping students view tests as temporary measures of knowledge acquisition that help the teacher and students make decisions about future methods, materials, and behaviors. Teachers can also minimize time limits placed on test taking and can help students learn how to manage stress in test situations and how to take tests effectively. Student goal setting and self-recording of learning gains can also provide structure that can make tests and other learning activities less threatening. The skilled teacher balances the value of structure in creating a safe, clearly understood classroom environment with the costs associated with too much teacher dominance or control. Chapter 9 presents methods for creating well-structured classrooms. Chapters 10–12 offer methods for increasing classroom order and safety by helping students modify their unproductive behavior.

Have Time to Integrate Learning

The school provides a busy and varied environment. During the day students may learn a new concept in math, master several new spelling words, discuss a new concept in social studies, sing a new song, complete a science experiment, and be involved in numerous social interactions in the classroom, in the lunchroom, and on the playground. This diversity and fast pace will often be stimulating and interesting, but it also presents a real problem to many if not all students. Students need time to integrate the new ideas they encounter.

In his work on how learning occurs, Jean Piaget (1952, 1970) points to the fact that the learner must take new information and either assimilate the material into existing cognitive structures or create new structures by accommodation. Piaget writes that, because the learner is actively involved in this restructuring, learning requires considerable time and energy.

Students need time during the school day to slow down and integrate what they have learned. All too often students are rushed from one activity to another, with no time allotted for summarizing the learning that has taken place in each activity. When this hurry occurs, students begin to feel confused and often experience a sense of failure, for they frequently have not understood what it was they were supposed to have learned from the preceding activity. As teachers, we are often lulled into believing that everyone has understood because several of our students who learn quickly indicate that the material has been learned and understood. Students learn at varying rates, however, and in different ways, and it is important to slow down and provide all students with an opportunity to organize the new ideas that have been presented. Effective teachers develop specific instructional activities designed to help students summarize new learning and relate this new knowledge to previous and future learning and the students' own lives.

Have Positive Contact with Peers

The need to interact with peers is an academic need as well as an important personal and psychological need. Piaget (1952) writes that social interactions are important in influencing learning. Numerous studies have supported this contention. Studies comparing the amount of learning that takes place when students work together, as opposed to working individually, indicate that initial learning, retention, and transfer of concepts tend to be higher when cooperative learning is used (Davis, Laughlin, & Komorita, 1976; Johnson & Johnson, 1987; Johnson, Johnson, & Johnson-Holubec, 1988). Students also seem to enjoy working together, and this approach to learning promotes positive attitudes toward instructional activities and subject areas (Dunn & Goldman, 1966; Wheeler & Ryan, 1973). In discussing the positive effects of cooperative learning, David Johnson, one of the leading researchers in the field, writes:

> The more cooperative students' attitudes and experiences, the more they see themselves as being intrinsically motivated, persevering in pursuit of clearly defined learning goals, believing it is their own efforts that determine school success, wanting to be good students and get good grades, and believing that ideas, feelings, and learning new ideas are important and positive. (Johnson, 1979, p. 151)

As discussed in chapter 2 and expanded on in chapter 5, creating positive peer relationships also appears to meet a basic personal need that serves as a prerequisite to productive involvement in the learning process (Lewis & St. John, 1974; Schmuck & Schmuck, 1983). This evidence makes it somewhat surprising to find that peer work groups are rare in U.S. schools (Clements, 1983; Goodlad, 1984; Stodolsky, 1983). Anyone who has worked with students knows that they find their peers to be perhaps the most consistently interesting aspect of the school environment. Educators can choose either to attempt to squelch the energy inherent in this interest or to channel this energy toward their learning goals.

Have Instruction Matched to Students' Level of Cognitive and Skill Development and Learning Style

Even though we recognize that the personal and academic needs described throughout this chapter apply to all children, we must also be aware that children differ considerably in their levels of cognitive development and learning styles. On the issue of teachers' responding to differences in students' achievement and ability levels, Deborah Stipek (1988) writes:

The educational implications of this principle are simple to state, but difficult to put into practice. Each child must be given tasks that are hard enough to require some effort and to result in increased competency, but easy enough to be completed with no more than a modest amount of assistance. . . .

The importance of tasks being matched to each child's skill level cannot be overemphasized. This is necessary for intrinsic motivation, and it is necessary for learning. As difficult a principle as this is to implement, it is the most important principle of motivation and learning. (pp. 55, 57)

Teachers who use the same instructional methods with every student or who use a limited range of instructional activities will create a situation in which some students become frustrated, experience failure, and respond by misbehaving.

Cognitive Development

Piaget's theories on the sequential stages of cognitive development suggest that teachers should consider the complexity of the subject matter as compared with students' current level of cognitive development. Piaget also presented the important concept that students construct knowledge. Therefore, when considering the concepts to be presented and the degree of abstractness with which they can be discussed, we should constantly monitor the degree to which students are able to understand and generalize—rather than merely mimic—the material being taught.

Figure 6.3 indicates the variability in cognitive development among students at each age from 5 to 18. The data indicate that fewer than one-quarter of 13-year-olds have reached even the onset of formal operational thought—the ability to consider abstract concepts apart from concrete examples. Consider the typical junior high school English, social studies,

FIGURE 6.3 Distribution of Percentages of Children at Piagetian Stages

Age (years)	Preoperational (%)	Concrete onset (%)	Concrete mature (%)	Formal onset (%)	Formal mature (%)
5	85	15			
6	60	35	5		
7	35	55	10		
8	25	55	20		
9	15	55	30		
10	12	52	35	1	
11	6	49	40	5	
12	5	32	51	12	
13	2	34	44	14	6
14	1	32	43	15	9
15	1	14	53	19	13
16	1	15	54	17	13
17	3	19	47	19	12
18	1	15	50	15	19

From Herman T. Epstein, Cognitive growth and development. *Colorado Journal of Educational Research*, 1979, *19*, 35. Reprinted by permission.

or math class that presents a wide range of abstract material without using concrete learning activities or relating material to students' own experience. When presented with material related to historical events or literary and mathematical abstractions, few seventh or eighth graders can truly understand the material. Though some higher-achieving students can provide correct answers to abstract questions, many of them do not understand what they have learned.

Toepfer (1979) offers evidence that many students with tested high IQs who have achieved well during the elementary school years experience school failure during early adolescence because the material is too abstract for them to comprehend. Unfortunately, his data suggest that many of these potentially fine students began to develop a sense of school failure and inadequacy during the sensitive early adolescent years and become behavior problems and dropouts. Dembo (1977) describes the key relationship between instruction and cognitive development:

> A teacher who uses the best textbooks available and develops the most interesting and stimulating lesson plans can still fail to reach a majority of students in his class who do not have the necessary structures (operations) to enable them to "understand" the presented material. This means that the classroom teacher must be able to (1) assess a child's level of cognitive development, and (2) determine the type of abilities the child needs to understand the subject matter. (p. 273)

Learning Style

In addition to attending to students' current level of cognitive development, teachers can increase students' motivation and success by responding effectively to students' learning styles. Students differ in their approaches to learning. Every student has a cognitive or learning style that represents the general approach he or she takes to learning and organizing material (Sigel & Coop, 1974). Reisman (1964) writes that teachers too often examine students' failure by considering personal and social problems and do not focus on the child's learning style and determine the best approach to providing instruction.

Research (deHirsch, Jansky, & Langford, 1966; Dunn & Dunn, 1987) suggests that students' learning can be enhanced by providing them with material that enables them to use the sensory modality with which they are most comfortable. Students also differ in their pace of learning (Kagan, Moss, & Siegel, 1963; Shumsky, 1968). In addition, Bernard (1973) comments that, though teachers have generally been aware of students' individual needs in amount of time needed to complete various tasks, they have generally ignored other aspects of students' learning styles. For example, several authors (Ramirez & Castaneda, 1974; Witkin & Moore, 1974) suggest that students differ according to whether they depend on personalized, social factors in learning (field-dependent students) or on more impersonal, abstract factors (field-independent students). Ramirez and Castaneda (1974) suggest that field-independent students are less concerned about relationships within the classroom and prefer abstract material. They enjoy independent work and competition. Conversely, field-dependent students seek teacher and peer approval and want learning material to be concrete and related to their own interests. Students also differ on such factors as their ability to attend to relevant cues and ignore inappropriate stimuli (Hagen & Hale, 1972), to accept new ideas and surroundings (Messick, 1970; Sperry, 1972), and the ability to reflect on questions before responding (Kagan, 1966; Messick, 1970). Artley (1981) reviewed many of the major techniques used in reading instruction during the past 80 years. He reports that all programs help the reading problems some students have, while at the same time creating (or at least failing to respond to) the difficulties other students experience.

Extensive research conducted by Rita Dunn and her colleagues provides support for the studies cited in the previous paragraph. Dunn's research demonstrates that a variety of elements differentially affect individuals' learning. Figure 6.4, a chart designed by Kenneth and Rita Dunn, demonstrates these variables or elements. Dunn (1983; Dunn & Dunn, 1987) reports various studies demonstrating that allowing students to work in classroom settings in which environmental, physical, and sociological factors were similar to those preferred by the student dramatically enhances student learning.

For example, studies, primarily by doctoral students working with Rita Dunn (Dunn & Dunn, 1987), suggest that many students learn material more effectively and score higher on tests when allowed to sit on comfortable materials rather than at standard desks and when allowed to work in noisy environments, and that some students, especially elementary children, learn more effectively and are less fidgity in low rather than in bright lights. In one study, half of all seventh-grade students in one junior high school learned more effectively when allowed to move about during learning activities. Student learning can also be enhanced by allowing students to eat when they need to, study material at a time of day best suited to their learning preference, and learn through modalities they prefer. Chapter 7 presents a number of methods teachers can use to respond to students' learning preferences within the context of regular classroom operation.

Researchers including Anthony Gregorc (1982), David Kolb (1978), Joseph Renzulli (1978, 1983), and Bernice McCarthy (1987; McCarthy, Leflar, & McNamara, 1987) categorized individual learning styles and found that when instructional methods match students' learning-style preference, student achievement is significantly enhanced. McCarthy developed the 4-MAT system, a cycle of learning that identifies four distinct styles of learning and four matching instructional roles that facilitate learning for each learning style. Figure 6.5 presents a model of learning styles based on these researchers' findings.

As discussed in chapter 7, McCarthy does not suggest that teachers need to individualize each lesson in order to incorporate the learning-style preference of each learner. Learning-style theory and research do suggest, however, that students will be more highly motivated and will learn significantly more when instructional methods are diversified so that opportunities exist for all learners to be regularly involved in instructional activities that emphasize their own learning-style preference.

It is interesting but not surprising that students can provide useful information about how they learn best. As part of a required audit, the Little Rock School District asked a random sample of 566 students in grades 7 to 12 to state what classroom factors helped them learn. The results (Mosley & Smith, 1982) showed the top five factors to be:

1. Clear, complete explanations and concrete examples;
2. Positive, relaxed learning environments in which students could talk to and learn from other students;
3. Individualized instruction, in which teachers know that the students are different, occasionally divide students into groups, check on students' progress, and assign varied tasks;
4. Adequate academic learning time in class; and
5. Motivation and interest by using a variety of instructional methods and teacher's enthusiasm.

FIGURE 6.4 Diagnosing Learning Styles

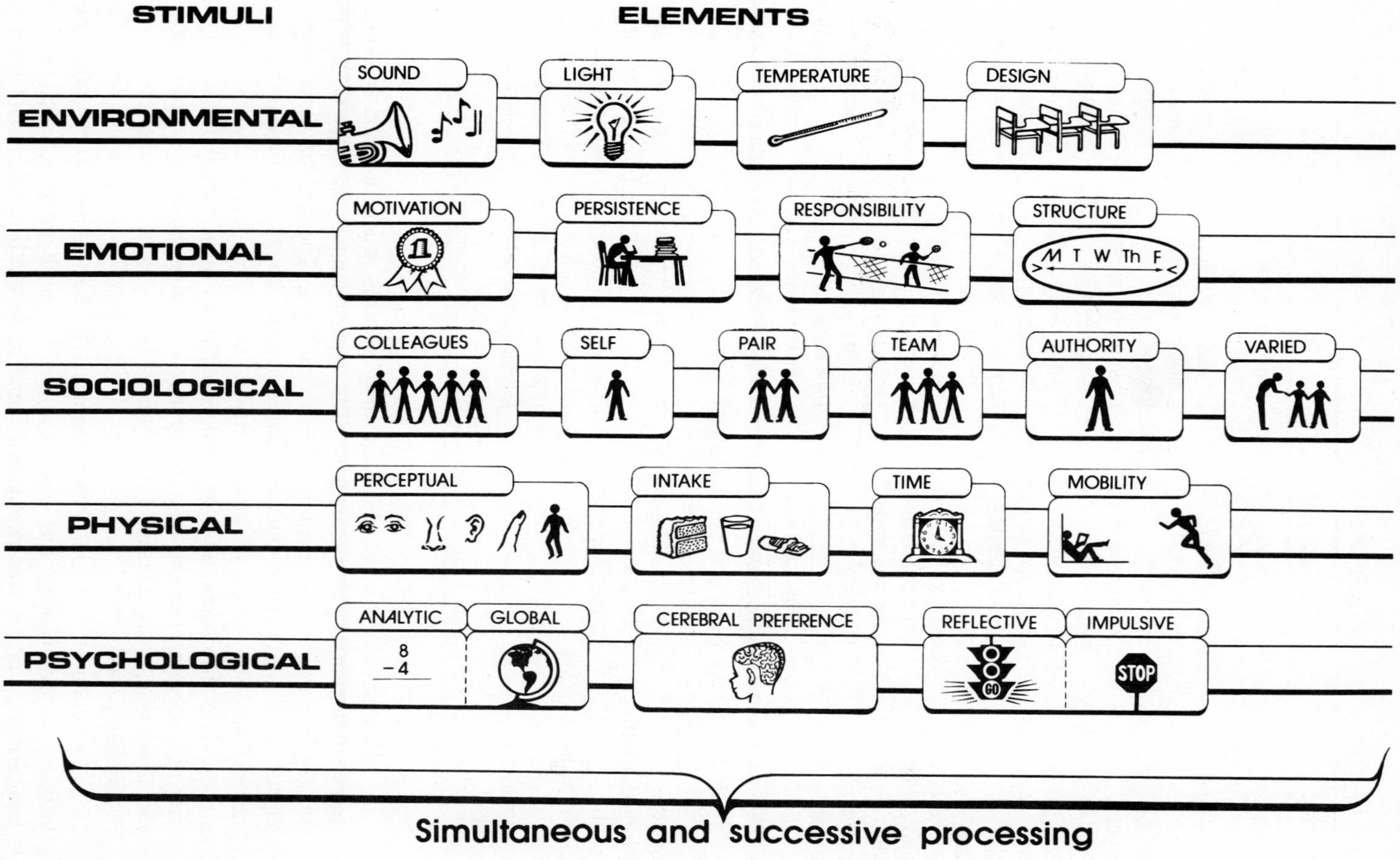
STIMULI
ELEMENTS
ENVIRONMENTAL
SOUND
LIGHT
TEMPERATURE
DESIGN
EMOTIONAL
MOTIVATION
PERSISTENCE
RESPONSIBILITY
STRUCTURE
M T W Th F
SOCIOLOGICAL
COLLEAGUES
SELF
PAIR
TEAM
AUTHORITY
VARIED
PHYSICAL
PERCEPTUAL
INTAKE
TIME
MOBILITY
PSYCHOLOGICAL
ANALYTIC
8
– 4
GLOBAL
CEREBRAL PREFERENCE
REFLECTIVE
GO
IMPULSIVE
STOP
Simultaneous and successive processing

Source: Rita Dunn and Kenneth Dunn. The Center for the Study of Learning and Teaching Styles. St. John's University. Reprinted by permission.

FIGURE 6.5 Learning Styles

Innovative Learner	Analytic Learner	Common-Sense Learner	Dynamic Learner
The Learner:	*The Learner:*	*The Learner:*	*The Learner:*
Seeks meaning	Wants to know the	Needs to know how	Needs to use the
Wants reasons for	facts	things work	self-discovery
learning new	Perceives	Seeks usability	method
material	information	Enjoys solving	Takes risks
Needs to be	abstractly,	problems	Is flexible
personally	processes it	Desires hands-on	Relishes change
involved in the	reflectively	experiences	Seeks action
learning process	Can create concepts	Wants ideas to be	Follows through with
Desires to work with	and build models	practical	plans
people	Enjoys collecting	Needs to know how	Enjoys the
Is highly imaginative	data	things that they	trial-and-error
Has good divergent	Needs to know what	are asked to do	method
thinking skills	the experts think	will help in real life	Receives
Perceives	Values sequential	Likes to practice	information
information	thinking	ideas	concretely,
concretely,		Perceives	processes it
processes it	*The Teacher:*	information	actively
reflectively		abstractly,	
	Provides information	processes it	*The Teacher:*
The Teacher:	by direct	actively	
	instruction		Is a resource
Is a motivator	Sees knowledge as	*The Teacher:*	Becomes an
Uses the discussion	increasing		evaluator
approach	comprehension	Becomes a coach	Serves as a
Incorporates a great		Models	facilitator
deal of		Involves the student	Encourages a
teacher-student		Gives immediate	variety of learning
interaction		feedback	approaches

Learning-style inventories can also provide teachers with information about students' learning-style preferences. The recommended readings at the end of this chapter include several learning-style inventories. The use of these inventories can support several important student learning needs. Assessment of learning styles can (1) increase students' sense of efficacy by helping them better understand the learning process (how they learn and why teachers make key instructional decisions), (2) increase student involvement in the learning process, (3) help students establish goals, and (4) encourage teachers to increase the amount of instructional activities that have meaning to the student.

The concept of brain hemisphericity is closely linked to the work on students' learning styles. During the past few years considerable research has been done supporting the notion that people who tend to be left-brain dominant learn in different ways and have different environmental and organizational needs in the classroom than do right-brain dominant people (Dunn, Cavanaugh, Eberle, & Lenhausern, 1982). Right-brain dominant people in general are bothered by noise when working; prefer dim lighting; are less persistent and motivated when doing detailed, logical, sequential kinds of tasks; prefer a tactile mode of learning; and like to learn while working with peers. Left-brain dominant students tend to learn best when it is quiet, and they like bright light, prefer to work by themselves, and learn visually, auditorily, or both. These students enjoy analyzing situations, like tasks to be logical and sequential, and pay attention to detail.

Most of the curriculum in the public school deals with facts and knowledge: logical, sequential, linear concepts; systems, rules, and symbols. "In elementary and many secondary classes, students spend two-thirds of their time doing seatwork with printed worksheets" (Doyle, 1983, p. 180). Durkin (1981) analyzed five basal reading programs and reported that they emphasized practice and assessment and included little instruction in comprehension. Findings from national studies by Boyer (1983), Goodlad (1984), Lipsitz (1984), and Sizer (1984) all reinforce the fact that most instruction is teacher-dominated and fact-oriented. This type of instruction favors left-brain dominant students. Many students are right-brain dominant, however, and learn best when they are actively involved in the realm of creativity, imagination, intuitiveness, spatial concepts, and inventiveness. Therefore, as discussed in chapter 7, when designing curriculum and instruction, it is important to create a balance of activities that focus on the learning-style preferences of right- and left-brain dominant students.

ACTIVITIES FOR EXAMINING STUDENTS' ACADEMIC NEEDS

As discussed in chapter 2, we can discover students' needs by analyzing the classroom environment in light of theories and research, by asking students to provide specific feedback, or both. In this section we provide four activities you can use to consider how effectively you are meeting students' academic needs. The first three activities are based on the theories and research described in this chapter; the fourth activity involves students' feedback.

ACTIVITY 6.1   Evaluating a Classroom Environment in Light of Students' Academic Needs

For each of the 13 student academic needs listed in Figure 6.1, list two ways in which you currently meet the need within the classroom. Be specific. For example: I use interest centers to respond to students' needs to follow their own interests. If you are not currently teaching, select a classroom that you have observed recently.

After completing chapter 7, return to this activity and list two specific ways in which you could alter your teaching methods in order to meet these needs more effectively.

ACTIVITY 6.2 Assessing Instructional Factors Related to Student Motivation

Select a recent lesson you taught. For the lesson you have selected, write a brief statement describing what you did or said to introduce the lesson. For this same instructional activity, write a brief statement indicating how you taught the material to the students. On a one-to-five scale (five being the highest) rate how effectively this lesson responded to the academic needs listed below.

Students' academic needs

____ Understand and value the learning goals
____ Understand the learning process
____ Be actively involved in the learning process
____ Relate subject matter to their own lives
____ Control the learning environment by setting goals or following their own interests
____ Experience success
____ Receive realistic and immediate feedback that enhances self-efficacy
____ Receive rewards for performance gains
____ See learning modeled by adults as an exciting and rewarding activity
____ Experience an appropriate amount of structure
____ Have time to integrate learning
____ Have positive contact with peers
____ Receive instruction matched to their skill level and learning style

ACTIVITY 6.3 Responding to Students' Academic Needs—Examining an Individual Case

Select a student who is having particular difficulty behaving appropriately in class. List at least two academic needs that are not being met for this student. After completing chapters 7 through 9, return to this activity and list at least one specific approach that can be used to ensure that each need you have listed can be more effectively met for this student.

ACTIVITY 6.4 Using Students' Input to Determine the Extent to Which Their Academic Needs Are Being Met in a Classroom

Students can provide us with helpful information on how well the classroom environment is meeting their academic needs. The questionnaire in Figure 6.6 is an example of an instrument that can be administered to discover how students feel about their classroom.

To complete this activity, administer the questionnaire provided or modify it to fit the skill level of the children completing the form. Tally the results as suggested in Figure 2.5. When the results have been tallied, analyze the data by completing these items:

1. List all the statements that more than five students responded to with the responses "Always true" or "Most of the time."

---

2. List all the statements to which a majority of students responded with the responses "Occasionally" or "Never true."
3. Write three responses to the statement: "I learned that. . . ."
4. Based on this new information, write three statements about changes you would like to make in your classroom.

FIGURE 6.6 Student Academic Needs Questionnaire

Please check the appropriate box	Always true 100%	Most of the time 75%	Half of the time 50%	Occasionally 25%	Never true 0%
Understand the teacher's goal					
1. Do you understand the goals for each lesson?					
2. Do you know the purpose of or reason assignments are given?					
3. Do I explain new material well enough to you?					
4. Are the directions in class clear?					
Actively involved in the learning process					
5. Do you frequently raise your hand to answer a question?					
6. Do you get a chance to share your ideas in class?					
7. Have you suggested changes for our classroom?					
8. Is there a good balance for you in the amount of time spent in small- and large-group activities?					
Relate subject matter to their own lives					
9. Do you see the skills taught in this class as being useful in some other area of your life?					
10. Are you asked to collect information or materials from outside of school to use in school assignments?					
Follow own interests					
11. Are you able to study subjects or ideas that interest you?					
12. Do you get to make choices about the topics you study?					
Experience success					
13. Do you feel good about how much you are learning?					
14. Do you experience success in your academic work?					

(continued)

FIGURE 6.6 (*continued*)

Please check the appropriate box	Always true 100%	Most of the time 75%	Half of the time 50%	Occasionally 25%	Never true 0%
15. Do you accomplish academic goals that you set?					
Receive realistic and immediate feedback					
16. Are my comments on your work helpful?					
17. Do tests give you information about what you have learned?					
18. Do tests and assignments help you see what skills you still need to practice?					
Experience an appropriate amount of structure					
19. Does this class seem organized?					
20. Do you know when work is due?					
21. Are deadlines reasonable?					
22. Are you aware of your progress in this class?					
23. Do you understand the class rules and procedures?					
Time to integrate learning					
24. Do I allow enough time for questions?					
25. Is there enough review time before a test?					
26. Is there enough practice on each skill before going on to a new one?					
Have positive contact with peers					
27. Are other students accepting of your ideas?					
28. Do people listen carefully to whoever is speaking?					
29. Do students in this class help each other?					
Receive instruction matched to skill level and learning style					
30. Are most of the assignments in class challenging to you?					
31. Do you feel that you have a variety of choices for exhibiting your knowledge?					
32. Does the way I teach help you learn the material?					

SUMMARY

Until recently, research, theory, and inservice education in the area of classroom management and school discipline ignored the relationship between student behavior and students' attitudes toward learning. Classroom management focused on how to increase on-task behavior with relatively little attention paid to whether the curriculum and instructional methods motivated students to learn. Fortunately, educators are becoming increasingly aware of the relationship between student motivation and students' behavior. Such well-known educators as Jere Brophy, William Glasser, John Goodlad, Joan Lipsitz, Ted Sizer, and Ernest Boyer emphasize that the motivational quality of the learning environment is a key factor influencing student learning and behavior. This chapter examines the key factors that influence the degree to which students are motivated to learn and will become positively engaged in instructional activities. When these factors are ignored, teachers find themselves spending much time attempting to control student behavior. When these student needs are met, however, a greater portion of students' classroom behavior becomes directed toward completing learning tasks.

RECOMMENDED READING

Ames, C., & Ames, R. (Eds.). (1984). *Research on motivation in education. Vol. I: Student motivation.* New York: Academic Press.

Ames, C., & Ames, R. (Eds.). (1985). *Research on motivation in education. Vol. II: The classroom milieu.* Orlando, Fla.: Academic Press.

Bybee, R., & Sund, R. (1982). *Piaget for educators.* Columbus, Ohio: Charles E. Merrill.

DeCharms, R. (1976). *Enhancing motivation.* New York: Irvington.

Deci, E., & Ryan, R. (1985). *Intrinsic motivation and self-determination in human behavior.* New York: Plenum.

Dewey, J. (1963). *Experience and education.* New York: Macmillan.

Dunn, R., & Dunn, K. (1978). *Teaching students through their individual learning styles: A practical approach.* Reston, Va.: Reston.

Edwards, B. (1979). *Drawing on the right side of the brain.* Boston: Houghton Mifflin.

Good, T., & Brophy, J. (1987). *Looking in classrooms, 4th ed.* (ch. 8). New York: Harper and Row.

Hart, L. (1983). *Human brain and human learning.* New York: Longmans.

Holt, J. (1967). *How children learn.* New York: Dell.

Johnson, D., & Johnson, R. (1987). *Learning together and alone: Cooperative, competitive, and individualistic learning,* 2nd ed. Englewood Cliffs, N.J.: Prentice-Hall.

McCarthy, B. (1980). *The 4-MAT system: Teaching to learning styles with right/left mode techniques.* Oak Brook, Ill.: Excel.

Rogers, C. (1969). *Freedom to learn.* Columbus, Ohio: Charles E. Merrill.

Rotalo, S. (1982). *Right-brain lesson plans for a left-brain world—A book of lesson plans for English and speech.* Springfield, Ill.: Charles C Thomas, Publisher.

Silberman, C. (1970). *Crisis in the classroom: The remaking of American education.* New York: Random House.

Slavin, R. (1983). *Cooperative learning.* New York: Longmans.

Stipek, D. (1988). *Motivation to learn: From theory to practice.* Englewood Cliffs, N.J.: Prentice-Hall.

CHAPTER 7

Instructional Methods That Motivate Students and Increase Learning

Certain skills or abilities are also essential to the educated man: the ability to learn for himself, to take hold of a subject and "work it up" for himself, so that he is not dependent upon his teacher's direction.

/ Charles E. Silberman (1970)
Crisis in the Classroom: The Remaking of American Education

All genuine learning is active, not passive. It involves the use of the mind, not just the memory. It is a process of discovery in which the student is the main agent, not the teacher.

/ Mortimer J. Adler (1982)
The Paideia Proposal: An Educational Manifesto

This important work of several decades ago, as well as much of what has since been in the forefront of educational thought, stresses the importance of teachers finding ways to make subject matter relevant to students, to involve students in setting their own goals, to vary the ways of learning to use approaches that employ all of the senses, and to be sure that there are opportunities for relating the knowledge to experiences or actually using it.

/ John I. Goodlad (1984)
A Place Called School: Prospects for the Future

A self-propelled learner is the goal of a school, and teachers should insist that students habitually learn on their own. Teacher-delivered knowledge that is never used is temporary.

/ Theodore Sizer (1984)
Horace's Compromise: The Dilemma of the American High School

198

Our research has also established that, when teachers offer several activities (not all worksheets or silent reading), are interactive in their instruction, and provide a supportive environment, then students are on-task a greater percentage of the time (90–95 percent) and students are absent less often.

/ Jane Stallings (1987)
(Personal correspondence)

Unfortunately, many students do not view school as a place for learning important academic knowledge and skills but rather as a place they are required to be in order to acquire a certificate . . .
Effective teachers are clear about what they intend to accomplish through their instruction, and they keep these goals in mind both in designing the instruction and in communicating its purpose to the students. They make certain that their students understand and are satisfied by the reasons given for why they should learn what they are asked to learn.

/ Andrew Porter and Jere Brophy (1988)
"Synthesis of Research on Good Teaching," *Educational Leadership*

"Productive time" is the time spent on suitable lessons adapted to the learner—in contrast to "engaged" or "allocated" time, which may be futile if content or method of instruction is inappropriate for individual students.

/ Herbert J. Walberg (1988)
"Synthesis of Research on Time and Learning," *Educational Leadership*

It is difficult to separate effective classroom management from effective instruction. Students learn more and behave better in classrooms in which teachers use instructional methods appropriate to the learning goals and students' learning needs. At all grade levels, effective teachers are skilled in providing direct instruction to large and small groups. Effective teachers also incorporate methods that help students become actively involved in the learning process and develop skill in taking responsibility for their own learning.

During the past several years leading educators have increasingly emphasized that the quality of instruction is a key factor influencing students' behavior and achievement. Research and practice focusing on the quality of instruction have followed two general paths. First, a group of researchers (Anderson, Evertson, & Brophy, 1979; Good & Grouws, 1979) have examined the specific instructional skills and amounts of time spent on various instructional tasks displayed by teachers whose students achieved higher scores on standardized tests. Stimulated by these process-product studies relating students' acquisition of basic skills to a variety of teacher behaviors that increase students' engaged learning time, several leading educators, including Thomas Good (1979), Madeline Hunter (1981), and Jane Stallings (1984), have developed teacher-training programs aimed at increasing students' achievement by improving teachers' skills in providing direct instruction to students. Because recent national studies indicate that many students are not mastering fundamental knowledge in basic skills, it is imperative that teachers learn instructional skills that will increase students' gains in acquiring basic skills. Furthermore, attaining higher-level cognitive goals depends heavily on students' having mastered basic skills.

A second group of educators, including John Goodlad (1984), David and Roger Johnson (1987), Bruce Joyce and Marsha Weil (1986), Bernice McCarthy (1987), McCarthy, Leflar, and McNamara (1987), Robert Slavin (1983a), and Robert Soar (1983), emphasize instructional approaches that actively involve students in instructional activities aimed at acquiring not only important basic skills but also higher level cognitive skills and interpersonal skills. This work coincides with increasing interest in student responsibility and self-control (Brophy, 1985; Duke & Jones, 1985; Glasser, 1986, 1988; Good, 1983). As discussed in chapter 6, research supports the concept that increased choice and feelings of personal responsibility enhance academic achievement. Thomas Good (1983) summarizes the focus on students' involvement:

> In particular, researchers should examine how teachers' classroom management styles influence student initiative and self-control. Students need structure and purposeful direction, but they must also have opportunities to learn to determine their own objectives and to develop strategies for evaluating progress in self-chosen goals. Such abilities become increasingly important as students get older. (p. 63)

Taken together, the research described above suggests that teachers must possess the skills (outlined in chapters 8 and 9) for organizing and managing classrooms and for systematically presenting material to students. Teachers must also, however, have skill in helping students establish learning goals, initiate and evaluate their own learning, work cooperatively in the learning process, and develop skills in higher-level cognitive processes such as analysis, synthesis, and research methodology. "Since no single teaching strategy can accomplish every purpose, the wise teacher will master a sufficient repertoire of strategies to deal with the specific kinds of learning problems he or she faces" (Joyce & Weil, 1986, p. 20). This concept is echoed by Thomas Good (1983, p. 62): "Effective managers in the research reviewed here thought about the needs of their students and adjusted their teaching to particular classes. These teachers appeared to be good decision makers." We believe that, as professionals, teachers must be introduced to a broad range of knowledge and be provided with assistance in learning to make thoughtful decisions about how to integrate various methods of instruction and classroom management.

This chapter provides a practical overview of many instructional skills (Figure 7.1) that can improve students' acquisition of basic skills and increase their motivation, interest,

FIGURE 7.1 Instructional Methods for Improving Students' Motivation and Achievement

1. Improving the quality of direct and active instruction
2. Teaching more than facts
3. Incorporating students' interests
4. Responding to students' individual learning styles
5. Taking into account students' level of cognitive development
6. Involving students in academic goal setting
7. Using learning centers
8. Implementing self-evaluation
9. Using cooperative learning
10. Using peer tutoring

and higher-level cognitive skills. It is obviously not possible in one chapter to describe in detail the increasing amount of excellent work available for helping teachers improve and diversify the quality of their instruction. Therefore, although we refer to much available literature and materials, we focus on aspects we have found most useful in our own teaching and our work with teachers. This chapter can help you develop a variety of practical skills as well as directions for further professional growth.

Research consistently indicates that the choice of the most effective teaching method varies according to such context variables as student's age, student's ability, instructional goals, and student's personal characteristics and learning styles. Some teacher behaviors, such as giving clear instructions, seem to be desirable in all settings, but our choice of teaching methods varies considerably depending on the context variables.

EFFECTIVE DIRECT INSTRUCTION

Barak Rosenshine (1978) describes direct instruction as "Teaching activities focused on academic matters, where goals are clear to students; time allotted for instruction is sufficient; content coverage is extensive; student performance is monitored; questions are at a low cognitive level and produce many correct responses; and feedback is immediate and academically oriented" (p. 46). Direct instruction is a teacher-controlled approach to instruction. It is most effective in reaching objectives that require students to memorize, practice, and master basic factual information. Direct instruction is effective because it is based on behavioristic learning principles, such as obtaining students' attention, reinforcing correct responses, providing corrective feedback, and practicing correct responses. Direct instruction also is effective because it tends to increase the amount of ALT (academic learning time) or the amount of instructional time during which students are attending to the task and performing at a high success rate.

Many studies have found that students learn basic skills more rapidly when they receive a greater portion of their instruction directly from the teacher (Brophy, 1979; Evertson, Emmer, & Brophy, 1980; Fisher, Berliner, Filby, Marliave, Cahen, & Dishaw, 1980; Good, 1979; Good & Grouws, 1979; Rosenshine, 1976; Stallings, 1980).

These studies reinforce the value of teachers' working directly with the entire class and with small groups of five or more students rather than assigning large amounts of seatwork and assisting individual students. This research also indicates that students learn best when teachers actively engage them by asking questions, expecting responses, and increasing accountability by calling on all students and frequently monitoring completed work.

We believe direct instruction involves four key components: (1) clear determination and articulation of goals, (2) teacher-directed instruction, (3) careful monitoring of students' outcomes, and (4) consistent use of effective classroom organization and management methods. During classroom supervision and consultation with more than 300 preservice and experienced teachers over 15 years, we have consistently found failure to implement effective, direct instruction to be a major cause of classroom-management problems. Likewise, every skilled classroom manager with whom we have worked has possessed good skills in direct instruction. Madeline Hunter and Jane Stallings are two researchers who have been particularly successful in devising inservice training programs aimed at helping teachers at all grade levels improve their direct instruction.

Madeline Hunter's Instructional Theory into Practice (ITIP)

Madeline Hunter and her associates at the University Elementary School at the University of California at Los Angeles have spent two decades analyzing educational research and specifying the instructional skills possessed by effective teachers. This work has led to the finding that, to be effective, teachers need skill in seven basic areas:

1. Content,
2. Materials,
3. Planning,
4. Classroom management,
5. Human relations,
6. Human growth and development, and
7. Instructional methods.

Acknowledging the value of the first six areas, Hunter's work nonetheless has focused primarily on the elements of effective instruction. Hunter describes four of these elements:

1. Teaching to an objective,
2. Selecting an objective at the correct level of difficulty,
3. Monitoring and adjusting, and
4. Employing principles of learning.

It is beyond the scope of this book to describe the four elements of instruction. More nearly complete descriptions of these skills are found in teacher-training material developed by Madeline Hunter (1976, 1981), in Carol Cummings's (1980) *Teaching Makes a Difference*, and in an article by Barak Rosenshine (1983).

These instructional elements have been incorporated into a lesson design teachers can use for presenting almost any type of lesson (Figure 7.2). Our experience strongly supports

FIGURE 7.2 Lesson Design

1. Anticipatory set
   a. Focus the students' attention
   b. Provide tie with prior learnings
   c. Develop readiness for instruction
2. The objective and its purpose: What the learners will be doing and why they will be doing it.
3. Instructional input (sometimes called direct or active instruction)
   a. Present material in small steps
   b. Focus on one point at a time
   c. Present varied and specific examples
4. Modeling
   a. Visual input accompanied by verbal input
   b. Criteria for a correct performance are known
5. Monitoring to check for understanding
   a. Sampling: Question whole group and take responses from individuals
   b. Signaled responses: Thumbs up if you agree
   c. Private response: Written or whispered to teacher
6. Guided practice: The initial practice stage in which the response of the learner must be monitored by the teacher to make certain it is accurate.
7. Summary
   a. Students state or write what they have learned from the lesson
   b. Students record their progress toward a learning goal
8. Independent practice: The student can perform the task without major errors, discomfort, or confusion, and with a minimum of teacher supervision.

the value of developing lessons organized around this design. Students find lessons that follow this format to be clear, and they respond by demonstrating high rates of on-task behavior during these lessons.

A sample lesson will help you understand and implement this lesson design. The lesson, taught by one of us, involved teaching the water cycle to fourth-grade students. As an anticipatory set, the teacher asked the class, "Why does rain fall though clouds do not?" After soliciting answers from the class, the objective and purpose were provided by informing the students that when they went home in the evening, they would be able to tell the adult(s) at home how rain was formed and how water was recycled. The teacher then asked students to list any specific questions they wished answered about rain and water. The instructional input and modeling involved presenting the information with a model prepared on a felt board. A film, filmstrip, or overhead projector could also have been used. Monitoring was accomplished by several methods. Students were periodically asked orally to summarize points the teacher had made. On several occasions students were asked to tell an answer to the student next to them and, after the teacher gave the answer, students whose partner had answered correctly raised their hands. Guided practice had students label and describe phases in the water cycle presented on a worksheet. Independent practice was accomplished by having students work in groups to research specific problems associated with the water cycle.

Research (Goodlad, 1984) supports what Madeline Hunter has said for many years. Most teaching involves only steps three and six in the eight-step lesson design presented in Figure 7.4. Teachers too often merely present information and then assign individual seatwork. Furthermore, research (Anderson, 1981; Doyle, Sanford, & Emmer, 1982) suggests that teachers who use large amounts of seatwork often fail to provide students with adequate procedures and assign tasks that are poorly matched with student ability. This instructional approach fails to provide students with a sense of purpose or direction, ignores the reality that a significant number of students do not understand the material, and does not provide for students' involvement in using the information they have acquired.

Many school districts across the country have trained teachers in Madeline Hunter's procedures. One of us recently observed a creative supplement to this type of staff training. The staff at a middle school nationally recognized for its excellence taught students a variation of the eight elements in an effective lesson. These elements were then posted on the front wall of each classroom and students were asked to inform the teachers any time they omitted a step. This procedure not only ensured consistently more effective teaching, but also provided students with a sense of meaningful involvement in the instructional process. Another middle school staff with whom we have worked decided that even though they valued the basic components of direct instruction, they wanted to develop their own form to apply the criteria of effective direct instruction to evaluate their teaching effectiveness. Their form (Figure 7.3) provides a good example of how teachers can relate theory to practice and take an active role in their own evaluation process.

Even though we believe the strategies described by Madeline Hunter are important ingredients in effective instruction, there have been very few studies concerning the effectiveness of teachers' implementing this model. The limited data available indicate no measurable advantages in achievement gains for students taught by teachers who have received training in these methods (Donovan, Sousa, & Walberg, 1987; Slavin, 1986; Stallings & Krasavage, 1986). Therefore, while we encourage teachers to include these components in their instruction, we also suggest that teachers and administrators consider the benefits associated with the other instructional methods presented in this chapter and that inservice training and teacher evaluation focus on a variety of instructional skills rather than on one model.

Research carried out and summarized by Jere Brophy simultaneously supports many ideas presented by Madeline Hunter and suggests a somewhat different orientation. Both Brophy and Stallings emphasize active teacher involvement with students. In summarizing the results of research on this type of instruction, Jere Brophy (1986a) writes:

> These classes include frequent lessons (whole class or small group, depending on grade level and subject matter) in which the teacher presents information and develops concepts through lecture or demonstration, elaborates this information in the feedback given following responses to recitation or discussion questions, prepares the students for follow up assignments by giving instructions and going through practice examples, monitors progress on assignments after releasing students to work independently, and follows up with any needed feedback or reteaching. The teacher carries the content to the students personally rather than depending on curriculum materials to do so, but conveys information mostly in brief presentations followed by recitation or application opportunities. There is a great deal of teacher talk, but most of it is academic rather than procedural or managerial, and much of it involves asking questions and giving feedback rather than extended lecturing. (p. 4)

FIGURE 7.3 Teacher Designed Questions to Help Analyze a Lesson

Teacher _____

Date _____

1.0 *Standards*

Did the students seem to know what was expected of them in terms of behavior? ____ Yes ____ No

Did the teacher have difficulty getting students into a learning atmosphere? ____ Yes ____ No

Were all materials and equipment necessary for the class session in place and ready for use? ____ Yes ____ No

Was time wasted during taking of attendance and/or record keeping? ____ Yes ____ No

2.0 *Introduction—Purpose*

Was the learning for that session clearly stated to students? ____ Yes ____ No

Were students shown how the learning related to previous learning they had experienced or to needs in their lives? ____ Yes ____ No

3.0 *Teaching*

Did the teacher give an adequate explanation of the learning before students were expected to put it into practice? ____ Yes ____ No

What strategy did the teacher use to put across the learning?

____ lecture ____ group discussion ____ student input
____ inquiry (questions) ____ role playing ____ other

Did the teacher model the learning and its application for the students? ____ Yes ____ No

Did the teacher check regularly to make sure that all students understood the learning? ____ Yes ____ No

4.0 *Practice*

Did the students practice the learning through some form of overt behavior? ____ Yes ____ No

Was the practice directly related to the learning? ____ Yes ____ No

Did the teacher monitor each student's practice of the learning? ____ Yes ____ No

Did the teacher reteach the learning when and where necessary? ____ Yes ____ No

5.0 *Closure*

Did the teacher close the class by having students identify what the session's learning was? ____ Yes ____ No

(continued)

FIGURE 7.3 (continued)

Did the students leave the class knowing and understanding what the learning for that session was? ___ Yes ___ No

6.0 *Follow up* (unguided practice)

Did the teacher assign homework based on the day's learning? ___ Yes ___ No

7.0 *Motivation*

During the class session, did the teacher use any of the following forms of motivation?

___ increasing/decreasing anxiety
___ adding notes of interest
___ granting rewards
___ maintaining friendly atmosphere
___ giving students knowledge of their results
___ allowing students moments of success

Source: *Teacher Handbook*, Gregory Heignts Middle School, Portland, Ore., Portland Public School District #1, n.d., pp. 21, 22.

The Work of Jane Stallings

Research conducted by Jane Stallings supports a similar concept of direct instruction. Stallings found that teachers who were most effective in helping low-achieving secondary students gain from 1.5 to 2.0 years in reading skills in one academic year spent at least 60 percent of their time in direct instruction and allocated only 20 percent to seatwork activities. Figures 7.4 and 7.5 provide an overview of Stallings's findings on the effective use of time for secondary basic skill classes.

Stallings (1987) states that the research on teaching indicates that effective teachers:

1. Spend about half (50 percent) of class time on interactive academic activities: explaining new material, discussing and reviewing assigned work, question and answer sessions, etc.

2. Spend about one-third (35 percent) of class time on actively monitoring silent reading, written work, lab work.

3. Spend less than 15 percent of class time on classroom management and organization: passing papers, explaining activities, arranging desks, lesson transitions, taking roll, making announcements, etc.

4. Have a system of behavior rules that are clear, posted in view, and consistently enforced.

5. Spend very little in-class time socializing with students, visitors, or aides.

6. Plan daily activities in advance and make them clear to students (e.g., by writing the day's schedule on the board).

7. Plan a variety of academic activities using differing modalities during one class period.

8. State objectives and purpose of lesson.

9. Have students read for understanding and content.

FIGURE 7.4 Effective Use of Time in Secondary Basic Skills Classes

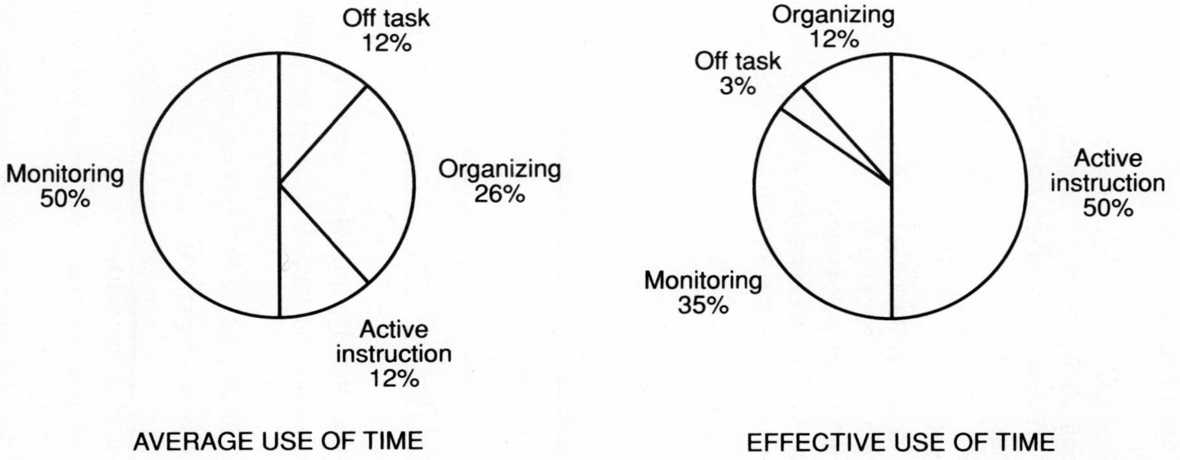

Organizing
12%

Off task
3%

Active
instruction
50%

Monitoring
35%

EFFECTIVE USE OF TIME

Off task
12%

Organizing
26%

Active
instruction
12%

Monitoring
50%

AVERAGE USE OF TIME

Source: Jane Stallings, University of Houston.

FIGURE 7.5 Time Allocations for Secondary Basic Skills Classes

Organizing/Management Activities (15% or less)
(E) Take roll, sponge activities
(E) Make announcements
(E) Make expectations *clear* for the period: 15% non-academic
     quality and quantity of work
(S) Organize groups
(E) Clarify and enforce behavior expectations
Interactive Instructional Activities (50% or more)
(E) Review/discuss previous work objectives (long and short range)
(E) Inform/instruct new concept
     Demonstrate/give examples
     Link to prior knowledge   85% academic
(E) Question/check for understanding
(S) Reteach small group (if necessary)
(S) Oral drill and practice (as necessary)
(E) Evaluate/summarize (Did we meet objectives?)
Teacher Monitoring/Guiding Seatwork (35% or less)
(I) Written work
(I) Silent reading

Key
E = Total class
S = Small group
L = Large group
I = Individual

Source: Jane Stallings, University of Houston.

10. Give short quizzes and give immediate feedback.

11. Focus most instruction on the whole class or small groups rather than on individuals.

12. Distribute opportunities for verbal response equally among students.

13. Praise student success and effort.

14. When a student answers incorrectly, give him/her another chance to get it right by rephrasing the question or giving hints.

15. Have an overview or review before presenting new material and a summary and explanation at the end. (pp. 17, 18)

Like the work of Hunter, research by Brophy and Stallings highlights the integral relationship between classroom management and instruction. These three leading educators also highlight the importance of students' understanding learning objectives and being made aware of their progress. However, especially in the work of Jere Brophy, we see a major focus on motivating students to learn and finding methods to involve students more actively in the learning process. We believe this crucial issue is a major influence on student behavior and learning.

EFFECTIVE ACTIVE INSTRUCTION

Tom Good (1986) suggests that the term *active instruction* is preferable to direct instruction because it is broader and less tied to one set of research findings. Good states that active instruction includes many key instructional factors associated with direct instruction, but that active instruction encompasses more diverse instructional methods. He summarizes this research:

> Teachers who present information accurately, pay attention to the meaning and conceptual development of content, look for signs of student comprehension and confusion, and provide successful practice opportunities appear to have more achievement gains than do teachers who are less active and who rely more upon seatwork and other classroom activities. . . . In active teaching, the initial style may be inductive or deductive, student learning may be self-initiated or teacher-initiated (especially if thorough critique and synthesis activities follow students' learning attempts). Active teaching also connotes a broader philosophical base (it may occur in classrooms using a variety of organizational structures) and should become somewhat less direct as students become more mature and instructional goals more focused on affective and process outcomes. (Good, 1986, p. 59)

We strongly support the training of teachers to provide effective direct instruction and believe it provides the foundation for effective teaching, and yet we also believe that Good's conceptualization of the difference between direct and active instruction exposes an important issue. Like most of the methods presented throughout this book, direct instruction has too often been presented in isolation and offered as the solution to teachers' instructional and management problems. In his *Freedom to Learn,* Carl Rogers (1969) defines significant learning as including four components: (1) personal involvement, (2) self-initiation, (3) pervasiveness—making a difference in the learner's life, and (4) self-evaluation. Piaget's theoretical work on the learning process also points to the importance of actively involving the child in the learning process. Teachers of middle school and high school students often find that even basic facts are better learned by actively involving students in games, group work, or discovery learning.

Unfortunately, too few teachers actively involve students in learning either basic facts or higher-level cognitive skills. In lamenting the lack of exciting instruction in American schools, Theodore Sizer (1984) writes:

> No more important finding has emerged from the inquiries of our study than that the American high school student, as student, is too often docile, compliant, and without initiative. (p. 54)

He goes on to note that "most high school students perceive the course of study to be a large collection of unambiguously specific data to be memorized and sometimes manipulated" (p. 93). In *High School: A Report on Secondary Education in America,* Ernest Boyer (1983) wrote, "Classes are at times inspired, occasionally dreadful, and most often routine" (pp. 15, 16). Many instructional activities are ignored because they are more difficult for most teachers to manage than are teacher presentation or seatwork. Although high rates of student engagement can occur during instructional activities involving extensive student input and interaction (Johnson & Johnson, 1987; Jones, 1980; Silverstein, 1979), this technique appears to require greater classroom management skills than does obtaining on-task behavior during teacher-dominated lessons. Teachers are also reinforced by students for offering high rates of teacher presentation. Even in first grade, students tend not to take risks and instead use strategies that encourage teachers to provide the answer (Mehan, 1974). To no one's surprise, studies with high school students also suggest that students are hesitant to shift away from teacher-directed learning focusing on memory of basic facts (Brause & Mayher, 1982; Davis & McKnight, 1976). In fact, in secondary schools in which students are developmentally more capable of benefiting from active involvement and cooperative work, classes are characterized by less instructional variety than in elementary classes (Rounds, Ward, Mergendoller, & Tikunoff, 1982).

In middle schools, teachers' beliefs about students' cognitive limitations combine with teachers' worries about classroom management to increase the likelihood that teacher-controlled direct instruction will be the preferred instructional mode. In her *Successful Schools for Young Adolescents,* Joan Lipsitz (1984) discusses this issue:

> The quality of discourse in the classrooms is characterized by a surprising lack of intellectual rigor. While school administrators stress inquiry into ideas, teachers for the most part stress the transmission of facts. There is relatively little inquiry. The tone of classroom discussion reflects an assumption that young adolescents are developmentally incapable of grappling with concepts. . . . However, two points are being overlooked in the stampede to concrete thinking and learning for all students. First, it is as much a failure to deny the diversity of development during early adolescence by making teaching predominantly concrete and atheoretical as by making it predominantly abstract. Second, sensitivity to the majority of students' limited capacity for theoretical ideation does not preclude the teacher from extracting general principles from the factual, making connections among concrete examples, or encouraging preliminary examination of ideas and values. (pp. 189, 190)

From an instructional point of view, the problem with overemphasis on control-oriented teaching is that it often (although not necessarily) emphasizes passive student behavior and acquisition of factual knowledge at the expense of students' creativity, responsibility, and comprehension. In an analysis of case studies in science education, Stake and Easley (1978) observed that students seemed primarily interested in grades. "They did not think of themselves as mastering a certain body of knowledge, but more of mastering (or not mastering) those things being required by the teacher or the test" (Ch. 15, p. 29). Studies in elementary schools indicate a similar trend for students to complete work without concern for understanding what the content means (Anderson, 1981; Blumenfeld, Pintrich, Meece, & Wessels, 1982).

These studies should not be interpreted as suggesting that all teachers should dramatically reduce the amount of time they allot to presenting information to students. As Brophy and Stallings note, teacher-directed instruction that actively involves students in responding to content presented by the teacher can, especially during the elementary school years, be very effective in increasing students' scores on standardized tests.

There are a variety of methods for incorporating active teaching. At one end of the continuum, active teaching can look like effective direct instruction in that it includes effective teacher presentation that engages students in answering questions and responding to their classmates' comments. Active teaching can also involve much more than effective lecture, demonstration, and recitation. It also incorporates a variety of instructional methods intended to involve students actively in the learning process. Therefore, active instruction can also include cooperative learning, student goal setting, student projects, field trips, and numerous other activities. The following sections offer specific suggestions for using nine approaches (see items 2 to 10 in Figure 7.1) for more actively and meaningfully involving students in the learning process.

Teaching More Than Facts

The teaching of factual material is a major function of the public schools. Schools serve society by transmitting information and providing children with basic skills in reading, writing, and arithmetic. The acquisition of basic factual information and skills is, especially in the primary grades, a very important component of a child's learning.

It is equally true, however, that children increasingly need skills to analyze their environment and make important personal decisions. Between 1981 and 1982, the National Assessment of Educational Progress examined the reading, mathematical, and writing skills of 106,000 9-, 13-, and 17-year-olds. In a report presented in November 1982, the agency concluded that even though American schools have been quite successful at teaching basic facts, students could not write statements to explain or defend their answers. Students' work was described as generally shallow and superficial.

In a society characterized by rapid changes in technology and information processing, the acquisition of facts is increasingly a means to an end rather than an end in itself. Schools must begin early to help children use their basic skills for more analytic and creative purposes. Basic skills are important prerequisites to higher-level cognitive functioning. Especially at the secondary level, though, curriculum and instructional techniques used with students who possess basic skills too often focus on memorization and low-level cognitive skills.

Respondents to the 1984 Gallup Poll of the Public's Attitudes Toward the Public Schools (Gallup, 1984), gave high rankings to numerous goals other than acquisition of basic skills. Slightly more than half of the respondents gave a 10 (the highest rating) to the education goal "to develop the ability to live in a complex and changing world." John Goodlad reported similar findings from his *A Study of Schooling* (1983a):

> Second, analysis of documents regarding goals for U.S. schools reveals a steady evolution from narrow academic skills to a far wider array of concerns—and to citizenship, vocational, and personal goals as well. All 50 states endorse them, as did most of the 8,600 parents surveyed in *A Study of Schooling*. Are we to brush these aside as impractical idealism simply because, for the most part, they elude our ability to measure them? (p. 553)

Incorporating material that goes beyond the factual level also greatly influences students' motivation and behavior. Students enjoy acquiring factual information; they also have a strong need to become emotionally involved in the learning process.

Levels of Instruction

In their *Clarifying Values through Subject Matter,* Harmin, Kirschenbaum, and Simon (1973) suggest that instruction can take place at the fact, concept, or personal application level. Additional models were presented by Bloom (1956) in his *Taxonomy of Educational Objectives, Handbook I: Cognitive Domain* and Krathwohl, Bloom, and Masia (1964) in their *Taxonomy of Educational Objectives, Handbook II: Affective Domain*. In developing curricula, we have found it most helpful to categorize instruction into the four levels: facts, concepts, generalizations, and personal application. The relationship between these four levels and Bloom's taxonomy is shown in Figure 7.6.

The facts level involves providing students with basic information. When developing a unit on ecology, we would include information on the chemicals that are associated with pollution, what causes pollution, and the effects various pollutants have on the human body. This level is similar to the knowledge level described by Bloom (1956).

The concepts level focuses on the relationships among facts and examines major themes associated with facts. An ecology unit might examine the concept of people's relationship to their environment, the benefits and costs associated with progress, or our responsibility to future generations. This level incorporates what Bloom describes as *comprehension* and *analysis*.

The generalizations level provides students with an opportunity to use the information they have obtained and the concepts they have developed to solve problems or interpret situations. In the context of an ecology unit, students might be asked to write legislative proposals dealing with ecology or to develop a model city. The educational objectives associated with these activities are similar to those Bloom labels *application*, *synthesis*, and *evaluation*.

At the final level is personal application. Here, students are asked to relate their learning to their own beliefs, feelings, and behaviors. In an ecology unit we might ask them to discuss their own behavior regarding such topics as litter, recycling, or water usage. This level relates to the learning objectives in the affective domain described by Krathwohl et al. (1964). Because it is at this level that students relate learning directly to their own lives, we should, whenever possible, incorporate this level into our instruction. No other level has greater potential for stimulating students' interest and increasing on-task behavior.

It is obvious that older students will be better able to become involved in instruction associated with higher levels. Nevertheless, primary teachers should attempt to help children develop simple concepts, think creatively about generalizations and applications, and, most important, view learning as something that relates to their own lives. Though this approach may not be the major emphasis during the primary grades, failure to incorporate higher levels indicates to children that learning is merely the acquisition of often

FIGURE 7.6 Comparison of Bloom's Taxonomy of Educational Objectives and Teaching More Than Facts

Teaching More Than Facts	Bloom's Taxonomy
Facts	Knowledge
Concepts	Comprehension analysis
Generalizations	Application Synthesis Evaluation
Personal application	Affective domain

unrelated facts. When this failure occurs, it is more difficult for teachers in subsequent grades to introduce higher levels of instruction.

An Example

An example of a lesson used by one of us in a fourth- grade class can help to clarify how each level can be incorporated into an instructional unit. The example, involving a unit on the Northwest Indians, begins with students learning numerous *facts* about the lives and history of these Indians. Individual student interests are accommodated by having each student choose a topic of special interest, obtain relevant material, and make a presentation to the class. As students learn about the beliefs Indians held and how their lives have changed over the years, we incorporate discussions of such *concepts* as prejudice, progress, and "might makes right." In this lesson, instruction at the *generalization* level takes two forms. First, students are asked to discuss such topics as what legislators could do to assist the Indians, how society should handle such current problems as salmon-fishing rights, and whether Indians should live their own life-style separately or be integrated into society. Second, students design and perform a Potlatch. This performance involves creating costumes, learning authentic songs and dances, making dried food, and decorating the room.

One of us and a colleague have also developed a method for incorporating the *personal application* level by providing students with an intense personal experience related to this unit. The activity has one class move out of the classroom on the pretext that the other class needs the room to complete some useful research. The displaced class is placed in a corner in the hall behind a chalkboard. When students become uncomfortable and complain, it is suggested that they petition the principal to change the situation. The principal's refusal almost inevitably provokes anger associated with a sense of impotence. Once students have been allowed to experience these feelings, they return to their classroom and are assisted in sharing their feelings with the class that displaced them. The teachers then help the students draw the analogy between their experience and that of the American Indian. The activity ends by the two classes having a small party to reduce any negative feelings that may have been created by the experience.

It is likely that students will remember this activity and the basic concept taught. Although this example provides a rather dramatic approach to incorporating students' feelings into a lesson, there are numerous less time-consuming approaches. Figure 7.7 outlines a high school unit that incorporates all four levels. If you are interested in obtaining additional suggestions, consult Harmin, Kirschenbaum, and Simon's (1973) *Clarifying Values through Subject Matter*.

Informing Students about the Learning Process

Regardless of what or how one is teaching, we must consider whether students understand why they are studying the material and why the instructional method has been selected. Many, if not most, students do not really understand the learning process. They study to obtain good grades, please their parents or teacher, or avoid punishment. For many students, school becomes a game. As one adolescent stated:

> School is just like roulette or something. You can't just ask: Well, what's the point of it? . . .
> The point of it is to do it, to get through and get into college. But you have to figure the system
> or you can't win, because the odds are all on the house's side. (Silberman, 1970, pp. 146–147)

FIGURE 7.7 Teaching More Than Facts: A Lesson Design for Teaching *Romeo and Juliet*

Factual Level

Activities

1. Read the play aloud, with students taking parts and the teacher reading the more difficult parts and explaining as they progress through the play.
2. Discuss what happens in each act, using a guide sheet.
3. Introduce students to the structure of a Shakespearean tragedy.
4. Introduce major themes and elements of a Shakespearean tragedy.
5. Give quizzes after the completion of each act and at the end of the play.

Concept Level

Activities

1. Relate the plot of *Romeo and Juliet* to movies they have seen or books they have read. (A shortened version of *West Side Story* might be taught at the end of this unit in which character-by-character and scene comparisons are done.)
2. Discuss the problems Romeo and Juliet had in communicating with their parents. (Relate to Romeo's tragic flaw—impetuousness.)
3. Discuss the effects of hate and prejudice.
4. Discuss the concept of fate.
5. Introduce students to Elizabethan concepts relevant to a greater understanding of the play.
6. Point out universality of themes, characters, and situations to show their relevance to students.
7. By reading the play in class students will study it as a literary work and dramatic performance but they also will be viewing the Franco Zepherelli version of *Romeo and Juliet* to analyze his interpretation.
8. Discuss the plot complication of Juliet's impending marriage to Paris.

Generalization Level

Activities

1. Relate the specific problem of Romeo and Juliet to adolescents today.
2. Discuss alternatives to the outcome of Romeo and Juliet.
3. Discuss examples of hate and prejudice today.
4. Help students realize that reading Shakespeare's plays, like reading any great works of literature, is both a demanding and a rewarding experience.
5. Do environmental situations influence prejudice? Would there be more prejudice against gays in a small rural town or San Francisco?
7. Give examples of prejudice against nationalities, beliefs, appearance, and values.

Personal Application Level

Activities
1. What could Romeo and Juliet have done differently?
2. Do you think their death justifies the ending of the feud? (Do the means justify the end?)
3. Are Juliet's parents hypocrites?
4. How do you view the nurse's relationship to Juliet and did she betray Juliet?
5. Has the friar done the right thing for Romeo and Juliet?
6. What prejudices do you think you have?
7. How did you arrive at those prejudices? Did anyone or any situation influence you?
8. What can you and society do to help eliminate or lessen prejudice?

As noted earlier, studies (Anderson et al., 1984; Brophy, 1986b; Brophy & Kher, 1987; Doyle, 1983) suggest that students do not understand why they are learning the material presented to them or why it is being presented in the manner selected by the teacher. Given students' need for a sense of efficacy and clarity, it is not surprising that studies indicate that when students are informed about the learning process, they become more productively involved in the learning environment.

For example, Maher (1987) found that when inner-city high school students who were experiencing persistent behavior and academic problems were given opportunities to meet with teachers and discuss the material and methods to be used in the classroom each week, the students completed significantly more work. Roehler, Duffy, and Meloth (1984) found similar results when teachers were taught to call students' attention to the purpose of the learning material. Jones (1986) found that after being introduced to the concept of teaching students about the learning process and requesting students' feedback about how effectively teachers were implementing designated instructional methods, 80 percent of teachers indicated they used this process, and 87 percent stated that it had a positive effect on student learning.

One of the authors worked in a middle school that found student achievement and attitudes about school were increased when students were informed of their teachers' instructional methods and allowed to provide teachers with feedback concerning how effectively teachers followed these stated methods. The authors know of a middle school and high school that administer a learning-styles inventory to all students. The students and their teachers discuss the results, and the teachers explain how these results will influence their instructional decisions. The district has discovered that students find this information exciting and motivational and that it has been associated with both improved student behavior and academic performance. Our work with alternative schools suggests that increased opportunities for teacher-student dialogue concerning the instructional content and process is a major factor influencing reduced student behavior problems and increased student motivation when compared to students' efforts in the regular school setting.

As a professor of educational psychology, one of the authors is consistently surprised at the extremely limited amount of knowledge bright college juniors have about the learning process. Despite having spent fifteen years involved in the process, these students have virtually no understanding of the factors influencing learning and generally do not appreciate that their teachers make intentional decisions concerning the methods they use to present material. Because these students have been highly successful, they have remained in school and mastered academic content despite their lack of understanding of the learning process. Their peers who were less motivated by grades and parental pressure or who were more interactive and demanding of involvement and power in the learning process have not faired so well in their academic pursuits.

Incorporating Students' Interests

Children are incredibly curious. Anyone who has raised or taught children has variously been exhilarated, exhausted, and annoyed by their frequent "Why?" questions. Likewise, as they become able to examine abstract concepts and develop new skills in taking different perspectives (Selman, 1980), adolescents are, when given the opportunity, inquisitive, challenging learners.

One of the authors recently observed a high school physics teacher introduce a difficult concept. The teacher asked the class how many of them had, at the beginning of the year, listed understanding flight as an interest and learning goal for the class. Most students raised their hands, and the teacher reinforced this response by providing the data that had been generated during the first week of class. He then informed the class that the next two weeks would be spent on some difficult material that, by itself, had little meaning. He noted, however, that when combined with one additional skill, this material would allow them to figure trajectories and other factors associated with flight. He then asked how many of the students were interested in delving into this difficult but important material. All the students in the class raised their hands, and the stage was set for a productive series of lessons.

We are making a major mistake and creating many problems for ourselves when we fail to provide productive outlets for students' interests. Although teaching at more than the facts level will stimulate students' interest and involvement in the learning process, we can increase their motivation and learning by using a wide range of strategies that directly incorporate students' interests into the curriculum. The following methods suggest various approaches to incorporating students' interests.

Methods

1. *Early in the school year, have students build a list of things they would like to learn about each major curriculum area to which they will be exposed.* This activity provides you with valuable information and stimulates students' interest by showing that some of their learning will relate directly to their interests. You may choose to create a unit on one or more topics that received widespread interest. Topics of interest can also be incorporated into the regular school curriculum. Finally, you may integrate these interests into several of the other strategies presented in this section.

2. *When introducing a unit, have the students list questions they have about the topics that will be covered.* In addition to providing you with useful information, this activity creates for the students an association (often lacking) between their interests and the material they are asked to learn.

3. *Teach students how to order films so they can order films on topics that interest them.* Students can watch these films during study times when they have completed their work, in place of recess, or when you structure time for exploring individual interests. If a film is of particular interest because it relates to a topic being examined by the entire class or because many students share an interest, the film can be shown to the entire class.

4. *Teach students how to invite guest speakers (including parents) to discuss a topic of interest to students.* You will, of course, always want to confirm younger students' contracts, but they can learn to take major responsibility for obtaining interesting guests.

5. *Create a unit on biographies.* Students can be asked to choose a person about whom they would like to know more and acquire information about this person. Each student can then dress up like the person they have researched and make a presentation to the class as that person.

6. *Allow individual students to choose special topics they would like to study.* When presenting a unit, have students choose different aspects of the topic and report their findings to the class.

7. *Create opportunities for structured sharing.* Each day of the week can be designated as a time for sharing what students have read or accomplished in a particular area. Monday might be set aside for sharing written compositions, Tuesday for newspaper articles, Wednesday for something positive students did for someone else, and so on.

8. *Have students develop special-interest days or weeks.* Students can decide on a topic they would like to study. All subject matter for the day (or week) can be related to this topic. If they selected whales, lessons in math, reading, creative writing, science, and social studies could be constructed around whales.

9. *When involving students in creative writing, do not always assign topics.* Instead, allow them to write stories related to experiences that have been meaningful to them.

10. *Use learning logs.* In their learning logs, students write in their own words what they are learning, what it means to them, and how it relates to their own life.

11. *Begin a unit by having students write what they already know about the topic.* In addition to providing diagnostic information, you can use these data to involve students who have special interest and knowledge in instructing small groups or the entire class.

12. *Allow students to develop their own spelling list.* Teachers who use this approach often find that students who have previously learned very few spelling words make dramatic gains and select words more difficult than those they had been misspelling.

Responding to Students' Individual Learning Styles

A less obvious and relatively new approach to involving students in the learning process is to let students use an approach to learning that they find most beneficial. As mentioned in chapter 6, individual students vary considerably in the manner in which they learn most effectively, and several authors have attempted to list the factors that influence students' learning and to categorize individual learning styles.

Writers disagree on how effectively teachers can diagnose students' learning styles. Knowing the quality of knowledge available in this area and the demands individualization places on teachers, it seems reasonable that rather than attempt to individualize according to each student's preferred learning style, we should use instructional methods that respond to obvious differences in students' learning styles. Although teachers often view this as a herculean task, there are two reasonable and realistic approaches to accommodating various student learning styles.

Adjusting Environmental Factors to Meet Students' Learning Needs

One approach to responding to students' learning styles has been developed by Rita and Kenneth Dunn (see chapter 6). Research (Dunn, 1989) indicates that most students are significantly affected by approximately 6 of the 26 factors that influence students' learning (Figure 6.4). By adjusting the classroom environment and some instructional methods, we can easily create a learning environment more conducive to many students' unique learning needs.

The following methods have been implemented by ourselves and by many teachers with whom we work.

Methods

1. *When presenting material, use visual displays, such as writing on the overhead projector, to assist students who are visual learners.* Dunn (1983) states that approximately 40 percent of students learn more effectively when they can read or see something. Interestingly, Price (1980) suggests that most children are not good visual learners until they reach third or fourth grade.

2. *Allow students to select where they will sit.* Students vary in the amount of light, sound, and heat they prefer and may, in fact, self-select seats that provide more productive learning environments for them. Teachers often comment that, especially during junior high school, some students may abuse this privilege. We have found that they seldom do so if they are taught the concept of learning styles and if classroom procedures such as allowing students to select their own seats are presented as part of a procedure to make learning more personalized and effective for all students.

3. *Permit students to choose where they wish to study.* Some students work most effectively at a table, others in a soft chair, and others seated at a traditional school desk. We have taught children who worked best when they could move around the room and do their work on a clipboard.

4. *Be sensitive to individual students' needs to block out sound or visual distractions.* Discuss differences in learning style with the class and allow students to select a quiet study carrel. Also, observe students to see whether they appear easily distracted during seatwork. We have observed that teachers frequently move easily distracted students nearer to the teacher's desk. Because this is often the busiest place in the classroom, however, this move may aggravate the problem by creating more distractions for the student to cope with.

5. *Make healthy snacks available to students or allow them to bring their own.* Because many students fail to eat an adequate breakfast, mid-morning is a key time for allowing them to have a snack. Teachers who try this tactic generally find that initially all students take a cracker, carrot, or celery stick. Soon, however, only students who are hungry or who work best when they can eat will choose to eat.

6. *Provide opportunities for students to select whether they will work alone, in pairs, or with a small group.* Students can work with peers to complete assignments, study for tests, work on long-term projects, or critique each other's work.

7. *Provide adequate structure for both short-term and long-range assignments.* Students learn more effectively when seatwork is preceded by substantial direct instruction. Likewise, students need the structure provided by periodic conferences with the teacher or an assignment checklist and timetable for longer assignments.

8. *Give students instruction in study skills.* Both reflective and impulsive learners can benefit from learning to organize material prior to writing a formal paper. Some students organize material best using an outline format. More right hemisphere-oriented students may prefer to organize by mapping—a process of making connections in nonlinear fashion. Likewise, visual and kinesthetic learners profit from learning how to take notes.

9. *Provide learning activities that require use of both sides of the brain.* Figure 7.8 lists a variety of traditional instructional activities that emphasize use of either the right or left hemisphere as well as activities that tend to require use of both hemispheres.

10. *Employ individual goal setting, self-monitoring, and contracts.* These devices can assist students who require structure and concrete evidence to enhance motivation.

11. *Realize that some students require more frequent breaks than do others. Teach students how to take short breaks without disrupting the class.*

12. *Consider that students doing poorly in a subject might perform better if that subject were taught at a different time of day.* It is somewhat difficult to make this adjustment, but we have worked with several teachers who have had dramatic results by switching a student's basic-skill lesson from morning to afternoon. Secondary school schedules that rotate the periods at which classes are taught allow students to study all subjects at a time when they work best.

13. *Increase the length of time you wait before calling on a student to answer a question.* This time assists more reflective learners. Again, it is important to explain and teach this procedure to the class before implementing it.

14. *Develop learning centers that incorporate a variety of learning modalities.* Learning centers can be created that allow students to learn visually, auditorially, and kinesthetically. Learning centers also enable students to make decisions concerning light, sound, and design preferences, whether to work independently or with other students, and to select activities that allow them to deal with the material supportive of their own cognitive learning-style preference.

Incorporating a Variety of Instructional Techniques

A second approach to accommodating various student learning styles has focused on training teachers to use a wide range of instructional methods when presenting information

FIGURE 7.8 Learning Activities Related to the Right and Left Hemispheres of the Brain

LEFT

workbooks, worksheets
drill and repetition
repetitive learning games
demonstrations
copying
following directions
collecting facts
computations
record keeping
making displays
making scrapbooks

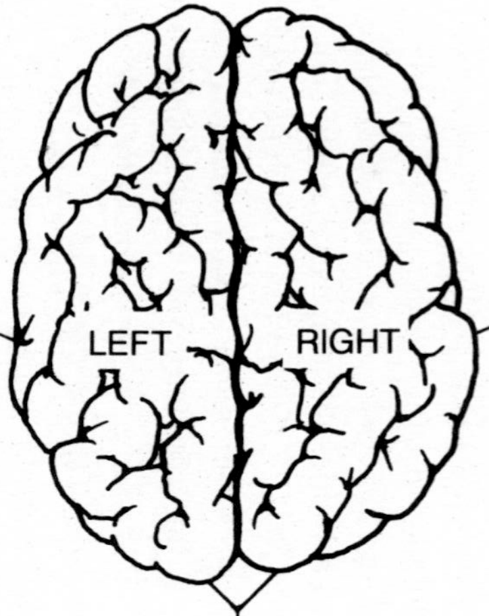

RIGHT

creative art activities
boundary breakers
guided imagery
creative writing
values clarification
use of metaphors
designing
solving old problems new ways
mythology
open-ended discussions
self-expressive activities

INTEGRATIVE

problems of logic
acting
interpreting data
hypothesizing
simulation games
dramatic presentations

directed art activities
brainstorming
oral reports
independent research
word problems
research methods

role-plays
evaluating alternatives
"show and tell"
developing plans
group projects
organizing and directing

group sharing
writing essays
being read to
reading aloud
designing an experiment
personal journals, logs

to students. A number of models have been developed to help us create more diverse instructional methods; of these, we have found three approaches most useful.

Before presenting these methods, we offer a word of caution. The methods described in the remainder of this section are quite complex, and it is likely that only the experienced teacher will be able to incorporate them from the limited exposure that can be provided here. These methods are offered because our experience indicates that their use can increase students' motivation and learning. Most readers, however, will want to consult the original source material or take a workshop on these methods in order to incorporate them consistently and effectively into their instructional repertoire.

First, in their book *Models of Teaching,* Bruce Joyce and Marsha Weil (1986) present 22 models of teaching. The presentation of each model includes a description of the instructional goals the model is best suited to meet, the student and teacher roles and relationships encouraged by the model, and the special conditions and materials needed to implement the model. Teachers with whom we have worked state that the addition of several models to their repertoire has had dramatic effects on their enjoyment of teaching as well as on students' motivation and behavior.

Second, Anthony Gregorc describes four types of learners. His work suggests that students learn best when teachers include optional approaches that students can select for practicing material or demonstrating their understanding. Figure 7.9 provides a lesson plan with options for students who have each learning-style preference described by Gregorc (1982) (see chapter 6). If you are interested in additional ideas, you can consult work by Kathleen Butler (1984).

Like Gregorc, Bernice McCarthy (1987; McCarthy, Leflar, & McNamara, 1987) states that students' learning styles can be described by four categories (see chapter 6). Rather than emphasizing the importance of determining each student's preferred category, McCarthy encourages teachers to develop lesson plans that include learning activities that systematically respond to all four student learning styles. In each unit, this approach provides some instruction matched to each student's preferred approach to learning, but it also requires that students experience and hopefully develop further skills in the other three styles of learning. Figure 7.10 offers activities for each of the four quadrants or learning styles as well as for right and left brain-dominated learners within each style.

Taking into Account Students' Level of Cognitive Development

We cannot in this book provide a comprehensive discussion of the relationship between instructional strategies and students' level of cognitive development, but we emphasize two key points. First, research (Rosenshine, 1983) indicates that many strategies associated with direct instruction are particularly important when teaching primary students. Specifically, instruction should be broken into small segments with frequent practice and the goal of overlearning; discussions should be teacher-led with an attempt to elicit primarily correct answers; material should be reviewed frequently; and most material should be presented and many numerous questions asked in order to monitor students' understanding.

Second, early adolescence is another stage that has received considerable attention in terms of desired instructional strategies. Many writers point to the need for young adolescents to deal with concrete material, be actively involved in the learning process,

FIGURE 7.9 Adjusting to Students' Learning Styles

Unit: Advertising
Goals: Students will:

1. Become aware of propaganda techniques.
2. Learn how to introduce and market an item.
3. Understand the five myths of advertising.
4. Become more aware of consumerism.
5. Become aware of careers in the field of advertising.

Possible learning activities for each learning style presented by Anthony Gregorc

Abstract sequential

1. Describe the history and growth of the advertising field in the past fifty years.
2. Interpret the meaning of the phrase *honesty in advertising.*
3. List myths about advertising.
4. Devise a theory for the recent changes in commercials that are viewed during prime time.
5. Research each advertising technique.
6. List careers in the field of advertising.

Abstract random

1. Create a taste test for the public on a new product.
2. Devise and conduct a survey about what consumers want in a fast-food restaurant.
3. Write a jingle for a product.
4. Write, then role play a commercial.
5. Design a bulletin board about advertising.

Concrete random

1. Brainstorm many ways in which advertising influences people in their daily lives.
2. Create and design a new product and its logotype.
3. Describe the types of products consumers might buy in the year 2000.
4. Write a poem or story about how toothpaste became popular.
5. Design a board game to teach facts and information about advertising.
6. Identify 25 products by their logotypes.

Concrete sequential

1. Design a storyboard using sequential procedures.
2. Write a computer game about advertising.
3. Design a wall display showing a past advertisement for a product, a current advertisement, and a future advertisement for the same product.
4. Make a collage of advertisements from various magazines by classifying them according to an advertising technique.
5. Take a field trip to an advertising agency.

FIGURE 7.10 Sample Activities for a Unit on Water Supply

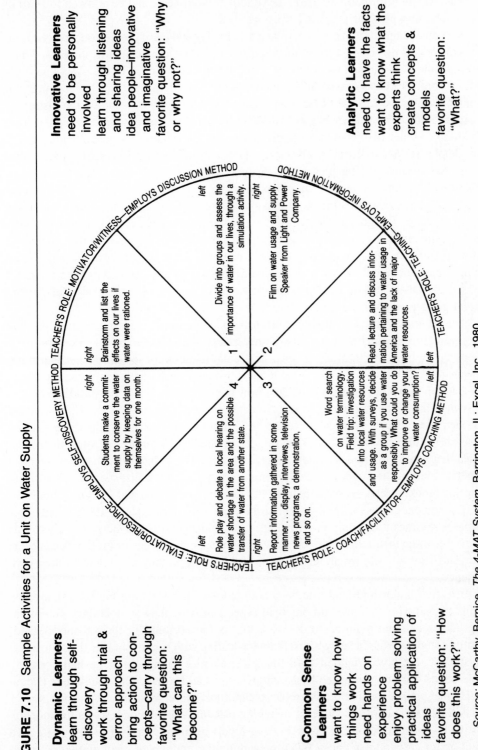

Innovative Learners
need to be personally
involved
learn through listening
and sharing ideas
idea people–innovative
and imaginative
favorite question: "Why
or why not?"

Analytic Learners
need to have the facts
want to know what the
experts think
create concepts &
models
favorite question:
"What?"

Dynamic Learners
learn through self-
discovery
work through trial &
error approach
bring action to con-
cepts–carry through
favorite question:
"What can this
become?"

**Common Sense
Learners**
want to know how
things work
need hands on
experience
enjoy problem solving
practical application of
ideas
favorite question: "How
does this work?"

TEACHER'S ROLE: MOTIVATOR/WITNESS–EMPLOYS DISCUSSION METHOD

TEACHING–EMPLOYS INFORMATION METHOD

SELF-DISCOVERY METHOD TEACHER'S ROLE: EVALUATOR/RESOURCE–EMPLOYS

TEACHER'S ROLE: COACH/FACILITATOR–EMPLOYS COACHING METHOD

TEACHER'S ROLE: TEACHING–EMPLOYS INFORMATION METHOD

right Brainstorm and list the effects on our lives if water were rationed.

left Divide into groups and assess the importance of water in our lives, through a simulation activity.

right Film on water usage and supply. Speaker from Light and Power Company.

left Read, lecture and discuss infor- mation pertaining to water usage in America and the lack of major water resources.

right Students make a commit- ment to conserve the water supply by keeping data on themselves for one month.

left Role play and debate a local hearing on water shortage in the area and the possible transfer of water from another state.

right Report information gathered in some manner . . . display, interviews, television news programs, a demonstration, and so on.

left Word search on water terminology. Field trip: investigation into local water resources and usage. With surveys, decide as a group if you use water responsibly. What could you do to improve or change your water consumption?

1
2
3
4

Source: McCarthy, Bernice. *The 4-MAT System.* Barrington, Il.: Excel, Inc., 1980.

223

study high-interest material they can relate to their own lives, work cooperatively with peers, investigate information outside the school environment, and be allowed to learn in ways congruent with their preferred learning styles.

Several examples from our experience can display and clarify these concepts. Several years ago, one of us visited a sophomore history class for low-achieving students. Three of the students were labeled emotionally disturbed and spent much of the school day in a resource room. The class also included many behavior-problem students. The lesson being presented was on the League of Nations. The class had previously studied the history of this organization. The teacher began his lesson by dividing the class into groups of five. Each group was then given the five-square game, which provides each group with a variety of puzzle pieces. When distributed properly, the pieces can be arranged so that each group member has a square. The pieces are designed, however, so that there is only one combination that enables all five members to make a square. A variety of other combinations will allow several members to make a square, but will prevent all members from building a square. The goal of the game is for each group to arrive at the situation in which each group member has a perfect square. The major rules of the game are that no talking is allowed and that although a group member can give away one or more pieces, no one can take a piece or signal to have a piece given. These rules are intended to put a premium on observing others' needs and on being willing to give up something of value for the eventual greater good of the group.

The students worked feverishly at this task for approximately fifteen minutes. By that time, several groups had finished and two other groups were blocked by members' refusing to break up their square in order to open new combinations for the group. At that time, the teacher asked the students to put aside their task and form one large circle. He began the discussion by asking students to discuss how they felt about the activity and to examine their own behavior during the exercise. Students listened carefully as their peers talked about their experiences. After approximately 15 minutes of discussion, the teacher asked the class how this activity related to the League of Nations. A number of students offered the idea that when individuals or nations protect their private interests, this act adversely affects the goals of the larger group. Students were then asked to list specific instances in which this blocking had occurred both in the League of Nations and at their school.

The student on-task level throughout the class period was nearly 100 percent. This example is not meant to imply that in every case students will respond positively to this form of classroom instruction. It does, however, indicate that behavior problems can often be prevented by actively involving students in lessons that they can relate to their own experience.

Effective junior high and middle school teachers use teaching methods that allow students to deal with concrete and practical aspects of what they are learning. Too often, young adolescents are required to do work that is too abstract for them to understand. Recently, a student brought home an assignment dealing with adverb phrases. Despite being an *A* student, the boy struggled with the material all evening. After he had correctly completed the task, he was asked to explain what he had learned. The young man had no idea. He had simply studied the example in the book and consistently replicated it.

A final example of the value of matching teachers' instructional styles to students' cognitive level occurred during our year-long involvement in a project to study effective instruction for early adolescence. When presenting the findings of a committee report to his colleagues, a junior high school teacher, who was well regarded by his colleagues, said that he wished to make a personal comment. He informed his colleagues that he had discovered he was a ''closet elementary teacher.'' He proceeded by saying that for years he had proudly kept his door open while lecturing to students. Whenever students worked in groups, were involved in gamelike activities, or in other ways studied using an active, experiential approach, though, he had closed his door. The teacher reported that over the years he had observed that students were happier and learned best when involved in the more active learning. He also commented that he went home more satisfied and relaxed on days when students had been actively involved. He reported, however, that before being involved in the district's study, he had always been embarrassed to admit that he taught in a mode other than lecture followed by seatwork. He concluded by stating that he would now proudly open his door during lessons in which students were actively involved in the learning process.

Young adolescents enjoy games, their peers, and activity. They need material to be concrete and need to see its usefulness. A significant portion of disruptive behavior (Jones, 1980) and failure (Toepfer, 1979) in secondary schools is caused by instruction that is too abstract and teacher-dominated. The following methods suggest ways in which we can adjust instruction to meet the developmental and cognitive needs of early adolescence. Many of these methods are frequently used in elementary schools.

Methods

1. *Increase active student participation.* Students should be involved in cooperative group work, competitive teams, group discussions, debates, and role playing.

2. *Learning should be concrete.* When abstract concepts are presented, use concrete activities to develop the concepts. The example of student participation in five-square, presented in this chapter, used a personalized, experiential, concrete activity to teach an abstract concept. You can also make your presentations more concrete by following the lesson design shown in Figure 7.2. Students need clear statements about goals as well as frequent summaries that help them understand the purpose of what they are learning.

3. *Use games whenever possible.* Young people are avid game players. The use of computers is successful partially because students enjoy the graphics and gamelike quality of the experience. We know a highly successful eighth-grade social studies teacher who teaches her subject by incorporating material into many types of television games.

4. *Whenever possible, relate material to students' lives.* Because they are just developing a sense of past and future, young adolescents are very here-and-now oriented. They are motivated by seeing how what they learn can help solve real problems. They will neither benefit from nor be excited about learning, in isolation, three causes of the civil war, the leading export of Australia, or adverb phrases.

5. *Bring community resources into the school and allow students to collect information in the community.* A ninth-grade teacher with 20 years of experience recently told us that if someone wanted to see his students at their best, they should be observed during field work in the community. He reported his constant amazement at the difference in energy, attitude, and behavior displayed by his 15-year-olds in class compared to the amount they showed in the community.

6. *Allow students to teach their peers.* Young adolescents are extremely peer oriented, and much positive behavior can be generated by involving them in goal-directed peer activities.

7. *Involve students in evaluating their own work as well as your instruction.* Young adolescents have a strong developmental need to experience a sense of responsibility and control over their environment. They are motivated by sincere and consistent efforts to involve them in goal setting and evaluation.

8. *Provide adequate structure for learning activities.* Because early adolescents are experiencing extreme physical, personal, and cognitive changes in their lives, they need structure in their school experience. Assignments should be clear and must be frequently checked by the teacher. Students should know exactly how they will be graded, and they benefit by keeping records of their assignments and grades. We can also instruct students on taking notes and other key study skills.

Involving Students in Academic Goal Setting

As discussed in chapter 6, students will be more motivated by instructional tasks when they experience a sense of control over their environment and perceive themselves as mastering material. Students who perceive themselves as directing their own learning work harder and take greater pride in the outcome than do students who are less involved in decision making.

Individual goal setting is perhaps the most effective method for enabling students to experience a sense of understanding and controlling their own learning while incorporating their own interests. This method also has potential for helping students select learning activities that are congruent with their learning style.

Teachers need to help students develop goals that are both realistic and directed at improving skill deficits revealed by diagnostic testing and observation, but students' involvement in establishing goals and recording progress can also significantly enhance their motivation and reduce acting-out or withdrawal behavior.

An academic goal statement or contract should include (1) what material the student plans to learn, (2) what activities the student will engage in to develop these skills, (3) the degree of proficiency the student will reach, and (4) how the student will demonstrate that the learning has occurred. We can use several approaches when implementing academic goals. Each student can be involved in working toward one or more academic goals associated with a personal skill deficit or interest. This emphasis on goals can be expanded to incorporate term-length goal statements. Because most schools provide an academic report to parents (and, we hope, to students) following a nine-week term, students can be aided in setting several academic goals on a term basis. Nine weeks will be too long for primary children, but most intermediate-grade and secondary students with whom we have worked say they find nine-week goal setting provides a sense of direction and commitment. At the beginning of each term you and the student can examine the student's current performance level and the material he or she will study during the term. The student can be helped to write several goals for the term, perhaps stating that by the end of the term he or she will be able to solve two-place multiplication problems with 80 percent accuracy. It is obviously important that we help each student choose goals that are attainable but that will require some additional effort by the child. Although children are motivated to achieve goals that require some real effort, they are also frequently intimidated by goals that seem impossible to reach. Furthermore, continued failure tends to reduce students' achievement orientation and self-concept.

Figure 7.11 is an example of a high-interest form an elementary or middle school teacher could use to help students commit themselves to specific academic goals.

When working with students who have difficulty organizing their work and who have a history of school failure, it is often helpful to use a detailed goal-planning sheet that helps the students make very specific decisions. Figure 7.12 presents an example of such a form. When working with students who possess fairly good study skills and who have a history of average or above-average school success, teachers will generally want to use less detailed goal setting forms. At the beginning of each unit, students might be asked to list such things as the grade they wish to earn, the percentage of assignments they plan to complete on time, and specific new information they wish to possess following the lessons. It is important that teachers support this process by clearly stating their goals in terms of student learning outcomes. Teachers can also help by providing students with forms that ask specific questions about students' learning goals. Student responses should be collected, responded to, and returned to students as soon as possible. Teachers should confer with students whose goals seem unrealistically high or low.

Another approach to employing academic goal setting involves designing assignments that allow students to choose the type of work they will complete, and, if appropriate, the grade they will earn for completing the designated amount of work. The most common format for using this method involves listing assignments for earning each grade and having students sign a contract indicating which assignments they plan to complete. This approach is particularly effective when we wish to involve all students in an assignment on which lower-achieving students might experience considerable difficulty with more complex aspects of the assignment. A contractual approach enables each student to choose an appropriate level of difficulty, and we can ensure that the basic concepts are learned by incorporating them within the lowest acceptable level. Students respond positively to this approach because it is a clear statement of what they will learn and what they must accomplish.

The benefits of this approach were highlighted in a recent study involving behavior problem adolescents (Maher, 1987). In this study, 49 high school students identified under special education classification as behavior disordered were placed in mainstream classes. Half the students and their mainstream teachers were involved in jointly setting academic goals and specifying the instructional methods that would be used to reach these goals. The remaining students were placed with teachers who were required to set instructional goals but who did not work with students in setting these goals or discussing instructional methods. Results indicated that students involved in goal setting and a discussion of instructional methods learned more, felt more positive about school, and felt that this approach would be useful with other handicapped students. Teachers involved in the experimental group used a greater diversity of instructional methods, were positive about the approach, and stated that they could incorporate the approach within their normal planning.

Implementing Self-Evaluation

Involving students in self-evaluation not only saves us much time and energy, but it also provides students with an opportunity to understand their academic performance better and to experience a sense of personal responsibility. When students evaluate and record their

FIGURE 7.11 Goal-Setting Form

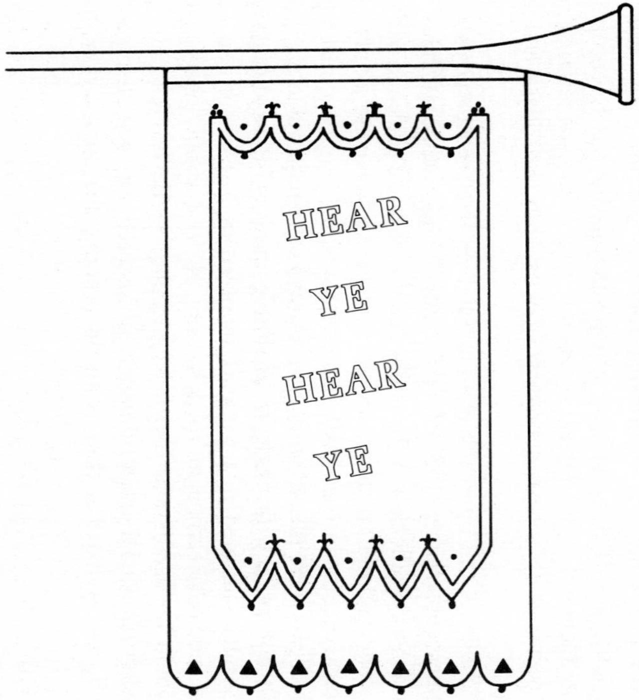

HEAR YE HEAR YE

My Goal in _____ for
(subject)

today is to _____

_____

I will have my goal completed

by _____ with _____ %
(time)

accuracy.

_____
student

_____
date

_____
teacher

FIGURE 7.12   Goal Planning Worksheet

Name _____ Class _____ Date _____

1. Goal: _____
   _____

2. Reason(s) for working on goal: _____
   _____

3. Where will you work on the goal: _____
   _____

4. Time needed to finish goal: _____
5. Materials needed: _____
   _____

6. Steps used to reach goals:
   a. _____
   b. _____
   c. _____
   d. _____
   e. _____
   f. _____

7. Prediction of my success:
   Choose one: Grade _____   Points _____
               Percent (70) _____   Other_____

8. Records:
   Goal Sheet _____   Checklist _____
   Graph/Chart _____   Timeline _____
   Products _____   Other _____

9. Reward: _____

Source: Van Reusen, A. K., & Bos, C. S. (1988), The Goal Regulation Strategy

own work, they are more likely to develop an internal locus of control and view their progress as based on their own efforts. Similarly, self-evaluation enables students to acknowledge areas that need improvement. In working with third-grade students from an inner-city public school, Klein and Schuler (1974) found that when students were allowed to evaluate their own performance contingent on passing skill tests in math, their performance improved markedly. Apparently, the ability to be autonomous was motivating to these students. Allowing students to score their own work also demonstrates our respect for them, which in turn enhances students' sense of significance and competence, and the associated increase in self-esteem often has a positive effect on students' behavior.

Students are impressed with displays of data, especially when the data deal with their own performance. Data provide immediate, concrete reinforcement for learning. Students often fail to associate their seemingly herculean efforts with actual increased knowledge or changes in behavior. Data make the learning or behavior change a concrete experience, which alone often provides more reinforcement than any free time or praise from us. Surprisingly, the benefits associated with monitoring progress may be particularly great for students who are progressing slowly. These students often view themselves as making no progress or actually falling behind (as indeed they may be when the basis for comparison is their peers' work). Providing these students with specific data that demonstrate their progress is perhaps the most effective and honest motivational strategy.

Student goal setting provides an ideal opportunity for introducing regular data collection into the classroom. Students need periodic checks to determine how they are progressing toward their goals. One method for monitoring students' progress is to teach them to chart their own improvements. We can do so by instructing them in using graph paper to display results. Because bar graphs involve simple counting, students will have little difficulty in acquiring this skill. In fact, one of us worked with a teacher who successfully taught primary grade, emotionally disturbed children to use six-cycle graph paper.

Once students have learned how to chart data, they can begin to monitor their own progress. The graphs can be kept in their desk or notebook and should be attached to the associated contract or statement of goals. Students can be asked to contact the teacher or a peer with whom they are working if their graph suggests that they are having difficulty reaching their goal. We should, of course, periodically check students' results to see whether they are making satisfactory progress in reaching their goals. Figures 7.13 and 7.14 are examples of charts students can use to record their academic progress.

Students can use the form in Figure 7.14 to combine goal setting and self-evaluation. Each week students take a spelling pretest (students of varying ability have different numbers of words and therefore use a longer or shorter form). The students record the pretest score and, based on this score, select a goal for the number of words they will spell correctly on the posttest. A visual image also is provided by having the students color in the number of words spelled correctly on the pretest and (in a different color) the posttest. Of equal importance, the teacher also has students record the number of words they learn each week. This helps students learn the critical distinction between how their learning compares to that of other students and their own learning gains. On a separate chart students record the number of words they have learned each week and the cumulative total for the year. It is possible that some of the least-skilled spellers will learn more spelling words (based on formal spelling tests) than the better spellers in the class, who miss very few words on their pretests.

Another approach to student self-evaluation is to involve students either in pre-parent conferences or to include students in parent-teacher conferences. Teacher-student conferences held prior to parent-teacher conferences can be a chance for students to evaluate their own behavior and academic performance and compare this to the marks we have prepared. Teacher and student can discuss any differences, which can lead either to a compromise or to our helping the student better understand his or her marks and setting specific goals for obtaining the desired marks during the next marking period. Another obvious advantage to this type of teacher-student conference is that it can reduce the anxiety many students experience in parent-teacher conferences. The fear of the unknown is eliminated when students know their marks and the issues we plan to discuss with their parents.

Cooperative Learning

As children become less egocentric and more social, they increasingly enjoy and benefit from working with their peers to achieve learning goals. Considerable research evidence indicates the value of students' working in groups. David Johnson discusses this work:

FIGURE 7.13 Spelling Record

Name________________________

Pretest ____	Pretest ____	Pretest ____	Pretest ____	Pretest ____	Review Week Score ______
Goal ____	Goal ____	Goal ____	Goal ____	Goal ____	
Posttest ____	Posttest ____	Posttest ____	Posttest ____	Posttest ____	Units Goal Was Reached
Learned ____	Learned ____	Learned ____	Learned ____	Learned ____	Unit __ ____
					Unit __ ____
					Unit __ ____
					Unit __ ____
					Unit __ ____

20			20			20			20			20		
19			19			19			19			19		
18			18			18			18			18		
17			17			17			17			17		
16			16			16			16			16		
15			15			15			15			15		
14			14			14			14			14		
13			13			13			13			13		
12			12			12			12			12		
11			11			11			11			11		
10			10			10			10			10		
9			9			9			9			9		
8			8			8			8			8		
7			7			7			7			7		
6			6			6			6			6		
5			5			5			5			5		
4			4			4			4			4		
3			3			3			3			3		
2			2			2			2			2		
1			1			1			1			1		

FIGURE 7.14 Monitoring Acquisition of Skills

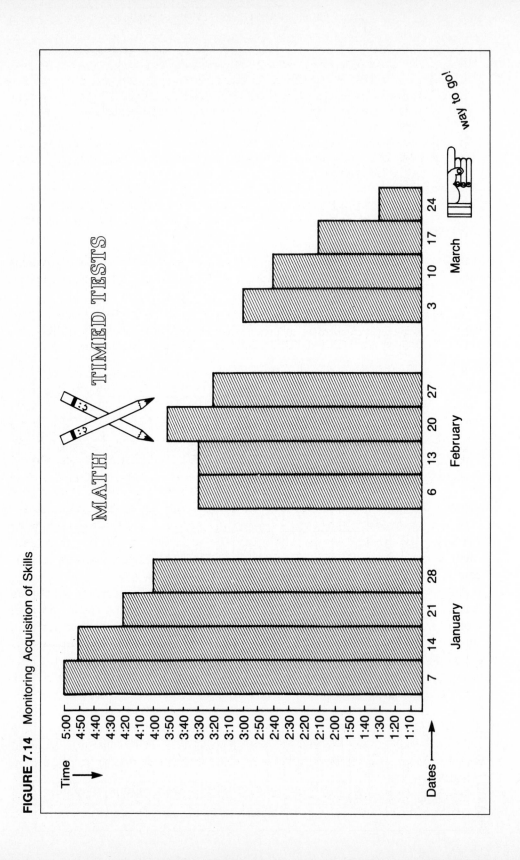

The successful mastery, retention, and transfer of concepts, rules, and principles is higher in cooperatively structured learning than in competitive or individualistic learning. . . . Members of cooperative groups evolve superior strategies for conceptual learning, seek and utilize others' information more effectively, cognitively rehearse and formulate in their own words the material being learned, and cover more material in a shorter period of time. . . .

The more cooperative students' attitudes and experiences, the more they see themselves as being intrinsically motivated, persevering in pursuit of clearly defined learning goals, believing it is their own efforts that determine school success, wanting to be good students and get good grades, and believing that ideas, feelings and learning new ideas are important and positive . . . students experiencing cooperative instruction like the teacher better and perceive the teacher as being more supportive and accepting (academically and personally) than do students experiencing competitive or individualistic instruction. (Johnson, 1979, pp. 149–151)

As mentioned in chapter 6, working cooperatively with peers not only enhances learning and positive attitudes toward both subject matter and school in general, but it also creates positive peer relationships and enhances students' self-esteem.

Teachers interested in implementing cooperative learning can choose from a wide variety of methods. Cooperative learning methods, however, generally fall into three types or approaches: (1) simple structure, (2) process, and (3) extended structure.

Simple Structure Activities

Simple structures refer to activities teachers can use periodically to stimulate discussion and review materials. In his book *Cooperative Learning: Resources for Teachers,* Spencer Kagan (1989) presents a number of simple structure activities that can be used in any subject matter. Roundtable is one activity in which the teacher asks a question that has numerous possible answers—such as to list all the possible causes of the Civil War or all the common denominators for 24 and 42. Students then make a list on one sheet of paper, with each student adding one answer and passing the paper to the left. Numbered head together is another activity. Students are again asked a question and placed in small groups to develop an answer. Each student in the group is assigned a number. The students work until the teacher signals them to stop. The teacher then calls out a number and each student assigned that number raises his or her hand. This student is the group's representative and can be called on to present the group's answer.

Another simple structure activity called Stars is used to review material and prepare students for a quiz or test. After the teacher has presented the material, study groups of three or four students of mixed abilities are assigned. Each group is asked to develop five questions related to the material being studied and to provide the correct answer for each question. Each member of the group makes a copy of this material. The next task (usually occurring the following day) involves creating quiz groups consisting of students from different study groups. In the quiz group one person at a time reads a question from his or her list and the other students write down the answer they think is correct. The person who read the question then provides the correct answer and the person to the right asks the next question. This process continues until each person has read all the questions prepared by the study group. The questions are then collected and the teacher prepares a test from these questions.

Teachers interested in developing simple structure cooperative activities can find excellent ideas in *Cooperative Learning: Resources for Teachers* by Spencer Kagan (1989) (available by writing Resources for Teachers, Suite 201, 27402 Camini Capistrano, Laguna Niguel, CA 92677), and in Johnson and Johnson's (1985) *Cooperative Learning: Warm-Ups, Grouping Strategies and Group Activities.*

Process Approach

David and Roger Johnson from the University of Minnesota have conducted numerous research studies and written extensively on cooperative learning. We term their approach the *process approach* because it highlights a process or series of steps teachers can apply to implement cooperative learning with any subject matter. The Johnsons state that there are five basic elements of this process (Johnson, Johnson, & Johnson-Holubec, 1988):

1. *Positive interdependence.* This element involves structuring goals and activities so that students must be concerned about the performance of all members of the group. This can be accomplished through such methods as providing only one copy of the material (materials interdependence), assigning each group member a role (role interdependence), making success dependent on all members' reaching a specified goal (goal interdependence), assigning the same grade or reward to each group member (reward interdependence), or providing each member only a portion of the information necessary to complete the task (resource interdependence). The key is that the group members know that they are in it together and that they sink or swim together.

2. *Individual accountability.* This means that every student is accountable for mastering the material. This can be accomplished through the traditional means of having each student take a quiz or otherwise demonstrate competence. It can also be created by indicating to students that any group member can be asked to demonstrate mastery of the content by being called to the overhead or by being called on in some other way.

3. *Face-to-face interaction.* Students are arranged in such a manner that they are knee to knee and eye to eye and are involved in actively sharing and discussing the content.

4. *Teaching collaborative skills.* To function effectively in groups, students must learn how to work cooperatively in a small group. Figure 7.15 lists specific group skills the authors have found it important to teach students. Figure 7.16 presents the steps Johnson and Johnson (1987) have outlined for teaching students cooperative skills.

5. *Processing group skills.* Once students have been introduced to cooperative group skills, it is necessary to monitor and reinforce these skills consistently. This task will initially be accomplished by the teacher, but it can be transferred to students as they develop proficiency in the skills. When initially teaching and monitoring group skills, it is best to focus on one or two skills at a time. As students become more familiar with group skills,

FIGURE 7.15 Group Collaborative Skills

1. State the assignment.
2. State the group process goal(s).
3. Call attention to the time limit.
4. Assign group roles (if used).
5. Proceed with the assignment.
6. Summarize the activity.
7. Evaluate the group process skills.

FIGURE 7.16 Helping Students Develop Collaborative Skills

1. Do students believe the skill is needed and useful?
2. Do students understand what the skill is, what the behaviors are, what the sequence of behaviors is, and how it looks when it is all put together?
3. Have students had an opportunity to practice the skill?
4. Have students received feedback that is immediate, descriptive, and specific?
5. Have students persevered in practicing the skill?
6. Have students had the opportunity to use the skill successfully?
7. Have students used the skill frequently enough so that they have integrated the skill into their natural behavior?
8. Do the classroom norms support the use of the skill?

they can be monitored on three to five skills at a time. Figure 7.17 provides an example of a form the authors have found helpful for monitoring group skills.

Figure 7.18 presents the steps Johnson, Johnson, & Johnson-Holubec (1988) suggest for teachers who are interested in incorporating cooperative learning into their classroom. Teachers interested in incorporating the Johnsons' approach to cooperative learning into their classrooms can find a variety of materials available and can also attend well-designed workshops to develop the needed experience and skills. The materials the authors have found most helpful are *Learning Together and Alone, Circles of Learning, Cooperation in the Classroom*, and *Cooperative Learning: Warm-Ups, Grouping Strategies and Group Activities*. (These materials can be ordered through Interaction Book Company, 7208

FIGURE 7.17 Teacher Observation Sheet

Tally the number of times students demonstrate a skill.							
	Group One				*Group Two*		
Skill	*Bob*	*Nancy*	*Tariq*		*Rolando*	*Marissa*	*Beryl*
Contributes ideas							
Encourages others							
Listens							
Participates							
Checks for understanding							
Organizes the task							

FIGURE 7.18 The Teacher's Role in Cooperation

Make Decisions

Specify Academic and Collaborative Objectives. What academic and/or collaborative skills do you want students to learn or practice in their groups? Start with something easy.

Decide on Group Size. Students often lack collaborative skills, so start with groups of two or three students; later advance cautiously to fours.

Assign Students to Groups. Heterogeneous groups are the most powerful, so mix abilities, sexes, cultural backgrounds, and task orientations. Assign students to groups randomly or select groups yourself.

Arrange the Room. The closer the students are to each other, the better they can communicate. Group members should be "knee to knee and eye to eye."

Plan Materials. Materials can send a "sink or swim together" message to students if you give only one paper to the group or give each member part of the material to learn and then teach the group.

Assign Roles. Students are more likely to work together if each one has a job which contributes to the task. You can assign work roles such as Reader, Recorder, Calculator, Checker, Reporter, and Materials Handler or skill roles such as Encourager of Participation, Praiser, and Checker for Understanding.

Set the Lesson

Explain the Academic Task. Prepare students by teaching them any material they need to know, then make certain they clearly understand what they are to do in the groups. This might include explaining lesson objectives, defining concepts, explaining procedures, giving examples, and asking questions.

*Structure Positive Interdependence. Students must feel that they need each other to complete the group's task, that they "sink or swim together." Some ways to create this are by establishing mutual goals (students must learn the material and make certain group members learn the material), joint rewards (if all group members achieve above a certain percentage on the test, each will receive bonus points), shared materials and information, and assigned roles.

*Structure Individual Accountability. Each student must feel responsible for learning the material and helping the group. Some ways to ensure this feeling include frequent oral quizzing of group members picked at random, giving individual tests, having everyone in the group write (pick one paper at random to grade), or having students do work first to bring to the group.

Structure Intergroup Cooperation. Having groups check with and help other groups and giving rewards or praise when all class members do well can extend the benefits of cooperation to the whole class.

Explain the Criteria for Success. Student work should be evaluated on a criteria-referenced rather than a norm-referenced basis. Make clear your criteria for evaluating the groups' work.

Specify Expected Behaviors. The more specific you are about the behaviors you want to see in the groups, the more likely students will do them. Make it clear that you expect to see everyone contributing, helping, listening with care to others, encouraging others to participate, and asking for help or clarification. Younger students may need to be told to stay with their group, take turns, share, ask group members questions, and use quiet voices.

Teach Collaborative Skills. After students are used to working in groups, pick one collaborative skill they need to learn, point out the need for it, define it carefully, have students give you phrases they can say when using the skill, post the phrases (praise, bonus points, stars), and observe for and encourage the use of the skill until students are doing it automatically. Then teach a second skill. Consider praising, summarizing, encouraging, checking for understanding, asking for help, or generating further answers.

Monitor and Intervene

Arrange Face-to-Face Interaction. The beneficial educational outcomes of cooperative learning groups are due to the interaction patterns and verbal exchanges that take place among students. Make certain there is oral summarizing, giving and receiving explanations, and elaborating going on.

Monitor Students' Behavior. This is the fun part! While students are working, you circulate to see whether they understand the assignment and the material, give immediate feedback and reinforcement, and praise good use of group skills.

Provide Task Assistance. If students are having trouble with the task, you can clarify, reteach, or elaborate on what they need to know.

Intervene to Teach Collaborative Skills. If students are having trouble with group interactions, you can suggest more effective procedures for working together or more effective behaviors for them to engage in. You can ask students to figure out how to work more effectively together. If students are learning or practicing a skill, record on an observation sheet how often you hear that skill, then share your observations with the groups.

Evaluate and Process

Evaluate Student Learning. Assess how well students completed the task and give them feedback on how well they did.

Process Group Functioning. In order to improve, students need time and procedures for analyzing how well their group is functioning and how well they are using collaborative skills. Processing can be done by individuals, small groups, or the whole class. To start, have groups routinely list three things they did well in working together today and one thing they will do better tomorrow. Then summarize as a whole class.

Provide Closure. To reinforce student learning you may wish to have groups share answers or paper, summarize major points in the lesson, or review important facts.

---

*Essential Elements of Cooperative Learning Groups

Source: D. Johnson, R. Johnson, and E. Johnson-Holubec, *Cooperation in the Classroom* (Edina, Minn.: Interaction Book Co., 1988), pp. 2-38–2-39.

Cornelia Drive, Edina, MN 55435. Additional information can be obtained through the Cooperative Learning Center, the University of Minnesota, (612) 624–7031.)

Extended Structure Approach

Robert Slavin and his colleagues at Johns Hopkins University have produced several approaches and a variety of methods that combine cooperation and competition with a game or tournament activity. These methods are referred to as Student Team Learning. The most popular are Teams Games Tournament (TGT) and Student Teams—Achievement Division (STAD).

Teams Games Tournament (TGT) includes four steps. First, the teacher presents material to the whole class. Second, students study together in heterogeneous groups of four or five to master content and prepare for a tournament at the end of the week. Third, students are assigned to tables comprising three students of similar ability and from different teams. The three students compete at academic games (usually questions on cards or dittos prepared by the teacher) to demonstrate mastery of material covered that week. By answering questions, students earn points for their team. Fourth, the points earned by team members at their various tables are totaled to determine the team's weekly score. These scores are often published in a weekly newsletter as a means to provide students with recognition for their efforts. In addition, depending on individual performance in the weekly tournament, the teacher may rearrange the groups to ensure that all groups have an opportunity to experience success.

Student Teams—Achievement Division (STAD) is a modified form of TGT. In this approach, weekly individual quizzes replace the tournaments, but points are still totaled for the group and recognition is provided for group scores. STAD has become increasingly popular because it is easier to implement than TGT. Also, because it does not include face-to-face competition, it is less competitive; this is important for some students. (Information on the use of these methods can be obtained by writing The Johns Hopkins Team Learning Project, Center for Research on Elementary and Middle Schools, The Johns Hopkins University, 3505 N. Charles Street, Baltimore, MD 21218.)

Summary of Cooperative Learning

In general, research seems to indicate that cooperative learning activities that include some form of competition and group rewards are more effective than those that depend on the benefits of students' working together. However, the benefits of cooperative learning are considerable even when these variables are not a major focus of the activity. Given the problems associated with competition and rewards, we encourage teachers to focus as much as possible on the benefits of improved learning for all students, to help individual students and the class keep records of learning gains, and to emphasize the joy in assisting one another. Also, as discussed in chapter 11, teachers should emphasize social and activity reinforcement and minimize the use of concrete, tangible rewards for achievement gains.

It is also important to realize that none of the authors or trainers involved in cooperative learning believes it should replace teacher-directed instruction. Even though cooperative learning can be used to generate ideas or can serve as a pretest to determine students' knowledge, students need to learn material from teachers and in many cases do not have the skill to develop new information or a new concept. Therefore, cooperative learning is most effective when it is used to practice or work on the application of material first introduced by a teacher. As noted earlier in this chapter, cooperative learning can be used in the context of different learning activities intended to meet the needs of students with varying learning styles. Cooperative learning is a technique that supports and enhances a number of instructional decisions, but it is not intended to be an end in itself. Nevertheless, the benefits of using cooperative learning are considerable, and we encourage readers not currently using this method to consider incorporating it into their instructional repertoire. Good and Brophy (1987) effectively summarize the value of cooperative learning:

Achievement effects appear to be positive for all types of students, although there are some indications that black and Hispanic students gain even more from cooperative learning arrangements than Anglo students do.

Effects on outcomes other than achievement are even more impressive. Cooperative learning arrangements promote friendship choices and prosocial patterns of interaction among students who differ in achievement, sex, race, or ethnicity, and they promote the acceptance of mainstreamed handicapped students by their nonhandicapped classmates. Cooperative methods also frequently have positive effects, and rarely have negative effects, on affective outcomes such as self-esteem, academic self-confidence, liking for the class, liking and feeling liked by classmates, and various measures of empathy and social cooperation. (p. 438)

Our own work in training elementary, middle school, and high school teachers in cooperative learning has reinforced these findings. Teachers with whom we have worked have been extremely impressed with the benefits related to student attitudes toward the subject matter and their peers and with the achievement gains made by lower-achieving students.

When implementing cooperative learning, teachers should, however, realize that having students work in groups, even when the teacher has structured the activity to encourage positive interdependence and individual accountability, will not ensure a productive learning environment. As with any other activity (see chapter 9), teachers need to instruct students in the classroom procedures to be followed when involved in cooperative learning activities. For example,

1. Do the students clearly understand their task and the associated learning goals?
2. Do the students understand why you have chosen to use group work to facilitate their learning the content?
3. Do the students find intrinsic, achievement, or utility value in the material?
4. Do the students possess the skills necessary to complete the task; that is, do they know how to use the materials, and can at least several students in each group read any written material associated with the task?
5. Are all materials readily available, and has a procedure been established so they can be easily obtained?
6. Do the students know how much time they have to complete the task?
7. Do the students know what they should do if they require assistance?
8. Do the students know what to do if they finish early or what options are available if they cannot complete the task in the allotted time?
9. Have you established a method for gaining the students' attention should it be necessary to add an instruction, clarify a problem, or ask the groups to stop their work?
10. Do the students know the behaviors that will be expected of them while they work in the group?

Using Peer Tutoring

A number of benefits can be derived from implementing peer tutoring in a classroom. First, tutoring fosters the concept that asking for and offering help are positive behaviors. This act encourages cooperation and concern for peers and thereby creates a more supportive, safe learning environment. Second, the opportunity to instruct another child can provide a student with a sense of competence and personal worth. Third, in assisting another student, the student frequently learns the material more thoroughly. The combination of increased understanding and the act of instructing another student frequently makes a student a more excited and confident learner. Finally, peer tutoring helps the teacher monitor and individualize instruction. By allowing students to serve as resources for other students, we increase the availability of individual attention and thereby reduce students' frustration and the accompanying acting-out behavior.

Although peer tutoring has many benefits, it can become a frustrating and counterproductive activity if students are not provided with skills in how to assist each other. Therefore, it is important that if we plan to implement peer tutoring we then provide our students with instruction in how to assist another student. We can do so by listing and discussing the dos and don'ts of helping someone with the work. We can then model appropriate behavior, and we should allow students to practice this behavior and receive feedback from us. If the equipment is available, students can be videotaped while assisting other students, and the tape can be viewed and discussed. An exciting aspect of providing students with instruction in how to teach another student is that this activity helps them better understand the learning process.

There are numerous approaches to implementing peer tutoring. Students can be provided with green and red 8½-inch-square cards attached to their desks so that they can be displayed in front of the desk. Students who need help during seatwork can display a red card, and students who understand this material and are willing to assist other students can display a green card. This procedure can be particularly helpful when we are busy working with a small group and are not available to assist students. A similar approach involves our listing on the board the names of students who are able to assist their peers on a project.

Assigning individual students to work with a student who needs assistance is another common approach to peer tutoring. This activity may involve students in the same class or students from higher grades. Another method involves arranging students' desks in groups of four and informing students that they may assist their peers as long as they follow previously learned procedures for effective teaching.

Recently one of us observed a young teacher presenting an art lesson to a group of eighth-grade students. The teacher was working with a particularly difficult class. The class included several students whom the school had characterized as behavior problems, as well as a very withdrawn, emotionally handicapped boy. The teacher indicated that she was somewhat concerned about the day's lesson because she had a very limited background in the material she was presenting. She also said that the last period of the day on a particularly nice spring day was not the ideal time to be teaching eighth graders a concept as difficult as depth perception. With this introduction, I was prepared to observe chaos and to have numerous opportunities for observing the teacher's skills in dealing with behavior problems.

The teacher began the lesson by briefly reviewing the material she had presented on the previous day. She appeared comfortable responding to a variety of students' questions. On one occasion, a student pointed out a major flaw in something she had presented. The teacher indicated that she did not see his point and asked the student if he would be willing to come up to the board and clarify his point for both her and the class. The student did so, and the class responded politely to his brief instruction.

After perhaps ten minutes of instruction, the teacher indicated that the students should continue working on their assignments. She commented that some students were finding the tasks more difficult than others and suggested that when they had a problem, they find another student to help them. As students began working on their projects, the teacher circulated around the room answering students' questions and reinforcing students' work.

It soon became apparent, however, that she could not possibly answer all the questions that were being fired at her. Her interventions then changed from direct work with students to serving as a clearing center for resources available within the classroom. As she moved around the room, she made comments such as, ''Why don't you ask John? He does a good job with two-point perspective.'' ''It might help, Bill, if you could explain to him why you. . . . '' ''I really appreciate your helping, Sue. You did a really good job of teaching because you helped him to discover the answer for himself.''

As I observed the class, I was impressed with the extremely high percentage of on-task behavior displayed by the students. In addition, the teacher's role as facilitator freed her to spend much time with her most severely disturbed student. Because she had structured students' responses to be positive and supportive, students' interactions through-out the class period were extremely positive. In addition to assisting each other, students frequently showed their work to their peers and almost always received either compliments or constructive suggestions.

In examining the dynamics of this class period, it is interesting to recall Postman and Weingartner's (1969) statement that teachers should perhaps teach subjects outside of their area of academic preparation. When teaching subjects they understand extremely well, teachers often do all the teaching, while the students are forced into the role of passive learner. On the other hand, when teachers are learning the material or are somewhat unsure of the content, it may be easier to allow students to become involved as co-learners and team teachers. It may appear that material is being covered more slowly (and perhaps more noisily) when using this format, but the theoretical considerations and research results presented earlier in this section point to many advantages associated with this form of instruction.

An increasingly popular approach to peer tutoring involves creating support groups outside the classroom for students who have the ability to complete their work but who have experienced serious and persistent achievement problems. Sullivan (1988) reports the results of a special study groups program for middle school students whose ability levels indicated that they could pass their courses but who were failing one or more courses. Students were involved in weekly study skills meetings with the vice-principal, met with their group to work on assignments several times a week, and received a progress report every Friday. Results indicated that 50 percent of the total number of grades received by students in the study skills groups went up at least one grade, and only 10 percent of the grades went down. Results for a control group showed that only 14 percent of the grades went up.

A Case Study

This case study, taken verbatim from a project completed by a high school English teacher as part of her work in a graduate education course, typifies how you can incorporate ideas found throughout this book to help individual students reach their potential. We chose this example because:

1. It was carried out and written by a teacher who deals with 140 students each day.
2. The teacher developed and carried out the project with no assistance.
3. The teacher has just completed a course using this text as the major sourcebook.

At first I didn't take much notice of Bill in my freshman and sophomore-level writing class. He's one of those quiet, unobtrusive students, the kind you love to use in a seating chart as a barrier between the class clown and a social butterfly. Rarely, if ever, did he call attention to himself. He never raised his hand to volunteer an answer, and when called on, would struggle so to come up with an appropriate response that I would too frequently—to avoid his obvious embarrassment—cut short his efforts and recognize one of the hands waving excitedly around him. He is never late to class; he has never asked for a hall pass; he never questions directions or instructions for an assignment; he seldom visits in class with his neighbors; he always appears to listen attentively to lectures. Therefore, next to the 140 other students who come to me daily with varying levels of ability and enthusiasm for "creative writing," Bill, at first, didn't demand a lot of my attention.

A couple of weeks into the term, however, I began to notice that in fact Bill was becoming a problem of the subtler type: he was not doing his assignments. In fact, his pattern of behavior seemed suspiciously close to what has been categorized as "failure syndrome"—a feeling of defeatism and helplessness resulting from repeated failure. Therefore, after three weeks of inconsistent, below-class-average performance, I decided to investigate Bill's history as a student in our district.

I discovered that in his elementary years he was apparently a pleasure to his teachers. Their comments on his conduct and citizenship grades suggested he was a model of exemplary behavior, and his academic marks were "satisfactory" or better. In junior high school, however, his grades began to slip; notably, those earned in English dropped to a "D" average throughout his seventh and eighth grades. As a result, his junior high English teachers recommended that he be placed in Sentences (our low-level remedial-writing class) during the first term of his freshman year in high school. Let there be no doubt that, as well-intentioned as this program may be, a stigma is attached to this placement as surely as if these students wore a badge that proclaimed their lack of proficiency and their below-average performance. At any rate, in Sentences he earned a term grade of "C minus" and was promoted the next year to Paragraphs. That is where our paths crossed.

Next, I checked into Bill's current C.A.T. scores. The grade-level score for overall comprehension for his age group is 9.7; Bill's score was 7.7—two years below grade level. On the Gates Reading Test he had scored 8.3 on comprehension; the grade-level score is 9.3. He scored about a year below grade level, no small consideration in a class such as writing, which is a complex activity requiring mature, advanced mental operations. Therefore, his scores indicated that many of the writing tasks I required of him were quite possibly beyond his level of competence.

I wondered about his other classes. So I sent a Progress Report form to his other teachers to determine how successful he was in his other courses. The results were that in classes requiring incremental, concrete, mechanical exercises he was doing above-average work. But in the majority of his classes—those requiring more abstract, complex cognitive processes—his grades were below average. Unfortunately, the beginning of a pattern seemed to be developing that, without intervention, sooner or later would probably lead to resignation on his part.

Glasser's theory indicated what my first move should be: provide a caring atmosphere. I decided to make a point of casually noticing him, smiling and saying hello as he entered the classroom daily. I routinely do this to my students at random, and so this notice didn't cause him to be unduly curious. But each day I made sure I spoke to him until it became a habit for both of us. The next step he provided. He received the "Outstanding Athlete of the Week" award, for which I, of course, complimented him and placed his newspaper picture on a bulletin board in my room where "Class Heroes" who have received such an honor get recognition of some sort. On seeing his picture in this spot and receiving accolades from his classmates, I believe his chest size must have expanded three inches.

While he was feeling more comfortable and "invited" in the classroom, he seemed to be gaining confidence in himself, which was reflected in his assignments. (And was I also—albeit unconsciously—giving him more credit as a struggling student who deserved the benefit of the doubt?) I used as many opportunities as possible to reaffirm these signs of success—praised his improved writing, included a well-written narrative paper (on soccer, naturally) as a class model for effective writing. As research on attribution theory suggests, low-achieving students need to be reminded that their success is due to their efforts. A "Happy-Gram" sent home mentioning specifically his particularly good narrative paragraph, followed two weeks later by his "Goal Completion Award" seemed to be the turning points that altered his downward slide in my class.

During this intervention I made some academic changes as well as the social ones. First, I allowed more flexibility in the topics I assigned for writing projects so that Bill (and the other students) had more options to choose from. The more interested he was in a topic, the more knowledgeable he was about it, and the more motivated he became to write. I also began to assess his learning style—both by analyzing the type of assignments he did well on and by conversations with him when I asked for feedback. As a result, after giving directions for an assignment, I used my "roaming" time for private contact with him to clarify his understanding and review his independent work, making solicited suggestions so that I could spot misunderstandings and frustrations and offer followup assistance. I also began to use a different approach to grading his writing. Martin and Lauridsen (1974) suggest in *Developing Student Discipline and Motivation* that students needs to be graded on an individual basis. Consequently, I allowed him to compete against himself and not his more academically mature classmates, so that his continuous progress merited praise. Then, because he was growing in confidence and self-esteem, the next step seemed to be to try the suggestions of Johnson and Johnson (1987) and allow Bill to work in a group. Their research suggests that successfully orchestrated group work increases confidence in one's ability. And so I arranged for Bill to participate in a peer editing group in which he was both academically and socially compatible. In this setting, a feeling of interdependence grew between him and members of the group, fostering sociability, responsibility, and self-esteem.

Meanwhile, research by Jones (1980) suggests that students should share the responsibility in behavior modification by some type of self-monitoring. Therefore, it became Bill's responsibility to keep personal records on a weekly Progress Report form I filled out. He also continued to keep a class notebook in which he copied daily assignments from the board and kept them in front of his notebook as a type of table of contents. The completed assignment then, after it was graded and returned, was kept chronologically in his notebook and a check mark was made on the assignment page. As a back-up reminder, in case an assignment did not get turned in by the deadline, we agreed that a "Homework Alert" notice was to be sent home, signed by his parent, and returned to me within two days. If the card was not returned within the time limit, Bill was aware I would be calling home to discuss the situation with his parent. This back-up strategy was never necessary, however. In fact, during the past five weeks, Bill has missed only one assignment (because of a late soccer game and a long bus ride home).

A statement by Jere Brophy (1982b) summarizes my intervention best:

For example, in dealing with failure-syndrome students who have essentially given up attempts to cope with classroom demands, effective teachers refuse to cave in by reducing task demands and treating these students as if they are really unable to succeed in the classroom. Instead, they approach such students with a mixture of sympathy, encouragement, and demands. These teachers reassure the students that they do have ability and that work given will not be too difficult for them. Then, the teachers help them to get started when they are discouraged or need some support, reinforce their progress, and perhaps offer contracts providing rewards for accomplishments and allowing opportunities for students to set goals. In general, the emphasis is on encouragement and help rather than prodding through threat of punishment. Failure-syndrome students are not merely *told* that they can succeed, but *shown* convincingly that they can, and helped to do so. (p. 23)

These suggestions seemed to have worked in providing more realistic expectations, building self-confidence, and in creating a more comfortable classroom in which Bill could become the student he can be.

IMPLEMENTATION ACTIVITIES

A major problem with listing numerous teaching methods is that you will feel overwhelmed and will respond by failing to implement or even consider any of the methods. The following activities can help you implement and assess methods presented in this chapter.

ACTIVITY 7.1   Designing a Lesson

Select a lesson you plan to teach in the next few days. Using the outline in Figure 7.2, develop a lesson design. When teaching the lesson, make sure to use all eight steps. After the lesson is complete, answer these questions:

Compared to recent lessons I have taught, students were more. . . .
Compared to recent lessons I have taught, students were less. . . .
The element I think helped make the lesson go well was. . . .
One thing I would do differently if I taught this lesson again is. . . .
Compared to recent lessons, during this lesson I felt more. . . .
One thing I learned from this activity is. . . .

ACTIVITY 7.2   Responding to Variations in Learning Styles

Create a chart like the one presented below. List the instructional activities you have used (or those you have seen used if you are currently observing a classroom rather than teaching) during the past two days. Behind each activity indicate the type of cognitive skill it emphasizes.

		Abstract sequential (AS)
	Right brain (RB)	*Abstract random* (AR)
	Left brain (LB)	*Concrete sequential* (CS)
Instructional activity	*Integrative* (I)	*Concrete random* (CR)

1.
2.
3.
4.
5.
6.
7.

Tally the responses to provide yourself with an indication of the number of activities that fell into each category (e.g., 10 left-brain activities, 2 right-brain, and 7 integrative).

   Within the lessons you have planned (if you are not in a classroom, design a set of lesson plans), attempt for two days to use instructional activities that fall into each category. You may also wish to design a lesson that incorporates Bernice McCarthy's four learning-style types.

After teaching these lessons, answer these questions:

Did you notice any differences in students' behavior during the two days in which the lessons were more balanced? Describe these differences.

Were any particular students noticeably more involved or better behaved or both during these two days? If so, which students were they?

How did you feel during these two days?

Complete these sentences:

I learned that. . . .

I was surprised that. . . .

In the future I will try to. . . .

ACTIVITY 7.3 Implementing Methods for Increasing Students' Involvement in the Learning Process

1. List two additional methods you can use to increase students' involvement in the learning process.
   a.
   b.
2. Select one method discussed in this section and incorporate it into your classroom. After completing the activity or implementing it for several weeks, answer these questions:
   a. How have students responded to the activity?
   b. Has any student become particularly involved in the activity?
   c. Has involvement in the activity seemed to bring about a more positive attitude for any student(s)?
3. Develop a short form on which students can express their reaction to the new activity.

ACTIVITY 7.4 Analyzing Students' Behavior Problems

If you are having problems with the behavior of a student or group of students, it is important to consider instructional factors that may be causing the problem. First, write the name of the student or students who are creating the most difficulty for you in a class. Next, complete the form in Figure 7.19 for each student you have listed. After carefully examining your responses, answer these questions:

One reason this student(s) may be acting out in my class is. . . .

This activity made me realize that. . . .

In order to help this student(s) behave more appropriately in this class, I will need to. . . .

Two specific things I will change in this class or with this specific student are. . . .

FIGURE 7.19 Analyzing the Classroom Environment

As you present your next lesson or assignment in an area in which a student or group of students has had trouble, notice:

	Almost always	Sometimes	Almost never
1. Is the subject area one in which the student has always failed?			
2. Can the student read at whatever level the material is presented?			
3. Is the assignment clear enough so the student knows exactly what is expected?			
4. Is the task at a level of difficulty that is challenging but which offers a chance of successful completion for the individual (rather than for the class average)?			
5. Is the material presented in a manner which seems to interest the student: written, lecture, audiovisual, programmed workbook, independent work, group assignments, etc? Is the material content of interest?			
6. Is enough time allowed to get into the assignment and develop an interest and complete the task satisfactorily?			
7. Will the student be graded on an individual basis so that successful completion will get a good grade?			
8. Is there a pleasant consequence that you know appeals to the student (possibly chosen by the student) that will follow successful completion of the task?			
9. Is there some motivating consequence to at least complete part of the assignment, even if the student cannot complete all of it?			
10. Do you give the student another chance to do the assignment correctly and to improve the grade?			
11. Do you give more attention to the student when he tries a task than you do when he refuses to try?			

From *Developing Student Discipline and Motivation* by Reed Martin and David Lauridsen. © 1974 by Research Press, Champaign, Ill. 61820. Reprinted by permission.

ACTIVITY 7.5   Student Feedback to the Teacher

As suggested throughout this book, students can provide teachers with useful feedback on how consistently they are implementing effective teaching methods. Figure 7.20 is a sample form that you can administer to students to assess how effectively you are using many of the methods presented in this chapter.

FIGURE 7.20   Student's Assessment of Teacher's Instructional Skills

I believe students are knowledgeable both about how they learn best and in describing effective teaching. Therefore, I am asking you to give me some feedback on what I believe to be important aspects of my teaching. Please be serious, fair, and honest when completing this form. Also, please do not put your name on the form. Place an *X* in the box that best describes the question.

What's the Score?

FORE!

	Hole in one	Birdie	Par	Bogey	Out of bounds
1. Are the goals and objectives for each lesson clear?					
2. Do you value what you are learning in this class?					
3. Do I use different ways to teach lessons (films, projects, discussions, guest speakers, and so on)?					
4. Do you get to study subjects or ideas that interest you?					
5. Is there a good balance for you in the amount of time spent in large- and small-group activities?					
6. Do you think the skills taught in this class are useful in some other areas of your life?					
7. Do you accomplish goals you set in this class?					
8. Do tests give you information about what you have learned?					
9. Do tests help you to see what skills still need to be practiced?					
10. Do you feel pressured to finish work in this class?					
11. Are you comfortable sharing your ideas with other students in this class?					

(continued)

FIGURE 7.20 (continued)

	Hole in one	Birdie	Par	Bogey	Out of bounds
12. Are the goals of each new assignment clear?					
13. Are you aware of how you are doing in this class?					
14. Are most of the assignments challenging but not too hard for you?					
15. Do I allow enough time for questions and discussion?					
16. Does the class allow you to express yourself creatively?					
17. Do you think the grading is fair?					
18. Do you feel you have a chance to be actively involved in learning?					
19. The best thing about this class is. . . .					
20. If I were teaching this class I would. . . .					
22. The way I learn best is to. . . .					

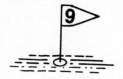

Administer Figure 7.20 (or a revision you develop) to at least two of your classes. Tally the results as suggested in Figure 2.5. After carefully examining this tally, answer these questions:

Students rate me very highly on my ability to. . . .
Students' feedback suggests that I may need to. . . .
I was pleasantly surprised to find that students believe I. . . .
I was disappointed that students rated me somewhat low on. . . .
One specific change I will make in my teaching is. . . .

SUMMARY

The areas of curriculum and instruction have increasingly been recognized as key factors influencing student behavior. Regardless of how effectively a teacher has organized a classroom, disruptions are more likely to occur and achievement is more likely to be lower if instructional activities fail to engage students meaningfully and actively. The late 1970s and early 1980s were characterized by a focus on direct instruction as a way to increase on-task behavior and student achievement. Throughout the 1980s an increasing emphasis was also placed on incorporating diverse instructional methods that more effectively met the learning needs of students with varying learning styles. Cooperative learning also became a popular and well-researched approach for increasing student involvement and learning.

This chapter has presented an applied overview of the major instructional methods that have been used to increase positive student engagement in the learning process. We are increasingly impressed by the importance of incorporating these instructional methods as an integral part of an effective classroom management, schoolwide student management, or at-risk program.

RECOMMENDED READING

Carin, A., & Sund, R. (1978). *Creative questioning and sensitive listening techniques.* Columbus, Ohio: Charles E. Merrill.

Cummings, C. (1980). *Teaching makes a difference.* Edmonds, Wash.: Teaching.

Dunn, R., & Dunn, K. (1972). *Practical approaches to individualizing instruction: Contracts and other effective teaching strategies.* West Nyack, N.Y.: Parker.

Dunn, R., & Dunn, K. (1978). *Teaching students through their individual learning styles: A practical approach.* Reston, Va: Reston.

Gibbs, J., & Allen, A. (1978). *Tribes: A process for peer involvement.* 3702 Mt. Diablo Blvd., Lafayette, Calif.: Center for Human Development.

Harmin, M., Kirschenbaum, H., & Simon, S. (1973). *Clarifying values through subject matter.* Minneapolis, Minn.: Winston Press.

Huggins, P., & Hansen, P. (1986). *The ASSIST program: Teaching friendship skills.* 7024 N. Mercer Way, Mercer Island, Wash., 98040.

Hunter, M. (1976). *Improved instruction.* El Segundo, Calif.: TIP.

Johnson, D., & Johnson, R. (1987). *Learning together and alone: Cooperative, competitive, and individualistic learnings,* 2nd ed. Englewood Cliffs, N.J.: Prentice-Hall.

Johnson, D., & Johnson, R. (1984). *Cooperation in the classroom.* Edina, Minn.: Interaction Book Company.

Johnson, D., Johnson, R., & Johnson-Holubec, E. (1986). *Circles of Learning: Cooperation in the classroom.* Edina, Minn.: Interaction Book Company.

Johnson, R., & Johnson, D. (1985). *Cooperative learning: Warm-ups, grouping strategies and group activities.* Edina, Minn.: Interaction Book Company.

Johnson, R., & Johnson, D. (Eds.). (1984). *Structuring cooperative learning: Lesson plans for teachers.* Edina, Minn.: Interaction Book Co.

Jones, V. (1980). *Adolescents with behavior problems: Strategies for teaching, counseling, and parent involvement.* Boston: Allyn and Bacon.

Joyce, B., & Weil, M. (1986). *Models of teaching,* 3rd ed. Englewood Cliffs, N.J.: Prentice-Hall.

Kagan, S. (1987). Cooperative learning: Resources for teachers. Printed by the author—Suite 201, 27402 Camino Capistrano, Laguna Niguel, Calif., 92677.

McCarthy, B. (1987). *The 4-MAT system: Teaching to learning styles with right/left mode techniques.* Barrington, Ill.: Excel, Inc.

McCarthy, B., & Leflar, S. (1983). *4-MAT in action: Creative lesson plans for teaching to learning styles with right/left mode techniques.* Barrington, Ill.: Excel, Inc.

McCarthy, B., Leflar, S., & McNamara, M. (1987). *The 4-MAT workbook: Guided practice in 4-MAT lesson and unit planning.* Barrington, Ill.: Excel, Inc.

McElmurry, M. (1985). *Cooperating: Alternatives to competition in the home and classroom.* Carthage, Ill.: Good Apple.

Postman, N., & Weingartner, C. (1969). *Teaching as a subversive activity.* New York: Delacorte.

Rogers, C. (1969). *Freedom to learn.* Columbus, Ohio: Charles E. Merrill.

Slavin, R. (1980). *Using student team learning.* The Johns Hopkins University, 3505 N. Charles Street, Baltimore, Md.: The Center for Social Organization of Schools.

Slavin, R. (1983a). *Cooperative learning.* New York: Longman.

Slavin, R. (1983b). *Working together and learning together.* Saskatchewan Department of Cooperation and Cooperative Development, The Stewart Resources Center, S.T.F. Box 1108, Saskatoon, Saskatchewan, S7K3N3.

Stanish, B. (1981). *Hippogriff feathers: Encounters with creative thinking.* Carthage, Ill.: Good Apple.

Minimizing Disruptive Behavior and Increasing Learning by Effective Classroom Organization and Management

In his chapter on classroom organization and management in the *Handbook of Research on Teaching* (3rd ed.), Walter Doyle (1986) wrote:

> Broadly speaking, classroom teaching has two major task structures organized around the problems of (a) learning and (b) order. Learning is served by the instructional function. . . . Order is served by the managerial function, that is, by organizing classroom groups, establishing rules and procedures, reacting to misbehavior, monitoring and pacing classroom events, and the like. (p. 395)

In the previous unit we examine the major findings on instructional methods that teachers can use to increase the likelihood that students will be motivated by learning tasks and will benefit from instruction. This unit focuses on the second major task associated with classroom teaching: maintaining order in the classroom.

Studies indicate that the amount of time students are engaged in instructional activities vary from less than 50 percent in some classes to more than 90 percent in others (Fisher et al., 1978). This unit helps you increase the time students spend actively engaged in learning. More effective teachers use their management time wisely and thereby enhance the time available for instruction and monitoring student work. In a study of eight secondary schools, Stallings and Mohlman (1981) found that effective teachers spent less than 15 percent of their time organizing and managing their classes. Teachers who effectively use the time needed to organize and manage classrooms can minimize the time required for these important functions.

Chapter 8 lists in detail strategies that effective teachers use when presenting material to students and monitoring students' seatwork. Researchers have demonstrated that use of these strategies is associated with higher rates of on-task student behavior and greater academic achievement.

Chapter 9 presents the methods effective teachers use at the beginning of the school year. We emphasize strategies for teaching classroom rules and ensuring that all students learn such key classroom procedures as what to do during the first few minutes of class, how to request assistance with seatwork, when it is appropriate to talk, and how to request permission to leave the room. In this chapter we also examine methods effective teachers use when students fail to follow accepted rules or procedures.

Classroom Management Skills That Increase Learning by Maximizing On-Task Behavior

We also found that student engagement in lessons and activities was the key to successful classroom management. The successful teachers ran smooth, well-paced lessons with few interruptions, and their students worked consistently at their seatwork.

/ Jere Brophy and Carolyn Evertson (1976)
Learning from Teaching

More than two decades ago, Jacob Kounin discovered that effective teachers could be distinguished not by their way of dealing with students' misbehavior but by the classroom management strategies they used to prevent classroom disruptions. Subsequent studies have reinforced and elaborated on Kounin's findings. To increase students' on-task behavior and achievement and to minimize disruptive behavior, you can consider implementing many proven methods of classroom management discussed in this chapter.

The importance of teachers' using the skills described in this chapter was emphasized by Kounin's (1970) research on classroom discipline. Kounin began his study by collecting several thousand hours of videotapes, both from classrooms of teachers who were acknowledged to be extremely effective in managing their classes and from classrooms of teachers who had serious, continuing management problems. Kounin expected to find significant differences in how teachers from these two groups handled discipline problems that occurred in their classrooms. Surprisingly, the results indicated that the successful teachers responded to control problems in much the same manner as did the teachers whose classrooms were often disorderly.

Based on these findings, Kounin and his colleagues reexamined the tapes, seeking any real differences between the teaching methods of teachers who were successful and those who experienced major management problems. They discovered that the differences lay in the successful teachers' ability to prevent discipline problems. These teachers used many types of management skills to ensure that students were more consistently and actively engaged in instructional activities. Successful teachers were better prepared and organized and moved smoothly from one activity to another. These teachers also maintained students' involvement in instructional activities by initially stimulating the students' interest and effectively holding their attention throughout the lesson. Similarly, successful teachers used seatwork that was individualized and interesting. Kounin also discovered that the more effective teachers had greater classroom awareness, constantly scanning the classroom so that they were aware of potential problems and could deal with these before any real difficulties arose. These teachers anticipated students' needs, organized their classrooms to minimize restlessness and boredom, and effectively coped with the multiple and often overlapping demands associated with teaching.

Research on teachers' effectiveness in producing gains in students' learning (Brophy & Evertson, 1976) indicates that the same teacher behaviors that reduce classroom disruption are also associated with increased student learning. In describing the findings of the two-year Teacher Effectiveness Project, which examined the relationship between various teacher behaviors and gains in students' learning, Brophy and Evertson (1976) stated, "Our data strongly support the findings of Kounin (1970). . . . That is, the key to successful classroom management is prevention of problems before they start, not knowing how to deal with problems after they have begun" (p. 127). Brophy and Evertson also wrote:

> Of the process behaviors measured through classroom observation in our study, the group that had the strongest and most consistent relationships with student learning gains dealt with the classroom management skills of the teachers. By "classroom management," we mean planning and conducting activities in an orderly fashion; keeping students actively engaged in lessons and seatwork activities; and minimizing disruptions and discipline problems. (p. 51)

In their study of 12 inner-London secondary schools reported in *Fifteen Thousand Hours*, Rutter et al. (1979) found teachers' classroom-management skills to be a key factor influencing students' achievement and behavior. They write:

> The measures we used touched on only a few aspects of classroom management and there are innumerable ways in which good management may be achieved. What is important is that teachers learn the skills involved. (p. 186)

FIGURE 8.1 Instructional Management Skills That Facilitate On-Task Behavior and Academic Achievement

1. Giving clear instructions
2. Beginning a lesson
3. Maintaining attention
4. Pacing
5. Using seatwork effectively
6. Summarizing
7. Providing useful feedback and evaluation
8. Making smooth transitions

The research on academic learning time (ALT) supports the idea that teachers should incorporate teaching methods that increase on-task student behavior. "If 50 minutes of reading instruction per day is allocated to a student who pays attention about one-third of the time, and only one-fourth of the student's reading time is a high level of success, the student will experience only about four minutes of ALT-engaged reading time at a high success level" (Berliner, 1984, p. 62).

Barak Rosenshine (1983) summarizes specific teacher behaviors found to be associated with students' achievement gains and includes many of the skills presented in this chapter. Research demonstrates that we can now provide teachers with training in specific instructional procedures and know that if these procedures are implemented, students will behave in more acceptable ways and learn more effectively (Anderson, Evertson, & Brophy, 1979; Borg & Ascione, 1982; Good & Grouws, 1979; Tharp, 1982).

METHODS FOR IMPLEMENTING DISRUPTION-FREE LESSONS

Our purpose in this chapter is to provide you with a wide variety of effective teaching methods that prevent students' misbehavior. If you are an experienced teacher you will undoubtedly find that many of these methods are already a part of your teaching behavior. Probably, however, many new methods can easily be added to this repertoire. These additions can be expected to significantly reduce disruptive student behavior and thereby make teaching more enjoyable while increasing students' achievement.

The chapter is organized around the eight general instructional management skills listed in Figure 8.1. Following a brief statement about each skill, we present numerous specific teaching strategies that will help improve your classroom management.

It is critical to understand how to use the methods in this chapter. They are not offered as gimmicks for increasing students' time on-task or your control. Instead, they are methods that can assist you in helping students better understand their schoolwork and enhance the quality of learning time. Neither are these methods offered as a cookbook of behaviors to be routinely followed. Like the neophyte cook, the beginning teacher may choose to implement many of these methods. Much as a cook alters and discards recipes depending on the outcome, the skilled teacher seasons standard methods with understanding how children develop and learn. We constantly need to monitor our own behavior and its relationship to students' learning in order to develop teaching methods that are maximally effective in our classrooms. In addition to the ideas and activities presented in this book, you will find Good and Brophy's (1987) *Looking in Classrooms* and Jane Stallings's (1983) work particularly useful in helping monitor and adjust classroom organization and management behavior.

Giving Clear Instructions

A key step in presenting a lesson is to provide clear instructions for the activities in which students will be engaged. A significant amount of disruptive student behavior stems from students' not knowing how they are to proceed or what they are to do when they require assistance or complete their work. Students are often poorly prepared for seatwork assignments. Teachers frequently fail to provide adequate information on why assignments are given or how work relates to past or future learning. Students often do not get enough procedural directions. Because seatwork accounts for nearly 70 percent of students' time in class (Doyle, 1983; Good, 1983), and students tend to take seriously only work for which they believe they will be held accountable (Doyle, 1983), it is critical that we improve our skill in providing students with clear directions on academic work. The following methods suggest ways of eliminating disruptions caused by lack of clear instructions.

Methods

1. *Give precise directions.* Instructions should include statements about (a) what students will be doing, (b) why they are doing it, (c) how they can obtain assistance, (d) what to do with completed work, and (e) what to do when they finish. It is also helpful to indicate how much time they will be spending on the task. This direction may include a statement about when the work can be completed if it cannot be finished within the designated time limits. Research (Brophy & Evertson, 1976; Kounin, 1970) clearly indicates that a significant amount of disruptive student behavior stems from students' not having enough information on these matters. Students respond to this uncertainty by interrupting us with multiple requests for information or by expressing their boredom or anxiety by acting out. We also should specify the aspects of the assignment that are most important, and we may even want to post these factors where students can refer to them. This information is valuable in reducing students' anxiety and helps them pace themselves. Some of these instructions are best taught as continuing procedures. For example, students should understand the procedure for obtaining assistance, handing in work, and selecting alternative activities after they complete seatwork.

2. *Describe the desired quality of the work.* This can increase students' sense of accountability and decrease their anxiety. Accountability without clarity, however, is often confusing and anxiety-provoking, and it is important to provide specific guidance on our expectations. A teacher of talented and gifted students recently told us that she tells students that there are three types of work: (1) "throwaway"—material that is for practice only and not to be handed in; (2) "everyday learning"—work that should be neat because it will be graded by the teacher, but not a perfect copy because the main purpose is to check students' understanding; and (3) "keepers"—work that will be displayed or which the student may wish to keep.

3. *Vary your approach to giving instructions.* Though we must consistently provide clear instructions, it is useful to employ different approaches in giving them. For example, changing one's voice from a soft to an excited tone (or vice versa) can heighten students' attention. We can also use different media, such as the chalkboard, overhead projector, or butcher paper, for writing instructions.

4. *Employ attending and listening games to improve students' receiving skills.* They must have clear instructions, but it is equally important that students develop skill in listening to and understanding instructions.

5. *After giving instructions, have students paraphrase the directions, state any problems that might occur to them, and make a commitment.* After giving instructions, ask such questions as, "What is one thing you will be doing?" "What will you do if you finish early?" or "What do I want you to do?" It is often useful to ask key questions of several students who normally have difficulty in following instructions. This tactic not only increases the likelihood that they will listen to instructions but also provides reinforcement for their attending skills. The next step is to ask students whether they see any problems that might arise. Students are very adept at listing potential difficulties, which can then be alleviated. Finally, we can look at various groups of students and ask, "Are you ready to start and follow these directions?" By obtaining a nod or verbal commitment from each student, we increase the likelihood that they will attempt to complete the activity in a satisfactory manner. If some students indicate that they are not interested in attempting the task, we can accept this statement and indicate that we need to meet briefly with them after the class has begun their work. We can then proceed to obtain a commitment from the remaining students.

6. *Positively accept students' questions about directions.* Employing the strategies described in this section will vastly reduce the number of questions about directions, but situations will arise in which students have questions. To create a safe, supportive atmosphere, it is important to respond positively to student questions. Reprimanding students in front of the class only creates a negative atmosphere. If one or more students consistently ask questions about directions that have already been clearly stated, we should discuss this problem privately with the student(s). This discussion should use the problem-solving approaches described in chapter 10. Examples of solutions that might result from discussing the problem include having the student write the directions, having the student choose a classmate to assist in clarifying directions, or calling on the student to paraphrase a portion of the directions.

7. *Place directions where they can be seen and referred to by students.* Accessibility is particularly useful when directions are complicated, when students will be working on an assignment over an extended period, or when students frequently repeat an activity. For nonreaders we can use pictures to describe the directions.

8. *Have students write out instructions before beginning an activity.* This method provides students with much-needed practice in thinking through the steps they should take before they begin their work. Students can be told that their directions must be checked by the teacher or aide before they begin the assignment. Though checking requires time and effort and should not be used with every lesson, it is especially useful when students will be working on a long-term project.

9. *When students seem to be having difficulty following directions, consider breaking tasks down into smaller segments.* Young children often have difficulty following a series of directions. Therefore, it is often necessary to give only one or two directions at a time or to have students complete one portion of a task before going on to the next activity.

10. *Give directions immediately prior to the activity they describe.* One of us recently observed a student-teacher give excellent directions about seatwork, then proceed to present fifteen minutes of direct instruction. By the time students were released for seatwork, most of them had forgotten the directions.

11. *Model the correct behavior.* If students have been asked to raise their hand before answering, we can raise our hand while asking the question.

12. *Hand out worksheets or outlines before taking a field trip.* Anyone who has visited British schools has seen excellent examples of this strategy. British children are frequently provided with worksheets to complete during a field trip. By helping students focus on relevant materials, this method reduces acting-out behavior and simultaneously helps students understand what they can learn from the activity.

Beginning a Lesson

Teachers frequently have difficulty in attracting students' attention and getting a lesson started. The reason is at least partly that students often attempt to postpone the beginning of a lesson by socializing or moving about the room. Students quite accurately realize that the best time for buying time is before the lesson begins. The material presented in this section suggests approaches you can use to reduce disruptions that occur while you are introducing a lesson. Before implementing any of these methods, however, you should carefully examine such factors as whether the previous lesson has been satisfactorily summarized so that students are ready to move on to a new lesson, and whether the problem may lie more in the transition between lessons than in the beginning of the new lesson. We refer you to sections later in this chapter for suggestions in summarizing lessons and facilitating smooth transitions.

Methods

1. *Select and teach a "cue" for getting students' attention.* Students benefit from having a consistent cue indicating that it is time to focus their attention. Students hear standard phrases such as "Okay, we are ready to begin" so often that these statements are often ineffective for eliciting attention. One of us has her class select a new cue each month. Students enjoy being involved and choose catchy phrases. During a recent year students chose "Boo" for October, "Gobble Gobble" for November, and "Ho Ho Ho" for December. While teaching a summer institute on classroom management, we demonstrated the value of using a catchy phrase by recording the time it took 40 teachers to pay attention quietly following the phrase "May I please have your attention?" The average time for five such requests was nearly two minutes (in each instance, students were involved in group work). The class was presented with this figure and asked to develop a less common phrase. They chose "Rain Rain Go Away." This phrase was practiced until the class could attend within ten seconds. Followup data gathered during the next two weeks showed that the group never took more than ten seconds to become completely quiet.

2. *Do not begin until everyone is paying attention.* Almost every teacher has heard this suggestion, and yet most teachers find it very difficult to follow. Worried about wasting time, we often begin a lesson even though we do not have several students' attention. Unfortunately, numerous disadvantages are associated with this decision. First, teachers inevitably spend much more time reprimanding students or repeating directions than they would waiting for students to be quiet. Second, it is impolite to talk over other people even if they are talking when they should be listening. Third, talking over students is poor modeling because it suggests that this is an acceptable method of gaining attention. Fourth, by beginning a lesson while students are talking or not paying attention, we indicate that we are not in control of the class. Finally, both we and the students who are behaving appropriately will be distracted by inappropriate student talk and consequently the lesson will be less effective. Because of these multiple disadvantages, it appears obvious that we will do well to delay our introductory comments until every student is quiet and attentive.

3. *Begin the lesson by removing distractions.* Many students—especially those with behavior problems—find it difficult voluntarily to screen out distracting stimuli. We can help students focus on the lesson by closing the door if noise is coming from the hallway or by asking students to clear their desks of everything except items they will need for the assignment.

4. *Clearly describe the goals, activities, and evaluation procedures associated with the lesson being presented.* Students are more highly motivated and learn more when they are aware of the specific goals toward which they are working (Bryan & Locke, 1967; Kennedy, 1968). Clear statements about the learning process meet students' needs for safety and control over their environment. Because students are often extremely concerned about such factors as whether they can complete the work on time and how it will be evaluated, we should respond to these issues at the beginning of the lesson. If these issues are not discussed, some students will be worrying about these factors rather than devoting their attention to the lesson.

5. *Stimulate interest by relating the lesson to the students' lives or a previous lesson.* It is extremely important to place content in perspective. Students often feel that they are being asked simply to learn a series of unrelated facts or concepts. Students' motivation can be increased dramatically by indicating why the material is being learned and by suggesting ways in which the learning can influence their lives. For example, division can become much more interesting if it is viewed as a method for determining a Little League batting average. We can reduce anxiety associated with learning a new skill by relating this material or its components to skills students already possess or information that has been learned previously. This approach increases students' sense of safety and enables them to approach the new task with greater confidence.

6. *Start with a highly motivating activity in order to make the students' initial contact with the subject matter as positive as possible.* One of us begins a unit on the Lewis and Clark expedition by dressing up as Meriwether Lewis and collaborating with a colleague to present a skit summarizing the lives of these two noteworthy explorers. Students find the skit entertaining and are motivated to learn more about the expedition. Students' interest can be similarly stimulated by a good film, an experiment, or by presenting interesting questions, such as "Why can birds fly though people cannot?"

7. *Hand out an outline, definitions, or study guide to help students organize their thoughts and focus their attention.* This material can be made more interesting by embellishing it with humorous cartoons or scattering thought-provoking questions or comments throughout.

8. *Challenging students to minimize their transition time.* Children enjoy games and are impressed by data. We can draw on this knowledge by presenting students with data indicating the amount of time it requires them to settle down and asking them to try to reduce this time. There are six basic steps to implementing this approach. First, we must collect baseline data (see chapter 11) and record them on a large and easy-to-read chart. Second, the data should be discussed with the students and their assistance requested. Third, we must help the students choose an appropriate and reasonable goal. Fourth, it is necessary to define exactly what we mean by being ready for class. Fifth, the class must develop a system for collecting and recording data. Finally, it may be necessary to determine a reward for reaching the stated goal.

Maintaining Attention

The amount of time students spend involved in instruction is significantly related to their achievement (Denham & Lieberman, 1980; Fisher et al., 1978). Classes vary dramatically in the percentage of time students are engaged in instructional tasks, with rates ranging from consistently less than 50 percent to 90 percent (Fisher et al., 1978).

Many teachers state that one of the most frustrating tasks associated with teaching is maintaining students' attention during group instruction. Although children and young adolescents do in fact have a somewhat shorter attention span than do adults, their ability to attend quietly to an interesting television program or video game suggests that the skilled teacher can stimulate more consistent attention to task than is seen in most classrooms.

Methods

1. *Arrange the classroom so that students do not have their backs to the speaker.* When a lesson involves the teacher as the center of attention, students should be seated so that everyone is facing the teacher. This arrangement can be accomplished using rows, a circle, or a U-shape. When students are seated in small groups, we should request that all students face us before beginning a lesson. Similarly, if we wish students to talk to each other, desks must be arranged in a circle, square, or U-shape so that students can comfortably see and hear each speaker. Teachers who use a variety of instructional activities should consider teaching students a procedure for quickly and quietly moving desks. We have found that with a small amount of instruction, students in all grades can learn to rearrange desks in approximately one minute. Figure 8.2 presents a seating arrangement we have found particularly useful in elementary school classrooms because it allows for easy monitoring of seatwork as well as for effective group discussion.

2. *Employ a seating arrangement that does not discriminate against some students.* Teachers spend nearly 70 percent of their time in front of the classroom (Adams & Biddle, 1970). Therefore, it is no surprise that students at the back of the room contribute less to class discussions (Adams & Biddle, 1970; Delefes & Jackson, 1972), are less attentive and on-task (Schwebel & Cherlin, 1972), and achieve less (Daum, 1972) than do students seated near the front of the class.

Considering these findings, it is interesting that teachers tend to place higher-achieving students nearer the teacher and provide them with more contact (Rist, 1970). Fortunately, research also indicates that teachers can encourage more evenly distributed student responding. Daum (1972) demonstrated that when low-ability students were moved to the front of the room, their achievement improved more than that of low-ability students who remained at the back of the room. Interestingly, the high-achieving students' achieve-

FIGURE 8.2 Classroom Arrangement

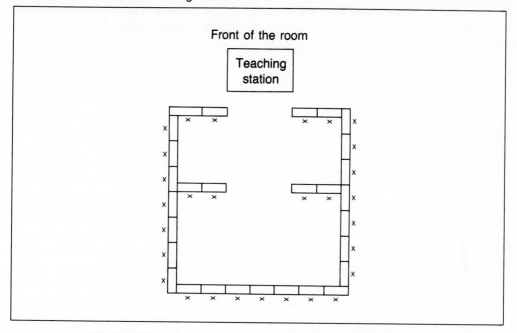

ment did not suffer when they were moved farther from the teacher. Similarly, Adams and Biddle (1970) discovered that students' involvement is more evenly distributed when high- and low-achieving students are interspersed throughout the room. These studies suggest that teachers can increase on-task student responses by adjusting seating arrangements and moving around the room so that all students become actively involved in meaningful classroom interaction.

3. *Use random selection in calling on students.* When we call on students by progressing up and down rows or around a circle, students who have just responded or who know they will not have to respond for several minutes often become bored and disruptive. Students can be kept attentive if we select them randomly and occasionally return to a student who has recently answered a question. When employing random selection we must be careful not to provide significantly more response opportunities to high-achieving students. Research (Brophy & Good, 1974; Cooper & Good, 1983) indicates that teachers provide high-achieving students with more response opportunities than their low-achieving peers. One strategy for preventing this bias is to place a tally beside each child's name as he or she is called on. It is a good idea periodically to explain to students why we choose to call on every student. Students who always volunteer answers have probably received numerous response opportunities during their school career and may become frustrated when these opportunities are distributed more equally. We can reduce this frustration by informing the class that calling on all students allows us to find out whether most people understand the material and helps everyone to learn by giving everyone a chance to respond.

One danger in involving all students is that we are less likely to receive an immediate correct answer to every question. Studies (Brophy & Evertson, 1976; Stallings, 1976; Ward & Tikunoff, 1976) indicate that, especially in the primary grades and when working with children from lower socioeconomic classes, students' achievement is enhanced when we provide information, ask focused questions, and receive correct answers from students. Therefore, we should carefully consider when to involve lower-achieving students. For example, these students might be called on when they raise their hands during skill-acquisition lessons and might be encouraged to become actively involved during lessons that involve personal issues or opinions.

4. *Ask the question before calling on a student.* When we select the student before asking the question, other students may become less interested in the question. By asking the question, looking around the room, and providing students with an opportunity to consider the question, we create greater interest and anticipation and thereby increase attending behavior. We can also take this opportunity to reinforce the procedure of students' raising their hands to answer questions. We might say, ''Raise your hand if you can answer this question,'' or, ''John, you have your hand raised. What is the answer?''

5. *Wait at least five seconds before answering a question or calling on another student.* Most teachers are surprised to learn that research (Rowe, 1974) indicates that, on the average, teachers wait only one second for a student to respond before answering a question themselves or calling on another student. To make this finding more believable and relevant, consider a typical question you might ask in your classroom and silently count to ten in order to experience a ten-second wait. You may be surprised at how long ten seconds seems. Consider, however, the process students must go through when asked a question. First, they must hear the question and decide whether they understand it. Second, they must search for the information. Third, they must consider whether their response will be accepted. Fourth, they must decide whether they will receive reinforcement or rebuke for their response (in some situations a correct response will be reinforced by the teacher but punished by peers). This process may occur very rapidly for bright students, but most students require considerably longer than one second to complete it.

As with most strategies, teachers need to consider the context when increasing their wait time. For example, during a whole-class oral drill review on math facts a teacher would probably wait only one or two seconds before calling on a student. Perhaps the main reason we fail to wait following a question is that many students' hands are raised before we complete the question and the class moves along smoothly if we simply call on a student whose hand is raised.

Research (Rosenthal, 1973) indicates that teachers tend to wait longer for answers from students they view as brighter. The study also suggests, though, that when teachers do wait longer for lower-achieving students, they are rewarded with greater responsiveness from the students. Rowe (1978) reported that when teachers increase their waiting time, a variety of positive things occur. Figure 8.3 summarizes her findings. In a review of studies involving wait time, Tobin (1987) found that when average teacher wait time was greater than three seconds, teacher and student discourse changed and higher cognitive level achievement occurred at all grade levels.

If we wish to maintain students' attention and increase their willingness and ability to answer questions, we must provide all students adequate time to answer. When we fail to provide this time, students soon learn that they can maintain their uninvolvement simply by failing to respond immediately.

6. *Use games that encourage attentive listening.* Children often find it difficult to sit quietly and listen when the teacher or their peers are talking. This important skill can

FIGURE 8.3 Advantages of Increasing Teachers' Wait Time

1. Length of students' responses increases
2. Number of unsolicited but appropriate answers increases
3. Failure to obtain a response decreases
4. Children's confidence increases
5. Teacher-centered teaching decreases
6. Students' questions increase
7. Lower-achieving students contribute more
8. Students' proposals increase
9. Students give more evidence to support their answers
10. The variety of students' responses increases

be taught by involving students in activities that encourage listening. One strategy that students enjoy is the yarn activity. Before leading a group discussion, we inform the class that they will use a ball of yarn to facilitate the discussion. The students are told that only the person holding the ball of yarn can speak. When a student finishes speaking, he or she is to roll the yarn to another student who has raised his or her hand. Before releasing the ball, the speaker holds on to the yarn. This act indicates that he or she has been involved in the discussion; as the yarn is passed from student to student a sociogram-like matrix is created by the yarn. Another good activity is to use paraphrasing during a group discussion. Before stating a point, each speaker must accurately paraphrase the point made by the previous speaker. Students quickly learn that they are often thinking about their own response rather than listening to the speaker, and they quickly learn to become better listeners.

7. *Ask students to respond to their classmates' answers.* We often inadvertently reinforce the idea that students do not need to listen to their classmates' answers. By asking students a series of independent (though often related) questions, we create a situation in which students can, with no immediate consequences to themselves, become inattentive to their peers' responses. We can alleviate this problem by occasionally asking students to comment on an answer provided by a classmate. It is important, however, that we not use this approach as a method for catching and embarrassing inattentive students. When calling on such a student, we should ask a question that he or she can answer. You might say, "John says that when we do not give this plant any light it will die. Do you agree, Bill?"

8. *Do not consistently repeat students' answers.* Many teachers parrot nearly every answer provided by a student. This practice is intended to ensure that all students hear the correct answer. But it also teaches students that (1) they do not need to speak loudly because the teacher is the only one who needs to hear their answer, (2) they do not need to listen to their peers because the teacher will repeat the answer, and (3) the teacher is the source of all learning in the classroom. All these negative side-effects reduce students' motivation, involvement, and attention.

9. *Model listening skills by paying close attention when students speak.* Children model their behavior after adults who have a significant role in their lives. If we want students to listen attentively to their peers, we must model good listening skills. We should concentrate on looking at the speaker and using nonverbal cues that indicate sincere interest.

Unfortunately, teachers often find that their attention is distracted by disruptive student behavior. We should initially attempt to deal with this distraction by employing a quick glance or gesture to indicate displeasure. If the behavior requires a more extensive diversion of attention from the speaker, we may wish to apologize to the speaker by making a statement such as, "I'm sorry that I did not hear the last part of your answer, John, but I had to ask several students to check themselves. Would you mind repeating your answer?"

10. *Be animated.* In his classic work on classroom discipline, Kounin (1970) writes, "teachers who maintain a group focus by engaging in behaviors that keep children alert and on their toes are more successful in inducing work involvement and preventing deviancy than are teachers who do not" (p. 123). Studies indicate not only that students like enthusiastic teachers, but that our enthusiasm facilitates students' achievement (Coats & Smidchens, 1966; Mastin, 1963; Rosenshine & Furst, 1973). We can demonstrate enthusiasm and animation by moving around the room, varying our voice level, using interested facial expressions, and maintaining a high energy level. If we wish to examine our behavior periodically to see whether it appears animated we can use audio- or videotape recordings of our teaching. Though every teacher must develop a personal own style and few teachers want to put on a performance all day every day, some animation is extremely helpful in keeping students' attention.

11. *Reinforce students' efforts and maintain a high ratio of positive to negative verbal statements.* Students will feel safer and more willing to be involved in a classroom characterized by warmth and support. Though they do not want overly affected or unrealistically positive feedback, they are motivated by straightforward and sincere praise. When teachers fail to provide frequent, clear, and varied reinforcement, students begin to lose interest and often attempt to acquire more interesting responses by engaging in inappropriate behavior.

12. *Vary instructional media and methods.* Anyone who has sat through a two-hour monotone lecture is aware of the need to vary the stimuli used during instruction. Because they spend a great deal of time watching television, youngsters may be particularly sensitive to changing stimuli. Though we cannot match television's diversity, we should nevertheless concentrate on adding diversity to instruction. We can use various media, such as an overhead projector, chalkboard, butcher paper, and film, as we move from lesson to lesson. Similarly, different instructional approaches can be used for different lessons. We may use seatwork for math, small groups for social studies, and a presentation during science. Teachers and students can also invite guests into their classrooms. During a recent school week guests in one of the author's classes included a local folk-singing group, an ambulance driver who demonstrated the equipment in her ambulance as well as mouth-to-mouth resuscitation and cardiopulmonary resuscitation, and a mother who spoke about nutrition. Students enjoy and are almost always attentive to adults from their community. Finally, teachers can add surprises such as using different-colored chalk or writing larger and smaller in the same sentence to attract students' attention.

13. *Create anticipation.* We can create a sense of interest by making statements such as, "This is a tough one," or "I'm not sure we've talked about this but maybe someone can answer it." Anticipation can also be created by leaving an interesting lesson without attaining closure. People tend to recall unfinished tasks and are more likely to forget completed tasks. By stimulating interest but moving on to a new activity, we can increase students' interest. This increased interest may also generalize to other subjects. When using this approach, however, you will want to attain some closure by examining possible answers and will also want to assure students that they will be able to return to the subject the following day.

14. *Use silences effectively.* Research on teachers' waiting time suggests that most teachers are uncomfortable with silence: we seem to believe that silences will be filled with disruptive behavior. Silences, however, offer several advantages that enhance students' learning and may reduce disruption. Silence can create suspense and anticipation. It can also give students time to slow down and assimilate material. Similarly, silence often clarifies information by breaking it into smaller segments. Finally, it can be used to emphasize an important point or to signal students to attend to the next statement or action. If we fall into the habit of employing rapid, nonstop talking to prevent students from interrupting, they often develop strategies for taking their own breaks. Unfortunately, these strategies often include disruptive, attention-getting behavior. Students who are poor auditory learners will find rapid, uninterrupted talk frustrating and will frequently respond by tuning out or acting out. As we saw in discussing random questioning, it is helpful to inform students why silences are being used and to provide them with assistance in using silences productively. We may state, "Before answering, I would like each of you to think about the question and see if you can find the answer," or "Please sit quietly for a minute and think about the slide we just saw."

15. *Ask questions that relate to students' own lives or similar situations.* Students find learning more meaningful when it can be related to their own lives and interests. We should therefore include questions such as, "Have you ever felt this way?" "How would your parents feel about this?" or "Do you believe that it is right to . . .?" Similarly, we can incorporate aspects of students' daily lives into our instruction. During creative writing, students can write stories in which others in the class are characters.

16. *Provide work of appropriate difficulty.* Students' misbehavior is often a response to work that is either too easy or too difficult. Students prefer work that is moderately difficult over tasks that are too easy (Kleinfeld, 1975; Maehr & Sjogren, 1971). When work is too difficult, though, students become discouraged. Failure also causes students to lower their expectations of their own performance.

Research (Brophy & Evertson, 1976) suggests that when the teacher is available to provide assistance (as during monitored seatwork or recitation), students should be able to answer 70 to 80 percent of questions correctly. When students must work independently (as on independent seatwork or homework), students should be able to answer 95 percent correctly (Brophy, 1982a; Fisher et al., 1980). Seatwork must not only allow for these high success rates but must also be different enough from previous work to challenge students.

Similarly, teacher questions to students should also elicit a relatively high rate of correct responses. Brophy (1986a) states that approximately three-fourths of teachers' questions should elicit correct responses and the remainder should elicit some form of incorrect or incomplete answer rather than failure to respond. Success rates can be expected to be lower when new material is being introduced but higher during reviews. Brophy notes that, "Consistently low success rates (below about 65 percent), however, suggest that the teacher is 'teaching over the students' heads' or has not prepared them effectively for the questions" (p. 9).

17. *Provide variability and interest in seatwork.* Seatwork can be made more interesting by developing units that relate to current events, such as sports or students' other interests (animals, entertainment figures, and so on), or by creating seatwork that is based on some form of board game. Students can also be involved in working cooperatively with peers or presented with a competitive situation.

18. *When presenting difficult material, clearly acknowledge this fact, set a time limit for the presentation, and describe the type of follow-up activities that will clarify the lesson.* Students are less likely to become discouraged and subsequently act out when we provide this type of information. Though we must not create a self-fulfilling prophecy, students benefit from knowing that the presentation involves a new and complicated concept. We can simultaneously stimulate interest and acknowledge the difficulty of the material by comments such as, "We're going to work on a new math skill today. I'll talk about it for fifteen minutes and then give you some problems. If you have difficulty, I will help you with the problems."

Pacing

Undoubtedly, you have experienced many examples of both effective and ineffective pacing. People who have sat through a dull movie or a long meeting in which they were neither interested in the topic nor asked to be involved have experienced ineffective pacing. Conversely, teachers have all experienced lessons that presented an ideal blend of active involvement and presentation of new ideas. Take a moment and recall a specific situation in which you felt the pacing was optimal. Now, recall an instance in which the pacing was very poor. Reflect on how you felt and behaved in each situation. If you are like most people, you were much more comfortable and attentive in the well-paced setting. Students' behavior is also dramatically influenced by the quality of their teacher's pacing. Disruptive student behavior can often be linked directly to poorly paced lessons.

Methods

1. *Develop awareness of your own teaching tempo.* Students' behavior and performance are affected by their teacher's tempo (Yando & Kagen, 1968). We can learn to generate interest and enthusiasm effectively or to create a calming effect by adjusting our own personal pace in the classroom. The best method for examining your own pace is to videotape yourself during large-group instruction. As you watch the replay, ask yourself such questions as, "Did I talk too fast?" "Was I animated?" "Did I repeat myself too often?" and "Would I enjoy listening to my own presentations?"

Another method for obtaining feedback on pacing involves incorporating questions about pacing into questionnaires given to students to assess the teacher's instruction. Students can respond to questions such as, "Do I speak slowly enough?" "Do I notice when you are not understanding the material and stop to explain?" or "Do you have time to complete the work I require?" Following a workshop presented by one of us, an experienced high school teacher decided to improve his pacing by teaching his students several signals they could use to provide him with feedback. Students were asked to make the common chattering movement with their hand to indicate that the teacher was repeating himself, place their hand up in a stop motion when he was going too fast, and make a circle with their index finger when they were confused. The teacher reported to his colleagues that students thoroughly enjoyed providing him with feedback and that he believed his teaching was more effective.

2. *Watch for nonverbal cues indicating that students are becoming confused, bored, or restless.* We often become so involved in presenting our material that we fail to attend to indications that several or even many students are becoming increasingly inattentive. Kounin (1970) discovered that teachers who had fewer discipline problems effectively scanned their rooms and responded to potentially disruptive student behavior before it became a major problem. When students appear restless, we have several options. First, we can state our perception and ask the children to express their feelings. We might say, "A number of you seem to be having difficulty paying attention. Can someone tell me what is causing the problem?" If students have become accustomed to sharing feelings and solving problems, it is likely that one or more can pinpoint the problem. Another option that may be used separately or may follow the intervention above is to speculate about the cause of the problem and change the pace accordingly. Therefore, we might decide that too much material is being covered and may shorten the lesson and incorporate several personalized questions to increase students' involvement and attention. The teacher who continues undaunted in the face of students' restlessness is inviting further disruptive behavior.

3. *Break activities up into short segments.* The use of films as instructional aids helps demonstrate this strategy. Teachers almost always allow a film to run all the way to the end before discussing its content. There are, however, several advantages to stopping the film at important points and discussing the ideas being presented. First, major points of information can be highlighted. Second, this procedure allows students to assimilate smaller amounts of information at a time. Many students simply cannot process the material offered in a half-hour film. Third, this method differentiates viewing a film at school from watching a movie or viewing television. Students can begin to learn that movies shown in school are meant to convey specific information and ideas rather than simply to entertain.

4. *Provide structured short breaks during lessons that last longer than 30 minutes.* Disruptive behavior is sometimes merely students' method of obtaining a short respite from the rigors of a long school day. Because many students do not have the skill to refresh themselves quietly and productively during extended periods of study, we can reduce disruptions either by providing structured breaks or by teaching children how to take their own breaks. We can provide a break by asking the class to put their pencils aside and take a minute to stand and stretch. We can also create a break by involving students in a short (three to five minutes is the optional length for such break activities) game such as Twenty Questions, Seven-up, or Simon Says. It is important to inform the students that this activity is being used to provide a brief break and that they will be expected to return to work as soon as the activity is completed. Students can be taught how to relax using deep muscle relaxation. We can then encourage them to respond to the need to wander around the room or disrupt another student by taking a moment to relax themselves before continuing with their work. We can reinforce this approach by occasionally employing it as a structured break activity.

5. *Vary the style as well as the content of instruction.* Students often become restless when faced with extended instructional periods using only one type of instruction. If students have completed a large-group discussion in social studies, it is best not to move directly to a large-group science presentation. Teachers with good classroom-management skills learn to move smoothly among a variety of instructional approaches.

6. *Do not bury students in a "purple plague."* Students' misbehavior is not infrequently an attempt to add a little entertainment and relief to a day filled with innumerable worksheets. Students may act out because they are given 30 problems to complete when only 5 were needed to indicate mastery of a new skill or when they are confronted with a continuous procession of worksheets.

Using Seatwork Effectively

Research in hundreds of elementary school classrooms shows that students spend more than half their time working privately at seatwork (Angus, Evans, & Parkin, 1975; Good & Beckerman, 1978; McDonald, 1976). Data from some of the classes of the Beginning Teacher Evaluation Study (Fisher et al., 1978) also show that in some classes students make nearly 100 percent errors during 14 percent of the time they are involved in seatwork. Given findings suggesting that during seatwork students learn best when experiencing approximately 90 percent success rates (Rosenshine, 1983), it is critical that we learn to structure seatwork effectively to ensure students' involvement and success.

Methods

1. *Make seatwork diagnostic and prescriptive.* Seatwork should be designed to provide students with meaningful practice while enabling teacher and student to assess the student's progress. Therefore, seatwork should be checked by the teacher or student, recorded and filed by the student, monitored by the teacher, and discussed in periodic teacher-student conferences. When this procedure is followed, students view seatwork as meaningful and are much less likely to act out during instructional periods designated for seatwork.

2. *Develop a specific procedure for obtaining assistance.* Students will inevitably require assistance when engaged in seatwork assignments. Because teachers are often engaged in small-group instruction or helping other students while all are doing seatwork, it is necessary to establish a procedure whereby children can obtain assistance without interrupting the teacher. If such procedures are not established and students are instructed not to disturb the teacher, they will become frustrated when they need assistance and are likely to respond by acting out. The most effective method of providing assistance is peer tutoring.

3. *Establish clear procedures about what to do when seatwork is completed.* It is helpful to display a poster reminding students what to do with their completed work (for example, we may remind them to score, record, and file their work), and what alternatives are available once these tasks have been completed. Learning centers and puzzles or other challenging activities provide useful and necessary alternatives for students.

4. *Add interest to seatwork.* Include cartoons, puzzles, or personalized questions on worksheets.

5. *Monitor seatwork by moving around the room systematically.* Teachers often inadvertently spend a disproportionate amount of time in one or more areas of the classroom. During seatwork instruction, it is important to monitor each student's work. We can ensure that this is done by carrying a clipboard and noting when each student's work is monitored, or by having a colleague or student draw a map of our walking pattern during a seatwork period.

When involved with a small group, we can assign the group a task and leave briefly to monitor students involved in seatwork. By teaching a procedure for obtaining assistance, we can reduce the need to provide lengthy assistance to students involved in seatwork and can simply remind them to follow the procedure.

6. *Monitor students' seatwork and make needed adjustments.* One of us recently observed a student teacher in a fifth-grade class. Students in the class completed seatwork at varying rates, and the teacher's failure to adjust seatwork or provide optional learning activities meant that many students were free to wander and disrupt the class. To bring out this point for the teacher, I coded at five-minute intervals the number of students who had completed one-quarter, half, three-quarters, or all their work. The results (Figure 8.4) clearly indicate the inappropriateness of giving all students the same seatwork task.

In addition to monitoring the time required to complete seatwork, we should monitor the percentage of students who complete their work with at least 75 percent accuracy (a higher percentage should be selected if we are not available to monitor the seatwork). This information as well as a group average score should be recorded as a basis for determining future seatwork assignments for individual students or the class as a whole.

7. *Work through the first several seatwork problems with the students.* All students will then understand the procedure to be followed and will be able to ask questions if they do not understand the work.

8. *Spend considerable time in presentation and discussion before assigning seatwork.* Students learn more effectively when they have been well prepared for this work.

9. *Relate seatwork directly to material presented immediately prior to it.* Students will have more difficulty with seatwork assignments related to material discussed on the previous day or stemming from individualized work.

10. *Keep contacts with individual students relatively short (30 seconds or less).* Longer contacts minimize your ability to scan the room or to provide assistance to all students.

11. *Provide short segments of seatwork.* Rather than making one long presentation followed by an extended period of seatwork, break the instruction into smaller segments and follow each with a short period of seatwork.

12. *Have students work together during seatwork.* Students can jointly develop solutions or can cooperatively prepare for group competition.

FIGURE 8.4 Number of Students Who Had Completed Various Amounts of Seatwork at Five-Minute Intervals

	Percentage of work complete			
	0–25%	*26–50%*	*51–75%*	*76–100%*
5 minute	11	12	8	2
10 minute	6	10	10	7
15 minute	4	6	13	10
20 minute	3	4	7	9

Summarizing

Many children view the school day as a series of tasks to be completed and do not understand what they have learned or how the learning relates to specific learning goals or their own lives. Try to recall a course you found particularly difficult. Take a moment to consider how you went about studying for the course and how well you understand the material. It is likely that you studied specific facts and that you did not fully understand the central concepts of the discipline or the relationship between what you were studying and your own life. It is also very likely that you found the course frustrating and confusing. Unfortunately, many students experience similar feelings about much of the school day. We should not be surprised that acting-out behavior replaces appropriate on-task behavior. Many of the methods presented in this chapter are effective in producing more positive student behavior precisely because they reduce students' frustration. Helping students understand what they have learned is a key factor in clarifying the school experience. When combined with clearly stated goals and useful feedback, the methods presented in this section provide students with a sense of accomplishment and meaning in their school experience.

Methods

1. *At the end of a lesson or a school day, ask students to state or write in a journal one thing they have learned.* Not only does this activity help clarify what they have learned, but it also provides each student with a sense of accomplishment. Students should be informed that if they have difficulty stating what they have learned, they can seek assistance from the teacher or a peer.

2. *Have students play the role of a reporter and summarize what has been learned.* We can introduce a student as a news reporter who will highlight the information from a lesson. We might say, "This is NBC reporter Billy Williams, who will report on the Nez Perce conflict that caused the tribe's flight to Canada. Come in, Billy."

3. *Have students create a skit to act out what they have learned.* In a unit on fur trappers, students can play the role of trappers building a bull boat. During their work the trappers can discuss how the boat is built and how it applies to their livelihood. Similarly, when studying parts of speech, students can be given cards listing various parts of speech and asked to organize themselves into meaningful sentences.

4. *Ask students to create learning displays.* Students can develop a collage, outline, newspaper article, and so on, to display their learning. They might write an article reporting on how plants grow. Students could also draw a chart that demonstrates this process.

5. *Encourage students to present their learning to others.* Students can share what they have learned with their classmates, other classes, or their parents. This sharing can take the form of reporting results of science experiments, performing skits, or showing the results of art projects, and so on. Students can also share their learning by actually teaching their newly acquired information to other students.

6. *Display students' work.* Displaying students' work provides students with a sense of pride and accomplishment and also provides closure to an activity. Students can view the result of a unit or lesson, which reinforces the fact that the various steps led to an observable final product.

7. *Relate material to students' lives and interests.* An effective summary involves clarifying how the new material relates to students' lives or can be useful to students. When completing a unit on division, students can be asked to calculate their Little League batting averages, their teams' won-lost percentages, or whether they would save money on certain items by purchasing them in larger quantities. Similarly, at the completion of a unit on how plants grow, students could be asked to list the ways in which their new knowledge will help them to grow a better garden or keep their house plants alive longer.

8. *Provide frequent review sessions.* It is helpful frequently to review previous learning and relate this information to current or future lessons. When presenting a daily, continuing lesson, we should begin the day's lesson with a brief review of the material covered on the previous day. This refresher not only enhances retention but also reinforces the concept that learning builds on previous learning. Students too often perceive each lesson as an isolated hurdle to be jumped rather than a step in a sequential learning process. Frequent reviews increase the likelihood that learning will be seen as a connected series of events.

9. *Use tests as tools for summarizing learning.* Teachers should treat tests like any other summary or learning experience. Students need to be informed that tests are a means for discovering how much they have learned and what material may need to be covered more thoroughly. When they have completed a test, answers should be discussed so that students receive a review of the correct answers.

Providing Useful Feedback and Evaluation

Evaluation of students' performance is an area that causes much worry among students, teachers, and parents. Teachers worry about their ability to evaluate students accurately and whether their feedback is fair and helpful. Students worry not only about what evaluations indicate about their own competence, but also about their parents' reactions to teachers' evaluations. Finally, parents worry about reports on their child's performance, not only because they hope their child will be successful and happy and because a good evaluation reflects favorably upon them, but also because consistently poor evaluations may suggest either poor parenting or limited academic potential. Because of the interest and potential anxiety associated with evaluation, it is clear that by using effective methods in this area we can create greater clarity and safety and thereby reduce disruptive behavior. Many years ago Regan (1966) wrote in *Modern Elementary Curriculum* that the six basic purposes of evaluation are:

1. To reveal to teachers what is happening to each child.
2. To motivate learning through furnishing pupils with information concerning success in various areas of the curriculum.
3. To furnish teachers with a means of appraising teaching methods, textbook, and other instrumentalities of the educative process.
4. To provide a basis for continuous improvement of the curriculum.
5. To give pupils experience in evaluating their own progress.
6. To reveal the progress the school program is making toward the achievement of the accepted objectives. (p. 452)

The methods presented below reinforce these purposes and offer practical ideas for effectively using evaluation in the classroom.

Methods

1. *Help students view evaluation as part of the learning process.* We need to place no greater emphasis on tests or report cards than on any other instructional activity. Children should be encouraged to view evaluation as simply an integral part of learning. This understanding can be enhanced by employing many of the methods described in this section.

2. *Tell students the criteria by which they will be evaluated.* When working with specific skills, students should know what they are to learn and what level of performance is acceptable. Similarly, when they are assigned projects in subjects from art to social studies, they should be informed about the specific goals for the lesson, and, if their work will be evaluated, what specific criteria will be used. The importance of sharing information with children was powerfully stated by Herbert Kohl (1967):

> The easiest way to bring this up in class was to tell the children exactly where they stood. I braced myself, and defying all precedent as well as my own misgivings, I performed the unforgivable act of showing the children what their reading and IQ scores were according to the record cards. I also taught a lesson on the definition of IQ and of achievement scores. The children were angry and shocked; no one had ever come right out and told them they were failing. It was always put so nicely and evasively that the children never knew where they stood. (p. 176)

3. *Relate feedback directly to individual or teacher goals.* Feedback should help students understand how effectively they are progressing toward clearly specified goals. This clarification makes the learning process much more concrete and clear. Studies (Burrows, 1973; Collins, 1971) indicate that providing students with the results of diagnostic tests and then providing instruction aimed at achieving mastery of specific objectives leads to dramatic increases in learning.

4. *Record data so that students can monitor their progress.* Students can benefit immensely from the realization that they are able to learn. One of us once worked with a seventh-grade boy who viewed himself as a totally inept learner. One day while the boy was working in a room that included a two-way mirror, the boy was videotaped during a period in which he worked diligently for 50 consecutive minutes. When the videotape was shown to the student he responded with disbelief. He simply could not believe that he could study for 50 minutes. The student asked to have the principal and his own mother view the tape. This incident proved to be a watershed in the boy's school life.

Students should be taught how to record their academic progress. We can do so by teaching simple graphing skills. We may also wish to provide interesting data displays, such as a football field with strings to which cardboard football players are attached. The players can be moved down the field to represent individual or group acquisition of skills. Chapter 7 provides specific techniques for employing academic goal setting and student self-monitoring.

5. *Provide immediate and specific feedback.* Page (1958) found that students' learning was enhanced when they were provided with specific positive and negative information about their performance. Generalized feedback such as a grade or comments such as "Good" or "Nice work" do not tend to improve students' performance on subsequent tests.

6. *Attempt to focus on positive accomplishments.* Whenever possible, we should help students record their accomplishments rather than focus on their failures. We can initially focus on the items students have answered correctly and then help them correct mistakes. Effective feedback encourages students to describe both the strengths and weaknesses of their work.

7. *Provide honest feedback.* It is important to focus on students' success, but students' performance is not aided by feedback that is inaccurately positive. Students resent feedback they perceive as fake (Travers, 1967). Furthermore, providing students with too much praise for work that does not meet acceptable standards only confuses them and reduces their motivation and performance.

8. *Ask students to list factors that contributed to their success.* Students need assistance in specifying behaviors that enabled them to succeed. Low-achieving students often view their successes as based on luck or outside forces rather than on their own efforts. Helping children focus on the relationship between their effort and performance can help them feel a greater sense of competence and power. This confidence will in turn increase the likelihood that they will begin to accept greater responsibility for their own behavior.

9. *Deemphasize comparisons between students and their peers.* Though it is helpful for students to know how they stand in relation to grade-level norms, we should not evaluate how well they perform in relation to their peers. In addition to placing some children in a no-win situation, comparative evaluations suggest that the goal of learning is to outperform one's peers rather than to master the material. Students should be evaluated on criterion-referenced tests and their performance compared to their own earlier work.

10. *Deemphasize grades as feedback on students' work.* Grades by themselves provide almost no useful information. When it is important or necessary to provide students with information about the quality of their performance as compared to an external criterion such as grade-level norms, it is best to have a teacher-student conference and outline specific skills the student will need to improve in order to score at grade level. Detailed teacher's comments and supportive statements are much more effective than grades in motivating students' performance.

> Grades tend to motivate those students who least need it; that is, those who are already successful; while, perversely, the very students who need motivating the most (poor students) are most put off and threatened by grades. . . .
>
> When it comes to motivating school achievement, it appears that the type of learning structure is by far the more important factor, with grades playing a secondary, even negligible, role. (Covington & Beery, 1976, pp. 116, 117)

Making Smooth Transitions

A surprisingly large amount of classroom time is spent in transition from one activity to another. The approximately 30 major transitions each day in elementary classrooms account for nearly 15 percent of classroom time (Gump, 1967; Rosenshine, 1980). Most experienced teachers acknowledge that the beginning and end of class periods, or the transition between subjects or activities during the period, are the times when students are most likely to be disruptive. Therefore, as we would expect, the handling of transitions distinguishes skilled from less-skilled classroom managers (Arlin, 1979; Doyle, 1984).

Students' disruption during transitions often leads to extended periods of off-task behavior, which drains teachers' energies and reduces students' achievement. Because students' learning is directly related to the amount of time they spend studying a subject (Borg, 1980; Rosenshine, 1976; Sirotnik, 1982), we must develop skill in making smooth transitions. It is equally important, however, that we realize that the quality of learning time is more important than time itself (Berliner, 1979; Doyle, 1983; Good, 1986; Peterson & Swing, 1982). Therefore, the goal of an effective transition is not so much getting students immediately on task as it is preparing students to be productively involved in the coming instruction.

Methods

1. *Arrange the classroom for efficient movement.* The classroom should be arranged so that areas through which students move frequently are wide and cleared of materials. Desks should be arranged so that students and teacher can move around the room without disturbing students who are working. We encourage you to make a detailed map of your classroom and mark areas where students frequently move or congregate. Are these large enough to prevent overcrowding and its accompanying disruption? Are pathways clear and wide? Is space used so that the classroom has a sense of openness?

2. *Create and post a daily schedule and discuss any changes in schedule each morning.* Numerous low-level discipline problems arise when students are confused over scheduling issues, such as a change in their violin lesson or not attending reading due to the specialist's absence. These difficulties can be minimized by discussing the classroom schedule each morning. This activity also provides a clear and task-oriented transition into the school day.

3. *Have material ready for the next lesson.* It is often helpful to have an outline of the lesson written on the chalkboard or on butcher paper. Similarly, having a filmstrip or film set up and ready to go or having materials ready for distribution allows us to make a smooth transition rather than attempting to prepare materials while monitoring students' behavior and dealing with disruptions that often occur during transition periods. Students' behavior is dramatically affected by our behavior. If we are well prepared, relaxed, and make smooth transitions, students will almost always follow by moving calmly from one activity to the next. Conversely, when we become frustrated or anxious while attempting to arrange an activity, students inevitably follow suit.

4. *Do not relinquish students' attention until you have given clear instructions for the following activity.* We can prevent numerous problems by moving from a summary of one lesson immediately into a transition activity (such as a brief game of Seven-Up) or the next lesson. All too often, we allow the class to become disruptive while we prepare for the next lesson, only to find that it requires considerable time and energy to regain the students' attention.

5. *Do not do tasks that can be done by students.* We can free ourselves to monitor the class and can reduce the demands on our own time and energy by having students do a wide variety of tasks, such as handing out and collecting materials, running filmstrips, and taking the roll. In addition to freeing us for more important instructional and management tasks, involving students in organizational tasks can provide them with a sense of competence and power.

6. *Move around the room and attend to individual needs.* Being prepared and allowing students to handle many small tasks can free us to scan the classroom more effectively and handle any minor problems that, if ignored, could expand into major disruptions. Having a moment to notice and say a few words to a student who is frustrated by an inability to complete the previous activity may prevent a major disruption by that student during the next lesson.

7. *Provide students with simple, step-by-step directions.* Younger students especially benefit from being given specific directions asking them to do one thing at a time. Rather than asking students to "get ready for lunch," we might break this task into the smaller steps of clearing their desks, sitting quietly, one group at a time getting their lunches, and so forth.

8. *Remind students of key procedures associated with the upcoming lesson.* If the next lesson requires some students to work independently while you instruct a small group or have conferences with students, remind students of the procedures they should follow during this type of activity. This is best handled by first describing the learning activity and its goal and then asking students to describe the procedures they are to follow during this type of activity.

9. *Use group competition to stimulate more orderly transitions.* We can involve the class in attempting to reduce the amount of time required to make a transition. Similarly, small groups or rows of students can be involved in competition to see who can make the quietest and fastest preparation for the next lesson.

10. *Develop transition activities.* Students often find it difficult to make the transition from home to school or from lunch or physical education back to a quieter setting. We can facilitate smooth transitions by implementing structured activities that help students make these transitions. We can ask them to begin the school day by writing in their journals or by discussing the daily schedule. Transitions from active periods such as lunch into quieter learning activities can be facilitated by transition activities such as our reading to the students or leading students in deep muscle relaxation. When these activities are used consistently, students not only find safety and comfort in this structure, but also can learn how to monitor transitions for themselves.

IMPLEMENTING AND ASSESSING NEW TEACHING METHODS

A major problem associated with reading a long list of methods is the tendency to acknowledge their value but not slow down long enough to implement any one method systematically. You may feel stimulated or overwhelmed by the many methods presented in the previous section. Unfortunately, neither of these feelings has a direct, positive effect on students' behavior. To improve students' learning and behavior, you must take time to use several of these methods thoughtfully in the classroom.

ACTIVITY 8.1 Implementing and Assessing New Teaching Methods

Label each of eight sheets of paper with one of the eight approaches to reducing disruptions during a lesson (see Figure 8.1). Next, under each topic write one specific method you do not currently use and that you believe would help you reduce classroom disruptions. On the page labeled *Giving Clear Instructions,* you might write: Place directions where they can be seen and referred to by students. The next step involves writing and completing these statements on each page:

I will begin using this method (give a specific date) _____ .
I will know that I have implemented this method when I have. . . .
After _____ days I will evaluate this method by. . . .

After thoughtfully and specifically completing these statements for each of the eight methods, write the following statement near the bottom of each page and complete it after you have implemented and evaluated the new method.

Based on my evaluation, I believe the new method. . . .

In addition to selecting specific methods that will help improve students' learning and behavior, you will develop professionally by attempting the following activity that helps to demonstrate the value of collecting data on your use of new teaching methods.

ACTIVITY 8.2 Monitoring Students' Hand Raising

Part I: During a question-and-answer period, select five questions varying in difficulty. When asking these, stop approximately two-thirds of the way through each question and quickly count the number of hands that are raised. Also, try to notice which students have their hands up. It may help to involve a colleague or parent in collecting these data. After the lesson, complete these questions:

How many students had their hands raised when you stopped during each question?
Were considerably more hands raised for the less difficult question?
What did you notice about the students whose hands were raised? Did they tend to be your higher-achieving students?

Part II: During a question-and-answer period in the same subject with the same students, select five questions varying in difficulty. Wait five full seconds after completing each question. Count the number of hands that were raised to answer each of these questions. Again, try to notice which students raised their hands.

After the lesson, complete these questions:

How many students had their hands raised to answer each question?
Were considerably more hands raised for the less difficult questions?
What did you notice about students who raised their hands?

Now compare the results of your two experiments. Make the task easier by completing this form for each set of questions.

Question	Number of students' hands raised	Type of student raising hand
1. Most difficult		
2.		
3.		
4.		
5. Least difficult		

Finally, complete these sentences.

I learned that . . .
I was surprised that . . .
When I waited longer . . .

This is only one example of how you can collect data to assess the results obtained by implementing new teaching methods. Whenever possible, we encourage you to generate some form of evaluation to assess the results of using new methods.

SUMMARY

The original research on classroom management focused on the noninstructional aspects of teacher behavior that prevented disruptive student behavior. Jacob Kounin discovered that what differentiated effective from less effective classroom managers was what these teachers did before, not after, students became involved in unproductive behavior. This chapter presents eight areas of teacher behavior that are related to student behavior and achievement. For each area, we present both a brief overview of the research findings and a number of specific suggestions teachers can use in order to increase positive student behavior. Even though we now know that this is only one aspect of effective classroom management, you can find that by using a variety of the methods presented here you can create a more smoothly run, efficient classroom in which student behavior is significantly more goal-directed.

RECOMMENDED READING

Brophy, J., & Evertson, C. (1976). *Learning from teaching*. Boston: Allyn and Bacon.

Good, T., & Brophy, J. (1987). *Looking in classrooms*, 4th ed. New York: Harper and Row.

Hosford, P. (1984). *Using what we know about teaching*. Alexandria, Va.: Association for Supervision and Curriculum Development.

Kounin, J. (1970). *Discipline and group management in classrooms*. New York: Holt, Rinehart and Winston.

Smith, D. (1984). *Essential knowledge for beginning educators*. Washington, D.C.: American Association of Colleges for Teacher Education.

Squires, D., Huitt, W., & Segars, J. (1984). *Effective schools and classrooms. A research-based perspective*. Alexandria, Va.: Association for Supervision and Curriculum Development.

Wlodkowski, R. (1978). *Motivation and teaching: A practical guide*. Washington, D.C.: National Education Association.

CHAPTER 9

Developing Productive Student Behavior by Effectively Teaching Rules and Procedures

Although the rules and procedures used by effective classroom managers vary from teacher to teacher, we do not find effectively managed classrooms operating without them.

/ Edmund Emmer, Carolyn Evertson, Julie Sanford,
Barbara Clements, and Murray Worsham (1982)
Organizing and Managing the Junior High School Classroom

And teachers can't expect students to follow rules they perceive only as arbitrary challenges to their freedom and dignity. When teachers take the time to explain the rationale underlying rules, student compliance increases.

/ *Today's Education*, 1983–84. Annual Edition

Teaching is a demanding, fast-paced job. Each day the typical elementary school teacher has more than a thousand teacher-student interactions and teaches 10 subjects. Secondary teachers often teach 150 or more students with only 4 minutes between classes. These demanding working conditions can cause confusion and frustration and limit students' learning time. Research indicates that effective teachers take time early in the school year to develop classroom rules and procedures that help their classrooms run smoothly and minimize disruptions, and thus maximize students' learning time.

Research in teacher effectiveness has increasingly stressed that effective teachers organize their classrooms so as to prevent disruptive behavior. Nearly 20 years ago, Good and Brophy (1973) wrote:

> Teachers who take time early in the year to listen to students and to explain carefully the rationales underlying rules and assignments are making a wise investment. This ultimately will establish teacher credibility and reduce the students' tendencies to continue to test the teacher throughout the year. (p. 168)

Three years later Brophy and Evertson (1976) reported a similar result:

> Much of the behavior that distinguished the most effective teachers from the less effective ones was behavior that could be called ''proactive.'' That is, it was behavior initiated by the teachers themselves, often prior to the beginning of the school year or the beginning of a particular school day. (p.142)

Research reviews by Soar and Soar (1979,1980) also suggest that students' learning is enhanced by teachers' developing basic classroom structure. Soar and Soar (1979) write that research indicates that ''unless a teacher has established a minimum of structure, relatively strong interactions that are not functional for pupil learning are likely to occur''(p.117).

Research conducted at the Research and Development Center for Teacher Education at the University of Texas at Austin (Emmer, Evertson, & Anderson, 1980; Evertson & Emmer, 1982a, 1982b) provides specific information on techniques that effective teachers use during the first few weeks of school. Effective classroom managers at both the elementary and junior high school level spend time teaching students classroom rules and procedures. Emmer, Evertson, Sandford, and Worsham (1981) describe *rules* as ''written rules which are either posted in the classroom, given to students on ditto or other copy, or copied by students into their notebooks'' (pp. 18, 19). *Procedures* are defined as, ''Procedures, like rules, are expectations for behavior. They usually apply to a *specific* activity, and they usually are directed at accomplishing, rather than forbidding some behavior'' (p.19). Effective teachers do more than post rules or present procedures. Especially in elementary classrooms, teachers work with students to ensure that they understand and can demonstrate rules and procedures. This is an important point. Students' behavior needs to be dealt with much like their academic skills. Teachers spend considerable time during the first few weeks of school assessing students' knowledge, reviewing material, and reteaching academic skills students have forgotten. Similarly, when effective teachers first introduce important academic material, they attempt to provide clear instruction, carefully monitor students' progress, and provide immediate corrective feedback if a student or group of students are having difficulty with the material. In the same manner, teachers must begin the school year by teaching the classroom rules and procedures, carefully monitoring students' behavior, informing students of mistakes, and reteaching rules or procedures that students are frequently failing to follow.

The initial studies involving teacher behavior at the beginning of the school year were correlational; teachers whose students made greater achievement gains were observed establishing rules and procedures and carefully monitoring student work. Following these discoveries, however, several studies were conducted to determine whether teachers trained in the materials in this chapter were more effective in increasing student on-task behavior and learning than were teachers who did not receive this training and implement these new teacher behaviors. Results from these studies (Evertson, 1985; Evertson, Emmer, Sanford, & Clements, 1983) clearly demonstrate that providing training in these methods can lead to changes in teacher behaviors that are associated with improved student behavior. In addition, Evertson (1985) found that even when provided to teachers who had recently received systematic training to improve their instructional skills, training in effectively developing, monitoring, and reinforcing classroom rules and procedures was associated with improved student behavior. Figures 9.1 and 9.2 outline the content presented in the elementary and secondary teacher training sessions.

We must keep in mind that many behaviors that are undesirable in the classroom are not inherently bad and in fact may be encouraged in other settings. For example, neither student chatter nor attention-seeking behavior is bad or destructive in itself. We

FIGURE 9.1 Major Components Presented in Beginning-of-Year Treatment

1. *Readying the classroom.* Be certain your classroom space and materials are ready for the beginning of the year.
2. *Planning rules and procedures.* Think about what procedures students must follow to function effectively in your classroom and in the school environment: decide what behaviors are acceptable or unacceptable; develop a list of procedures and rules.
3. *Consequences.* Decide ahead of time consequences for appropriate and inappropriate behavior in your classroom, and communicate them to your students; follow through consistently.
4. *Teaching Rules and Procedures.* Teach students rules and procedures systematically; include in your lesson plans for the beginning of school sequences for teaching rules and procedures, when and how they will be taught, and when practice and review will occur.
5. *Beginning-of-school activities.* Develop activities for the first few days of school that will involve students readily and maintain a whole-group focus.
6. *Strategies for potential problems.* Plan strategies to deal with potential problems that could upset your classroom organization and management.
7. *Monitoring.* Monitor student behavior closely.
8. *Stopping inappropriate behavior.* Handle inappropriate and disruptive behavior promptly and consistently.
9. *Organizing instruction.* Organize instruction to provide learning activities at suitable levels for all students in your class.
10. *Student accountability.* Develop procedures that keep the children responsible for their work.
11. *Instructional clarity.* Be clear when you present information and give directions to your students.

Source: C. Evertson, E. Emmer, J. Sanford, and B. Clements."Improving Management: An Experiment in Elementary School Classrooms," *Elementary School Journal,* 84 (1983): 173–188. Copyright © 1983 by The University of Chicago.

FIGURE 9.2 Outline of Workshop Content for Secondary Teachers in the Experimental Group

I. *Planning* (before school starts)
   A. Use of space (readying the classroom)
   B. Rules for general behavior
   C. Rules and procedures for specific areas
      1. Student use of classroom space and facilities
      2. Student use of out-of-class areas
      3. Student participation during whole class activities/seatwork
      4. Student participation in daily routines
      5. Student participation during small-group activities
   D. Consequence/incentives for appropriate/inappropriate behavior
   E. Activities for the first day of school
II. *Presenting Rules, Procedures, and Expectation* (beginning of school)
   A. Teaching rules and procedures
      1. Explanation   3. Feedback
      2. Rehearsal   4. Reteaching
   B. Teaching academic content
   C. Communicating concepts and directions clearly
III. *Maintaining the System* (throughout the year)
   A. Monitoring for behavioral and academic compliance
   B. Acknowledging appropriate behavior
   C. Stopping inappropriate behavior
   D. Consistent use of consequences/incentives
   E. Adjusting instruction for individual students/groups
   F. Keeping students accountable for work
   G. Coping with special problems

Source: Carolyn M. Evertson,"Training Teachers in Classroom Management: An Experimental Study in Secondary School Classrooms,"*Journal of Educational Research,* 79 (1): 54, 1985. Reprinted with permission of the Helen Reid Educational Foundation. Published by Heldref Publications, 4000 Albermarle St., N.W., Washington, D.C. 20016. Copyright © 1985.

would expect 30 children placed in close quarters to make a considerable amount of noise. Similarly, children often show off in front of adults or their peers. In fact, adults encourage children to seek the limelight in sporting events or other competitive activities. Therefore, we should not be surprised to discover that we must help children develop attitudes and skills that support behavioral norms that are most adaptive in a school environment.

We offer several words of caution before discussing approaches to establishing productive classroom rules and procedures. Rules and procedures should be developed in conjunction with teaching strategies that help students meet their personal and academic needs. In his *Culture against Man*, Jules Henry (1963) vividly depicts an example of a classroom procedure that violates students' personal needs.

Boris had trouble reducing "12/16" to the lowest terms, and could only get as far as "6/8". The teacher asked him quietly if that was as far as he could reduce it. She suggested he "think."

Much heaving up and down and waving of hands by the other children, all frantic to correct him . . . . She then turns to the class and says, "Well, who can tell Boris what the number is?" A forest of hands appears, and the teacher calls Peggy. Peggy says that four may be divided into the numerator and the denominator.

Thus Boris' failure has made it possible for Peggy to succeed; his depression is the price of her exhilaration; his misery the occasion for her rejoicing. This is the standard condition of the American elementary school, and is why so many of us feel a contraction of the heart even if someone we never knew succeeds merely at garnering plankton in the Thames: because so often somebody's success has been bought at the cost of our failure. (pp. 295, 296)

Unfortunately, students are often expected to behave in compliance with rules and procedures even though the learning environment does not respond sensitively to their needs and interests. When we find this condition in a classroom, it is understandable that students' behavior begins to oppose the classroom rules. The educational exchange must function effectively in both directions. Students can be expected to support rules and procedures that enhance learning only if the learning process shows respect for students and their needs.

Another concept that can help you thoughtfully develop classroom rules is that rules should not be designed to catch children misbehaving so that they can be punished. Instead, rules should provide guidelines or benchmarks that help children examine their behavior, considering its effects on themselves and others. Consequently, behavior that violates accepted rules should be dealt with by discussing the matter with the child. This does not mean that reasonable punishments should not be used, but when dealing with unproductive behavior, we must help children examine both their motivations and the consequences of their actions. Overemphasis on punishment often obscures the issue of motivation and attitude and simultaneously limits the child's attention to the immediate negative consequences of his or her behavior. This pressure tends to limit thoughtful consideration of either the effect the behavior has on others or the long-term consequences associated with continuing the behavior. In a real sense, a punishment orientation reinforces a low level of moral development and does not help children develop a higher, more socially valuable level of morality.

DEVELOPING CLASSROOM RULES

Several factors increase the likelihood that students will accept and consistently follow classroom rules. First, students need to be involved in developing the rules that apply in the classroom. Second, rules need to be clearly stated. Students have difficulty responding to glittering generalities such as "behave appropriately." Third, although it is important to state expectations clearly, it is just as important to keep the rules as few as possible. Fourth, students must clearly indicate their acceptance of the rules agreed on by the classroom group. Fifth, because rules established in the school setting may conflict with rules children experience outside of school, it is important that student behavior be monitored and frequently discussed to ensure that it is consistent with the classroom rules. Finally, students will be more likely to behave in accordance with rules if they know that the rules are accepted by significant others, such as their parents and peers.

The specific methods presented in the remainder of this chapter apply most directly to elementary school classrooms or other relatively small, self-contained settings, such as a special education class or a small alternative school. The basic ideas, however, describe the essential ingredients in establishing classroom rules and responsibilities. Whenever significant variations are needed for secondary classrooms, they are included.

Discussing the Value of Rules

The first step in developing classroom rules is to help students discuss why it is important to develop rules that all members of the class agree to follow. We may want to introduce or stimulate the discussion by asking students why adults have rules such as obeying traffic signals, paying their taxes, or not crowding in lines. Throughout this discussion, we reinforce the concept that the classroom group and the school are a society, and, like larger societal groups, they will function more effectively when people decide to create and follow rules. We can help students consider how rules benefit people who must work together. This topic places the focus clearly on the advantages each child derives from class members' accepting the rules. For example, students may state that rules are important because if everyone did whatever he or she wanted, the classroom might become too disruptive for effective studying.

Students' statements on why it is important to develop classroom rules can be written on the chalkboard or a large piece of butcher paper. The latter approach has the advantage of making the list easier to save and discuss later should the group have difficulty in following its rules. Secondary teachers generally use a less elaborate discussion of why rules are needed. Nevertheless, we should elicit students' comments about why rules are needed when a group of people work for some time together in a relatively small space.

Developing a List

The next step in developing functional classroom rules is to have the students list all rules they believe are important. These can include rules related to academic as well as behavioral expectations. An academic rule might include working quietly during study periods or attempting to complete all homework on time. During this stage, we should help the students state all rules in a positive manner. If a student states, "Don't talk while others are talking," we can help the student phrase this rule thus: "Each student should listen quietly while another person is talking." Similarly, the rule: "Students should not steal from each other, the teacher, or the school," could be stated as: "If anyone needs something he or she will ask to borrow it." Once the students and you have completed their list of rules, help them cross out any that do not apply and combine as many as possible.

Secondary teachers may not want to develop a separate list for each of five or six classes; two optional strategies are available. First, we know teachers who have each class select one rule. These rules are combined to form the teacher's class rules. Second, we may present our own rules and ask each class if they believe one or two additional rules might help their class.

Figure 9.3 lists classroom rules that can be used in either an elementary or secondary classroom. Rules need to be general and all encompassing. When developing such a list with young children, teachers can increase students' understanding by discussing, role playing, and initially displaying (pictorially or in writing) several specific behavioral examples of following and violating each rule. Activity 9.1 (at the end of the chapter) offers

FIGURE 9.3 Classroom Rules

1. Speak politely to others.
2. Treat each other kindly.
3. Follow teacher requests.
4. Be prepared for class.
5. Make a good effort at your work and request help if you need it.
6. Obey all school rules.

you an opportunity to practice developing classroom rules that would be appropriate and effective with the students with whom you work.

Getting a Commitment

When the final list has been developed, lead a discussion to clarify each rule and ask students to state whether they can accept each rule. During this important stage several students may state that they do not believe they can abide by a particular rule. You can then ask the students whether the rule seems to be one that does not help people or whether they agree that it is a good rule but do not believe they can consistently act in accordance with it. If they express the latter, you can explain that they are not expected to be able to act perfectly all the time. Just as they will learn how to solve new math problems and read more efficiently, they will also learn how to behave in ways that are more effective. The initial question is not whether the students can already solve all their math problems or consistently behave appropriately, but whether they believe that these skills are helpful to them and if they will attempt to improve these skills. If the students state that a rule is not acceptable, you can help them clarify why they believe it to be undesirable. In most cases, students will quickly acknowledge the basic value of the rule. If one or more students persist in stating that a rule is unacceptable, however, you have the option of deleting the rule or asking to postpone further discussion of the item until you have had an opportunity to discuss it with the small group of students who disagree.

We work with a number of teachers who have their students take the list of rules home (usually with an accompanying statement about how the teacher will handle persistent rule violation) for parents to sign and return. This strategy is particularly useful when working with young adolescents or a group of students who a teacher expects may have difficulty consistently demonstrating responsible behavior. The fact that everyone responsible for the students' behavior understands the rules and consequences can have a positive effect on student behavior and can minimize the confusion and tension associated with instances when parents must be contacted about a student's inappropriate behavior.

When sending a list of rules and consequences home, it is important to include a general philosophy statement about your classroom management and instruction. This lets you present the issue of rules in a positive manner that indicates their relationship to effective instruction and student learning. For example, your statement might begin:

As an educator I believe all students can learn, demonstrate concern for others, and choose to act responsibly in the classroom. My goals as a teacher are to help all students learn to the best of their capabilities and to assist students to work effectively with others. My goal is to create a classroom environment that encourages mutual respect and cooperation and that provides opportunities for students to make choices regarding their behavior. In order to create a positive and productive learning environment in which all students can achieve and learn to take responsibility for themselves, I have worked with the students to create a list of rules and procedures that will guide our behavior. Because I know you share my deep concern for the quality of your child's learning, I would appreciate your discussing the attached material with your child, signing it, and returning it to me by _____. I look forward to working with your child and to communicating with you concerning his or her progress, special achievements, and any concerns that may arise.

Monitoring and Reviewing Classroom Rules

Once students have developed reasonable rules and agreed to behave in accordance with them, the next step is to help them recognize and monitor their behavior. One approach helpful with primary-age children is to have them take turns acting out the rules. Each child can be asked to role-play both the appropriate and inappropriate behavior, and you can ask their peers to raise their hands whenever the student is behaving appropriately and place their hands in their lap when the student is behaving inappropriately. This activity is helpful in ensuring that every child clearly understands the rules.

At all grade levels it is important to review the rules frequently for several weeks. A good approach is to review them every day for the first week, three times a week during the second week, and once a week thereafter. It is also helpful to have the rules displayed in a prominent place in the classroom. During the first week it is desirable to discuss them briefly at the beginning of each day and to end the day by having the class evaluate their behavior and consider whether improvement in any area is needed. If the entire class consistently displays appropriate behavior or shows considerable improvement over the previous day, you may want to send a positive note or award home with each student. Significant individual improvements can be similarly rewarded.

For students beyond the third grade, it is often useful to give periodic quizzes on the classroom and school rules. You can ask students to list the rules and write a description for each. You can also ask them to rate themselves on how consistently they follow the rules.

After the first month of school, there are several occasions on which the rules should be brought to the class's attention. First, it is a good idea to review these rules every two weeks to determine whether they are still meaningful and whether any rules need to be added or deleted. Not only does this refresher provide a helpful review of the rules, but it also acknowledges that students' needs and skills change; therefore, students may be allowed more freedom as the year progresses. For example, if an initial rule was for students to remain seated unless given permission to leave their seats, you may decide after several weeks that they have demonstrated enough responsibility that this rule can be altered or eliminated.

Classroom rules also need to be reviewed with each new student who enters the class. Many students who transfer during the school year come from highly mobile families. Some of these students have often had a pattern of difficulties in school. It is important that these students get off to a good start, which can be facilitated by their knowing the expectations for classroom behavior. A student who does well in class and is respected by other students can be assigned to help new students learn classroom rules and procedures.

Rules should also be discussed when a student or the teacher indicates that violation of one or more of the rules is detracting from learning or is infringing on a student's rights. One of us recently found that her classroom was becoming quite noisy during an afternoon study period. Despite several clear "I" messages from the teacher as well as several students, the classroom continued to be unproductively loud during this time. Consequently, at the beginning of the study period the next day, the teacher asked the class to discuss the rule of maintaining a noise level that was conducive to studying. The class decided that they often became too loud and agreed to reduce their noise level. At the end of the period the teacher asked the students to examine the amount of work they had completed. Most students acknowledged that they had accomplished much more work. We brought the issue to their attention again the next day and every other day for six days. Because the noise level appeared to maintain an acceptable level the discussions were terminated. The rule had been reestablished.

The benefits accrued from reviewing classroom rules can also be seen in association with schoolwide rules. Anyone who has taught for even one year is aware that students become restless and tend to lapse into unacceptable behavior near the end of the school year. We have worked with several school staffs who have dealt with this problem by meeting during the latter part of the school year to review the school rules. The teachers then set a time when all discuss the school rules with their classes. Finally, the teachers agree to monitor the rules in a uniform manner. The clarity and structure provided by this uniform approach help students behave more productively and make the final weeks of the year more enjoyable for everyone.

CLASSROOM PROCEDURES

As we mentioned earlier in this chapter, research indicates that effective teachers not only work with students to develop classroom rules but also teach the procedures they expect students to follow during specific classroom activities. This research also provides specific information on the types of classroom activities for which effective teachers develop procedures. In their research in elementary classrooms, Evertson and Emmer found five general areas in which effective teachers taught students how to act:

1. Students' use of classroom space and facilities
2. Students' behavior in areas outside the classroom, such as the bathroom, lunchroom, drinking fountain, and playgrounds
3. Procedures to follow during whole-class activities, such as whether to raise a hand to speak, where to turn in work, or how to get help during seatwork
4. Procedures during small-group work
5. Additional procedures, such as how to behave at the beginning and end of the school day, or when a visitor arrives.

Effective Procedures

Figure 9.4 outlines the major classroom activities for which elementary teachers who are particularly effective managers develop and teach procedures.

FIGURE 9.4 Elementary Classroom Procedures

I. *Room Areas*
   A. Student desks, tables, storage areas
   B. Learning centers, stations
   C. Shared materials
   D. Teacher's desk, storage
   E. Fountain, sink, bathroom, pencil sharpener
II. *School Areas*
   A. Bathroom, fountain, office, library
   B. Lining up
   C. Playground
   D. Lunchroom
III. *Whole Class Activities/Seatwork*
   A. Student participation
   B. Signals for student attention
   C. Talk among students
   D. Making assignments
   E. Passing out books, supplies
   F. Turning in work
   G. Handing back assignments
   H. Make up work
   I. Out-of-seat policies
   J. Activities after work is finished
IV. *Small-Group Activities*
   A. Student movement into and out of group
   B. Bringing materials to group
   C. Expected behavior of students in group
   D. Expected behavior of students out of group
V. *Other Procedures*
   A. Beginning of school day
   B. End of school day
   C. Student conduct during delays, interruptions
   D. Fire drills
   E. Housekeeping and student helpers

For junior high school classrooms, researchers found four key areas in which effective teachers developed procedures:

1. Beginning the class
2. Whole class activities
3. Procedures related to academic accountability
4. Other activities, such as the end of the class period, interruptions in the class, and fire drills.

Figure 9.5 outlines the major classroom activities for which secondary teachers who effectively manage their classrooms develop and teach specific procedures. Figure 9.6 outlines the areas in which effective classroom managers teach specific procedures related to student accountability for academic work.

An example from our experience teaching in junior high school can clarify the concept of procedures. Most junior high school students have only four or five minutes between classes. Therefore, they usually enter the classroom excited or agitated, having had little time to review what they learned in their previous class or to get mentally prepared for the coming class. I discussed this problem with the students in my class and worked with them to develop procedures for making a smooth transition when entering the classroom. First, the class and I listed warm-up activities for the first four minutes of class. These activities, which changed every month, included:

1. An instructional warmup activity
2. Sharing something you had learned in school during the past day
3. A relaxation activity
4. Listening to music selected by the teacher
5. Listening to music selected by the students.

FIGURE 9.5 Secondary Classroom Procedures

I. *Beginning Class*
  A. Rollcall, absentees
  B. Tardy students
  C. Behavior during PA
  D. Academic warm-ups or getting ready routines
  E. Distributing materials
II. *Instructional Activities*
  A. Teacher-student contacts
  B. Student movement in the room
  C. Signal for student attention
  D. Headings for papers
  E. Student talk during seatwork
  F. Activities to do when work is done
III. *Ending Class*
  A. Putting away supplies, equipment
  B. Organizing materials for next class
  C. Dismissing class
IV. *Other Procedures*
  A. Student rules about teacher's desk
  B. Fire drills
  C. Lunch procedures
  D. Bathroom, water fountains
  E. Lockers

FIGURE 9.6 Accountability Procedures

I. *Work Requirements*
   A. Heading papers
   B. Use of pen or pencil
   C. Writing on back of paper
   D. Neatness, legibility
   E. Incomplete papers
   F. Late work
   G. Missed work
   H. Due dates
   I. Make-up work
II. *Communicating Assignments*
   A. Posting assignments
   B. Requirements/grading criteria for assignments
   C. Instructional groups
   D. Provisions for absentees
   E. Long-term assignments
III. *Monitoring Student Work*
   A. In-class oral participation
   B. Completion of in-class assignments
   C. Completion of homework assignments
   D. Completion of stages of long-term assignments
IV. *Checking Assignments in Class*
   A. Students' exchanging papers
   B. Marking and grading papers
   C. Turning in papers
V. *Grading Procedures*
   A. Determining report card grades
   B. Recording grades
   C. Grading stages of long-term assignments
   D. Extra credit
VI. *Academic Feedback*
   A. Rewards and incentives
   B. Posting student work
   C. Communication with parents
   D. Students' record of their grades

Students daily selected the transition activity, each activity being used once each week. I also developed a procedure for tardy students to report to class, a procedure for taking roll, and a signal for gaining the students' attention at the end of the transition activity. Similar procedures were developed for summarizing the day's lesson and leaving the classroom. Activity 9.2 gives you an opportunity to consider the procedures you wish to establish in your classroom.

Teaching and Monitoring Classroom Procedures

A procedure is best taught by:

1. Discussing the need for the procedure
2. Possibly soliciting student ideas
3. Having students practice the procedure until it is performed correctly
4. Reinforcing the correct behavior.

When introducing the procedure of developing a signal to obtain students' attention, you might work with the class to develop the signal, set a goal (everyone facing the teacher and quiet within five seconds), use the procedure while students are engaged in an activity, and reinforce them when they respond within the determined time limit. For a procedure such as lining up, you might elicit ideas for behaviors students display when lining up, practice lining up, and reinforce the class when they line up in the desired manner.

Classroom procedures must be carefully monitored during their initial acquisition. Early in the school year, teachers should respond to almost every violation of a rule or procedure. When you notice that the class or an individual student is not correctly following a procedure, the best approach is to ask the student to state the correct procedure and then to demonstrate it. If a class lines up poorly after having once demonstrated the correct procedure, you should politely comment that you know the class can line up more effectively and ask them to return to their seats so that they can practice the procedure. You might then ask students to describe the behaviors associated with lining up correctly. The class could then be asked to demonstrate their skill and be reinforced for their improved effort. Effectively teaching procedures to students is similar to good athletic coaching. The skilled coach first demonstrates the new procedure—often having the athlete perform the maneuver in slow motion. The athlete is then asked to perform the task and receives feedback on the performance, sometimes in the form of videotape replay. The coach has the athlete practice until the feat is performed satisfactorily. Later, perhaps under game conditions, if the athlete performs the task incorrectly, the coach reteaches it in a subsequent practice session. Figure 9.7 lists a number of interesting and fun methods for teaching classroom rules and procedures to students.

There are situations in which you will need to do more than provide additional instruction to ensure that an individual or class follows a procedure. The key concept to keep in mind is that your response should help students take responsibility for their behavior. The following section examines methods for responding to situations in which students continue to violate classroom rules and procedures despite your efforts to teach and monitor these.

WHAT TO DO WHEN A RULE OR PROCEDURE IS NOT FOLLOWED

One question we are frequently asked during workshops and classes is, "What do I do when students misbehave?" Our first response is to ask teachers to consider their goals related

FIGURE 9.7 Creative Ways to Teach Rules and Routines

1. *Puppet Plays:* Use puppets to role play responsible behaviors. Have students discuss what was appropriate. Have students identify what behaviors were not appropriate; what rules relate to the behaviors, and what behaviors should have happened instead.
2. *Storytime:* In September, read books to students that teach lessons on following rules and procedures and the rewards from self-discipline.
3. *Posters:* Have students make good behavior, good study habit, safety rule, etc. posters for the classroom, school hallways, cafeteria, and so on. Hang them where appropriate to remind students of your expectations.
4. *Letters:* Teach how to write friendly letters. Have students write letters to playground aides, bus drivers, cooks, custodians, the principal, etc., regarding the rules and their plans to be self-disciplined in the area of interest to whom the letter is written.
5. *Oops, I Goofed!:* Conduct a class discussion on student experiences when they broke a rule. Have students share a personal experience when they goofed in their behavior. Have students share what they should have done instead. Focus in on the idea that we all make mistakes and it is OK if you learn from the mistake and don't repeat it.
6. *Create a Play:* Have students write and produce a play on rules and procedures. Have students present the play to other classes in the school.
7. *School in Relation to Community Rules:* Have students share how school rules and the reasons for following them relate to community rules and their responsibilities as citizens.
8. *Rule Unscramble:* Have your class/school rules stated in phrases. Mix up the words in the phrase. Have students put the words in correct order so they make sense. Or mix up the letters of the words in a rule and have students put the letters of each word back in order so rules make sense.
9. *Rule Bingo:* Make bingo cards with classroom/school rules listed in each square. Have a student or the teacher act out the rule. Students cover the square if they have the rule listed that is being acted out.
10. *Wrong Way:* Have students role play the wrong way to behave or the wrong way to follow procedures. Videotape the role playing and have the whole group review and discuss not only what was done wrong but also how to do it the right way.
11. *Hug or Handshake:* When the teacher or students "catch" others following the rules, ask them if they want a hug or handshake and reward them with their wish.
12. *Contract for Success:* Have students write a letter to their parents listing the rules for the class and their plan for successful behavior and self-discipline for the school year. Have students take the letter home and review it with their parents. All persons sign the Contract for Success. Student returns the contract to school the next day.
13. *Picture Signals:* Have pictures as signals for each classroom rule. For example, ears for the rule "We listen politely." or chair for "Sit correctly in

your chair." Then use the pictures to signal students if they are not following the rule. The picture signals allow silent management rather than having to stop teaching to tell students what they are doing wrong.

14. *Rules in the Sack:* Write rules on cards and put them into a paper sack. Have a student draw out a rule from the sack and explain it to the rest of the class.

15. *Hidden Rules:* Fold paper. On the inside write the class rule. On the outside of the folded paper give clues to the rule. Students read clues and guess the rule. They open the folded paper to see if they are correct. This also works well for a bulletin board display.

16. *Numbered Rules:* Give each classroom rule a number. When a student is following a rule correctly, ask students to hold up the number of fingers which related to the rule being followed. Or when teaching rules, give clues for a specific rule and students hold up the correct number of fingers for the correct numbered rule.

17. *Discrimination:* Develop a list of correct and incorrect behaviors relating to the rules and routines of the classroom and school. Have students read through the list and separate the correct from the incorrect, thus making two lists from the one. Use this discrimination activity during a reading class.

18. *Wheel of Fortune:* Play *Wheel of Fortune* where rules are the puzzles to be solved. Students guess letters of the puzzle and try to guess the rule in the puzzle.

19. *Awards:* Design certificates or bookmarker awards for classroom rules. Give students the awards when their behavior reflects appropriate behavior in relation to the specific rule.

20. *Picture Posters:* Have students bring a picture of themselves to school. Use student pictures on posters to highlight a school rule. "The following students believe it is important to respect all teachers." Show their pictures listing their names and grades. Post the posters throughout the school. Use positive peer pressure for pride in school.

Source: Deborah Johnson, Lidgerwood Elementary School, Spokane, Wash.

to classroom management. Hosford (1984) reports that when hundreds of teachers and administrators were asked to rate the most important objectives of education they consistently listed as the top four objectives:

1. Desire for learning
2. Improved self-concept
3. Basic skill acquisition
4. Respect for others.

Similarly, in collecting data for *A Place Called School,* Goodlad (1984) and his colleagues examined educational goal statements from every state and interviewed 8,600 parents. Statewide statements consistently included numerous goals related to personal and civic skills, and parents voiced their support for these goals. Therefore, it seems ironic that teachers so often accept classroom-management methods such as assertive discipline (Canter, 1976) that emphasize immediate control and order but fail to provide children with skills needed to become responsible citizens. These control-oriented solutions also fail to help teachers examine the possible causes of misbehavior or to adjust the learning environment to prevent future student failure and misbehavior. If we sincerely wish to help students become motivated learners and responsible citizens, we must respond to their misbehavior in a manner that encourages students' participation and responsibility.

Before discussing a specific approach to handling student violations of rules, we stress that students should be clearly informed about any approach you select. Students do not respond well to surprises. They rebel against arbitrary, unexpected consequences. The teacher must take time to discuss and even practice with students his or her response to disruptive student behavior. This is particularly true for middle school and high school teachers. Adolescents are sensitive to issues of equality and justice. They are experiencing the developmental task of becoming responsible for their own behavior and demonstrating their competence. When approaches to classroom management directly conflict with these needs, they will be met with varying degrees of resistance.

Tips for Handling Minor Disruptions

Misbehavior often occurs because students find acting out to be more interesting than a boring lesson or a better option than another failure experience. Similarly, unproductive student behavior often occurs because students do not understand a task, are not involved in the learning activity, or are unable to obtain assistance when it is needed. Therefore, most minor discipline problems can be alleviated by implementing the instructional methods discussed in Part III of this book. Nevertheless, when 30 people are required to work for approximately 6 hours a day in a 30-x-30-foot area, minor problems will inevitably occur. As Kounin (1970) discovered, a major factor in effective classroom management is teachers' ability to deal with minor disruptions before they become major problems.

The following sections present ideas for responding to persistent student misbehavior or situations in which students do not respond to teachers' effective initial interventions. The nine methods presented here provide techniques for initially responding to minor classroom disruptions.

Methods

1. *Arrange seating patterns so that you can see and easily move to be near all students.* During small-group work the students should have their back to the class and you should face the class. By maintaining awareness of what is going on and being able to move around the room without disturbing children, you can solve minor problems more quickly.

2. *Scan the class frequently in order to notice and respond to potential problems or minor disruptions.* One of the most difficult tasks for beginning teachers to learn is how to attend to more than one thing at a time. Teachers frequently become so engrossed in working with a group or an individual student that they fail to notice potential problems stemming from a frustrated student or a minor argument. Though it is important to attend to the student(s) being taught, we can learn to scan the room quickly.

3. *The disruptive influence of the teacher's intervention should not be greater than the disruption it is intended to reduce.* Teachers often create more disruptions with their attempts to discipline students than the students are causing themselves. We should, whenever possible, ignore such minor disruptions as a dropped book or overuse of a pencil sharpener. If an individual student continually creates minor disruptions, this problem can be dealt with more effectively by discussing the issue privately with the student. If many class members are involved in low-key disruptive behavior, the behavior should be discussed during a class meeting.

4. *An inappropriately angry teacher response creates tension and increases disobedience and disruptive behavior.* Both Kounin (1970) and Brophy and Evertson (1976) found evidence of a "negative ripple effect" associated with harsh teacher criticism. Rather than improving student behavior, students tend to become more anxious and disruptive in classes characterized by overly harsh discipline. Therefore, though firmness can have a positive effect on classroom behavior, it should be associated with teacher warmth, politeness, and explanations.

5. *A positive ripple effect is associated with a calm and immediate response to a problem.* When teachers react calmly and quickly to a student's disruptive behavior, other students respond by improving their own behavior.

6. *When misbehavior occurs, the first step is to make contact quietly with the student.* We can do so with a glance, by moving close to the student, by touching the student on the shoulder, or by asking the student for an on-task response. When asking the student to respond, we should always ask a question the student can answer. If the student has obviously not been listening to the discussion, we will embarrass the student by asking "Sam, what do you think about Tom's answer?" Asking Sam a new question, however, or paraphrasing Tom's statement and asking Sam for his opinion can productively reintegrate Sam into the mainstream of the classroom activity. Another approach to making a positive initial contact with the student is to praise a positive behavior that competes with the negative behavior. Rather than criticize a student's off-task behavior, we can praise the student the moment he or she begins to work on his or her assignment or focus on the class discussion.

7. *Use effective communication skills when resolving conflicts.* Rather than criticizing students, use paraphrasing to defuse their anger and anxiety. If a student states angrily, "This work is stupid!" we can respond by paraphrasing, "The work doesn't seem to make any sense. Would you like some help with it?" Similarly, if a student is off-task, rather than criticize, simply describe the student's behavior and offer assistance. We might say, "Pat, you seem to be wandering around the room a lot during this math assignment. Would you like someone to help you with the work?" Another communication skill involves sending an "I" message rather than criticizing a student. When a student consistently interrupts during a lesson, we can say, "Excuse me Bill, but when you interrupt without raising your hand, I get distracted and it is harder for me to teach. Would you please raise your hand next time?"

Teachers should also avoid threats and appeals to authority when stopping misbehavior through direct intervention. By simply stating how they want the student to behave, teachers communicate the expectation that they will be obeyed. However, if they add a threat ("Do it or else . . . ''), they place themselves in a position of conflict with the student, and at the same time, they indirectly suggest that they are not sure he is going to obey. (Good & Brophy, 1973, p. 204)

It is often difficult to remember to use these skills when confronted with annoying or aggressive student behavior. When we can train ourselves to employ these skills, however, we model appropriate behavior for our students, create a calmer, more positive classroom environment, and feel considerably more positive about ourselves and less resentful toward our students.

8. *Remind students of the classroom rule or procedure they are not demonstrating.* Rather than yelling, ''Chris, stop bothering Mary while she is working!'' we can simply walk over to Chris and ask quietly, ''Chris, do you know which rule you are not following?'' Similarly, if an entire class is becoming disruptive or lining up without having cleared their desks, we can ask the class to describe their behavior and mention any classroom procedures that are being neglected.

9. *When one or two students are being extremely disruptive it is best to focus the other students' attention on their task and then talk privately with the disruptive students.* We could say, ''Would you all please help me by working quietly on your spelling sentences while I help Tom and Bob solve their problems?'' By handling the situation calmly and positively, we indicate our competence, which in turn will have a calming effect on the other students.

Even though these methods are very effective, every teacher knows there are instances when, even in the most positive and effectively instructed and managed classrooms, a student does not respond productively to these methods. To handle this inevitability positively, teachers must develop a procedure for responding to serious or continuous disruptive student behavior. The next section presents methods for such situations. It also discusses the use of punishment in school settings.

Appropriate and Effective Responses to Student Misbehavior: Punishment or Logical, Instructional Consequences?

How do teachers respond to inappropriate, irresponsible student behavior? The answer most often seems to be, with punitive responses. By punitive responses, we refer to the use of verbal threats and putdowns, a loud voice, sarcasm, the placing of a student's name on the board, removal of a privilege, assignment of additional work or writing sentences, time out or other isolation with no associated skill development activity (such as being responsible for developing a plan), or physical punishment or suspension. Englander (1982) conducted two studies to determine how teachers responded to disruptive student behavior. In the first study 40 teachers were observed for one week to determine their responses to three rule-violating behaviors. Of the 120 incidents, teachers responded punitively 108 times while ignoring the other 12 behaviors. In another study Englander asked 176 teachers to select from 15 responses to misbehavior those they would use for 20 specific student misbehaviors. In 78 percent of the cases teachers listed punitive responses to student misbehavior. The popularity of assertive discipline with its focus on controlling students through punishments and rewards is another indication that teachers support the use of punishment as a major response to irresponsible student behavior.

The focus on punishment in schools is further supported by the frequency with which corporal punishment is used. Rose (1984) surveyed 324 principals randomly selected from 18 states to examine the extent of corporal punishment in school. Seventy-four percent of the principals stated that corporal punishment was used in their schools. Reardon and Reynold (1979) found widespread support for corporal punishment from samples of parents, principals, teachers, and school board members. Finally, the rate at which students are suspended from school in the United States supports the focus on punishment.

Disadvantages of Punishment

Punishment for misbehavior has several serious problems. First, and perhaps foremost, it does not teach the student alternative methods of behavior that can be used to prevent future behavior problems. Because schools are educational institutions, it seems contradictory that children who have difficulty would be punished rather than receiving instruction in how to behave more productively. Second and perhaps of equal importance in school settings, punishment appears to inhibit learning (Englander, 1986). Kounin and Gump (1961) conducted a study involving competent first-grade teachers who differed in their use of punitive behavior with students. The findings indicated that the students of the more punitive teachers expressed less value in learning, were more aggressive, and were more confused about behavior problems in school. This finding was substantiated by the work of Kounin (1970). Studies suggest that schools in which students learn more effectively are characterized by high rates of positive reinforcement and also by somewhat lower rates of punishment (Mortimore & Sammons, 1987; Rutter, Maughan, Mortimore, Ouston, & Smith, 1979). Nash (1963) has reported on a study of corporal punishment in British schools:

> It is notable that the schools where corporal punishment was absent had the best records of behavior and delinquency, despite being in areas with the lowest average ratable value. It is also notable that behavior deteriorates and delinquency increases as corporal punishment increases. (p. 401)

Third, research suggests that punishment is not an effective method for changing student behavior. Emmer and Aussiker (1987) examined the literature on the results of research evaluations associated with four approaches to discipline—teacher effectiveness training, reality therapy, Assertive Discipline, and Adlerian-based approaches. They also contacted 120 school districts in the United States and Canada to obtain evaluation studies about these programs. Their findings indicated that the most punitive-oriented approach (assertive discipline) was ineffective. They summarize the results on Assertive Discipline:

> Evidence on *student* behavior and attitudes is *not* supportive of AD training; that is, many more studies found no effects, or mixed and negative effects, than found that AD training resulted in improved student behavior and attitudes. (pp. 15, 16)

Similar findings concerning the impact of punitive responses to student misbehavior were reported by Becker, Engelmann, and Thomas (1975). These researchers found that when teachers were asked to increase their use of punitive control methods of responding to disruptive student behavior that misbehavior in the classes actually increased from 9 to 31 percent of student behavior.

Fourth, punishment allows the student to project blame rather than to accept responsibility for the behavior. Punishment tends to create a situation in which the student becomes angry or blames the individuals responsible for the punishment rather than examining personal responsibility for the problem. Glasser (1988) believes that 95 percent of all student discipline problems in schools are caused by students' lack of power and that misbehavior is an attempt to gain some sense of power. Punitive responses to student misbehavior detract from rather than enhance students' sense of power and efficacy and often lead to withdrawal or actively destructive and confrontational responses.

Fifth, using such activities as writing sentences, assigning additional homework, and lowering a student's grade as punishment may create a negative attitude regarding these activities. Activities and settings in which one is involved when receiving punishment tend to become aversive. We do not want this connection made with homework or writing.

Englander (1986) states that even though responding to student misbehavior with punishment is both common and natural, it is nonetheless impractical. Based on his extensive background in the field and his thorough review of the research, he summarizes his assessment of punishment:

> If punishment works it does so only under very precise and complicated conditions, much too complicated for us to consistently use in classrooms. The controls that one must utilize to optimize the effectiveness of punishment are not possible in day-to-day operations either within families or schools. (pp. 40, 41)

Corporal Punishment

The disadvantages of punishment described above apply to all forms of punishment—particularly to corporal punishment. Corporal punishment allows the student to place blame outside himself or herself rather than to accept responsibility for a problem and learn to develop new skills. Also, corporal punishment is extremely poor modeling; research has consistently shown that aggression tends to beget aggression. It is interesting how often the authors have heard someone respond to a criticism of corporal punishment by stating that this is what the student experiences at home and thus this is what needs to be implemented at school. Would educators apply the same logic to a child whose family is illiterate and who has never been read to or learned to read? Schools are educational institutions; their goal is to provide students with new skills that can open healthy and productive options for future life. Educators cannot justify using any method that demeans and hurts children while failing to provide them with healthy alternatives.

It is interesting to note that during the past 20 years public opinion has gradually moved toward a less favorable view of physical punishment. Gallup and Elam (1988) note that in 1988, 50 percent of those surveyed for the Annual Gallup Poll of the Public's Attitudes Toward the Public Schools responded *yes* and 45 percent responded *no* to this question:

> Spanking and similar forms of physical punishment are permitted in the lower grades of some schools for children who do not respond well to other forms of discipline. Do you approve of this practice? (p. 42)

This response compared with 62 percent who favored such actions and 33 percent who opposed physical punishment in 1970. It is also interesting to note that the poll question suggests that other forms of discipline have been tried and that this practice is used only with young children. Therefore, it is likely that there is considerably less public support for physical punishment with upper elementary and older children and for the use of physical punishment when other methods have not been effectively and systematically employed.

If the use of corporal punishment, time out with no task assigned, screaming, threatening, and ridiculing are not recommended by current research and theory, what options are available to help teachers cope effectively with the increasing number of at-risk students whose school behavior negatively effects their own learning and that of other students? The next section presents a classroom management procedure teachers can use to handle classroom disruptions calmly and productively. The final section in this chapter presents a model for how teachers can handle situations in which students' behavior does not improve despite the teachers' use of an effective classroom management procedure.

Options to Punishment: A Classroom Procedure for Handling Disruptive Student Behavior

Even though teachers and schools should attempt to minimize their use of punishment in responding to student behavior, this does not imply that students should not receive consequences for misbehavior. Teachers are responsible for ensuring that classroom and school environments are safe, productive places in which to learn, and, like most of us, students need structure and limits to assist them in making responsible choices about their behavior.

As indicated earlier, we strongly believe that responses to disruptive, irresponsible student behavior are most effective and professionally responsible when they serve the dual function of (1) ensuring a safe and orderly classroom and school environment and (2) providing an educational intervention that helps students develop new skills. Additionally, the response to student misbehavior is most effective when it maintains or enhances the student's dignity and self-esteem and invites the student to be responsible for his or her behavior and to become a productive member of the classroom group. Methods that focus primarily on control and punishment do not help youngsters develop new skills and tend to alienate and isolate rather than invite students.

Several key factors are involved in developing professionally responsible, effective responses to unproductive, irresponsible student behavior.

1. Students must be clearly aware of the rules and procedures and the consequences for violating them.
2. Students must be given clear cues indicating that continuation of a behavior will evoke the specified consequences.
3. It is important to be as consistent as possible in employing consequences.
4. Students should be informed that they are choosing the consequence.
5. The consequence should be educational in nature.

Figure 9.8 outlines a procedure for responding to a procedure violation that we have used as teachers and have taught to hundreds of teachers. This method involves first using a predetermined signal to help the student become aware of his or her behavior. If the student does not see this action or fails to respond to it, we can say the student's name and politely request that he or she follow our classroom rules. If the student continues an unacceptable behavior, we can inform him or her that should this behavior continue, the student will be choosing to take time to develop a solution to the problem. Ideally, this work will occur in the classroom, where the student can benefit from instruction and also realize that the problem can be resolved among those involved. Students who have adequate writing skills can be provided with an area in which to work and materials necessary for them to complete a problem-solving form.

Figure 9.9 is an example of a problem-solving form that elementary and secondary teachers can use in their classrooms. Once a student has completed the form, it is placed in a designated spot or shown to the teacher; the student then returns to his or her seat. It is, of course, important to have a brief discussion with the student about the responses on the form. This can be done near the end of class or at the beginning of the next class period. With elementary school students, it is particularly important that they feel invited back to the class and that they realize that even though you could not accept the behavior that necessitated the problem solving, you care about them, respect their ability to be responsible for their behavior by completing the form, and are glad that they have rejoined the class.

It is essential that students clearly understand each step in this sequential process. This can be accomplished by role playing each step in Figure 9.8 and then asking a student to violate a classroom rule (such as talking to a neighbor while you are talking). You then ask the student to stop the inappropriate behavior when you employ the second step. This procedure can be continued until several students had been involved in responding to each of the first three steps. You can then instruct the students in writing solutions and plans. Each student writes a plan, you check these, and you subsequently discuss them with the class.

Several years ago during a graduate seminar, one of us commented that it was probably not necessary to teach the problem-solving step to students in college pre-

FIGURE 9.8 Steps in Responding to Students' Violation of Rules and Procedures

Step	Procedure	Example
1.	Nonverbal cue	Raised index finger
2.	Verbal cue	"John, please follow our classroom rules."
3.	Indicate choice student is making	"John, if you continue to talk while I am talking, you will be choosing to develop a plan."
4.	Student moves to a designated area in the room to develop a plan	"John, you have chosen to take time to develop a plan."
5.	Student is required to go somewhere else to develop a plan	"John, because you are choosing not to be responsible, you will need to see Mrs. Johnson to develop your plan."

FIGURE 9.9 Problem-Solving Form

CHOOSE TO BE RESPONSIBLE

Name_____ Date_____

Rules we agreed on

1. Speak politely to others
2. Treat each other kindly
3. Follow teacher requests
4. Be prepared for class
5. Make a good effort at your work and request help if you need it
6. Obey all school rules

Please answer the following questions:

1. What rule did you violate?_____
_____

2. What did you do that violated this rule?_____
_____

3. What problem did this cause for you, your teacher, or classmates?_____
_____

4. What plan can you develop that will help you be more responsible and
   follow this classroom rule?_____
_____

5. How can the teacher or other students help you?_____
_____

I, _____, will try my best to follow the plan I
have written and to follow all the other rules and procedures in our classroom
that we created to make the classroom a good place to learn.

---

paratory junior and senior high school classes. A seminar participant who had been in a course we taught five years earlier disagreed with this statement. He said that he role-played the procedures described above with all his juniors and seniors in chemistry and physics. He noted that students and parents frequently commented on the value of this process. This teacher was convinced that despite needing to use the fourth step only about a dozen times each year, it was a vital aspect of an effective classroom-management program.

As with all methods suggested in this book, you should carefully consider its applicability to your own teaching setting and should critically assess results when you use the new method. Should you choose to implement the method above for responding to rule violations, it is critical to ensure that it is not used in a manner unduly emphasizing disruptive behavior. Studies show that teachers often attend more frequently to disruptive than to on-task behavior, and that this action tends to increase off-task student behavior (Becker, Engelmann, & Thomas, 1975; Walker, Hops, & Fiegenbaum, 1976). Therefore, when implementing this method, attend to desired student behavior frequently and monitor behavior to assess whether the new approach was indeed associated with an increase in on-task behavior.

Should a student refuse to go to the designated area or to complete the form, the teacher needs to express a belief that the problem can be resolved and that he or she sincerely wishes the student to remain. For example, the teacher might say, "Sam, I'm sure we can work this out and I would like to have you remain in the class. If you will start work on the form, I'll come over as soon as I can and I'm sure we can work this out together." If the student continues to be defiant, the teacher needs to indicate that the student is making a choice. For example, the teacher can say, "Sam, if you choose not to work this out here, you are choosing to do it in the office. I would like to have you remain here, but it is your choice." Some students will continue to view this as a challenge and defy the teacher; this will almost never happen in classrooms in which the teacher has consistently demonstrated concern and respect for students and in which students have been made aware of the sequence of consequences to be followed.

We are occasionally asked whether the method described above adequately allows for individual differences because it suggests that teachers respond to disruptive behavior by using the same consequence for every child and for every rule violation. We believe that students want and need consistency and fairness. We also believe that establishing clarity and incorporating an educational component in the procedure for responding to classroom disruptions are so important that it is best to use a single method. This does not mean, however, that the teacher is limited to this one intervention when helping students develop more responsible behavior. As we discuss in chapter 11, there exist a number of exciting and effective methods for working with individual students to help them develop or increase the frequency of behaviors critical to their success in school and the community.

Case Study

Recently, a teacher who had studied with us wrote to share an idea she had developed for combining problem solving with consistent record keeping about students' rule violation. She had a number of at-risk students in her classroom and believed her sixth-grade students responded better when they had a very structured response to misbehavior.

Her method involves beginning each week by placing six 3/4- × 2-inch strips of masking tape on the upper right hand corner of each student's desk. The students label each strip with their name. Each time a student is informed that he or she has broken a classroom rule, that student is responsible for waiting for an appropriate time to place one piece of tape in his or her page in a looseleaf binder and to complete the information on date and unacceptable behavior. A student who fails to act responsibly and does not file the tape, writes illegibly, or writes something inappropriate in the book is choosing to give up another tape. This system provides a record made by the students in their own writing about their behavior. Students who lose more than two tapes in a day must give up lunch recess and complete a problem-solving form. After losing all six tapes, a student receives one bonus tape each day for the remainder of the week. A child who loses a bonus tape receives another lunch recess detention and problem-solving form. If this happens more than four times, the student is referred to a team to develop a special plan for the student. Students who keep their tapes can earn special privileges and the class can also earn special events by meeting certain goals for total tapes retained.

Note that the authors prefer a less structured system and believe that the use of structured reinforcement for appropriate behavior (as opposed to positive verbal feedback and notes home) has serious problems. Nevertheless, in cases in which good classroom management and instruction are occurring and social reinforcement is not eliciting desired results, some form of structured activity reinforcement may be necessary and may encourage students to use acceptable behavior.

Handling Violent Student Behavior

Even though most teachers are not confronted with violent student behavior, all teachers should be prepared for this possibility. When such behavior occurs, the teacher first needs to make a firm yet polite statement that he or she expects the behavior to stop. The teacher might say, "I understand that you two are angry, but we have other ways to solve problems here. I expect you to stop immediately." If the student(s) fail to respond, the teacher should send a student for assistance. If the behavior involves only a student throwing a temper tantrum or a classroom fight between two students, the teacher may ask other students to leave the room and go to a supervised area such as the library or even the hallway. Sometimes students act aggressively in order to impress other students, and they may calm down much more easily when no audience is available.

In rare cases when a teacher must restrain a student, it is important that the teacher not step between the fighting students. Instead, the teacher can select the student with whom he or she has the better rapport and physically attempt to remove that student from the fight. This is best done from the side of or behind the student by grabbing a belt or shirt, which leaves the student's hands free for self-protection. While doing this, the teacher should talk to the student, stating that he or she may have a right to be angry and will have an opportunity to resolve the conflict as soon as he or she calms down. Talking to students helps to calm them down and can help them save face by indicating that they will be involved in solving the problem. With some students it is also helpful to remind them that this behavior is against agreed on rules and to note the consequence they will be choosing if they continue the fight. Even some angry high school students quiet down considerably when reminded that their parents will have to become involved if they cannot calm down and settle the problem in a more productive and acceptable manner.

In those rare instances in which a student must be restrained, it is helpful if the teacher has had some training in methods of restraint. In addition, the teacher should continue to talk calmly to the child, saying that it is all right to be upset and that he or she can be released and have a chance to talk about the frustration or anger as soon as he or she can stop struggling and talk calmly.

METHODS FOR SOLVING MAJOR AND CONTINUING STUDENT BEHAVIOR PROBLEMS

The methods described above are designed as responses for individual incidents of disruptive classroom behavior. A more serious concern involves the student who continues to disrupt the classroom despite the use of professionally responsible responses. When this occurs, several options are available to the teacher:

1. The teacher should examine the classroom environment to determine what factors may be causing the misbehavior and what, if any, adjustments can be made to increase the likelihood that the student will behave productively in the classroom.
2. The teacher can meet with the student to discuss the problem and attempt to generate a solution.
3. The teacher can contact the parent(s) and inform them of the problem and of the attempts being made to improve the student's behavior.
4. The teacher can implement some form of behavioral intervention to help the student improve his or her behavior.
5. The teacher can refer the student to the office for consequences associated with the schoolwide student management program

It is our firm belief that, whenever possible, we should take these steps in the order listed.

The last section in this chapter examines methods for assessing the environment. Chapter 10 focuses on methods for problem solving with students. Chapter 5 provides ideas for contacting parents about a student's behavioral problem. Chapter 11 presents methods for implementing behavioral interventions to alter students' behavior. Finally, chapter 12 presents methods for ensuring that building level support is available, consistent, and effective in responding to persistent or extremely disruptive student behavior.

Completing an Environmental Assessment

In a study of suspension and expulsions from various schools serving similar student populations, Galloway and Goodwin (1987) found that

1. Whether a pupil is considered disruptive or maladjusted depends at least as much on factors within the school as on factors within the pupil or the family.
2. In general, schools that cater successfully for their most disturbing pupils also cater successfully for the rest of their pupils. (p. 132)

As discussed in chapter 2, students seldom misbehave or choose to fail in classroom or school settings in which their academic and learning needs are being consistently met. Therefore, when faced with continuing disruptive classroom behavior by one or more students, it is our responsibility as teachers to (1) assess our use of effective classroom management and instructional methods and (2) determine which classroom factors seem to be associated with the student's irresponsible behavior. Figure 9.10 is a form we have used with hundreds of teachers to help them examine their own classroom management and instructional responsibilities as a factor in the unproductive behavior of an individual student or group of students. This form is not intended to be used as an evaluative instrument. Instead, it is to be used by a teacher or a teacher and colleague/consultant to consider whether changes may be warranted in one or more general area(s) related to management and instruction. Activity 9.4 provides an opportunity for you to use this form.

In addition to examining our own behavior, it can be extremely valuable to analyze a student's classroom behavior systematically and specifically. Figure 9.11 presents a form

FIGURE 9.10 Interventions before Removing a Student from the Classroom or Referring a Student for Special Education Services

Level 1: Classroom Management and Instruction	Yes	No
1.1 The teacher interacts positively with the student		
1.2 The teacher communicates high expectations to the student		
1.3 The student is actively involved with peers either through cooperative learning or peer tutoring		
1.4 Classroom procedures are taught to students and this student demonstrates an understanding of the procedures		
1.5 There is a consistent routine in the classroom that is understood by the student		
1.6 The student's instructional program is appropriate to his or her academic needs		
1.7 The student has been involved in some form of academic goal setting and self-recording		
1.8 Rules for managing student behavior are posted in the classroom		
1.9 Rules are appropriate, succinct, stated positively, and all-inclusive		
1.10 Consequences for inappropriate behavior are clear to all students		
1.11 Consequences are appropriate, fair, and implemented consistently		
1.12 The student demonstrates that she or he understands the rules and consequences		
1.13 The teacher has met privately with the student to discuss the problem and jointly develop a plan both parties agree to implement in order to assist the student		
Level 2: Individual Behavior Program		
2.1 An academic and/or behavior program has been developed and consistently implemented and corresponding data collected for at least four weeks		
2.2 An alternative program was implemented if the original plan (2.1) proved to be ineffective		

the authors have used with hundreds of teachers to assist in determining the classroom factors that may be influencing a student's behavior. Teachers with whom we have worked have found this to be extremely helpful and on a number of occasions have adopted it as a model for providing information to colleagues at staffings held to develop intervention plans for students. Activity 9.5 provides an opportunity for you to use this form for obtaining information on a particular student whom you have observed or with whom you work. The elementary case study presented in the following section used this form to obtain the data necessary to develop the successful interventions described.

FIGURE 9.11   Analyzing Environmental Factors That Influence Students' Behavior

Student _____

Date_____

Staff member_____

Part I   Student's misbehavior(s)
  1. Describe misbehavior(s)
     a.
     b.
     c.
  2. How frequent is each type of misbehavior?
     a.
     b.
     c.
  3. What time of day does it occur?
     a.
     b.
     c.
  4. In what physical surroundings?
     a.
     b.
     c.
  5. With which peers or adults?
     a.
     b.
     c.
  6. In what kinds of activities is student engaged before misbehavior occurs?
     a.
     b.
     c.

Part II Teacher (or other) actions
  1. What do you do when student misbehaves?
     a.
     b.
     c.
  2. How does student respond?
     a.
     b.
     c.
  3. When are your actions most successful?
  4. When are these actions least successful?

Part III   Student motivation
  1. What responsibilities (assignments, tasks, or orders) does student fulfill?

2. What types of reinforcement (positive and negative) does student receive?
   a. positive (and/or encouragement)
   b. negative (and/or logical consequences)
3. How does student respond to reinforcement?
   a. positive (and/or encouragement)
   b. negative (and/or logical consequences)
4. How does student relate to the group (physical aggression, verbal aggression, passivity, or other behaviors)?

Part IV When student is not misbehaving
1. Describe positive behaviors.
   a.
   b.
   c.
2. How frequent is each type of positive behavior?
   a.
   b.
   c.
3. What time of day does each behavior occur?
   a.
   b.
   c.
4. In what physical surroundings?
   a.
   b.
   c.
5. With which peers or adults?
   a.
   b.
   c.
6. In what kinds of activities is student engaged before positive behavior occurs?
   a.
   b.
   c.

Part V Additional questions
1. What does student enjoy doing (hobbies or subjects)?
2. What does student do well (hobbies or subjects)?
3. Are there any reasons to suspect health or physical disabilities?

Case Study: Middle School

Several years ago one of the authors was asked to help a first-year band teacher in an inner-city school. The teacher was having serious problems with a last period eighth-grade beginning band class. The class met in a portable building, and the teacher worked in an elementary building until the last two periods of the day. The class consisted of 33 students including 11 drummers (there were 4 drums in the classroom). Students were extremely disruptive, and the on-task rate was less than 30 percent.

After discussing the situation, the teacher agreed to involve the students in presenting their concerns about the class. Students were very open about their frustration with a variety of classroom procedures. For example, the teacher often worked for an extended period with one section of the band while expecting all other students to sit quietly. Students also expressed confusion about a variety of procedures, including obtaining their instruments, warm-ups, music selection, and discipline. The author and teacher spent 5 days working with students to establish and practice procedures for each of the 25 areas the students and teacher determined needed clarity. This included changing the discipline system from assertive discipline to the use of a form similar to those in Figures 9.8 and 9.9.

Pre- and postobservations showed dramatic changes in on-task behavior and an almost complete reduction in serious acting-out behavior. By involving students in the process and by creating clarity and consistency in classroom procedures, students felt a sense of safety, security, and belonging that had been lacking. They responded dramatically to this change by demonstrating more responsible behavior.

Case Study: Elementary School

This case involved a fourth-grade girl who transferred into a new school in February. Within 7 weeks she had been involved in 15 serious incidents of physical violence with peers and had on several occasions been suspended from school. The school used assertive discipline, and the severe clause had been invoked on numerous occasions.

When asked to be involved in helping the school in working with this student, one of the authors first asked the teacher to complete the environmental analysis form found in Figure 9.11. Much to everyone's surprise, the results suggested that all but one of the student's physical assaults on peers had occurred during periods of reading or math. Further analysis showed that these two periods were consecutive and involved 1 hour and 50 minutes of continuous seatwork and small-group work. Additionally, the student was completing her work at only 24 percent accuracy, was only in a small group 21 minutes during this time, and no procedures existed for students to obtain help if they experienced difficulty with seatwork. Interviews with students suggested that the pattern preceding the attacks was that the student became frustrated with her seatwork and sought to obtain answers from another student (often using inappropriate methods such as grabbing the paper or looking over a student's shoulder). Because the girl had a slight body odor, was not as well dressed as most of her peers, and had not been accepted into the classroom group, these attempts at assistance were frequently met with rebuffs, putdowns, and complaints to the teacher.

Before the author's involvement in the class, the use of assertive discipline and a behavior contract were the only interventions employed to alter the child's behavior. Before reading any further, set the book aside and jot down the possible interventions you might make based on the information you have about this situation.

The author suggested that the teacher consider five interventions. First, the student's seatwork was altered so she could successfully complete more than 80 percent of her assignments. Second, the student was asked if she would like to work with a peer tutor. She selected three students, two of whom agreed to work with her. The girl was taught several statements to use when requesting assistance, and the tutors were given instruction in methods for providing help. Third, a number of aquaintance activities were implemented to help the girl become integrated into the classroom. Fourth, the school health nurse made a home visit to discuss the girl's personal hygiene with the mother. Fifth, it was suggested that the teacher schedule the reading and math groups differently.

The first three interventions were implemented successfully. The last two interventions were not successful because of the mother's inability to become productively involved and the teacher's decision to continue her instructional schedule. Nevertheless, the girl had only one aggressive behavior during the remaining three months of school—and this occurred when she was intentionally tripped on the playground. The following year the girl did not have a physically aggressive school behavior before transferring out of the school near the end of the first semester.

This case study provides an excellent example of the importance of analyzing the classroom environment and of developing proactive interventions before using control methods (such as the assertive discipline and the behavior contract that the school was using). Our experience in working with dozens of similar cases is that when provided with proactive methods for creating a more positive learning environment for a student, teachers can and will implement these methods, and that these methods are almost always associated with significant positive changes in the student's behavior.

ACTIVITIES FOR EXAMINING YOUR METHODS OF ESTABLISHING CLASSROOM RULES AND PROCEDURES

The activities in this section give you an opportunity to work with several of the major skills presented in this chapter. The value of these activities can be enhanced if you discuss them with a colleague. These activities may suggest changes you wish to incorporate in your classroom. If you make changes, keep a record of them. One week after implementing the change(s), take time to write about and share with a colleague the results of these changes.

ACTIVITY 9.1   Selecting Your Classroom Rules

List five classroom rules you would choose for your class. When you are satisfied with the rules, discuss them with a colleague who teaches or has recently taught at your grade level.

ACTIVITY 9.2 Deciding on Your Key Classroom Procedures

For this activity refer to Figures 9.4 and 9.6 if you are an elementary teacher and Figures 9.5 and 9.6 if you are a middle school or high school teacher. For each area in which effective teachers teach classroom procedures, list a procedure you would feel comfortable using in your classroom. The material below provides an example of this activity.

General area	Needed procedures	Specific procedure
Beginning the class	1. Getting students' attention 2. Entering the class 3. Obtaining materials 4. What to do if tardy 5. Where to put slips that need signing 6. 7.	Students determine a signal
Whole-class activities	1. How to leave the room 2. What to do when work is completed 3. Voice level 4. How to get help on an assignment 5. Using the pencil sharpener 6. When students can leave their seats 7. 8. 9.	Take the hall pass
Student assignments	1. How to find work missed while absent 2. How late work will be handled 3. Heading papers 4. Where to hand in work 5. Credit for late work 6. 7.	Notebook on the back table
Other activities	1. Dismissing 2. Public address system announcements 3. Fire drill 4. Guest entering the class 5. 6. 7.	Everyone must be seated and quiet.

ACTIVITY 9.3 Examining Your Methods of Establishing Rules and Procedures

Evaluate your use of various methods of developing classroom rules and procedures by completing the following form. If you are not currently teaching, respond by recalling a classroom in which you previously taught or observed.

	Yes	Somewhat	No

1. Do clear classroom rules apply in your class?
2. Are the rules listed in the form of positive statements?
3. Are there five or fewer rules?
4. Can every student list these rules from memory?
5. Are the rules clearly displayed in your room?
6. Are students involved in developing the rules?
7. Does each student make a clear commitment to follow these rules?
8. Do you discuss these rules frequently when they are first developed?
9. Do you review the rules every three weeks?
10. Do students clearly understand your approach to handling rule violations?
11. Do you teach students the important procedures related to classroom activities?
12. Do you teach students the major procedures related to behaviors outside the classroom?
13. When students fail to follow a procedure do you immediately reteach the procedure?
14. Does every parent know the classroom rules that apply in your class?
15. Does every parent know your methods of handling discipline problems?

Carefully examine your responses to the above questions and then complete the following statements:

I learned that. . . .
I am pleased that I. . . .

Three approaches I will implement in order to develop more productive classroom rules and procedures are:
1.
2.
3.
I will also consider the possibility that next year I could. . . .

ACTIVITY 9.4 Assessing Your Classroom Management Behavior

Think of a student whose behavior has created a problem for himself or herself and/or for the class. With this student in mind, complete the interventions form in Figure 9.10 and then answer the following questions.

1. What changes could you make in your classroom that would create a more clearly structured, inviting environment for this student?
2. What interventions have you already attempted to assist this student in behaving more responsibly?
3. Based on the data you have collected, how effective do you believe you have been in assisting this student?

ACTIVITY 9.5 Completing an Environmental Assessment

Think of a student whose behavior has created a problem for himself or herself and/or for the class. With this student in mind, complete the form in Figure 9.11 and then respond to the following items.

1. List as many specific things as possible that you learned about this student's unproductive behavior.
2. Based on these discoveries, what changes could you make in the classroom to assist this student in behaving more responsibly?

SUMMARY

Successful teachers create procedures involving both proactive and corrective approaches to student behavior. In the proactive area, teachers whose students have higher rates of on-task behavior spend time early in the school year developing and teaching classroom rules and procedures. This provides students with a much needed sense of structure and security. More effective classroom managers also develop and teach clear methods for responding to unproductive student behavior that emphasize helping students take responsibility for their own behavior and learn alternative ways for handling frustrating situations. These more successful teachers are also able to analyze their classroom environment and implement changes that allow students more readily to meet their personal and academic needs in the classroom.

RECOMMENDED READING

Cummings, C. (1983). *Managing to teach.* Snohomish, Wash. Snohomish Publishing.

Emmer, E., Evertson, C., Sanford, J., Clements, B., & Worsham, M. (1984). *Classroom* management for secondary teachers. Englewood Cliffs, N.J.: Prentice-Hall.

Evertson, C., Emmer, E., Clements, B., Sanford, J., & Worsham, M. (1984).Classroom management for elementary teachers. Englewood Cliffs, N.J.: Prentice-Hall.

Fox, R., Luszki, M., & Schmuck, R. (1966). Diagnosing classroom learning environments. Chicago: Science Research Associates.

Good, T., & Brophy, J. (1987). Looking in classrooms, 4th ed. New York: Harper and Row.

Jones, V. (1980). Adolescents with behavior problems: Strategies for teaching, counseling, and parent involvement. Boston: Allyn and Bacon.

Schmuck, R., & Schmuck, P. (1983). Group processes in the classroom, 4th ed. Dubuque, Iowa: William C. Brown.

Fellers, P., & Gritzmacher, K. (1985a). Alphabet soup: A curriculum for your first week of school. Canby, Ore.: Tops Learning Systems. (10970 S. Mulino Rd., 97013)

Fellers, P., & Gritzmacher, K. (1985b). A summer start: How to organize your best school year ever. Canby, Ore: Tops Learning Systems.

Fellers, P., & Gritzmacher, K. (1987). Peaceful procedures: A master teacher's approach to peaceful classroom management. Canby, Ore.: Tops Learning Systems.

When Prevention Fails: Methods for Altering Unproductive Student Behavior

When sensitively and consistently used, the methods presented in Parts II, III, and IV can result in increased student achievement and the elimination of a significant amount of disruptive student behavior. A few students, however, will cause major or consistent behavior problems despite our efforts to create positive, supportive, well-organized, and stimulating learning environments. Furthermore, the pressures and inevitable frustrations of learning and working in a relatively small area with 30 or so classmates create a situation in which some students will occasionally misbehave and require assistance in controlling and improving their behavior.

In Part V, we present many types of intervention strategies that teachers, counselors, child development specialists, and administrators can use to help pupils better understand and control their behavior. When examining and implementing these strategies, educators should keep in mind that these methods will be more effective when used in conjunction with the methods discussed in the previous chapters. In fact, we believe that adults harm youngsters by implementing behavior-control strategies to ensure that young people act passively and positively in environments that do not meet their basic psychological and academic needs.

Several key concepts underlie the materials presented in chapters 10, 11, and 12. First, we will be most effective in our efforts to help students develop new skills and demonstrate responsible behavior when everyone in the school understands his or her responsibility and works cooperatively. As discussed in chapter 1, we use the term *systems approach* to describe this coordination of efforts. Chapter 12 presents a detailed look at this concept.

Second, we believe that all interventions made in response to student behavior problems should be educational in nature. As educators we will be most effective in assisting students if we view student misbehavior as based on the dual factors of student responses to the environment and skill deficits. Therefore, once we have made every attempt to adjust the environment, the next step is to assist students in developing new skills.

Third, we believe there exists a hierarchy for responding to irresponsible, unproductive student behavior. This hierarchy (presented in Figure 10.1) suggests that it is most beneficial to students if we first implement interventions emphasizing the creation of positive learning environments followed by interventions that focus primarily on student involvement and responsibility for resolving problems. Methods that depend on external reinforcers or that place outside restrictions on students' behavior are used as a last resort.

Fourth, underlying the behavior-change interventions presented in Part V is the belief that students should be actively involved in all attempts to alter their behavior. Students should be involved in solving problems, helped to collect and understand data about their own behavior, and be instrumental in developing contracts aimed at altering their behavior. Finally, although it may not be desirable to have students present during all discussions of their behavior, they should be included in many such discussions and should always be aware of the problems being discussed and the programs being implemented.

When you use the methods presented in chapters 10 and 11, be careful not to view problem-solving and behavioristic interventions as mutually exclusive. Problem-solving approaches do emphasize students' involvement in the behavior-change process, but we should recognize that with some students it may be necessary to incorporate a behavioristic approach such as self-observation or the creation of a contract. Consistent with our belief that educational interventions should meet students' needs, maintain their integrity, and teach them to control their own behavior, Part V begins with a chapter about helping students solve their own problems.

CHAPTER 10

Reducing Unproductive Student Behavior with Problem Solving

Philosophically, there is little question about the desirability of extending autonomy and freedom of choice to everyone; the problem is determining when and how much. The ability to act independently and make wise and appropriate choices is learned just like any other facet of behavior. . . . A child needs not only experience but the right kind of experience. And he needs a wise guide who can steer him clear of danger and who encourages, prompts, and reinforces behavior that is adaptive and successful.

/ Garth Blackham and Adolf Silberman (1975)
Modification of Child and Adolescent Behavior

Regardless of how effectively we create positive learning environments and implement varied instructional methods, some disruptive student behavior is almost inevitable. At all grade levels, students' developmental needs conflict with an environment that requires large groups of students to engage in learning new skills for an extended time. Skilled teachers prevent most disruptions by using methods of classroom management and instruction that encourage positive interpersonal relationships and academic success. They also, however, possess a repertoire of methods for helping students responsibly solve minor conflicts that arise.

The ultimate goals of implementing methods to reduce unproductive or disruptive student behavior are (1) to increase the achievement of both the individual student and his or her classmates, and (2) to help youngsters develop positive social skills. As stated in the introduction to Part V, the fact that schools group 30 or more students for instruction creates a situation in which some minor conflicts are likely to occur. Unfortunately, many teachers lack training and skill in helping students solve their problems (Brophy & Rohrkemper, 1981; Brown, 1975). Teacher-training programs have frequently failed to provide teachers with either prerequisite communication skills or specific methods for involving students in solving problems. Consequently, teachers all too often find themselves resorting to the authoritarian models they experienced as students. This point was brought home recently when a young teacher told one of us, ''My voice is one octave lower than it was at the beginning of the year. I really hate myself for yelling at the students, but I don't know what else to do.''

Regardless of the approach we take, working with students whose behavior is disruptive requires time and energy. Research (Walker & Buckley, 1973; Walker, Hops, & Fiegenbaum, 1976) indicates that teachers spend a lot of time attempting to control acting-out students. Teachers often, however, misdirect their energies:

> It often appears that the harder a teacher tries to control an acting-out child's behavior, the less effective she/he is. This process can be physically draining and emotionally exhausting. (Walker, 1979, p. 18)

Teachers will be more effective if they spend less energy attending to and trying to control disruptive behavior and considerably more energy implementing the methods described in Parts II, III, and IV. When disruptions occur in spite of our using effective interpersonal, organizational, and instructional strategies, we should focus our energies on involving students in examining their behavior and developing mutually agreed on methods for changing the behavior.

Whenever confronted with the decision to use an authoritarian or problem-solving approach to discipline, one of us is reminded of a comment made by a veteran junior high school teacher with whom he taught. When talking to a group of young teachers about the teaching profession, the teacher stated that it was impossible to be a teacher and not go home tired every night. The teacher said, however, that there were two ways to go home tired. The first was to leave the school building and sigh with relief that another day was over and the students had been kept in line relatively well. He stated that this feeling usually stemmed from teachers' taking an authoritarian, power-oriented approach to discipline; this type of teacher frequently spent evenings worrying about whether the students would behave the next day and what could be done if they did not. The second type of fatigue, he stated, was based on using a problem-solving approach to discipline. He described it as caused by having interacted openly with students all day. Because he experienced the latter type of fatigue, he almost always felt good about his work and generally looked forward to seeing the children the next day.

In his *Teacher Effectiveness Training*, Gordon (1974) stated the issue in a similar manner in discussing the problems associated with teachers' attempting to control students by using power methods of influence:

Teacher-student relationships at the upper-elementary and secondary levels are much more strained and stressful because teachers relied so heavily upon power (backed up by rewards and punishment) when the children were younger. Then, when students are older, they begin to react to these techniques to an ever-increasing degree with anger, hostility, rebellion, resistance, and retaliation. . . .

Students do not naturally have to rebel against adults in the schools. But they will rebel against the adults' use of teacher power. Drop the use of teacher power, and much of the student rebellion in schools disappears. (Gordon, 1974, p. 198)

A basic assumption that teachers must accept before using a problem-solving approach is that they can reduce their authoritarian control and replace it with natural authority. Natural authority is the logical and readily accepted leadership associated with obvious competence, interest, and concern.

Authoritarian or role-bound authority comes from the teachers' assigned role to maintain an orderly classroom environment and from the rewards and punishments teachers have access to in order to accomplish this end. Natural authority is the logical and readily accepted leadership associated with obvious competence, interest, and concern. In the school setting, natural authority can be based on the teacher's knowledge of subject matter, ability to develop interesting lessons, skill in working with the classroom group, and skill in problem solving.

There are three basic situations in which teachers must make a decision regarding the type of authority they will use: (1) in responding to student concerns about issues of curriculum, instruction, and matters of classroom operation; (2) in efforts to alter persistent problems concerning student behavior and learning; and (3) in attempts to stop disruptive or inappropriate student behavior. In all three situations, natural authority will be more effective because students are more likely to accept it. In addition, natural authority allows the teacher to serve as a role model for students, an increasingly important factor as schools are responsible for working with many youngsters who have not been exposed to effective adult role models. Arbitrary, authoritarian, role-bound authority should never be used in the first two situations listed above. In serious instances of aggressive student behavior toward another student, however, a teacher may need to assert authoritarian control if methods based on natural authority have failed. As discussed in the previous chapter, however, the teacher should continue to talk to the student in a manner that indicates a focus on caring for the student and the teacher's desire to be involved in problem-solving activities.

An important point to consider when deciding whether to give up authoritarian control is that this approach becomes noticeably less effective as students become older. Authoritarian control can be effectively used in the primary grades (although the effects on children are often destructive), but it is less effective with older students, who are beginning to enter a developmental stage whose main task is developing an individual identity and sense of independence.

As suggested by the teacher who discussed the two ways in which teachers can go home tired, giving up authoritarian control can have benefits for teachers as well as students. As teachers begin to involve students in solving classroom problems, the teacher's role changes from that of an all-knowing, totally responsible adult to that of an effective facilitator. Although teachers cannot abdicate their ultimate responsibility, they can create classroom settings in which they do not have to be constantly and totally in charge of every decision. The difficulty of maintaining an authoritarian role and the number of teachers who continue to accept it are two reasons for continuing high teacher turnover.

There are several advantages to using fewer teacher-directed, behavioristic interventions initially. First, though some young people will, in fact, respond only to very structured, controlling interventions, others will respond surprisingly well to effective problem-solving approaches presented in a safe, caring environment characterized by effective teaching. Because it is impossible to determine which students will respond to less control-oriented methods, it is always desirable to try these first. Second, students know when they are being singled out from their peers. Students view adults as powerful and knowledgeable, and so they internalize much of what adults' words and actions say about them. Consequently, when adults use behavioristic methods for controlling a student's behavior, students may learn that they are different from and less capable than their peers. Although this situation is sometimes inevitable, its influence can be reduced by initially employing problem-solving interventions with all students. Students who perceive that a more behavioristic intervention is a response to their inability to respond to a problem-solving approach will understand more clearly why they are being provided with a structured program than will students who are initially confronted with such a program. Third, by providing acting-out students with an introduction to problem-solving approaches, educators increase the likelihood that the youngster who must be temporarily removed or controlled by a structured behavioristic program will be more knowledgeable about and able to adjust to less controlled methods when these become appropriate. Finally, because they are quite effective in controlling behavior, teachers sometimes use behavioristic interventions without first examining such important variables as the quality of teacher-student and peer relationships or the instructional materials and techniques being used in the classroom. Therefore, behavioristic approaches are sometimes used to manipulate pupils into behaving passively in environments that are not meeting their basic needs. Because problem-solving approaches give students an opportunity to discuss the environment, they are an important precursor to behavioristic interventions.

PLACING PROBLEM SOLVING IN CONTEXT

When considering when and how to implement problem solving, teachers must answer two important questions: Where does problem solving fit into my responsibilities for managing student behavior and my classroom management plan? and How does problem solving relate to other corrective behavior management interventions I may choose to employ?

Figure 10.1 can help answer the first question. As indicated in Figure 10.1, problem solving is used one or more times when a student continues to act unproductively in the classroom despite the teacher's best efforts to create a positive, well-structured learning environment. As discussed in chapter 9, problem solving may take the form of having the student complete a problem-solving form as a consequence for violating a classroom rule or procedure. It may also involve the teacher's taking time to meet with the student and verbally problem solve with the student. Additionally, as discussed in chapter 12, we believe that effective schoolwide student management programs also involve the student in problem solving when a persistent or serious misbehavior has led to an office referral.

FIGURE 10.1 Behavior Intervention Sequence

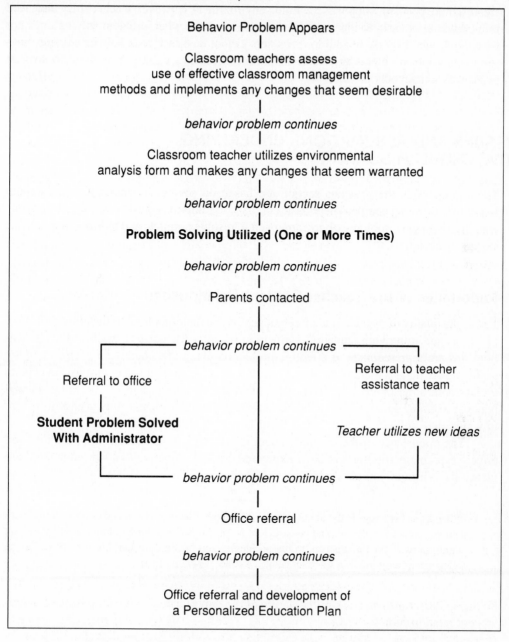

Even teachers skilled in involving students in solving their own problems find that some students have major skill deficits and/or personality disorders that prevent them from responding to interventions requiring the establishment of a trusting relationship and an ability to evaluate one's behavior in light of its effect on others. When faced with such students, teachers need to provide greater structure than is provided by the problem-solving methods presented in this chapter. Problem solving is the intervention teachers should use following or in conjunction with attempts to alter the classroom environment in order to create a more positive, supportive learning environment. However, teachers may also need to incorporate other individualized intervention methods when problem solving does not have the desired results. In addition, teachers cannot be effective in helping students with serious behavior problems unless the school incorporates a variety of methods to provide assistance and support to teachers.

BASIC ISSUES AND ASSUMPTIONS UNDERLYING EFFECTIVE PROBLEM SOLVING

The comments in the previous section are based on several fundamental beliefs about working with young people. These basic beliefs or assumptions must be accepted by anyone who plans to use a problem-solving approach to resolve conflicts and reduce inappropriate student behavior.

Importance of the Teacher-Student Relationship

Just as the quality of teacher-student relationships is a major factor in preventing discipline problems and improving students' motivation (chapter 3), positive teacher-student relationships are a prerequisite to effective problem solving. Teachers who wish to employ problem solving as a method for dealing with disruptive student behavior must first create a classroom atmosphere characterized by warmth, openness, and safety. Students will honestly examine their own behavior and sincerely attempt to change only in an atmosphere in which they are cared for and their input is consistently valued.

The importance of the teacher-student relationship in facilitating responsibility and effective problem solving has been expressed by numerous well-known educators and therapists. Virginia Axline wrote:

> When a teacher respects the dignity of a child, whether he be 6 or 16, and treats the child with understanding, kindliness, and constructive help, she is developing in him an ability to look within himself for the answers to his problems, and become responsible for himself as an independent individual in his own right. (Axline, 1947, p. 156)

William Glasser presented a similar picture of the importance of a warm, positive teacher-student relationship:

> [Students] can't make better choices, more responsible choices, unless they are strongly and emotionally involved with those who can. . . . teachers and therapists too often stand aloof from children; they do not get emotionally involved; they are not warm, personal and interested; they do not reveal themselves as human beings so that the children can identify with them. Thus they fail to alleviate the loneliness of the many children who need human warmth so desperately. Only in a school where a teacher and student are involved with each other and

equally involved with the curriculum through thinking and problem solving does education flourish—an education that prepares students to live successfully in the world. (Glasser, 1969, p. 19)

Respect for Students' Abilities

Closely related in importance to the teacher-student relationship is the fact that the implementation of individual and group problem-solving methods is based on the assumption that young people want to control their own behavior and to experience a sense of competence. Not all youngsters have the skill to solve their own problems. Rather, youths are seen as having the potential and desire to be involved in solving their own problems and therefore can be expected to respond enthusiastically to teachers' sincere efforts to involve them in this process.

Unfortunately, teachers often give up after one or two attempts at problem solving have failed to bring about a satisfactory solution. Before rejecting this approach, we should first consider whether students have really been involved in the procedure or whether the problem-solving intervention was, in reality, a disguised teacher's solution. Furthermore, even when we effectively use problem-solving approaches, students cannot be expected to resolve all conflicts effectively and immediately. Not only do students need to learn problem-solving skills or begin to apply these skills in a new setting, but students who have experienced several years of teacher-dominated solutions may also initially be skeptical of our sincerity in involving students. We frequently need to prove that we respect young people and their abilities before students will apply themselves in helping to solve problems.

The extensive research on the powerful effect of teachers' expectations (Brophy, 1983; Good, 1981) indicates that pupils' behavior is influenced by the expectations adults communicate to them. Therefore, when we express our respect for students' ability to solve their own problems, students often respond by living up to these expectations. It appears that students would benefit more from our erring slightly in the direction of expecting too much in this area than expecting too little.

Desire to Help Students Learn Responsibility

A frequent complaint heard in school staff rooms is, "Students are not responsible. They must be constantly reminded and cannot do things on their own. I have to tell them what to do every step of the way." Teachers understandably bemoan this situation, and yet it is one they have often inadvertently created or reinforced. It is unrealistic to expect students to be independent and responsible learners when they have received limited assistance in developing problem-solving skills and few opportunities to display their independence.

Students need problem-solving skills if they are to become productive members of society. Ruth Benedict (1954) presented the concept that societies should provide young people with gradually increasing amounts of responsibility rather than suddenly inundating young adults with new responsibilities. Schools should make a concerted effort to teach students how to solve their problems and to provide them with opportunities to practice these skills. When teachers implement this approach they are usually surprised to find that it significantly reduces the amount of negative discipline they use in the classroom. Thomas Gordon placed the relationship between discipline and responsibility in an interesting perspective:

> When teachers say, "I don't have enough authority in the classroom," they mean they need more power to reward and punish. When teachers complain, "Kids these days have no respect for authority," they mean that the rewards and punishments are too few or too ineffective.
>
> Paradoxically, most teachers genuinely reject dependence and fear as desired traits in the students in their classes. Here is their dilemma. Teachers say they want unafraid, independent, self-reliant, self-disciplined students, but when they have students with those qualities they find that power will not work well with such students. (Gordon, 1974, pp. 195–196)

The work on attribution theory referred to in chapter 6 has important implications about methods required to help students develop responsibility. Skinner (1971) stated that individuals will feel accountable for their behavior only if they are not being controlled by external factors. Attribution theory states that individuals will be more likely to make a continued personal effort when they believe results are attributable to their effort rather than to luck, basic ability, or the difficulty of the task. Harter and Connell (1981) found that students' sense of understanding of whether control was internal or external was an important factor influencing their achievement, self-concept, and intrinsic motivation. If we want students to have a sense of controlling and taking responsibility for their own behavior, it is critical that we involve students in discussing and actively resolving individual and classroom problems. A problem-solving approach facilitates this process.

Helping Students Assume Responsibility for Their Behavior

Students, especially those experiencing problems, tend to blame other people for their difficulties. Schools often inadvertently reinforce this unproductive attitude by using discipline policies and ways of talking to students that do not emphasize students' responsibility for their own behavior. In our work with disruptive youth, we have found it useful to teach students a conceptual framework on which they can base their own decision making and responsibility. This conceptual framework involves applying the curriculum of responsibility (described in chapter 1) to student behavior. When using the curriculum of responsibility with students we include five factors: (1) knowledge, (2) limits, (3) options, (4) choices, and (5) consequences.

Students need to realize that in order to make good decisions (choices), they need to understand their environment. They need to know how the people around them wish to be treated, what behaviors other people value, and their expectations regarding student behavior. Although children may not be able to change other people, understanding others' wants and needs can help youngsters make informed, productive decisions.

Students also need to know the limits that exist regarding behavior. In a school setting this means knowing the rules and the consequences associated with rule violation. It also means knowing the personal limits of those with whom they interact. Teachers vary in the degree to which they will permit certain types of student behavior before invoking consequences.

Students should be helped to understand the various options available to them. Many behavior-problem youngsters feel almost totally controlled by external factors, and their acting out is to some extent an attempt to gain or demonstrate their control. With these students it is particularly useful to point out that they have options. For example, the student who is frustrated in class has, among others, the option to discuss the problem with the teacher, talk to a counselor, passively accept the frustration, or disrupt the class.

Students constantly need to be reminded that they make their own choices about their behavior. Within the context of a situation with varying options, *they* make the choice to act. The student who is frustrated in class makes the decision to seek help, suffer silently, or respond disruptively.

Finally, adults need to help students understand that individuals choose the consequences they receive. Because students have the opportunity and responsibility to understand their environment and the limits involved, and because they always have options available to them, their behavior indicates their choice of positive or negative consequences.

It is critical that adults help students understand these issues. Just as they require assistance in learning mathematical and reading skills, students need instruction in and reinforcement of the skills in taking responsibility for their own behavior. When adults respond with simple punishment, young people may develop the incorrect idea that adults are responsible for student behavior. When adults talk to young people in terms of the youngsters' options and choices, students learn responsibility.

METHODS FOR SOLVING PROBLEMS WITH INDIVIDUAL STUDENTS

Several writers have developed methods for helping students resolve problems and take responsibility for their own behavior. In his *Teacher Effectiveness Training,* Tom Gordon (1974) offers a six-step approach to problem solving. Frank Maple's (1977) *Shared Decision Making* describes a variety of skills needed to resolve problems effectively. For teachers working with students who have serious problems, the method of life space interviewing developed by Fritz Redl and expanded by William Morse and Nicholas Long (Long, Morse, & Newman, 1971) provides a method for helping the student understand and resolve conflicts within a structured, supportive approach. Similarly, Mary Wood's (1975) *Developmental Therapy* and Betty Epanchin and James Paul's (1982) *Casebook for Educating the Emotionally Disturbed* offer methods for working with seriously disturbed students.

Although we have at various times used each method described above, the remainder of this chapter presents the approaches we have found most useful in our own teaching and counseling experience. If you are interested in examining other methods, we refer you to the recommended readings at the end of this chapter.

Glasser's Seven Steps to Effective Discipline

Many teachers find the issue of dealing unsuccessfully with persistent student behavior problems to be one of the most frustrating and time-consuming aspects of teaching. Though most teachers are well trained in subject-matter methods, many are untrained or feel uncomfortable with the role of problem solver and disciplinarian. Furthermore, with the increased emphasis on competencies and achievement-test scores, we frequently feel anxious about time spent solving problems. Therefore, we need to develop skills in solving problems in a positive yet rapid manner. Most teachers have neither the inclination nor the expertise to become involved in extensive counseling with their students. We are, however, confronted daily with individual problems that must be resolved in order for students to benefit from our instruction.

The simplest and most effective method of helping children solve their problems and alter their behavior was described by William Glasser (1965, 1969) in his *Reality Therapy* and *Schools without Failure*. Though Glasser provided several step-by-step approaches to discipline, the method we have found most effective involves these seven steps: (1) be warm and personal and willing to get emotionally involved; (2) deal with specific, current behavior; (3) help the youngster make a value judgment about his or her behavior; (4) work out a plan for changing the behavior; (5) get a commitment from the student to carry out the plan; (6) follow up by checking to see how the plan is working; (7) do not punish the student by being negative or sarcastic, and do not accept excuses if the inappropriate behavior continues. Figure 10.2 outlines Glasser's seven steps.

Advantages of Glasser's Method

Four factors make Glasser's model extremely useful for school personnel. First, the problem solving can be accomplished in a short time. Most conflicts can be resolved in

FIGURE 10.2 Glasser's Problem-Solving Method

Step 1: Be warm and personal and willing to become emotionally involved
"I am glad you're here and I care about you as a person and a learner."

Step 2: Deal with the present behavior
"What did you do?"

Step 3: Make a value judgment
"Is it helping you?"
"Is it helping others?"
"Is it against a rule?"

Step 4: Work out a plan
"What can you do differently?"
"What do you need me to do to help?"
"Do you need any assistance from others?"

Step 5: Make a commitment
"Are you going to do this?"

Step 6: Follow up
"Let's check later and see how the plan worked."

Step 7: No put downs but do not accept excuses
"It's O.K. Let's keep trying. I trust that you can develop a plan that will work."
"I know things happen, but you made a plan. Do we need a new plan?"

less than five minutes, and frequently a solution can be developed in only a minute or two. Therefore, though it is often desirable to remove the student from the group so that the discussion can take place privately, you do not need to become involved in a lengthy discussion that diverts your attention from other instructional or supervisory duties. Second, because the model employs a step-by-step procedure, it is easy to learn. Furthermore, if a problem-solving session does not go well, you can analyze each step and discover what needs to be improved to make the session more effective.

Third, by actively involving the student in the problem-solving process, the model responds to a variety of students' needs. Rather than establishing a teacher-versus-student debate or a situation in which you manipulate the student by offering rewards for changed behavior, the student is meaningfully involved in examining his or her behavior and developing a plan for changing the behavior. Finally, because the model focuses on specific, observable behavior, data can be collected and the student is accountable for the results. The focus on observable behavior also enables you and the student realistically to analyze the effectiveness of the plan. To become competent at using Glasser's approach, you need to understand each step and then frequently use the approach with students.

Step One
The first step is presented in chapter 3. If we employ the communication skills and other strategies for improving teacher-student relationships described in chapter 3, students will sense that we care and will almost always be willing to examine and attempt to change their behavior.

Step Two
The second step is to ask the student to describe his or her behavior. Awareness of actions is an important component in any behavior-change program. Indeed, a simple increase in children's awareness of their behavior is often accompanied by major changes in their behavior. We can help students describe their behavior by asking questions such as, ''What did you do that upset Sally?'' It is important to focus the student's attention on what he or she did, not on what the other person did. The emphasis should be placed on specific, observable behavior. If a student states that he or she was bad or didn't obey us, we should help the child specify how he or she was bad or what request he or she did not obey and what he or she said or did when rejecting the request. If the student begins to answer the question by discussing what the other person did, we should indicate that, although this subject can be discussed later and the other person may even become involved, the student knows what he or she did and we would like to discuss this act.

Students will sometimes respond to our question about what they did by saying ''nothing'' or ''I don't know.'' Then we have several options. First, we can respond by stating, ''John, I'm not trying to blame you or get you in trouble. What I want to do is help you solve the problem, and I need to know what you did so I understand what happened.'' When we focus on the problem rather than threaten the student or focus on the punishment, students are often willing to discuss their behavior. A second approach is to ask if the student would be willing to hear what we observed or, if we were not present, to have someone else share what they saw. It is important that this option be presented positively and not as a threat. When confronted with this option, students will normally discuss their behavior. If a student does not respond positively to either of these options, it usually means that he or she is quite emotional and may need time to calm down and think about the problem. We can deal with this situation by saying, ''John, it seems you don't feel comfortable talking about the problem right now. Why don't we talk about it during recess.'' Providing the student with time to relax often facilitates a positive resolution of the problem.

Step Three

Once the student has described his or her behavior, we should help him or her determine whether the behavior is desirable. Students will not make meaningful, lasting changes in a behavior unless they decide that the behavior should be altered, particularly older students. When directing a program for seventh- and eighth-grade students who exhibited serious behavior problems, one of us was surprised when a number of the students stated that when they changed their behavior to earn the rewards offered by a contract, they thought they were being bribed and earned the rewards only to ''play the system.'' The students resented not being involved in assessing their behavior. Consequently, behavior changes occurred only as long as the staff could devise adequate rewards or punishments. Based on this information subsequent behavior-change interventions used more dialogue and a less unilateral approach to solving problems. Research results (Jones, 1973) indicate that this approach was more successful.

Glasser suggests that, when helping youngsters make a value judgment about their behavior, we ask them: ''Is the behavior helping you? Is it helping me? Is it helping the other students?'' When children are involved in obviously unproductive behaviors, they will almost always answer ''no'' to these questions. If they answer, ''yes,'' we can ask, ''How is it helping you?'' or ''How is it helping the others?'' Finally, if the student insists that the behavior is helping him or her and his or her peers, we can describe how the behavior is causing problems for him or her. If we have established a positive relationship with the student, this will often provide the impetus for the student to acknowledge that the behavior needs to be changed.

Another approach to helping youngsters make a value judgment is to have them list the advantages and disadvantages or payoffs and costs of their behavior. When working with older students, we can ask them to put the payoffs and costs in writing. Figure 10.3 provides a form that can be used to facilitate this process.

If a student continues to state that an unproductive behavior is helping him or her and that he or she wishes to continue the behavior, it is likely that he or she is feeling backed into a corner or is testing our resolve. It is usually best to postpone the discussion for a short time. If a student continues to insist that an unproductive behavior is acceptable, we may need to confront the student with the logical consequences of the behavior. We should be very careful not to rush to this point without exhausting all possible approaches to helping the student decide to alter the behavior. If it is necessary to use this intervention, however, it should be discussed in a matter-of-fact, nonthreatening manner, and we should clearly explain to the student why the behavior must be altered. We might say, ''I am sorry that you do not see the behavior as harmful. It is my job, though, to make sure that students follow school rules. Therefore, if you do not choose to be responsible for your behavior, I must take responsibility.'' If the student continues to insist that the behavior does not need to change, we should inform the student of the specific consequences that will occur if the behavior continues.

FIGURE 10.3 Payoff-Cost Model of Behavioral Counseling

	Short term	Long term
Payoffs		
Costs		

From Vernon F. Jones, *Adolescents with Behavior Problems: Strategies for Teaching, Counseling, and Parent Involvement*, p. 200. Copyright © 1980 by Allyn and Bacon. Reprinted with permission.

Step Four

After the student has decided that the behavior really does need to be changed, the next step is to help him or her develop a workable plan for making the change. We should start by asking the student a question such as, "What do you think you can do so that you can study without bothering other students?" or "What kind of plan could you work out so that you don't get in trouble in music?" We must not accept a superficial plan such as the statement, "I won't do it again" or "I'll try harder." We might be relieved to hear these promises, but they do not provide the student with a specific approach for dealing more effectively with the situation. Consequently, we can respond to promises by saying, "I'm glad that you are going to try not to do it. That will certainly help. But what else can you do? What can you do when you start to get frustrated with your work?"

Students are refreshingly creative at devising useful plans for solving their own problems. Nevertheless, students sometimes state that they cannot think of a solution. Our first response should be to encourage them to think about the situation and report back to us at a designated time. Students have frequently become so accustomed to having adults provide answers that at first they are confused by having the burden placed on them. When given time to think about the situation, though, they often devise thoughtful plans. If the student is unable to develop a workable plan, we can offer several ideas for the student to consider. We must offer several suggestions so that the student will make the final decision. This involvement in choosing the solution increases the likelihood that the student will accept and follow through on the plan.

Plans should initially be relatively simple and unstructured, such as a student's deciding to work with another student in order to stay on task and complete his or her work. Plans may, however, involve a somewhat more structured approach. In fact, when less structured solutions have failed, many of the procedures described in chapter 11 can serve as methods for implementing a plan to help a child alter his or her behavior. For example, students might be involved in writing a formal contract or self-monitoring their behavior.

Step Five

The next step is to ensure that both we and the student clearly understand the plan and ask the student to make a commitment to the plan. We can say, "All right, that seems like a good plan. Now, just to be sure that we both understand it, what are you going to do when you become frustrated with your work?" After the student describes the plan we can paraphrase the student's decision and acknowledge our role in the plan. We might say, "Okay, whenever you get frustrated you're going to raise your hand. If I'm busy and can't help you, you're going to quietly walk over and ask Sally for help. Then, it is my responsibility to come over and check your work as soon as I get a chance." Although it is often adequate simply to obtain an oral agreement, it is sometimes helpful to put the plan in writing. This contract is especially valuable when students are first introduced to problem solving or when the final plan is developed in the form of a contract in which both parties agree to behave in a specified manner.

Once the plan has been clarified, the student should make a commitment to try the plan. This *compact* can be accomplished by asking, "Do you believe this is a good plan? Will you give it a try?" Although this step is often part of the final negotiation of a plan, it is important to elicit a clear commitment to the plan.

Step Six

The sixth and seventh steps involve our followup. In devising a workable solution to a problem it is necessary to designate a time when the two parties will meet to discuss how the plan is working. This step provides us with an opportunity to reinforce the student's efforts and to discuss any problems that might arise. If the plan involves a behavior that occurs frequently throughout the day, we should meet briefly with the student on the same day as the plan is made. Furthermore, if we see the student successfully implementing the plan, we should praise the student for his or her efforts. If the plan involves a behavior that occurs only occasionally—as during the student's music class—we can agree to meet the student as soon as possible following the class. Followup sessions need not take long. We can simply ask, "How did your plan work?" If the plan worked well, we should express our pleasure and ask the student how he or she felt about the results. If it would reinforce the student, we may choose to provide additional followup by asking the principal to praise the student or by sending a positive note home with the student.

Step Seven

The final step in Glasser's plan deals with what we should do if a plan does not work. First, we should not be critical or sarcastic or punish the student. A major assumption underlying the use of a problem-solving approach is that in a positive, supportive environment students will want to be responsible and behave appropriately. Therefore, the student's inability to carry out a plan should not be punished. At the same time, we should not accept excuses. Students often defend their failure to change their behavior by blaming other people. Rather than allowing the student to describe what other people did that caused her or his failure to follow her or his plan, we should begin another problem-solving conference. Because the student will already have examined the behavior and made a decision to change it, the first three steps will usually take only a minute or two to complete. The conference should then focus on asking the student to consider why the plan did not work and helping her or him develop another plan. If the behavior is one that is harmful to other students, such as pushing children on the playground, we may need to inform the student of the consequences that will be incurred should the behavior continue. Although the emphasis should always be on devising a plan rather than on punishing the student, situations in which it is necessary to incorporate a punishment into a plan do occur.

Examples

The following examples of first an upper elementary and then a middle school teacher using Glasser's model with a student indicates how effective communication skills can be combined with Glasser's step-by-step procedure to create a positive resolution to a problem.

Example 1

STEP **1.**   TEACHER: Darby, can I talk to you by my desk for a little bit?

DARBY: Okay.

STEP **2.**   TEACHER: After we corrected math today, I went over everyone's paper. Can you tell me what I found on your paper?

DARBY: I didn't get finished.

STEP **3.**   TEACHER: That's right. Is it helping you to not get your work done on time?

DARBY: I guess not.

TEACHER: What happens when you don't have your work ready?

DARBY: Jon doesn't have a paper to correct.

TEACHER: Yes, can you think of any other things that happen?

DARBY: I'll get a bad grade and have to do my work again.

TEACHER: Okay, and does it make it even harder for you to have to complete this assignment and then begin working on the one for tomorrow?

DARBY: Yeah.

TEACHER: Well, Darby, would you like to start having your work done on time, so that you don't get behind, and so that you can feel good about giving Jon a completed paper to correct?

DARBY: Yeah.

STEP **4.**   TEACHER: All right. Can you think of a plan that can help you get your work done on time?

DARBY: No—I'll just try to get it done.

TEACHER: Well, that's super to hear, but can you think of some way really to succeed in getting this work completed?

DARBY: Oh, I guess I could do it after I get home from school, before my mom gets home from the beauty shop each night. But I like to play, too.

TEACHER: Well, let's plan it out. What time does your mother get home?

DARBY: 5:30.

TEACHER: And what time do you get home from school?

DARBY: 3:15.

TEACHER: Now, do you think you can play for a while . . .

DARBY: Oh, I know. I'll play until 4:30 and then do my work from 4:30 to 5:30!

STEP 5.   TEACHER: Darby, that sounds like a great idea! I'm sure that most days you won't even need a whole hour to finish your work, especially when you get into such a good habit! And won't it be nice to be all done when your mother gets home! How long do you think you could make this plan work?

DARBY: Forever!

TEACHER: Oh, whoa!! I'm excited, too, but let's take it a little at a time!

DARBY: Okay. I will do it tonight and tomorrow night.

TEACHER: Great! Then Jon and I can expect to see completed assignments on Thursday and Friday!

Thursday

STEP 6.   DARBY: It worked! I played, got my math done in 30 minutes (it was easy!) and was watching TV when Mom got home. Boy, was she surprised when I showed her my work!

TEACHER: Oh, Darby. I knew you could do it! I really am proud of you! Keep up the good plan!

Example 2

STEP 1.   TEACHER: Horace, may I please speak with you for a few minutes?

HORACE: Okay.

STEP 2.   TEACHER: What did you do that upset Larry?

HORACE: I didn't do anything.

TEACHER: Horace, I'm not trying to blame you or get you in trouble. What I want to do is try to help you solve the problem. But before we can solve it, I need to know what you did so that I understand what happened.

HORACE: Well, I pushed Larry's books off his desk and onto the floor and his papers got all messed up.

STEP 3.   TEACHER: Thank you for being honest with me. It sounds like you are really making an attempt to try to figure this problem out. Is this helping you or Larry in any way?

HORACE: No, but he marked in ink on my assignment sheet that I was just about to hand in, and he ruined it. And so, now I have to do it all over again.

STEP 4.   TEACHER: I will talk to Larry about this problem after we get finished dealing with your part of the problem. What kind of plan do you think you could work out so that you won't retaliate against anyone the next time something like this happens to you?

HORACE: I won't do it again.

TEACHER: I'm glad that you are going to try to not do it again. That will certainly help. But what else can we do?

HORACE: I don't know.

TEACHER: Well, how about if I make a few suggestions and you pick one of my plans to try to work with?

HORACE: Well, okay.

TEACHER: How about sending that person an "I" message telling them how you feel. Like, "It angers me when you ruin my homework and I have to do it over again." Or you could just get up and move away from that person, showing them that you don't appreciate what they've done. Do you like either one of these plans, Horace?

HORACE: Well, because we've worked on "I" messages and you want us to work out our own problems, I will try an "I" message next time.

STEP **5.** **TEACHER:** Great; now, just to be sure we both understand, what are you going to do the next time somebody bothers you and your work?

HORACE: Send that person an "I" message.

TEACHER: Good; I'll check back with you in a couple of days to see how your plan is working.

A couple of days later:

STEP **6.** **HORACE:** It worked!! Gary ripped one of my papers yesterday and I sent him an "I" message, and he actually apologized to me. I couldn't believe it.

TEACHER: I'm proud of you for working out your plan. I can see by your reaction that you are happy with your results.

Implementing Glasser's Model in the Classroom

As discussed in chapter 7 and earlier in this chapter, we believe problem solving should be an integral part of a teacher's classroom management plan. You must decide for yourself how this method will be incorporated into your plan. Some teachers choose to focus almost exclusively on a written form of problem solving. Other teachers prefer to have students go to a time-out area, think about the problem, generate a plan, and share the plan verbally when time permits. Many teachers use a combination of these methods in which written responses are the consequence for continued rule violation and verbal problem-solving is used to deal with problems that do not involve serious violation of classroom rules or when the student misbehaves frequently but always responds to warnings and thus infrequently chooses to receive the consequence of a written problem-solving form.

As with any procedure we use in the classroom, it will be dramatically more effective and efficient if students are taught how to use the procedure. The following ten activities are those the authors and many teachers with whom we work use in teaching Glasser's method to students.

1. Provide the students with a handout and write the steps on the overhead.
2. Discuss each step and provide an example.
3. Role play several situations in which a student misbehaves and the teacher uses this method for assisting the student in taking responsibility for his or her behavior.
4. Lead a discussion following each role play.
5. Have the students practice by taking the role of both student and teacher and role playing several situations.
6. Process these interactions.
7. Provide the class with an example of a violation of a classroom rule and have each student write a problem-solving plan on a form such as that in Figure 9.9.
8. Have students share and assist the class in evaluating and if necessary modifying several plans.
9. Explain how the problem-solving process relates to the classroom management plan and the difference between verbal and written plans.
10. Quiz students on the steps in the sequence and the classroom management plan.

When implementing Glasser's approach, it is important not to skip any of the seven steps listed in Figure 10.2. We often see teachers working with a student to develop a plan when the student has yet to make a value statement about his or her behavior. Regardless of the student's age or the nature of the problem, it is critical that the adult involved use each step and proceed in the order presented. The authors have used this method (embedded in the curriculum of responsibility) with their own children beginning at age 2, with students at every age and grade from 4-year-olds to high school seniors, and with students ranging from talented and gifted to incarcerated delinquents. We firmly believe that it is a central factor in creating positive learning environments and helping students learn personal responsibility. The teacher who uses Glasser's approach will find that student attitudes about the teacher and school in general will improve and that students will learn to take more responsibility for their behavior.

METHODS FOR SOLVING PROBLEMS BETWEEN STUDENTS

Teachers too seldom allow students to work out their own solutions to conflicts involving two or more students. By the third or fourth grade most children have considerable experience in resolving interpersonal conflicts. Furthermore, students' disagreements are often short-lived. It is not unusual to see younger children who were fighting one minute, playing happily together several minutes later. Indeed, adults' attempts to involve children in extensive problem solving about peer conflicts often tend to extend, compound, and intensify the problem. Similarly, when adults punish children for peer conflicts, they often inadvertently intensify the conflict. Rather than being forgotten, conflicts may linger on as students recall the punishment they received.

Teachers' involvement in solving peer conflicts may also reinforce the undesirable behavior. Students often enjoy the attention they receive when the teacher or counselor spends time helping them solve a peer conflict. This reinforcement may be especially powerful if the discussion takes place during time the students would normally be involved in academic tasks.

Excessive teacher involvement in resolving peer conflicts also suggests that students are unable to resolve their own conflicts. By reinforcing the concept that teachers alone possess the knowledge and skill for solving problems, we inadvertently encourage students to be more dependent. This situation affects both teacher and student negatively. Students are prevented from developing a sense of industry, competence, and power. This interference negatively affects their self-esteem, and students will often find less productive means of demonstrating their power. The effect on teachers is less pronounced but nevertheless notable. Teachers who attempt to solve every minor problem are often inundated with student concerns. This flood not only drains energy but also detracts from the teacher's ability to assist children with their academic tasks.

Knowing the considerable disadvantages associated with teachers' too frequently intervening in peer conflicts, it is useful to examine how we can go about increasing students' involvement in this process. The first factor to consider before encouraging students to solve their own conflicts is the degree to which students in the classroom know and like one another. If you have employed a variety of peer relationship activities such as those presented in chapter 4, and if you have implemented cooperative learning, students will be much more likely to work together to solve their own problems. If students are highly competitive, however, or have not been assisted in establishing a positive peer culture, they will normally be much less effective in solving their own problems. Similarly, even when positive peer relations have been established, we should be careful about having two students resolve a conflict if one student has considerably more power or prestige than the other. Unless the more powerful student is very sensitive and willing to use his or her power to help facilitate a positive solution, the situation may be characterized by negative manipulation. When we have good reason to question the students' ability to obtain a positive resolution, it may be best for us to serve as a third-party facilitator during the discussion.

The actual process of involving students in solving their own conflicts is quite simple. The first step is to discuss the procedure with the class. We can introduce the topic by asking students how they think problems are solved most effectively. When working with older students, we may wish to incorporate a brief discussion of the ways in which nations or individuals in the larger society solve their differences of opinion. The purpose of a discussion is to increase students' involvement in the process while making the point that disagreements are usually most effectively solved by direct communication between the parties. Even when a third party is involved, this person's role is merely to facilitate a productive dialogue between the disagreeing parties. Once the students have discussed this issue, we should inform them that whenever a student comes to us with a problem or we are required to intervene temporarily in an angry interchange between students, they will be asked to set a time to meet to resolve their differences.

It is important that we provide adequate structure for these student meetings. We should designate an area of the room where such meetings will take place. We know a teacher who tapes two lines on the floor so that students will discuss their differences while remaining far enough apart so that physical contact is discouraged. We may also wish to designate a time when conflict-resolution conferences will take place. Students can be informed that these will occur during recess periods, lunch breaks, or after school. Similarly, especially if students are allowed to meet during classroom activities, we may wish to set a time limit for such meetings. We can also provide students with a worksheet that helps them structure their meeting and clearly report their solution. Figure 10.4 is a form we have used with children in grades 4 through 8. Finally, we can help students develop the skills necessary for productive conflict resolution. Students can be taught to use "I" messages and active listening. We can also model an effective conflict resolution and can involve the class in role playing several typical conflicts. This skill building takes very little time, is an enjoyable activity for students, and significantly increases the percentage of conflict-resolution meetings that result in two happy students and a positive solution.

During the 1980s, much progress was made toward implementing peer conflict resolution in the schools. This progress stemmed from the work in the area of community mediation. Finding the courts glutted with cases, lawyers and concerned citizens established community mediation programs to reduce court cases dealing with minor neighborhood disputes. Today there are more than 350 dispute resolution programs in existence. Concern about world peace is another factor that stimulated interest in student-conflict resolution. Organizations such as Educators for Social Responsibility and programs such as Brooklyn Community School District 15's Model Peace Education Program have extended the concept of world peace to conflict resolution in schools.

In the spring of 1987, the Chicago School District introduced a curriculum on dispute resolution in all of its high schools. The 6-week unit includes a focus on interpersonal as well as global conflict resolution. The Conflict Manager Program developed by the Community Board Center in San Francisco is another widely used program. It provides students with 16 hours of training in communications and problems-solving skills. Students then serve as mediators in their schools. In elementary school buildings, student mediators wear bright Conflict Manager T-shirts to designate their role. Cahoon (1988) reports developing a similar program in her elementary school that, while using less training time, has had positive results. Roderick (1988) reports that more than 300 schools have implemented student mediation programs and that by 1991 75 percent of the public schools in San Francisco will have student mediator programs. Roderick's article is an excellent reference for resources in this area.

While it is often possible for students to resolve their own conflicts, there are times when teachers will be involved either because students have not yet been trained or because the conflict cannot be resolved by the students—either with or without a student mediator. When this occurs teachers will benefit from developing skill in mediating conflicts.

Most teachers find that when first implementing a new approach it is helpful to have a model to follow. The model we find most useful in helping teachers resolve peer conflicts with students is the Think—Feel—Act model, introduced to us by Cory Dunn, coordinator for the Program for Emotionally Handicapped Students in Linn and Benton Counties, Oregon. Figure 10.5 illustrates this method. In implementing this approach, the teacher's role is to allow each student to state his or her account of what happened, how he or she felt, and what he or she believes needs to be done, and to have the other student paraphrase each statement so each person experiences a sense of having been heard and understands

FIGURE 10.4 Problem-Solving Form

WORKING
TOGETHER
to
Solve
Problems

1. What happened that caused the other person to become upset?

Before	During	After
_____	_____	_____
_____	_____	_____
_____	_____	_____
_____	_____	_____

2. Did the behaviors described above violate a school or classroom rule?

_____ _____ if so which one _____

    no   yes

_____

3. Did the behaviors help you to positively resolve the problem?

____   ____

  no   yes

4. What agreement or plan can you create to resolve the problem? Complete the sentence.

We have decided that we will _____

_____

_____

5. What plan can you develop for preventing future problems? Complete the sentence.

The next time one of us does something that bothers the other we will

_____

_____

Student #1 signature	Student # 2 signature	Date

FIGURE 10.5 Think—Act—Feel Method of Conflict Resolution

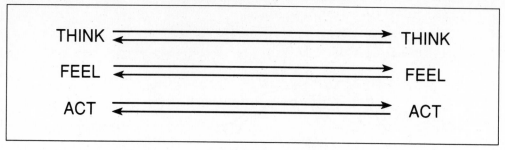

the other student's point of view. This process will be much easier to implement if students have been taught and practiced the method prior to its implementation.

The following dialogue occurred on the playground following an incident in which a small, emotionally disturbed third grader was accidently hit in the face with a ball and had his glasses knocked off. When teaching students to use this method and, whenever convenient, when using it with students, we have found it useful to draw the arrows (as seen in Figure 10.5) to indicate who is speaking and to demonstrate that each student has had an opportunity to speak and be heard.

Teacher facilitating a student problem

PETER: (Crying) He hit me with the ball and broke my glasses.

TEACHER: (Puts arm around Peter) I'm sorry you're hurt. That must have been a surprise to have that ball fly over and hit you. Let's talk to Bill and see what happened. Bill, would you please come here for a minute? (Bill leaves his game and joins the teacher and Peter.) Peter, can you tell Bill what happened?

PETER: You threw a ball and broke my glasses.

TEACHER: Bill, what did Peter tell you he thinks happened:

BILL: I didn't break his glasses. He's just being . . .

TEACHER: (interrupts Bill) Remember our method for problem solving, Bill. What I need you to do is tell us what you heard Peter say.

BILL: He said I threw a ball and it hit him in the face and broke his glasses.

TEACHER: Thank you, Bill. I appreciate your being responsible and helping us by using the problem-solving method. Now, Bill, would you please tell Peter what you thought happened.

BILL: We were playing catch with the football and John threw it over my head and it hit Peter. I jumped as high as I could to catch it, but it was too high.

TEACHER: Peter, can you tell us what Bill just said?

PETER: He said he didn't hit me with the ball.

TEACHER: What did he say happened?

PETER: He said John threw it over his head and he tried to catch it.

TEACHER: Peter, that was a very good job of stating what Bill said. Now, Peter, can you tell me how you are feeling?

PETER: I'm sad that my glasses are broke and I'm mad that someone broke them.

TEACHER: Bill, can you state back to us how Peter is feeling?

BILL: He's feeling mad and sad because his glasses are broken.

TEACHER: Thank you, Bill. Now, can you tell Peter how you are feeling?

BILL: I don't know.

TEACHER: Well, are you happy, sad, angry?

BILL: I guess I'm sad that his glasses got broken, but I didn't do it.

TEACHER: Peter, can you tell us how Bill said he is feeling?

PETER: He said he is feeling sad but that it's my fault the glasses are broken.

TEACHER: You're right that he said he was sad that your glasses were broken, but he didn't say it was your fault; he said that he did not break them. O.K., Peter, can you tell us what you think we need to do to solve this problem?

PETER: Yes, somebody has to buy me new glasses. My mom will kill me if I come home with broke glasses.

TEACHER: Bill, what did Peter say about what we need to do?

BILL: He said I have to buy him new glasses, but I didn't even break them.

TEACHER: Well, he said someone ought to pay for new glasses. I will take care of checking on the glasses. Bill, what do you think will help to solve this problem?

BILL: Well, I think John and me could apologize and I think we could be more careful about where we throw the ball. But Peter needs to be more careful about where he stands.

TEACHER: Peter, what did Bill just say?

PETER: He said him and John would apologize and be more careful.

TEACHER: Anything else?

PETER: Yah, he said I should look where I stand.

TEACHER: Peter, does that sound like a fair solution to the problem?

PETER: Yah, as long as someone pays for my glasses.

TEACHER: Bill, do you think we've solved the problem?

BILL: Yah.

TEACHER: O.K., boys, why don't you shake hands and then Bill will go over and get John so they can apologize to you, Peter.

The boys shook hands and Bill walked over to explain the situation to John. At this point Peter took his glasses and started to bend them. In doing this he realized that he had flexible stems and the stem popped back into place.

PETER: Hey look, they're not busted. They just got bent.

TEACHER: That's great, Peter. I'm really glad. Let's tell Bill and John that when they come over.

Even though using this method takes some time, it is very effective. Not only does this approach allow students to feel heard and help them develop problem-solving skills, but it also helps students understand others' points of view and develop skill in identifying their feelings. As we mention earlier in this chapter, all interventions in response to behavior problems should be educational in nature. This approach helps students develop a number of skills in which most students with behavior problems are deficient.

METHODS FOR GROUP PROBLEM SOLVING

Class Meetings

Class meetings allow both teacher and students to resolve problems openly and before they become major issues that negatively affect learning. Whenever people live close together for many hours every day, it is mandatory that time be taken to resolve minor conflicts openly. Like an automobile engine that may appear to run smoothly but will suddenly boil over unless properly lubricated, classrooms require proper maintenance checks and minor tune-ups. When implemented in a positive, supportive atmosphere, class meetings serve as the lubricant for a smoothly running classroom.

Class meetings are an integral part of a program designed to involve students in solving their own problems. By implementing these meetings, we clearly acknowledge our respect for students' ability to solve their own problems. Class meetings not only support the use of individual problem-solving conferences but can also provide students with opportunities for improving their social and problem-solving skills. When a youngster is positively reinforced for a behavior, another student is more likely to model the behavior (Bandura, 1969; Kazdin, 1973). Class meetings provide a setting in which this type of positive modeling can be encouraged.

Parents and educators frequently state that schools should do more to teach students to be responsible. Teachers often bemoan the fact that students cannot take responsibility for their own learning and behavior. This situation will not and cannot be changed unless students are meaningfully and consistently involved in monitoring their own behavior and solving their own problems. Responsible problem solving is as much a teachable skill as is math or reading, but it will not be learned unless we take time to facilitate the learning of the skills thoughtfully and skillfully.

The use of class meetings will vary with grade level. The ideas presented in the following section are most appropriate for relatively self-contained classrooms in which teachers have major responsibility for the social and academic skill development of 25 to 35 students. Class meetings can also be an important component in middle and high school classrooms. Because students at this age spend less time with one group of students, however, and are more sensitive to peer responses, it is generally best to focus on instructional or behavioral matters affecting the entire class, while handling individual student problems in private meetings with the teacher and one or a few students. Class meetings will generally be held less often in secondary classrooms, and the agenda will usually be presented by the teacher. Students can be encouraged, though, to bring problems to our attention and request that the problem be discussed by the class.

Guidelines for Implementing a Class Meeting

The first step in implementing class meetings is to discuss the concept with students. Students should be informed that class meetings will provide them with an opportunity to discuss things they like about the class as well as things that may need to be changed in order for the class to run more smoothly. We can ask students to develop their own list of reasons meetings are important. It is important now for us to display enthusiasm and express interest in holding class meetings.

Once students have discussed why class meetings are helpful and are excited about holding their first meeting, we should present the general guidelines for class meetings. You may add your own guidelines; we have found the following guidelines to be useful for elementary and middle school class meetings.

1. Class meetings will be held in a tight circle with all participants (including the teacher) seated in the circle. The circle must not be too large or it will detract from students' involvement and encourage off-task behavior.

2. All problems relating to the class as a group can be discussed. Problems between two or three individuals, however, will be resolved outside the class meeting unless this problem has an effect on the class.

3. An agenda will be created prior to every class meeting. The agenda is created by students' writing the topic on the chalkboard. Students must sign their name behind the agenda item. (If the children cannot write, they can tell us the item and we can place it on the board.) The items will be discussed in the order in which they appear on the board. If an agenda item no longer applies when the meeting is held, however, it will be from the deleted list.

4. Discussions during class meetings are always directed toward arriving at a solution that is not a punishment. The goal of class meetings is to find positive solutions to problems and not to criticize people or occurrences in the classroom.

5. If an individual student's behavior is listed on the agenda, the item will not be discussed without the student's permission. If the student agrees to have his or her behavior discussed, we should emphasize that the goal of the meeting is to help the student. We must be sure that students' statements focus on the youngster's behavior and are presented as ''I'' messages rather than as judgmental statements about the youngster or his or her behavior. The focus should always be on providing the student with sensitive, thoughtful feedback and positive suggestions for altering behavior.

Students should be informed that several options are available to those who choose not to have their behavior discussed at a class meeting. First, the student may leave the room while the other students attempt to devise an approach for helping the student. We may then wish to tape-record the discussion and share it with the student during an individual conference. Second, the student may choose to discuss the problem with us and a small group of concerned students. With the student's permission the results of this discussion can be shared with the entire class at the next class meeting. Finally, the student can discuss the problem with us and design a plan for alleviating the problem.

6. Students' responsibilities during class meetings include (1) raising hands and being called on to speak, (2) listening to the speaker and not talking while someone else is speaking, (3) staying on the topic until it has been completed, and (4) being involved by sharing ideas that will help the group.

7. The teacher will initially serve as facilitator for the class meetings.

Meeting Frequency and Length

It is best to hold class meetings whenever the agenda indicates that a meeting is necessary. Students should be assisted in listing only issues that are important to the smooth functioning of the classroom. Nevertheless, it is possible that a class meeting may be held every day. Because unresolved issues will only create problems that will significantly detract from students' learning, time spent in class meetings is usually rewarded with increased on-task behavior and the associated academic gains. A class meeting should be held at least once a week regardless of whether an agenda exists. A weekly meeting is necessary to maintain students' interest and skills as well as to reinforce the concept that the group is a valuable source of ideas and solutions. If no agenda exists, we can involve the class in a discussion of the positive aspects of the week. Similarly, we may wish to instigate a positive sharing activity and praise the class for having a positive, problem-free week.

The length of class meetings will vary according to the students' attention spans. Most primary-grade teachers find that their meetings can last between 10 and 30 minutes, and intermediate-grade teachers find between 30 and 45 minutes optimal. Middle school teachers or specialists in elementary schools who meet with a class 5 hours or fewer a week often choose to hold class meetings on a biweekly basis or to limit weekly meetings to 15 minutes so that meetings will not take up a significant portion of instructional time.

Starting Class Meetings

Begin the first class meeting by reviewing the purpose and general guidelines for class meetings.

During the initial meetings it is very important to monitor students' behavior carefully to ensure that general procedures and responsibilities are followed so that meetings run smoothly and students develop good habits. In order to ensure that initial meetings are viewed as positive and useful, be sure each agenda item is clearly resolved. Do so by asking several students to paraphrase the solution and ask for the group's commitment to carry out any plans that are developed. You may even initially wish to record each decision and post it in a prominent place in the room so that the class is reminded of their decision. A positive feeling can also be enhanced by closing each meeting on a positive note. You can do this by asking each student to state one nice thing that has happened to him or her or that he or she did for someone since the last meeting. Similarly, the group can be asked to say one nice thing about each member of the group.

Reinforce the value of students' solutions by beginning each meeting with a discussion on the results of solutions developed at the previous meeting. Unless students feel that their solutions are useful, they will understandably soon lose interest in class meetings.

Furthermore, because class meetings are designed to teach problem-solving skills, it is important to reinforce students' successful efforts, analyze their failures, and help them develop increasingly effective solutions.

Increasing Students' Involvement in Class Meetings

Because a major goal in implementing class meetings is to teach students skills involved in functioning effectively in a problem-solving group, it is desirable gradually to increase their responsibility for facilitating class meetings. This is difficult to do with primary-grade children, but third-grade students can be taught to run their own class meetings. We have found that these four steps provide a successful approach to having students take over the class meeting:

1. After leading approximately ten class meetings, present students with a handout describing the major functions a leader serves when facilitating a group meeting (Figure 10.6). Discuss each function and behavior with the class and inform them that they will soon be asked to lead their own meetings by having students serve these important functions.

2. Introduce an agenda item or classroom problem. While the class discusses this situation, point out and define each intervention you make. Because you continue to serve all three functions, the discussion will be interrupted on numerous occasions. Students are usually excited about learning the new skills, however, and enjoy your instructional interventions.

3. After running three or four actual class meetings in which you consistently point out the function of each intervention, meet with and teach one student the role of discussion leader. At the next meeting this student serves as the discussion leader while you maintain the other roles. Prior to the following meeting you meet with another student who learns the role of task observer. At the next meeting the student serves this function. Following this meeting, you instruct a third student in the role of behavior and feeling observer, and at the following meeting you become a group member who abides by the group responsibilities while the students run the meeting.

4. Each student should function in a role for five or six meetings so that he or she can master the skills associated with the role and effectively model it for other students. If a student has difficulty with a role, take time between meetings to instruct the student in the skills associated with the role. Providing students with this type of experience requires a small amount of time and considerable restraint and patience, but students respond to their new skills by becoming more positive, productive class members. Indeed, behavior-problem children often respond especially well, for they gain self-esteem and peer acceptance when serving as productive participants in class meetings.

IMPLEMENTATION ACTIVITIES

As mentioned earlier, one advantage to using a systematic approach to solving problems is that the adults can evaluate their use of the process. Activity 10.1 can help you analyze your effectiveness in employing Glasser's model.

FIGURE 10.6 Class-Meeting Jobs

Discussion Leader

1. Make sure everyone is comfortable and all distracting things are out of the way.
2. Make sure everyone can see all others in the circle.
3. Give the speaker time to get his or her point across.
4. Give the speaker a nod or a smile.
5. Ask clarifying questions:
   a. Are you saying that . . . ?
   b. Do you feel that . . . ?
6. Summarize:
   a. Is there anything else you would like to say?
   b. Would someone briefly summarize what has been said?

Task Observer

1. Make sure the task gets finished on time.
2. Watch the time.
3. Make suggestions of alternatives to solve the problem.
4. Point out behaviors that don't help in solving a problem.
5. Listen carefully and understand what the discussion leader is doing.
6. Understand the agenda and call out each agenda item.

Behavior and Feeling Observer

1. How did this discussion make you feel?
2. What could we do now? What might help us?
3. Was anything asked that caused you _____ (name of person) to be concerned?
   Can you tell us what it was and how you felt about it?
4. _____ (person's name) you usually help us out. Do you have any ideas for this problem?
5. Has anyone thought of new ideas for improving our discussions?
6. How many of you feel that the discussion was of value to you? Why?

ACTIVITY 10.1 Analyzing a Glasser Problem-Solving Dialogue

Choose a student who is acting inappropriately in the classroom and solve the problem using Glasser's model. Do not choose the most disruptive student, for the model will be learned more effectively if it is initially used to solve less serious problems. At a later time it may be useful to employ this approach with an extremely disruptive youngster and incorporate one or more of the strategies presented in chapter 11 into the plan.

Analyze your problem-solving interaction by answering the questions listed below. This examination will help clarify exactly how the interchange progressed. Although it will be impossible to report the dialogue verbatim, summarize the essence of each stage as specifically and accurately as possible.

Step 1 What activities or approaches have you used to help the student feel that you care about him or her?

Step 2 Record the dialogue that occurred as you attempted to help the student describe his or her behavior. Try to recall accurately the questions you asked and the answers you received.

Step 3 Record the dialogue that occurred as you attempted to help the student make a value judgment.

Step 4 Record the dialogue that took place while you helped the student make a plan, and write the plan that was finally developed.

Step 5 Record the manner in which you asked the student to make a commitment to the plan. Was the student's agreement enthusiastic? Why or why not?

Step 6 How soon after the plan was made did you follow-up? Record the interaction that took place during the followup.

Step 7 Did you use sarcasm or punish the student? If so, explain the circumstances. If the plan was not effective, record the dialogue that occurred when you confronted the student with the problem. Did you start at Step 1? Were you nonpunitive?

If your intervention was successful, write three reasons you think the model worked for you and the student.

If the use of this method was not effective, carefully examine your analysis of each step. Also, ask yourself these questions:

Do you accept the basic assumptions presented at the beginning of this chapter?

Were you helping the students solve the problem or were you solving the problem for them?

Were you positive and nonpunitive?

Having analyzed the dialogue and answered these questions, list three reasons the approach did not work for you in this case. Do not list factors involving the student; focus on your own behavior.

ACTIVITY 10.2 Assessing Your Classroom Meetings

> If you currently use class meetings, complete these evaluation items. If you do not currently use class meetings, use the general guidelines presented above to implement class meetings in your classroom. Hold at least five class meetings before evaluating the results.
>
> List two classroom problems that have been positively resolved using this approach.
> List two ways in which class meetings have helped to improve students' attitudes or behavior in your classroom.
> Write a brief statement about how your students have responded to or feel about class meetings.
> Write a brief statement about your reactions to class meetings.
> List two problems you see associated with class meetings.
> List two things you could do to improve your class meetings.
> If you are having difficulty with class meetings, ask a colleague who uses them effectively to observe at least one meeting and give you suggestions.

SUMMARY

The concept of problem solving as a major focus for responding to inappropriate student behavior has existed for more than 25 years. However, our experience as well as reviews of the research suggest that it has been systematically implemented into a surprisingly small percentage of teachers' classroom management plans and schoolwide student management systems. This is unfortunate because, when properly applied, problem solving responds to a number of important socioemotional needs of students and helps remediate a wide range of skill deficits experienced by many students who consistently behave unproductively in school.

Fortunately, an increased emphasis on conflict resolution and the continued efforts of leaders like William Glasser have helped create a positive climate for the use of problem solving. This chapter describes several specific methods for incorporating problem solving into a classroom management plan as well as ideas for using this approach to resolve peer conflicts. Our experience indicates that teachers who use these approaches are impressed with the positive student attitudes they generate as well as with their students' ability to solve problems and take more responsibility for their behavior.

RECOMMENDED READING

Dreikurs, R., Grunwald, B., & Pepper, F. (1982). *Maintaining sanity in the classroom: Classroom management techniques*, 2nd ed. New York: Harper and Row.

Fagan, S., Long, N., & Stevens, D. (1975). *Teaching children self-control: Preventing emotional and learning problems in the elementary school.* Columbus, Ohio: Charles Merrill.

Glasser, W. (1965). *Reality therapy.* New York: Harper and Row.

Glasser, W. (1969). *Schools without failure.* New York: Harper and Row.

Glasser, W. (1986). *Control theory in the classroom.* New York: Harper and Row.

Gordon, T. (1974). *Teacher effectiveness training.* New York: Wyden.

Jones, V. (1980). *Adolescents with behavior problems: Strategies for teaching, counseling, and parent involvement.* Boston: Allyn and Bacon.

Kraft, A. (1975). *The living classroom: Putting humanistic education into practice.* New York: Harper and Row.

Kreidler, W. (1984). *Creative conflict resolution: More than 200 activities for keeping peace in the classroom K–6.* Glenview, Ill.: Scott, Foresman.

Maple, F. (1977). *Shared decision making.* Beverly Hills, Calif.: Sage.

Wood, M. (1975). *Developmental therapy.* Baltimore: University Park Press.

CHAPTER **11**

Behavioristic Management Procedures

The classroom teacher is the most powerful influence in any classroom. One reason for this is that the teacher has such direct control of the antecedents and consequences that precede and follow child behavior. . . . Further, the more deviant and disruptive a child's behavior, the more likely it is that reinforcement and punishment will be required to effectively change the child's overall behavior.

/ Hill Walker (1979)
The Acting-Out Child: Coping with Classroom Disruption

Students occasionally need highly structured programs to help them change specific behaviors. A few students require our continuing efforts to help them acquire and demonstrate acceptable behavior. We cannot be expected to spend large amounts of time implementing behavior-change programs, but to be effective, we must be able to implement behavior-management methods that have proven effective in the classroom. When implemented in classroom settings characterized by supportive interpersonal relationships and instruction matched to students' needs, these methods frequently have dramatic effects on students' behavior.

The first responses to unproductive student behavior should be to examine the learning environment and attempt to alter the student's behavior by creating an environment that more effectively meets the students' personal and learning needs. When children behave unproductively in positive learning environments, adults should first help them examine their behavior and solve their problems. Unfortunately, a few children continue to behave in ways that harm themselves and others despite our efforts to create positive learning environments and effectively use problem-solving strategies. These children require special assistance in controlling their behavior so that they can take advantage of the positive school environment created for them.

Public Law 94–142, with its emphasis on mainstreaming exceptional children, and the fact that many children come from families that are experiencing serious turmoil or adjustment problems, have created a situation in which teachers face an increasing number of children who require considerable help in developing appropriate behaviors. Therefore, we need the skills described in this chapter. Teachers should not, however, use these methods unless they have first created a classroom in which all students are accepted by the teacher and their peers, classroom rules and procedures have been carefully taught and consistently monitored, effective instructional methods are being used, and students are involved in interesting work at which they can succeed. Employing behavioristic interventions to manipulate students into behaving docilely in an environment that does not meet their personal-psychological and academic needs is morally wrong. Employing behavioristic interventions to help students adjust to a positive learning environment, on the other hand, is an important part of being a competent teacher.

We begin this chapter with a brief presentation of the key assumptions associated with behavior modification and a discussion of the advantages and disadvantages of using behavioristic methods. In the remainder of the chapter we offer specific techniques for collecting and recording data, involving young people in monitoring their own behavior, and writing contracts with pupils.

BEHAVIOR MANAGEMENT IN PERSPECTIVE

Behavioristic interventions have, in many ways, been misunderstood by teachers. On the one hand, some teachers have viewed behavioristic methods as a complex, time-consuming approach that nevertheless held the answer to all their discipline problems. Conversely, many teachers have viewed behaviorism as a manipulative, overly repressive approach to working with students. As we often find, the answer lies somewhere between these extremes. Behavioristic methods cannot and should not solve all discipline problems. There is no substitute for effective teaching in a caring environment. Behaviorism, though, is also not necessarily a mechanistic, manipulative science. Rather, it can be used to help teachers better understand students' behavior and improve it by applying consistent positive and logical consequences to students' behavior. Furthermore, many behavioristic interventions are relatively simple and can be applied quickly and comfortably in a classroom setting.

Keep in mind that the methods described in this chapter need not and, indeed, should not be used with most students. Most teachers will find that at any given time these methods will be used with only 5 to 10 percent of their students. Moreover, most teachers indicate that these techniques are extremely helpful in assisting students with serious or persistent discipline problems positively alter their behavior. The time spent in developing an effective behavioristic intervention is almost always repaid many times over by reduction in the student's disruptive behavior.

Basic Assumptions Underlying Behavioristic Interventions

Behaviorism is really more a rationale and a methodology than a specific set of procedures. It is based on examining specific data and applying experimentally validated procedures in order to alter behavior. Quite simply, behaviorism is a scientific approach to changing behavior. This approach is based on three major assumptions: (1) behavior is influenced by the consequences following the behavior; (2) behavior-change programs must be focused on specific, observable behavior; and (3) data collection is necessary in order to alter behavior thoughtfully and systematically.

Behavior Is Influenced by the Consequences Following the Behavior

Behaviorists acknowledge the importance of antecedent conditions (the stimulus), but they emphasize the consequences of a behavior. We can see this emphasis in three basic rules of behaviorism developed through careful studies of human behavior: (1) a behavior followed immediately by a reward will occur more frequently, (2) a behavior will be extinguished when it is no longer reinforced, and (3) a behavior followed closely by a punishing consequence will occur less often. Although behavioristic interventions emphasize changing behavior by systematically influencing the rewards or punishments that follow a behavior, behaviorists do not ignore antecedent or stimulus conditions. Students cannot be reinforced for producing a behavior unless they possess the ability to emit the behavior. Therefore, we must create positive environments in which students will risk trying new behaviors and must systematically provide children with assistance in gradually developing new skills.

Behavior-Change Programs Must Focus on Specific, Observable Behavior

If we wish to help students develop new skills or eliminate undesired behaviors thoughtfully and systematically, we must deal with specific, observable behavior. It is not helpful to either teacher or student to state that the student is disruptive and incorrigible. It is much more helpful if we state that the student will learn more and be better liked by peers if he or she can reduce the number of times he or she interrupts the teacher and other students and can decrease the number of times he or she hits others. Focusing on observable behavior that can be counted is the first step in developing a program for systematically altering a student's behavior.

Data Collection Is Necessary in Order to Alter Behavior Thoughtfully and Systematically

It is surprising that this basic approach is so often criticized by teachers who state that data collection is too time consuming. Effective teachers base their academic instructional program on pretests that indicate the specific skills their students possess. This step is followed by activities specifically designed to develop new skills. Finally, another test is given or an observation is made to determine how well the skill has been learned and what activities should follow. Collecting data on students' behavior serves a similar purpose. It allows us to determine whether a problem exists, how serious the problem is, and whether the interventions being used are significantly affecting the behavior. When teachers fail to collect some form of data, they often fail to assess a student's behavior accurately. Without data, we cannot objectively determine whether a student's behavior is in reality significantly different from that of his or her peers, or what behavior most needs changing.

Data collection also allows us to evaluate a treatment designed to change a student's behavior. Unless we collect data, it is easy to become frustrated when a new program or intervention does not bring about an immediate change in the behavior. By collecting data, we can notice small but significant changes in a student's behavior. Because behaviors often change slowly, we may misinterpret the effect of our interventions. An excellent example is found in the criticism trap (Becker, Englemann, & Thomas, 1975): Teachers use criticism or reprimands because these cause an immediate, although usually temporary, change in students' behavior. In the long run, however, the negative behavior often increases because it is reinforced by the teacher's attention. Collecting and analyzing data can prevent teachers from continuing an ineffective behavior-change strategy or terminating an approach that is having significant but gradual success.

Perhaps the most systematic and data-based attempt to provide teachers with specific alternatives to specific types of disruptive or dysfunctional student behavior was conducted by Robert Spaulding (1982; Spaulding & Spaulding, 1983). Based on observations of 1,066 K–12 students and several hundred effective teachers, Spaulding identified eight common styles of unproductive student behavior and seven treatment methods. Spaulding then described specific treatment approaches that were most effective with each of the eight types of unproductive student behavior.

Advantages of Behavioristic Interventions

There are several advantages to using behavioristic interventions to alter students' behavior. First, some youngsters need special assistance in controlling their behavior. Anyone who has worked extensively in special education or child psychotherapy is aware that a few youngsters do not initially respond to the types of interventions that are effective in helping most children change their behaviors. Although the research suffers from failure to examine the quality of the teacher-student relationship, it does indicate that some children do not respond to adults' praise (Sgan, 1967; Thomas, Becker, & Armstrong, 1968; Walker, Hops, Greenwood, Todd, & Garrett, 1977). Similarly, though the studies have examined the presentation of rules but not students' involvement in the development or monitoring of these rules, research suggests that some students do not change their behavior when presented with rules (Madsen, Becker, & Thomas, 1968; O'Leary, Becker, Evans, & Saudargas, 1969). Therefore, research suggests that there are situations in which it is necessary to provide structured, concrete reinforcement or a systematic monitoring of behavior to help some youngsters change their behavior.

A second advantage of behavioristic interventions is that extensive research clearly demonstrates these interventions can be effective. Research shows that, when systematically applied, reinforcers ranging from simple teacher praise (Hall, Lund, & Jackson,

1968) to a combination of praise, token reinforcers, and response cost (Walker, Hops, & Fiegenbaum, 1976) can effectively alter students' behavior.

Third, although behavioristic intervention does require our time and effort, it frequently requires less time than we anticipate and less time than we currently spend attempting to control the student's behavior. Furthermore, the behavioristic intervention may have a positive effect on other students in the classroom (Drabman & Lahey, 1974; Kazdin, 1973), whereas reprimands often create a negative ripple effect that increases classroom disruption (Kounin, 1970).

Teachers who are especially worried about students' self-concepts and peer relationships often state that behavioristic interventions isolate and alienate children. However, research (Drabman & Lahey, 1974) suggests that, by helping students improve their behaviors, behavioristic treatment programs may improve students' relationships with their peers.

Disadvantages of Behavioristic Interventions

The major disadvantage associated with behavioristic interventions is that, because the focus is on changing students' behavior by systematically manipulating consequences, teachers are less likely to examine their own teaching methods or other classroom factors as possible causes of students' unproductive behavior.

One of us recalls a teacher who referred 17 of her students for special assistance because they were emotionally disturbed. Even though students were placed in classes randomly, only 1 student from the adjacent classroom was referred. Observations indicated that the referred children were significantly more active and aggressive toward their peers than their counterparts across the hall. The observations suggested, however, that the frequency and intensity of the teacher's critical statements to students was a major factor influencing the students' behavior. Before we attempt to modify students' behavior with behavioristic methods, we should carefully examine how extensively our own teaching strategies and style of interacting with students are negatively affecting their behavior.

A second disadvantage to behavioristic strategies for changing students' behaviors is that, except for self-management interventions, behavioristic approaches emphasize external controls. This emphasis is in opposition to children's need for a sense of competence and power and dramatically conflicts with adolescents' desire to be autonomous. The use of external rewards also tends to reinforce lower levels of moral development. Therefore, particularly when working with adolescents, overemphasis on behavioristic methods may detract from the important developmental tasks of understanding others' perspectives and learning to make decisions based on the effect one's behavior has both on oneself and on others (Selman, 1980). Working with youngsters who are experiencing serious behavior problems can be viewed as a reparenting process. These young people have not learned the social skills or acquired the positive feelings about themselves that enable them to function effectively. Like caring, effective parents, adults who work with these students need to provide them with love and self-respect and with skills in controlling their own environment. Although this may need to be supplemented by behavioristic interventions aimed at controlling the students' behavior, these interventions should never become the major treatment program. If emphasis on behavioristic interventions sidetracks us from incorporating a wide range of less restrictive, less control-oriented treatment interventions

A stopwatch can be used to record any continuous behavior. The teacher or coder records the starting and stopping time and the behavior to be monitored. If we wish to know the percentage of time a student is out of his or her seat, we start the stopwatch whenever the student leaves the seat and stop the watch when the student is seated. At the end of the observation period we have an immediate record of the behavior we were observing. This figure can then be recorded on a chart as time out of seat or translated into a percentage by dividing the time out of seat by the total observation time and multiplying by 100. Figure 11.3 presents a form we might use to record out-of-seat behavior and translate it into the percentage of time the student was out of his or her seat.

Recording Data

Recording data is a simple task, and students can be taught to record their own data. Data can be recorded using either a bar graph or a line graph. If all the observations took place in the same setting, we write the behavior being recorded on the vertical axis and the day or time when the observations occurred on the horizontal axis. The data are then recorded, and a line is drawn to connect the points, or a bar graph is created.

If we have collected data at different times of the day and during different activities, it is important to record this information so that the graph helps us determine whether the student's behavior is influenced by certain conditions. These data can be displayed by using a bar graph with different colors. The vertical axis again contains the behavior being recorded, and the horizontal axis indicates the time interval or days. A code can be made to indicate the activity during which the behaviors occurred. Figure 11.4 is an example of data graphed in this manner.

One major advantage to collecting and displaying data is that it allows adults to determine whether their efforts to help a student are being successful. Therefore, the final ingredient in an effective data display is to include a record of any changes we have made to alter the student's behavior.

The most common procedure for recording our attempts to alter a student's behavior is initially to record the behavior for a time (often five days) during which no special

FIGURE 11.3 Form for Monitoring Continuous Behavior

Behavior: Out-of-seat behavior   *Observation start time:* _____10:20_____
                                              Observation stop time: _____10:45_____
                                              Total observation time: 25 minutes

Activity: Language arts seatwork

Out-of-seat behavior time recorded on stopwatch: 10 minutes
                                                          22 seconds

    Total seconds in observation (number of minutes x 60):   1500
        Total seconds recorded (number of minutes x 60
                           + number of seconds):   622

Percentage of time off task: $\dfrac{\text{number of seconds recorded}}{\text{total number of seconds}} \times 100$

               $= \dfrac{622}{1500} \times 100 = .41 \times 100 = 41\%$

that help students to accomplish important developmental tasks, behaviorism can have a negative effect on students' ability to become competent and positive individuals.

A final disadvantage associated with behavioristic interventions is that they may place a negative connotation on the very goal they are intended to make more desirable. Several studies have found that when people are offered an extrinsic reward for performing a task they view as interesting, the task soon becomes perceived as less interesting and on-task behavior and task performance decrease (Deci, 1971, 1972; Lepper & Greene, 1975). Consequently, whenever possible, we should use the least externally control-oriented approach to changing a student's behavior. In the long run this restraint will encourage a greater sense of personal competence and a more internalized commitment to the values inherent in the desired behaviors.

DATA COLLECTION

As we have mentioned, there are numerous benefits to collecting data on students' behavior. Data enable us to determine whether a problem exists, how serious it is, and the effectiveness of any attempts to alter the behavior. Data also help us effectively and professionally discuss students' problems with parents and colleagues. Finally, clearly displayed data motivate students to change their behavior.

Despite the multiple advantages of collecting data, teachers frequently indicate that data collection is too complex and too time consuming to be used in the classroom. In this section we attempt to dispel these myths by describing the types of data we can collect and presenting practical methods for collecting data in the classroom.

Defining Students' Behavior

Teachers often define students' behavior in very general terms. A teacher may state that a student acts out or is unmotivated. These descriptions express the teacher's concern and suggest that a problem may exist, but they do not provide the teacher, student, parent, or consultant with any indication of the specific problem or the behaviors the teacher wants the student to change. Therefore, the first step in collecting data is to define the behavior in specific, observable terms. A specific behavioral description about an ''angry'' youngster might include the fact that the youngster hits other students or will not obey the teacher's requests. Similarly, behavioral descriptions about an ''unmotivated'' pupil might include the fact that the youngster turns in only 15 percent of assignments or is on-task only 20 percent of the time during seatwork. To reinforce this concept, take a minute to complete Activity 11.1 at the end of the chapter.

When we consider collecting data on students' behavior, it is helpful to decide whether the behavior is discrete or continuous. Discrete behavior can be easily counted, and its occurrence is more important than its duration. The number of assignments handed in by a student is a discrete behavior. Likewise, though the behavior may last for a time, handraising or talk-out behavior can be defined as discrete behavior because it can be counted and we generally care more about its occurrence than its duration.

Continuous behavior is difficult to count, and the duration of the behavior is the important factor. Out-of-seat and on-task behavior are examples of continuous behavior.

We can count the number of times a student leaves his or her seat, but the important factor is the amount of time the student is actually out of his or her seat. Similarly, we can count the number of times a student is off-task, but it would be a difficult chore and the data would not be very useful. It would be much more useful to know the percentage of time the student was on-task during a lesson. To determine your understanding of this concept, complete Activity 11.2 at the end of the chapter.

Some behaviors can be described as either discrete or continuous. In Activity 11.2, it would be possible either to count the number of times a student sharpened a pencil during a two-hour period (discrete behavior) or to record the number of minutes the student was out of his or her seat while sharpening the pencil (continuous behavior). In a situation such as this we should decide what aspect of the behavior is causing the problem. If the out-of-seat behavior were creating a problem for us or the student or both, we would want to define the behavior as continuous. If the loud grinding of the pencil sharpener were the major problem, though, we would choose to focus on the actual number of times the student used the pencil sharpener.

Defining a behavior as discrete or continuous helps us determine how the behavior should be counted and recorded. Discrete behavior can be counted by making a tally each time the behavior occurs. Continuous behavior is monitored with a stopwatch or a time sample.

Tallying Discrete Behavior

Once a behavior has been clearly defined and labeled as discrete, we need to develop a method for tallying the behavior. We can keep a tally by placing a mark on a chart each time the student emits the behavior being counted. Depending on where we will be when the behavior occurs and how frequently it occurs, this chart can be placed on our desk, carried on a clipboard, or placed on the student's desk. Figure 11.1 shows a typical form we might use for tallying behavior. For situations in which marking a tally on a sheet of paper can be distracting to us or students, we can record the behavior by carrying a golf counter and depressing the button each time the behavior occurs.

FIGURE 11.1 Form for Monitoring Discrete Behavior

Behavior: Talks without raising hand			Time: 9:30–10:05	
Activity: Social Studies				
Tally				
Monday	Tuesday	Wednesday	Thursday	Friday

The only difficulty we may experience when attempting to count student behavior is that it is sometimes difficult to watch a student carefully enough to record every incidence of a behavior. Though somewhat less a problem when recording discrete behavior, it often becomes a major factor when collecting data on continuous behavior. In either case, teachers can request the assistance of parents, aides, or even of older students. Because behavioral data are usually associated with programs designed for extreme acting-out children, this process will be used sparingly and most teachers will have little difficulty obtaining assistance.

Discrete data gathering can be a simple tally, but it can also be expanded to incorporate information about the antecedent conditions that precipitated the behavior. When determining how often a student hits peers, we might find it useful to know what occurs immediately prior to the student's striking a peer. Similarly, it might be useful to know the time of day when each incident occurs. Does it always occur late in the morning (perhaps the student does not eat breakfast and is especially irritable by late morning) or during a specific subject? Figure 11.2 presents a form we might use to record this type of information.

Time Sampling: Tallying Continuous Behavior

A time sample can be obtained by using a time-interval approach in which the coder records what the student is doing at designated intervals. The coder looks at the student every 15 seconds and records his or her behavior.

This method can be used when a stopwatch is not available. It has numerous disadvantages compared to timing the student's behavior. Employing a time-interval method requires the coder to look at the student at exact time intervals, which is almost impossible for a teacher to do while helping other students. This method is also less accurate than using a stopwatch, for whatever the student is doing as the coder looks up is recorded as the behavior that occurred during the entire interval. Finally, a stopwatch is somewhat less obtrusive than a coder with a pad and pencil who makes a tally every 10 or 15 seconds.

FIGURE 11.2 Form for Monitoring Environmental Factors Associated with Students' Behavior

Behavior: Hitting other students				Date:_____
Occurrences				
Time	Student hit	What occurred immediately before the hitting?	Recipient's reaction	Teacher's reaction

FIGURE 11.4 Bar Graph for Recording Data from Observations Occurring in Different Settings

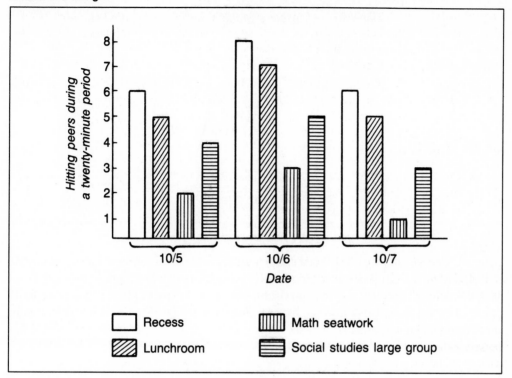

intervention is made and we continue using whatever approaches we have been using. The result is called baseline data, and it allows us to determine the effect our current method of handling classroom behavior has on the student. The next step is to implement a new approach to help the student change, and to record the behavior under the new conditions. The change in our approach and the subsequent student behavior can be recorded as shown in Figure 11.5. This figure presents a hypothetical case in which the teacher collected baseline data for five days, used Glasser's model for two weeks, and then implemented a contract with the student.

A major advantage associated with collecting data and developing concise data displays is that they help us determine when an intervention is necessary and how effectively a program is working. In addition, data clearly indicate to parents, administrators, and specialists that we are approaching the student's disruptive behavior in a conscientious and professional manner. This evidence increases parents' and administrators' willingness to accept the teacher's judgments and to become involved in helping us work with the student. In an age characterized by increasing emphasis on accountability, collecting and displaying data are an important ingredient of effective teaching.

SELF-MANAGEMENT

As we discuss throughout this book, the approach that is most beneficial in helping students change their behavior is one that provides the greatest amount of student involvement and

FIGURE 11.5 A Complete Data Display

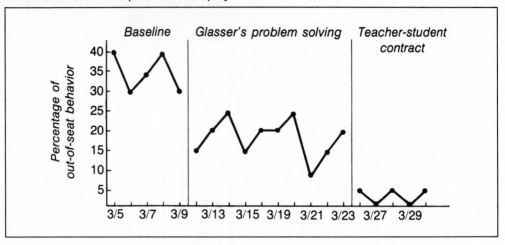

helps students develop new skills that can be transferred to other settings. The behavioristic strategies that best fulfill these criteria involve students in monitoring their own behavior. In addition to the problem-solving approaches discussed in chapter 10, there are two basic approaches to helping students monitor and control behavior. The first method is to help them count and record their own behavior. A second approach is to implement cognitive-behavior therapy.

Self-Monitoring

Students have a basic need to be viewed positively and to demonstrate their competence and power by controlling their own behavior. Often, however, students are not aware of the extent of their unproductive behavior. Some youngsters have difficulty controlling their emotions and behaviors without the assistance of external cues (Patterson, 1971). Involving students in collecting data on their own behavior can, in some instances, provide enough external structure to produce dramatic improvements in their behavior.

Students can be taught to record their own behavior (Anderson & Prawat, 1983). This procedure not only involves students in their own behavior-change program, but also significantly reduces the amount of time we must spend in collecting data. Furthermore, perhaps because self-monitoring helps create an internalized locus of control, changes in behavior associated with this approach seem more likely to generalize both to other situations and to other behaviors (Johnson, 1970; Johnson & Martin, 1973).

Self-monitoring procedures have proven effective in a variety of settings and with both normal and exceptional children (McLaughlin & Gnagey, 1981). McKenzie and Rushal (1974) report that having youngsters record their behavior on a bulletin board was effective in improving the behaviors of those who were consistently late, absent, or uninvolved in activities at a swim club. Broden, Hall, and Mitts (1971) demonstrated that self-recording attending and nonattending behavior and receiving praise for improvement was an effective intervention with an eighth-grade girl who was failing history. The girl's attending behavior increased from 30 percent to 80 percent under this treatment condition.

Hutzell, Platzek, and Logue (1974) reported similar success in reducing head jerking and distracting guttural vocal sounds in an 11-year-old boy.

Procedures

When first instructing students in counting their own behavior, we must ensure that they can accurately describe the behavior. We can teach this skill by asking them to demonstrate the desirable and undesirable behaviors. The next step is to develop a method for tallying the data. Especially when working with young children, it is helpful to start by incorporating a visual display of the behavior being counted. A *countoon* can serve this purpose. A countoon includes a picture of the behavior being tallied and a place for the student to make a tally each time the behavior occurs. Figure 11.6 is an example of a countoon used to help a student become aware of how often he talks out without raising his hand. Older students may not be willing to make checks on a chart each time they emit inappropriate behaviors. A talented junior high school counselor uses the form shown in Figure 11.7 to help students take more responsibility for their behavior.

Although most students will accurately monitor their own behavior after these two steps have been accomplished, seriously acting-out students will usually require more assistance. There are two additional steps that we can implement to encourage students to count their own behavior accurately.

We can start by reinforcing the student for obtaining data that closely match those we or another adult coder obtain. As they learn to record their behavior accurately, reinforcement for accuracy can be replaced by rewarding decreases in the unproductive behavior. This procedure can be effective in reducing disruptive behavior in seriously acting-out children (Drabman, Spitalnik, & O'Leary, 1973).

Another procedure involves initially having the student receive reinforcement for improving behaviors that are being recorded by an adult. As the student's behavior improves, he or she can be allowed to monitor his or her own behavior and receive designated reinforcements for improved behavior. Finally, the reinforcement is withdrawn and the student simply receives praise for controlling and recording his or her behavior. Bolstad and Johnson (1972) demonstrated that this approach could be effectively used with disruptive first- and second-grade children.

Regardless of the methods we use to encourage students to monitor their own behavior accurately, the student must record his or her own data and the results must be placed where the student can refer to them. In a creative study in which emotionally disturbed junior high school students were taught to influence their teachers' behaviors positively, Gray, Graubard, and Rosenberg (1974) reported that students' involvement in collecting data was a major factor in the program's effectiveness. Youngsters who have experienced numerous failures are reinforced and motivated by data indicating that they are improving their behavior. Conversely, when these data are lacking, these students frequently become unmotivated and depressed, even though their efforts are producing meaningful results.

Case Study: Elementary

This study was conducted by a first-grade teacher who was confronted with a particularly difficult class in an inner-city school. Most of her students had been late registrants for kindergarten and, because of overcrowding, had spent their kindergarten experience in an

FIGURE 11.6 Countoon

COUNTOON

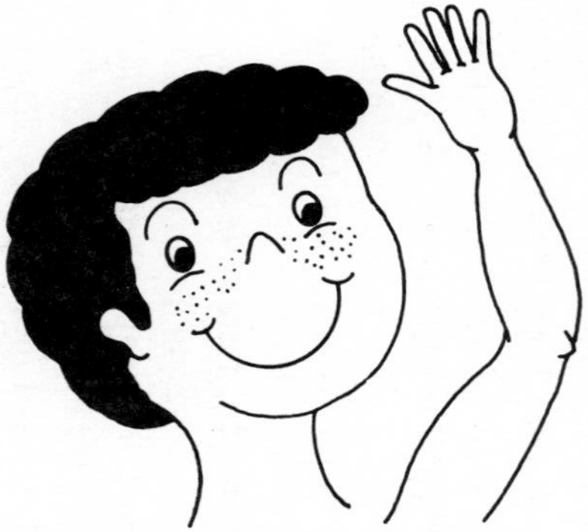

Count your hand raising

1	2	3	4	5	6	7	8	9	10
11	12	13	14	15	16	17	18	19	20
21	22	23	24	25	26	27	28	29	30
31	32	33	34	35	36	37	38	39	40
41	42	43	44	45	46	47	48	49	50

Count your talk outs

1	2	3	4	5	6	7	8	9	10
11	12	13	14	15	16	17	18	19	20
21	22	23	24	25	26	27	28	29	30
31	32	33	34	35	36	37	38	39	40
41	42	43	44	45	46	47	48	49	50

FIGURE 11.7   Student Self-Monitoring Form

Time	What the class is <u>supposed</u> to be doing	What good ol' (student's name) is doing . . . (+ or o)
9:55		
10:00		
10:05		
10:10		
10:15		
10:20		
10:25		
10:30		
10:35		

Student's Name_____

Teacher's signature

isolated room in the district's administrative office building. Consequently, the children arrived in first grade having had few interactions with older schoolchildren. In addition, their kindergarten class had started nearly a month late and they had had several teachers during the year. They were also generally a particularly immature, unskilled group, more than half living in single-parent homes. The following material is taken directly from the teacher's report of her study.

Many distractions within my classroom were caused by students who were not attending to my instructions. My students needed to learn to sit and work without talking, opening and closing their desks, walking to someone else's desk to talk, and so on. I decided to attempt a self-management technique, or a countoon, with my class. This group wanted to please me and be viewed positively by me, but they lacked the inner skills to control their behavior on their own. This technique would let them demonstrate their competence at monitoring and controlling their own behavior. I do not think they were aware of the extent of their off-task behavior. Some children have difficulty controlling their behavior without assistance from an external cue. When children are involved in collecting data on their own behavior, sometimes this act can provide enough external structure to produce dramatic results.

I started my study by collecting baseline data on five children in my group, to determine their off-task frequency. I chose five students who varied greatly in ability, behavior, background, and so forth. I recorded their behavior during seatwork three times at ten-minute intervals, and the results (Figure 11.8) showed that during a ten-minute interval, the frequency

FIGURE 11.8 Elementary Classroom Self-Monitoring Program

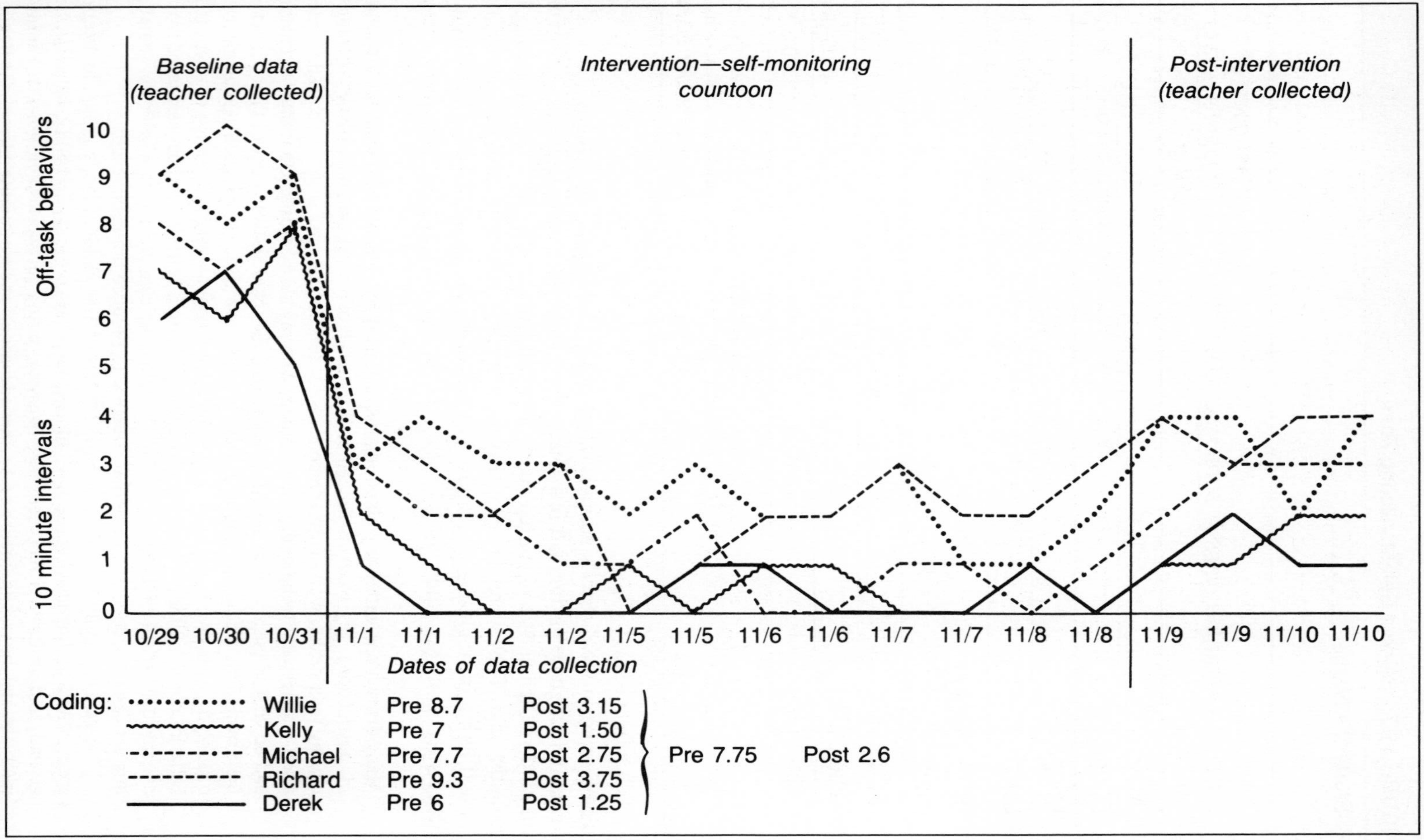

of off-task behavior averaged eight per student. I then individually informed the students that I had collected data on them and then I informed the entire group of my results without mentioning the names of the students I had observed. I tried to emphasize to them that I did not think they realized the extent of their off-task behavior. I told them I was going to set up a program whereby they would keep track of their own off-task behavior, with the hope that it would help them to increase their time on task. We then discussed, modeled, and role-played those behaviors which would be considered off-task behaviors. This behavior included talking out loud either to oneself or to a peer; doing any other activity than what I had instructed them to do; getting up from one's desk to wander around the room; or making distracting noises, either by mouth or by opening desks, rolling pencils; and so on. They realized that if they needed assistance from me, they should raise their hand, and because I have a free bathroom-break policy, they could use the bathroom if it was necessary. Students need to be taught how to record their own behavior, and so I spent considerable time in this phase of the project. Also, with students involved in collecting their behavioral data, the time I had to spend on behavior monitoring was lessened. Self-monitoring ideally helps create an internalized source of control, and changes in behavior associated with this approach are expected to be more likely to generalize both to other situations and to other behaviors.

After we had sufficiently practiced and discussed behaviors, I gave each student a countoon. My countoon had a picture of desirable behavior on it, showing an animal deeply involved in doing a worksheet. Originally I had decided to involve only five students in the study, but after a discussion with the class, I decided to give every student a countoon. My results in this study will include only the five students described in the baseline data, but I really felt that it could not hurt to have all the students involved, making them all aware of their talking and behaviors, and keeping track of their off-task times. I then instructed the students when to keep track of their behavior. Each box on the countoon was for tallying off-task behavior. After each ten-minute interval, we circled the box with a crayon so that the children could keep track of how many intervals we had done. In that way, if a student had no off-task behavior, the box was still circled to show that we had kept track of that interval. I ran the program for six days, monitoring behavior twice each day for ten minutes each. Generally this monitoring was done during math or science, in which we were working on booklets about baby animals. Several of the children almost completely quit off-task behaviors. They were excited about the program and requested that we keep track of behaviors more often. I think they really did feel they had some control over their situation. Because the results were favorable, they also received praise and points for a class party, and the atmosphere in the room improved significantly during use of the countoons. The five students for whom I had collected baseline data went from an average of eight off-task behaviors to less than three per ten-minute interval during data collection. When I did the followup data collection, without their knowledge, they did regress a little, and were a little more talkative, but overall their off-task behavior was cut in half.

Case Study: Mainstreaming a Junior High School Student

The following study was implemented by a teacher concerned about the behavior of a student in her last-period study hall. She implemented the study with no assistance and as a project for a course in classroom management.

Background

Samuel (not the student's real name) is a retained seventh grader who has been identified as seriously emotionally disturbed. He has been receiving special education services since the first grade and has attended the same school district since kindergarten. He is functioning in the average range on both the verbal and performance scales of the WISC. His academic achievement does not match his potential. The Woodcock-Johnson Psycho-Educational Battery shows an average knowledge score, low average reading, a mild deficiency in math, and a severe deficiency in written language.

Further testing shows that he has a weakness in visual motor tasks and in visual memory. He gains most of his knowledge auditorily as he has good hearing comprehension. Language is adequate for his age. He expresses his thoughts and ideas appropriately and has good conversational skills. He placed below the fifth percentile on the Piers Harris Children Self-Concept Scale.

Classroom Problem

Samuel is in my ninth-period study hall. He has an extremely high percentage of off-task behavior, which includes talking out, drawing pictures on his assignments, distracting other students, and just generally wasting time. I have tried a variety of interventions through the quarter, including changing his seat, having him stay after school, and glaring at him. The problem continued despite these efforts.

Intervention Plan

For three days I collected baseline data on Samuel and three other students in the same study hall. The results showed that the three control students were off task an average of 6.7 percent during the 40-minute period, whereas Samuel was off task 50 percent during the same period.

I showed the graph to Samuel and told him of my concerns with his off-task behavior. We had a good informative talk, part of which was a pep talk to let him know of his cognitive and academic strengths. I told him about the class I was taking and the project I wanted to involve him in. I showed Samuel the countoon (similar to Figure 11.7) I wanted him to use for the next five days. He was to watch the clock (without having it interfere with his work) and put a plus at the end of each five-minute period that he was on task or a zero if he was off task. I would be doing the same thing, and at the end of the period we would discreetly compare our results. No one in the class would know about our project. This was extremely important to Samuel. The self-monitoring recording sheet was to be kept in his folder each day, and he would stay after school to discuss it.

Results

The first day of self-monitoring Samuel was extremely aware of the clock; it really did distract him. We discussed this after class. The next day was better, and he continued to improve the third day. During the fourth and fifth days, he had only one incident each of off-task behavior. Our comparison data were very similar. A lot of verbal feedback went along with the plan, and Samuel responded well to the praise and individual attention.

The next week Samuel knew I was taking data on him but he was no longer self-monitoring. We discussed his behavior every day and looked at the data. The results (Figure 11.9) were very gratifying to us both. Samuel actually maintained an average of 5 percent of off-task behavior the third week. He was getting an incredible amount of homework done and was receiving positive feedback from his other classroom teachers as well.

Afterthoughts

I am really excited about the results of this project. With it I was able to do in three weeks what I thought was impossible. I thought Samuel was my most difficult student and really did not think I would get dramatic results using this approach.

FIGURE 11.9 Self-Monitoring Project with a Handicapped Seventh-Grade Student

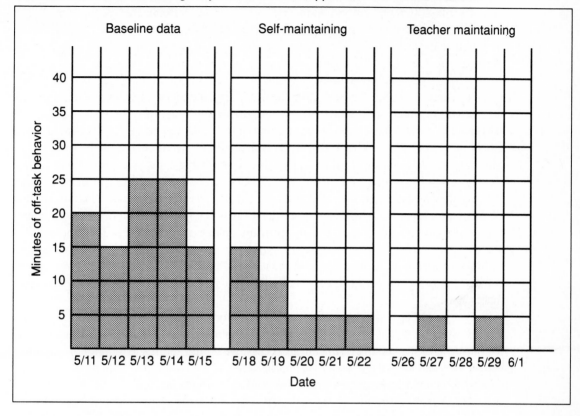

Self-Instruction

Students who consistently act out in a school setting are often characterized by their inability to express or control their emotions productively. Partially because these students have had numerous failure experiences and lack confidence, they frequently respond with intense emotions when confronted by situations their peers handle quite comfortably.

One approach to helping students respond more effectively to frustration and stress is to teach them to give themselves verbal instructions that cue them to behave more appropriately. This approach is based on the concept that students who are labeled *hyperactive* or *impulsive* are less skilled than normal youngsters in using silent speech to monitor their behavior (Epstein, Hallahan, & Kaufman 1975; Meichenbaum & Cameron, 1974). When faced with a difficult problem, a normal student might say to herself or himself, "Okay, I'll try it once more and if I can't do it I'll ask the teacher for help." Behavior-problem students may lack the ability to monitor their behavior in this manner and therefore respond actively and unproductively when faced with a frustrating task. Behavior-problem students may also use negative silent speech. A student might say to herself or himself, "I'm stupid and I can't do this." This internalized statement compounds the student's problem and intensifies negative emotions.

According to the principles of rational-emotive therapy, students' behaviors can be changed by helping them make positive, thoughtful internalized statements in place of the negative, unproductive statements they often make. Research indicates that this approach can be successful in reducing students' anxiety (Warren, Deffenbacher, & Brading, 1976), improving academic performance of behavior-problem students (Lovitt & Curtiss, 1968), reducing rule-breaking behavior (Monohan & O'Leary, 1971), and responding less aggressively to oral taunts from peers (Goodwin & Mahoney, 1975).

The basic procedure involves teaching students to use silent statements to control their behavior more effectively. We can do so by providing students with specific statements that they can make when confronted with specific, frustrating situations. Students who become frustrated when attempting to solve math problems can be taught to say, "I can do this if I slow down and relax. What I have to do is first add the two numbers on the right. . . ." Similarly, a student who becomes aggressive when losing a game can be taught to say, "Okay, I didn't win this time, but that's all right. The other students will like me better if I give the ball back and go to the end of the line." We can help students develop these skills by providing them with opportunities to practice self-instruction under our supervision and on tasks they can already perform. While working on fairly simple tasks, students may initially be encouraged to make statements we provide. The students can then be asked to repeat these statements on their own. Next, they can be asked to whisper the words as they complete the task. Finally, they can be encouraged to say the words to themselves.

We should provide students with social reinforcement for behavior changes that accompany the use of self-instruction. When implementing this approach with a student who has had difficulty accepting losing during recess, we should attempt to monitor the student's behavior. When the student responds appropriately when confronted with the problem situation, we should immediately praise the student's efforts and discuss the process he or she used to replace irrational, negative self-talk with more facilitative self-statements.

If you are interested in examining these procedures in more detail, you can find additional practical suggestions in Kranzler's (1974) *You Can Change the Way You Feel: A Rational-Emotive Approach,* and Workman's (1982) *Teaching Behavioral Self-Control to Students.*

A similar approach focuses both on self-talk and developing alternative methods for dealing with problem situations. Students can be asked to role play situations in which they consistently respond in an inappropriate manner. As the role playing unfolds, students are encouraged to replace unproductive self-talk with statements that help them control their behavior. Likewise, the teacher and/or other students provide alternative methods of responding. For example, a boy who consistently responds angrily to not being chosen immediately at recess may be asked to replace self-talk such as "Nobody likes me" or "I'm no good" with the statement, "I'll be chosen soon. I guess some students are a little better at this game than I am." The student may also be taught how to send an "I" message in a class meeting to express his hurt over not being chosen or given help in learning positive social skills that make it more likely that peers will choose him to be on their team.

A final approach to self-instruction involves teaching students skills in self-relaxation. This can be accomplished by the teacher or counselor initially providing direct instruction in how to relax. Students can learn to relax using the Jacobson (1938) method of relaxing and tensing different muscle groups. More simple and less obvious methods involve teaching youngsters yogalike breathing skills or asking them to let their bodies go limp and imagine a warm, relaxing substance flowing through their body. After students have learned relaxation methods, they can be encouraged to use these methods when they experience feelings of tension or anxiety. We can assist acting-out students by providing them with cues when it is necessary for them to use relaxation procedures. We can reinforce use of these skills by using them with the entire class before or following tension-producing or exciting activities, such as tests, recesses, or assemblies.

Relaxation can also be used in association with cognitive rehearsal (a strategy similar to self-talk). Before an activity that might evoke anxiety or inappropriate student behavior, we can have students close their eyes and go into a relaxed state. We then describe the upcoming situation and the desired student behavior. Before an assembly, we might have the students envision themselves walking quietly to the gymnasium, sitting quietly during the performance, and applauding at appropriate times. When students visually practice behavior in a relaxed state before performing the activity, their behavior can be significantly improved.

DEVELOPING CONTRACTS

A behavior contract is an agreement between two or more parties that indicates the manner in which one or more of the parties will behave in a given situation. Behavior contracts provide a specific, often written, agreement designating the exact behavior(s) each individual will emit. Furthermore, behavior contracts frequently indicate the specific reinforcement or punishment associated with performing or failing to perform the behaviors listed in the contract. Therefore, behavior contracting is a more structured intervention than either problem solving or self-management. Behavior contracting provides students with a structure that encourages them to perform behaviors they have been unable to display consistently without some form of external, concrete payoff or negative consequences.

> Because the behavior contract . . . is definitive, interaction among the parties is highly predictable, and each person is therefore encouraged to assume his responsibilities. The specificity of the terms makes people face up to ''the games they play'' and prevents the conscious use of defensive posturing, such as readily invoked excuses. Since the interaction among parties is clearly structured, a sense of security and safety appears to be an important by-product of the stratagem. (Blackham & Silberman, 1975, p. 127)

Negotiating a Contract

Unless a contract is sensitively and concisely negotiated, we may find that it fails regardless of the type of consequence involved. Contracts should ideally result from a teacher-student discussion in which we help the student describe his or her behavior, decide that it needs to be changed, and suggest a plan for making the change. When students are unable to devise a plan or when previous plans have failed to bring about the desired change, we can help them develop a more structured behavior contract.

An effective behavior contract includes a statement about each of these variables.

1. What is the contract's goal? Why has the contract been developed?
2. What specific behaviors must the student perform in order to receive the rewards or incur the punishment?

3. What reinforcers or punishers will be employed?
4. What are the time dimensions?
5. Who will monitor the behavior and how will it be monitored?
6. How often and with whom will the contract be evaluated? (Jones, 1980, p. 230)

Behavior contracts can be presented to students in many forms. Short-term contracts with elementary school children need not include each of the six components listed above. The important factor is that the child clearly understand the contract. Figure 11.10 is an example of a form you can use to present a contract to a primary-grade child, and Figure 11.11 is a form for intermediate-grade or secondary students. Though it is not necessary to develop a written contract, putting an agreement in writing tends to clarify each party's responsibilities. Whenever possible, students should be involved in determining the terms of a contract. Teachers should also help students express their feelings about a contract. Finally, once the contract has been negotiated, the student should be able to paraphrase clearly the conditions outlined in the contract.

Selecting Reinforcement Procedures and Consequences

Once we know when a contract should be used and how to negotiate a contract with a student, the next step involves understanding the various types of consequences (reinforcers and punishers) that can be incorporated into a behavior contract.

Just as the preventive measures discussed in Parts II and III of this book should precede the corrective measures outlined in Part IV, and problem-solving approaches should be implemented before using behavioristic methods, we should begin our contractual interventions with the least restrictive and most natural types of consequences. Figure 11.12 presents a hierarchic approach to consequences used in behavior contracts. We should start by trying to use contractual agreements based on the types of reinforcers and controls at the bottom of the hierarchy. Only if these fail should we develop a contract based on higher-level reinforcers.

Examining Figure 11.12, we see that teachers should initially use reinforcers that are a normal part of the school day and are available to all students. Although token reinforcers may appear to be less natural than curtailment of activity, we constantly provide token reinforcers in the form of grades, points earned on tests, or promises to provide a reward if students behave appropriately for a designated period. Furthermore, we should, whenever possible, focus on positive behavior. Punishment in the form of curtailments of activity should be used only after natural reinforcers have proven ineffective in helping a student change a behavior. Curtailment of activity is listed as more desirable than implementing a response cost (the procedure of taking away points or other rewards when a student misbehaves) primarily because response cost is a complex intervention and should not be used unless simpler interventions fail. Curtailment of activity is placed lower on the hierarchy than are tangible reinforcers because restricting a student's behavior by requiring that he or she stay in from recess in order to complete required work is a more logical intervention than is providing the student with candy for completing a task. Furthermore, the use of tangible reinforcements suggests that the desired behavior is not valuable enough to warrant being displayed without a tangible payoff. This statement has subtle but potentially powerful negative consequences for long-term improvement in the student's behavior.

FIGURE 11.10 Primary-Grade Contract

I'm Leaping in to say

If:

I Can Play Four Square

Without Getting In a

Fight At Recess

Then:

I Can Play With

The Gerbil For

Ten Minutes

My Friend's Name Who Will Help Me

Teacher's Name

My Name

Date

FIGURE 11.11   Upper Elementary or Middle School Contract

I've got the POWER!

_____Matt_____

IS GREAT!
NOT LATE!

I WILL be on time to P.E. class, 11:00 a.m. sharp

FOR 5 consecutive days. Allan HAS OFFERED

TO HELP BY walking to class with Matt. MY

TEACHER WILL HELP BY telling me how well I did

each day I am on time.

TO CELEBRATE I WILL BE ABLE TO be a student

helper in P.E. and referee/umpire activities.

_____   _____
DATE   GREAT PERSON

                                            _____
                                            HELPER

                                            _____
                                            TEACHER

In the remainder of this chapter, we provide procedures for implementing the first four types of consequences listed in Figure 11.12. Because few teachers use response-cost or tangible reinforcers, these consequences are not discussed. If you are interested in these, refer to Hill Walker's (1979) book, *The Acting-Out Child*.

Social Reinforcement
Social reinforcement refers to behaviors of other people that tend to increase the frequency with which a student emits a behavior. If a smile from us is followed by a student's

FIGURE 11.12 Behavior-Contract Hierarchy

Tangible reinforcement
Social, token, and activity reinforcement and response cost
Curtailment of activity
Social, token, and activity reinforcement
Activity reinforcement
Social reinforcement

continuing to work on an assignment, the smile has served as a social reinforcer. Similarly, if a child consistently returns to a group after having been chased away, the attention inherent in being chased may be viewed as a social reinforcer. Social reinforcement can be used either as a spontaneous teaching strategy for influencing students' behavior or as a consequence in a contract.

When systematically using social reinforcement as a method for improving students' behavior, we should develop skill in employing a wide range of reinforcers, learn how to give reinforcement, and learn when to use it.

Among the many types of social reinforcement, the most obvious involves saying positive things to students. When giving social reinforcement, we should be careful not to use the same word or phrase constantly. Students appreciate different, creative expressions of encouragement and appreciation. Figure 11.13 lists social reinforcers we can use at a variety of grade levels.

Words are not the only type of social reinforcement. We can use many types of nonverbal social reinforcers. We can share our positive feelings about students' behavior by smiling, laughing, winking, or looking interested in what a youngster is doing. We can also reinforce students by spending time with them. Many behavior-problem students receive little attention and affection from adults and are starved for positive attention. We can reinforce these children by walking with them, eating lunch together, joining them in playground games, or asking them to stay after school and help us with a classroom task. Physical touch is another important and effective nonverbal social reinforcer. Research (Kazdin & Klock, 1973) has demonstrated that nonverbal reinforcement in the form of smiles and touch can positively influence students' on-task behavior.

When using social reinforcement, we must be especially careful to reinforce specific behaviors. We often use words such as *great, good, nice,* and *super* when referring to students' work or behavior. Unfortunately, this form of reinforcement does not provide the student with specific information on which aspect of behavior is being reinforced. Therefore, it is important that we describe the behavior being praised. Rather than saying, "That's nice, Bill," when Bill listens attentively, we might say, "Bill, I appreciate the way you are listening to the discussion. It should help you do well on the assignment."

Although we must develop an extensive repertoire of social reinforcers and learn to praise specific behavior, it is perhaps even more important that we learn when to reinforce students. The reason social reinforcement is frequently ineffective in changing students' behavior is that it is so often ineffectively used by teachers. Several studies have demonstrated that we often dispense social reinforcement at the wrong time. Walker, Hops, and Fiegenbaum (1976) observed the interactions between five acting-out children and their

FIGURE 11.13 Social Reinforcers

Praising words and phrases	
Good	That's interesting
That's right	That's really nice
Excellent	Wow
That's clever	Keep up the good work
Good job	Terrific
Good thinking	Beautiful
That shows a great deal of work	I appreciate your help
You really pay attention	Now you've got the hang of it
You should show this to your father	Now you've figured it out
Show Grandma your picture	Very interesting
That was very kind of you	That's an interesting point
Thank you; I'm pleased with that	Nice going
Great	You make it look easy
I like that	What neat work
Exactly	I like the way you got started on your homework

Expressions	Nearness	Physical contact
Smiling	Walking together	Touching
Winking	Sitting together	Hugging
Nodding up and down	Eating lunch together	Sitting in lap
Looking interested	Playing games with student	Shaking hand
Laughing	Working after school together	Holding hand

teachers. The results showed that though the five teachers praised the acting-out child's appropriate behavior about once every hour, they attended to inappropriate behavior nine times each hour. Similarly, Walker and Buckley (1973) observed an elementary classroom teacher and found that although 82 percent of the teacher's interactions with normal children followed appropriate behavior, 89 percent of the responses to acting-out children followed inappropriate behavior. Taken together, these and other studies suggest that we should attempt to increase our use of positive social reinforcement and make this reinforcement contingent on acceptable student behavior. When an acting-out child demonstrates a positive behavior, we should try to reinforce this behavior immediately.

Social reinforcement is usually viewed as a spontaneous approach to changing students' behavior, but it can also be incorporated into behavior contracts. Because social reinforcement is inexpensive, readily available, and easy to give, we should attempt to incorporate this type of reinforcement into our initial contracts with a student. There are several approaches we can take when using social reinforcement in this manner. A contract can be developed in which a student receives social reinforcement from peers or us as a consequence for making a desirable behavior change. We can also involve parents in providing social reinforcement when their child behaves appropriately at school. A contract might indicate that if a student reaches a specified behavioral or academic goal, we will send a note home to the parent and the parents will respond by providing the student with a designated number of specific positive statements.

Activity Reinforcement

Because social reinforcement is not a powerful enough reinforcer to bring about prompt or significant change for all students, we need to use other forms of reinforcers. Involvement in various preferred activities is another natural and easily dispensable reward for desirable behavior.

PROCEDURES. The first step is to list activities that students find reinforcing. Students enjoy being involved in this process and often offer creative and surprising ideas. Figure 11.14 lists classroom-activity reinforcers.

The second step is to develop a contract stipulating what the child must do to obtain the activity reinforcer. Figure 11.10 is an example of a simple contract. Whenever activity reinforcers are used, they should be paired with social reinforcement so that the social reinforcement may gradually acquire some of the reinforcing properties associated with the activity reinforcer.

The problem of delayed gratification (the student becomes frustrated because he or she must wait for the reinforcement) that is frequently associated with activity reinforcers can be dealt with by gradually extending the time a student must wait in order to receive the reward. When first implementing a contract, the student can be informed that he or she can be involved in the activity immediately after performing the desired behavior. As the student's behavior improves, he or she can be informed that he or she will have to demonstrate increasingly appropriate behavior as well as wait longer before the reinforcement is provided.

An interesting approach to using activity reinforcers involves allowing students to take home school equipment they find particularly interesting. A student's contract might indicate that he or she can take a tape recorder home for two days if he or she meets the conditions of the contract. Although this type of reinforcement may at first glance appear to be a tangible reinforcer, the student uses the borrowed item but neither consumes nor acquires permanent possession of the reinforcer. The reinforcer provides the student with an opportunity to reinforce himself or herself by participation in an activity involving school property. In essence the student is involved in the reinforcing event at home rather than at school.

Social, Token, and Activity Reinforcement

Token reinforcement refers to a system in which students receive immediate reinforcement in the form of a check, chip, or other tangible item that can be traded in for reinforcement at a future time.

PROCEDURES. There are seven basic steps to implementing a token reinforcement system in the classroom. Before introducing a token system, we should determine specifically how each step will be accomplished.

FIGURE 11.14 Activity Reinforcers

Being group leader	Performing for parents
Going first	Taking a class pet home for the
Running errands	weekend
Collecting materials	Leading the songs
Helping clean up	Being team captain
Getting to sit where he or she wants	Reading to the principal
to	Seeing a filmstrip
Taking care of class pets	Getting to read a new book
Leading the flag salute	Seeing a movie
Telling a joke to the class	Listening to music
Being in a skit	Playing games in class
Having a party	Write on chalkboard: white or colored
Making puppets and a puppet show	chalk
Doing artwork related to studies	Play with magnet or other science
Spending special time with	equipment
the teacher	Solve codes and other puzzles
Choosing the game for recess	Listen to a song
Getting to make puzzles	Perform before a group: sing a song;
Earning an extra or longer recess	tell a poem or riddle; do a dance,
Choosing songs to sing	stunt, or trick
Work puzzle	Be hugged, tickled, kissed, patted
Draw, paint, color, work with clay, and	Choose book to review for class
so on	Select topic for group to discuss
Choosing group activity	Read to a friend
Take a "good" note home to mom	Read with a friend
(arrange a reward with the mother)	Right to tutor a slower classmate
Extend class recess by specified	Free time in the library
number of minutes	Ask child what he or she would like to
Visit another class	do
Help teacher	Listen to record or radio with
10-minute break to choose game and	earphones
play with a friend, QUIETLY	Plan a class trip or project
Build with construction materials	Work in school office
Time to read aloud	Work in school library
Play short game: tic-tac-toe, easy	
puzzles, connect the dots	

1. Determine when and with whom the program should be implemented. We might choose to employ a token system with two acting-out children whose behavior during seatwork continues to be extremely disruptive despite our attempts at instigating other types of interventions.

2. Select the specific behaviors to be reinforced. When working with an individual student, we might state that the student will receive a token for every two minutes he or she is in his or her seat, not talking to peers, and working on the assignment. When working with several students or the entire class it is desirable to generate a list of behaviors (the classroom rules may be suitable) that will be reinforced. It is desirable to involve students in determining the behaviors and to post the behaviors in a prominent place.

3. Decide when tokens will be dispensed. When working with a seriously acting-out student you will usually have to dispense the tokens whenever the desired behavior occurs. As the student begins to gain control of his or her behavior, teacher and student can tally the occurrence of the desired behaviors (the tallies serve as tokens), and this total can be recorded or actual tokens can be given to the student at the end of a designated time. When employing a token system with an entire class, it is best to distribute tokens randomly. Thus, as you move around the room or work with a group, you present tokens to students who are behaving appropriately. Though you must be careful not to overlook students or unfairly focus on some students, a random reinforcement schedule is easy to administer and maintains acceptable behavior at a high rate.

4. Determine how to dispense tokens. There are numerous methods for dispensing tokens. Each student involved in the program can have a card taped on the corner of his or her desk and you can make a mark on the card each time the student displays the desired behavior. When working with small children, teachers occasionally choose to place a jar or box on each participant's desk so that tokens can be dropped into the container when the student behaves appropriately. When working with students who change classes or teachers during the day, a travel card (Figure 11.15) can be used. The desired behaviors are written on the card, and at the end of each period the student receives a check for each desired behavior displayed throughout the period.

5. Select a procedure for recording tokens earned. Because most token systems involve earning tokens over a specified period, it is necessary to devise a system for recording the number of tokens each child has accumulated. Likewise, because children can trade tokens in for preferred activities, a record of tokens spent and remaining must be kept.

Curtailment of Activity

Activity curtailment refers to any situation in which inappropriate student behavior is followed by removal of a desired activity. This method of altering students' behavior has been used since time began, but it has received considerable attention with formal time-out procedures.

Procedures

1. Students should understand the behaviors that will lead to curtailment of activity, what activities will be curtailed, and how long the restriction will be in effect. Punishment should never be presented arbitrarily.

2. Rules on curtailment of activity should be used consistently and fairly. If fighting on the playground is followed by sitting out the next recess, this restriction should be applied to all students in every instance. We should also consider, however, whether playground facilities and activities support positive play, whether rules are clearly understood, and whether students have been taught methods for resolving inevitable playground conflicts.

3. Be aware of cases in which curtailment of activity provides a more desirable alternative than the activity itself. Students may behave inappropriately in order to receive what appears to us to be a punishment but the student views as a relatively positive

FIGURE 11.15 Travel Card

Student _____ Grade _____ Date _____

Desired behaviors

Period	On time to class	Brought necessary materials	Handed in assignment	Obeyed class rules	Participated in class	Teacher's signature
1						
2						
3						
4						
5						
6						
7						

consequence. A student may dawdle at work in order to stay in from recess, either because recess is perceived as undesirable or the time in the room is viewed as pleasant. Continuing to use a curtailment of activity in this situation might prevent the child from dealing with important social skill deficits that are causing problems on the playground. Therefore, the punishment would be detrimental rather than helpful.

4. Present the negative consequences in a nonpunitive, interested manner. We should communicate sincere regret that a punishment is necessary. This attitude helps students accept responsibility for their behavior rather than project the blame onto the teacher. Punishment should never be presented in anger, which only encourages the student to feel persecuted and to transfer the blame to the teacher.

5. When presenting a curtailment of activity to a student, always inform the student which specific behavior(s) were responsible for bringing about the undesirable consequence. The student should also be reminded of the desirable behaviors that could prevent the consequences.

6. When presenting a punishment, inform the student what must be done to terminate the punishment. You might inform a student that he or she can return to the class activity after quietly completing a problem-solving form.

7. Whenever possible, a curtailment of activity should logically relate to the behavior that necessitated the punishment. If a child could not play on the playground without fighting, it is logical that he or she should miss recess until he or she can develop a plan for interacting more appropriately with peers. It is not logical, though, to have children stay after school and write sentences because they fought on the playground.

8. Activity curtailment should, whenever possible, be consolidated with activities aimed at helping the student develop new skills that will prevent repeated performance of the undesirable behavior. Therefore, when being excluded from a desired activity, the student should be involved in examining the problem and developing a plan for solving it.

9. We should collect data to help us determine whether the curtailment of activity is effective in reducing the undesirable behavior or increasing the desired behavior. Because punishment in any form may have numerous negative side effects, it should be discontinued if data indicate that it is ineffective.

10. Punishment methods of changing students' behavior should be phased out as soon as possible and replaced by more positive approaches, such as problem solving, self-management, or social or activity reinforcement.

Group Contracts

A group contract involves a situation in which the entire group earns a reward or loses previously awarded points or privileges contingent on the entire group's behaving in a desired manner. Some writers define group contracts as including programs in which an individual student's behavior is reinforced by a desired activity for the entire group, but this technique is more accurately labeled an activity reinforcer.

PROCEDURES. In an attempt to reduce talking out and out-of-seat behavior in a fourth-grade class, Barrish, Saunders, and Wolf (1969) developed a group contract called the Good Behavior Game. The class was divided into two teams, and students were informed that it was possible for either or both teams to win or lose. The winning team(s) received a 30-minute free period at the end of the school day as well as an opportunity to wear victory tags and be first in line for lunch. The game was played by having the teacher make a mark on the board each time a team member talked out or was out of seat without permission. The team with the fewest points was designated the winner. Both teams could win, however, if neither team had more than five marks. Results of this activity showed marked decreases in the undesirable behavior.

Schmidt and Ulrich (1969) report successful implementation of a similar program in which a class was reinforced with free time when they maintained an acceptable noise level and remained in their seats. In their program, though, the class could also lose free time for violating these rules.

A more formal procedure for reinforcing on-task behavior involves providing a group reinforcement contingent on the entire group's being on task for a designated percentage of the class period. A method for implementing such a procedure has been developed and extensively researched by Greenwood, Hops, Delquadri, and Walker (1974). This systematic program, entitled PASS (Program for Academic Survival Skills) is aimed at helping students learn and demonstrate specific skills that are necessary for academic success.

In its simplest form, the PASS Program involves these components: (1) a list of class rules (survival skills); (2) daily charting of the percentage of time these rules are followed by all class members; (3) a group reward for improvement; and (4) gradual removal of the major program components, such as the visible timing device, rules, and data display.

The PASS Program was initially designed for use with elementary school children, but it has also been successfully employed with young adolescents (Jones, 1980). The program involves the class in developing class rules stated in terms of specific, observable behaviors. The class is then informed that they will receive a group-activity reinforcement if they can improve the percentage of time during which all members of the class are obeying all the rules. The students receive feedback about their on-task behavior by means of a clock operated by the teacher. The clock shows a green light whenever the entire class is on task and the clock is recording, and a red light indicates that the clock has stopped because at least one student is violating one of the rules. As the class begins to follow the rules consistently more than 80 percent of the time, the frequency of reinforcement is systematically reduced and the clock light is replaced by a stopwatch. Eventually the reinforcement becomes entirely verbal except for periodic maintenance checks and occasional activity reinforcers associated with a particularly positive check.

Group competition and group rewards have also proved effective in reducing disruptive behavior in a school cafeteria (Sherman, 1973). In this program, rules were established, and each day the class that was judged as following the rules most effectively received praise and had a star placed on a chart posted in the cafeteria. Further reinforcement was provided in the form of a special prize offered each month for the class with the most stars. Teachers on lunchroom duty were asked to ignore inappropriate behavior and praise students who followed the rules. Implementation of this program was followed by immediate reduction in disruptive behavior.

One problem that occasionally arises when implementing a group contract is that one or several students subvert the group's chance for success. When they do so, the teacher might initially implement a Glasser problem-solving discussion in order to help the student acknowledge the situation, decide whether to make a change, and develop a plan. If the student either indicates unwillingness to change or is simply unable to control his or her behavior adequately in response to a group contract, the student can be placed on an individual contract and the class can be informed that his or her behavior will not influence the class's chances of earning a reward. Although this intervention may be necessary, it tends to isolate the student. Therefore, we should periodically discuss the situation with the student with the goal of including the student in the group contract.

A final approach to devising a group contract is to develop the contract during a class meeting. An excellent example of this method occurred when one of our graduate students expressed concern because students in her eighth-grade math class were averaging nearly ten minutes before they were all seated and ready to begin the day's lesson. The teacher's initial idea was to present the students with an offer to take the entire class out for an ice cream cone on Friday if they could be ready to start class within two minutes after the bell rang for five consecutive days. We suggested, however, that students would be more likely to accomplish the goal and might need less reinforcement if they solved the problem themselves. The teacher accepted this logic and decided to present the problem to the class along with a large chart indicating the number of minutes it had taken them to settle down during the past ten days.

Because the teacher was well liked by her students and had demonstrated her competence by coming prepared with a data display, the students acknowledged that a problem existed and decided to solve it. The initial solution offered by a student and enthusiastically supported by the class was simply for everyone to be prepared every day when the bell rang. Fortunately, the teacher realized that this was an overly ambitious goal and informed the class that she would be delighted if the class could be prepared to start two minutes after the bell rang. The class then decided to clearly define the term ''ready to start'' and determined that it meant the entire class (1) being in their seats, (2) having a paper and pencil on their desk, (3) being quiet, and (4) looking at the front of the room. Finally, the class decided to borrow a stopwatch from the physical education department and to allow each member of the class to time the class for one day and mark the results on the large chart the teacher had prepared.

Not surprisingly, the student involvement served as its own reinforcement, and no one suggested any form of extrinsic reward. Results indicated that during the 5 weeks the class marked the chart, they never required more than 1 minute 45 seconds to become prepared for class. Furthermore, followup data collected 2 weeks after students had ceased to mark the chart indicated that this behavior had been maintained.

The effectiveness of this group contract was based on the fact that the solution responded sensitively to students' needs for competence and power while using a problem-solving approach that incorporated the basic components of a sound behavioristic intervention. When teachers are able to integrate these approaches, they will consistently find themselves able to work with their students to develop productive solutions to classroom problems.

CASE STUDY: A CONTRACT WITH A HIGH SCHOOL BAND CLASS An excellent example of a group contract was recently presented by a high school band teacher who used a contract to reduce talking during class. In this incident the students decided that a consequence and reward would help them change their behavior. They agreed to give up 1 minute of the break following band class for every minute they were off task. They also decided that if they could meet the goal of 30 minutes off task in 8 days they would have a buffet luncheon as a reward. Figure 11.16 presents the data associated with this intervention. The data indicate that off-task behavior reduced from 17.2 minutes per class period to 2.88 minutes per period. This teacher also found that when students are presented with the data and asked to be involved in determining the solution, dramatic results can often be obtained.

A Contract for Teaching Student Responsibility

One problem with contracts is that they too often focus on controlling student behavior rather than on helping students develop responsibility. As mentioned earlier, this problem can be minimized by using contracts as step 5 (developing a plan) in Glasser's reality therapy approach. In addition, as presented in the section on group contracts, involving students in developing the contract and monitoring the results can also increase the

FIGURE 11.16 Group Behavior Contract

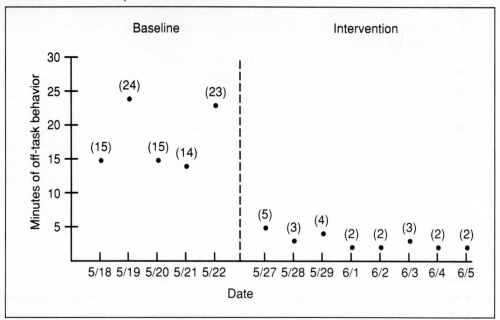

likelihood that students will develop a sense of responsibility while being involved in a contract. Another method for using a contract to control student behavior while simultaneously focusing on student responsibility and an internal locus of control is to develop a contract that uses language related to responsibility. Figure 11.17 presents the form we use for such contracts, complete with an actual example involving an eighth-grade girl. Consistent with the curriculum of responsibility discussed in chapters 1 and 10, this contract helps students realize that they are responsible for their own behavior and that they can control their environment. It also clarifies and specifies the choices they are making and the consequences for these choices.

While we have worked with teachers who use this type of contract, it is most often used in conjunction with a counselor or special education teacher or consultant. The next section presents a model for helping a group of educators develop a specific plan to assist a student who has failed to respond to a teacher's best efforts to implement a variety of proactive and corrective behavior change interventions.

FACILITATING AN EFFECTIVE STAFFING AND DEVELOPING A PERSONALIZED EDUCATION PLAN

Even though current technology provides teachers with a variety of proactive and corrective methods they can implement to help students develop productive behaviors, there are obviously times when teachers need assistance. Chapter 12 provides a sequential systems approach for determining when to involve various individuals in working with a behavior-problem student. This section presents the model we use to develop a specific behavior change plan for students who continue to act irresponsibly despite teachers' efforts to implement many of the methods described in this book.

FIGURE 11.17 Behavior Contract Emphasizing Student Responsibility

Name of Student: ___Suzy Jones_____ Grade: _8th___ *Date:* _____

School: _____Middle School_____ Contract Monitor*: __Mrs. Smith____

Reason for Contract: __Demonstrates difficulty controlling anger with regards to peer__ __interaction__

Student Expectations for Responsible Behavior

1. Follow all classroom and school rules.
2. Expectations requiring additional instructions and clarification.
    A. When angry, Suzy is expected to remain in control by making responsible choices to handle her anger. This applies in the classroom so students can continue working and applies to unstructured time outside the classroom.

Student Choices

Responsible choices
(ways to meet expectations)

A. Ignore situation
B. Remove self from situation
C. Ask for five minutes time out at desk
D. Do deep breathing or relaxation exercises at desk
E. Write down feelings until I can talk the situation over with teacher or counselor

Irresponsible choices
(choosing negative consequences)

A. Not doing work
B. Refusing to continue working
C. Distracting classmates from work
D. Yelling at peers or teachers
E. Running away
F. Fighting

Student Consequences

Consequences for Responsible Behavior
At School:

A. Stay in class
B. Be with friends
C. Learn new things
D. Have a boyfriend
E. Feel good about my ability to control my anger

At Home:

If Suzy chooses to control her anger all week at school, she will earn an extra half-hour on the weekend to have private time with mother.

Consequences for Irresponsible Behavior

A. If the behavior occurs, Suzy will go to the office and fill out a Problem-Solving Worksheet; she must be able to control herself prior to returning to class.

B. If the behavior occurs during unstructured time, she will be expected to sit on the curb until end of free time and then will be expected to go to office to fill out Problem-Solving Sheet.

Contract Monitor agrees to:

1. Consistently apply stated consequences for both responsible and irresponsible behavior.
2. Regularly review contract with student every three weeks.
3. Review contract at staffings as appropriate.

(continued)

FIGURE 11.17 (continued)

> *Contract Termination Criteria:* Contract will be terminated when student consistently makes responsible choices to deal with her anger for a three-week period.
>
> Student Signature: _____ Date: _____
> Contract Monitor Signature: _____ Date: _____
> Parent Signature: _____ Date: _____
>
>   _____
>   *Staff member responsible for contract development, application, and review
>   From Linn-Benton ESD, Abany, Ore. Reprinted with permission.

Like most experienced teachers, we have attended hundreds of staffings. The problem with many of these is that they sound more like soap operas than well-organized attempts to develop specific plans to assist a student. We know family factors influence student behavior; we also believe that school factors have a significant impact and that educators need to place a primary emphasis on school factors. If home factors appear to be a major issue in a particular case, this should be noted and a person can be assigned to contact the school or community agent responsible for coordinating services for families. The staffing can then return to a focus on school variables that can be altered to help the student.

To emphasize the focus on developing a specific plan for the student, we prefer to call staffings Personalized Education Plan (PEP) meetings. The development of such plans can be expedited by using a structured approach to staffings. We have found that an effective process includes these five steps:

1. Focusing on specific student behaviors needing change
2. Determining specific interventions to bring about these changes
3. Assigning responsibility to staff for implementing each intervention
4. Determining the data to be collected for the purpose of assessing the effectiveness of interventions
5. Setting a date to review the program.

We recommend focusing on no more than two behaviors and developing no more than two interventions for each behavior, and in most cases we develop no more than two interventions during any one PEP meeting. Figure 11.18 presents the outline we recommend for facilitating a PEP meeting. To demonstrate a potential outcome of a PEP meeting, Figure 11.18 includes the PEP form completed for the case study presented in the following section. The intervention plan involves five components, three of which have to do with the one topic of clarifying limits and procedures.

CASE STUDY: A DISRUPTIVE HIGH SCHOOL STUDENT

The following example occurred when one of us was asked to assist a high school staff develop a program for a disruptive student. The student had received dozens of office referrals for relatively minor but persistent classroom disruptions and had finally been

FIGURE 11.18 Personalized Education Plan

Behavior to Change	Intervention Plan	Person Responsible	Evaluation Method	Review Date
Disrupting class by talking out, inappropriate comments, and failing to follow responsible teacher requests	1. Provide Randy with a clear statement concerning how teachers will respond to any inappropriate classroom behavior (to follow the sequence in Figure 9.6) 2. Develop a clear sequential set of consequences for inappropriate behaviors that lead to an office referral (to include a problem-solving form) 3. Ensure that Randy understands these new procedures by role playing them and having him write them out 4. Provide more consistent reinforcement for appropriate behavior—this will include phone calls and the use of up slips 5. Provide a weekly opportunity for Randy to monitor and discuss his progress	1. Randy's counselor will inform him of the sequence determined during the PEP staffing 2. Randy's special education agent responsible working with the school vice-principal 3. The counselor will role play for understanding of the new procedures 4. Teachers will provide reinforcement and will provide Randy's special education teacher with a copy of any written reinforcement and a note about any phone calls home 5. Randy will meet weekly with his counselor to discuss his progress	a. Teacher tallies of disruptive classroom behavior b. Data on office referrals c. Percentage of assignments handed in	Two weeks from the initial PEP meeting

383

pulled out of two of his classes. The student was identified under P.L. 94–142 and had serious social cognition deficiencies. He demonstrated limited ability to understand others' perspectives and limited sense of his own efficacy and responsibility and attributed his successes and failures to external factors. He also had few skills in developing specific plans to alter his behavior. Based on observations and interviews with parents, teachers, administrators, counselors, and the student, the following recommendations were made to the school staff to help them respond to this young man more productively. These recommendations highlight the importance of following the ten procedures for effective curtailment of activity. They also reinforce the value of collecting data, examining the learning environment, helping students become responsible for their own behavior, and systematically assessing the effectiveness of a program developed to change a student's behavior.

Recommendations

1. The current and past IEPs available to me did not include any specific educational program that would assist Randy in remediating or circumventing his handicap. The IEP merely listed several obvious goals and an evaluation component to several but not all of the goals. Randy's school history, psychological assessment, and comments from school staff all support my belief that Randy has deficiencies in impulse control, social cognition, judgment, and problem solving. It seems necessary and appropriate that an ongoing program be developed for remediating these deficiencies. A peer counseling group, focusing on social skills and conflict resolution, or at minimum, ongoing counseling, focusing on responsibility and enhancing social cognition, would seem desirable. Additionally, the school's response to Randy's behavior problems should be adjusted so that it consistently serves a behavior change function in light of Randy's handicap. (See items 3 and 5.)

2. The school staff should keep more accurate records of Randy's behavior problems. Available records are possibly acceptable for nonidentified students but are not adequate for making IEP decisions. For example, the vice-principal indicated that during the past semester, Randy had been referred to his office "every other day." His records, however, were kept on a five-by-seven card with no trend analysis made on an ongoing or summative basis. Additionally, I was informed that Randy had been suspended once, yet Randy stated unequivocally that he had not been suspended during the previous term. I believe it is important to have a good record concerning the behavior, the class in which it occurred (and thus time of day), the time during the class (early, middle, or late), the activity in which the class was involved, preceding events, and responses by the teacher. These data can help those involved in writing the IEP determine the environmental factors influencing Randy's behavior.

3. The school should develop a clear, concise policy regarding consequences for office referrals. It appears that most of the behaviors for which Randy is referred fall into the category of minor discipline problems. The student handbook is vague concerning the consequences for these behaviors. There is no indication as to how many referrals result in a Saturday school, suspension, or expulsion. While this policy has the advantage of providing administrative flexibility, it creates a response that can be confusing and countertherapeutic for some students. Last semester Randy spent numerous hours sitting in the office. It is very likely that besides being moderately reinforcing, the lack of clear, precise, predictable consequences was confusing for Randy and was a factor affecting his continued disruptive behavior. Indeed, the vice-principal mentioned that at one point Randy's mother was informed that "Randy would be expelled if he continued to be referred." Randy continued, however, and these consequences did not follow. An expulsion certainly would not have been the correct response given the lack of a systematic program prior to this serious consequence. The point, is, however, that no predetermined guidelines were established and followed.

I recommend that a program be developed that provides Randy with a clear statement that X number of referrals will result in a Saturday school, Y number of Saturday schools will result in the next referral's being a suspension, and Z number of suspensions will mean that the next referral will result in a change of placement. This consistent policy will provide clarity, limits, and structure for Randy—important components in a responsible educational plan for him.

4. Similar to the schoolwide program, teachers should provide Randy with a clear statement about how they will respond to his violations of classroom rules. It is important that this discussion not take place unless Randy begins to develop a pattern of disruptive behavior. At this point, Randy appears to be behaving well in all of his classes. It would be undesirable and unfair to treat him in a manner suggesting that problems are expected. However, if problems arise, Randy should have a clear understanding about how they will be handled. Generally, this should involve making a polite request to stop the behavior. If Randy continues to be disruptive, he should again politely and calmly be informed that further disruptions will mean *he is choosing* to receive an office referral. If he persists, he should be informed that he has chosen a referral.

5. If Randy receives an office referral, he should not be allowed to chat with the vice-principal or sit in the office. Instead, he should be required to complete a worksheet in which he responds to a series of questions such as (1) What did you do? Be specific. Describe *your* behavior, not the behavior of others. (2) Did your behavior violate a classroom rule or disrupt the class? Describe the possible negative effect your behavior might have had on the teacher and other students. (3) Do you believe this behavior needs to be changed? (4) What can you do to help prevent this from happening again? (5) Is there any way the teacher can help you prevent this behavior and have a better class? (6) Will you attempt to follow the suggestions you have made?

Completing such a form will help Randy consider his actions in a concrete way and thus respond to the goals that should be written into his IEP. Randy needs assistance in understanding others' perspectives, taking responsibility for his own behavior, and developing plans to improve his behavior. Consequences for misbehavior should be aimed at teaching these needed skills, not merely making him sit or complete custodial work.

6. Randy needs to receive attention and praise for his positive efforts and performance. At the time of my visit, he had gone 12 days without a referral and had received only one up slip (note indicating improved behavior or achievement). Staff—including the vice-principal, who could serve as a good model for Randy—should be encouraged to provide Randy and his mother with specific statements about Randy's improvement.

7. The change to a 2–1–2–1–2 schedule was a wise decision. Randy begins his day with two academic courses, followed by a study hall, two more courses, lunch, and completes the day with two courses. The only possible problem I envision would be the last period.

8. Randy appears to be influenced by his peers. He admits that much of his acting out involves peers who encourage and reinforce these behaviors. When planning Randy's schedule, an attempt should be made to place him in classes with students who value appropriate behavior. It may be better to err slightly in terms of placing Randy in more challenging courses than to place him in lower courses with more disruptive peers. At this point, however, I would continue on his current schedule. He seems particularly pleased with the quality and sensitivity of his current teachers.

9. Randy should be involved in a weekly monitoring of his academic and behavioral progress in each class. His assessment should be shared and discussed with a counselor with the goal of reinforcing progress and accomplishment and developing plans for dealing with any problems.

ACTIVITIES FOR DEVELOPING SKILL IN DATA COLLECTION AND USING BEHAVIORAL INTERVENTIONS

The following activities can help you improve your skills in data collection and the use of behavioral interventions.

ACTIVITY 11.1 Clearly Defining Students' Behavior

For each of the five adjectives listed in the left-hand column, write three specific observable student behaviors that might be displayed by a student described by the adjective.

General descriptor	Specific behavioral descriptor
Angry	1. 2. 3.
Unmotivated	1. 2. 3.
Hyperactive	1. 2. 3.
Uncooperative	1. 2. 3.
Lacks social skills	1. 2. 3.

ACTIVITY 11.2   Discriminating between Discrete and Continuous Behavior

Determine whether each of the ten behaviors listed is a discrete or continuous behavior. Indicate your choice by placing an *X* under the appropriate word in the right-hand column.

Behavior	*Discrete*	*Continuous*
Example: On-task		X
Sharpens pencil		
Requests to go to the bathroom		
Talks out without raising hand		
Sits with chair tilted backward		
Out-of-seat		
Refuses to obey teacher's request		
Spends time alone on playground		
Scratches arm while sitting at desk		
Hits other children		
Talks to other students during seatwork		

When asked to collect data on students' behavior, teachers frequently state that the advantages of possessing specific data are outweighed by the complexity of collecting them. The only fair way to evaluate the payoffs and costs associated with collecting data is to attempt the procedure. Activity 11.3 offers a systematic approach to taking this step. When evaluating this procedure, keep in mind that, like most skills, data collection becomes easier and less time consuming with practice.

ACTIVITY 11.3   Practicing Data Collection

Select a student whose behavior in your classroom has been disruptive. Write a brief narrative statement about the extent of the student's behavior and its effect on the class.

After completing this statement, write a specific behavioral description of the student's behavior. Categorize this behavior as discrete or continuous and write the appropriate term beside your description.

Choose a method for collecting data on the behavior and collect these data during a minimum of two one-half–hour periods during which the student frequently tends to engage in the undesirable behavior.

Next, choose a student whose behavior is generally not a problem (do not choose a model student but merely an average student with few problems) and collect the same data on this student. If possible, collect the data simultaneously. If you cannot do so, collect the data during a similar activity and at the same time of day.

Record the data on a graph. Use a different color of line or bar for each student so that behaviors can be readily compared.

ACTIVITY 11.3 (continued)

Based on your data, write a brief statement about the problem student's behavior.

Finally, complete these statements:

I learned that . . . .
I was surprised that . . . .
When I compared the first narrative statement to my last statement I found that . . . .
One advantage to collecting data is . . . .

As suggested throughout this book, the only way to determine whether a procedure is effective or fits your teaching style is systematically to implement the method and evaluate the results. Activity 11.4 provides an opportunity to implement a method that deals directly with a specific disruptive student behavior.

ACTIVITY 11.4 Implementing and Assessing a Behavioristic Intervention

Select an individual student's behavior that is detrimental to the student as well as the class. Describe the behavior in behavioral terms, collect baseline data for at least two one-half–hour periods, and graph the results.

Next, select one of the procedures for developing a contract described in this chapter and develop a written contract with the student.

Implement the contract for five days. Collect and record data during all times when the contract is in effect.

At the end of five days, discuss the results with the student and determine whether to (1) continue the contract, (2) alter the contract by requiring improved behavior while reducing the reinforcement or employing a reinforcer lower on the hierarchy, or (3) discontinue the contract.

Finally, complete these statements:

The student's behavior . . . .
At the end of the five days the student said that he or she . . . .
I was surprised that . . . .
I was pleased that . . . .
I was displeased that . . . .
We changed the contract so that it . . . .
The reason for changing the contract was . . . .

SUMMARY

Even though teachers are not responsible for developing a series of sophisticated behavior change interventions, there are a variety of effective, efficient methods teachers can implement in their classroom management and instructional methods that can dramatically influence student behavior. As teachers work with an increasing number of at-risk students, they will benefit from being able to implement a variety of these methods.

Teachers will increasingly be asked to document both student behavior problems and their interventions aimed at altering student behavior. This chapter provides methods for accomplishing this important task. The chapter describes methods for helping students become involved in the data collection process and become more aware of and responsible for their own behavior through self-monitoring. Methods for involving students in setting goals and becoming more aware of the consequences associated with their behavior through the use of contracts have also been explored.

Our experiences and research (Jones, 1986) with teachers who have implemented these methods show that nearly 80 percent find they can use them in their classrooms and that the methods are effective approximately 80 percent of the time. While these teachers realize that the quality of their proactive classroom management and instruction are their major responsibility, they find that using the methods discussed in chapters 10 and 11 can have a major positive impact on individual problem students; this is professionally rewarding and also has a positive impact on the behavior and learning of other students.

RECOMMENDED READING

Alberto, P., & Troutman, A. (1986). *Applied behavior analysis for teachers,* 2nd ed. Columbus, Ohio: Charles E. Merrill.

Algozzine, B. (1987). *Problem behavior management: Educator's resource service.* Rockville, Md.: Aspen.

Axelrod, S. (1983). *Behavior modification for the classroom teacher,* 2nd ed. New York: McGraw-Hill.

Becker, W., Engelmann, S., & Thomas, D. (1975). *Teaching I: Classroom management.* Chicago: Research Press.

Blackham, G., & Silberman, A. (1975). *Modification of child and adolescent behavior.* Belmont, Calif.: Wadsworth.

Camp, B., & Bash, A. (1985). *The think aloud series: Increasing social skills—a problem-solving program for children.* Champaign, Ill.: Research Press.

Canter, L. (1976). *Assertive discipline: A take-charge approach for today's educator.* Los Angeles: Canter.

Cartledge, G., & Milburn, J. (Eds). (1986). *Teaching social skills to children: Innovative approaches.* 2nd ed. New York: Pergamon.

Duke, D., & Meckel, A. (1984). *Teacher's guide to classroom management.* New York: Random House.

Gardner, W., (1977). *Learning and behavior characteristics of exceptional children and youth: A humanistic behavioral approach.* Boston: Allyn and Bacon.

Gloeckler, T., & Simpson, C. (1988). *Exceptional students in regular classrooms.* Mountain View, Calif.: Mayfield.

Goldstein, A. (1988). *The prepare curriculum: Teaching prosocial competencies.* Champaign, Ill.: Research Press.

Goldstein, A., & McGinnis, E. (1988). *The skillstreaming video: How to teach students prosocial skills*. Champaign, Ill.: Research Press.

Hazel, J., & Pederson, C. *Social skills for daily living*. Circle Pines, Minn.: American Guidance Service.

Jackson, N., Jackson, D., & Monroe, C. (1983). *Getting along with others: Teaching social effectiveness to children*. Champaign, Ill.: Research Press.

Jones, V. (1980). *Adolescents with behavior problems: Strategies for teaching, counseling, and parent involvement*. Boston: Allyn and Bacon.

Jones, V., & Jones, L. (1981). *Responsible classroom discipline*. Boston: Allyn and Bacon.

Long, J., & Frey, V. (1977). *Making it till Friday: A guide to successful classroom management*. Princeton, N.J.: Princeton Book.

McCarney, S., & Cummins, K. (1988). *The pre-referral intervention manual: The most common learning and behavior problems encountered in the educational environment*. Columbia, Mo.: Hawthorne Educational Service.

McGinnis, E., & Goldstein, A. (1984). *Skillstreaming the elementary school child: A guide for teaching prosocial skills*. Champaign, Ill.: Research Press.

O'Leary, D., & O'Leary, S. (Eds.). (1977). *Classroom management: The successful use of behavior modification*, 2nd ed. New York: Pergamon Press.

Sloan, H., Buckholdt, D., Jenson, W., & Crandall, J. (1979). *Structured teaching*. Chicago: Research Press.

Spaulding, R., & Spaulding, C. (1982). *Research-based classroom management*. San Jose, Calif.: Maple Press.

Strain, P., Guralnick, M., & Walker, H. (Eds.). (1986). *Children's social behavior*. Orlando, Fl.: Academic Press.

Walker, H. (1979). *The acting-out child: Coping with classroom disruption*. Boston: Allyn and Bacon.

Walker, H., McConnell, S., Holmes, D., Todis, B., Walker, J., & Golden, N. (1987). *The ACCEPTS program: A curriculum for children's effective peer and teacher skills*. Austin, Tex.: Pro-Ed.

Walker, H., Todis, B., Holmes, D., & Horton, G. (1988). *The ACCESS program: Adolescent curriculum for communication and effective social skills*. Austin, Tex.: Pro-Ed.

Wolery, M., Bailey, D., & Sugai, G. (1988). *Effective teaching principles and procedures of applied behavior analysis with exceptional students*. Boston: Allyn and Bacon.

CHAPTER 12

Schoolwide Discipline Programs

Field research we have conducted suggests that educators often fail to consider all the possible control strategies available to them before they decide on a particular course of action. If failure to review alternative strategies characterizes other schools besides the ones we have investigated, it would help explain the contemporary crisis in school discipline and the seeming inability of educators to control dysfunctional behavior. The likelihood of making an effective decision is increased by expanding the number of alternatives that are considered.

/ Daniel L. Duke (1980)
Managing Student Behavior Problems

Teachers need the support provided by a clear, fair, consistent, schoolwide discipline policy. It is the teachers' responsibility to prevent and deal with minor student misbehavior in the classroom effectively, and they must have assistance in dealing with serious or persistent behavior problems. Students need to know that even though they have a right to attend skillfully taught classes, they will not be allowed to disrupt the learning process. School programs for handling discipline must be based on the creation of positive, productive learning environments, and a commitment to helping students develop skills they need to become responsible self-managers.

Factors outside the classroom influence our ability to establish positive learning environments and respond effectively to disruptive student behavior. What we do in classrooms cannot be considered in isolation from the values, norms, climate, and discipline procedures operating within the school at large. Research and theory on schoolwide factors that influence students' behavior have taken several directions. In an effort to determine schoolwide factors that are associated with high student achievement and low rates of disruptive behavior, researchers have compared schools that are more and less effective in attaining desired student outcomes (Edmonds, 1979, 1982; Rutter et al., 1979). Based partially on findings that the quality of administrative leadership is consistently a significant variable affecting school effectiveness, numerous studies have examined the role administrative leadership plays in creating effective schools (Greenfield, 1982; Lightfoot, 1983; Lipsitz, 1984). In addition, considerable research and prescription have focused on the quality of school climate (Anderson, 1982). Finally, work has been generated on the influence associated with developing systematic schoolwide discipline systems (Duke, 1980).

Because this book focuses on classroom-management methods that influence students' behavior within classrooms, we do not examine school organizational factors that influence teachers' and students' attitudes and behavior. Because the study of classroom management involves teachers' skills in responding to disruptive student behavior, however, it is important to consider ways in which teachers can be supported in dealing with extreme or persistent disruptive student behavior. Therefore, in this chapter we examine major concepts and practical methods related to creating this needed support.

A SYSTEMS APPROACH TO MANAGING STUDENT BEHAVIOR

Disruptive students evoke responses in adults that tend to limit their patience and creativity in managing these students. Unlike students with visual impairments or learning disabilities who may evoke empathy, concern, and other sensitive responses, a student who consistently or aggressively acts out often evokes feelings of fear, anger, frustration, and confusion. These feelings are understandably associated with the desire to have the student removed from the setting for which the adult is responsible and to have someone else assume responsibility for the student. However, this response runs counter to the needs of students and fails to comply with the requirement that all students receive the greatest possible amount of educational services in regular education classes.

The passage of P.L. 94–142 placed pressure on schools to provide adequate services for handicapped students. Unfortunately, in many instances, teachers and schools have too hastily referred students for special education services rather than first exploring how the classroom teacher and building staff could be involved in helping improve the student's achievement and behavior. Studies examining the quality of efforts made to assist students prior to referral for a special education evaluation and eligibility decision indicate that schools too seldom provide adequate services before placing students in special education settings (Smith, Frank, & Snider, 1984; Walker, Reavis, Rhode, & Jensen, 1985).

To serve students who experience behavior and learning difficulties and also to provide assistance for teachers who work with these students, it is important to clarify the various roles and responsibilities all educators have in managing student behavior. Likewise, it is imperative that rules and consequences for rule violation be clear and educationally sound. In their study of 50 elementary schools in London, Mortimore and Sammons (1987) found that "Much of the variation among schools in their effects on students' progress and development is accounted for by differences in school policies and practices" (p. 6). In their reanalysis of the High School and Beyond Study, Wehlage and Rutter (1986) found that "marginal students" viewed school discipline policies as ineffective and unfair. A report published by the Northwest Regional Educational Laboratory entitled "Effective Schooling and At-Risk Youth: What the Research Shows" (Druian & Butler, 1987) states a similar finding:

> Finally, it should be noted that one of the strongest criticisms of schools made by dropouts is that the *discipline* is unfair and arbitrary. Successful programs that serve drop-outs are characterized as having fair—though sometimes tough—programs of discipline. The programs clarify what offenses are and what the punishment is. (p. 6)

Our experience in working with school districts to establish a clear, fair system that creates shared responsibility for helping students with behavior problems suggests that this can best be accomplished by creating a systems approach to managing student behavior. Nine major concepts serve as the foundation for effectively implementing a systems approach.

MAJOR CONCEPTS IN DEVELOPING A SYSTEMS APPROACH

Concept 1: School policies for responding to irresponsible student behavior will be most effective when they are supported by clear school-board policies and administrative regulations.

Because a systems approach requires that a variety of individuals be actively involved in assisting students with behavior problems, it is likely to meet with some resistance. Our experience indicates that this model will be dramatically more effective if it receives support and legitimacy from the highest administrative level. For example, a school board or local educational service district can draft policy that supports a systems approach. This central administrative support places principals and other support staff in a more solid and positive position. Instead of being the instigator or supporter of a policy that asks all staff to be responsible for working effectively with behavior problem students, everyone involved is in the position of implementing school-board policy. This will enhance relationships between staff members and between staff and administration—factors shown to be associated with more effective responses to behavior-problem students (Anderson, 1985; Gottfredson & Gottfredson, 1985). The appendix provides an example of a well-designed school-board policy and the associated administrative regulations.

Concept 2: The teacher must initially assess his or her classroom management and instructional methods to determine whether they are consistent with best accepted practice.

As mentioned earlier, Figure 9.10 presents a form for helping teachers assess their use of effective classroom management methods. Teachers also need to determine whether the use of the instructional and motivational methods described in chapters 6 and 7 and particularly the implementation of academic goal setting can have a significant positive impact on student learning and behavior.

Concept 3: The teacher has a responsibility to use behavior change methods aimed at altering students' behavior.

The material in chapters 10 and 11 highlights what we believe are the most effective and practical methods teachers can use to fulfill this obligation. These methods relate directly to the bottom section of Figure 9.10. It is important that teachers keep a record of their efforts in this area.

Concept 4: Teachers need to receive assistance from peers in examining their efforts to help youngsters who persist in their learning and behavioral difficulties.

Because continued student failure, acting out, or withdrawn behavior evoke in teachers feelings of frustration and inadequacy, resources need to be available to assist teachers with these problems. These resources can include (a) inservice opportunities to improve their management or instructional skills; (b) observation by building, district, or contracted professionals to observe the teacher and student and to provide suggestions on how to work more effectively with the student; or (c) the creation of teacher assistance teams that offer a forum for colleagues to provide teachers with ideas for working with students who are experiencing behavior or academic difficulties (Chalfant, 1983; Chalfant, VanDusen Pysh, & Moultrie, 1979). The authors have recently been involved with a number of school districts that have established teacher assistance teams and have found the collegial support to be extremely valuable.

Concept 5: Teachers will be more effective in helping students develop responsible behavior when the school has a clearly written and effectively communicated schoolwide student management system.

The remaining sections of this chapter focus on this component. Research on school organization that influences student behavior has consistently pointed to the importance of clearly stated school rules and consequences for irresponsible behavior. The most effective programs, however, go beyond a focus on controlling students; they attempt to examine the quality of relationships and instruction in the building and the options provided to students experiencing difficulties.

Concept 6: An effective response to students who experience ongoing problems includes a procedure for holding staffings aimed at developing specific plans to assist the student.

Whenever behavior problems persist to the point at which the student has received several office referrals or is uninvolved in the classroom despite all efforts associated with concepts 1 through 5, it is desirable to have a staffing at which teachers meet to develop a specific plan for assisting the youngster in having a more successful school experience. Even though most schools use staffings, they are seldom built into the schoolwide student management plan as a systematic method for intervening to help the student. One way to ensure that staffings occur is to indicate within the schoolwide student management plan the specific stage at which a staffing will be held. Ideally, each staffing will lead to a specific intervention plan involving several school staff. As presented in chapters 10 and 11, we call these plans Personalized Education Plans (PEPs). Unlike an IEP, required for students identified as eligible for special education services, a PEP is not a legal document nor does it involve special education services. However, like IEPs, PEPs are specific plans developed to respond to the unique educational needs of a student.

Concept 7: Outside consultation should be provided when a student continues to have behavioral difficulties despite concepts 1 through 6 being employed.

School staff are often stretched to their limits and may not always be able objectively to assess attempts to help students whose behavior has consistently caused the staff frustration and anger. In addition, even though their concern and efforts may be commendable, school staff may lack skill in developing alternative interventions with students whose behavior is difficult to manage or extremely withdrawn. Because these factors may cause school staff to refer to special education or to exclude students who could function in a regular school environment, assistance should be provided to staff once it has been documented that the staff has followed district guidelines for assisting behavior-problem students.

Assistance can be provided by a variety of sources. District or regional service district school psychologists or behavioral specialists can be asked to review the situation and make recommendations. Our experience suggests that it is usually desirable to have the consultant spend a sizable portion of a school day observing the behavior-problem student in classroom settings. The consultant will also need to examine the student's school file and review PEP plans and the associated data. Finally, it is often useful for the consultant to interview the student. Following this evaluation the consultant can meet with the teachers involved and make recommendations concerning any additional interventions that appear likely to assist the student in improving behavior. The consultant might make suggestions concerning classroom management and instruction, modifications in the schoolwide student management plan, an individualized contract for the student, or additional school counseling services. The consultant may also indicate that the existing program appears to be a well-designed and reasonable response to the student's behavior and may suggest that the staff instigate a referral for special education services.

Concept 8: School personnel will better serve behavior-problem students when procedures are in place for coordinating with community resources.

A significant number of children experience emotional problems and difficulties outside of school that warrant interventions from community agencies. It is important for educators to realize that these at-risk children are viewed differently by schools and community agencies. In general, the term *at-risk* implies the threat of impending negative consequences for a child. Educational definitions of at-risk suggest a student may potentially drop out of a school program entirely. Within community agencies using clinical definitions, the term *at-risk* suggests the potential injury to a child of an emotional or mental nature that would require clinical intervention to remediate. While many students may meet criteria in both groups, there are important distinctions between them that have significant implications. One important difference is that the educational definitions imply educational interventions, whereas clinical definitions imply clinical interventions. It is, therefore, important for educators and social service agency staff to be aware of the variation in definitions and the implications for services.

For example, if educators assume a clinical definition of the term, they may decide that there is little they can do in the way of interventions with the student. In reality, as presented throughout this book, a wide range of preventive and corrective approaches for at-risk students are available to educators that are unavailable if clinical definitions are employed. On the other hand, due to the educational nature of their primary responsibility and the training of their staff, educational institutions have a limited ability to respond to the clinical needs that some students present in the school setting. It is therefore important for school systems to understand and be able to access the community resources that exist for the at-risk student.

A concept designed to respond to the needs of these students and the institutions that serve them is interagency cooperation and collaboration. More specifically, the Youth Service Team (YST) provides a format for promoting more productive services to at-risk students. These teams provide for networking and liaison among schools, social service agencies, law enforcement, the juvenile department, and other community resources. School personnel are often in a prime position to become aware of a variety of student needs that increasingly seem to be beyond the scope of appropriate intervention in the educational system. By staffing students among a variety of agency representatives, information is shared and alternatives can be developed. This process is effective in preventing a duplication of services as well as in identifying children who might otherwise never receive services.

Interagency collaboration and cooperation provide for a more comprehensive view and coordinated planning for at-risk children and their families. They also provide for the appropriate delivery of services and promote a much more responsible model for children who have the greatest need for being held accountable for their actions.

Concept 9: Referral for special education services should be considered when other interventions have failed.

One important benefit of using a systematic continuum of services approach to responding to unproductive student behavior is that if it becomes necessary to refer the student for special education identification, much of the most important groundwork will already have been completed. Research (Smith, Frank, & Snider, 1984) indicates that when making eligibility decisions regarding seriously emotionally disturbed or behavior disordered students, the most frequently missing data involve information on students' actual behavior and interventions that have been implemented to alter the inappropriate behavior. At least seven states currently require that such information be available prior to a student's being identified as behavior disordered or emotionally disturbed. Several other states recommend that this process be followed (Jones & Waksman, 1985). A continuum of services approach ensures that appropriate prior interventions will already have been made. Because this dramatically expedites referrals to special education, it helps alleviate a common teacher concern about the delays in processing such referrals.

SCHOOLWIDE STUDENT MANAGEMENT PLANS

What Are They?

The most widespread response to student behavior problems in this country has been the development of schoolwide plans for managing student behavior (Duke, 1986; Duke & Jones, 1984). In the early 1980s the State Board of Education in New York City required every city school to have a comprehensive disciplinary code listing unacceptable behaviors and the punishments teachers and administrators would administer when these occurred. A 1987 survey conducted for the Center for Educational Statistics showed that 93 percent of teachers in all grade levels stated that their school had a written discipline policy.

Two-thirds of teachers indicated that the policies were strict enough, 72 percent said they were comprehensive enough, and 80 percent said the policies were clear.

> While these differences clearly indicate that teachers viewed their schools' discipline policy more favorably in 1986–87 than they did in 1980, 34 percent of teachers in 1986–87 still regarded their schools' discipline policy as not strict enough; 25 percent regarded the policy as not comprehensive enough; and 50 percent indicated it was not consistently applied. (Ashwick, 1987, p. 7)

Schoolwide student management plans are essential ingredients in effective class-room management. These plans provide students with important clarity and safeguards concerning behavioral expectations and consequences. As mentioned earlier, many students who are doing poorly in school view school discipline policies as ineffective and unfair (Wehlage & Rutter, 1986). Students' attitudes toward school and their behavior can be improved by providing clarity and fairness in schoolwide student management policies (Stedman, 1985). Likewise, teachers must have the support of consequences that occur when students fail to respond to teachers' professionally responsible efforts to ensure acceptable student behavior.

When developing a schoolwide student management plan, it is essential that school personnel frame the plan within the context of a clear philosophy or goal statement. Duke (1986) highlighted an important aspect of a productive goal statement when he commented on the importance of viewing schoolwide student management plans as a method for increasing responsible student behavior rather than as a method for controlling behavior.

> Overemphasis on student control may result in a number of undesirable by-products, ranging from the alienation of responsible students to the preoccupation of teachers with rule enforcement. Clarity about the mission of the school and the purposes of the Student Discipline Plan (SDP) is probably the best precaution against goal displacement. Staff agreement, for example, that the main goal for the SDP is to increase the likelihood of responsible student behavior, rather than minimize the likelihood of irresponsible student behavior, can lead to a significant redirection of energies. (p. 231)

Figure 12.1 provides an example of a middle school philosophy statement that introduces their schoolwide student management plan (SSMP). Notice the focus on assisting students to be responsible as opposed to controlling students.

In addition to a philosophy statement that focuses attention on the positive goals related to student management, an effective schoolwide student management plan has eight operational components (Jones, 1984).

Major Components of an Effective Schoolwide Student Management Program

Component 1: A focus on positive school climate and positive consequences for responsible behavior.

Numerous writers and researchers point to the relationship between students' behavior and the quality of personal relationships in the school environment (Glasser, 1988;

FIGURE 12.1   Student Responsibilities and Rights

Philosophy
School discipline policies and procedures are established to create the best possible safe and healthy environment to promote learning and to protect and develop the physical, social, intellectual, and emotional growth of each student. They specifically limit the opportunity of an individual to interfere with the educational rights of other students, as well as those of the individual. The policies and procedures reflect an understanding of the developmental characteristics of the middle school age students in transition from childhood to adolescence.

   The school will also create an environment to encourage mutual respect and cooperation, while providing opportunities for students to make choices regarding their behavior. We believe that as students mature they will develop more self-direction; the discipline policies and procedures will encourage that development. Each student has dignity, worth, and rights—with these rights also go responsibilities. The students are responsible for their choices and the consequences of their behavior. Thus, the discipline policies and procedures are designed to teach and reinforce behavior that is conducive to learning, living, and working together in a harmonious manner in the school's society.

Source: Stanwood Middle School, Stanwood, Wash.

Purkey & Novak, 1984; Rutter, Maughan, Mortimore, Ouston, & Smith, 1979; Schmuck & Schmuck, 1983). Students who feel safe, accepted, cared for, and involved in school seldom exhibit consistent disruptive behavior. Other studies suggest that students perform more effectively and behave more appropriately in schools that provide reinforcements for positive student behavior (Mortimore & Sammons, 1987; Rutter, 1979). Therefore, schools should consider including statements in their SSMP about the importance of creating a positive school climate. Figure 12.2 presents the statement of consequences for responsible behavior listed in one elementary school's SSMP.

   Because of the high student turnover rate in many schools experiencing significant problems in student management, a positive school climate program should include methods for integrating new students into the school. These methods should include activities for helping new students develop friendships, become familiar with school and classroom expectations and procedures, and learn how to obtain assistance with academic, peer relationship, or other school-related problems.

   Middle schools often facilitate this integration of new students by creating structures to extend the time students remain with a teacher and a group of students. Specifically, middle schools that emphasize the guide or advisory program create a situation in which student problems are expected to be handled by a teacher who has developed a relationship with a group of students. In her summary of four outstanding middle schools, Joan Lipsitz (1984) reinforces this point:

   The relationships students have with adults are important to the comparative calm that is characteristic of these schools. Young adolescents are not ready for the atomistic independence

FIGURE 12.2 Consequences for Responsible Behavior

Appropriate student behavior in the common areas of the school (playground, cafeteria, hallways, and buslines) will be rewarded with positive recognition.

Students will be encouraged to develop positive behaviors through such activities as the following:

1. An honors board recognizing students for positive actions and achievement in such areas as:
   P.E. Library Bus
   Art   Music   Cafeteria
2. Special tokens for responsible and positive actions.
3. Monthly events recognizing responsible behavior.
4. Letters from principal and teachers to parents to recognize positive deeds and achievements.

Each classroom will establish its own system of consequences for responsible behavior within that classroom.

Source: Fairplay Elementary School, Corvallis, Ore.

foisted on them in secondary schools, which is one of the causes of the behavior problems endemic in many junior high schools. (p. 181)

One of us has worked with a middle school of approximately 650 students that does not have a schoolwide discipline policy, has no locks on students' lockers, and yet has high achievement gains and minimal discipline problems. This school is in a middle- and lower-middle-class neighborhood and has only adequate physical facilities. The quality of instruction, teacher-student relationships, and peer relationships facilitated by adults provides the basis for developing a positive school climate in which formal discipline procedures are not needed. The vice-principal uses a problem-solving approach on an individual basis and reports that this approach is consistent with the methods teachers are expected to use before any referral is made. Students are actively involved in instructional activities, frequently evaluate these activities, and are expected to work with their teachers—and with their guide teacher for a more serious or continuing problem—to resolve problems.

One of the authors recently worked with a middle school whose approach to managing student behavior included the creation of a plan to assist at-risk students. Figure 12.3 presents an outline of the activities developed by this creative and committed faculty to create a positive, inviting, supportive school environment for students who struggle to do well in school.

Component 2: A program must place the initial emphasis on the teacher's responsibility for adjusting students' instructional programs and implementing productive classroom management interventions.

As stated throughout this book, teachers make a difference. In addition, teachers now have access to proven methods for effectively intervening in irresponsible student behavior. Therefore, as suggested in the material on a systems approach earlier in this

FIGURE 12.3   Components of the Monroe Middle School At-Risk Plan

---

Philosophy and Goals

At Monroe Middle School we are committed to provide for the success of all students. Failing to meet the needs of any student, by default, is a failure for all. For an increasing number of students, schools and teachers make the difference between their success and failure. These students we define as being *at-risk*.

Providing for the opportunity for all students to succeed is the only way for a school to achieve excellence. To achieve this kind of excellence requires special understanding and extra time and effort with the at-risk student.

To meet our commitment to provide success for our students, we intend to focus on the following goals. These goals are the basis of the programs and activities described in the rest of this plan. Our entire program focuses on meeting the needs of our students, but the specific programs described in this document will be coordinated by our administrators and counselor in such a way as to particularly focus on at-risk students.

1. To improve the self-esteem of all students.
2. To provide a program where students feel a sense of belonging and success.
3. To provide for students' academic success realizing that to do this we must concern ourselves with those social and psychological factors that largely control the ability or readiness to achieve academically.
4. To work with parents in an effort to increase students' success in school.
5. To seek additional time and resources for staff allocation and budgeting.
6. To increase the quality of at-risk students' lives and potential for their futures.
7. To join with the community at large to work for the success of at-risk students.
8. To develop a closely monitored system for coordination of programs within our school community and the community at large for at-risk students.

Selected Program Components

1. Guide groups that include a study skills curriculum, notebook monitoring, community projects, etc.
2. A mentor program that encourages staff to serve as a mentor for a student experiencing ongoing school difficulties.
3. Homework assignments given only on Friday, Tuesday, and Thursday, with teachers being available before school on Monday, Wednesday, and Friday to provide students with assistance on homework.
4. Continuous progress monitoring in math and reading for all students.
5. A peer tutoring program
6. Mini-classes to provide short-term high-interest learning experiences.
7. The use of a "K" grade—"a grade that can be awarded to those students who, in the judgment of the teacher, are working to the best of their

abilities, but have fallen below a grade average of 'C' in a noncontinuous progress class. By awarding a passing grade rather than a 'D' or 'F,' we hope to communicate to the student and parent(s) that we appreciate and applaud the student's sustained efforts to do his/her best work commensurate with his/her ability."

8. Weekly attendance staffings for students absent 5 out of any 20 school days.
9. A variety of incentive and reward programs.
10. An extensive drug and alcohol program.
11. Teachers "shadow" students for a day and report on their perception of how it felt to be a student.
12. Home visits for all incoming sixth graders and all new students.
13. A student "buddy"/guide program for all new students.
14. Followup interviews with new students at the end of the first, second, and sixth weeks and with their parents after the first two weeks.
15. A focus on heterogeneous grouping in all block classes with an emphasis on adjusting assignments to students' ability levels.
16. A 5-day summer day camp for 20 at-risk entering sixth graders to give them a head start on school.
17. Weekly and daily academic and behavior monitoring for students who benefit from this added structure.
18. Team meetings include an agenda item focusing on individual students needing special assistance.
19. An "Attendance Club"—a weekly support group for students experiencing attendance problems.
20. In-school suspension utilized whenever possible in lieu of out-of-building suspension.
21. Extensive home contacts concerning students' positive progress.
22. A parenting class to teach parents basic parenting skills.
23. A home-school liaison staff member
24. Twice yearly parent-student-staff breakfast.
25. Extensive programs for transitioning students from elementary to middle school and from middle school to high school.

Source: James Monroe Middle School, Eugene, Ore.

chapter, it is essential that teachers be expected to implement effective instructional and management methods in their classroom. Many schools have formalized the focus on the teacher's central role by stating this in their SSMP. Figure 12.4 presents an example of such a statement taken from a middle school SSMP. Figure 12.5 presents the form this same school uses to ensure that teachers have documented their interventions prior to referring a student to the office. Figure 12.6 presents a form that a junior high school in which one of the authors worked used to communicate both teachers' and administrators' interventions.

Component 3: A program should emphasize training that provides students and staff with new personal and educational skills.

FIGURE 12.4 Classroom Intervention Procedures

The key to effective discipline is an effective classroom management plan which includes a variety of intervention strategies that help create a good learning environment.

When a student disrupts the learning environment and the teacher feels formal action is needed to correct the inappropriate behavior, the teacher will fill out the *Classroom Intervention Form* and *Intervention #1*. If the behavior continues, the teacher will try another strategy and complete *Intervention #2;* the back copy of the form will be *mailed home.* The teacher will use a third strategy to attempt to modify the student's inappropriate behavior if it has continued and will fill out *Intervention #3*. If the behavior still has not been corrected after three different intervention strategies, the teacher will fill out the *evaluation of intervention attempts section* and send *the top two (2) copies of the form to the office;* the teacher will keep one copy.

Future incidents of this inappropriate behavior will be reported directly to the office by the teacher for administrative action on the appropriate discipline level.

Source: Stanwood Middle School, Stanwood, Wash.

Schoolwide discipline systems too often are focused on developing systematic procedures for monitoring and disciplining students. Instead, discipline should be viewed as a process for teaching students and teachers alternative methods for meeting their personal and intellectual needs. When a school accepts this definition of discipline, its student-management program is focused on training teachers and students in new methods for structuring the learning environment, presenting information, learning, interacting, and solving problems. The emphasis is shifted away from controlling students and toward creating methods that increasingly involve both parties in mutually positive educational and personal experiences in the school setting.

Training for students may include instruction in communication skills, study skills, or problem-solving methods.

As discussed in chapter 2, student misbehavior is almost always related to students' lacking skills for meeting their needs within the school environment. Responses to students' misbehavior should assist students in developing new behaviors that will help them have a more positive school experience. Therefore, students should never merely sit in time-out as a consequence for irresponsible behavior. Instead, they should be involved in examining their behavior and considering options they can implement on returning to the classroom or the next time they are in a situation similar to that in which they misbehaved. Figures 12.7 and 12.8 provide examples of problem-solving forms that can be given to students who receive an office referral.

An excellent example of responding in an educational manner to irresponsible student behavior was recently implemented by an elementary school staff with whom one of the authors worked. A number of students at the school were involved in very aggressive playground behavior. The initial response of the staff was to respond with short-term suspensions for anyone who fought. Unfortunately, this did not appear to reduce the behavior. The staff decided that the misbehavior was likely caused by the students' lack

FIGURE 12.5 Classroom Intervention Form (Stanwood Middle School)

Student Name: _____ Teacher: _____
Subject: _____ Period: _____

The student's behavior has become a concern; specifically, the problem(s) is:
_____
_____

Intervention History
Intervention #1 Date: _____
Description of Intervention Attempted: _____
_____
Student Signature: _____

Intervention #2 Date: _____
Description of Intervention Attempted: _____
_____
Student Signature: _____

*Send back copy to parent after Intervention #2
Intervention #3 Date: _____
Description of Intervention Attempted: _____
_____
Student Signature: _____

Evaluation of Intervention Attempts: _____
_____

Office Referral Date: _____

of skills in playing in a nonaggressive manner. The teachers decided to implement a lunch recess class for students who consistently demonstrated aggressive playground behavior that violated clearly posted playground rules. Students referred for this behavior were assigned to a series of noon detention sessions in which they practiced following playground rules and procedures and received reinforcement for applying these rules in structured play situations. When students received a designated number of points for appropriate behavior, they graduated back to the playground for their lunch recess. Results indicated that student behavior improved dramatically following these sessions.

While it is important to assist students in developing new skills, it is also essential to provide professional development for teachers. Teacher training may involve a review of human development theory and research, new ideas for instructional methods appropriate for the age group, curriculum-evaluation workshops, and new approaches to handling disruptive student behavior. If educational leaders wish to retain the best teachers and increase students' achievement, they must place a high priority on high-quality inservice training. This training should be provided during release time so that teachers view it as

FIGURE 12.6 Student Referral Form

Yellow Copy: Gr. Level Counselor
Pink Copy: Teacher
Gold Copy: Main Office

Student _____ Grade __ Period __ Teacher _____
Describe the specific problem: _____
_____
_____

Step 2
Summary of step two conference with student __ /__ /__ (Date)
_____
_____

Parent contacted __ /__ /__ (Date) at _____ AM or PM
Response _____
_____

Step 3
Referred to administrator on __ /__ /__ (Date)
Administrative action: __ Conference __ Detention __ Paper __ Suspension
__ Parent notified __ Parent conference __ /__ /__ (Date)
_____
_____

Counselor contacts were made on __ /__ /__   __ /__ /__ (Dates)
Summary of counselor contact _____
_____

(Office and staff use only—not a part of student's behavioral or cumulative files)

---

a legitimate aspect of their job. Equally important, this training must actively involve teachers in small groups in which they can share their expertise, generate new methods, and be accountable for reporting the results obtained when implementing new methods. Teaching is a highly demanding profession that requires support, skill improvement, and periodic opportunities to sit back and assess one's work.

Component 4: A program must include clear, concise school rules that are systematically communicated to students, parents, and staff.

Because middle school and high school students are particularly sensitive to such issues as fairness, democracy, and individual rights, an effective program involves these students in developing school rules. Once rules have been established, everyone involved must understand and must have had an opportunity to question and discuss the rules and procedures. Most adults would be angry if they received a ticket for speeding when the speed-limit sign was hidden behind a row of bushes. Likewise, students and parents wish to know what is expected of students. Figure 12.9 lists expectations developed by an elementary school staff.

Component 5: A program should include a clear statement about consequences associated with violating school rules.

Consequences for violating school rules should be communicated to students and parents. Methods of disseminating this information include printing it in a parent-student

FIGURE 12.7 Power of Choice Project

A plan for _____ Date ____ Time ____
           (*student*)

1. What rule or procedure did I break? _____
_____

2. a. What did I choose to do that got me into time out? _____
_____

   b. What else could I have done? _____
_____

3. What should I be doing now instead of being in time-out?
   a. Type of work _____
   b. Place _____

4. What is my plan for getting back to work and improving my school life?
   a. What will I stop doing? _____
   b. What will I start doing? _____
   c. When will I begin? _____

                                                Plan approved by:

_____   _____
        (*student signature*)   (*staff signature*)

handbook, making presentations in classes attended by all students, posting it in prominent places around the school, and discussing the program's components at an evening community meeting. Figure 12.10 presents the sequential consequences used at a middle school where one of the authors was a vice-principal. Figure 12.11 presents a sequence used at an elementary school where one of the authors has consulted.

Component 6: A program must provide a consistent response to students referred by a staff member.

FIGURE 12.8 Problem-Solving Form

This assignment is designed to help *you* be in control of your own behavior and to decide what you can do to make school a better place for you.
What did *you* do to earn this assignment? _____
_____

Did this behavior violate a classroom or school rule? ____   ____
                                                     yes   *no*

If you violated a rule, which one? _____
What problems did your behavior cause for a teacher or for other students?
_____

What could you choose to do next time so you would not break a rule or create a problem? _____
_____

What do you need changed here at school so you can keep from repeating this problem and enjoy school more? _____
_____

FIGURE 12.9 Expectations

Goal

In order to work toward becoming productive citizens at school and in their future lives, students must:

1. Learn to make appropriate choices.
2. Learn to be in control of their behaviors.

Responsibilities

At all times and in all parts of the school students are expected to:

1. Respect the rights and property of others.
2. Follow directions from those in charge.
3. Keep hands, feet, and objects to selves.
4. Use polite language.

On the playground
1. Use all equipment in the proper manner. (Guidelines for safe and proper use of equipment will be posted.)
2. Stay in designated play areas.
3. Play in a safe manner.
4. Use passes for drinking fountain and restroom use.

In the cafeteria
1. Enter and wait in line quietly.
2. Use acceptable table manners. (Guidelines for acceptable manners will be posted.)
3. Wait quietly to be excused.
4. Leave through proper exit.

At arrival and dismissal
1. Arrive no sooner than 8:00 A.M. (noon for P.M. Kg students)
2. Leave promptly at 2:40 P.M. (10:40 for A.M. Kg students)
3. Walk to, wait for, and board buses quietly.
4. Walk bicycles on the blacktop and past bus lines.
5. Wait for parents on the sidewalk.
6. Act responsibly when walking to and from school.
7. Follow bus rules on the bus and at bus stops.

In the hallways
1. Walk quietly, keeping hands and feet to selves.
2. Carry passes in the hallway during morning and noon breaks.

In classrooms
1. Follow classroom expectations

Source: Fairplay Elementary School, Corvallis, Ore.

FIGURE 12.10 Secondary Schoolwide Student Management Consequence Sequence

Step 1: The teacher informs the student that the behavior is against a classroom rule and requests that the student follow agreed upon rules.

Step 2: The teacher meets with the student to discuss the behavior problem and assist the student in developing a plan for altering his/her behavior.
  a. The teacher may also refer the student to a counselor or other appropriate school personnel such as the guide teacher.
  b. The teacher can use classroom detention.
  The teacher must keep a record of the plan developed during this step.

Step 3: *(1st office referral)* The teacher sends the student to the office with (if possible) a completed referral form. If the referral form is to follow, the teacher sends a brief note with the student or calls the office.
  a. The teacher completes the referral form before 4:00 P.M. that day.
  b. The administrator will give feedback to the staff member within 24 hours of the referral.
  Administrative action: The administrator will meet with the student and assign
  a. An administrative detention
  b. A problem-solving form
  c. Some form of restitution activity (such as clean-up) if appropriate
  d. Notify the parent (by phone and in writing) of the incident, the consequence, and the next step in the consequence sequence.

Step 4: *(2nd referral)* Any behavior warranting a second office referral within four weeks of the previous referral (whether from the same or a different teacher or for the same or a different behavior) will result in the following administrative action:
  a. A repeat of Step 3 actions.
  b. At any step when the referral represents a second referral by a teacher, the administrator will be responsible for arranging a conference with the referring teacher and the student.

Step 5: *(3rd referral)* A referral within four weeks of the previous referral will lead to the following administrative action:
  a. Assignment of a 1/2-day in-building suspension.
  b. A telephone conference with the parent(s) and a followup letter stating the consequence associated with another referral within four weeks.
  c. A problem-solving plan.

Step 6: *(4th referral)* Another referral within four weeks of the previous referral will lead to the following administrative action:
  a. Assignment of a 1-day in-building suspension.
  b. A personal conference with the parent if possible and a followup letter stating the consequence associated with another referral within four weeks.
  c. A problem-solving form.
  d. Convening a staffing to devise a personalized education plan (PEP) to provide interventions aimed at assisting the student in developing the skills needed to succeed in the school setting.

(continued)

FIGURE 12.10 (continued)

Step 7: (5th referral) Another referral within four weeks of the previous referral will lead to the following administrative action:
    a. Assignment of a 3-day in-building suspension.
    b. Conference (in person or on the telephone) with the student's parent(s) and a followup letter stating the consequence associated with another referral within four weeks.
    c. A problem-solving form.

Step 8: (6th referral) Another referral within four weeks of the previous referral will lead to the following administrative action:
    a. Assignment of a 1-day out-of-building suspension.
    b. Conference (in person or on the telephone) with the student's parent(s) and a followup letter stating the consequence associated with another referral within four weeks.
    c. Require that a problem-solving form be completed prior to the student's being allowed to return to school.
    d. Reconvene the staffing to examine the personalized education plan developed for the student.

Step 9: (7th referral) Another referral within four weeks of the previous referral will lead to the following administrative action:
    a. Assignment of a 3-day out-of-building suspension.
    b. Conference (in person) with the student's parent(s) and a followup letter stating the consequence associated with another referral within four weeks.
    c. Require that a problem-solving form be completed prior to the student's being allowed to return to school.
    d. Discuss the case with the building special education teacher to determine whether the situation warrants consideration for referral to special education.

Step 10: (8th referral) Another referral within four weeks of the previous referral will lead to the following administrative action:
    a. Assignment of a 5-day out-of-building suspension.
    b. Conference (in person) with the student's parent(s) and a followup letter stating the consequence associated with another referral within four weeks.
    c. Require that a problem-solving form be completed prior to the student's being allowed to return to school.
    d. Inform the parents that the next student referral within a four-week period will lead to the student's being recommended for expulsion from the school setting for the remainder of the academic semester.

Step 11: (9th referral) Another referral within four weeks of the previous referral will lead to the following administrative action:
    a. Recommendation for expulsion from school for the remainder of the academic semester.

Each time a student goes four weeks without a referral, he/she moves one step back on the consequence sequence. Therefore, if a student at Step 6 had gone eight weeks without a referral and then received an office referral, he or she would be at Step 4 in the sequence.

FIGURE 12.11 Elementary School Discipline Policy

I. *Teacher Level* (consequences for inappropriate student behavior)

Step 1 Teacher/student conference to discuss inappropriate behavior and message, "not again." Staff member tells expected behavior, listens to student's side of the story, and comes to agreement that expected behavior will be followed.

Step 2 Step 1 procedure plus implementation of a problem-solving plan.

Step 3 Parent contact and implementation of a problem-solving plan.

Step 4 Step 1 plus teacher completes environmental analysis form and makes one change in student's instructional program and one other intervention.

II. *Principal Level* (to be used after the above four steps **if** teacher wants assistance for student misconduct and for immediate situations where the student poses immediate and continuing danger to self or others or substantial disruption of program)

Step 1 Principal/student conference.

Step 2 Step 1 plus a noon detention with written problem-solving assignment. The completed paper will be taken to teacher and home for signature.

Step 3 Steps 1 and 2 plus a parent conference; phone or in person.

Step 4 Steps 1–3 plus a staffing.

Step 5 Steps 1–3 including a fourth noon detention.

Step 6 Step 5 including a fifth noon detention.

Step 7 One-day out-of-school suspension.

A discipline program must place a premium on fairness and consistency. Most students are willing to accept a system in which reasonable rules that facilitate learning apply equally to all individuals. Consistency also meets our need to have clear support in matters involving students' misbehavior. Teachers' morale and willingness to be productively involved in working with misbehaving students are strongly influenced by the clarity, consistency, and quality of the support they receive in dealing with consistent or serious student misbehavior. Therefore, an effective program includes written referrals from the teacher followed by written feedback from the administrator or staff member responsible for handling the referral. The response should verify that the situation was handled according to the designated procedure and inform teachers of additional methods being used to assist the student or potential sources of assistance for helping us work with the student.

A program will not work effectively if individuals responsible for dealing with consistent or serious misbehavior do not feel comfortable with the approach they must use. Both teachers and students will become confused or angered if students referred for serious misbehavior are not dealt with skillfully within the expectations created by the school's discipline procedures. When a program is being developed, staff, students, and the administration must work together to design a program that is acceptable to all.

Component 7: A program should include a systematic procedure for involving parents in working with the school to alter their child's behavior.

Parents are extremely important to young people and play a significant role in influencing their behavior (Norman & Harris, 1981; Streit, 1980). To no one's surprise, studies show that parents can have a major positive influence on their children's school behavior (Jones, 1980; Walker, 1979). Therefore, an effective schoolwide discipline system that includes a component for dealing with continual or serious student misbehavior must involve parents in a consistent, predetermined manner that has been clearly articulated to staff, students, and parents. The type of parental involvement requested will differ depending on such factors as the student's age and the community in which the school is located.

Component 8: A program should be periodically evaluated by collecting and analyzing data related to key outcome variables.

School personnel too often spend time and money developing and implementing new procedures yet forget to assess the results. A schoolwide discipline program should be aimed at altering specific student behavior, and data are needed to assess program effectiveness. Data for evaluative purposes should consist primarily of repeated samples of the initial data. Dan Duke (1980) suggests that schools might collect these types of data:

1. Average daily attendance;
2. Average daily illegal absenteeism;
3. Average daily referrals to office;
4. Annual number of suspensions and breakdown according to reason;
5. Breakdown of number and type of student behavior problems;
6. Along with above breakdowns, data on race/ethnicity of students (to determine if a disproportionate number of certain groups of students are being suspended or reported for rule-breaking);
7. Breakdown of punishments applied to students and rate of repeated offenses;
8. Estimates by administrators, counselors, and teachers of time per day spent on discipline-related matters;
9. Breakdown of student behavior problems in special programs (i.e., alternative schools, continuation schools, etc.);
10. Sources of referrals to the office;
11. Comparative data on school discipline from (a) previous years and (b) nearby schools;
12. Number of student behavior problems occurring "in class" and "out of class" (before school, between classes, cafeteria, after school);
13. Number of students in disciplinary difficulty who transferred into the school after regular fall registration. (pp. 68–69)

POPULAR SCHOOLWIDE STUDENT MANAGEMENT PROGRAMS

Perhaps the two most widely implemented approaches to schoolwide student management (discipline) have been Assertive Discipline and Reality Therapy. The following sections briefly discuss these approaches and evaluate them in light of current research and the concepts developed in this book.

FIGURE 12.12 Glasser's Ten Steps to Discipline

1. What have I been doing when Johnny misbehaves?
2. Resolved: that whatever I've been doing I'm going to stop doing it.
3. Make at least one positive contact a day with the problem student.
4. Tell the student to stop his inappropriate behavior. Use variety and humor.
5. What are you doing? Is it against the rules?
   a. If you get no response, then you have to tell him what you saw him doing.
   b. If he doesn't answer the question, you have to answer it for him.
6. We've got to talk this over—develop a plan.
7. Teacher establishes a place where the student can go to develop the plan.
8. School establishes a place and a person to assist students who cannot develop a plan while in the classroom.
9. Send him home.
10. Referral to a community agency.

Glasser's Reality Therapy Approach to School Discipline

Glasser (1977) expanded his seven steps to Reality Therapy into a ten-step approach to school discipline (Figure 12.12). This approach incorporates the major aspects of Reality Therapy while providing school personnel with a systematic, hierarchic series of responses to student misbehavior.

The procedure for implementing Glasser's model on a schoolwide basis is quite simple. The entire staff is introduced to this approach and is asked to agree to use the model as the primary method for handling discipline. The staff then develops a form for recording plans made with students. This form not only encourages a uniform approach to problem solving but also allows plans to be clearly communicated.

An important aspect of implementing Glasser's model on a schoolwide basis is that if a student refuses to develop a plan or if several plans have failed, the student is sent to the principal's office to work out a plan. Because a record is kept of every plan, the principal knows what plans have failed. This information aids the principal in helping the student devise a successful plan. The principal keeps a copy of the plan he or she makes with the student, gives the student a copy, and has the student take a copy to the teacher. Students are informed that, should the plan they make with the principal fail, the principal will schedule a conference with the student and his or her parents and teacher to discuss the problem. This approach provides the principal with a positive role in handling discipline problems. School staffs with whom we have worked to develop such a program indicate that this procedure reduces acting-out behavior and is well received by parents.

Behavior problems on the playground are frequently a major concern of elementary and middle schools with whom we work. It is surprising how many of these schools use time out on a bench or against a wall as the disciplinary response for irresponsible playground behavior. The obvious problem with this response is that it does not help students develop skills for playing more positively. We have found it easy to help teachers and aides develop skills in using Glasser's problem-solving method (see chapter 10) on the playground. Students are informed that should they choose to violate a playground rule, they must sit in a designated area until they can responsibly work through the problem-solving approach and commit to a plan. When they are ready, they signal an adult who listens to them indicate what they did, the impact it had on other people, and the plan they have devised. Once the student commits to a plan, he or she returns to the playground. Students who have repeated problems can, as part of the schoolwide student management program, be sent to the office to develop a plan.

Assertive Discipline as a Schoolwide Procedure

Assertive Discipline was developed in the mid-1970s as a method for providing teachers with classroom control. In this system the teacher states nonnegotiable rules to students and informs them that violation of these rules will result in clear, negative consequences. When a student disobeys a rule, his or her name is written on the board. If the student misbehaves again, a check is placed behind the student's name, indicating that he or she must stay after school for 15 minutes. A second check means 30 minutes after school. A third check means 30 minutes after school and a call home. A fourth check involves removal from the room and a visit to a building administrator. In cases of serious misconduct, a *severe clause* is invoked and the student goes immediately to the office (Canter, 1976). Rewards for appropriate student behavior are also encouraged. The teacher might put a marble in a jar whenever he or she observes the entire class on task. When the jar is filled, the class receives a special activity as a reward.

Assertive Discipline has been used widely nationwide. It appeals to many teachers because it is easily implemented and places the teacher clearly in control. Administrators have supported the program because it requires minimal teacher training and provides a format that can be readily implemented by an entire staff.

We have worked with several large school districts and hundreds of teachers who have implemented Assertive Discipline. Though the approach was initially well received, these districts have moved away from it. Many teachers are frustrated because problem students seem to be relatively unaffected by the procedures, and students who do not need such repressive methods tend to find the method insulting or anxiety provoking. Our own concern is that too frequently the method creates a "sit down, shut up, or get out" philosophy in classrooms in which teaching methods are failing to meet students' basic personal and academic needs. Too often teachers use the Assertive Discipline procedures rather than examining their own teaching methods to consider how to prevent disruptive behavior. This issue is outlined by Sloane, Buckholdt, Jenson, and Crandall (1979) in discussing the use of token economies and similar behavioristic interventions:

> For relatively typical students the existence of problems suggests some failure in the current teaching procedures that can be remedied by the use of social reinforcement . . . the design of teaching tasks . . . or the pacing, planning, scheduling, or manner of presentation. . . . Inadequate diagnosis and prescription . . . may need attention. Adding a powerful reinforcement system may prevent the teacher from correcting these kinds of basic teaching deficiencies. Student gains are unlikely to be as great as they would be if other problems are first corrected. (p. 209)

Perhaps most important, we strongly agree with researcher Robert Spaulding:

A classroom management scheme that relies on strict teacher direction and a high degree of structure deprives reliable and responsible students of opportunities to learn self-management and problem-solving skills and to exercise their creativity and initiative. (Spaulding, 1983, p. 48)

Fortunately, with the increased emphasis on effective schools, effective teaching, and the teacher as a professionally informed decision maker, districts have begun providing teachers with more effective instructional and group-management methods rather than with behavior-control strategies.

Effects of Implementing Assertive Discipline or Reality Therapy

The most systematic analysis of the effectiveness of popular, packaged classroom management and school discipline approaches was presented by Emmer and Aussiker (1987). They used as a data source a review of articles and reports obtained from ERIC, Dissertation Abstracts, and the School Practices Information File. In addition, they sent letters to 1,200 school districts in the U.S. and Canada. They also sent requests for information to the developers of the studies they examined (including Canter and Glasser). They obtained data on 11 studies on Reality Therapy and 14 studies on Assertive Discipline. Emmer and Aussiker note that the methodology in most studies was very weak and in most cases failed to use control groups or to separate the implementation of the discipline program from other school variables. Keeping in mind the problems associated with generalizing from inadequately designed studies, the authors make the following summaries:

In summary, many of the studies of Reality Therapy that assessed effects on student variables had at least one student outcome variable that differed significantly for the experimental and control groups or from pre to post assessment. (p. 13)

In summary, studies of Assertive Discipline show consistent evidence of effects on *teachers'* perceptions of various aspects of discipline, including reduced problem behaviors. However, the evidence suggests only a small effect on teacher behavior itself. Evidence for effects on *student* behavior and attitudes is *not* supportive of AD training; that is, many more studies found no effects, or mixed and negative effects, than found that AD training resulted in improved student behavior and attitudes. (pp. 15, 16; emphasis in the original)

This statement about the ineffectiveness of Assertive Discipline was recently supported in an analysis of current data on this approach (Render, Padilla, & Krank, 1989). These authors examined all available studies "in which information was gathered in some systematic way" (p. 72). In the 16 studies they found, they were surprised to note that "not one study systematically investigated the program's effectiveness compared with any other specific approach" (p. 72). They concluded that "the claims made by Canter . . . are simply not supported by the existing and available research. . . . We found no evidence that Assertive Discipline is an effective approach deserving schoolwide or districtwide adoption" (p. 72).

Some writers (McCormack, 1989) suggest that the real issue is that practitioners believe Assertive Discipline is helpful; this can be said for any training. In addition, such claims fail to consider that many teachers and districts have become frustrated with the approach, finding that it did not meet their needs or the needs of their students. In the final analysis, we hope educators base their decisions on sound educational theory and on the best available research. The best research seems to indicate no support for Assertive Discipline, and our analysis of research on human motivation suggests that the model is theoretically unsound. We concur with Curwin and Mendler (1989):

> We see Assertive Discipline as little more than an attractive, well-marketed behavior mod- ification program in which one person (teacher or administrator) has all the power to define the rules while offering group and individual rewards for compliance. . . . Assertive Disci- pline does not address the known relationships between discipline and teaching, discipline and motivation, or discipline and stress. . . .
> His program implicitly sees students as the cause of all problems, so there are not demands on anybody else in the system to change. (p. 83)

These findings support our own observations in schools that have implemented one of these approaches. Our major concern is that school staff need to consider their goals carefully in establishing a schoolwide student management program and to develop strat- egies congruent with these goals. Our concern with Assertive Discipline is that it places the teacher control of students as a central goal with no focus on methods for improving the quality of instruction, personal relationships, or students' learning new behaviors. This approach runs counter to virtually everything we know about effectively responding to problematic student behavior.

As suggested in chapter 10, we strongly support Glasser's Reality Therapy approach to responding to unproductive student behavior. Obviously, however, as Glasser noted many years ago in *Schools without Failure* and has consistently stated in his work with school personnel, this approach must be part of a larger attempt to make schools good places for students to learn.

SUMMARY

Schoolwide student management is an important issue in many if not most schools. Students make better choices and take greater responsibility for their own behavior in schools that possess a systematic, clear, effectively communicated system for responding to inappropriate student behavior. Likewise, because a teacher's primary role is to provide excellent instruction, teachers need the support of a schoolwide student management system that removes and provides educational interventions for students who continue to disrupt classes when teachers have responsibly instructed and managed the class.

Unfortunately, schools have too often looked for and accepted simplistic, often unproven solutions for responding to unproductive student behavior. This chapter outlines the major components to a systems approach for involving a variety of school staff in accepting their responsibility for responding to disruptive student behavior. In addition, the chapter outlines and presents examples of the major components in an effective schoolwide student management (discipline) plan.

RECOMMENDED READING

Duke, D. (1980). *Managing student behavior problems*. Alexandria, Va.: Association for Supervision and Curriculum Development.

Duke, D. (1986). School discipline plans and the quest for order in American schools. In D. Tattum (Ed.), *Management of disruptive pupil behaviour in schools*. New York: John Wiley & Sons.

Emmer, E., & Aussiker, A. (1987, April). *School and classroom discipline programs: How well do they work?* Paper presented at the annual meeting of the American Educational Research Association, Washington, D.C.

Garden, J., Zins, J., & Curtis, M. (Eds). (1988). *Alternative educational delivery systems*. Washington, D.C.: National Association of School Psychologists.

Jones, V. (1984). An administrator's guide to developing and evaluating a building-wide discipline program. *National Association of Secondary School Principals Bulletin, 68,* 60–73.

Greater Albany Public Schools— Board Policies

PUPIL PERSONNEL

5200: Student Discipline

The Greater Albany Public School District recognizes its responsibility to students to provide a climate for their education which contributes to the orderly pursuit of learning. It also recognizes that all persons involved with the schools carry a responsibility to contribute to establishing and maintaining that orderly climate. There has been, however, a running debate regarding the students' role in maintaining discipline in schools. We believe the students' role is to fully contribute to the maintenance of the safe and orderly climate which is so necessary if all are to profit from the high quality education opportunities of our schools.

Establishing the disciplined educational climate requires also that we achieve the proper balance between protection of the teachers' right to teach and the students' right to learn how to correct their unproductive and inappropriate behavior under the guidance of caring school staff and parents. Teachers' rights to teach also encompass parents' rights to expect their children to be taught in a safe and encouraging environment. It also includes the students' rights to have their learning not disrupted by other students' inappropriate behavior.

Because teachers must deal most frequently and most directly with student behavior, they must plan to meet that part of their responsibilities. Teachers will continue to be the first to become aware when an imbalance occurs between their right to teach and the

---

Source: Greater Albany Public Schools: Albany, Oregon.

students' right to learn to correct inappropriate behavior. If this moment comes to the teacher's attention without forethought, there is a tendency to balance extreme student behavior with extreme teacher behavior. Pre-planning helps avoid extreme responses.

The growing emphasis on settling differences through the court system makes it increasingly necessary that the expectations we have for student behavior be made clear. The question "What behavior is expected of students?" must be answered in a way that recognizes students' right to learn how to correct inappropriate behavior.

Those experienced with dealing with student discipline issues have been able to extract some principles of prevention from their case studies. Those principles include:

1. Sharing behavior expectations with students and the reasons for those expectations. This includes sharing an understanding of why the expectations are reasonable.
2. Involved adults consistently applying a student behavior management procedure.
3. Communication of the consequences of inappropriate behavior.
4. Adjusting students' instructional programs to the appropriate level of difficulty whenever possible.
5. Maintaining a positive classroom climate and modeling positive peer and teacher-student relationships.
6. Providing positive reinforcement for appropriate behavior and negative/positive reinforcement for inappropriate behavior.
7. Developing a cooperative working relationship among the classroom teachers, school principal and parents to enable consistency throughout a young person's day.

The goal sought through use of these principles is that students will learn to make appropriate choices and develop the self-discipline necessary for independence beyond imposed authority. It is also incumbent upon the school district to protect the rights of all involved in disciplinary action to protect the students' constitutional rights. It must be remembered that students learn responsible behavior through practice.

Parents and students are expected to recognize their responsibilities and legal obligations in observing the attendance requirements and in adherence to the rules and regulations of the District and its schools. School/parent joint responsibility for appropriate behavior is outlined below:

AR 5200-A-1: Procedures for Student Behavior Management Program

The following progression of steps is to be used in Albany schools as Student Behavior Management Programs are developed and implemented. Under extreme conditions, however, the concern for safety understandably overrides these procedures.

At the beginning of each school year, all classroom teachers will develop, post in their rooms and teach their students the classroom rules for behavior they expect students under their supervision to follow. Since students are learning, rules for behavior are to be taught and reviewed in appropriate settings so students have the opportunity to learn them. The classroom behavior management program should stress positive student behavior.

Rules for behavior will be approved by the building principal to assure consistency with building and district behavior management plans.

The teacher's student management program should include the instructional and classroom management methods teachers will use in dealing with both appropriate and inappropriate student behavior. It is imperative that the teacher's classroom management methods be implemented early in the corrective process and before calling upon resources available beyond the teacher/classroom.

If, after a sufficient time period, the classroom teacher's corrective classroom methods are deemed insufficient to correct a problem, the counsel of other teachers, counselor and the principal within the building should be sought.

If the corrective methods are deemed insufficient after implementation of consultation advice by the classroom teacher and the principal, the student would be referred for the building-level student behavior management program and the principal would appoint a case worker.

At the beginning of each school year principals will review the building-level student behavior management plan with teachers, students and parents. The building-level student behavior management plan will be the vehicle through which corrective instruction can be provided to students referred from the classroom and through which the teachers' rights to teach will be supported. This plan is to be provided in writing to staff, students and parents. Appropriate reviews with these persons would be in order and records kept of reviews. The management plan should emphasize positive student behaviors.

> It is imperative that building-level intervention procedures be implemented before calling upon district support services for more than consultation.

If, after implementation and a sufficient trial period, it is felt that building-level corrective methods are deemed insufficient to correct a problem, the building principal should arrange for district consultation resources.

If, after consultation with district-level staff, implementation of consultation advice and a reasonable time period, it is felt that the methods applied at the building level are insufficient to correct the behavior *and the behavior is considered to be one which might lead to special education placement rather than further disciplinary action,* the building principal will follow the district's referral process to obtain assistance from the evaluation center. Upon completion of the evaluation a multi-disciplinary staff team composed of a building administrator or designee, involved teachers and a representative from the evaluation center will determine the eligibility of a student for placement in a special education program. If eligible for special education, the multi-disciplinary staff team would develop an I.E.P. and determine placement and programming. The building-level special education staff will provide and coordinate the service.

If the complete evaluation indicated in the preceding paragraph results in a recommendation of placement in a building-level special education program, placement proceeds. If the recommendation is for placement in a self-contained program, the recommendations from the evaluation center staff shall be reviewed with the Special Programs Coordinator.

If the student is placed in a self-contained program and after implementation and a sufficient trial period it appears that the placement is not appropriate, alternative placements shall be considered.

Bibliography

Adams, R., & Biddle, B. (1970). *Realities of teaching: Explorations with videotape*. New York: Holt, Rinehart and Winston.

Aikin, M. (1942). *The story of the eight-year study, Vol. 1.* New York: Harper and Row.

Akita, J., & Mooney, C. (1982). *Natural helpers: A peer support program.* Seattle, Wash.: Roberts and Associates.

Alberto, P., & Troutman, A. (1986). *Applied behavior analysis for teachers: Influencing student performance,* 2nd ed. Columbus, Ohio: Charles E. Merrill.

Alexander, C., & Campbell, E. (1964). Peer influences on adolescent aspirations and attainments. *American Sociological Review, 29,* 568–575.

Anderson, C. (1982). The search for school climate: A review of the research. *Review of Educational Research, 52,* 368–420.

Anderson, C. (1985). The investigation of school climate. In G. Austin & H. Garber (Eds.), *Research on exemplary schools.* New York: Academic Press.

Anderson, L. (1981, April). *Student responses to seatwork: Implications for the study of students' cognitive processing.* Paper presented at the annual meeting of the American Educational Research Association, Los Angeles.

Anderson, L., Brubaker, N., Alleman-Brooks, J., & Duffy, G. (1984). *Making seatwork work.* (Research Series No. 142). East Lansing: Michigan State University, Institute for Research on Training.

Anderson, L., Evertson, C., & Brophy, J. (1979). An experimental study of effective teaching in first grade reading groups. *Elementary School Journal, 79,* 193–223.

Anderson, L., & Prawat, R. (1983). Responsibility in the classroom: A synthesis of research on teaching self-control. *Educational Leadership, 12,* 62–66.

Andrews, G., & Debus, R. (1978). Persistence and the causal perception of failure: Modifying cognitive attributions. *Journal of Educational Psychology, 70,* 154–166.

Angus, M. J., Evans, K. W., & Parkin, B. (1975). *An observational study of selected pupil and teacher behavior in open plan and conventional design classrooms.* Australian Open Area Project (Tech. Rep. No. 4). Perth: Educational Department of Western Australia.

Arends, R. (1982). Beginning teachers as learners. *Journal of Educational Research, 76,* 235–242.

Arlin, M. (1979). Teacher transitions can disrupt time flow in classrooms. *American Educational Research Journal, 16,* 42–56.

Aronson, E., Blaney, N., Stephan, C., Sikes, J., & Snapp, M. (1978). *The jigsaw classroom.* Beverly Hills, Calif.: Sage.

Artley, A. (1981). Individual differences and reading instruction. *Elementary School Journal, 82,* 143–151.

Asher, S., & Markell, R. (1974). Sex differences in comprehension of high- and low-interest reading material. *Journal of Educational Psychology, 66,* 680–687.

Ashwick, H. (1987, April). Public school teacher perspectives on school discipline. *OERI Bulletin.* Washington, D.C.: U.S. Department of Education, Office of Educational Research and Improvement.

Aspy, D. (1969). The effect of teacher-offered conditions of empathy, congruence, and positive regard upon student achievement. *Florida Journal of Educational Research, 11,* 39–48.

Aspy, D. (1972). Reaction to Carkhuff's articles. *Counseling Psychologist, 3,* 35–41.

Aspy, D., & Buhler, J. (1975). The effect of teachers' inferred self-concept upon student achievement. *Journal of Educational Research, 47,* 386–389.

Aspy, D., & Roebuck, R. (1977). *Kids don't learn from people they don't like.* Amherst, Mass.: Human Resource Development Press.

Ausubel, D. (1968). *Educational psychology: A cognitive view.* New York: Holt, Rinehart and Winston.

Axline, V. (1947). *Play therapy.* Boston: Houghton Mifflin.

Bailey, R., & Kackley, J. (1980). *Positive alternatives to student suspensions: An overview*. St. Petersburg, Fla.: Pupil Personnel Services Demonstration Project, 1015 10th Ave. N.

Bandura, A. (1969). *Principles of behavior modification*. New York: Holt, Rinehart and Winston.

Bandura, A. (1977). *Social learning theory*. Englewood Cliffs, N.J.: Prentice-Hall.

Bandura, A. (1982). Self-efficacy mechanism in human agency. *American Psychologist, 37*, 122–147.

Bandura, A., & Schunk, D. (1981). Cultivating competence, self-efficacy, and intrinsic interest through proximal self-motivation. *Journal of Personality and Social Psychology, 41*, 586–598.

Barrish, H., Saunders, M., & Wolf, M. (1969). Good behavior game: Effects of individual contingencies for group consequences on disruptive behavior in a classroom. *Journal of Applied Behavior Analysis, 2*, 119–124.

Bar-Tal, D. (1979). Interaction of teachers and pupils. In I. Frieze, D. Bar-Tal, & J. Carroll (Eds.), *New approaches to social problems: Applications of attribution theory*. San Francisco: Jossey-Bass.

Bar-Tal, D., Bar-Tal, Y., & Leinhardt, G. (1975). *The environment, locus of control and feelings of satisfaction*. (LRDC Publication 1975/27). Pittsburgh: University of Pittsburgh, Learning and Research Development Center.

Bash, M., & Camp, B. (1981). *Think aloud: Increasing social and cognitive skills—A problem-solving program for children*. Champaign, Ill.: Research Press.

Bebermeyer, R. (1982). *Leadership for school climate improvement*. (A working paper prepared for the urban education network) St. Louis, Mo.: Cemrel.

Becker, W., Engelmann, S., & Thomas, D. (1975). *Teaching 1: Classroom management*. Champaign, Ill.: Research Press.

Bellack, A., Kliebard, H., Hyman, R., & Smith, F. (1966). *The language of the classroom*. New York: Columbia University Teachers College Press.

Benedict, R. (1954). Continuities and discontinuities in cultural conditioning. In W. Martin & C. Stendler (Eds.), *Readings in child development*. New York: Harcourt Brace.

Berenda, R. (1950). *The influence of the group on the judgments of children*. New York: King's Crown Press.

Berliner, D. (1979). Tempus educare. In P. Peterson and H. Walberg (Eds.), *Research on teaching: Concepts, findings and implications*. Berkeley, Calif.: McCutchan.

Berliner, D. (1984). The half-full glass: A review of research on teaching. In P. Hosford (Ed.), *Using what we know about teaching*. Alexandria, Va.: Association for Supervision and Curriculum Development.

Bernard, H. (1973). *Child development and learning*. Boston: Allyn and Bacon.

Blackham, G., & Silberman, A. (1975). *Modification of child and adolescent behavior*. Belmont, Calif.: Wadsworth.

Bloom, B. (Ed). (1956). *Taxonomy of educational objectives, handbook I: Cognitive domain*. New York: David McKay.

Blumenfeld, P., Pintrich, P., Meece, J., & Wessels, K. (1982). The formation and role of self-perceptions of ability in elementary classrooms. *Elementary School Journal, 82*, 400–420.

Bolstad, O., & Johnson, S. (1972). Self-regulation in the modification of disruptive classroom behavior. *Journal of Applied Behavior Analysis, 5*, 433–454.

Borda, M., and Borda, C. (1978). *Self-esteem: A classroom affair*. Minneapolis, Minn.: Winston Press.

Borg, W. (1980). Time and school learning. In C. Denham & A. Lieberman (Eds.), *Time to learn*. Washington, D.C.: National Institute of Education.

Borg, W., & Ascione, F. (1982). Classroom management in elementary mainstreaming classrooms. *Journal of Educational Psychology, 74*, 85–95.

Boyer, E. (1983). *High school: A report on secondary education in America*. New York: Harper and Row.

Bozsik, B. (1982, March). *A study of teacher questioning and student response interaction during pre-story and post-story portions of reading comprehension lessons*. Paper presented at the annual meeting of the American Educational Research Association, New York.

Brause, R., & Mayher, J. (1982). Teachers, students, and classroom organizations. *Research in the Teaching of English, 16*, 131–148.

Broden, M., Hall, R., & Mitts, B. (1971). The effect of self-recording on the classroom behavior of two eighth-grade students. *Journal of Applied Behavior Analysis, 4,* 191–199.

Bronfenbrenner, U. (1970). *Two worlds of childhood: U.S. and U.S.S.R.* New York: Russell Sage.

Brookover, W., Beady, C., Flood, P., Schweitzer, J., & Wisenback, J. (1979). *School social systems and student achievement: Schools can make a difference.* New York: Bergin.

Brookover, W., Patterson, A., & Thomas, S. (1965). *Self-concept of ability and school achievement.* (U.S. Office of Education, Cooperative Research Project No. 845) East Lansing: Office of Research and Publications, Michigan State University.

Brookover, W., Schweitzer, J., Schneider, J., Beady, D., Flood, P., & Wisenbaker, J. (1978). Elementary school social climate and school environment. *American Educational Research Journal, 15,* 301–318.

Brophy, J. (1979). Teacher behavior and its effects. *Journal of Educational Psychology, 71,* 733–750.

Brophy, J. (1981). Teacher praise: A functional analysis. *Review of Educational Research, 51,* 5–32.

Brophy, J. (1982). Classroom management and learning. *American Education, 18,* 20–23.

Brophy, J. (1983). Research on the self-fulfilling prophecy and teacher expectations. *Journal of Educational Psychology, 75,* 631–661.

Brophy, J. (1985). Classroom management as instruction: Socializing self-guidance in schools. *Theory into Practice, 24,* 233–240.

Brophy, J. (1986a, April). *Teacher effects research and teacher quality.* Paper presented at the annual meeting of the American Educational Research Association, San Francisco.

Brophy, J. (1986b, April). *Socializing students' motivation to learn.* Paper presented at the annual meeting of the American Educational Research Association, San Francisco.

Brophy, J. (1986c). Classroom organization and management. In D. Smith (Ed.), *Essential knowledge for beginning educators.* Washington, D.C.: American Association of Colleges for Teacher Education.

Brophy, J. (1987). Synthesis of research on strategies for motivating students to learn. *Educational Leadership, 45,* 40–48.

Brophy, J., & Evertson, C. (1974). *The Texas Teacher Effectiveness Project: Presentation of non-linear relationships and summary discussion* (Report No. 74–6). Austin: Research and Development Center for Teacher Education, University of Texas in Austin. (ERIC Document Reproduction Service No. ED 099 345).

Brophy, J., & Evertson, C. (1976). *Learning from teaching: A developmental perspective.* Boston: Allyn and Bacon.

Brophy, J., & Good, T. (1971). Teacher's communication of differential expectations for children's classroom performance: Some behavior data. *Journal of Educational Psychology, 61,* 365–374.

Brophy, J., & Good, T. (1974). *Teacher-student relationships: Causes and consequences.* New York: Holt, Rinehart and Winston.

Brophy, J., & Kher, N. (1986). Teacher socialization as a mechanism for developing student motivation to learn. In R. Feldman (Ed.), *Social psychology of education: Current research and theory.* Cambridge, Mass.: Cambridge University Press.

Brophy, J., & Rohrkemper, M. (1981). The influence of problem ownership on teachers' perceptions of and strategies for coping with problem students. *Journal of Educational Psychology, 73,* 295–311.

Brophy, J., Rohrkemper, M., Rashid, H., & Goldberger, M. (1983). Relationships between teacher's presentations of classroom tasks and students' engagement in those tasks. *Journal of Educational Psychology, 75,* 544–552.

Brown, G. (1975). *The training of teachers for affective roles.* In K. Ryan (Ed.), *The seventy-fourth yearbook of the National Society for the Study of Education.* Chicago: University of Chicago Press.

Brunkan, R., & Sheni, F. (1966). Personality characteristics of ineffective, effective and efficient readers. *Personnel and Guidance Journal, 44,* 837–844.

Bryan, J., & Locke, E. (1967). Goal setting as a means of increasing motivation. *Journal of Applied Psychology, 51,* 274–277.

Buike, S. (1981). *The shaping of classroom practices: Teacher decisions* (Research Series No. 97). East Lansing: Institute for Research on Teaching, Michigan State University.

Burrows, C. (1973). *The effects of a mastery learning strategy on the geometry achievement of fourth and fifth grade children.* Unpublished doctoral dissertation, Indiana University.

Bush, R. (1957). *The teacher-pupil relationship.* Englewood Cliffs, N.J.: Prentice-Hall.

Butler, K. (1984). Working your curriculum with style. *Challenge, 2,* 38–42.

Butler, R., & Nisan, M. (1986). Effects of no feedback, task-related comments, and grades on intrinsic motivation and performance. *Journal of Educational Psychology, 78,* 210–216.

Cahoon, P. (1988). Mediator magic. *Educational Leadership, 45,* 93–94.

Campbell, P. (1967). School and self-concept: A take-charge approach for today's educator. *Educational Leadership, 24,* 510–515.

Canfield, J., & Wells, H. (1976). *100 ways to enhance self-concept in the classroom: A handbook for teachers and parents.* Englewood Cliffs, N.J.: Prentice-Hall.

Canter, L. (1976). *Assertive discipline.* Los Angeles: Lee Canter Associates.

Cartledge, G., & Milburn, J. (1978). The case for teaching social skills in the classroom: A review. *Review of Educational Research, 48,* 133–156.

Casler, L. (1965). The effects of extra tactile stimulation on a group of institutionalized infants. *Genetic Psychology Monographs, 71,* 137–175.

Chaikin, A., Sigler, E., & Derlega, V. (1974). Nonverbal mediators of teacher expectancy effects. *Journal of Personality and Social Psychology, 30,* 144–149.

Chalfant, J. (1983). *Identifying LD students: Guidelines for decision making.* (ERIC Document Reproduction Service No. ED 258390).

Chalfant, J., VanDusgen Pysh, M., & Boultrie, R. (1979). Teacher assistance teams: A model for within-building problem solving. *Learning Disability Quarterly, 2,* 85–96.

Chandler, T. (1975). Locus of control: A proposal for change. *Psychology in the Schools, 12,* 334–339.

Chapin, M., & Dyck, D. (1976). Persistence in children's reading behavior as a function of N length and attribution retraining. *Journal of Abnormal Psychology, 85,* 511–515.

Charles, C. (1989). *Building classroom discipline: From models to practice,* 3rd ed. New York: Longman.

Clements, B. (1983). *Helping experienced teachers with classroom management: An experimental study* (R & D Report No. 6155). Austin: Research and Development Center for Teacher Education, University of Texas at Austin.

Coats, W., & Smidchens, U. (1966). Audience recall as a function of speaker dynamism. *Journal of Educational Psychology, 57,* 189–191.

Coleman, J. (1966). *Equality of educational opportunity.* Washington, D.C.: U.S. Department of Health, Education and Welfare, Office of Education.

Collins, K. (1971). A strategy for mastery learning in modern mathematics. In J. Block (Ed.), *Mastery learning: Theory and practice.* New York: Holt, Rinehart and Winston.

Combs, A., Avila, D., & Purkey, W. (1971). *Helping relationships: Basic concepts for the helping professions.* Boston: Allyn and Bacon.

Combs, A., & Taylor, C. (1952). The effect of the perception of mild degrees of threat on performance. *Journal of Abnormal and Social Psychology, 47,* 420–424.

Cooper, H., & Good, T. (1983). *Pygmalion grows up.* New York: Longman.

Coopersmith, S. (1967). *The antecedents of self-esteem.* San Francisco: W. H. Freeman.

Cormany, R. (1975). *Guidance and counseling in Pennsylvania: Status and needs.* Lemoyne, Pa.: ESEA Title II Project, West Shore School District.

Corno, L. (1979). A hierarchical analysis of selected naturally occurring aptitude-treatment interactions in the third grade. *American Educational Research Journal, 16,* 391–409.

Costello, C. (1964). Ego-involvement, success and failure: A review of the literature. In H. J. Eysenck (Ed.), *Experiments in motivation.* New York: Macmillan.

Covington, M., & Beery, R. (1976). *Self-worth and school learning.* New York: Holt, Rinehart and Winston.

Covington, M., Spratt, M., & Omelich, C. (1980). Is effort enough, or does diligence count too? Student and teacher reactions to effort stability in failure. *Journal of Educational Psychology, 72,* 717–729.

Culross, R. (1982). Developing the whole child: A developmental approach to guidance with the gifted. *Roeper Review, 5,* 24–26.

Cummings, C. (1980). *Teaching makes a difference*. Edmonds, Wash.: Teaching Publishing.

Currence, C. (1984, February 29). School performance tops list of adolescent worries. *Education Week, 3*, 8.

Curwin, R., & Fuhrmann, B. (1975). *Discovering your teaching self: Humanistic approaches to effective teaching*. Englewood Cliffs, N.J.: Prentice-Hall.

Curwin, R., & Mendler, A. (1989). We repeat, let the buyer beware: A response to Canter. *Educational Leadership, 46*, 83.

Darling-Hammond, L., Wise, A., & Pease, S. (1983). Teacher evaluation in the organizational context: A review of the literature. *Review of Educational Research, 53*, 285–328.

Davidson, H., & Lang, G. (1960). Children's perceptions of their teachers' feelings toward them. *Journal of Experimental Education, 29*, 109–118.

Davis, J., Laughlin, P., & Komorita, S. (1976). The social psychology of small groups: Cooperative and mixed-motive interaction. In M. Rosenzweig & L. Porter (Eds.), *Annual review of psychology, 27*, 501–542. Palo Alto, Calif.: Annual Reviews.

Davis, R., & McKnight, C. (1976). Conceptual, heuristic, and S-algorithmic approaches in mathematics teaching. *Journal of Children's Mathematical Behavior, 1* (Supplement 1), 271–286.

De Bevoise, W. (1981). Synthesis of research on the principal as instructional leader. *Educational Leadership, 41*, 14–20.

DeCharms, R. (1968). *Personal causation*. New York: Academic Press.

DeCharms, R. (1976). *Enhancing motivation*. New York: Irvington.

DeCharms, R. (1984). Motivation in educational settings. In R. Ames & C. Ames (Eds.), *Research on motivation in education, Vol. I: Student motivation*. New York: Academic Press.

Deci, E. (1971). Effects of externally mediated rewards on intrinsic motivation. *Journal of Personality and Social Psychology, 18*, 105–115.

Deci, E. (1972). The effects of contingent and noncontingent rewards and controls on intrinsic motivation. *Organizational Behavior and Human Performance, 8*, 217–229.

Deci, E. (1975). *Intrinsic motivation*. New York: Plenum.

Deci, E., Nezlek, J., & Sheinman, L. (1981). Characteristics of the rewarder and intrinsic motivation of the rewardee. *Journal of Personality and Social Psychology, 40*, 1–10.

deHirsch, K., Jansky, J., & Langford, W. (1966). *Predicting reading failure*. New York: Harper and Row.

Delefes, P., & Jackson, B. (1972). Teacher-pupil interaction as a function of location in the classroom. *Psychology in the Schools, 9*, 119–123.

Dembo, M. (1977). *Teaching for learning: Applying educational psychology in the classroom*. Santa Monica, Calif: Goodyear.

Denham, C., & Lieberman, A. (Eds.). (1980). *Time to learn*. Washington, D.C.: National Institute of Education.

Dennis, W. (1960). Causes of retardation among institutional children: Iran. *Journal of Genetic Psychology, 96*, 46–60.

Dewey, J. (1963). *Experience and education*. New York: Macmillan.

Diggory, J. (1966). *Self-evaluation: Concepts and studies*. New York: John Wiley.

Donovan, J., Sousa, D., & Walberg, H. (1987). The impact of staff development on implementation and student achievement. *Journal of Educational Research, 80*, 348–351.

Dooling, D., & Mullet, R. (1973). Locus of thematic effects in retention of prose. *Journal of Experimental Psychology, 97*, 404–406.

Dorman, G. (1981). *Middle Grades Assessment Program*. Chapel Hill, N.C.: Center for Early Adolescence.

Doyle, W. (1979). Classroom tasks and students' abilities. In P. L. Peterson & H. J. Walberg (Eds.), *Research on teaching*. Berkeley, Calif.: McCutchan.

Doyle, W. (1983). Academic work. *Review of Educational Research, 53*, 159–199.

Doyle, W. (1984). How order is achieved in classrooms. *Journal of Curriculum Studies, 16*, 259–277.

Doyle, W. (1986). Classroom organization and management. In M. C. Wittrock (Ed.), *Handbook of research on teaching*, 3rd ed. New York: Macmillan.

Doyle, W., Sanford, J., & Emmer, E. (1982). *Managing academic tasks in junior high school: Background, design, and methodology* (R & D Report No. 6185). Austin: Research and Development Center for Teacher Education, University of Texas at Austin.

Drabman, R., & Lahey, B. (1974). Feedback in classroom behavior modification: Effects on the target child and her classmates. *Journal of Applied Behavior Analysis, 7,* 591–598.

Drabman, R., Spitalnik, R., & O'Leary, K. (1973). Teaching self-control to disruptive children. *Journal of Abnormal Psychology, 82,* 10–16.

Dreikurs, R., & Cassel, P. (1972). *Discipline without tears: What to do with children who misbehave.* New York: Hawthorn.

Dreikurs, R., Grunwald, B., & Pepper, F. (1971). *Maintaining sanity in the classroom: Illustrated teaching techniques.* New York: Harper and Row.

Dreikurs, R., Grunwald, B., & Pepper, F. (1982). *Maintaining sanity in the classroom: Classroom management techniques,* 2nd ed. New York: Harper and Row.

Druian, G., & Butler, J. (1987). *Effective schooling and at-risk youth: What the research shows.* Portland, Ore: Northwest Regional Educational Laboratory.

Duckworth, E. (1964). Piaget rediscovered. In R. E. Ripple & V. N. Rockcastle (Eds.), *Piaget rediscovered: A report of the conference on cognitive skills and curriculum development.* Ithaca, N.Y.: Cornell University, School of Education.

Duffy, G., & McIntyre, L. (1982). A naturalistic study of instructional assistance in primary-grade reading. *Elementary School Journal, 83,* 15–23.

Duke, D. (1980). *Managing behavior problems.* New York: Columbia University Teachers College Press.

Duke, D. (1986). School discipline plans and the quest for order in American schools. In D. Tattum (Ed.), *Management of disruptive pupil behaviour in schools.* New York: John Wiley & Sons.

Duke, D., & Jones, V. (1984). Two decades of discipline—Assessing the development of an educational specialization. *Journal of Research and Development in Education, 17,* 25–35.

Duke, D., & Jones, V. (1985). What can schools do to foster student responsibility? *Theory into Practice, 24,* 277–285.

Duke, D., & Meckel, A. (1984). *Teacher's guide to classroom management.* New York: Random House.

Dunkin, M., & Biddle, B. (1974). *The study of teaching.* New York: Holt, Rinehart and Winston.

Dunn, K., & Dunn, R. (1987). Dispelling outmoded beliefs about student learning. *Educational Leadership, 44,* 55–62.

Dunn, R. (1983). Learning style and its relation to exceptionality at both ends of the spectrum. *Exceptional Children, 49,* 496–506.

Dunn, R., Beaudry, J., & Klavas, A. (1989). Survey of research on learning styles. *Educational Leadership, 46,* 50–58.

Dunn, R., Cavanaugh, D., Eberle, B., & Lenhausern, R. (1982). Hemispheric preference: The newest element of learning style. *American Biology Teacher, 44,* 291–294.

Dunn, R., & Goldman, M. (1966). Competition and noncompetition in relationship to satisfaction and feelings toward own group and nongroup members. *Journal of Social Psychology, 68,* 299–311.

Durkin, D. (1981). Reading comprehension instruction in five basal reader series. *Reading Research Quarterly, 16,* 515–544.

Dweck, C. (1975). The role of expectations and attributions in the alleviation of learned helplessness. *Journal of Personality and Social Psychology, 31,* 674–685.

Dweck, C. (1986). Motivational processes affecting learning. *American Psychologist, 41,* 1040–1048.

Edmonds, R. (1979). Effective schools for the urban poor. *Educational Leadership, 37,* 15–18.

Edmonds, R. (1982). Programs of school improvement: An overview. *Educational Leadership, 40,* 4–11.

Eisner, E. (1984). Can educational research inform educational practice? *Phi Delta Kappan, 65,* 447–452.

Eisner, E. (1988). The ecology of school improvement. *Educational Leadership, 45,* 24–29.

Elkind, D. (1967). Egocentrism in adolescence. *Child Development, 38,* 1025–1034.

Elkind, D. (1981). *The hurried child: Growing up too fast too soon.* Reading, Mass.: Addison-Wesley.

Emmer, E., & Aussiker, A. (1987, April). School and classroom discipline programs: How well do they work? Paper presented at the annual meeting of the American Educational Research Association, Washington, D.C.

Emmer, E., Evertson, C., & Anderson, L. (1980). Effective management at the beginning of the school year. *Elementary School Journal, 80,* 219–231.

Emmer, E., Evertson, C., Sanford, J., Clements, B., & Worsham, M. (1982). *Organizing and managing the junior high classroom.* Austin, Tex.: Research and Development Center for Teacher Education.

Englander, M. (1982). Teacher management of classroom misbehavior. In J. Harris and C. Bennett (Eds.), *Student discipline.* Bloomington: University of Indiana.

Englander, M. (1986). *Strategies for classroom discipline.* New York: Praeger.

Epanchin, B. C., & Paul, J. (1982). *Casebook for educating the emotionally disturbed.* Columbus, Ohio: Charles E. Merrill.

Epstein, H. (1979). Cognitive growth and development. *Colorado Journal of Educational Research, 19,* 34–35.

Epstein, J. (1981). *The quality of school life.* Lexington, Mass.: Lexington Books.

Epstein, M., Hallahan, D., & Kauffman, J. (1975). Implications of the reflectivity-impulsivity dimension for special education. *Journal of Special Education, 9,* 11–25.

Erikson, E. (1963). *Childhood and society,* 2nd ed. New York: Norton.

Erikson, E. (1968). *Identity, youth, and crisis.* New York: Norton.

Evertson, C. (1985). Training teachers in classroom management: An experimental study in secondary school classrooms. *Journal of Educational Research, 79,* 51–58.

Evertson, C., & Emmer, E. (1982a). Effective management at the beginning of the school year in junior high school classes. *Journal of Educational Psychology, 74,* 485–498.

Evertson, C., & Emmer, E. (1982b). Preventive classroom management. In D. Duke (Ed.), *Helping teachers manage classrooms.* Alexandria, Va.: Association for Supervision and Curriculum Development.

Evertson, C., Emmer, E., & Brophy, J. (1980). Predictors of effective teaching in junior high mathematics classrooms. *Journal of Research in Mathematics Education, 11,* 167–178.

Evertson, C., Emmer, E., Sanford, J., & Clements, B. (1983). Improving classroom management: An experiment in elementary school classrooms. *Elementary School Journal, 84,* 173–188.

Fagot, B. (1973). Influence of teacher behavior in the preschool. *Developmental Psychology, 9,* 196–206.

Farls, R. (1967). High and low achievement of intellectually average intermediate grade students related to self-concept and social approval. *Dissertation Abstracts, 28,* 1205.

Farquhar, W. (1968). *A comprehensive study of the motivational factors underlying achievement of eleventh-grade high school students* (U.S. Office of Education, Cooperative Research Report No. 846). East Lansing: Office of Research and Publications, Michigan State University.

Feather, N. (Ed.). (1982). *Expectations and actions.* Hillsdale, N.J.: Erlbaum.

Finlayson, D., & Loughran, J. (1978). Pupils perceptions in high and low delinquency schools. *Education Research, 18,* 138–145.

Firestone, W. (1989). Beyond order and expectations in high schools serving at-risk youth. *Educational Leadership, 46,* 41–45.

Fisher, C., Berliner, D., Filby, N., Marliave, R., Cahen, L., & Dishaw, M. (1980). Teaching behaviors, academic learning time, and student achievement: An overview. In C. Denham & A. Lieberman (Eds.), *Time to learn.* Washington, D.C.: National Institute of Education.

Fisher, C., Filby, N., Marliave, R., Cahen, L., Dishaw, M., Moore, J., & Berliner, D. (1978). *Teaching behaviors, academic learning time and student achievement* (Report of Phase III–B, Beginning Teacher Evaluation Study. Tech. Rep. V–1). San Francisco: Far West Laboratory for Educational Research and Development.

Fitzpatrick, K. (1982). *The effect of a secondary classroom management training program on teacher and student behavior.* Paper presented at the annual meeting of the American Educational Research Association, New York.

Flanders, N. (1963). Intent, action and feedback: A preparation for teaching. *Journal of Teacher Education, 14,* 251–260.

Flanders, N. (1970). *Analyzing teaching behavior.* Reading, Mass.: Addison-Wesley.

Flanders, N., & Amidon, E. (1967). *The role of the teacher in the classroom.* Minneapolis,

Minn.: Minneapolis Association for Productive Teaching.

Flanders, N., Morrison, B., & Brode, E. (1968). Changes in pupil attitudes during the school year. *Journal of Educational Psychology, 59,* 334–338.

Fowler, J., & Peterson, P. (1981). Increasing reading persistence and altering attributional style of learned helpless children. *Journal of Educational Psychology, 73,* 251–260.

Freiberg, J. (1989, March). *Turning around at-risk schools.* Paper presented at annual meeting of the American Educational Research Association, San Francisco.

Frericks, A. (1974, March). *Labeling of students by prospective teachers.* Paper presented at the American Educational Research Association Convention, Chicago.

Friedrich, L., & Stein, A. (1973). Aggressive and prosocial TV programs and the natural behavior of preschool children. *Monographs of the Society for Research in Child Development, 38* (4, Serial No. 151).

Gabriel, R., & Anderson, P. (1987). *Identifying at-risk youth in the Northwest states: A regional database.* Portland, Ore.: Northwest Regional Educational Laboratory.

Gall, M., Haisley, F., Baker, R., & Perez, T. (1982). *The relationship between inservice education practices and effectiveness of basic skills instruction.* Eugene, Ore.: Center for Educational Policy and Management.

Gallagher, J. (1965). Expressive thought by gifted children in the classroom. *Elementary English, 42,* 559–568.

Galloway, D., & Goodwin, C. (1987). *The education of disturbing children.* London: Longmans.

Gallup, A. (1984). The Gallup poll of teachers' attitudes toward the public schools. *Phi Delta Kappan, 66,* 97–101.

Gallup, A., & Clark, D. (1987). The 19th annual Gallup Poll on the public's attitudes toward the public schools. *Phi Delta Kappan, 69,* 17–30.

Gallup, A., & Elam, S. (1988). The 20th annual Gallup Poll of the public's attitudes toward the public schools. *Phi Delta Kappan, 70,* 33–46.

Gallup, G. (1984). The 16th annual Gallup Poll of the public's attitudes toward the public schools. *Phi Delta Kappan, 66,* 23–38.

Gambrell, L., Wilson, R., & Gantt, W. (1981). Classroom observations of task-attending behaviors of good and poor readers. *Journal of Educational Research, 74,* 400–405.

Gibb, J. (1964). Climate for trust formation. In L. Bradford, J. Gibb, & K. Beene (Eds.), *T-group theory and laboratory method.* New York: Wiley.

Glasser, W. (1965). *Reality therapy.* New York: Harper and Row.

Glasser, W. (1969). *Schools without failure.* New York: Harper and Row.

Glasser, W. (1977). Ten steps to good discipline. *Today's Education, 66,* 61–63.

Glasser, W. (1985). *Control theory in the classroom.* New York: Harper and Row.

Glasser, W. (1988). On students' needs and team learning: A conversation with William Glasser. R. Brandt (Ed.). *Educational Leadership, 45,* 38–45.

Goertzel, V., & Goertzel, M. (1962). *Cradles of eminence.* Boston: Little, Brown.

Goldberg, M., & Harvey, J. (1983). A nation at risk: The report of the National Commission of Excellence in Education. *Phi Delta Kappan, 65,* 14–18.

Goldstein, A., Sprafkin, R., Gershaw, N., & Klein, P. (1980). *Skillstreaming the adolescent.* Champaign, Ill.: Research Press.

Good, T. (1979). Teacher effectiveness in the elementary school. *Journal of Teacher Education, 30,* 52–64.

Good, T. (1981). Teacher expectations and student perceptions: A decade of research. *Educational Leadership, 38,* 415–423.

Good, T. (1983). Classroom research: A decade of progress. *Educational Psychologist, 18,* 127–144.

Good, T. (1986). Recent classroom research: Implications for teacher education. In D. Smith (Ed.), *Essential knowledge for beginning educators.* Washington, D.C.: American Association of Colleges for Teacher Education.

Good, T., & Beckerman, T. (1978). Time on task: A naturalistic study in sixth grade classrooms. *Elementary School Journal, 78,* 193–201.

Good, T., & Brophy, J. (1973). *Looking in classrooms.* New York: Harper and Row.

Good, T., & Brophy, J. (1974). Changing teacher and student behavior: An empirical investigation. *Journal of Educational Psychology, 66,* 390–405.

Good, T., & Brophy, J. (1984). *Looking in classrooms,* 3rd ed. New York: Harper and Row.

Good, T., & Brophy, J. (1987). *Looking in classrooms,* 4th ed. New York: Harper and Row.

Good, T., Ebmeier, H., & Beckerman, T. (1978). Teaching mathematics in high and low SES classrooms: An empirical comparison. *Journal of Teacher Education, 29,* 85–90.

Good, T., & Grouws, D. (1979). The Missouri mathematics effectiveness project. *Journal of Educational Psychology, 71,* 355–362.

Good, T., & Power, C. (1976). Designing successful classroom environments for different types of students. *Journal of Curriculum Studies, 8,* 47–52.

Goodlad, J. (1983a). A study of schooling: Some findings and hypotheses. *Phi Delta Kappan, 64,* 465–470.

Goodlad, J. (1983b). A study of schooling: Some implications for school improvement. *Phi Delta Kappan, 64,* 552–558.

Goodlad, J. (1984). *A place called school: Prospects for the future.* New York: McGraw-Hill.

Goodlad, J., & Oakes, J. (1988). We must offer equal access to knowledge. *Educational Leadership, 45,* 16–22.

Goodwin, S., & Mahoney, M. (1975). Modification of aggression through modeling: An experimental probe. *Journal of Behavior Therapy and Experimental Psychiatry, 6,* 200–202.

Gordon, T. (1970). *Parent effectiveness training: The tested new way to raise responsible children.* New York: Wyden.

Gordon, T. (1974). *Teacher effectiveness training.* New York: Wyden.

Gordon, T., & Breivogel, W. (1976). *Building effective home-school relationships.* Boston: Allyn and Bacon.

Gottfredson, G. (1983). From lunchroom larceny to assaults on teachers, it's a board problem, and it's big. *American School Board Journal, 170,* 19–21.

Gottfredson, G., & Gottfredson, D. (1985). *Victimization in schools.* New York: Plenum Press.

Gowan, J. (1960). Factors of achievement in high school and college. *Journal of Counseling Psychology, 7,* 91–95.

Gray, R., Graubard, P., & Rosenberg, H. (1974, November). Little brother is changing you. *Psychology Today, 7,* 42–46.

Greenfield, W. (1982). *Research on public school principals: A review and recommendations.* Paper presented at the NIE Conference on Principals for Educational Excellence in the 1980s, Washington, D.C.

Greenwood, C., & Hops, H. (1976). *Generalization of teacher praising skills over time and setting: What you teach is what you get.* Paper presented at the 54th Annual Convention of the Council for Exceptional Children, Chicago.

Greenwood, C., Hops, H., Delquadri, J., & Walker, H. (1974). *PASS: Program for academic survival skills.* Eugene: Center at Oregon for Research in the Behavioral Education of the Handicapped.

Gregorc, A. (1982). *An adult's guide to styles.* Maynard, Mass.: Gabriel Systems.

Gress, J. (1988). Alcoholism's hidden curriculum. *Educational Leadership, 45,* 18–19.

Gump, P. (1967). *The classroom behavior setting: Its nature and relation to student behavior.* (Report No. BR–5–0334). Washington, D.C.: Office of Education, Bureau of Research. (ERIC Document Reproduction Service No. EDO15515)

Hagen, J., & Hale, G. (1972). The development of attention in children. In A. D. Pick (Ed.), *Minnesota symposia on child psychology, Vol. 7.* Minneapolis: University of Minnesota Press.

Hahn, A., Danzberger, J., & Lefkowitz, B. (1987). Dropouts in America: Enough is known for action. Washington, D.C.: Institute for Educational Leadership.

Haley, P., & Berry, K. (1988). *Home and school partnerships: Helping parents help their children.* Andover, Mass.: The Regional Laboratory for Educational Improvement of the Northeast and Islands.

Hall, R., Lund, D., & Jackson, D. (1968). Effects of teacher attention on study behavior. *Journal of Applied Behavior Analysis, 1,* 1–12.

Hamby, J. (1989). How to get an "A" on your dropout prevention report card. *Educational Leadership, 46,* 21–28.

Hamilton, H., & Gordon, D. (1978). Teacher-child interactions in preschool and task persistence. *American Educational Research Journal, 15,* 459–466.

Hargreaves, D. (1967). *Social relations in a secondary school.* New York: Humanities Press.

Hargreaves, D. (1982). *The challenge for the comprehensive school*. London: Routledge and Kegan Paul.

Haring, N., & Phillips, E. (1972). Analysis and modification of classroom behavior. Englewood Cliffs, N.J.: Prentice-Hall.

Harlow, H. (1958). The nature of love. *American Psychologist, 13*, 673–684.

Harmin, M., Kirschenbaum, H., & Simon, S. (1973). *Clarifying values through subject matter*. Minneapolis, Minn.: Winston Press.

Harter, S., & Connell, J. (1981). A model of the relationship among children's academic achievement and their self-perceptions of competence, control and motivational orientation. In J. Nicholls (Ed.), *The development of achievement motivation*. Greenwich, Conn.: JAI Press.

Hawkins, D., Doueck, H., & Lishner, D. (1988). Changing teaching practices in mainstream classrooms to improve bonding and behavior of low achievers. *American Educational Research Journal, 25*, 31–50.

Hefele, T. (1971). The effects of systematic human relations training upon student achievement. *Journal of Research and Development in Education, 4*, 52–69.

Henry, J. (1963). *Culture against man*. New York: Random House.

Heward, W., & Orlansky, M. (1980). *Exceptional children*. Columbus, Ohio: Charles E. Merrill.

Hill, K., & Wigfield, A. (1984). Test anxiety: A major educational problem and what can be done about it. *Elementary School Journal, 85*, 105–126.

Hodgkinson, H. (1985). *All one system: Demographics of education, kindergarten through graduate school*. Washington, D.C.: Institute for Educational Leadership.

Holt, J. (1969). *The underachieving school*. New York: Pitman.

Holt, J. (1972). *What do I do Monday?* New York: Dell.

Horst, B., & Johnson, R. (1981). Brain growth periodization and its implications for language arts. *English Journal, 70*, 74–75.

Horton, L. (1988). The education of most worth: Preventing drug and alcohol abuse. *Educational Leadership, 45*, 4–8.

Hosford, P. (1984). *Using what we know about teaching*. Alexandria, Va.: Association for Supervision and Curriculum Development.

Howard, E. (1981). School climate improvement—rationale and process. *Illinois School Research and Development, 18*, 8–12.

Hudgins, B., & Ahlbrand, W., Jr. (1969). *A study of classroom interaction and thinking*. (Technical report series No. 8.) St. Ann, Mo.: Central Midwestern Regional Educational Laboratory.

Hunter, M. (1976). *Improved instruction*. El Segundo, Calif.: TIP.

Hunter, M. (1981). *Increasing your teaching effectiveness*. Palo Alto, Calif.: Learning Institute.

Hutzell, R., Platzek, D., & Logue, P. (1974). Control of symptoms of Gilles de la Tourette's Syndrome by self-monitoring. *Journal of Behavior Therapy and Experimental Psychiatry, 5*, 71–76.

Hyman, I., & D'Alessandro, J. (1984). Good old-fashioned discipline: The politics of punitiveness. *Phi Delta Kappan, 66*, 39–45.

Ince, L. (1976). The use of relaxation training and a conditioned stimulus in the elimination of epileptic seizures in a child: A case study. *Journal of Behavior Therapy and Experimental Psychiatry, 7*, 39–42.

Irwin, F. (1967). Sentence completion responses and scholastic success or failure. *Journal of Counseling Psychology, 14*, 269–271.

Jackson, N., Jackson, D., & Monroe, C. (1983). *Getting along with others: Teaching social effectiveness in children*. Champaign, Ill.: Research Press.

Jackson, P. (1968). *Life in classrooms*. New York: Holt, Rinehart and Winston.

Jacobson, E. (1938). *Progressive relaxation*. Chicago: University of Chicago Press.

Jencke, S., & Peck, D. (1976). Is immediate reinforcement appropriate? *Arithmetic Teacher, 23*, 32–33.

Johnson, D. (1979). *Educational psychology*. Englewood Cliffs, N.J.: Prentice-Hall.

Johnson, D. (1986). *Reaching out: Interpersonal effectiveness and self-actualization*, 3rd ed. Englewood Cliffs, N.J.: Prentice-Hall.

Johnson, D., & Johnson, R. (1975). *Learning together and alone: Cooperation, competition, and individualization*. Englewood Cliffs, N.J.: Prentice-Hall.

Johnson, D., & Johnson, R. (1985). *Cooperative learning warm-ups, grouping strategies and group activities*. Edina, Minn.: Interaction Book Co.

Johnson, D., & Johnson, R. (1986). Effects of cooperative and competitive learning experiences on interpersonal attraction between handicapped and non-handicapped students. *Journal of Social Psychology, 116,* 211–219.

Johnson, D., & Johnson, R. (1987). *Learning together and alone: Cooperative, competitive, and individualistic learning,* 2nd ed. Englewood Cliffs, N.J.: Prentice-Hall.

Johnson, D., Johnson, R., & Johnson-Holubec, E. (1986). *Circles of learning: Cooperation in the classroom.* Edina, Minn.: Interaction Book Co.

Johnson, D., Johnson, R., & Johnson-Holubec, E. (1988). *Cooperation in the classroom.* Edina, Minn.: Interaction Book Co.

Johnson, D., Marayama, S., Johnson, R., Nelson, D., & Skon, L. (1981). Effects of cooperative, competitive, and individualistic goal structures on achievement: A meta-analysis. *Psychological Bulletin, 89,* 47–62.

Johnson, R., & Johnson, D. (1983). Effects of cooperative, competitive, and individualistic learning experiences on social development. *Exceptional Children, 49,* 323–329.

Johnson, S. (1970). Self-reinforcement versus external reinforcement in behavior modification with children. *Developmental Psychology, 3,* 147–148.

Johnson, S., & Martin, S. (1973). Developing self-evaluation as a conditioned reinforcer. In B. Ashem & E. Poser (Eds.), *Behavior modification with children.* New York: Pergamon.

Jones, C. (1979). Dynamics of transcendence in the middle school setting. *Urban Review, 11,* 37–43.

Jones, V. (1973). A junior high school program for emotionally disturbed children. In J. McDonnel, H. Fredericks, V. Baldwin, W. Moore, R. Crowley, R. Anderson, & K. Moore (Eds.), *Impact 7 of the Title VI programs in the state of Oregon, September 1972–August 1973.* Monmouth: Teaching Research.

Jones, V. (1980). *Adolescents with behavior problems: Strategies for teaching, counseling, and parent involvement.* Boston: Allyn and Bacon.

Jones, V. (1982). Training teachers to be effective classroom managers. In D. Duke (Ed.), *Helping teachers manage classrooms.* Alexandria, Va.: Association for Supervision and Curriculum Development.

Jones, V. (1983). Current trends in classroom management: Implications for gifted students. *Roeper Review, 6,* 26–30.

Jones, V. (1984). An administrator's guide to developing and evaluating a building-wide discipline program. *National Association of Secondary School Principals Bulletin, 68,* 60–73.

Jones, V. (1986). *A model for preservice and inservice training in comprehensive classroom management.* Paper presented at the American Educational Research Association convention, San Francisco.

Jones, V. (1989). Classroom management: Clarifying theory and improving practice. *Education, 109,* 330–339.

Jones, V., & Waksman, S. (1985). *A suggested procedure for the identification of and provision of services to seriously emotionally disturbed students: Technical assistance paper 5.* Salem: Oregon State Department of Education.

Jorgenson, G. (1977). Relationship of classroom behavior to the accuracy of the match between material difficulty and student ability. *Journal of Educational Research, 69,* 24–32.

Joyce, B., Bush, R., & McKibbin, M. (1981). *Information and opinion from the California staff development study: The compact report.* Sacramento: California State Department of Education.

Joyce, B., & Clift, R. (1984). The Phoenix agenda: Essential reform in teacher education. *Educational Researcher, 13,* 5–18.

Joyce, B., & Weil, M. (1980). *Models of teaching,* 2nd ed. Englewood Cliffs, N.J.: Prentice-Hall.

Joyce, B., & Weil, M. (1986). *Models of teaching,* 3rd ed. Englewood Cliffs, N.J.: Prentice-Hall.

Kagan, J. (1966). Reflection-impulsivity. *Journal of Abnormal Psychology, 71,* 17–24.

Kagan, J., Moss, H., & Siegel, I. (1963). Psychological significance of styles of conceptualization. In J. C. Wright & J. Kagan (Eds.), *Basic cognitive processes in children. Monographs of the Society for Research in Child Development, 28,* 260.

Kagan, S. (1980). Cooperation-competition, culture, and structural bias in classrooms. In S. Sharan, P. Hare, C. Webb, & R. Hertz-Lazarowitz (Eds.), *Cooperation in education.* Provo, Utah: Brigham Young University Press.

Kagan, S. (1989). *Cooperative learning: Resources for teachers.* Suite 201, 27402 Camino Capistrano, Laguna Niguel, Calif.: Resources for Teachers.

Kazdin, A. (1973). The effect of vicarious reinforcement on attentive behavior in the classroom. *Journal of Applied Behavior Analysis, 6,* 71–78.

Kazdin, A., & Klock, J. (1973). The effect of nonverbal teacher approval on student attentive behavior. *Journal of Applied Behavior Analysis, 6,* 643–654.

Kelley, E. (1980). *Improving school climate: Leadership techniques for principals.* Reston, Va.: National Association of Secondary School Principals.

Kelley, E. (1981). Auditing school climate. *Educational Leadership, 39,* 180–183.

Kennedy, B. (1968). *Motivational effect of individual conferences and goal setting on performance and attitudes in arithmetic.* (Report No. UW–WRDCCL–TR–61). Washington, D.C.: Office of Education, Bureau of Research. (ERIC Document Reproduction Service No. ED 032113)

Kerman, S., & Martin, M. (1980). *Teacher expectations and student achievement.* Bloomington, Ind.: Phi Delta Kappa.

Kerr, M., & Nelson, M. (1983). *Strategies for managing behavior problems in the classroom.* Columbus, Ohio: Charles E. Merrill.

Klein, R., & Schuler, C. (1974, April). *Increasing academic performance through the contingent use of self-evaluation.* Paper presented at the annual meeting of the American Educational Research Association, Chicago.

Kleinfeld, J. (1972). *Instructional style and the intellectual performance of Indian and Eskimo students.* Project No. 1–J–027 (Final Report). Washington, D.C.: Office of Education, U.S. Department of Health, Education, and Welfare.

Kleinfeld, J. (1975). Effective teachers of Indian and Eskimo students. *School Review, 83,* 301–344.

Kohl, H. (1967). *36 children.* New York: New American Library.

Kohlberg, L. (1976). Moral stages and moralization. The cognitive-developmental approach. In T. Lickona (Ed.), *Moral development and behavior.* New York: Holt, Rinehart and Winston.

Kolb, D. (1978). *Learning style inventory technical manual.* Boston: McBer.

Kounin, J. (1970). *Discipline and group management in classrooms.* New York: Holt, Rinehart and Winston.

Kounin, J., & Gump, P. (1961). The comparative influence of punitive and non-punitive teachers upon children's concept of school misconduct. *Journal of Educational Psychology, 52,* 44–49.

Kranzler, G. (1974). *You can change the way you feel: A rational-emotive approach.* Eugene: Published by author, Counseling Department, University of Oregon.

Krathwohl, D., Bloom, B., & Masia, B. (1964). *Taxonomy of educational objectives, handbook II: Affective domain.* New York: David McKay.

LaBenne, W., & Green, B. (1969). *Educational implications of self-concept theory.* Pacific Palisades, Calif.: Goodyear.

Landry, R. (1974). *Achievement and self concept: A curvilinear relationship.* Paper presented at American Educational Research Association convention, Chicago.

Landry, R., & Edeburn, C. (1974, April). *Teacher self-concept and student self-concept.* Paper presented at the American Educational Research Association convention, Chicago.

LeCroy, C. (Ed.). (1983). *Social skills training for children and youth.* New York: Haworth Press.

Leinhardt, G., & Bickel, W. (1987). Instruction's the thing wherein to catch the mind that falls behind. *Educational Psychologist, 22,* 177–207.

Leonard, G. (1968). *Education and ecstasy.* New York: Dell.

Lepper, M. (1981). Intrinsic and extrinsic motivation in children: Detrimental effects of superfluous social controls. In A. Collins (Ed.), *Aspects of the development of competence: The Minnesota symposia on child psychology, Volume 14.* Hillsdale, N.J.: Erlbaum.

Lepper, M., & Greene, D. (1975). Turning play into work: Effects of adult surveillance and extrinsic rewards on children's intrinsic motivation. *Journal of Personality and Social Psychology, 31,* 479–486.

Lewis, R., & St. John, N. (1974). Contribution of cross-racial friendship to minority group achievement in desegregated classrooms. *Sociometry, 37,* 79–91.

Lightfoot, S. L. (1983). *The good high school.* New York: Basic Books.

Lindelow, J., & Mazzarella, J. (1981). *School climate*. (Contract No. 400–78–0007). Washington, D.C.: National Institute of Education. (ERIC Document Reproduction Service No. EA 014 193)

Lipsitz, J. (1984). *Successful schools for young adolescents*. New Brunswick, N.J.: Transaction Books.

Long, N., Morse, W., & Newman, R. (Eds.). (1971). *Conflict in the classroom*, 2nd ed. Belmont, Calif.: Wadsworth.

Lovitt, T., & Curtiss, K. (1968). Effects of manipulating an antecedent event on mathematics response rate. *Journal of Applied Behavior Analysis, 1*, 329–333.

Luce, S., & Hoge, R. (1978). Relations among teacher rankings, pupil-teacher interactions, and academic achievement: A test of the expectancy hypothesis. *American Educational Research Journal, 15*, 489–500.

McCarthy, B. (1987). *The 4-MAT system: Teaching to learning styles with right/left mode techniques*. Barrington, Ill.: Excel.

McCarthy, B., Leflar, S., & McNamara, M. (1987). *The 4-MAT workbook: Guided practice in 4-MAT lesson and unit planning*. Barrington, Ill.: Excel.

McClelland, D., & Alschuler, A. (1971). *The achievement motivation development project*. USOE Project No. 7–1231 (Final Report). Washington, D.C.: Office of Education, Bureau of Research.

McClelland, D., Atkinson, J., Clark, R., & Lowell, E. (1953). *The achievement motive*. New York: Appleton-Century-Crofts.

McCormack, S. (1989). Response to Render, Padilla, and Krank: But practitioners say it works! *Educational Leadership, 46*, 77–79.

McDill, E., Rigsby, L., & Meyers, E. (1969). Educational climates of high school: Their effect and source. *American Journal of Sociology, 74*, 567–586.

McDonald, F. (1976). *Research on teaching and its implications for policy making: Report on phase II of the beginning teacher evaluation study*. Princeton, N.J.: Educational Testing Service.

McGinley, P., & McGinley,. (1970). Reading groups as psychological groups. *Journal of Experimental Education, 39*, 35–42.

McGinnis, E., & Goldstein, A. (1984). *Skillstreaming the elementary school child*. Champaign, Ill.: Research Press.

McKenzie, T., & Rushall, B. (1974). Effects of self-recording on attendance and performance in a competitive swimming training program. *Journal of Applied Behavior Analysis, 7*, 199–206.

McLaughlin, T., & Gnagey, W. (1981, April). *Self-management and pupil self-control*. Paper presented at the annual meeting of the American Educational Research Association, Los Angeles.

McManus, M. (in press). *Troublesome behaviour in the classroom: A teacher's survival guide*. London: Routledge and Kegan Paul.

Madden, N., Slavin, R., Karweit, N., & Livermon, B. (1989). Restructuring the urban elementary school. *Educational Leadership, 46*, 14–18.

Madsen, C., Becker, W., & Thomas, D. (1968). Rules, praise, and ignoring: Elements of elementary classroom control. *Journal of Applied Behavior Analysis, 1*, 139–150.

Maehr, M. (1976). Continuing motivation: An analysis of a seldom considered educational outcome. *Review of Educational Research, 46*, 443–462.

Maehr, M., & Sjogren, D. (1971). Atkinson's theory of achievement motivation: First step toward a theory of academic motivation. *Review of Educational Research, 41*, 143–161.

Maher, C. (1987). Involving behaviorally disordered adolescents in instructional planning: Effectiveness of the GOAL procedures. *Journal of Child and Adolescent Psychotherapy, 4*, 204–210.

Mahoney, M. (1974). *Cognition and behavior modification*. Cambridge, Mass.: Ballinger.

Mannheim, B. (1957). An investigation of the interrelations of reference groups, membership groups and the self-image: A test of the Cooley-Mead Theory of the self. *Dissertation Abstracts, 17*, 1616–1617.

Maple, F. (1977). *Shared decision making*. Beverly Hills, Calif.: Sage.

Martin, R., & Lauridsen, D. (1974). *Developing student discipline and motivation*. Champaign, Ill.: Research Press.

Martorella, P. (1980). Social studies goals in the middle grades. *Journal of Research and Development in Education, 13*, 47–59.

Maslow, A. (1968). *Toward a psychology of being.* New York: D. Van Nostrand.

Mastin, V. (1963). Teacher enthusiasm. *Journal of Educational Research, 56,* 385–386.

Matheny, K., & Edwards, C. (1974). Academic improvement through an experimental classroom management system. *Journal of School Psychology, 12,* 222–232.

Mehan, H. (1974). Accomplishing classroom lessons. In A. V. Cicourel, K. H. Jennings, S. H. Jennings, K. C. Leiter, R. MacKay, J. Mehan, & D. Roth (Eds.), *Language use and school performance.* New York: Academic Press.

Meichenbaum, D., & Cameron, R. (1974). The clinical potential of modifying what clients say to themselves. In C. Mahoney & C. Thoresen (Eds.), *Self-control: Power to the person.* Monterey, Calif.: Brooks/Cole.

Mertens, S., & Yarger, S. (1981). *Teacher centers in action: A comprehensive study of federally funded teacher centers.* Syracuse, N.Y.: Syracuse Area Teacher Center.

Messick, S. (1970). The criterion problem in the evaluation of instruction. In M. C. Wittrock & D. E. Wiley (Eds.), *The evaluation of instruction: Issues and problems.* New York: Holt, Rinehart and Winston.

Meunier, C., & Rule, B. (1967). Anxiety, confidence and conformity. *Journal of Personality, 35,* 489–504.

Meyen, E. (Ed.). (1982). *Exceptional children in today's schools: An alternative resource book.* Denver: Love.

Moles, O. (1987, April). *Trends in student misconduct: The 70s and 80s.* Paper presented at the annual meeting of the American Educational Research Association, Washington, D.C.

Mongon, D., & Hart, S. (in press). *Improving classroom behaviour: Making a difference.* London: Cassell PLC.

Monohan, J., & O'Leary, K. (1971). Effects of self-instruction on rule-breaking behavior. *Psychological Reports, 29,* 1059–1066.

Morgan, M. (1984). Reward-induced decrements and increments in intrinsic motivation. *Review of Educational Research, 54,* 5–30.

Morris, J. (1978). *Psychology and teaching: A humanistic view.* New York: Random House.

Morrison, A., & McIntrye, D. (1969). *Teachers and teaching.* Baltimore: Penguin.

Morse, W. (1964). Self-concept in the school setting. *Childhood Education, 41,* 195–198.

Mortimore, P., & Sammons, P. (1987). New evidence on effective elementary schools. *Educational Leadership, 45,* 4–8.

Moskowitz, G., & Hayman, J. (1976). Success strategies of inner-city teachers: A year-long study. *Journal of Educational Research, 69,* 283–289.

Mosley, A., & Smith, P. (1982). What works in learning? Students provide the answers. *Phi Delta Kappan, 60,* 273.

Muldoon, J. (1955). The concentration of liked and disliked members in groups and the relationship of the concentration to group comprehensiveness. *Sociometry, 18,* 73–81.

Nash, R. (1963). Corporal punishment in an age of violence. *Educational Theory, 13,* 295–308.

Newmann, F., & Thompson, J. (1987). *Effects of cooperative learning on achievement in secondary schools: A summary of research.* Madison: The National Center on Effective Secondary Schools, School of Education, University of Wisconsin.

Nichols, P. (1984). Down the up staircase: The teacher as therapist. In J. Grosenick (Ed.), *Interventions in behavioral disorders.* Des Moines: Special Educational Division, State Department of Education.

Nickerson, C., Lollis, C., & Porter, E. (1980). *Miraculous me!* Seattle: The Comprehensive Health Education Foundation.

Norman, J., & Harris, M. (1981). *The private life of the American teenager.* New York: Rawson, Wade.

O'Leary, D., Becker, W., Evans, M., & Saudargas, R. (1969). A token reinforcement program in public school: A replication and systematic analysis. *Journal of Applied Behavior Analysis, 2,* 3–13.

O'Leary, D., & O'Leary, S. (Eds.). (1977). *Classroom management: The successful use of behavior modification,* 2nd ed. New York: Pergamon Press.

Page, E. (1958). Teacher comments and student performance. *Journal of Educational Psychology, 49,* 172–181.

Pascarella, E., Walberg, H., Junker, L., & Haertel, G. (1981). Continuing motivation in science for early and late adolescents. *American Educational Research Journal, 18,* 439–452.

Patterson, C. (1973). *Humanistic education*. Englewood Cliffs, N.J.: Prentice-Hall.

Patterson, G. (1971). Behavioral intervention procedures in the classroom and in the home. In A. E. Berzin and S. L. Garfield (Eds.), *Handbook of psychotherapy and behavior change: An empirical analysis*. New York: Wiley.

Peterson, P., & Swing, S. (1982). Beyond time on task: Students' reports of their thought processes during classroom instruction. *Elementary School Journal, 82*, 481–491.

Piaget, J. (1952). *The origins of intelligence in children* (M. Cook, Trans.). New York: International Universities Press.

Piaget, J. (1970). Piaget's theory. In P. H. Mussen (Ed.), *Carmichael's manual of child psychology, Vol. 1*, 3rd ed. New York: Wiley.

Piaget, J. (1977). The role of action in the development of thinking. In W. F. Overton & J. M. Gallagher (Eds.), *Knowledge and development, Vol. 1*. New York: Plenum Press.

Porter, A., & Brophy, J. (1988). Synthesis of research on good teaching. *Educational Leadership, 45*, 74–85.

Postman, M., & Weingartner, C. (1969). *Teaching as a subversive activity*. New York: Delacorte.

Price, G. (1980). Which learning style elements are stable and which tend to change? *Learning Styles Network Newsletter, 1*, 1.

Purkey, W. (1970). *Self-concept and school achievement*. Englewood Cliffs, N.J.: Prentice-Hall.

Purkey, W. (1978). *Inviting school success: A self-concept approach to teaching and learning*. Belmont, Calif.: Wadsworth.

Purkey, W., & Novak, J. (1984). *Inviting school success: A self-concept approach to teaching and learning*, 2nd ed. Belmont, Calif.: Wadsworth.

Quigley, B. (1987). *The registers: An analysis of non-participation in adult basic education*. Unpublished doctoral dissertation, Northern Illinois University.

Ramirez, M., & Castaneda, A. (1974). *Cultural democracy, bicognitive development, and education*. New York: Academic Press.

Ramsey, E., & Walker, H. (1988). Family management: Correlates to antisocial behavior among middle school boys. *Behavioral disorders, 13*, 187–201.

Reardon, F., & Reynolds, R. (1979). A survey of attitudes toward corporal punishment in Pennsylvania schools. In I. Hyman & J. Wise (Eds.), *Corporal punishment in American education*. Philadelphia: Temple University.

Regan, W. (1966). *Modern elementary curriculum*. New York: Holt, Rinehart and Winston.

Reisman, F. (1964). The strategy of style. *Teachers College Record, 64*, 484–495.

Render, G., Padilla, J., & Krank, H. (1989). What research really shows about Assertive Discipline. *Educational Leadership, 46*, 72–75.

Renzulli, J. (1983, April). *The assessment and applications of learning style preferences: A practical approach for classroom teachers*. Paper presented at the annual meeting of the American Education Research Association, Montreal.

Reynolds, D. (1976). Schools do make a difference. *New Society, 37*.

Rim, E., & Coller, R. (1979). In search of nonlinear process-product functions in existing schooling-effects data: A reanalysis of the first grade reading and mathematics data from the Stallings and Kaskowitz follow-through study. *JSAS Catalog of Selected Documents in Psychology, 9*, 92.

Rist, R. (1970). Student social class and teacher expectations: The self-fulfilling prophecy in ghetto education. *Harvard Educational Review, 40*, 411–451.

Robert, M. (1976). *School morale: The human dimension*. Niles, Ill.: Argus Communications.

Roberts, D. (1986). *Recognizing and reporting child abuse and neglect*. Salem, Ore.: Department of Human Resources.

Roderick, T. (1988). Johnny can learn to negotiate. *Educational Leadership, 45*, 86–90.

Roehler, L., Duffy, G., & Meloth, M. (1987). The effects and some distinguishing characteristics of explicit teacher explanation during reading instruction. In J. Niles (Ed.), *Changing perspectives on research in reading/language processing and instruction*. Rochester, N.Y.: National Reading Conference.

Rogers, C. (1958). The characteristics of a helping relationship. *Personnel and Guidance Journal, 37*, 6–16.

Rogers, C. (1969) *Freedom to learn*. Columbus, Ohio: Charles E. Merrill.

Rohrkemper, M., & Bershon, B. (1984). Elementary school students' reports on the causes and effects of problem difficulty in mathematics. *Elementary School Journal, 85,* 127–147.

Rose, S. (1983). Promoting social competence in children: A classroom approach to social and cognitive skill training. In C. W. LeCroy (Ed.), *Social skills training for children and youth.* New York: Haworth Press.

Rose, T. (1984). Current uses of corporal punishment in American public schools. *Journal of Educational Psychology, 76,* 427–441.

Rosenholtz, S., & Simpson, C. (1984). Classroom organization and student stratification. *Elementary School Journal, 85,* 21–37.

Rosenshine, B. (1970). Enthusiastic teaching: A research review. *School Review, 72,* 449–514.

Rosenshine, B. (1976). Classroom instruction. In N. Gage (Ed.), *The psychology of teaching methods.* National Society for the Study of Education. Chicago: University of Chicago Press.

Rosenshine, B. (1980). How time is spent in elementary classrooms. In C. Denham & A. Lieberman (Eds.), *Time to learn.* Washington, D.C.: National Institute of Education.

Rosenshine, B. (1983). Teaching functions in instructional programs. *Elementary School Journal, 83,* 335–351.

Rosenshine, B., & Furst, N. (1973). The use of direct observation to study teaching. In R. Travers (Ed.), *Second handbook of research on teaching.* Chicago: Rand McNally.

Rosenthal, R. (1973). The Pygmalion effect lives. *Psychology Today, 7,* 56–63.

Rosenthal, R., & Jacobson, L. (1968). *Pygmalion in the classroom: Teacher expectation and pupils' intellectual development.* New York: Holt, Rinehart and Winston.

Rotter, J. (1954). *Social learning and clinical psychology.* Englewood Cliffs, N.J.: Prentice-Hall.

Rotter, J. (1966). Generalized expectancies for internal versus external control of reinforcement. *Psychological Monographs, 80,* 1–28.

Rounds, T., Ward, B., Mergendoller, J., & Tikunoff, W. (1982). *Junior high school transition study: Vol. II—Organization of instruction* (Report EPSSP–82–3). San Francisco: Far West Laboratory for Educational Research and Development.

Rowe, M. (1974). Wait-time and rewards as instructional variables, their influence on language, logic, and fate control: Part one, Wait-time. *Journal of Research in Science Teaching, 11,* 81–94.

Rowe, M. (1978). Wait, wait, wait. *School Science and Math, 78,* 207–216.

Runkel, P., Lawrence, M., Oldfield, S., Rider, M., & Clark, C. (1971). Stages of group development: An empirical test of Tuckman's hypothesis. *Journal of Applied Behavioral Science, 7,* 180–193.

Rutter, M., Maughan, B., Mortimore, P., Ouston, J., & Smith, A. (1979). *Fifteen thousand hours.* Cambridge, Mass.: Harvard University Press.

Sadker, D., & Sadker, M. (1985). Is the o.k. classroom o.k.? *Phi Delta Kappan, 66,* 358–361.

Sanford, J., Emmer, E., & Clements, B. (1983). Improving classroom management. *Educational Leadership, 41,* 56–60.

Sanford, J., & Everston, C. (1981). Classroom management in a low SES junior high: *Three case studies. Journal of Teacher Education, 32, 34–38.*

Schmidt, G., & Ulrich, R. (1969). Effects of group contingent events upon classroom noise. *Journal of Applied Behavior Analysis, 2,* 171–179.

Schmuck, R. (1963). Some relationships of peer liking patterns in the classroom to pupil attitudes and achievement. *School Review, 71,* 337–359.

Schmuck, R. (1966). Some aspects of classroom social climate. *Psychology in the Schools, 3,* 59–65.

Schmuck, R., & Schmuck, P. (1974). *A humanistic psychology of education: Making the school everybody's house.* Palo Alto, Calif.: National Press Books.

Schmuck, R., & Schmuck, P. (1975). *Group processes in the classroom.* Dubuque, Iowa: Wm. C. Brown.

Schmuck, R., & Schmuck, P. (1983). *Group processes in the classroom,* 4th ed. Dubuque, Iowa: Wm. C. Brown.

Schunk, D. (1983). Reward contingencies and the development of children's skills and self-efficacy. *Journal of Educational Psychology, 75,* 511–518.

Schutz, W. (1966). *The interpersonal underworld.* Palo Alto, Calif.: Science and Behavior.

Schwebel, A., & Cherlin, D. (1972). Physical and social distancing in teacher-pupil relationships. *Journal of Educational Psychology, 63,* 543–550.

Seagoe, M. (1974). Some learning characteristics of gifted children. In R. Martinson (Ed.), *The identification of the gifted and talented.* Ventura, Calif.: Office of Ventura County Superintendent of Schools.

Selman, R. (1980). *The growth of interpersonal understanding: Developmental and clinical analyses.* New York: Academic Press.

Sgan, M. (1967). Social reinforcement, socioeconomic status, and susceptibility to experimenter influence. *Journal of Personality and Social Psychology, 5,* 202–210.

Sharan, S. (1980). Cooperative learning in small groups: Recent methods and effects on achievement, attitudes, and ethnic relations. *Review of Educational Research, 50,* 241–271.

Sharan, S., & Sharan, Y. (1976). *Small group teaching.* Englewood Cliffs, N.J.: Educational Technology.

Sharan, Y., & Sharon, S. (1987). Training teachers for cooperative learning. *Educational Leadership, 45,* 20–25.

Sherman, A. (1973). *Behavior modification: Theory and practice.* Belmont, Calif: Wadsworth.

Showers, B., Joyce, B., & Bennett, B. (1987). Synthesis of research on staff development: A framework for future study and a state-of-the-art analysis. *Educational Leadership, 45,* 77–87.

Shumsky, A. (1968). *In search of teaching style.* New York: Appleton-Century-Crofts.

Sigel, I., & Coop, R. (1974). Cognitive style and classroom practice. In R. H. Coop & K. White (Eds.), *Psychological concepts in the classroom.* New York: Harper and Row.

Silberman, C. (1970). *Crisis in the classroom: The remaking of American education.* New York: Random House.

Silverstein, J. (1979). *Individual and environmental correlates of pupil problematic and nonproblematic classroom behavior.* Unpublished doctoral dissertation, New York University.

Simpson, R. (1962). Parental influence, anticipatory socialization, and social mobility. *American Sociological Review, 27,* 517–522.

Sirotnik, K. (1982). The contextual correlates of the relative expenditures of classroom time on instruction and behavior: An explanatory study of secondary schools and classes. *American Educational Research Journal, 19,* 275–292.

Sizer, T. (1984). *Horace's compromise: The dilemma of the American high school.* Boston: Houghton Mifflin.

Sizer, T. (1988). On changing secondary schools: A conversation with Ted Sizer. R. Brandt (Ed.), *Educational Leadership, 45,* 30–36.

Skinner, B. (1971). *Beyond freedom and dignity.* New York: Alfred A. Knopf.

Slavin, R. (1983a). *Cooperative learning.* New York: Longman.

Slavin, R. (1983b). When does cooperative learning increase student achievement? *Psychological Bulletin, 94,* 429–445.

Slavin, R. (1986). The Napa evaluation of Madeline Hunter's ITIP: Lessons learned. *The Elementary School Journal, 87,* 165–171.

Slavin, R. (1987). Cooperative learning and the cooperative school. *Educational Leadership, 45,* 7–13.

Slavin, R. (1988). Cooperative learning: A best-evidence synthesis. In R. E. Slavin (Ed.), *School and classroom organization.* Hillsdale, N.J.: Erlbaum.

Slavin, R., & Madden, N. (1989). What works for students at risk: A research synthesis. *Educational Leadership, 46,* 4–13.

Slavin, R., Maddin, N., & Leavey, M. (1984). Effects on team-assisted individualization on the mathematics achievement of academically handicapped and non-handicapped students. *Journal of Education Psychology, 76,* 813–819.

Sloane, H., Buckholdt, D., Jenson, W., & Crandall, J. (1979). *Structured teaching: A design for classroom management and instruction.* Champaign, Ill.: Research Press.

Smith, C. (1983). *Learning disabilities—The interaction of learner, task and setting.* Boston: Little, Brown.

Smith, C., Frank, A., & Snider, B. (1984). School psychologists' and teachers' perceptions of data used in the identification of behaviorally disordered students. *Behavioral Disorders, 10,* 27–32.

Soar, R. (1977). An integration of findings of four studies of teacher effectiveness. In G. Borich (Ed.), *The appraisal of teaching: Concepts and process.* Reading, Mass.: Addison-Wesley.

Soar, R. (1983, March). *Impact of context variables on teacher and learner behavior.* Paper presented at the annual meeting of the American

Association of Colleges for Teacher Education, Detroit.

Soar, R., & Soar, R. (1972). An empirical analysis of selected follow-through programs: An example of a process approach to evaluation. In I. Gordon (Ed.), *Early childhood education.* Chicago: National Society for the Study of Education.

Soar, R., & Soar, R. (1975). Classroom behavior, pupil characteristics and pupil growth for the school year and the summer. *JSAS Catalog of Selected Documents in Psychology, 5,* 873.

Soar, R., & Soar, R. (1979). Emotional climate and management. In P. L. Peterson & H. J. Walberg (Eds.), *Research on teaching.* Berkeley, Calif.: McCutchan.

Soar, R., & Soar, R. (1980). Setting variables, classroom interaction and multiple pupil outcomes. *JSAS Catalog of Selected Documents in Psychology, 10,* 2110.

Soar, R., & Soar, R. (1986). Context effects in the teaching-learning process. In D. Smith (Ed.), *Essential knowledge for beginning educators.* Washington, D.C.: American Association of Colleges for Teacher Education.

Solomon, D., & Kendall, A. (1976). Individual characteristics and children's performance in "open" and "traditional" classroom settings. *Journal of Educational Psychology, 68,* 613–625.

Spaulding, R. (1983). A systematic approach to discipline, part 1. *Phi Delta Kappan, 65,* 48–51.

Spaulding, R., & Spaulding, C. (1982). *Research-based classroom management.* San Jose, Calif.: Maple Press.

Spencer-Hall, D. (1981). Looking behind the teacher's back. *Elementary School Journal, 81,* 281–289.

Sperry, L. (Ed.). (1972). *Learning performance and individual differences.* Glenview, Ill.: Scott, Foresman.

Squires, D. (1983). *Effective schools and classrooms: A research-based perspective.* Alexandria, Va.: Association for Supervision and Curriculum Development.

Squires, D., Huitt, W., & Segars, J. (1984). *Effective schools and classrooms: A research-based perspective.* Alexandria, Va.: Association for Supervision and Curriculum Development.

Stake, R., & Easley, J. (1978). *Case studies in science education* (Vol. 1). Urbana, Ill.: Center for Instructional Research and Curriculum Evaluation.

Stake, R., & Easley, J. (1978). *Case studies in science education,* Vol. 2. Urbana.: Center for Instructional Research and Curriculum Evaluation and Committee on Culture and Cognition, University of Illinois at Urbana-Champaign.

Stallings, J. (1975). Implementation and child effects of teaching in follow-through classrooms. *Monographs of the Society for Research in Child Development, 40,* 7–8.

Stallings, J. (1976). How instructional processes relate to child outcomes in a national study of the follow-through. *Journal of Teacher Education, 37,* 43–47.

Stallings, J. (1980). Allocated academic learning time revisited, or beyond time on task. *Educational Researcher, 9,* 11–16.

Stallings, J. (1983). *An accountability model for teacher education.* Paper presented at the annual meeting of the American Association of Colleges for Teacher Education, Detroit.

Stallings, J. (1984). *An accountability model for teacher education.* Nashville, Tenn.: George Peabody College for Teachers, Vanderbilt University, Stallings Teaching and Learning Institute.

Stallings, J. (1987). Personal correspondence.

Stallings, J., & Kaskowitz, D. (1974). *Follow-through classroom observation evaluation.* Menlo Park, Calif.: Stanford Research Institute.

Stallings, J., & Mohlman, G. (1981). *Principal leadership style, school policy, teacher change and student behavior in eight secondary schools* (Final Report). Washington, D.C.: National Institute of Education.

Stanwyck, D., & Felker, D. (1974). *Self-concept and anxiety in middle elementary school children: A developmental survey.* Paper presented at American Educational Research Association convention, Chicago.

Stedman, L. (1985). A new look at the effective schools literature. *Urban Education, 20,* 295–326.

Steiner, C. (1977). *The original warm fuzzy tale.* Sacramento, Calif.: Jalmar Press.

Stevens, D. (1971). Reading difficulty and classroom acceptance. *Reading Teacher, 25,* 52–55.

Stinchcombe. A. (1964). *Rebellion in a high school*. Chicago: Quadrangle.

Stipek, D. (1988). *Motivation to learn: From theory to practice*. Englewood Cliffs, N.J.: Prentice-Hall.

Stipek, D., & Weisz, J. (1981). Perceived personal control and academic achievement. *Review of Educational Research, 51*, 101–137.

Stodolsky, S. (1983). Frameworks for studying the uses of instructional groups in classrooms. In P. Peterson, L. Wilkinson, & M. Hallinan (Eds.), *Organization and processes of classroom groups*. New York: Academic Press.

Stoffer, D. (1970). Investigation of positive behavioral changes as a function of genuineness, non-possessive warmth and empathic understanding. *Journal of Educational Research, 63*, 225–228.

Streit, F. (1980). *Research review 1966–1980: Adolescent problems*. Highland Park, N.J.: Essence.

Sullivan, L. (1988). Special study groups: Motivating underachievers. *Middle School Journal, 19*, 20–21.

Sulzbacher, S., & Houser, J. (1968). A tactic to eliminate disruptive behaviors in a classroom: Group contingent consequences. *American Journal of Mental Deficiency, 73*, 88–90.

Swift, M., & Spivack, G. (1975). *Alternative teaching strategies: Helping behaviorally troubled children achieve*. Champaign, Ill.: Research Press.

Tanner, L. (1978). *Classroom discipline for effective teaching and learning*. New York: Holt, Rinehart and Winston.

Tharp, R. (1982). The effective instruction of comprehension: Results and description of the Kamehameha Early Education Program. *Reading Research Quarterly, 17*, 503–527.

Thomas, D., Becker, W., & Armstrong, M. (1968). Production and elimination of disruptive classroom behavior by systematically varying teacher's behavior. *Journal of Applied Behavior Analysis, 1*, 35–45.

Thomas, J., Presland, I., Grant, M., & Glynn, T. (1978). Natural rates of teacher approval and disapproval in grade 7 classrooms. *Journal of Applied Behavior Analysis, 11*, 91–94.

Thompson, R., White, K., & Morgan, D. (1982). Teacher-student interaction patterns in classrooms with mainstreamed mildly handicapped students. *American Educational Research Journal, 19*, 220–236.

Tobias, S. (1979). Anxiety research in educational psychology. *Journal of Educational Psychology, 71*, 573–582.

Tobin, K. (1987). The role of wait time in higher cognitive level learning. *Review of Educational Research, 57*, 69–95.

Toepfer, C. (1979). Brain growth periodization—A new dogma for education. *Middle School Journal, 10*, 18–20.

Toepfer, C. (1980). Brain growth periodization data: Some suggestions for re-thinking middle school education. *High School Journal, 63*, 222–227.

Torgerson, E. (1977, April 23–29). What teenagers watch and why. *TV Guide*, 4–7.

Torrance, E. (1960). Explorations in creative thinking. *Education, 81*, 216–220.

Travers, R. (1967). *Essentials of learning*, 2nd ed. New York: Macmillan.

Truax, C. & Tatum, C. (1966). An extension from the effective psychotherapeutic model to constructive personality change in pre-school children. *Childhood Education, 42*, 456–462.

Tuckman, B. (1965). Developmental sequence in small groups. *Psychological Bulletin, 63*, 384–489.

Turnbaugh, A. (1986). A view from the center. *National Center on Effective Secondary Schools Newsletter, 1*, 8–10.

Usher, R., & Hanke, J. (1971). The "third force" in psychology and college teacher effectiveness research at the University of Northern Colorado. *Colorado Journal of Educational Research, 10*, 3–10.

Veenman, S. (1984). Perceived problems of beginning teachers. *Review of Educational Research, 54*, 143–178.

Waksman, S., Messmer, C., & Waksman, D. (1987). *Those who leave early: A study of young people leaving Oregon schools prior to graduation*. Salem: Ore.: Oregon Department of Education.

Waksman, S., Messmer, C., & Waksman, D. (1988). *The Waksman social skills curriculum: An assertive behavior program for adolescents*. Portland, Ore.: Applied Systems: Instruction Evaluation Publishing.

Walberg, H. (1988). Synthesis of research on time and learning. *Educational Leadership, 45*, 76–85.

Walberg, H., & Anderson, G. (1968). The achievement-creativity dimension and classroom climate. *Journal of Creative Behavior, 2,* 281–292.

Walberg, H., & Waxman, H. (1983). Teaching, learning and management of instruction. In D. Smith (Ed.), *Essential knowledge for beginning educators.* Washington, D.C.: American Association of Colleges for Teacher Education.

Walker, H. (1979). *The acting-out child: Coping with classroom disruption.* Boston: Allyn and Bacon.

Walker, H., & Buckley, N. (1973). Teacher attention to appropriate and inappropriate classroom behavior: An individual case study. *Focus on Exceptional Children, 5,* 5–11.

Walker, H., & Buckley, N. (1974). *Token reinforcement techniques: Classroom applications for the hard-to-teach child.* Eugene, Ore.: E–P Press.

Walker, H., Hops, H., & Fiegenbaum, E. (1976). Deviant classroom behavior as a function of combinations of social and token reinforcement and cost contingency. *Behavior Therapy, 7,* 76–88.

Walker, H., Hops, H., Greenwood, C., Todd, N., & Garrett, B. (1977). *The comparative effects of teacher praise, token reinforcement, and response cost in reducing negative peer interactions* (CORBEH Report #25). Eugene: Center at Oregon for Research in the Behavioral Education of the Handicapped, University of Oregon.

Walker, H., McConnell, S., Holmes, D., Todis, B., Walker, J., & Golden, N. (1983). *The Walker social skills curriculum: The accepts program.* Austin Tex.: Pro-Ed.

Walker, H., Reavis, H., Rhode, G., & Jensen, W. (1985). A conceptual model for delivery of behavioral services to behavior disordered children in a continuum of educational settings. In P. Bornstein & A. Kazdin (Eds.), *Handbook of clinical therapy with children.* Homewood, Ill.: Dorsey Press.

Ward, B., & Tikunof, W. (1976). The effective teacher education program: Application of selected research results and methodology to teaching. *Journal of Teacher Education, 27,* 58–63.

Ware, B. (1978). What rewards do students want? *Phi Delta Kappan, 59,* 355–356.

Warren, R., Deffenbacher, J., & Brading, P. (1976). Rational-emotive therapy and the reduction of test anxiety in elementary school students. *Rational Living, 11,* 26–29.

Wayson, W., & Pinnell, G. (1982). Creating a living curriculum for teaching self-discipline. In D. Duke (Ed.), *Helping teachers manage classrooms.* Alexandria, Va.: Association for Supervision and Curriculum Development.

Weber, K. (1982). *The teacher is the key: A practical guide for teaching the adolescent with learning difficulties.* Denver: Love.

Wehlage, G. (1983). *Effective programs for the marginal high school students: PDK fastback 197.* Bloomington, Ind.: Phi Delta Kappa Educational Foundation.

Wehlage, G., & Rutter, R. (1986). Dropping out: How much do schools contribute to the problem? *Teachers College Record, 87,* 374–392.

Weiner, B. (1979). A theory of motivation for some classroom experiences. *Journal of Educational Psychology, 71,* 3–25.

Weinstein, R. (1976). Reading group membership in first grade: Teacher behaviors and pupil experience over time. *Journal of Educational Psychology, 68,* 103–116.

Wheeler, R., & Ryan, F. (1973). Effects of cooperative and competitive classroom environments on the attitudes and achievement of elementary school students engaged in social studies inquiry activities. *Journal of Educational Psychology, 65,* 402–407.

White, M. (1975). Natural rates of teacher approval and disapproval in the classroom. *Journal of Applied Behavior Analysis, 8,* 367–372.

White, R. (1959). Motivation reconsidered: The concept of competence. *Psychological Review, 66,* 478–481.

Williams, R., & Cole, S. (1968). Self-concept and adjustment. *Personnel and Guidance Journal, 46,* 478–481.

Willis, B. (1970). The influence of teacher expectations on teachers' classroom interaction with selected children. *Dissertation Abstracts, 30,* 5072–A.

Willis. H. (1987). *Students at risk: A review of conditions, circumstances, indicators, and educational implications.* Elmhurst, Ill.: North Central Regional Education Laboratory.

Wise, A., Darling-Hammond, L., & Berry, B. (1988). Selecting teachers: The best, the known and the persistent. *Educational Leadership, 45,* 82–85.

Witkin, H., & Moore, C. (1974, April). *Cognitive style and the teaching-learning process.* Paper presented at the annual meeting of the American Educational Research Association, Chicago.

Wittrock, M. (Ed). (1986). *Handbook of research on teaching,* 3rd ed. New York: Macmillan.

Wlodkowski, R. (1978). *Motivation and teaching: A practical guide.* Washington, D.C.: National Education Association.

Wolfgang, C., & Glickman, C. (1986). *Solving discipline problems: Strategies for classroom teachers,* 2nd ed. Boston: Allyn and Bacon.

Wood, F., & Johnson, G. (1982). *Staff development and the /I/D/E/A/ school improvement project.* Dayton, Ohio: Institute for Development of Educational Activities.

Wood, M. (1975). *Developmental therapy.* Baltimore: University Park Press.

Woods, P. (1976). Having a laugh: An antidote to schooling. In M. Hammersley & P. Woods (Eds.), *The process of schooling: A sociological reader.* London: Routledge & Kegan Paul.

Woolfolk, A. (1987). *Educational psychology,* 3rd ed. Englewood Cliffs, N.J.: Prentice-Hall.

Workman, E. (1982). *Teaching behavioral self-control to students.* Austin, Tex.: Pro-Ed.

Wragg, E. (Ed.). (1984). *Classroom teaching skills.* New York: Nichols.

Wylie, R. (1961). *The self-concept.* Lincoln: University of Nebraska Press.

Yamamoto, K., Thomas, E., & Karnes, E. (1969). School-related attitudes in middle-school age students. *American Educational Research Journal, 6,* 191–206.

Yando, R., & Kagan, J. (1968). The effect of teacher tempo on the child. *Child Development, 39,* 27–34.

Zumwalt, K. (1982). Research on teaching: Policy implications for teacher education. In A. Lieberman & M. McLaughlin (Eds.), *Policy making in education. Eighty-first yearbook of the National Society for the Study of Education.* Chicago: National Society for the Study of Education.

NAME INDEX

SUBJECT INDEX

ABOUT THE AUTHORS

Vern Jones, Ph.D., has taught high school students, been a junior high school teacher of emotionally handicapped students, and a junior high school vice-principal. He has written extensively, including *Adolescents with Behavior Problems* and *Comprehensive Classroom Management*. He also has written chapters in *Helping Teachers Manage Classrooms, Management of Disruptive Behavior in School,* and *Severe Behavior Disorders of Children and Youth* as well as many articles on classroom management in middle schools, with gifted children, and with seriously emotionally disturbed students. From 1986 to 1989 Vern was co-chair of the American Educational Research Association Special Interest Group on Classroom Management. He has consulted widely in classroom management, at-risk youth, and emotionally handicapped students. Vern is Professor of Teacher Education at Lewis and Clark College. During the 1987 to 1989 school years he was on leave in order to work as a consultant in schools.

Louise Jones, M.A.T., has been an elementary teacher for 19 years. She has taught grades 3 through 6 and also has taught both regular education and talented and gifted students. Currently, she consults with school districts in the areas of classroom management, student self-esteem, learning styles, and cooperative learning.